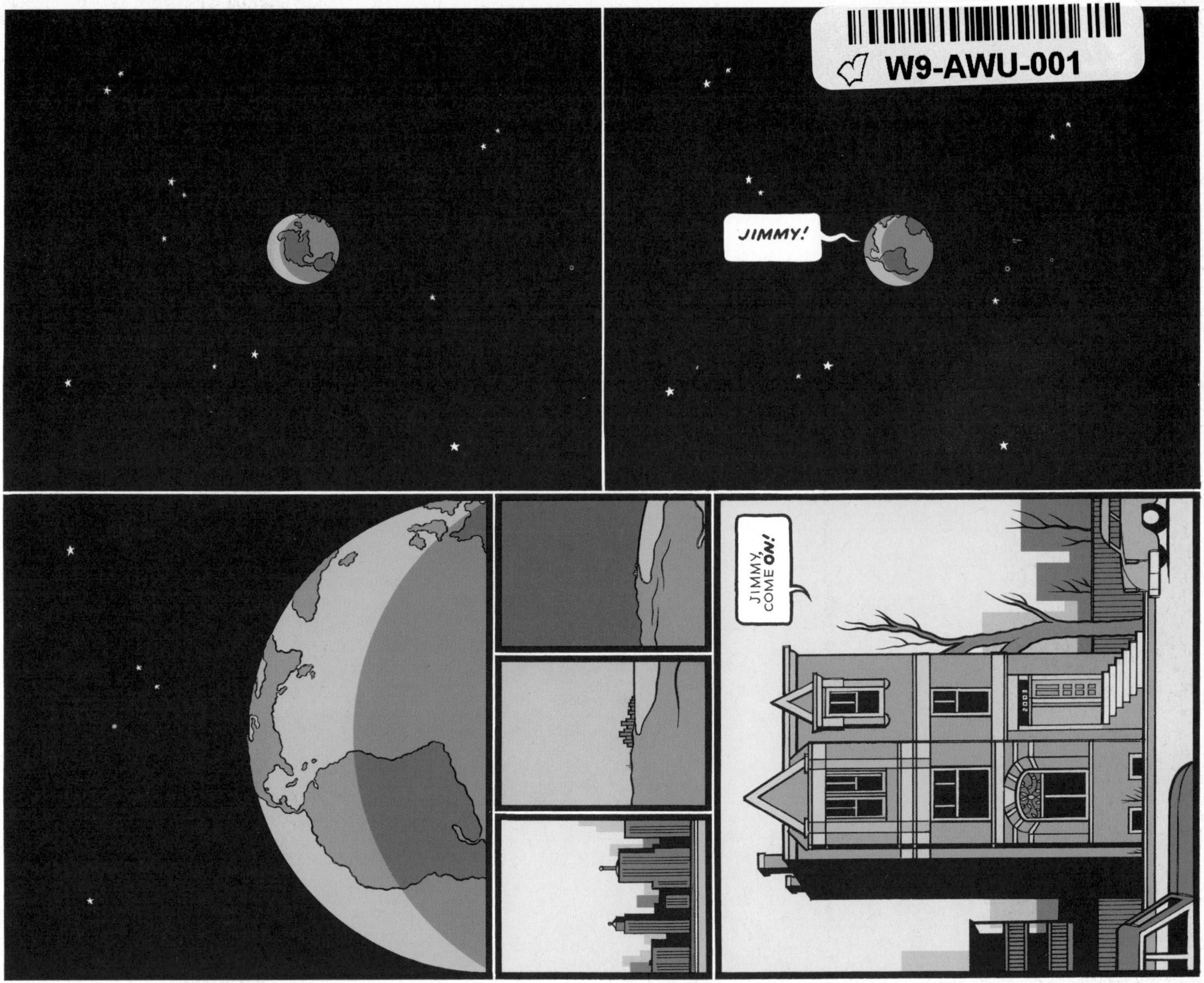
JIMMY!
JIMMY, COME ON!

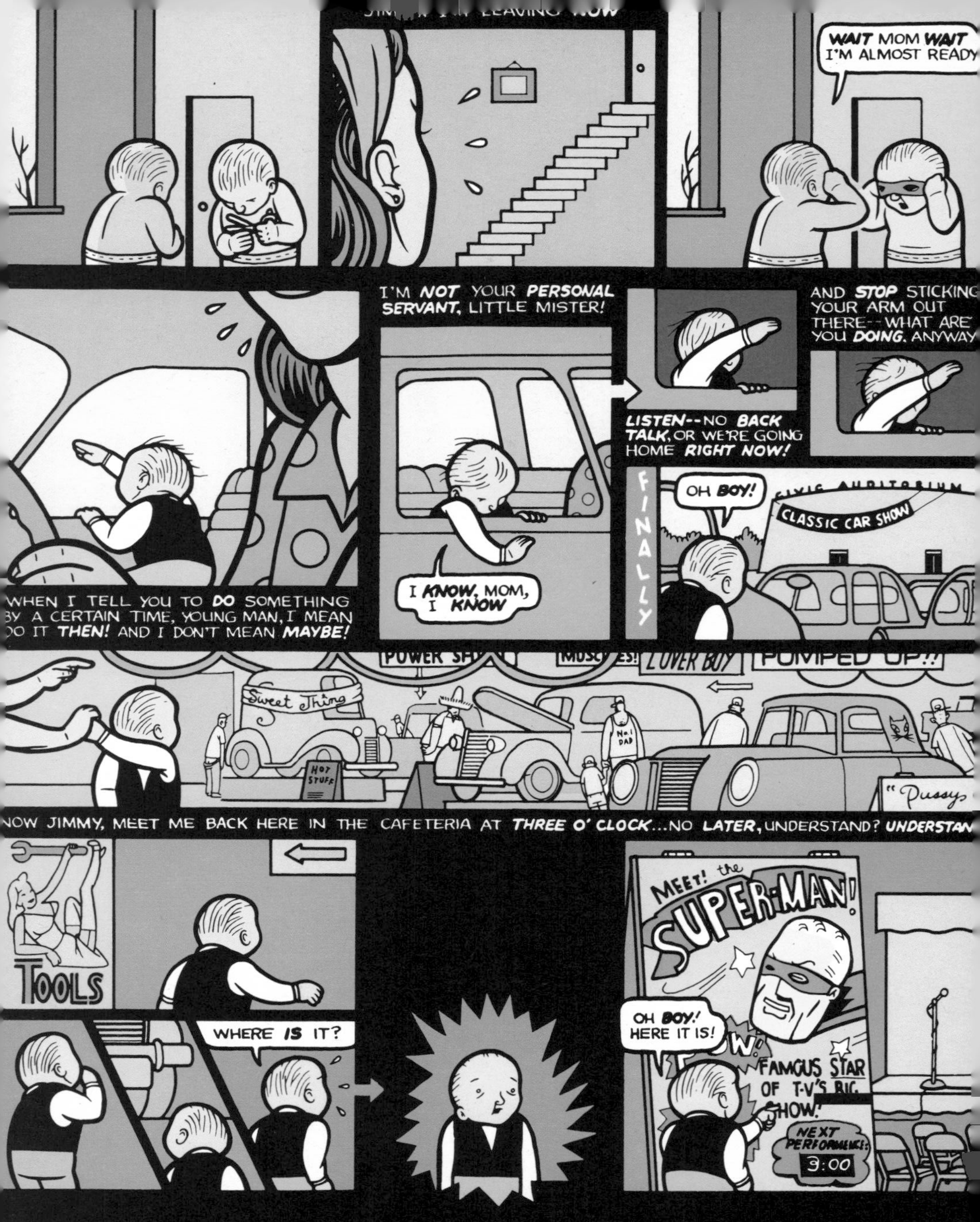
WAIT MOM WAIT I'M ALMOST READY
WHEN I TELL YOU TO DO SOMETHING BY A CERTAIN TIME, YOUNG MAN, I MEAN DO IT THEN! AND I DON'T MEAN MAYBE!
I'M NOT YOUR PERSONAL SERVANT, LITTLE MISTER!
I KNOW, MOM, I KNOW
LISTEN--NO BACK TALK, OR WE'RE GOING HOME RIGHT NOW!
AND STOP STICKING YOUR ARM OUT THERE--WHAT ARE YOU DOING, ANYWAY
FINALLY
OH BOY!
CLASSIC CAR SHOW
POWER
LOVER BOY
POMPED UP!!
Sweet Thing
HOT STUFF
No. 1 DAD
"Pussy
NOW JIMMY, MEET ME BACK HERE IN THE CAFETERIA AT THREE O' CLOCK...NO LATER, UNDERSTAND? UNDERSTAN
TOOLS
WHERE IS IT?
MEET! the SUPER-MAN!
FAMOUS STAR OF T-V'S BIG SHOW!
NEXT PERFORMANCE: 3:00
OH BOY! HERE IT IS!

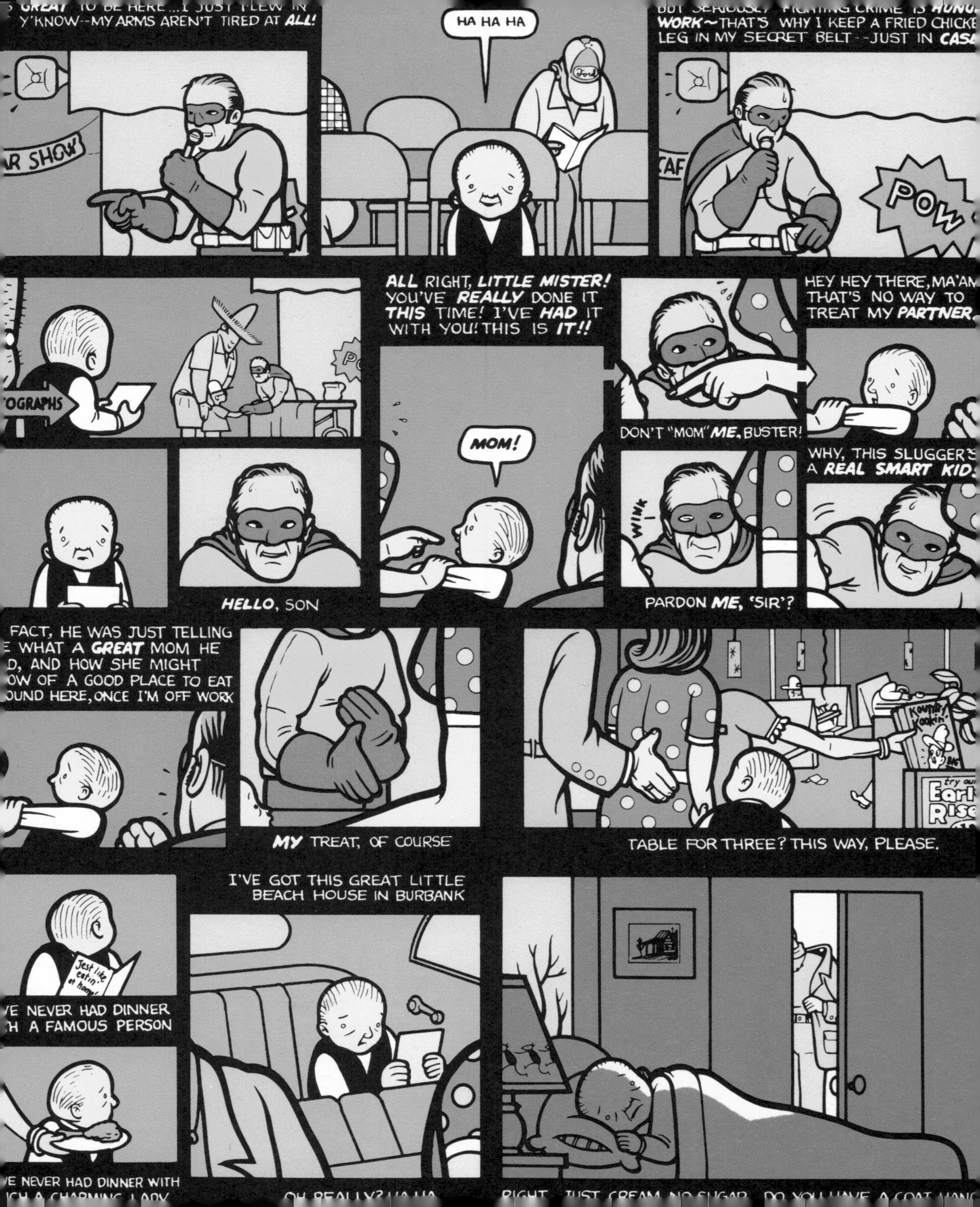
Y'KNOW--MY ARMS AREN'T TIRED AT ALL!
HA HA HA
WORK~THAT'S WHY I KEEP A FRIED CHICKE
LEG IN MY SECRET BELT--JUST IN CASE
POW
ALL RIGHT, LITTLE MISTER! YOU'VE REALLY DONE IT THIS TIME! I'VE HAD IT WITH YOU! THIS IS IT!!
HEY HEY THERE, MA'AM THAT'S NO WAY TO TREAT MY PARTNER
MOM!
DON'T "MOM" ME, BUSTER!
WHY, THIS SLUGGER'S A REAL SMART KID
WINK
HELLO, SON
PARDON ME, 'SIR'?
FACT, HE WAS JUST TELLING
WHAT A GREAT MOM HE
D, AND HOW SHE MIGHT
OW OF A GOOD PLACE TO EAT
OUND HERE, ONCE I'M OFF WORK
MY TREAT, OF COURSE
TABLE FOR THREE? THIS WAY, PLEASE.
I'VE GOT THIS GREAT LITTLE BEACH HOUSE IN BURBANK
Just like eatin' at home!
VE NEVER HAD DINNER
H A FAMOUS PERSON
VE NEVER HAD DINNER WITH

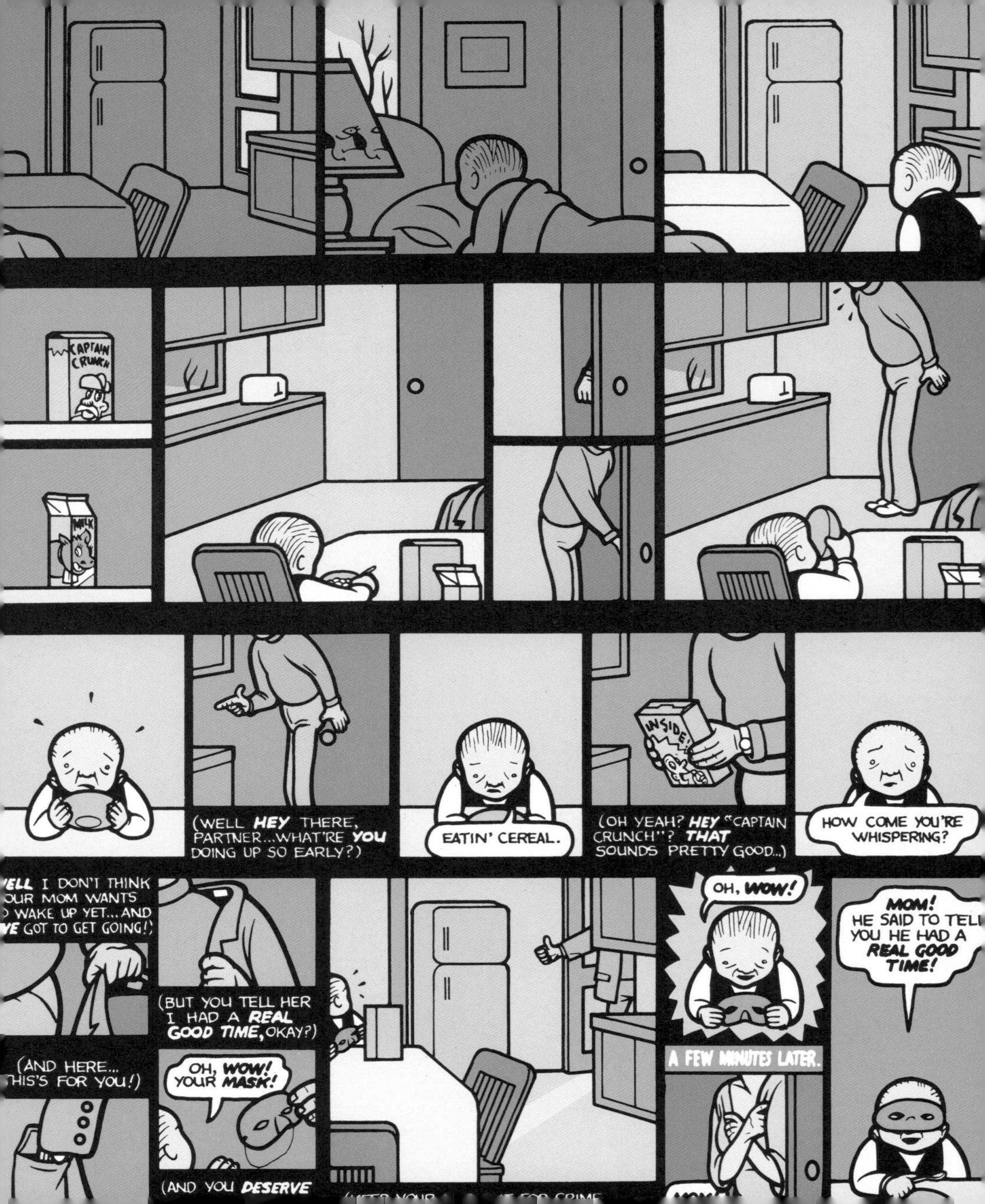

(WELL HEY THERE, PARTNER...WHAT'RE YOU DOING UP SO EARLY?)
EATIN' CEREAL.
(OH YEAH? HEY "CAPTAIN CRUNCH"? THAT SOUNDS PRETTY GOOD...)
HOW COME YOU'RE WHISPERING?
…I DON'T THINK …MOM WANTS …WAKE UP YET...AND …GOT TO GET GOING!)
(BUT YOU TELL HER I HAD A REAL GOOD TIME, OKAY?)
(AND HERE... …FOR YOU!)
OH, WOW! YOUR MASK!
(AND YOU DESERVE
OH, WOW!
A FEW MINUTES LATER.
MOM! HE SAID TO TEL… YOU HE HAD A REAL GOOD TIME!

Chris Greweling

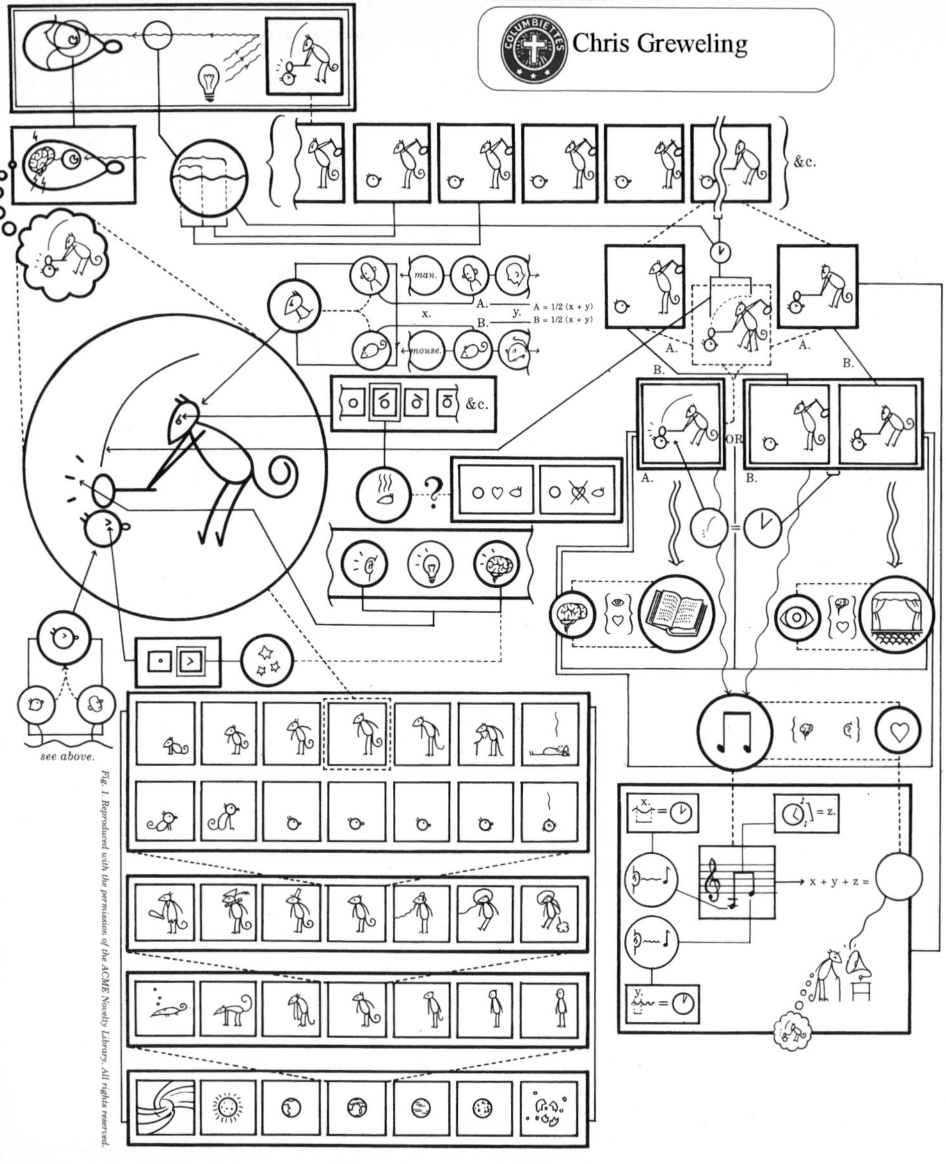

&c.
man.
mouse.
x.
y.
A.
B.
A = 1/2 (x + y)
B = 1/2 (x + y)
&c.
?
A.
B.
A.
B.
OR
A.
B.
x.
= z.
x + y + z =
y.
see above.

Fig. 1. Reproduced with the permission of the ACME Novelty Library.

New Pictorial Language Makes Marks.

Good for Showing Stuff, Leaving out Big Words.

Article reproduced with the permission of The Journal of Liberal Arts Degrees.

It is the natural inclination of children to describe events common to their lives through sequences of simple pictograms and images, for such "picture stories" serve to "make sense" and "order" the exciting and sometimes confusing new world which accosts them. However, with the onset of early education, social conditioning, and class circumstance, this congenital skill has been traditionally left to atrophy, kept alive only by the occasional prick to attention by the various "napkin gags" and "refrigerator clippings" which commonly litter the back pages of our newsdailies. Such an unfortunate cultural situation serves only to associate an otherwise potentially effective language with such juvenilia as lawn games, pony races, and gaily-costumed musclemen, thus greatly compromising both the maturity of material available for consumption and the happiness of those willing to submit to a life of companionless mockery in blind pursuit of its production. Despite these obstacles, a variegated loam for exciting stories and thrilling adventures has long lain untilled, yet now the seeds are being sewn, encouraged by a startling and seemingly unstoppable rise in illiteracy, and an accompanying dive in the general intelligence of the populace.

With the many recent technological breakthroughs in pictorial linguistics (as exemplified by airline safety cards, battery diagrams, and feminine protection directions), such heretofore-dormant skills of Comic Strip Apprehension (or CSA) are being reawakened in the adult mind, paving the way for the explosion of more complicated literature which almost certainly looms within the next decade. "CSA is here to stay," remarks a well-known and highly-decorated researcher of popular culture, "and all we can do is get ready. People can hardly form sentences that make any sense anymore; they're making nouns into verbs, and acronyming words out of the first letters of a lot of other words, and using words wrong all the time to mean things that they don't. So I guess little pictures are about the only way we're going to be able to tell stuff in the future, since most anybody can understand them. I think it'll be good, because people like looking at pictures, and I think words have had their day, anyway. It's a media-saturated world where media saturates everything and you can't think about anything except media saturation all the time." This same researcher added that adaptation of popular motion pictures, game shows, and installation art to this new language would also appear an inevitability. "I can see the whole of human culture being converted to CS – it's convenient, and saleable. Besides, people are getting less smart every day everywhere. It's a real world movement."

Certain publishing houses are experimenting with this new form of expression, test-marketing carefully demographed entertainments, and then strategically aiming them at a less-educated and/or intellectually blunted segment of the consumer pool. The results, thus far, are encouraging. "Dumb people are eating it up," says our researcher. "They love it. Especially people who buy a lot of stuff. This could be big." When queried as to the literary content of many of these projected releases, however, he is less forthcoming: "Uh, I dunno. Stories about people that people'll want to read. Fantasy stuff – y'know. Pretty girls, cars. We figure that'll take care of itself. We're working with a lot of content providers at the moment and so most of it's hush-hush. We're polling. You want to fill out a survey?"

Regardless, this "visual language" has secretly been in use by the military for many years, for its humorous, cross-cultural appeal to a wide variety of the ignorant made it the perfect means by which to explicate the mechanics of weaponry and killing. "It's like a movie, except without the popcorn," one articulate private offered. "I like it. Especially when there's naked chicks and stuff. It's like you're really there, except you're not."

It is expected that the earliest examples of such literature will appear in target economic regions later in the year, with a general release in the fall.

Addtional copies of this article may be procured by writing to the publisher, address below.

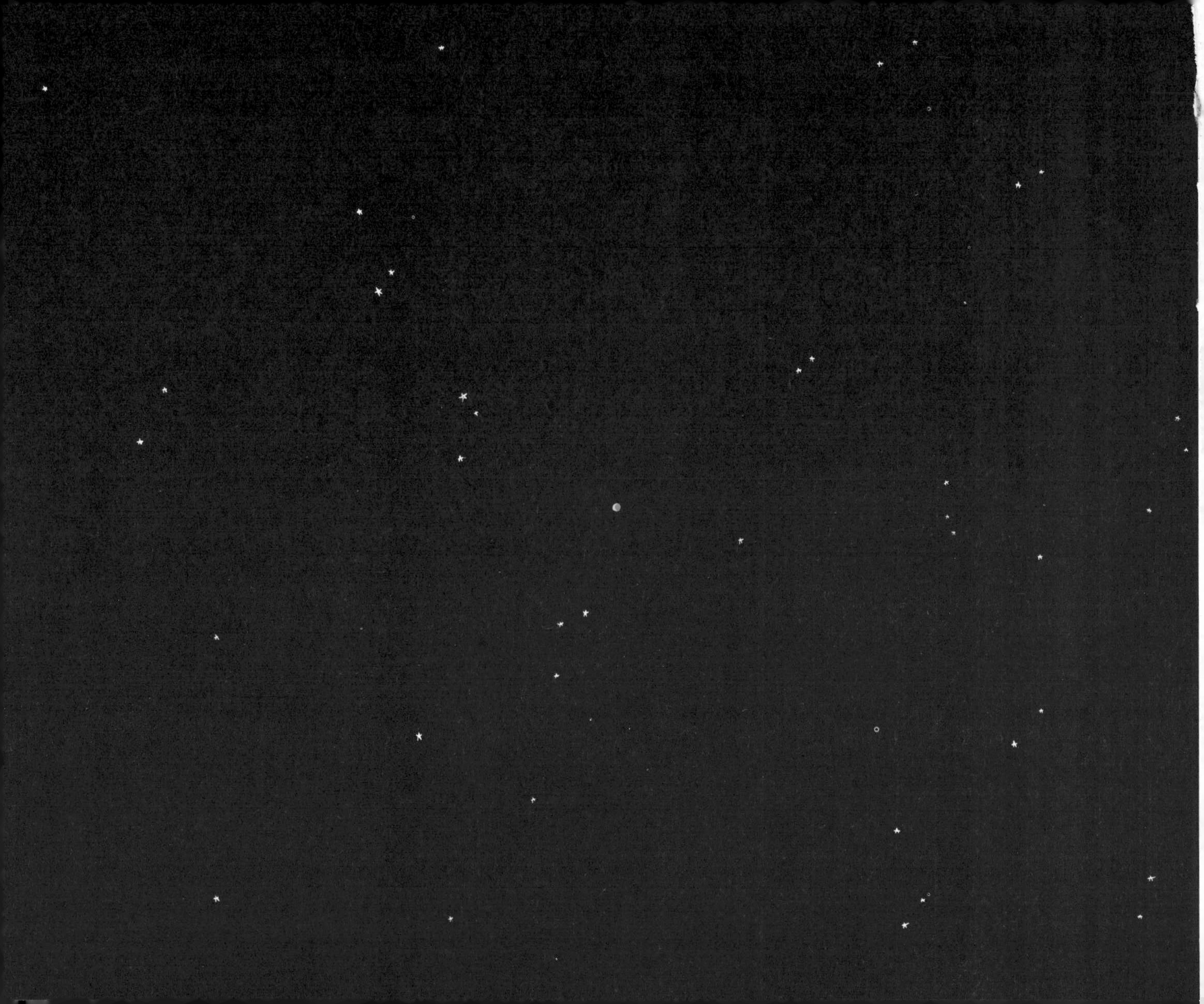

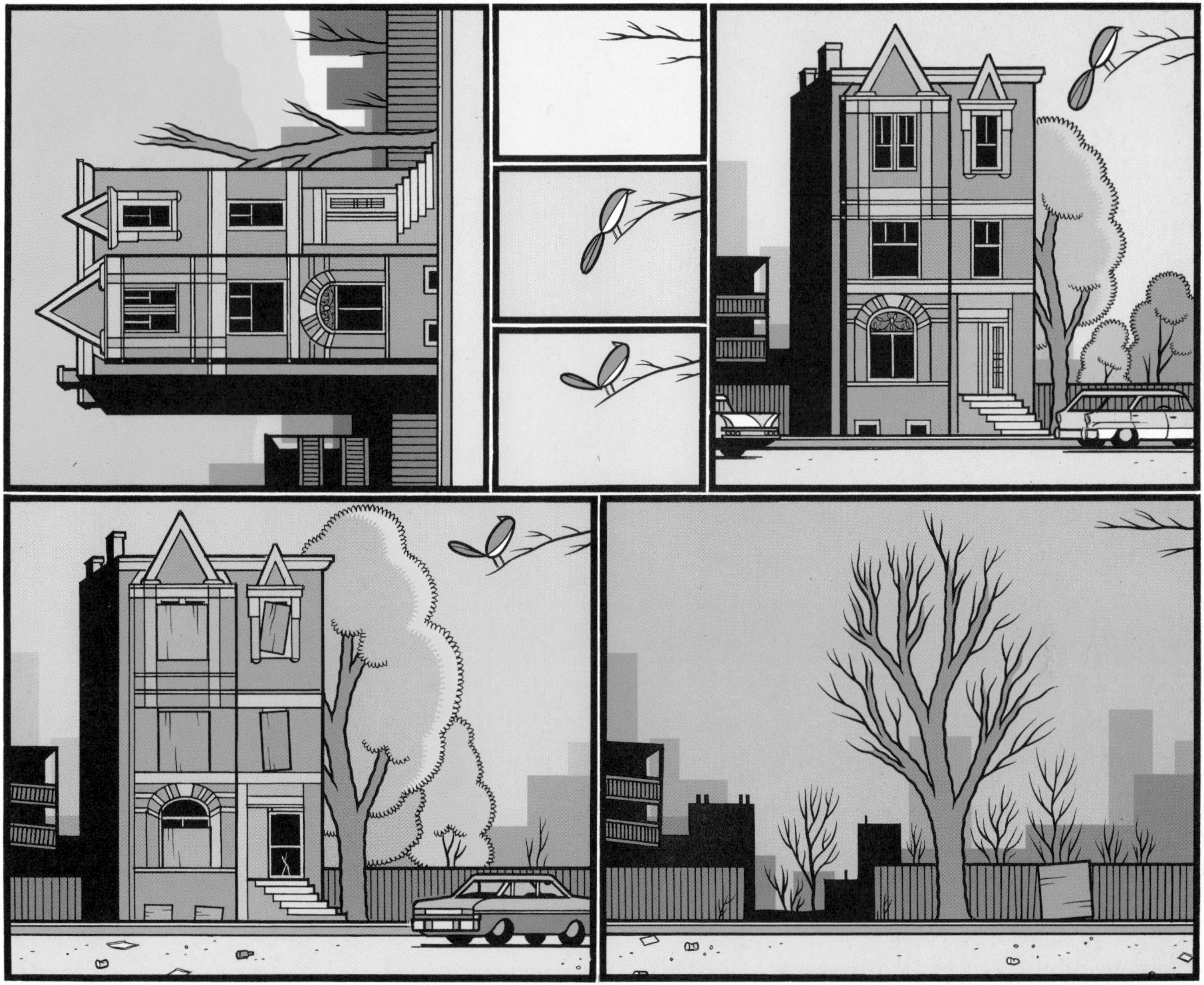

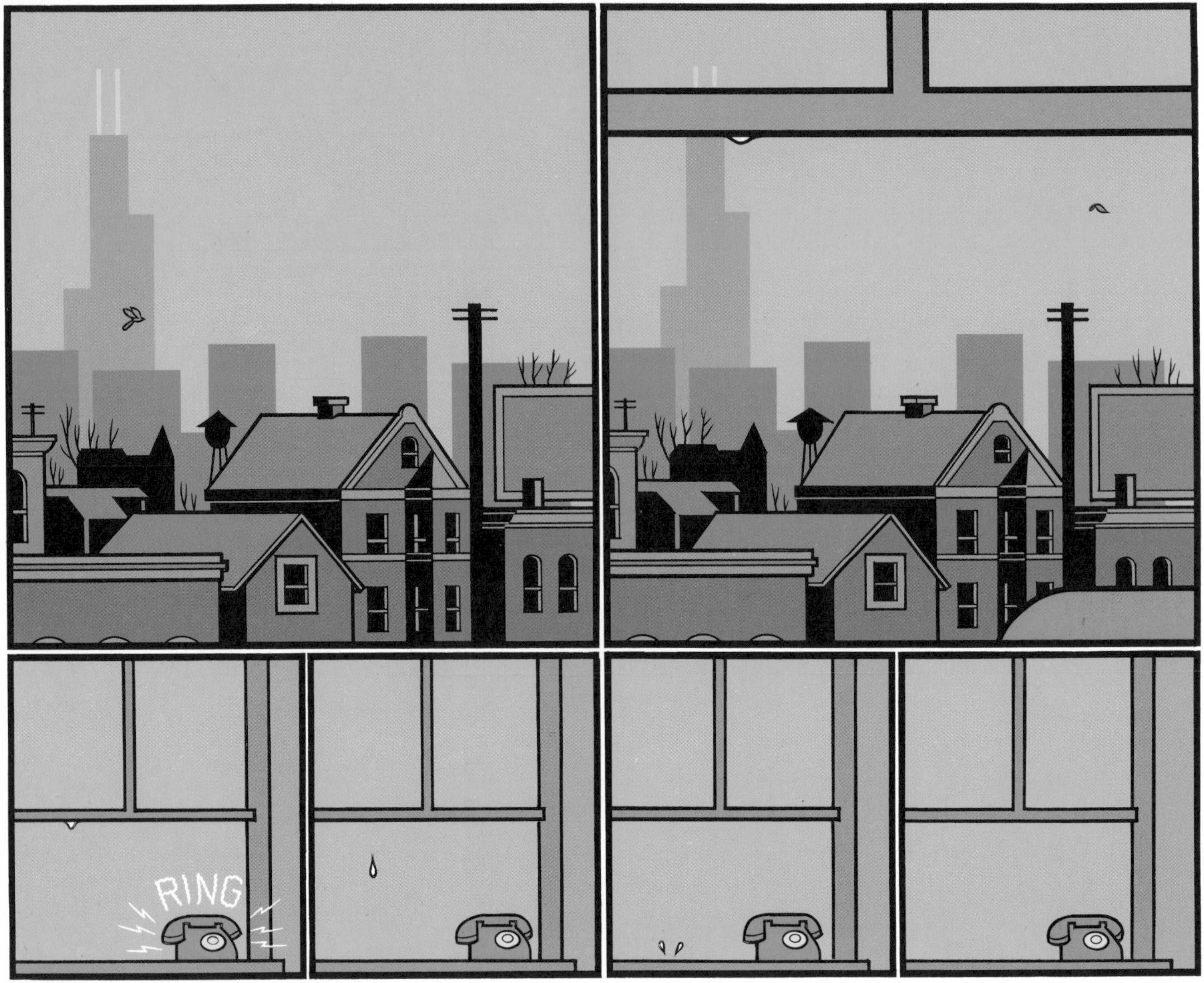
RING

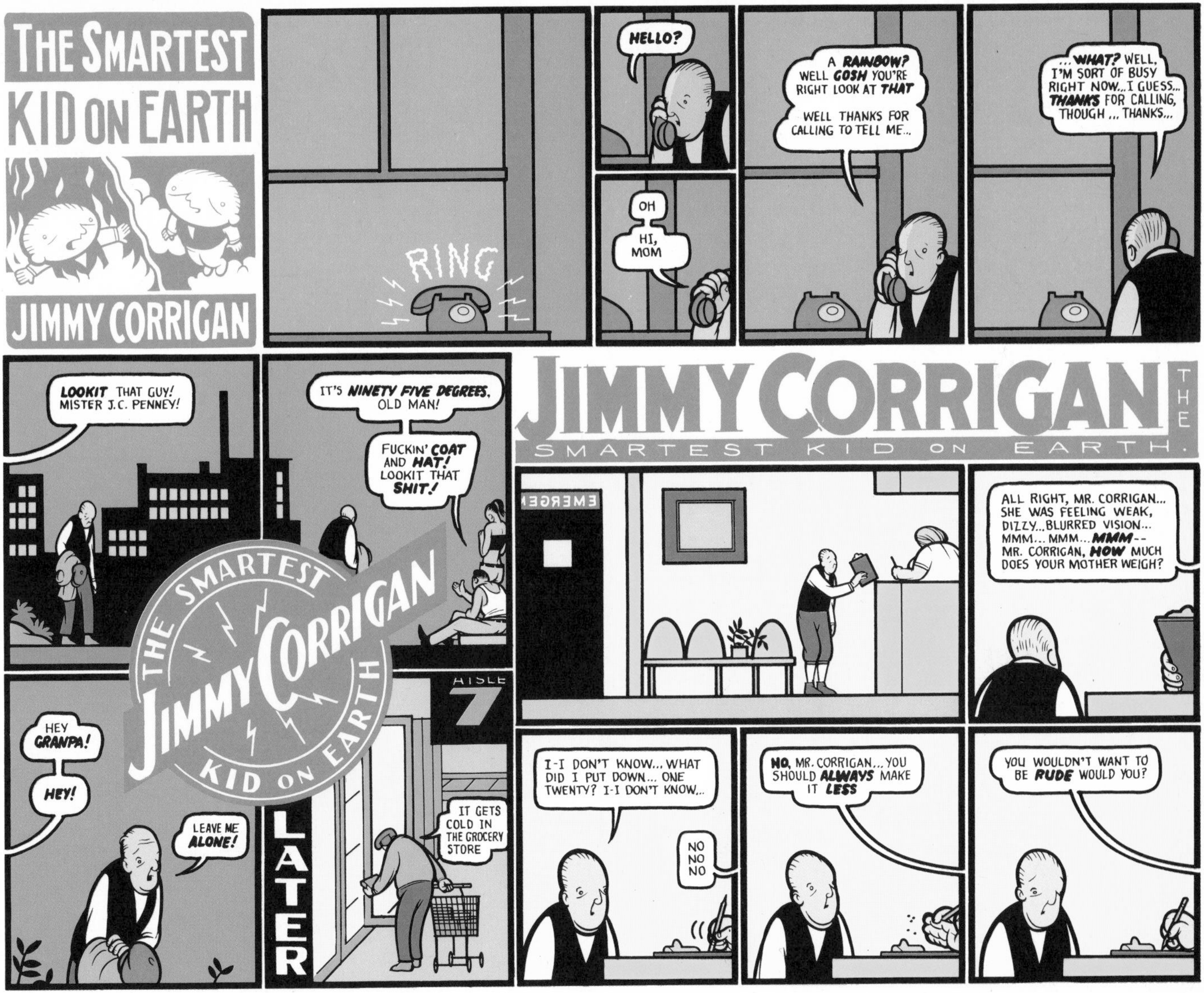

THE SMARTEST KID ON EARTH
JIMMY CORRIGAN
RING
HELLO?
OH
HI, MOM
A RAINBOW? WELL GOSH YOU'RE RIGHT LOOK AT THAT
WELL THANKS FOR CALLING TO TELL ME...
...WHAT? WELL, I'M SORT OF BUSY RIGHT NOW... I GUESS... THANKS FOR CALLING, THOUGH ... THANKS...
LOOKIT THAT GUY! MISTER J.C. PENNEY!
IT'S NINETY FIVE DEGREES, OLD MAN!
FUCKIN' COAT AND HAT! LOOKIT THAT SHIT!
THE SMARTEST JIMMY CORRIGAN KID ON EARTH
HEY GRANPA!
HEY!
LEAVE ME ALONE!
AISLE 7
LATER
IT GETS COLD IN THE GROCERY STORE
JIMMY CORRIGAN THE SMARTEST KID ON EARTH.
EMERGE
ALL RIGHT, MR. CORRIGAN... SHE WAS FEELING WEAK, DIZZY... BLURRED VISION... MMM... MMM... MMM-- MR. CORRIGAN, HOW MUCH DOES YOUR MOTHER WEIGH?
I-I DON'T KNOW... WHAT DID I PUT DOWN... ONE TWENTY? I-I DON'T KNOW...
NO NO NO
NO, MR. CORRIGAN... YOU SHOULD ALWAYS MAKE IT LESS
YOU WOULDN'T WANT TO BE RUDE WOULD YOU?

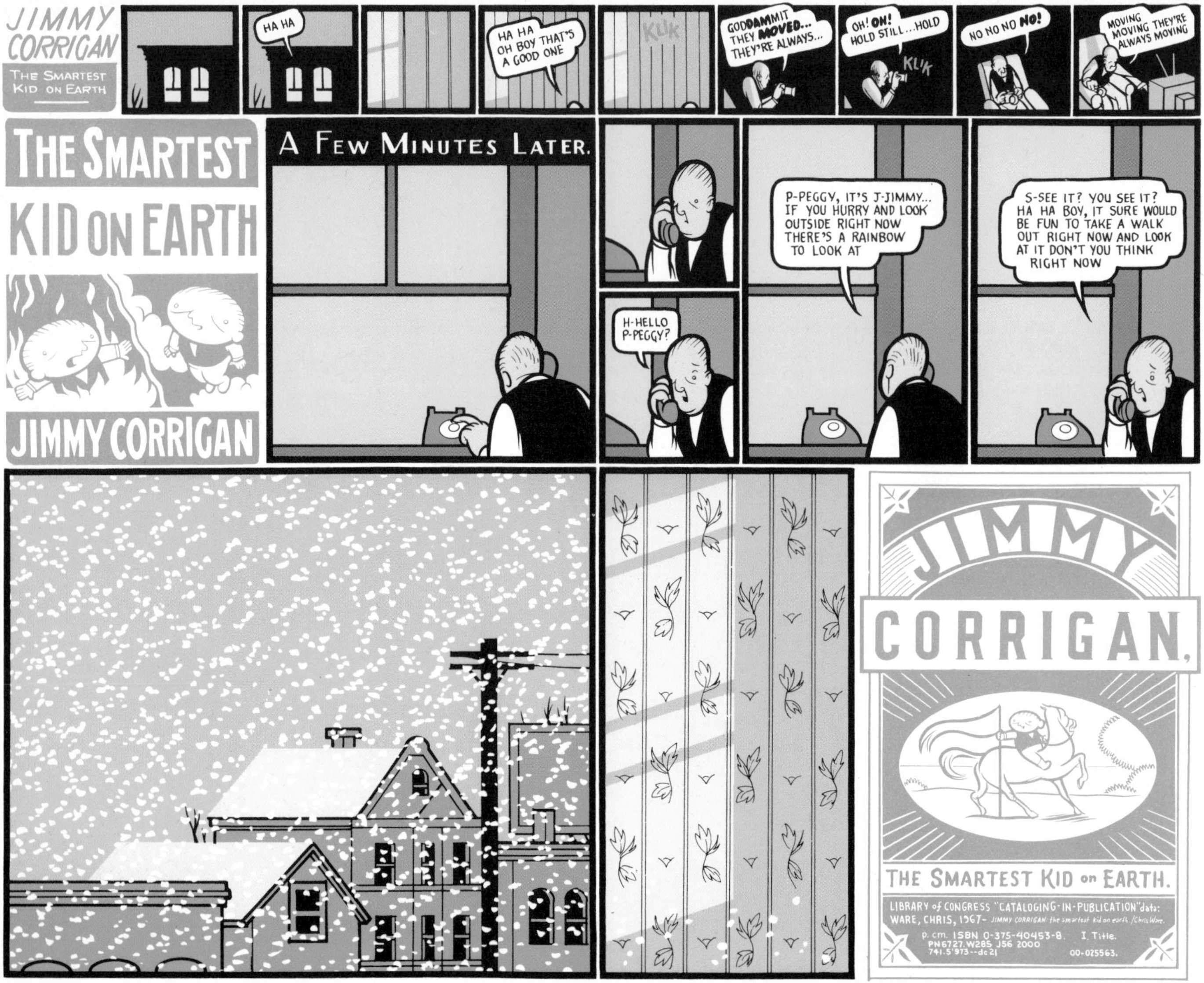
JIMMY CORRIGAN
THE SMARTEST KID ON EARTH
HA HA
HA HA OH BOY THAT'S A GOOD ONE
KLIK
GODDAMMIT THEY MOVED... THEY'RE ALWAYS...
OH! OH! HOLD STILL...HOLD
KLIK
NO NO NO NO!
MOVING MOVING THEY'RE ALWAYS MOVING
THE SMARTEST KID ON EARTH
JIMMY CORRIGAN
A FEW MINUTES LATER.
H-HELLO P-PEGGY?
P-PEGGY, IT'S J-JIMMY... IF YOU HURRY AND LOOK OUTSIDE RIGHT NOW THERE'S A RAINBOW TO LOOK AT
S-SEE IT? YOU SEE IT? HA HA BOY, IT SURE WOULD BE FUN TO TAKE A WALK OUT RIGHT NOW AND LOOK AT IT DON'T YOU THINK RIGHT NOW
JIMMY
CORRIGAN,
THE SMARTEST KID on EARTH.
LIBRARY of CONGRESS "CATALOGING-IN-PUBLICATION" data:
WARE, CHRIS, 1967- JIMMY CORRIGAN: the smartest kid on earth. / Chris Ware.
p. cm. ISBN 0-375-40453-8. I. Title.
PN6727.W285 J56 2000
741.5'973--dc21 00-025563.

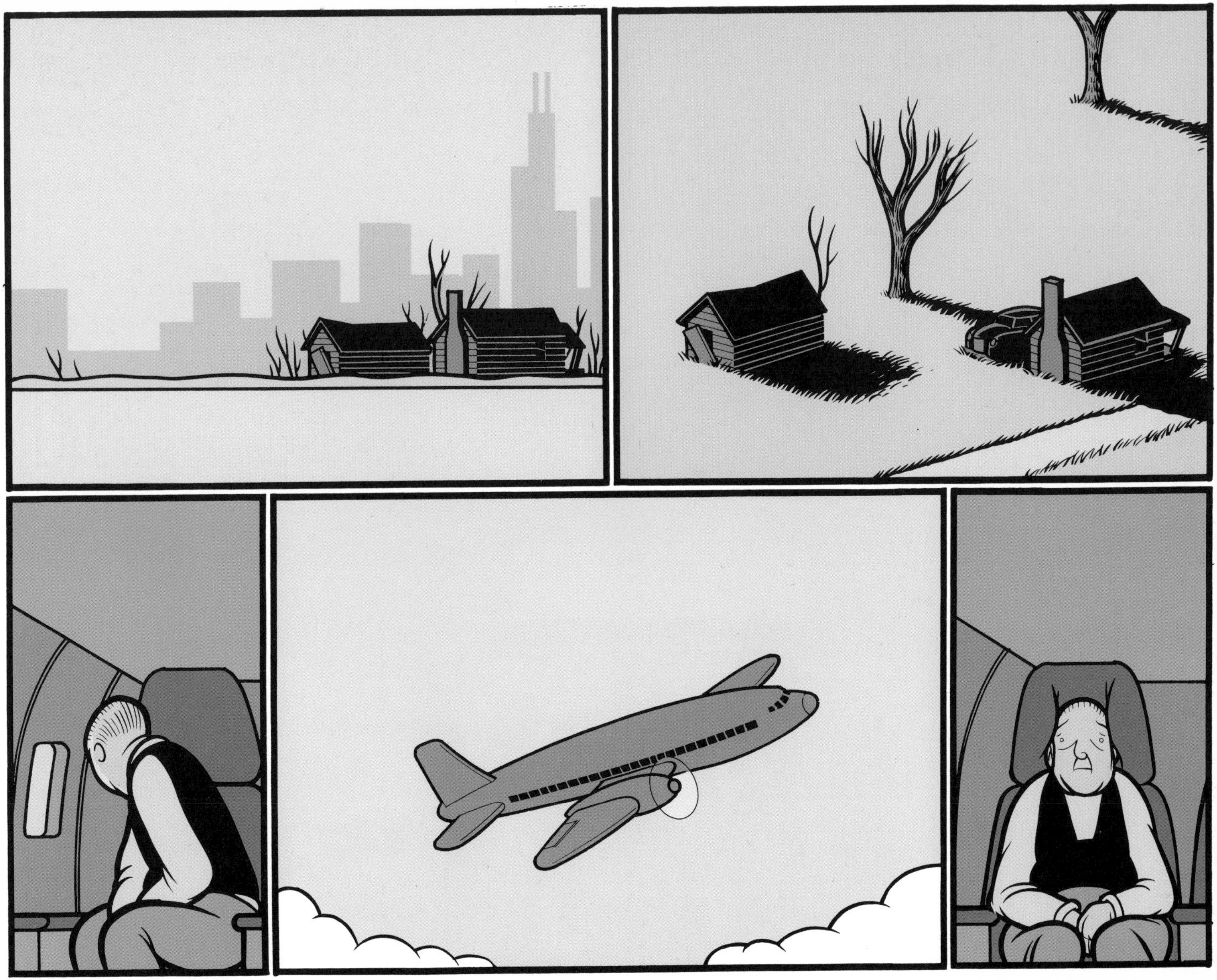

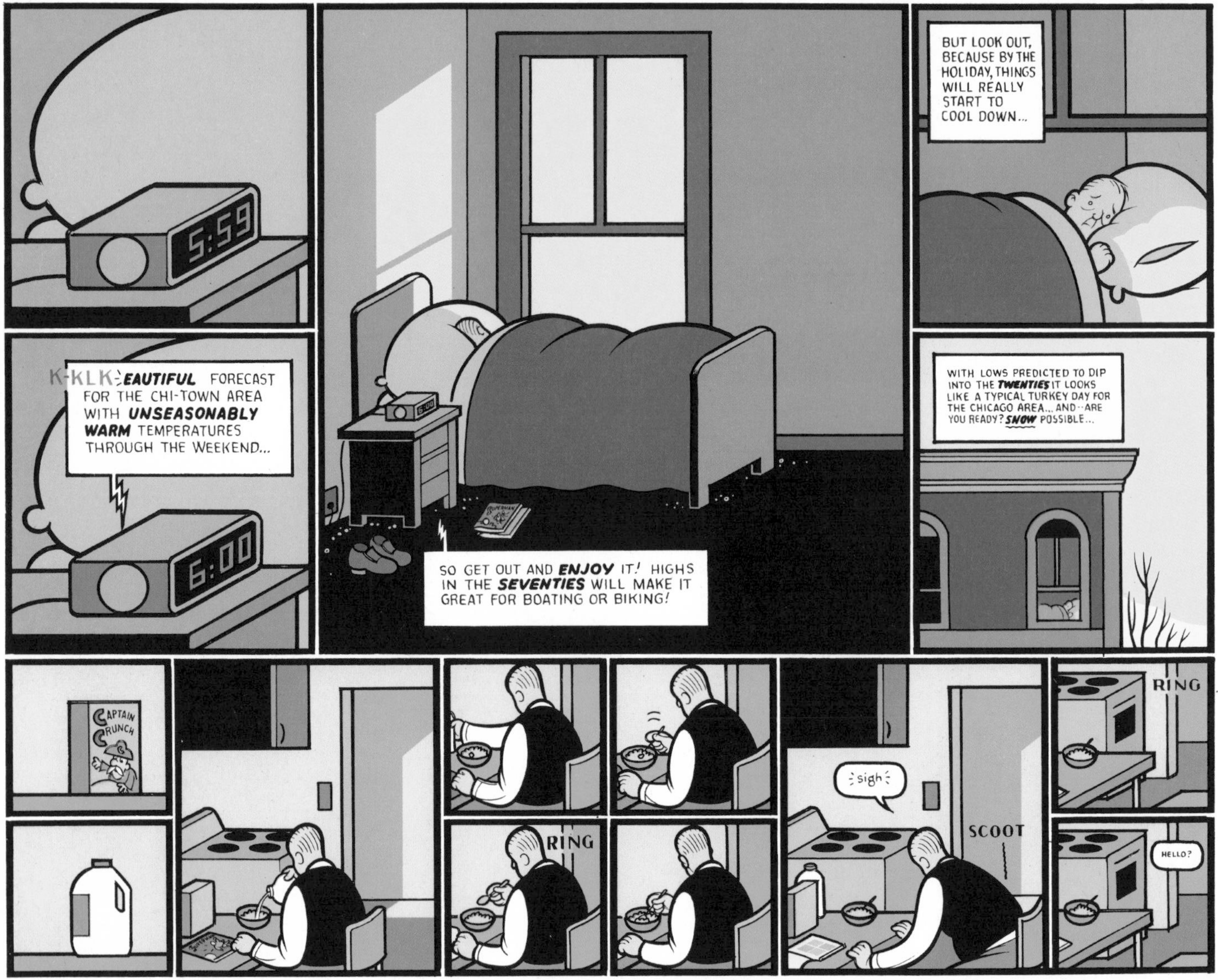
5:59
K-KLK-EAUTIFUL FORECAST FOR THE CHI-TOWN AREA WITH UNSEASONABLY WARM TEMPERATURES THROUGH THE WEEKEND...
6:00
SO GET OUT AND ENJOY IT! HIGHS IN THE SEVENTIES WILL MAKE IT GREAT FOR BOATING OR BIKING!
BUT LOOK OUT, BECAUSE BY THE HOLIDAY, THINGS WILL REALLY START TO COOL DOWN...
WITH LOWS PREDICTED TO DIP INTO THE TWENTIES IT LOOKS LIKE A TYPICAL TURKEY DAY FOR THE CHICAGO AREA... AND--ARE YOU READY? SNOW POSSIBLE...
CAPTAIN CRUNCH
RING
sigh
SCOOT
RING
HELLO?

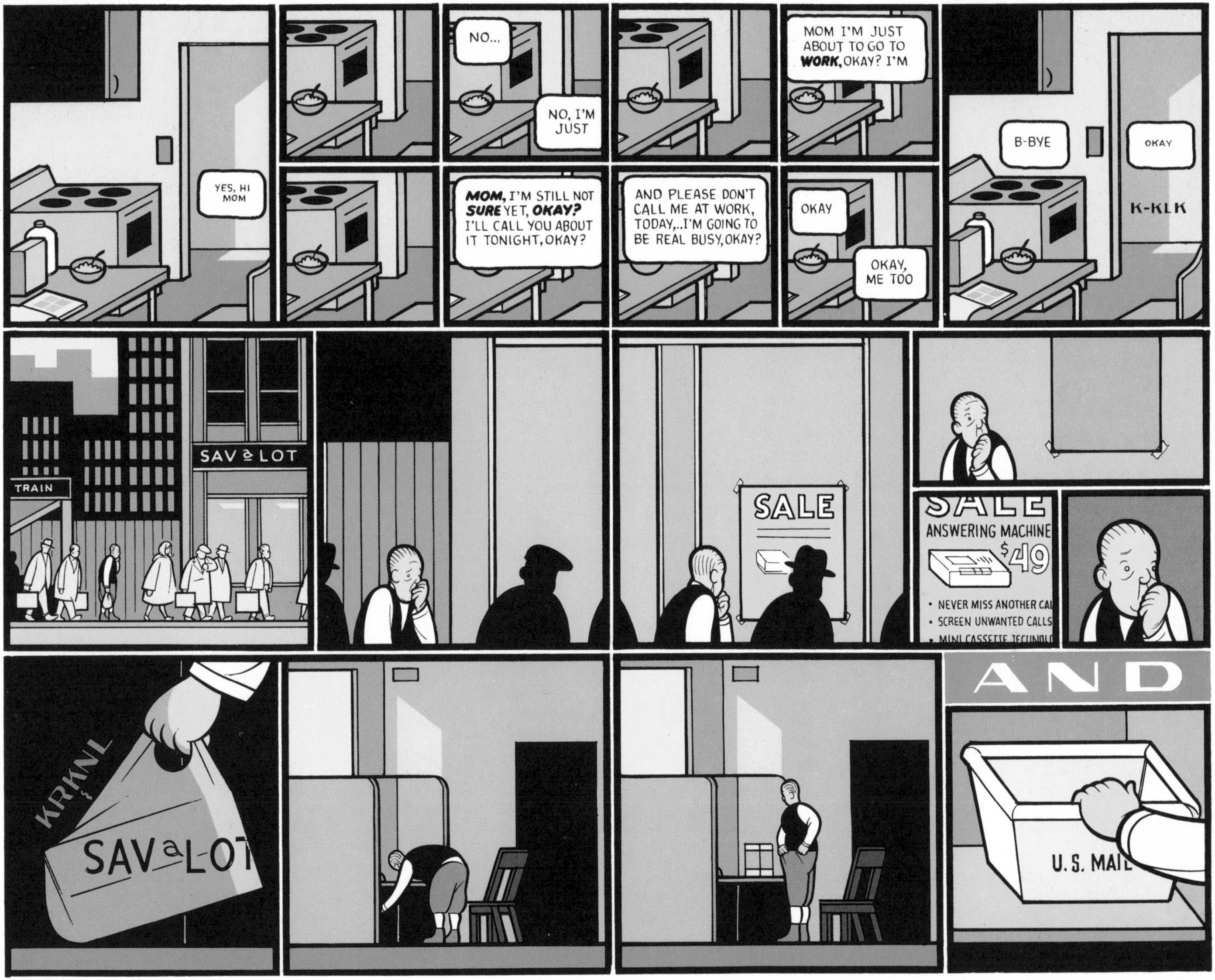
YES, HI MOM
NO...
NO, I'M JUST
MOM I'M JUST ABOUT TO GO TO WORK, OKAY? I'M
MOM, I'M STILL NOT SURE YET, OKAY? I'LL CALL YOU ABOUT IT TONIGHT, OKAY?
AND PLEASE DON'T CALL ME AT WORK, TODAY,..I'M GOING TO BE REAL BUSY, OKAY?
OKAY
OKAY, ME TOO
B-BYE
OKAY
K-KLK
SAV a LOT
TRAIN
SALE
SALE
ANSWERING MACHINE
$49
• NEVER MISS ANOTHER CAL
• SCREEN UNWANTED CALLS
KRKNL
SAV a LOT
AND
U.S. MAIL

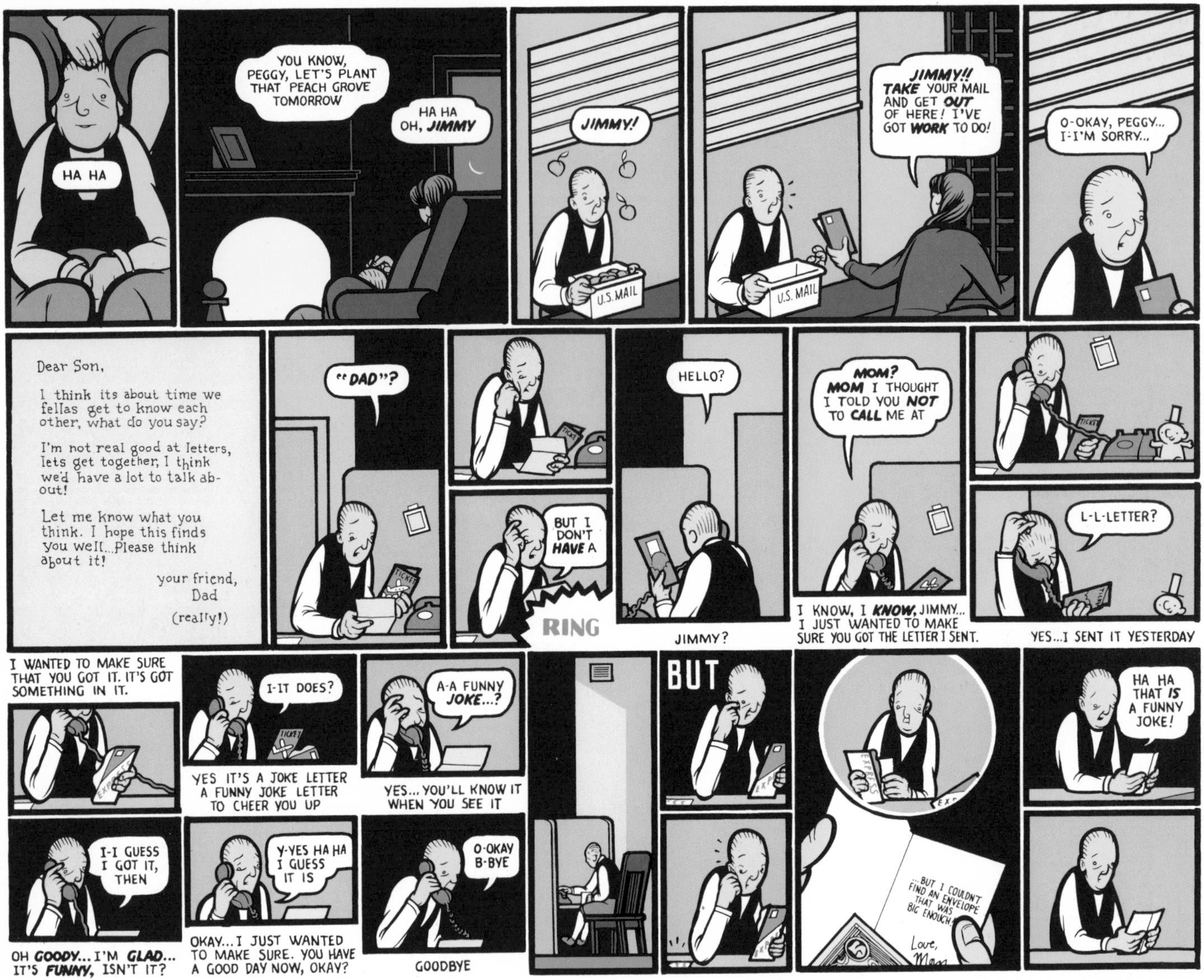
HA HA
YOU KNOW, PEGGY, LET'S PLANT THAT PEACH GROVE TOMORROW
HA HA OH, JIMMY
JIMMY!
JIMMY!! TAKE YOUR MAIL AND GET OUT OF HERE! I'VE GOT WORK TO DO!
U.S. MAIL
O-OKAY, PEGGY... I-I'M SORRY...
Dear Son,
I think its about time we fellas get to know each other, what do you say?
I'm not real good at letters, lets get together, I think we'd have a lot to talk about!
Let me know what you think. I hope this finds you well...Please think about it!
your friend, Dad
(really!)
"DAD"?
BUT I DON'T HAVE A
RING
HELLO?
JIMMY?
MOM? MOM I THOUGHT I TOLD YOU NOT TO CALL ME AT
I KNOW, I KNOW, JIMMY... I JUST WANTED TO MAKE SURE YOU GOT THE LETTER I SENT.
L-L-LETTER?
YES...I SENT IT YESTERDAY
I WANTED TO MAKE SURE THAT YOU GOT IT. IT'S GOT SOMETHING IN IT.
I-I GUESS I GOT IT, THEN
OH GOODY... I'M GLAD... IT'S FUNNY, ISN'T IT?
I-IT DOES?
YES IT'S A JOKE LETTER A FUNNY JOKE LETTER TO CHEER YOU UP
Y-YES HA HA I GUESS IT IS
OKAY... I JUST WANTED TO MAKE SURE. YOU HAVE A GOOD DAY NOW, OKAY?
A-A FUNNY JOKE...?
YES... YOU'LL KNOW IT WHEN YOU SEE IT
O-OKAY B-BYE
GOODBYE
BUT
...BUT I COULDN'T FIND AN ENVELOPE THAT WAS BIG ENOUGH!
Love, Mom
HA HA THAT IS A FUNNY JOKE!

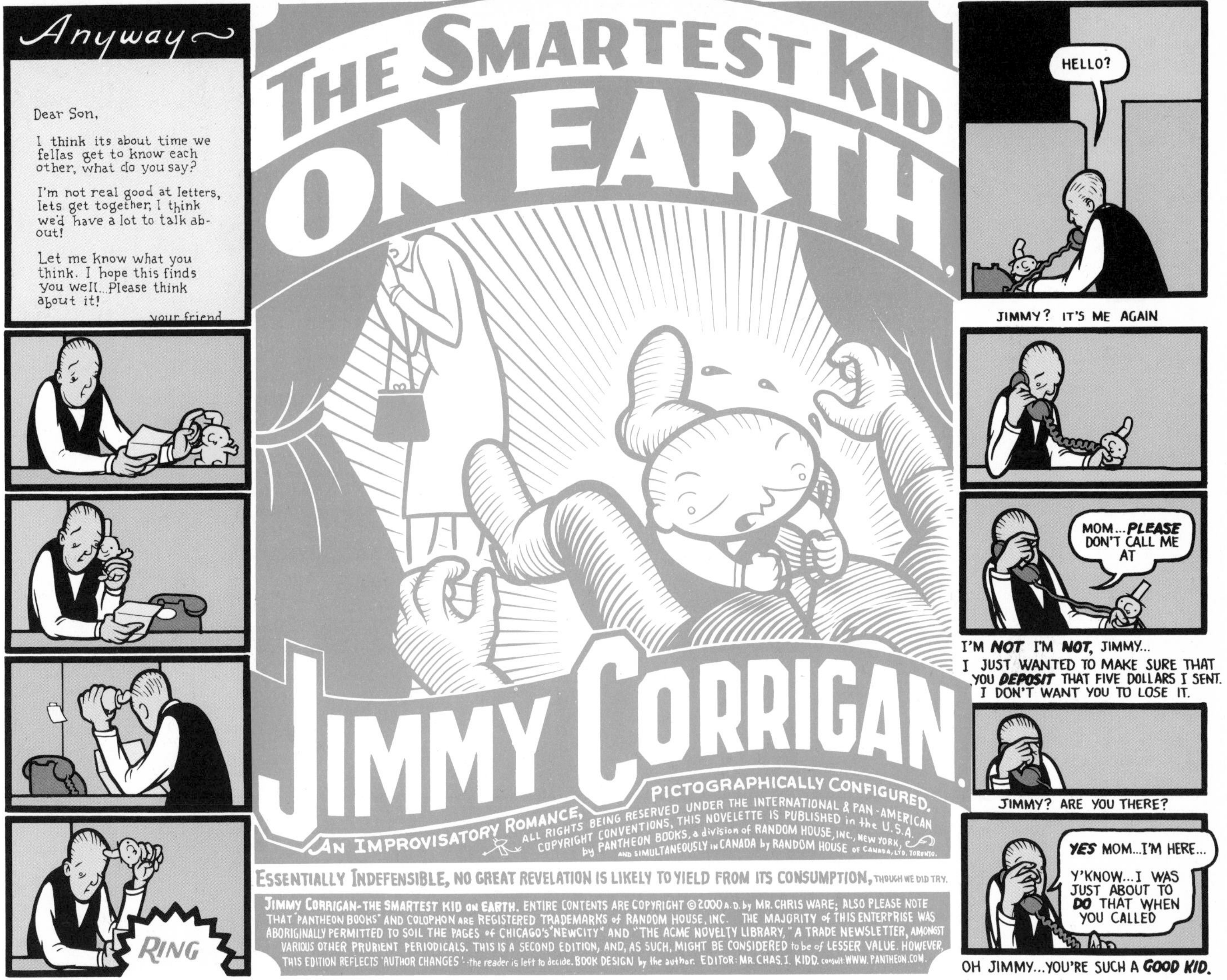
Anyway
Dear Son,
I think its about time we fellas get to know each other, what do you say?
I'm not real good at letters, lets get together, I think we'd have a lot to talk about!
Let me know what you think. I hope this finds you well...Please think about it!
your friend
RING
THE SMARTEST KID ON EARTH.
JIMMY CORRIGAN.
AN IMPROVISATORY ROMANCE, PICTOGRAPHICALLY CONFIGURED.
ALL RIGHTS BEING RESERVED UNDER THE INTERNATIONAL & PAN-AMERICAN COPYRIGHT CONVENTIONS, THIS NOVELETTE IS PUBLISHED in the U.S.A. by PANTHEON BOOKS, a division of RANDOM HOUSE, INC., NEW YORK, AND SIMULTANEOUSLY IN CANADA by RANDOM HOUSE OF CANADA, LTD. TORONTO.
ESSENTIALLY INDEFENSIBLE, NO GREAT REVELATION IS LIKELY TO YIELD FROM ITS CONSUMPTION, THOUGH WE DID TRY.
JIMMY CORRIGAN-THE SMARTEST KID ON EARTH. ENTIRE CONTENTS ARE COPYRIGHT © 2000 A.D. by MR. CHRIS WARE; ALSO PLEASE NOTE THAT "PANTHEON BOOKS" AND COLOPHON ARE REGISTERED TRADEMARKS of RANDOM HOUSE, INC. THE MAJORITY of THIS ENTERPRISE WAS ABORIGINALLY PERMITTED TO SOIL THE PAGES of CHICAGO'S "NEWCITY" AND "THE ACME NOVELTY LIBRARY," A TRADE NEWSLETTER, AMONGST VARIOUS OTHER PRURIENT PERIODICALS. THIS IS A SECOND EDITION, AND, AS SUCH, MIGHT BE CONSIDERED to be of LESSER VALUE. HOWEVER, THIS EDITION REFLECTS 'AUTHOR CHANGES'--the reader is left to decide. BOOK DESIGN by the author. EDITOR: MR. CHAS. I. KIDD. consult: WWW.PANTHEON.COM.
HELLO?
JIMMY? IT'S ME AGAIN
MOM...PLEASE DON'T CALL ME AT
I'M NOT I'M NOT, JIMMY... I JUST WANTED TO MAKE SURE THAT YOU DEPOSIT THAT FIVE DOLLARS I SENT. I DON'T WANT YOU TO LOSE IT.
JIMMY? ARE YOU THERE?
YES MOM...I'M HERE...
Y'KNOW...I WAS JUST ABOUT TO DO THAT WHEN YOU CALLED
OH JIMMY...YOU'RE SUCH A GOOD KID.

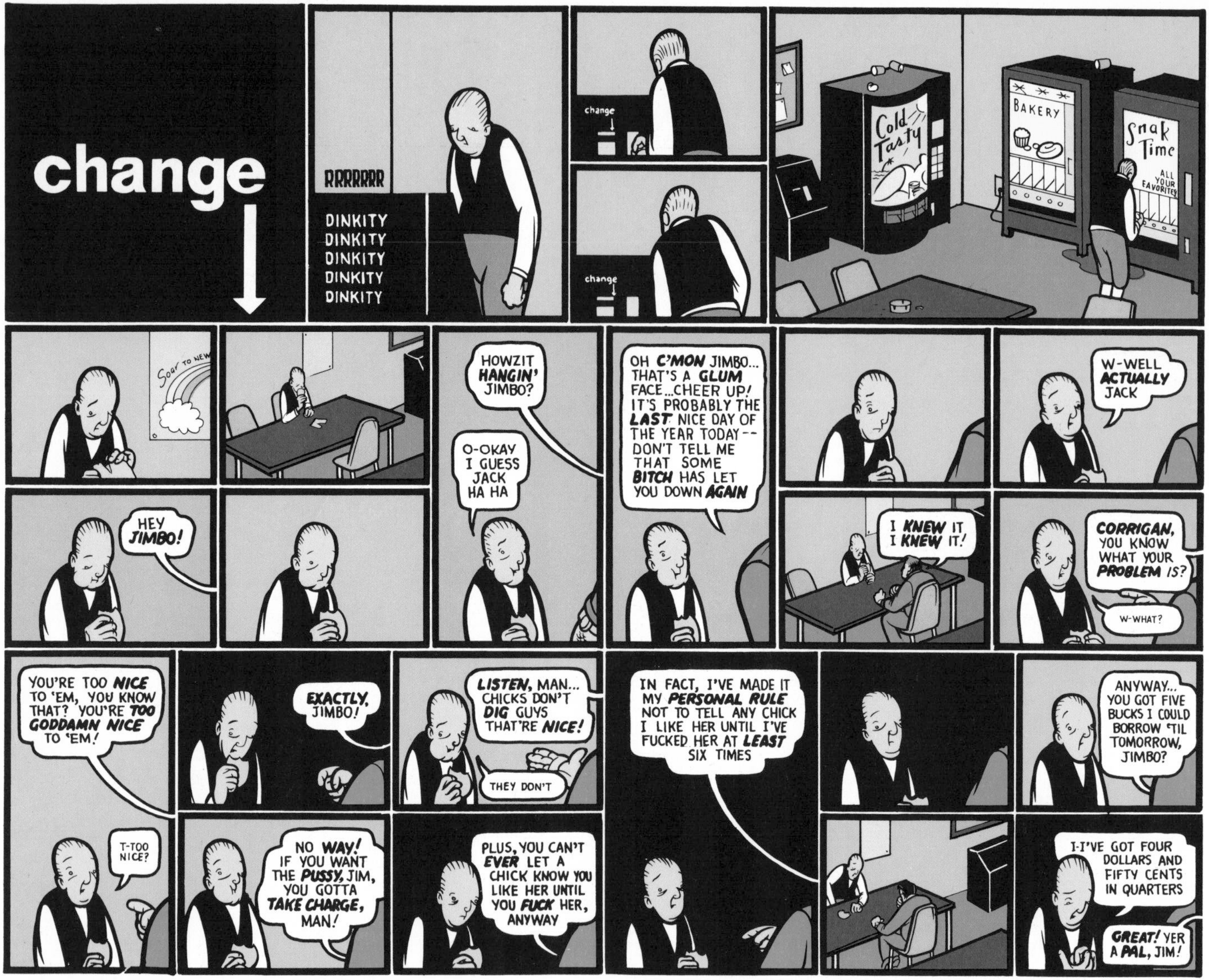

change
RRRRRRR
DINKITY
DINKITY
DINKITY
DINKITY
DINKITY
change
change
Cold Tasty
BAKERY
Snak Time
ALL YOUR FAVORITES
Soar TO NEW
HEY JIMBO!
HOWZIT HANGIN' JIMBO?
O-OKAY I GUESS JACK HA HA
OH C'MON JIMBO... THAT'S A GLUM FACE...CHEER UP! IT'S PROBABLY THE LAST NICE DAY OF THE YEAR TODAY-- DON'T TELL ME THAT SOME BITCH HAS LET YOU DOWN AGAIN
W-WELL ACTUALLY JACK
I KNEW IT I KNEW IT!
CORRIGAN, YOU KNOW WHAT YOUR PROBLEM IS?
W-WHAT?
YOU'RE TOO NICE TO 'EM, YOU KNOW THAT? YOU'RE TOO GODDAMN NICE TO 'EM!
T-TOO NICE?
EXACTLY, JIMBO!
NO WAY! IF YOU WANT THE PUSSY, JIM, YOU GOTTA TAKE CHARGE, MAN!
LISTEN, MAN... CHICKS DON'T DIG GUYS THAT'RE NICE!
THEY DON'T
PLUS, YOU CAN'T EVER LET A CHICK KNOW YOU LIKE HER UNTIL YOU FUCK HER, ANYWAY
IN FACT, I'VE MADE IT MY PERSONAL RULE NOT TO TELL ANY CHICK I LIKE HER UNTIL I'VE FUCKED HER AT LEAST SIX TIMES
ANYWAY... YOU GOT FIVE BUCKS I COULD BORROW 'TIL TOMORROW, JIMBO?
I-I'VE GOT FOUR DOLLARS AND FIFTY CENTS IN QUARTERS
GREAT! YER A PAL, JIM!

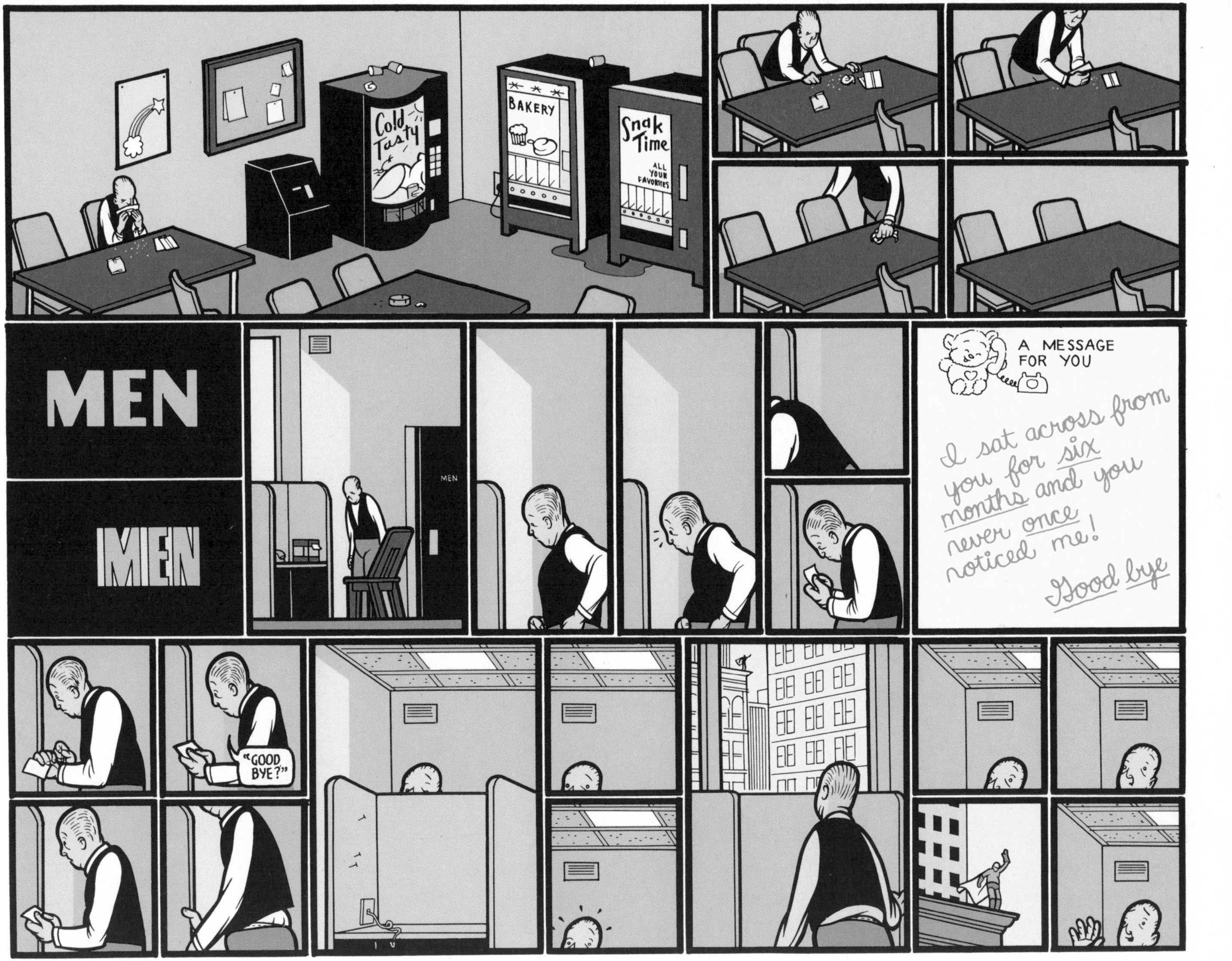
Cold Tasty
BAKERY
Snak Time
ALL YOUR FAVORITES
MEN
MEN
MEN
A MESSAGE FOR YOU
I sat across from you for six months and you never once noticed me!
Good bye
"GOOD BYE?"

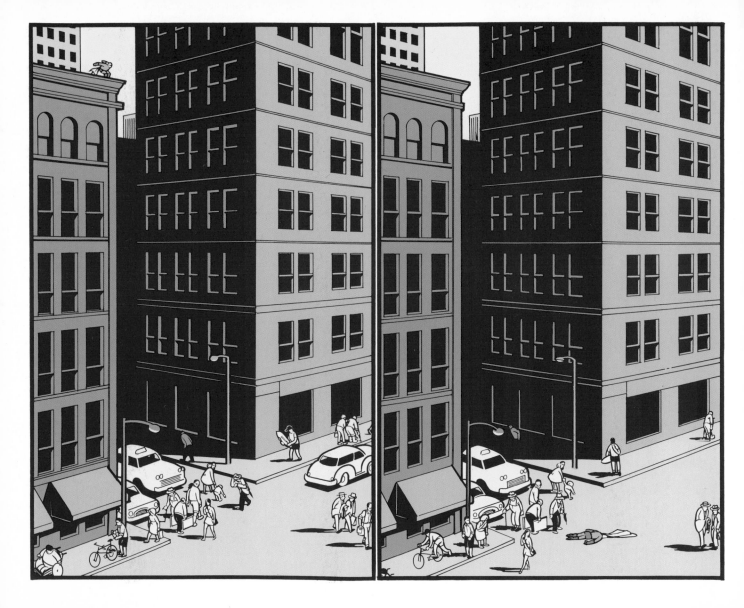

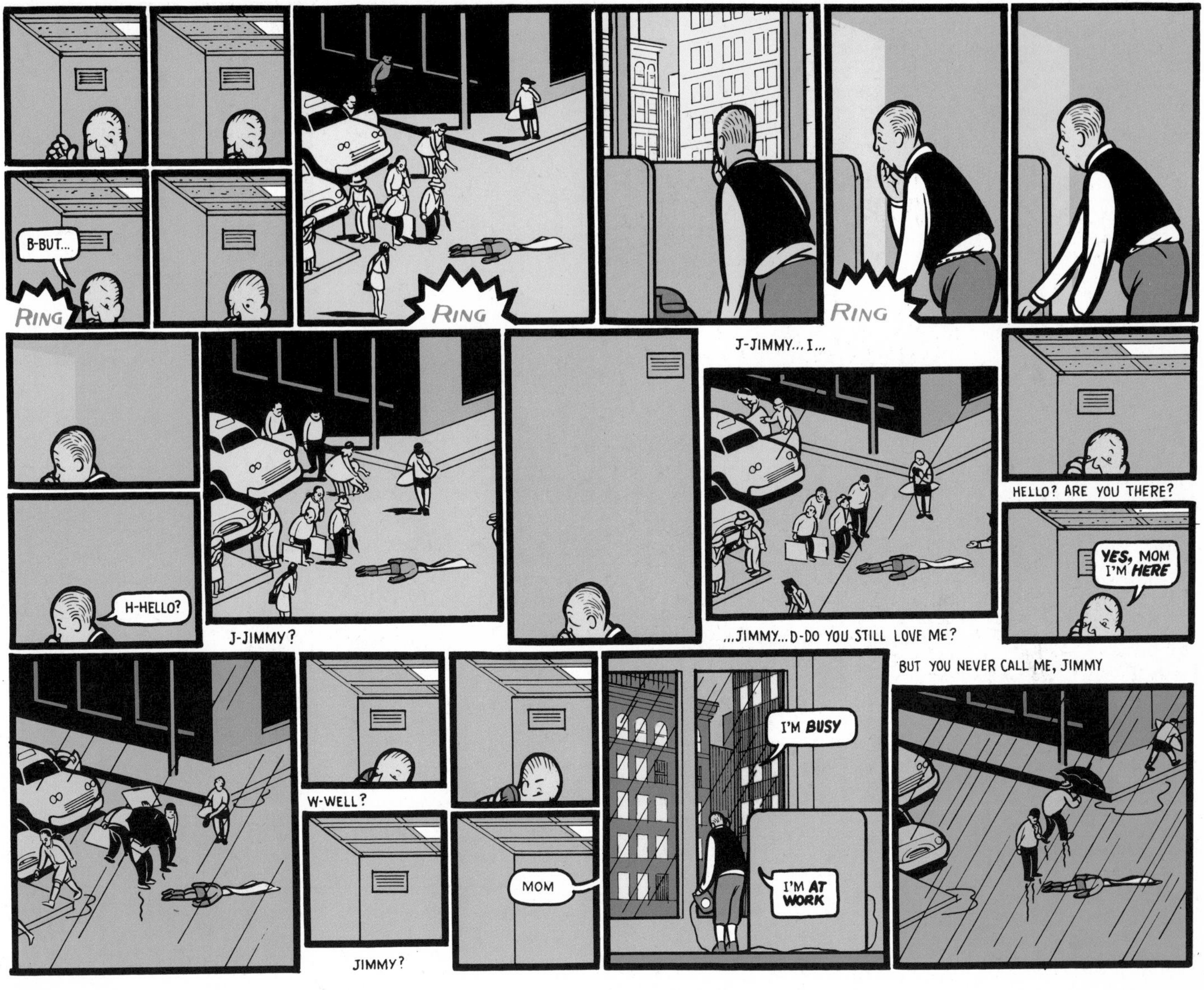
B-BUT...
RING
RING
RING
H-HELLO?
J-JIMMY?
J-JIMMY... I...
...JIMMY... D-DO YOU STILL LOVE ME?
HELLO? ARE YOU THERE?
YES, MOM I'M HERE
W-WELL?
JIMMY?
MOM
I'M BUSY
I'M AT WORK
BUT YOU NEVER CALL ME, JIMMY

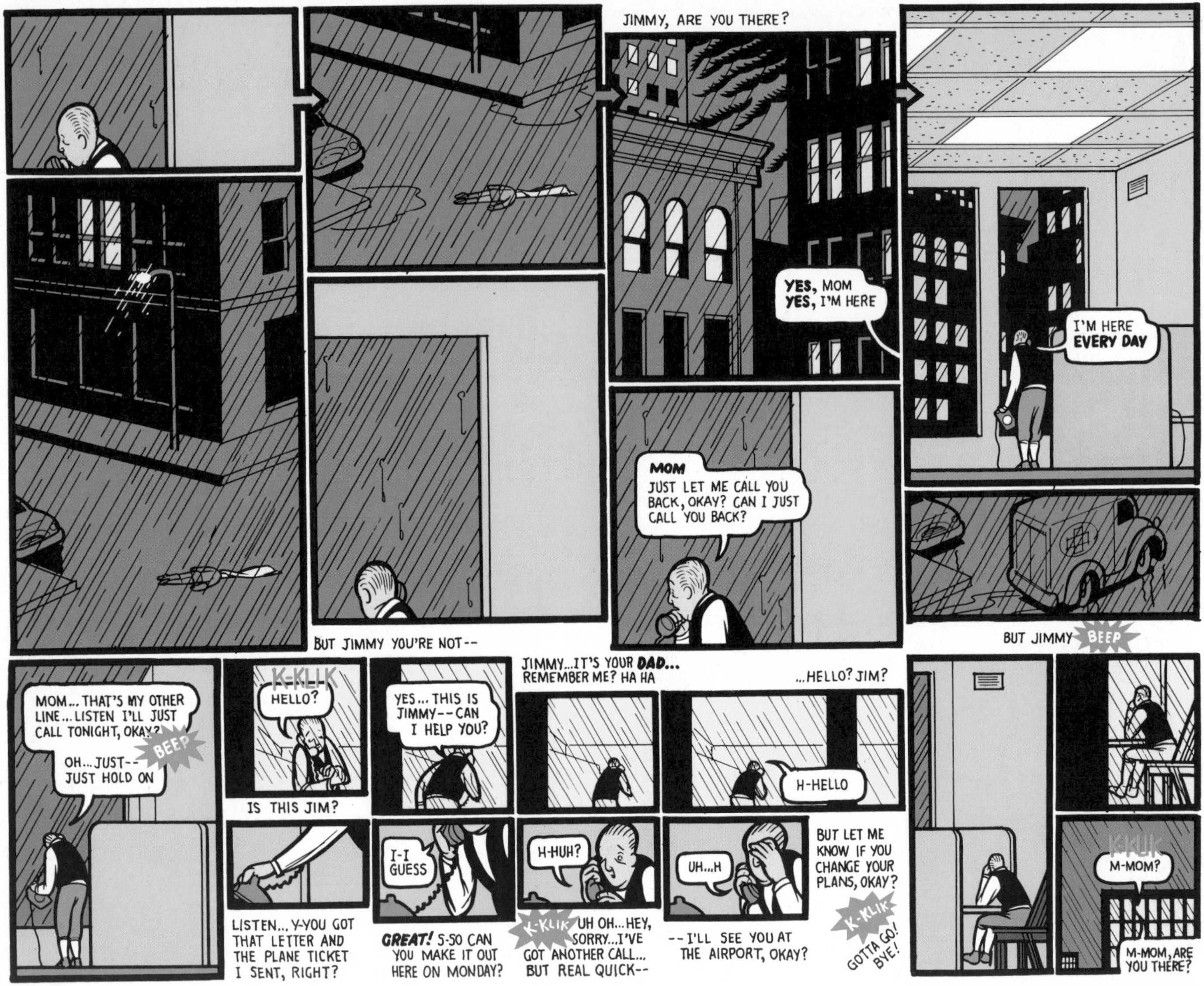

JIMMY, ARE YOU THERE?
YES, MOM
YES, I'M HERE
I'M HERE EVERY DAY
MOM
JUST LET ME CALL YOU BACK, OKAY? CAN I JUST CALL YOU BACK?
BUT JIMMY YOU'RE NOT--
BUT JIMMY
BEEP
MOM... THAT'S MY OTHER LINE... LISTEN I'LL JUST CALL TONIGHT, OKAY?
BEEP
OH... JUST-- JUST HOLD ON
K-KLIK
HELLO?
IS THIS JIM?
YES... THIS IS JIMMY-- CAN I HELP YOU?
JIMMY...IT'S YOUR DAD... REMEMBER ME? HA HA
...HELLO? JIM?
H-HELLO
LISTEN... Y-YOU GOT THAT LETTER AND THE PLANE TICKET I SENT, RIGHT?
I-I GUESS
GREAT! S-SO CAN YOU MAKE IT OUT HERE ON MONDAY?
H-HUH?
K-KLIK
UH OH... HEY, SORRY...I'VE GOT ANOTHER CALL... BUT REAL QUICK--
UH...H
-- I'LL SEE YOU AT THE AIRPORT, OKAY?
BUT LET ME KNOW IF YOU CHANGE YOUR PLANS, OKAY?
K-KLIK
GOTTA GO! BYE!
K-KLIK
M-MOM?
M-MOM, ARE YOU THERE?

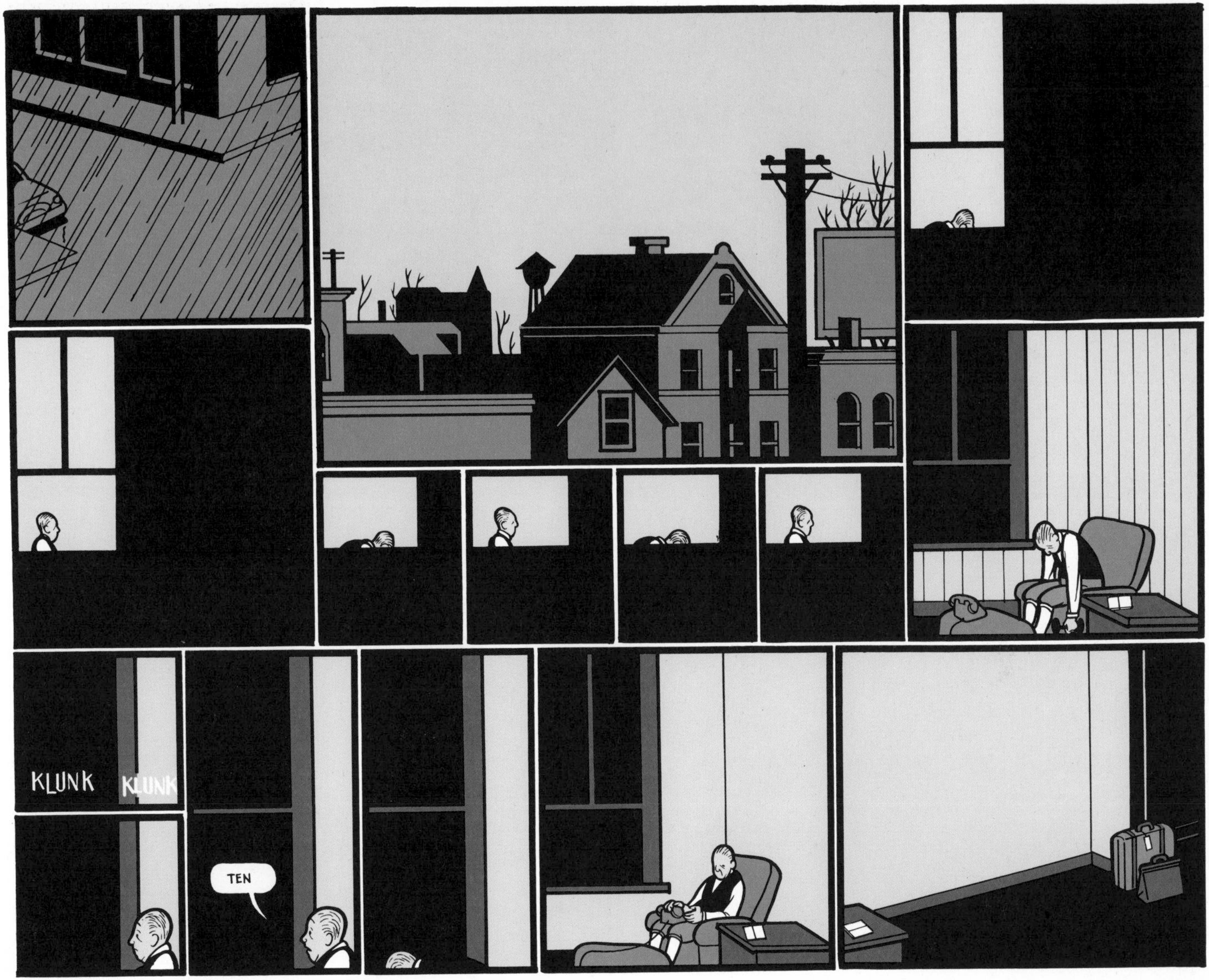

KLUNK
KLUNK
TEN

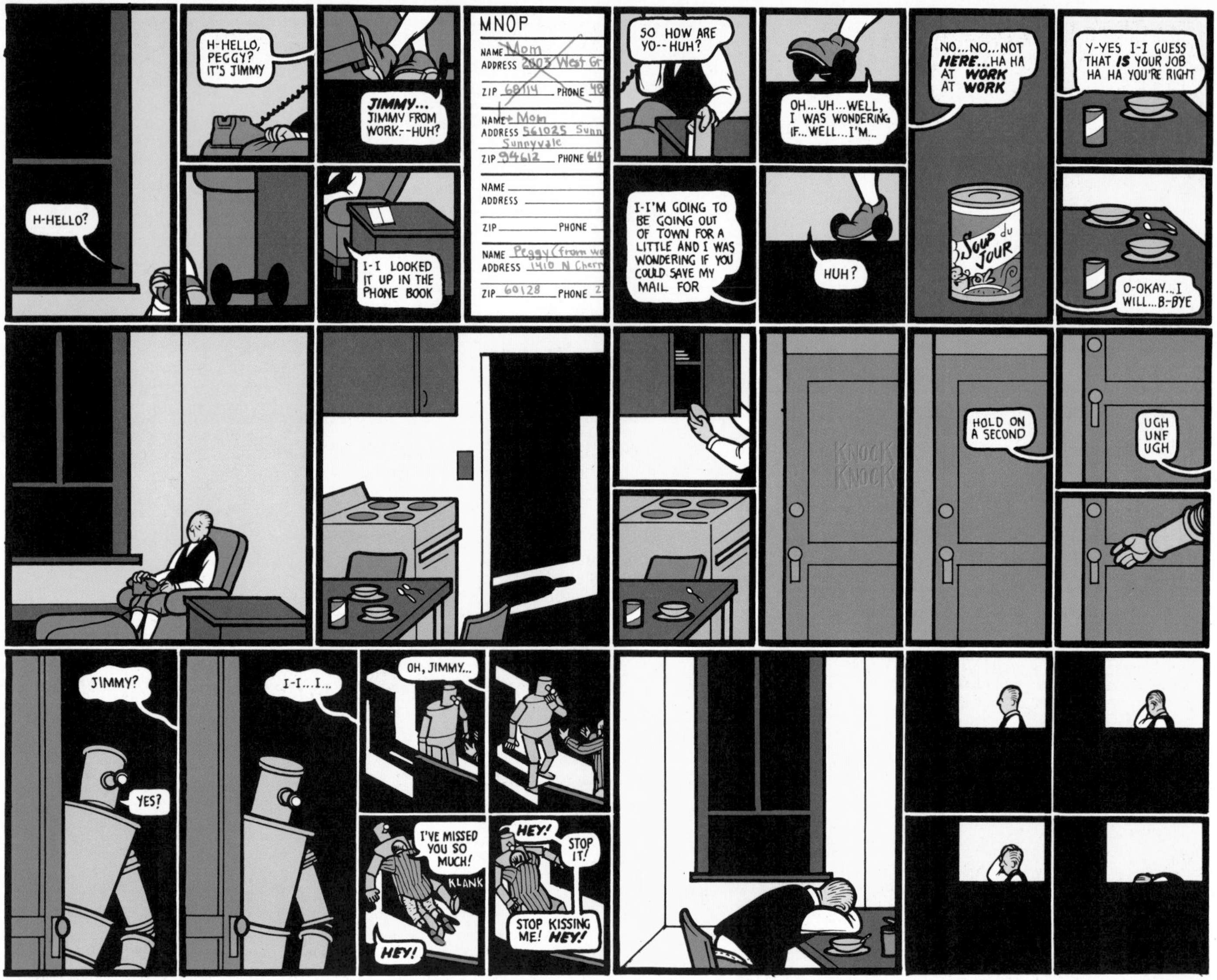
H-HELLO?
H-HELLO, PEGGY? IT'S JIMMY
JIMMY... JIMMY FROM WORK.--HUH?
I-I LOOKED IT UP IN THE PHONE BOOK
MNOP
NAME Mom
ADDRESS 2003 West Gr
ZIP 68114 PHONE
NAME Mom
ADDRESS 561025 Sunn
Sunnyvale
ZIP 94612 PHONE
NAME
ADDRESS
ZIP PHONE
NAME Peggy (from wo
ADDRESS 1410 N Cherr
ZIP 60128 PHONE
SO HOW ARE YO--HUH?
I-I'M GOING TO BE GOING OUT OF TOWN FOR A LITTLE AND I WAS WONDERING IF YOU COULD SAVE MY MAIL FOR
OH...UH...WELL, I WAS WONDERING IF...WELL...I'M...
HUH?
NO...NO...NOT HERE...HA HA AT WORK AT WORK
Soup du Jour
Y-YES I-I GUESS THAT IS YOUR JOB HA HA YOU'RE RIGHT
O-OKAY...I WILL...B-BYE
KNOCK KNOCK
HOLD ON A SECOND
UGH UNF UGH
JIMMY?
YES?
I-I...I...
OH, JIMMY...
I'VE MISSED YOU SO MUCH!
KLANK
HEY!
HEY!
STOP IT!
STOP KISSING ME! HEY!

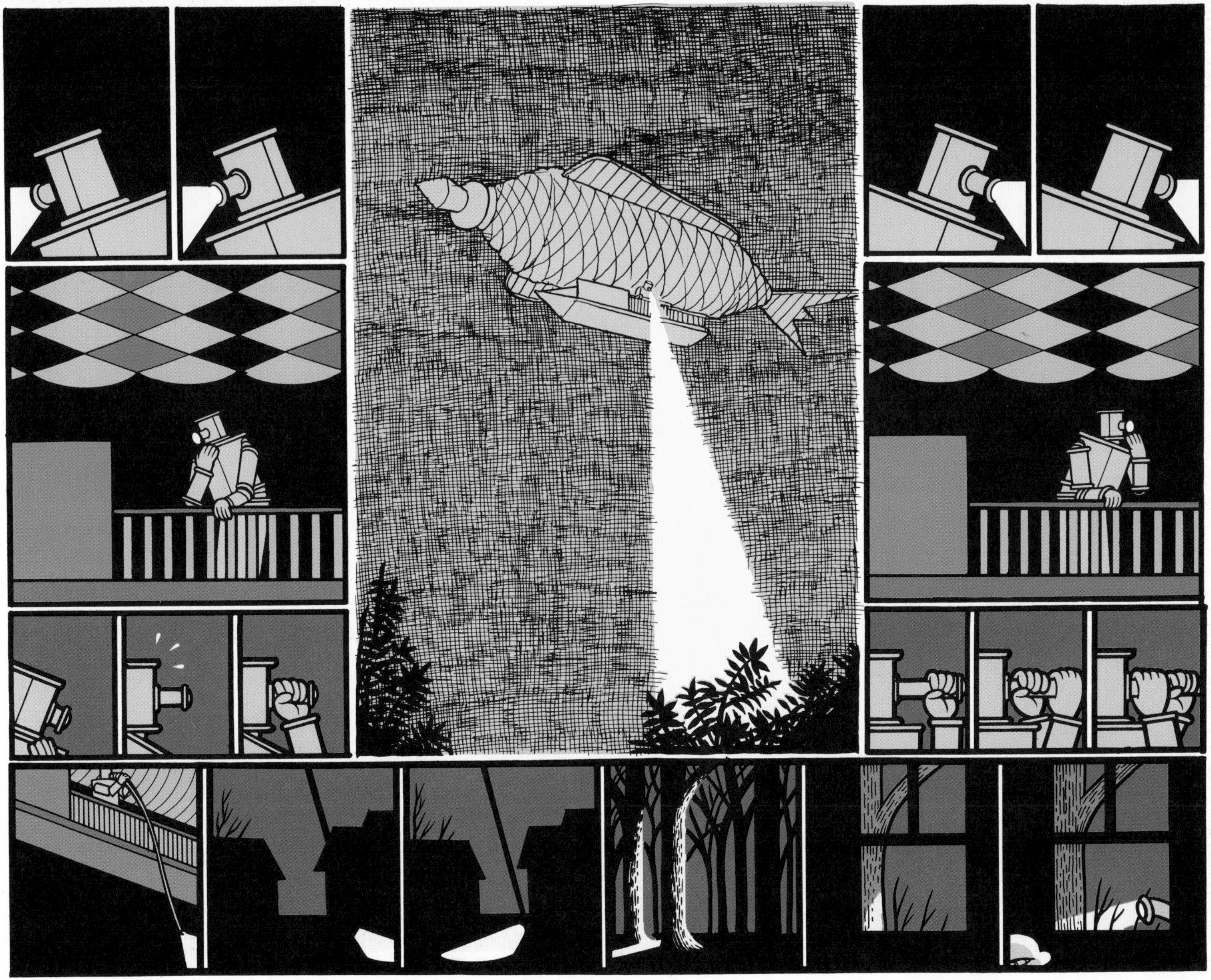

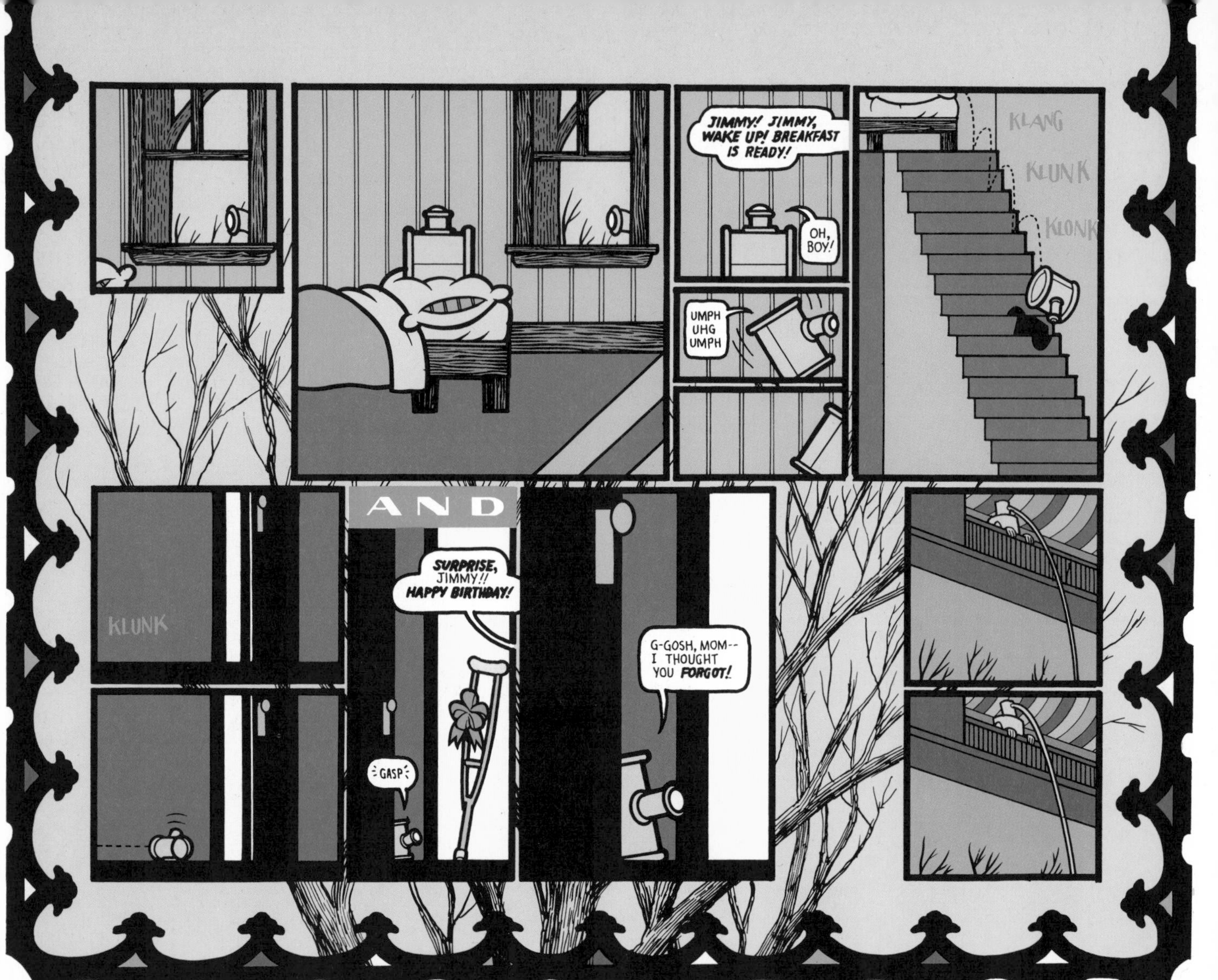
JIMMY! JIMMY, WAKE UP! BREAKFAST IS READY!
OH, BOY!
UMPH UHG UMPH
KLANG
KLUNK
KLONK
KLUNK
AND
SURPRISE, JIMMY!! HAPPY BIRTHDAY!
GASP
G-GOSH, MOM-- I THOUGHT YOU FORGOT!

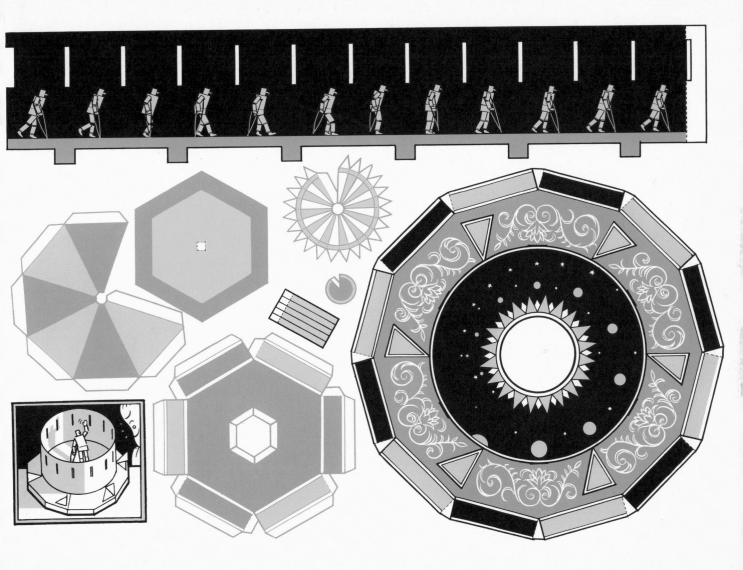

MEMORIZE ALL INSTRUCTIONS BEFORE WAKING UP THE PIECES ON OTHER SIDE.

● WELL HERE'S A FUN THING WHICH IS SURE TO APPEAL TO THE YOUNG BOY, GIRL, OR AIRSHIP PASSENGER IN ALL OF US. IT BEGS ONLY A SMALL AMOUNT OF EFFORT TO CONSTRUCT, AND THE ATTENTIVE STUDENT WILL BE REWARDED WITH A CONVINCING MODEL OF LIFE IN WHICH HE OR SHE MAY FIND SOME POETIC SYMPATHY. ALL THAT IS REQUIRED IS A SHARP HOBBY KNIFE, A METAL STRAIGHT EDGE, COMMON HORSE GLUE, AND THE SORT OF FREE LEISURE TIME THAT AIRPLANE PASSENGERS COMMONLY ENJOY. AS ALWAYS, GREAT PATIENCE AND A CLEAN WORK AREA ARE REQUIRED FOR FULFILLMENT OF THIS DIVERSION, AND IT SHOULD NOT BE ATTEMPTED IF EITHER ARE COMPROMISED.

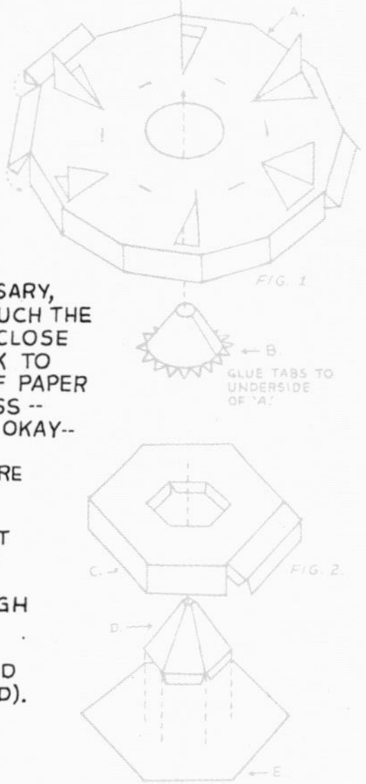
A.
FIG. 1
B
GLUE TABS TO UNDERSIDE OF 'A'.
C.
FIG. 2.
D.
E.

● GENERAL GUIDELINES - CUT OUT ALL PIECES ALONG HEAVY BLACK LINES, AND USE A BLUNT OBJECT SUCH AS THE SEAT POCKET CARD TO SCORE ALONG ALL FOLDS. DON'T USE ANY MORE GLUE THAN IS ABSOLUTELY NECESSARY, AND KEEP YOUR HANDS AND CLOTHING CLEAN. DON'T TOUCH THE PERSON NEXT TO YOU, OR YOURSELF, OR MOM. *NO!* PAY CLOSE ATTENTION TO THE WOMAN'S INSTRUCTIONING -- BACK TO BUSINESS. CLASS PASSENGERS -- CUT OUT -- CUT OUT OF PAPER LIKE BEFORE. *COME ON!* BACK TO BUSINESS. FIRST CLASS -- TELL YOU WHAT TO DO, AND HOW TO DO IT. THANK YOU. OKAY -- BACK TO BUCKLING PAPER -- IT BUCKLES WITH GLUE AND SO NOW YOU CAN START AND CONCENTRATE, FINALLY. WHERE WAS IT? YES! NOW...NOW:

1. *FIG 1.* ASSEMBLE THE WHEEL FUNDAMENT (A). CUT OUT CENTER CIRCLE, AND FOLD UP ALL SIX FLAG TABS WHICH CIRCLE IT. FOLD DOWN AND GLUE ALL TWELVE SIDES.
2. CURL UP AND GLUE CENTER CONE (B) AND AFFIX THROUGH BOTTOM OF WHEEL FUNDAMENT.

3. *FIG. 2.* FOLD UP BASE TOP (C). GLUE ALL SIX SIDES, AND FOLD DOWN CENTER TABS. ASSEMBLE SUPPORT CONE (D). GLUE SUPPORT CONE UP THROUGH BASE TOP, AFFIXING TABS TO EDGES OF CONE. GLUE THIS ASSEMBLY TO BASE (E). LET DRY AGAIN.

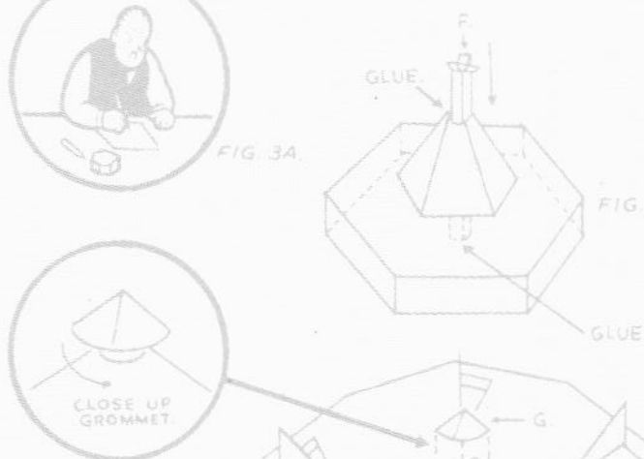
FIG. 3A.
F.
GLUE.
FIG. 3.
GLUE.
CLOSE UP GROMMET

4. *FIG. 3.* GLUE FOUR-SIDED SUPPORT ROD (F) TOGETHER. INSURE THAT IT INSERTS CLEANLY INTO THE SUPPORT CONE. IF NOT, SLIGHTLY ENLARGE THE OPENING OF THE CONE WITH A PENCIL.
5. PUT GLUE ON THE END OF THE SUPPORT ROD AND INSERT IT INTO THE SUPPORT CONE AS STRAIGHT AS POSSIBLE SO THAT IT SLIDES INTO THE BASE.
6. ADD GLUE WHERE THE ROD ENTERS THE CONE; ABOUT 1/8" SHOULD PROTRUDE FROM THE TOP. IF NOT, REMOVE, MAKE AN APPROPRIATELY-SIZED REPLACEMENT OUT OF SCRAP PAPER, AND WRITE AN ANGRY LETTER TO THE FATHER. *(FIG. 3A.)* LET DRY THOROUGHLY. DEAR DAD. STOP!

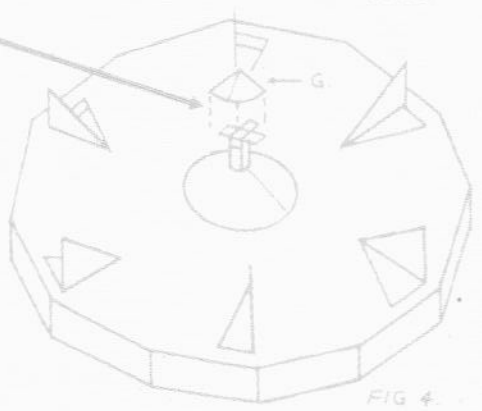
G.
FIG. 4.

7. *FIG. 4.* CURL UP AND GLUE GROMMET CONE (G). GINGERLY GLUE TO SUPPORT ROD TABS, TAKING CARE NOT TO SPREAD GLUE ANYWHERE ELSE SO THAT THE WHEEL FUNDAMENT MOVES FREELY. LET DRY FOR ONE FULL WEEK TO THE LETTER.

8. ONCE DRY, TEST BY HOLDING BASE IN HAND AND BLOWING AGAINST DAD. DEAR DAD. I DON'T EVEN KNOW DAD. DON'T KNOW, DON'T KNOW, DON'T KNOW. DON'T KNOW IF HE HATES ME -- DON'T WANT ME? AM I DONE NOW? DON'T KNOW!

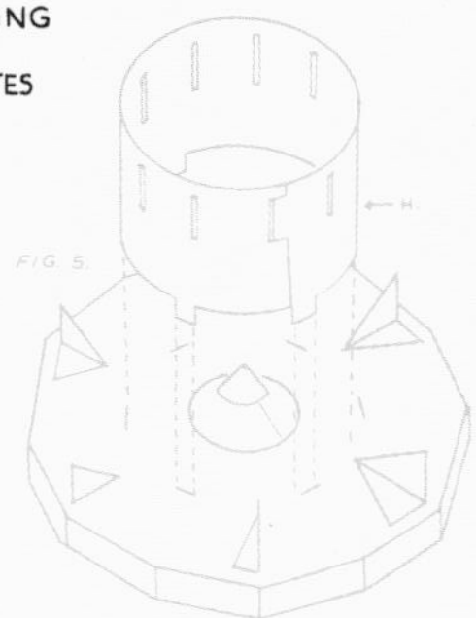
H.
FIG. 5.

9. NO -- NOW I KNOW... REMEMBER ALL ALONG NOW! DUMB -- RIGHT THERE ALL ALONG -- GET ALONG -- GET ALONG LITTLE DOGGIES, GET ALONG! HAW!

10. HAW! PAW I GET ALONG, PAW! IN THE PAW PAW PATCH, PAW. PLAYIN IN THE PAW PAW PATCH WITH PAW. DON'T -- HAW! GET ALONG PAW! TIME FOR DINNER -- *SUPPER.* ← WHAT THEY SAY, PAW ... SAY AMEN -- A-MEN, PAW!

AMEN! AY-MEN. PAW? AMEN! AY-**MEN**

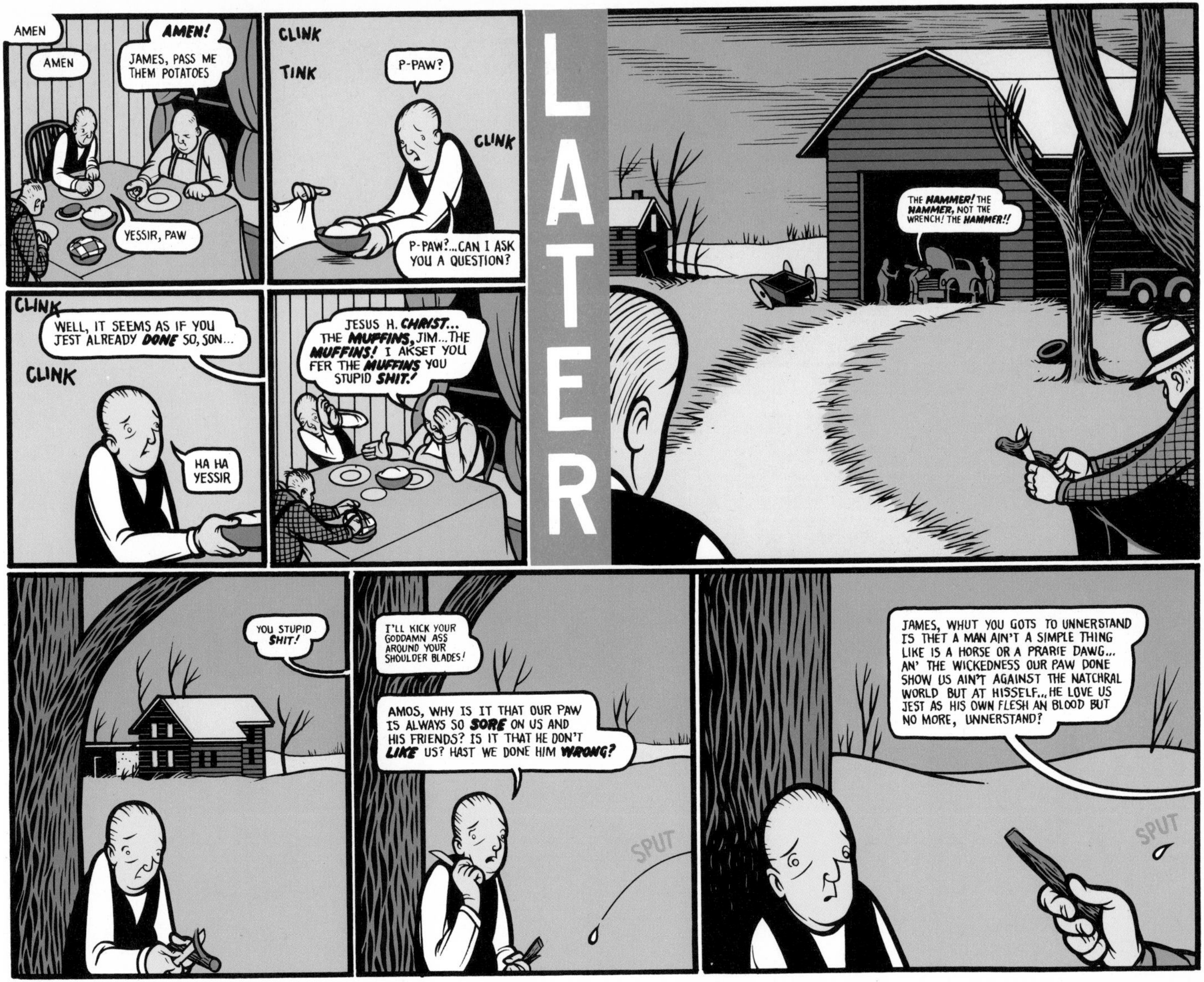
AMEN
AMEN
AMEN!
JAMES, PASS ME THEM POTATOES
YESSIR, PAW
CLINK
TINK
P-PAW?
CLINK
P-PAW?...CAN I ASK YOU A QUESTION?
CLINK
WELL, IT SEEMS AS IF YOU JEST ALREADY DONE SO, SON...
CLINK
HA HA YESSIR
JESUS H. CHRIST... THE MUFFINS, JIM... THE MUFFINS! I AKSET YOU FER THE MUFFINS YOU STUPID SHIT!
LATER
THE HAMMER! THE HAMMER, NOT THE WRENCH! THE HAMMER!!
YOU STUPID SHIT!
I'LL KICK YOUR GODDAMN ASS AROUND YOUR SHOULDER BLADES!
AMOS, WHY IS IT THAT OUR PAW IS ALWAYS SO SORE ON US AND HIS FRIENDS? IS IT THAT HE DON'T LIKE US? HAST WE DONE HIM WRONG?
SPUT
JAMES, WHUT YOU GOTS TO UNNERSTAND IS THET A MAN AIN'T A SIMPLE THING LIKE IS A HORSE OR A PRARIE DAWG... AN' THE WICKEDNESS OUR PAW DONE SHOW US AIN'T AGAINST THE NATCHRAL WORLD BUT AT HISSELF... HE LOVE US JEST AS HIS OWN FLESH AN BLOOD BUT NO MORE, UNNERSTAND?
SPUT

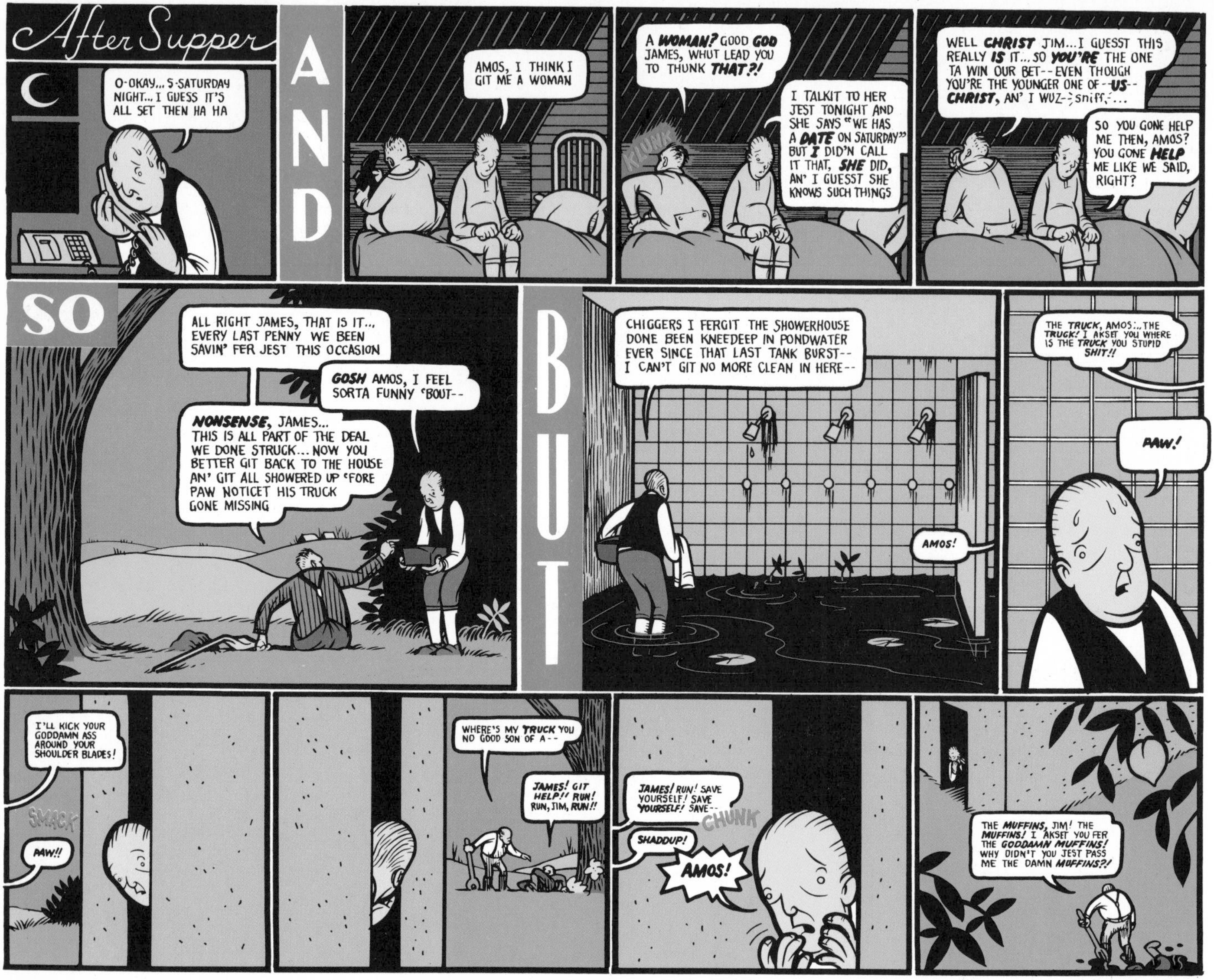
After Supper
O-OKAY... S-SATURDAY NIGHT... I GUESS IT'S ALL SET THEN HA HA
AND
AMOS, I THINK I GIT ME A WOMAN
KLUNK
A WOMAN? GOOD GOD JAMES, WHUT LEAD YOU TO THUNK THAT?!
I TALKIT TO HER JEST TONIGHT AND SHE SAYS "WE HAS A DATE ON SATURDAY" BUT I DID'N CALL IT THAT, SHE DID, AN' I GUESST SHE KNOWS SUCH THINGS
WELL CHRIST JIM... I GUESST THIS REALLY IS IT... SO YOU'RE THE ONE TA WIN OUR BET-- EVEN THOUGH YOU'RE THE YOUNGER ONE OF --US-- CHRIST, AN' I WUZ-- sniff...
SO YOU GONE HELP ME THEN, AMOS? YOU GONE HELP ME LIKE WE SAID, RIGHT?
SO
ALL RIGHT JAMES, THAT IS IT... EVERY LAST PENNY WE BEEN SAVIN' FER JEST THIS OCCASION
GOSH AMOS, I FEEL SORTA FUNNY 'BOUT--
NONSENSE, JAMES... THIS IS ALL PART OF THE DEAL WE DONE STRUCK... NOW YOU BETTER GIT BACK TO THE HOUSE AN' GIT ALL SHOWERED UP 'FORE PAW NOTICET HIS TRUCK GONE MISSING
BUT
CHIGGERS I FERGIT THE SHOWERHOUSE DONE BEEN KNEEDEEP IN PONDWATER EVER SINCE THAT LAST TANK BURST-- I CAN'T GIT NO MORE CLEAN IN HERE--
AMOS!
THE TRUCK, AMOS:.. THE TRUCK! I AKSET YOU WHERE IS THE TRUCK YOU STUPID SHIT!!
PAW!
I'LL KICK YOUR GODDAMN ASS AROUND YOUR SHOULDER BLADES!
SMACK
PAW!!
WHERE'S MY TRUCK YOU NO GOOD SON OF A--
JAMES! GIT HELP!! RUN! RUN, JIM, RUN!!
JAMES! RUN! SAVE YOURSELF! SAVE YOURSELF! SAVE--
CHUNK
SHADDUP!
AMOS!
THE MUFFINS, JIM! THE MUFFINS! I AKSET YOU FER THE GODDAMN MUFFINS! WHY DIDN'T YOU JEST PASS ME THE DAMN MUFFINS?!

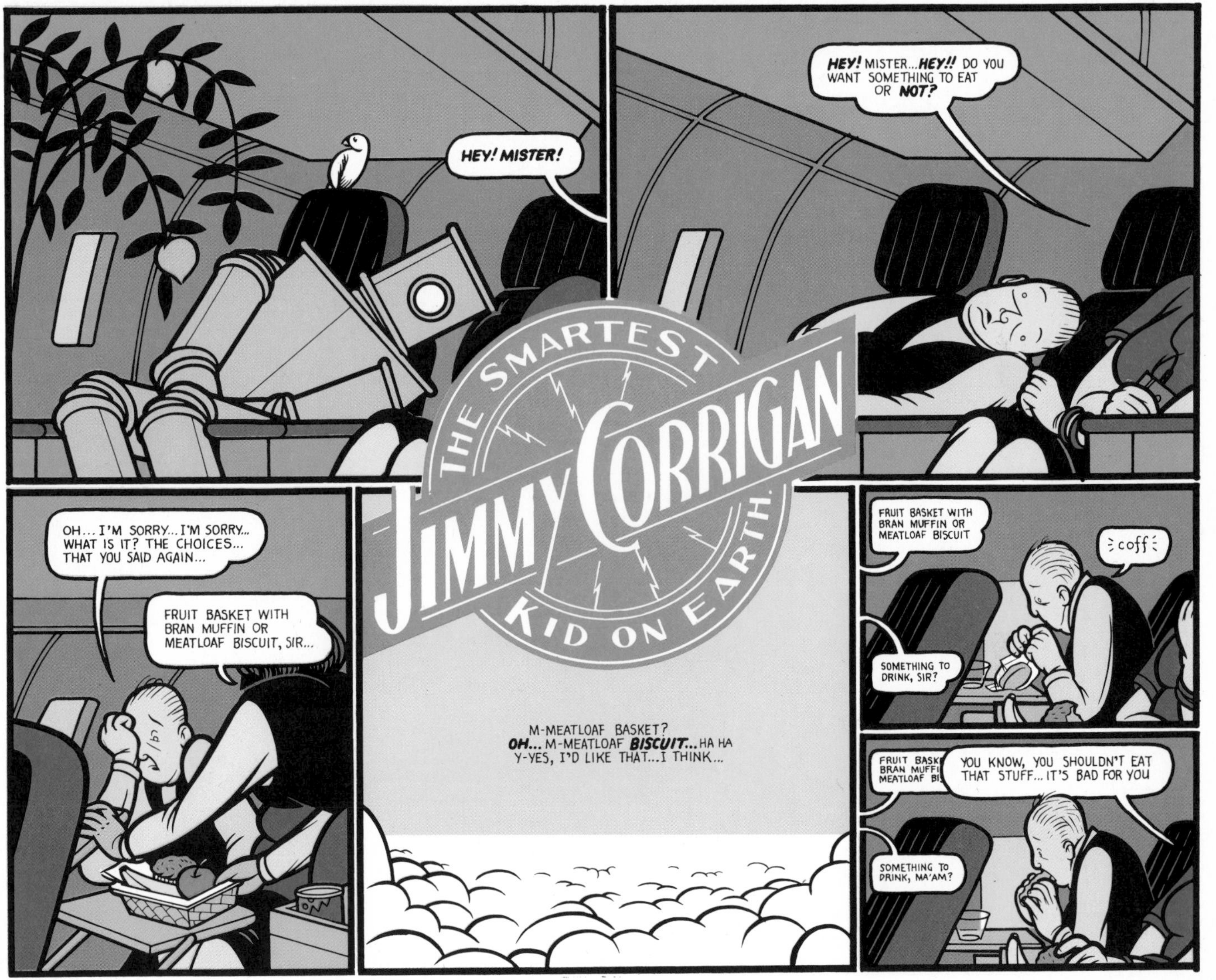
HEY! MISTER!
HEY! MISTER...HEY!! DO YOU WANT SOMETHING TO EAT OR NOT?
THE SMARTEST KID ON EARTH
JIMMY CORRIGAN
OH... I'M SORRY... I'M SORRY... WHAT IS IT? THE CHOICES... THAT YOU SAID AGAIN...
FRUIT BASKET WITH BRAN MUFFIN OR MEATLOAF BISCUIT, SIR...
M-MEATLOAF BASKET?
OH... M-MEATLOAF BISCUIT... HA HA
Y-YES, I'D LIKE THAT... I THINK...
FRUIT BASKET WITH BRAN MUFFIN OR MEATLOAF BISCUIT
coff
SOMETHING TO DRINK, SIR?
YOU KNOW, YOU SHOULDN'T EAT THAT STUFF... IT'S BAD FOR YOU
SOMETHING TO DRINK, MA'AM?

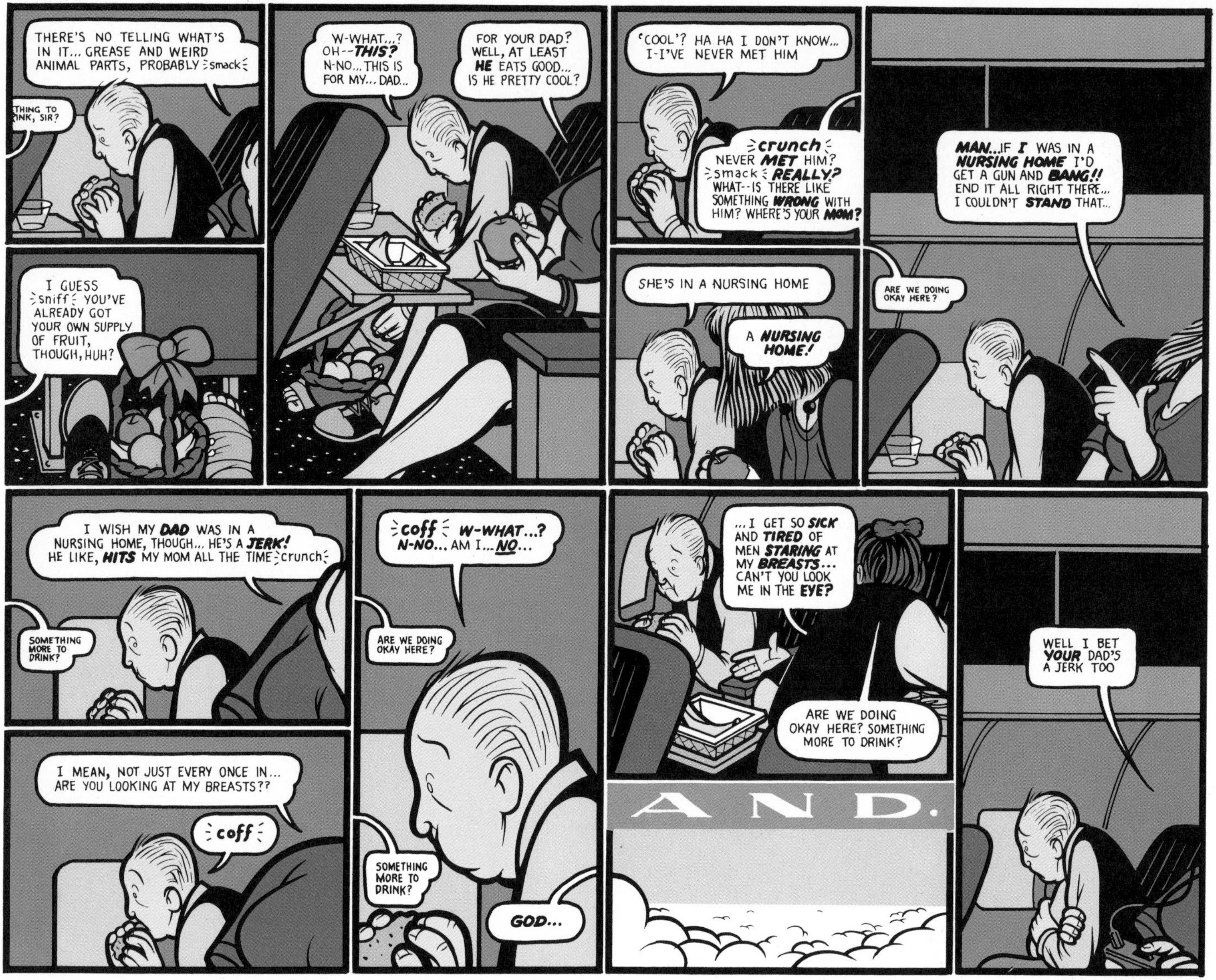
THERE'S NO TELLING WHAT'S IN IT... GREASE AND WEIRD ANIMAL PARTS, PROBABLY smack
THING TO INK, SIR?
W-WHAT...? OH--THIS? N-NO... THIS IS FOR MY... DAD...
FOR YOUR DAD? WELL, AT LEAST HE EATS GOOD... IS HE PRETTY COOL?
'COOL'? HA HA I DON'T KNOW... I-I'VE NEVER MET HIM
crunch NEVER MET HIM? smack REALLY? WHAT--IS THERE LIKE SOMETHING WRONG WITH HIM? WHERE'S YOUR MOM?
MAN...IF I WAS IN A NURSING HOME I'D GET A GUN AND BANG!! END IT ALL RIGHT THERE... I COULDN'T STAND THAT...
I GUESS sniff YOU'VE ALREADY GOT YOUR OWN SUPPLY OF FRUIT, THOUGH, HUH?
SHE'S IN A NURSING HOME
A NURSING HOME!
ARE WE DOING OKAY HERE?
I WISH MY DAD WAS IN A NURSING HOME, THOUGH... HE'S A JERK! HE LIKE, HITS MY MOM ALL THE TIME crunch
SOMETHING MORE TO DRINK?
I MEAN, NOT JUST EVERY ONCE IN... ARE YOU LOOKING AT MY BREASTS??
coff
coff W-WHAT...? N-NO... AM I... NO...
ARE WE DOING OKAY HERE?
SOMETHING MORE TO DRINK?
GOD...
...I GET SO SICK AND TIRED OF MEN STARING AT MY BREASTS... CAN'T YOU LOOK ME IN THE EYE?
ARE WE DOING OKAY HERE? SOMETHING MORE TO DRINK?
AND.
WELL I BET YOUR DAD'S A JERK TOO

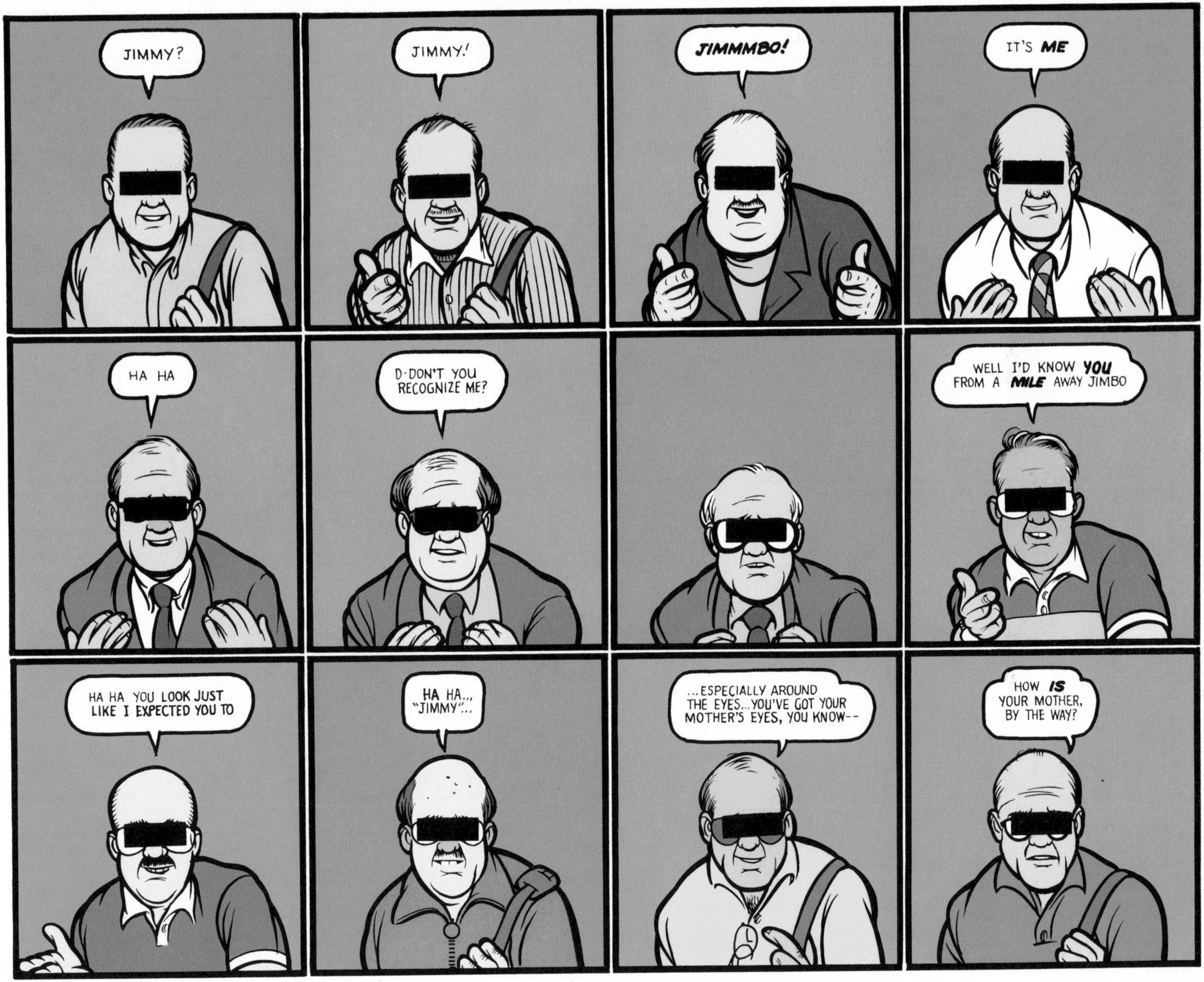
JIMMY?
JIMMY!
JIMMMBO!
IT'S ME
HA HA
D-DON'T YOU RECOGNIZE ME?
WELL I'D KNOW YOU FROM A MILE AWAY JIMBO
HA HA YOU LOOK JUST LIKE I EXPECTED YOU TO
HA HA... "JIMMY"...
...ESPECIALLY AROUND THE EYES...YOU'VE GOT YOUR MOTHER'S EYES, YOU KNOW--
HOW IS YOUR MOTHER, BY THE WAY?

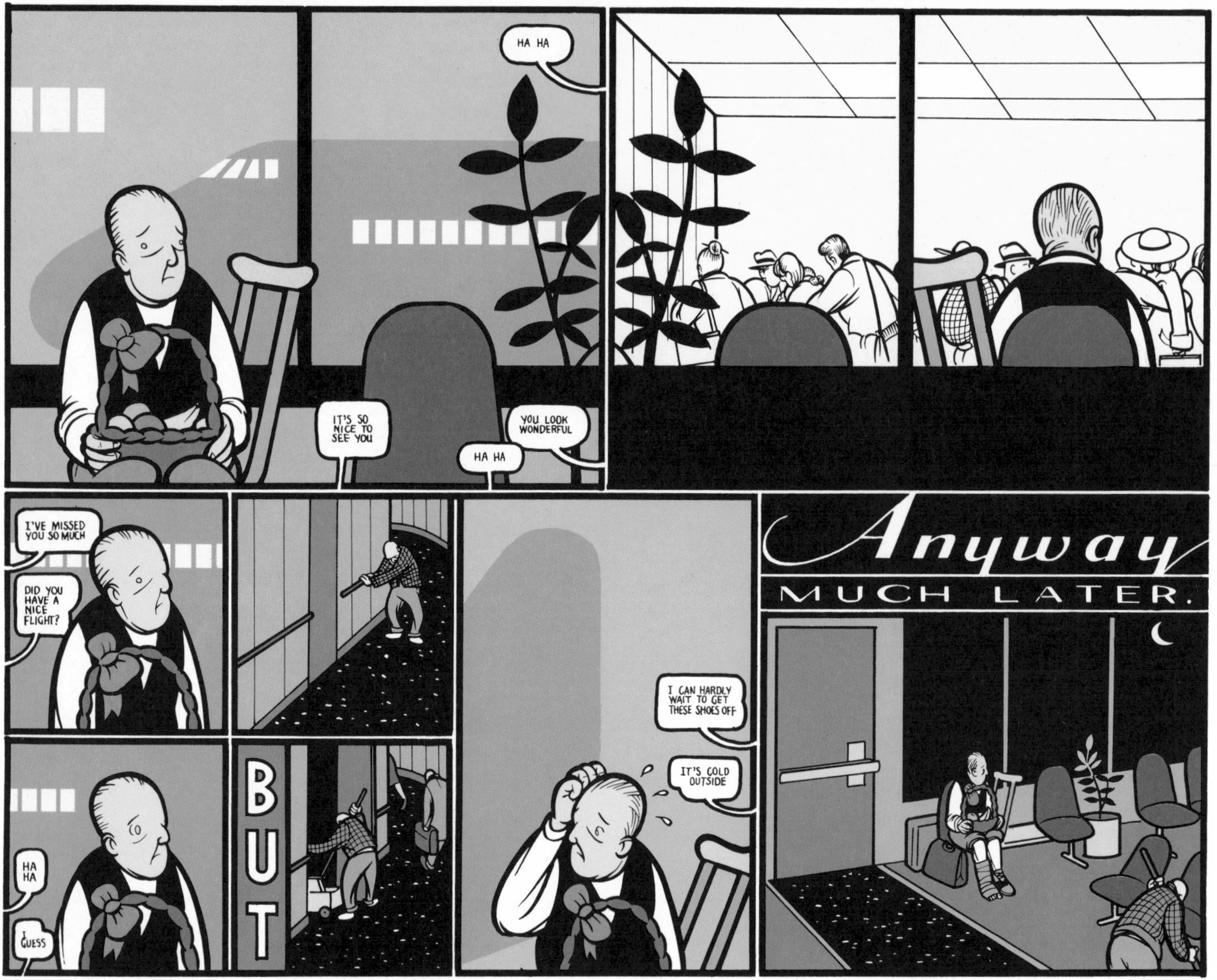
HA HA
IT'S SO NICE TO SEE YOU
HA HA
YOU LOOK WONDERFUL
I'VE MISSED YOU SO MUCH
DID YOU HAVE A NICE FLIGHT?
HA HA
I GUESS
BUT
I CAN HARDLY WAIT TO GET THESE SHOES OFF
IT'S COLD OUTSIDE
Anyway
MUCH LATER.

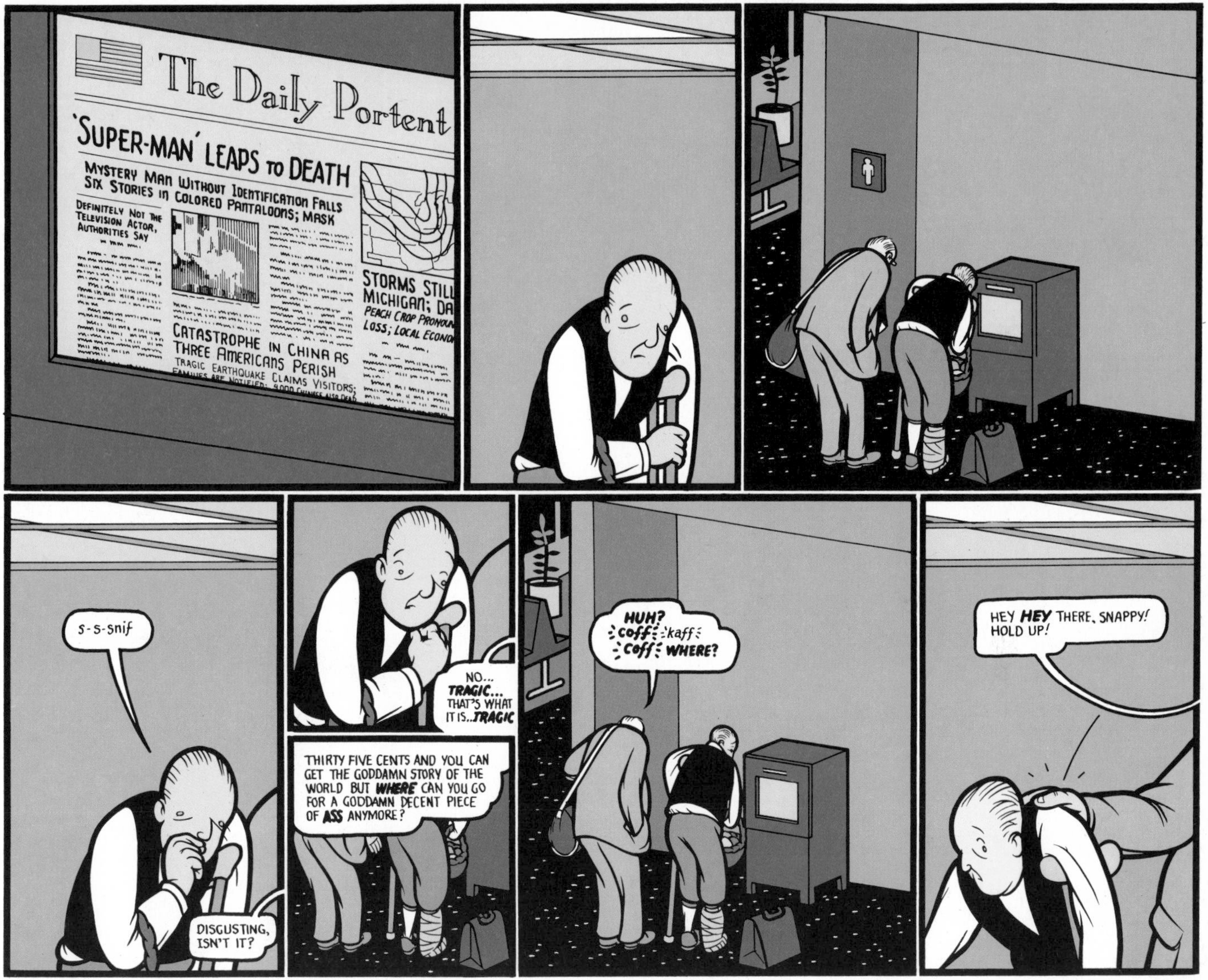
The Daily Portent
'SUPER-MAN' LEAPS TO DEATH
MYSTERY MAN WITHOUT IDENTIFICATION FALLS SIX STORIES IN COLORED PANTALOONS; MASK
DEFINITELY NOT THE TELEVISION ACTOR, AUTHORITIES SAY
CATASTROPHE IN CHINA AS THREE AMERICANS PERISH
TRAGIC EARTHQUAKE CLAIMS VISITORS;
STORMS STILL MICHIGAN; DA
PEACH CROP PRONOUN
LOSS; LOCAL ECONOM
s-s-snif
DISGUSTING, ISN'T IT?
NO... TRAGIC... THAT'S WHAT IT IS.. TRAGIC
THIRTY FIVE CENTS AND YOU CAN GET THE GODDAMN STORY OF THE WORLD BUT WHERE CAN YOU GO FOR A GODDAMN DECENT PIECE OF ASS ANYMORE?
HUH? coff kaff coff WHERE?
HEY HEY THERE, SNAPPY! HOLD UP!

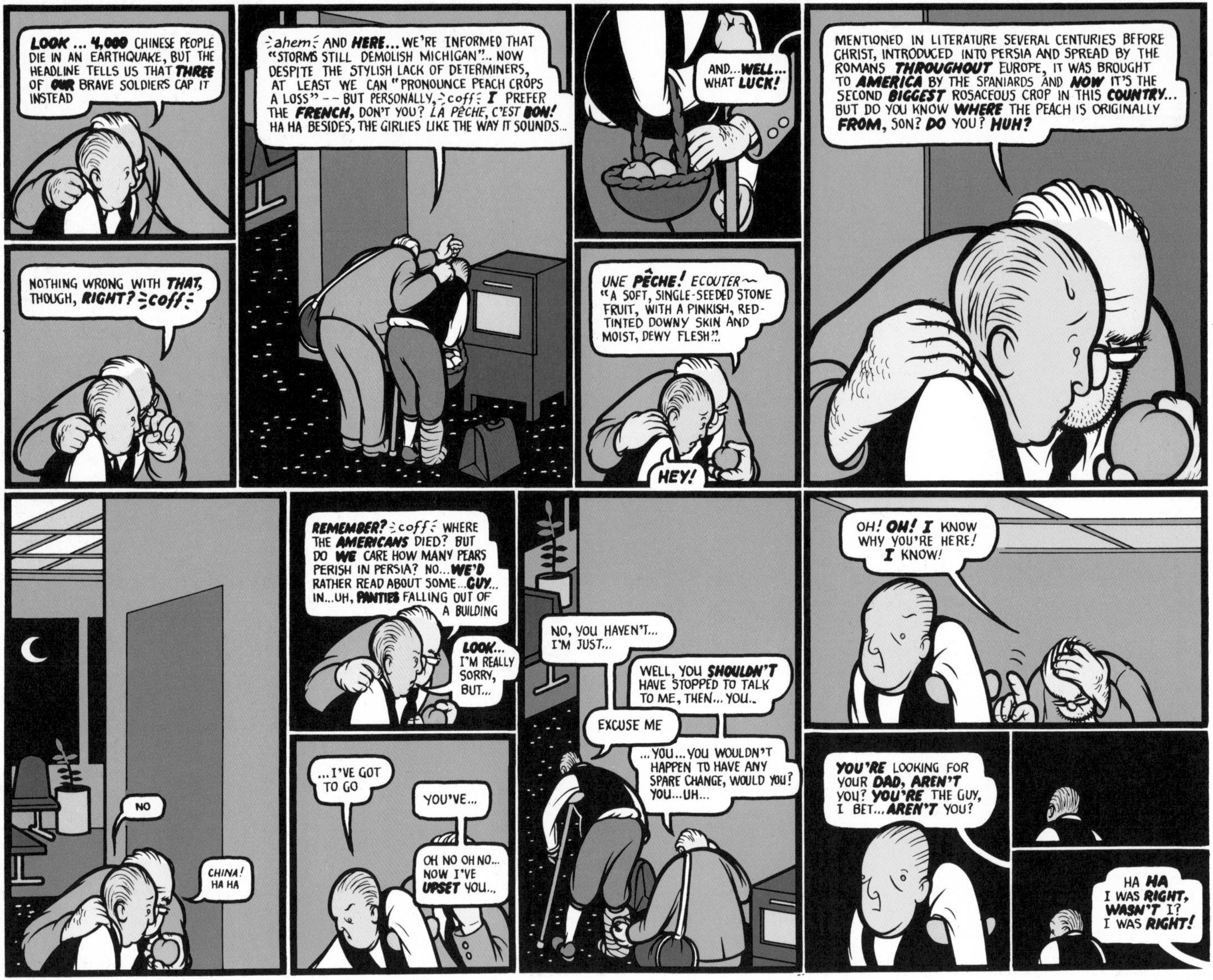
LOOK ... 4,000 CHINESE PEOPLE DIE IN AN EARTHQUAKE, BUT THE HEADLINE TELLS US THAT THREE OF OUR BRAVE SOLDIERS CAP IT INSTEAD
NOTHING WRONG WITH THAT, THOUGH, RIGHT? coff
ahem AND HERE... WE'RE INFORMED THAT "STORMS STILL DEMOLISH MICHIGAN"... NOW DESPITE THE STYLISH LACK OF DETERMINERS, AT LEAST WE CAN "PRONOUNCE PEACH CROPS A LOSS" -- BUT PERSONALLY, coff I PREFER THE FRENCH, DON'T YOU? LA PÊCHE, C'EST BON! HA HA BESIDES, THE GIRLIES LIKE THE WAY IT SOUNDS...
AND... WELL... WHAT LUCK!
UNE PÊCHE! ECOUTER~ "A SOFT, SINGLE-SEEDED STONE FRUIT, WITH A PINKISH, RED-TINTED DOWNY SKIN AND MOIST, DEWY FLESH"...
HEY!
MENTIONED IN LITERATURE SEVERAL CENTURIES BEFORE CHRIST, INTRODUCED INTO PERSIA AND SPREAD BY THE ROMANS THROUGHOUT EUROPE, IT WAS BROUGHT TO AMERICA BY THE SPANIARDS AND NOW IT'S THE SECOND BIGGEST ROSACEOUS CROP IN THIS COUNTRY... BUT DO YOU KNOW WHERE THE PEACH IS ORIGINALLY FROM, SON? DO YOU? HUH?
NO
CHINA! HA HA
REMEMBER? coff WHERE THE AMERICANS DIED? BUT DO WE CARE HOW MANY PEARS PERISH IN PERSIA? NO... WE'D RATHER READ ABOUT SOME... GUY... IN... UH, PANTIES FALLING OUT OF A BUILDING
LOOK... I'M REALLY SORRY, BUT...
...I'VE GOT TO GO
YOU'VE...
OH NO OH NO... NOW I'VE UPSET YOU...
NO, YOU HAVEN'T... I'M JUST...
WELL, YOU SHOULDN'T HAVE STOPPED TO TALK TO ME, THEN... YOU..
EXCUSE ME
...YOU... YOU WOULDN'T HAPPEN TO HAVE ANY SPARE CHANGE, WOULD YOU? YOU... UH...
OH! OH! I KNOW WHY YOU'RE HERE! I KNOW!
YOU'RE LOOKING FOR YOUR DAD, AREN'T YOU? YOU'RE THE GUY, I BET... AREN'T YOU?
HA HA I WAS RIGHT, WASN'T I? I WAS RIGHT!

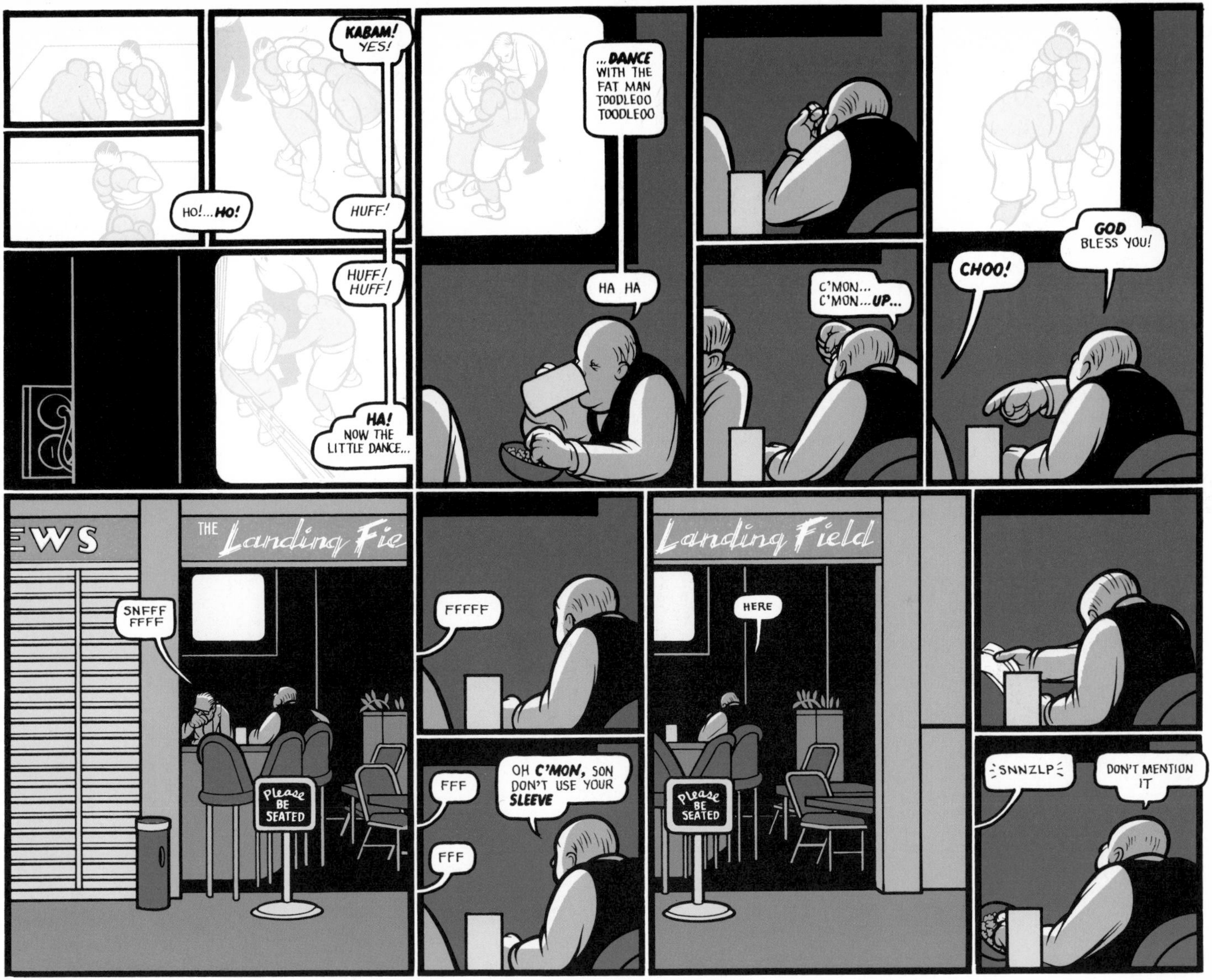

HO!...HO!
KABAM! YES!
HUFF!
HUFF! HUFF!
HA! NOW THE LITTLE DANCE...
...DANCE WITH THE FAT MAN TOODLEOO TOODLEOO
HA HA
C'MON... C'MON...UP...
CHOO!
GOD BLESS YOU!
EWS
THE Landing Fie
SNFFF FFFF
Please BE SEATED
FFFFF
FFF
OH C'MON, SON DON'T USE YOUR SLEEVE
FFF
Landing Field
HERE
Please BE SEATED
SNNZLP
DON'T MENTION IT

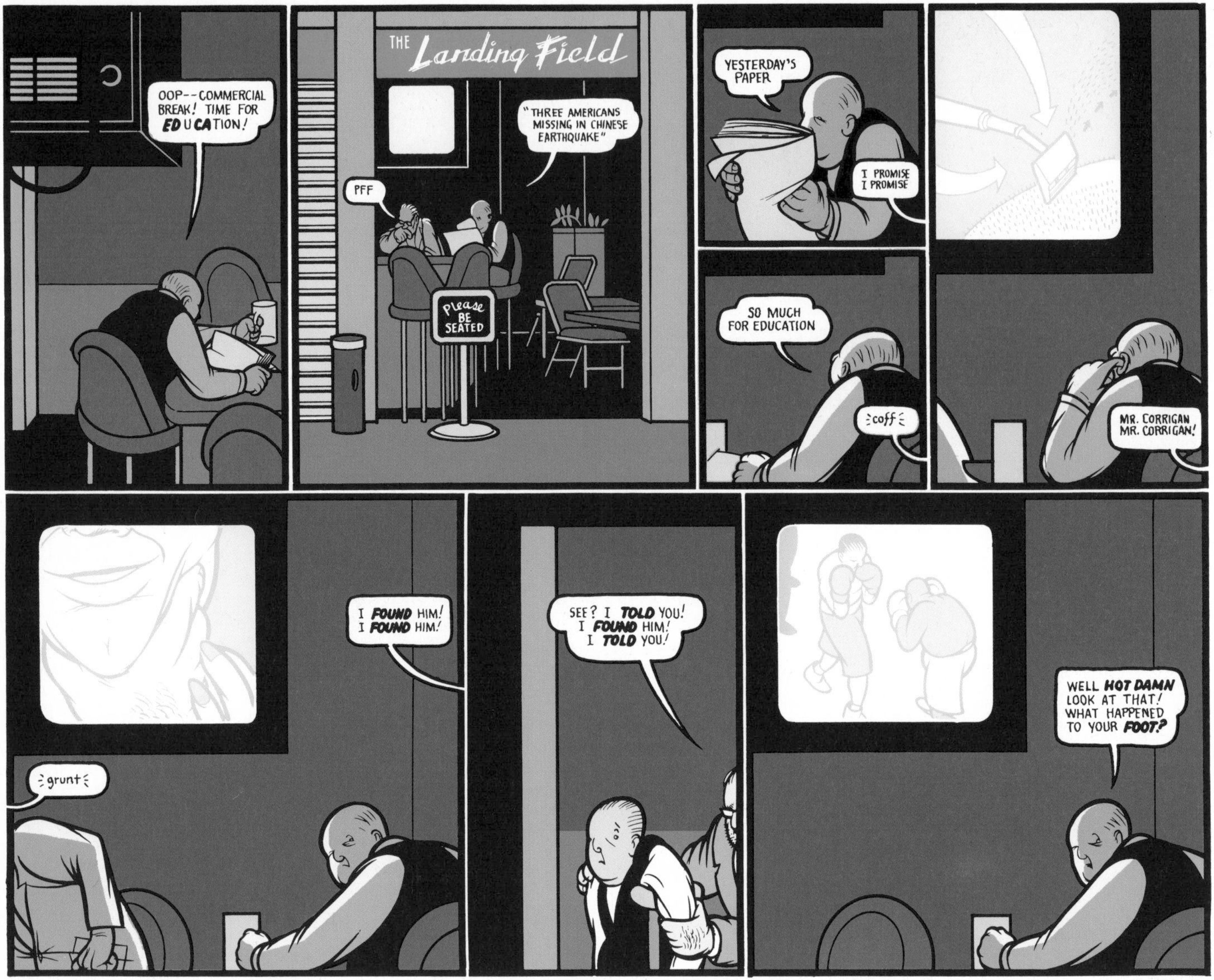
OOP--COMMERCIAL BREAK! TIME FOR EDUCATION!
THE Landing Field
"THREE AMERICANS MISSING IN CHINESE EARTHQUAKE"
PFF
Please BE SEATED
YESTERDAY'S PAPER
I PROMISE I PROMISE
SO MUCH FOR EDUCATION
coff
MR. CORRIGAN MR. CORRIGAN!
I FOUND HIM! I FOUND HIM!
grunt
SEE? I TOLD YOU! I FOUND HIM! I TOLD YOU!
WELL HOT DAMN LOOK AT THAT! WHAT HAPPENED TO YOUR FOOT?

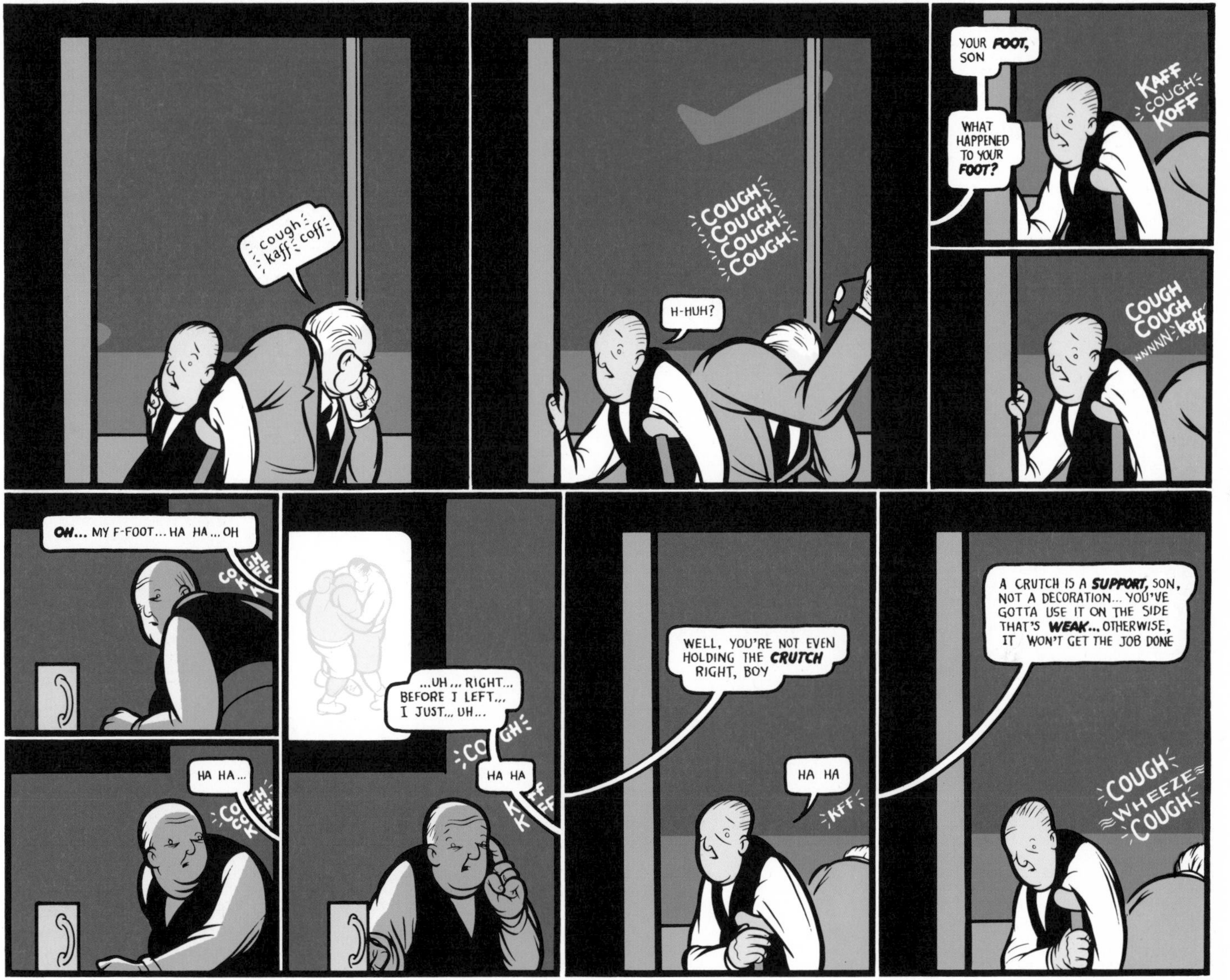
cough kaff coff
COUGH COUGH COUGH COUGH
H-HUH?
YOUR FOOT, SON
WHAT HAPPENED TO YOUR FOOT?
KAFF COUGH KOFF
COUGH COUGH NNNNN kaff
OH... MY F-FOOT... HA HA... OH
HA HA...
...UH... RIGHT... BEFORE I LEFT... I JUST... UH...
HA HA
WELL, YOU'RE NOT EVEN HOLDING THE CRUTCH RIGHT, BOY
HA HA
KFF
A CRUTCH IS A SUPPORT, SON, NOT A DECORATION... YOU'VE GOTTA USE IT ON THE SIDE THAT'S WEAK... OTHERWISE, IT WON'T GET THE JOB DONE
COUGH WHEEZE COUGH

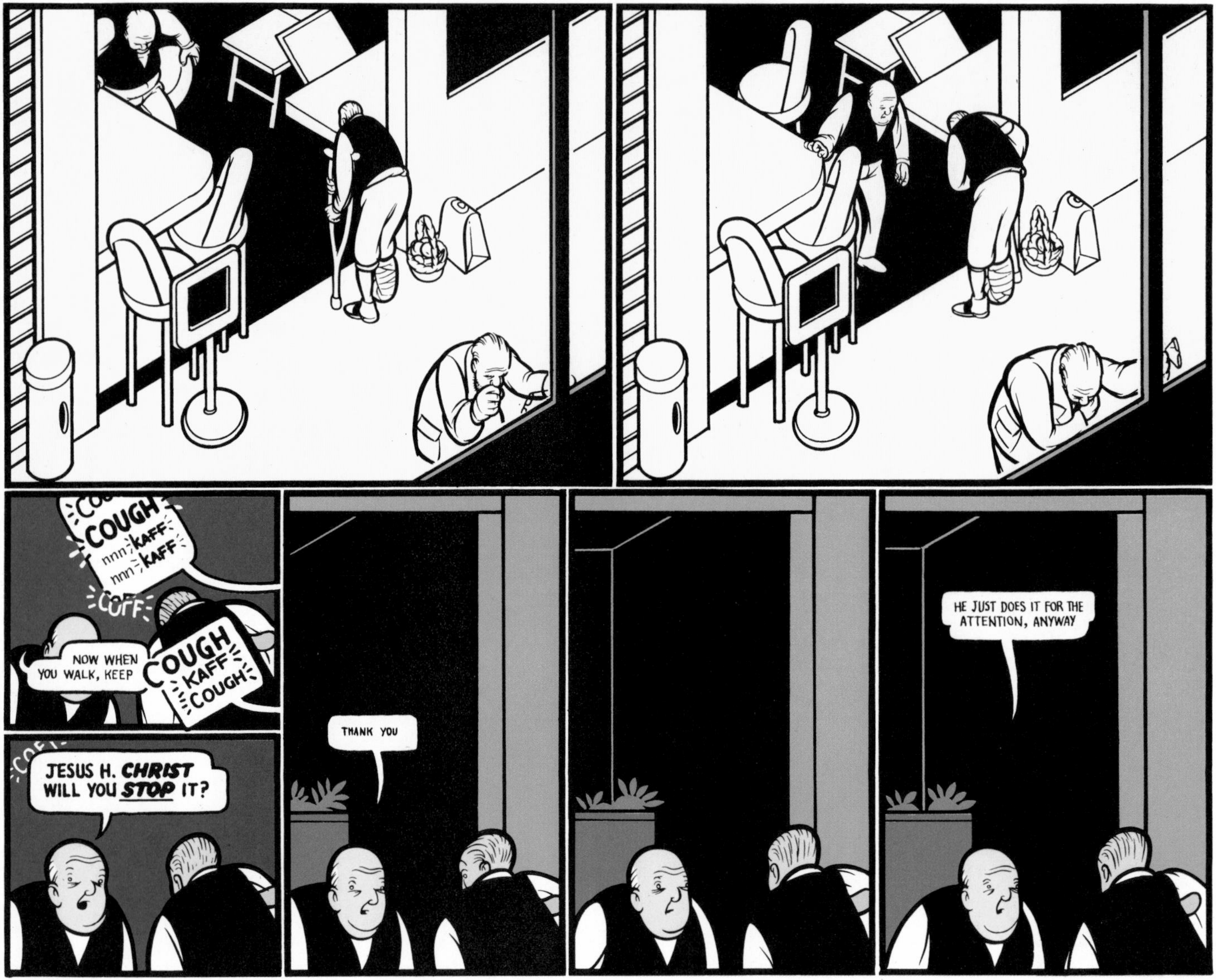
COUGH
nnn KAFF
nnn KAFF
COFF
NOW WHEN YOU WALK, KEEP
COUGH KAFF COUGH
JESUS H. CHRIST WILL YOU STOP IT?
THANK YOU
HE JUST DOES IT FOR THE ATTENTION, ANYWAY

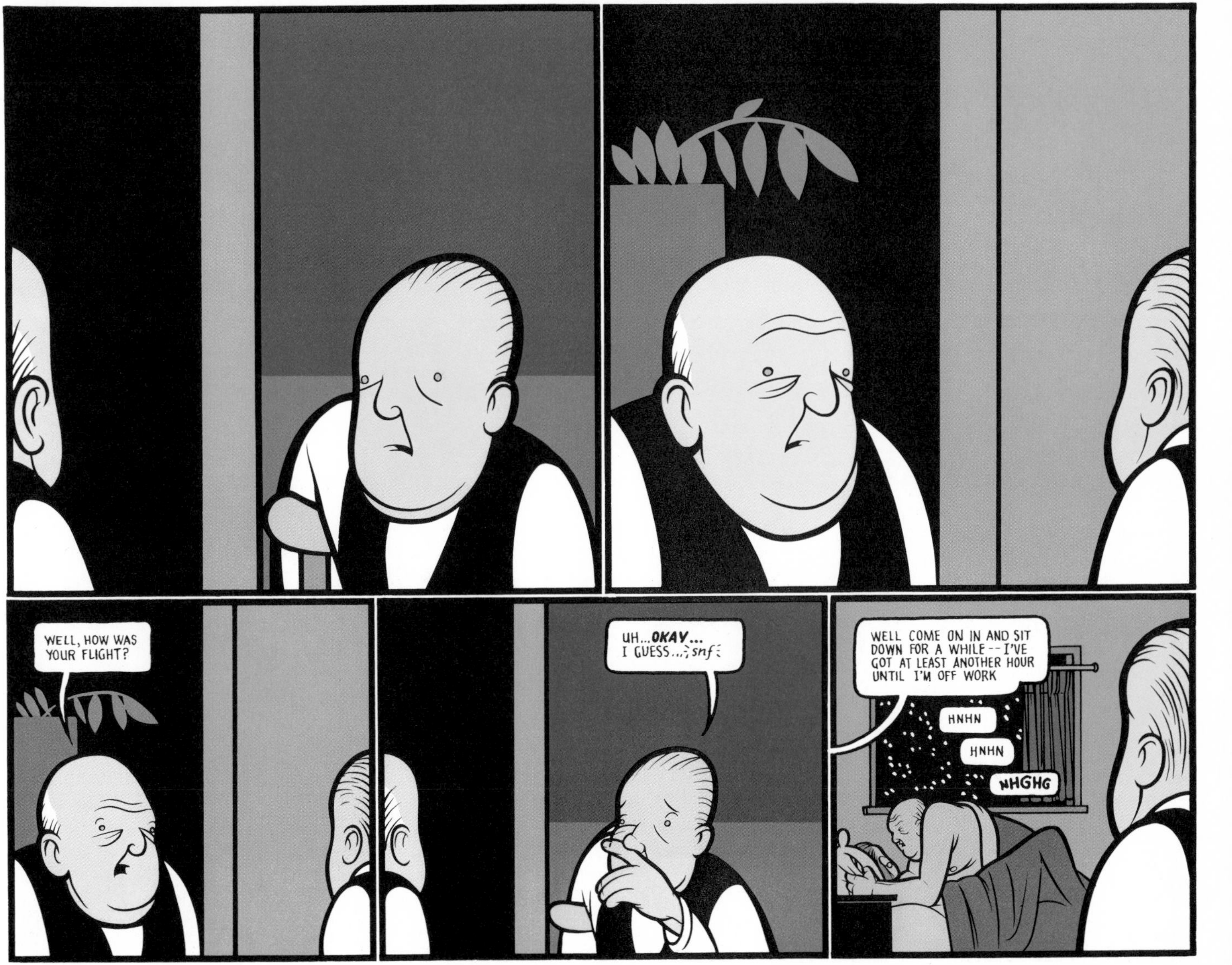
WELL, HOW WAS YOUR FLIGHT?
UH...OKAY... I GUESS... snf
WELL COME ON IN AND SIT DOWN FOR A WHILE--I'VE GOT AT LEAST ANOTHER HOUR UNTIL I'M OFF WORK
HNHN
HNHN
NHGHG

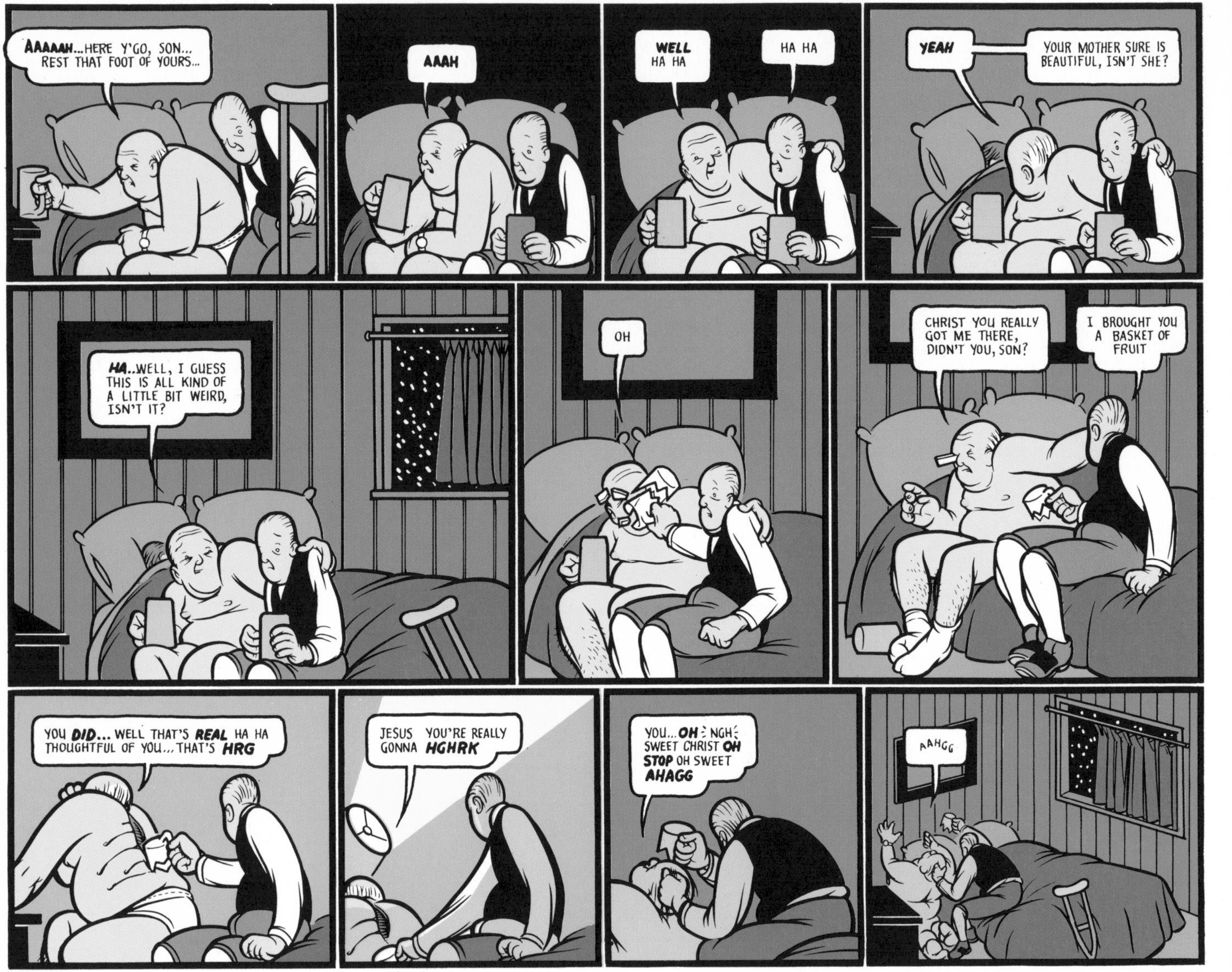
AAAAAH... HERE Y'GO, SON... REST THAT FOOT OF YOURS...
AAAH
WELL HA HA
HA HA
YEAH
YOUR MOTHER SURE IS BEAUTIFUL, ISN'T SHE?
HA.. WELL, I GUESS THIS IS ALL KIND OF A LITTLE BIT WEIRD, ISN'T IT?
OH
CHRIST YOU REALLY GOT ME THERE, DIDN'T YOU, SON?
I BROUGHT YOU A BASKET OF FRUIT
YOU DID... WELL THAT'S REAL HA HA THOUGHTFUL OF YOU... THAT'S HRG
JESUS YOU'RE REALLY GONNA HGHRK
YOU... OH NGH SWEET CHRIST OH STOP OH SWEET AHAGG
AAHGG

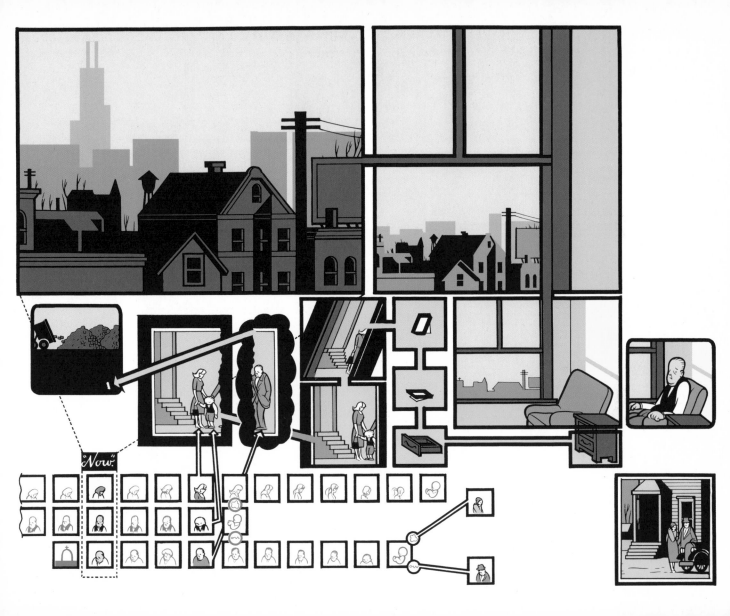

"Now"

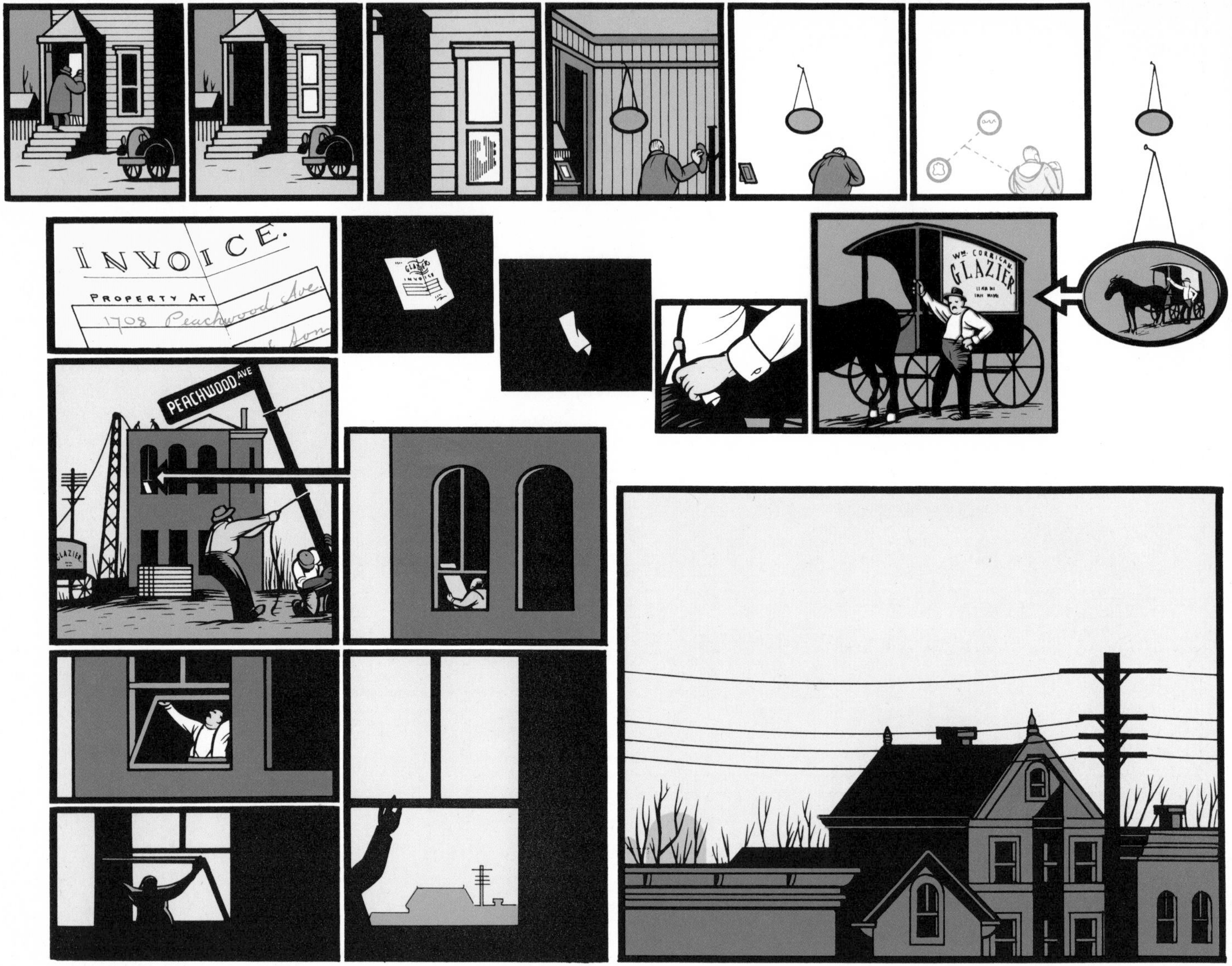
INVOICE.
PROPERTY AT
1708 Peachwood Ave.
& Son
Wm. CORRIGAN.
GLAZIER.
PEACHWOOD AVE
GLAZIER

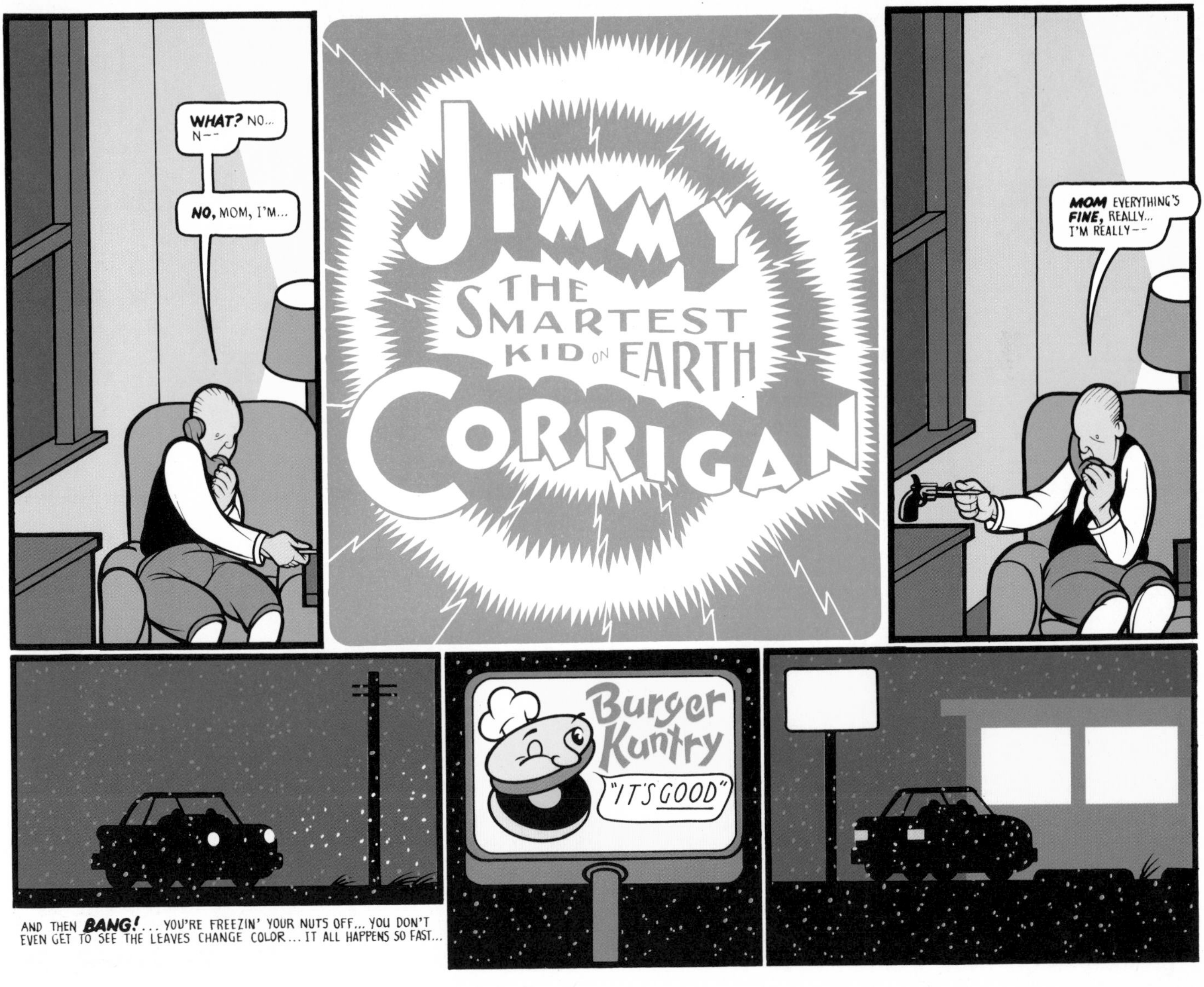
WHAT? NO... N--
NO, MOM, I'M...
JIMMY CORRIGAN
THE SMARTEST KID ON EARTH
MOM EVERYTHING'S FINE, REALLY... I'M REALLY--
AND THEN BANG!... YOU'RE FREEZIN' YOUR NUTS OFF... YOU DON'T EVEN GET TO SEE THE LEAVES CHANGE COLOR... IT ALL HAPPENS SO FAST...
Burger Kuntry
"IT'S GOOD"

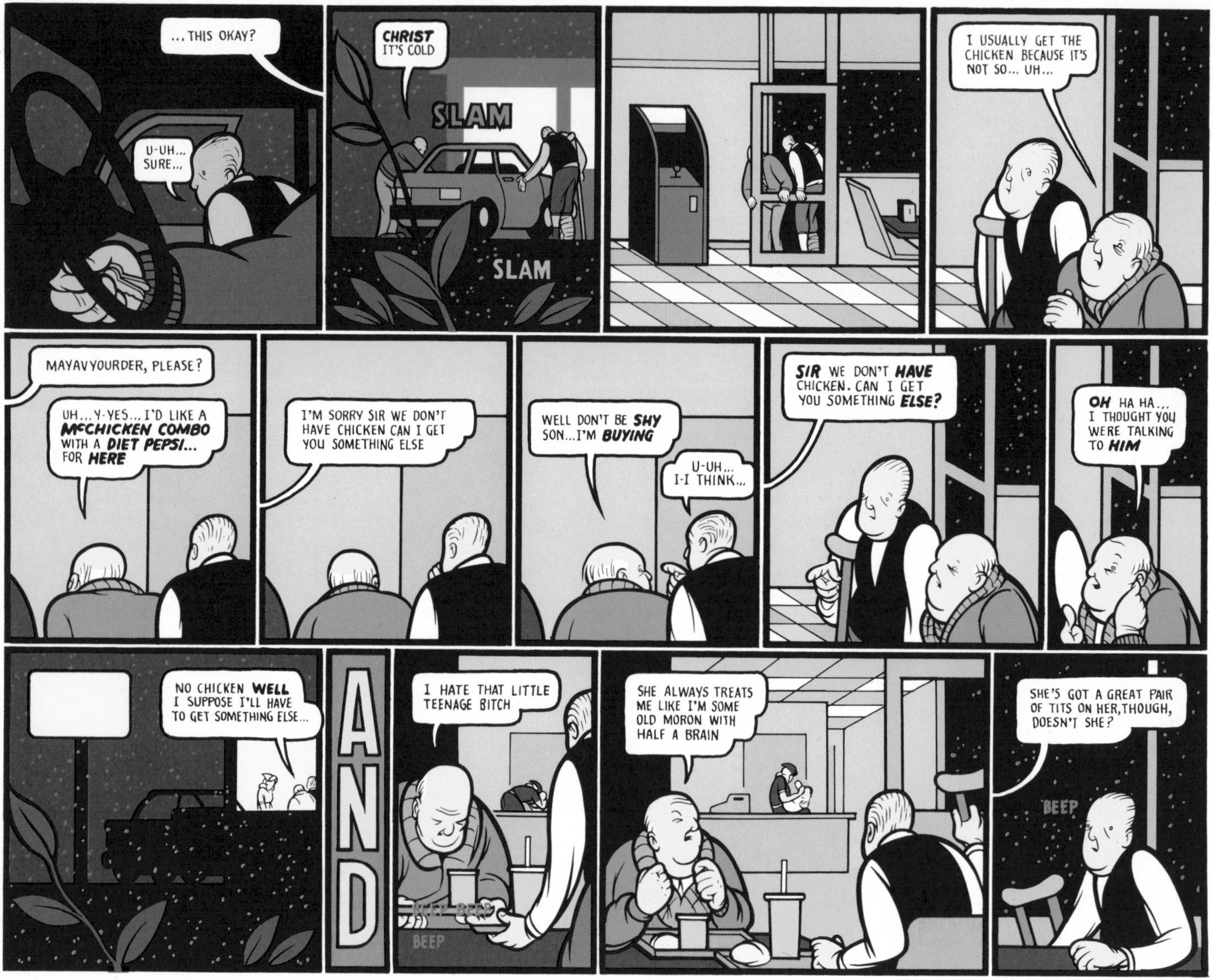
...THIS OKAY?
U-UH... SURE...
CHRIST IT'S COLD
SLAM
SLAM
I USUALLY GET THE CHICKEN BECAUSE IT'S NOT SO... UH...
MAYAVYOURDER, PLEASE?
UH... Y-YES... I'D LIKE A McCHICKEN COMBO WITH A DIET PEPSI... FOR HERE
I'M SORRY SIR WE DON'T HAVE CHICKEN CAN I GET YOU SOMETHING ELSE
WELL DON'T BE SHY SON...I'M BUYING
U-UH... I-I THINK...
SIR WE DON'T HAVE CHICKEN. CAN I GET YOU SOMETHING ELSE?
OH HA HA... I THOUGHT YOU WERE TALKING TO HIM
NO CHICKEN WELL I SUPPOSE I'LL HAVE TO GET SOMETHING ELSE...
AND
I HATE THAT LITTLE TEENAGE BITCH
BEEP
SHE ALWAYS TREATS ME LIKE I'M SOME OLD MORON WITH HALF A BRAIN
SHE'S GOT A GREAT PAIR OF TITS ON HER,THOUGH, DOESN'T SHE?
BEEP

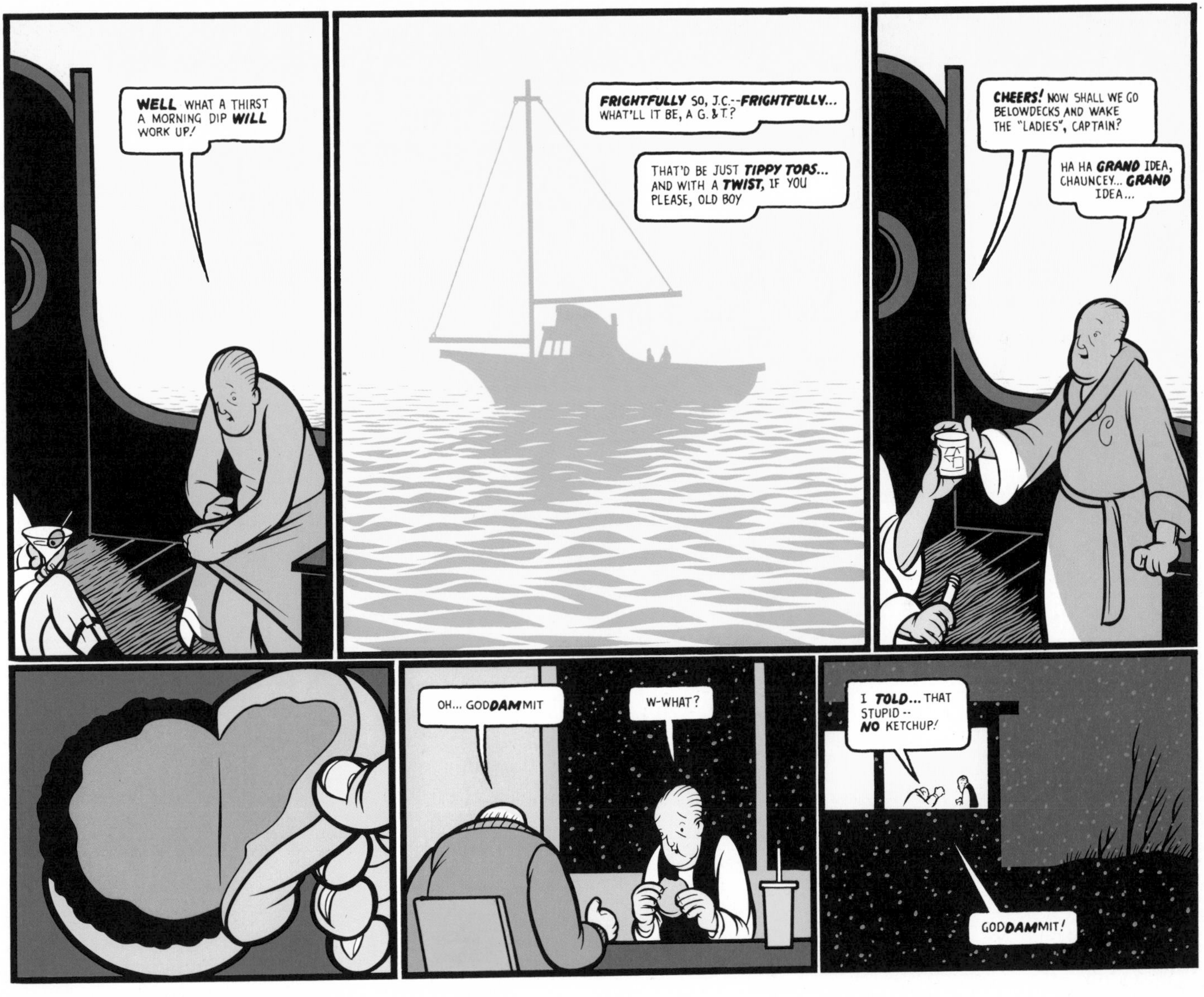
WELL WHAT A THIRST A MORNING DIP WILL WORK UP!
FRIGHTFULLY SO, J.C.--FRIGHTFULLY... WHAT'LL IT BE, A G.&T.?
THAT'D BE JUST TIPPY TOPS... AND WITH A TWIST, IF YOU PLEASE, OLD BOY
CHEERS! NOW SHALL WE GO BELOWDECKS AND WAKE THE "LADIES", CAPTAIN?
HA HA GRAND IDEA, CHAUNCEY... GRAND IDEA...
OH... GODDAMMIT
W-WHAT?
I TOLD... THAT STUPID -- NO KETCHUP!
GODDAMMIT!

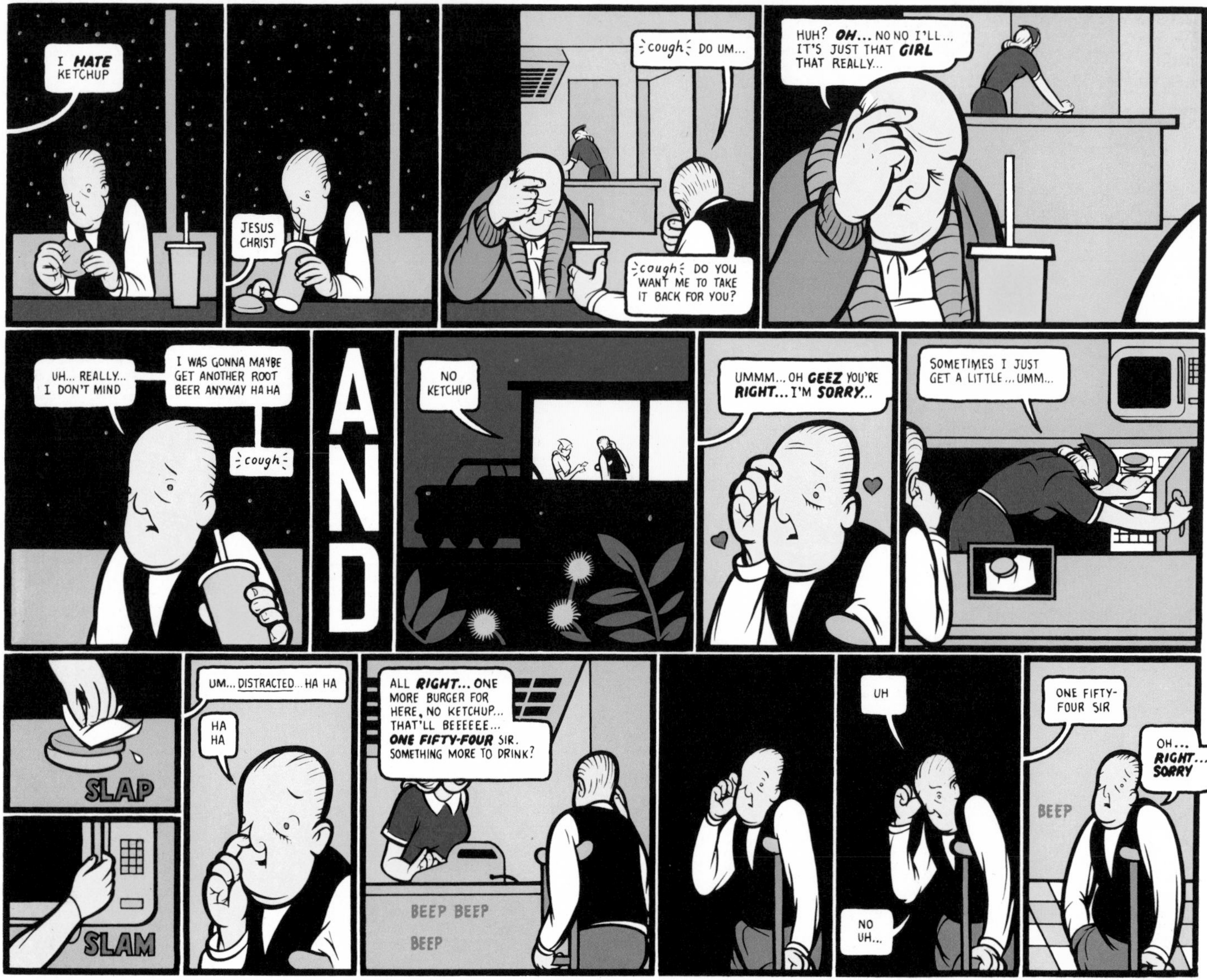
I HATE KETCHUP
JESUS CHRIST
cough DO UM...
cough DO YOU WANT ME TO TAKE IT BACK FOR YOU?
HUH? OH... NO NO I'LL... IT'S JUST THAT GIRL THAT REALLY...
UH... REALLY... I DON'T MIND
I WAS GONNA MAYBE GET ANOTHER ROOT BEER ANYWAY HA HA
cough
AND
NO KETCHUP
UMMM... OH GEEZ YOU'RE RIGHT... I'M SORRY...
SOMETIMES I JUST GET A LITTLE... UMM...
SLAP
SLAM
UM... DISTRACTED... HA HA
HA HA
ALL RIGHT... ONE MORE BURGER FOR HERE, NO KETCHUP... THAT'LL BEEEEEE... ONE FIFTY-FOUR SIR. SOMETHING MORE TO DRINK?
BEEP BEEP
BEEP
UH
NO UH...
ONE FIFTY-FOUR SIR
BEEP
OH... RIGHT... SORRY

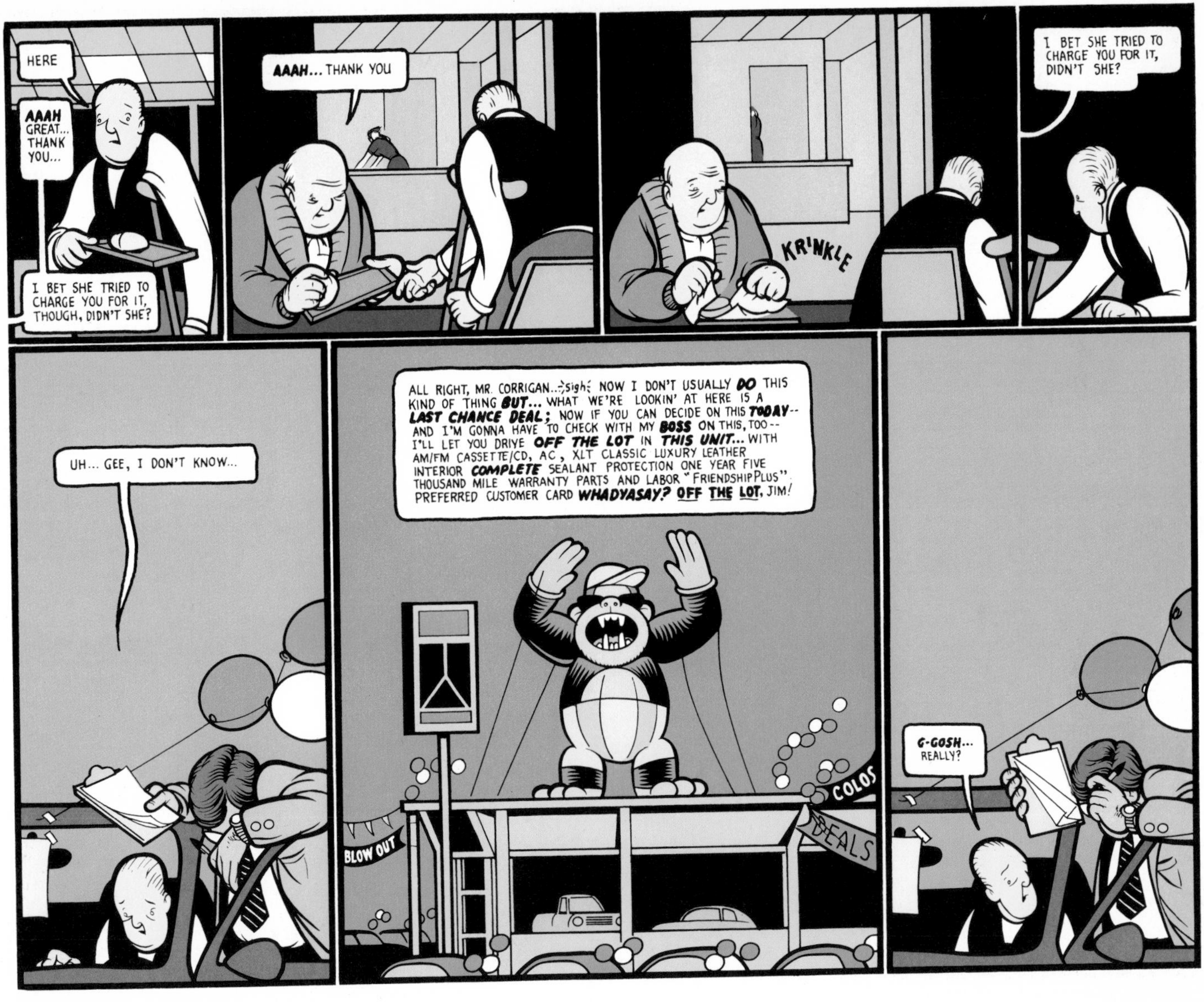

HERE
AAAH GREAT... THANK YOU...
I BET SHE TRIED TO CHARGE YOU FOR IT, THOUGH, DIDN'T SHE?
AAAH... THANK YOU
KRINKLE
I BET SHE TRIED TO CHARGE YOU FOR IT, DIDN'T SHE?
UH... GEE, I DON'T KNOW...
ALL RIGHT, MR. CORRIGAN... sigh NOW I DON'T USUALLY DO THIS KIND OF THING BUT... WHAT WE'RE LOOKIN' AT HERE IS A LAST CHANCE DEAL; NOW IF YOU CAN DECIDE ON THIS TODAY-- AND I'M GONNA HAVE TO CHECK WITH MY BOSS ON THIS, TOO-- I'LL LET YOU DRIVE OFF THE LOT IN THIS UNIT... WITH AM/FM CASSETTE/CD, AC, XLT CLASSIC LUXURY LEATHER INTERIOR COMPLETE SEALANT PROTECTION ONE YEAR FIVE THOUSAND MILE WARRANTY PARTS AND LABOR "FRIENDSHIPPLUS" PREFERRED CUSTOMER CARD WHADYASAY? OFF THE LOT, JIM!
BLOW OUT
COLOS
DEALS
G-GOSH... REALLY?

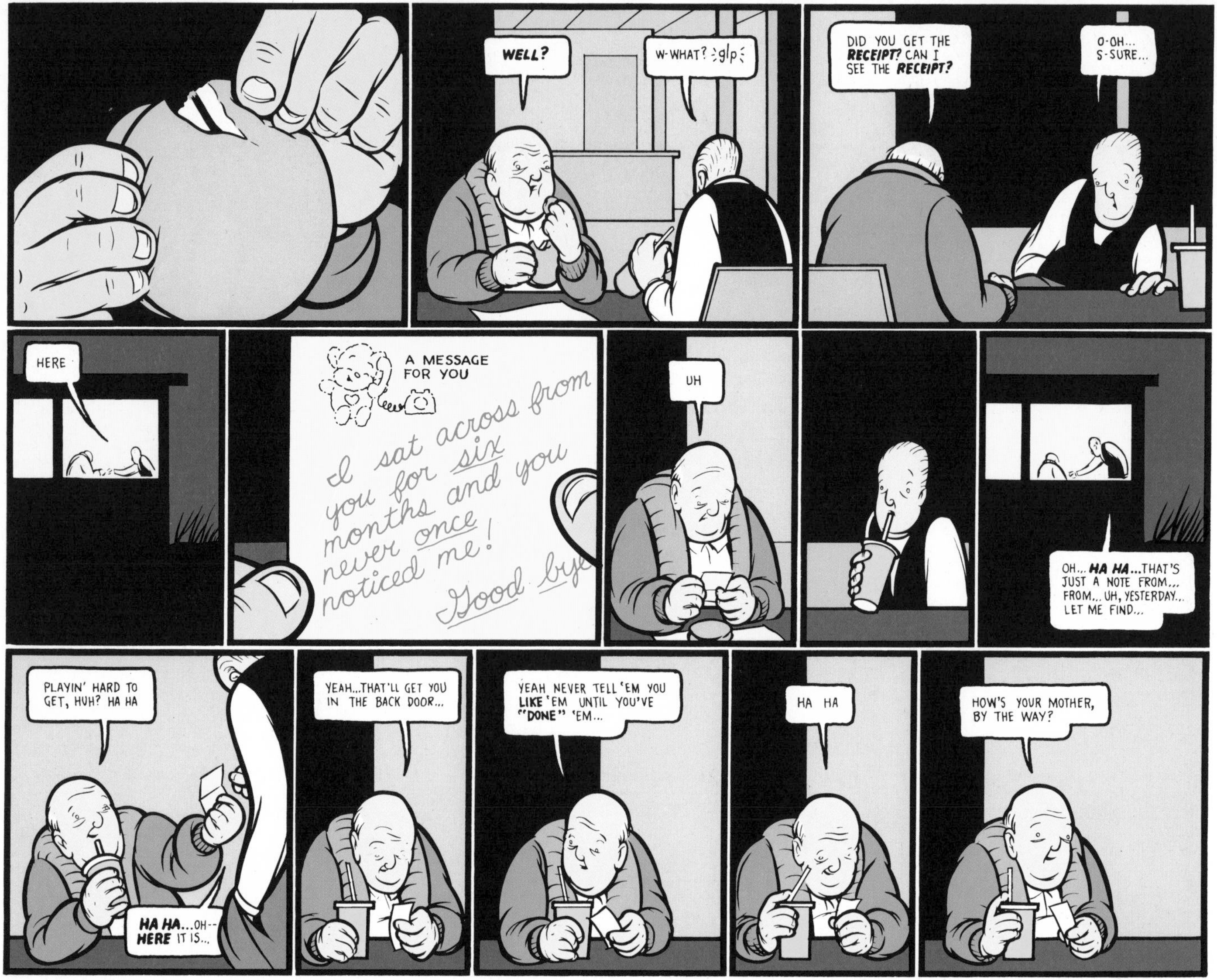
WELL?
W-WHAT? glp
DID YOU GET THE **RECEIPT?** CAN I SEE THE **RECEIPT?**
O-OH... S-SURE...
HERE
A MESSAGE FOR YOU
I sat across from you for six months and you never once noticed me!
Good bye
UH
OH... **HA HA...** THAT'S JUST A NOTE FROM... FROM... UH, YESTERDAY... LET ME FIND...
PLAYIN' HARD TO GET, HUH? HA HA
HA HA...OH-- **HERE** IT IS...
YEAH...THAT'LL GET YOU IN THE BACK DOOR...
YEAH NEVER TELL 'EM YOU **LIKE** 'EM UNTIL YOU'VE **"DONE"** 'EM...
HA HA
HOW'S YOUR MOTHER, BY THE WAY?

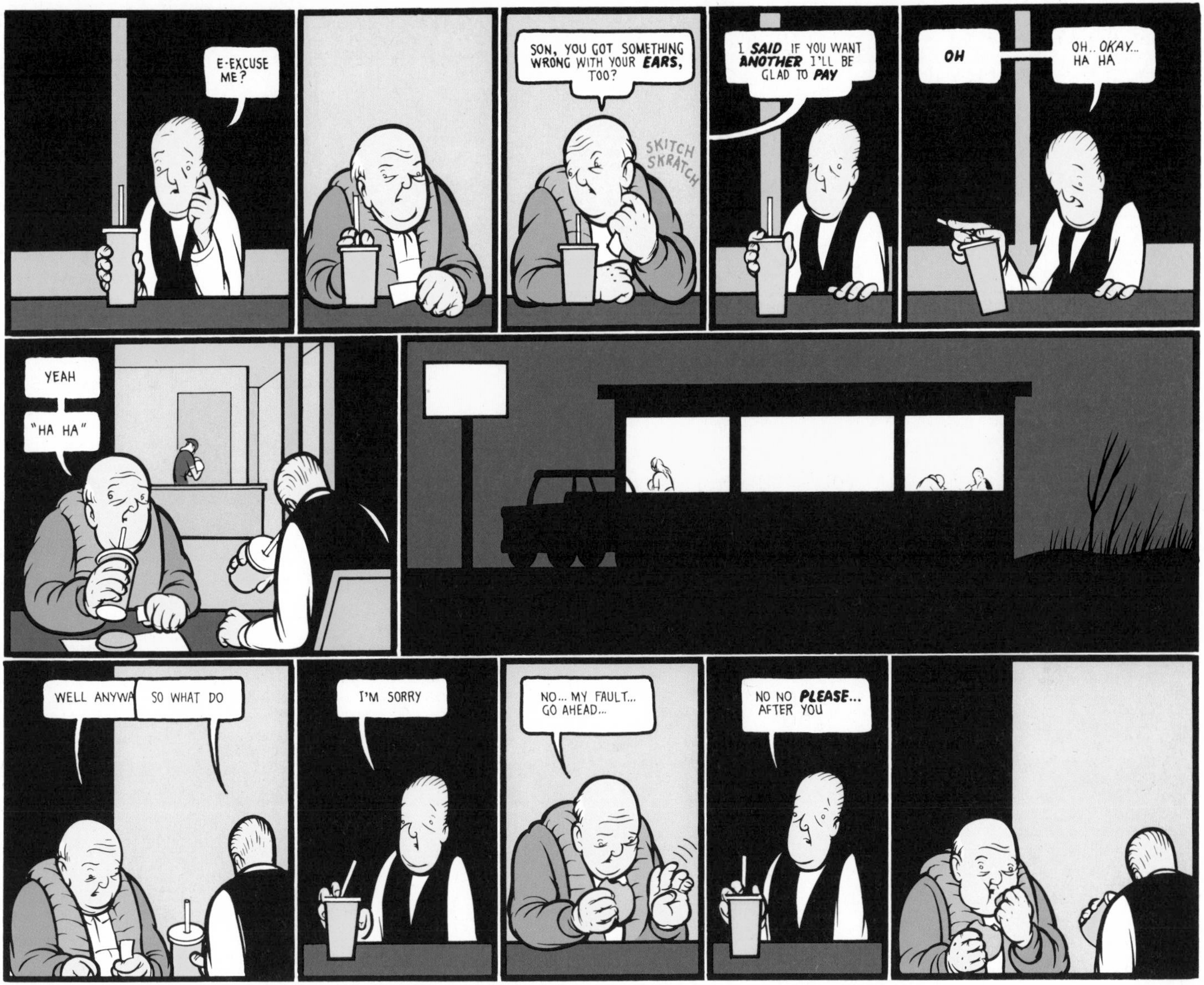
E-EXCUSE ME?
SON, YOU GOT SOMETHING WRONG WITH YOUR EARS, TOO?
SKITCH SKRATCH
I SAID IF YOU WANT ANOTHER I'LL BE GLAD TO PAY
OH
OH.. OKAY.. HA HA
YEAH
"HA HA"
WELL ANYWA
SO WHAT DO
I'M SORRY
NO... MY FAULT... GO AHEAD...
NO NO PLEASE... AFTER YOU

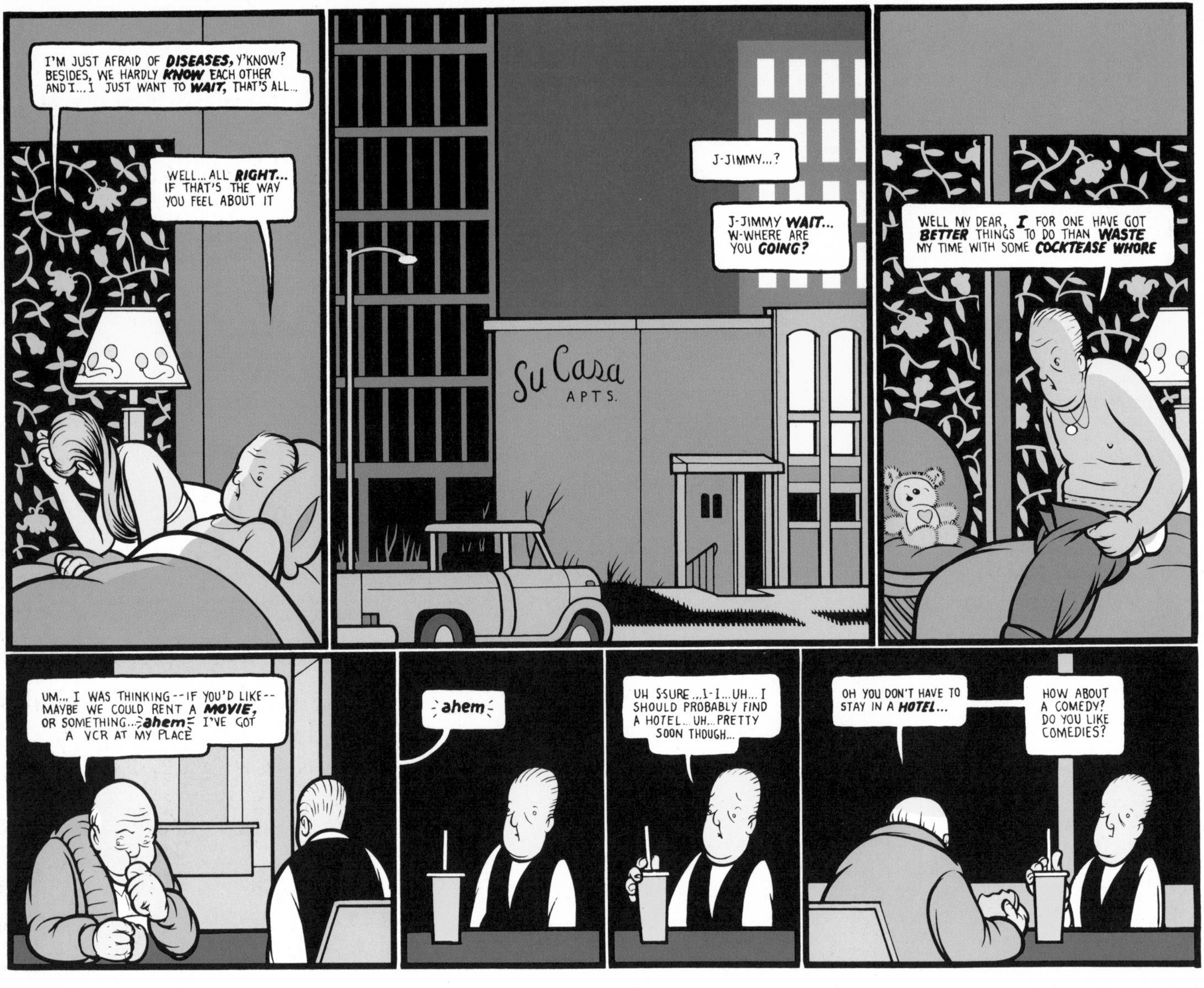
I'M JUST AFRAID OF DISEASES, Y'KNOW? BESIDES, WE HARDLY KNOW EACH OTHER AND I... I JUST WANT TO WAIT, THAT'S ALL...
WELL... ALL RIGHT... IF THAT'S THE WAY YOU FEEL ABOUT IT
Su Casa APTS.
J-JIMMY...?
J-JIMMY WAIT... W-WHERE ARE YOU GOING?
WELL MY DEAR, I FOR ONE HAVE GOT BETTER THINGS TO DO THAN WASTE MY TIME WITH SOME COCKTEASE WHORE
UM... I WAS THINKING--IF YOU'D LIKE--MAYBE WE COULD RENT A MOVIE, OR SOMETHING... ahem I'VE GOT A VCR AT MY PLACE
ahem
UH S-SURE... I-I... UH... I SHOULD PROBABLY FIND A HOTEL... UH... PRETTY SOON THOUGH...
OH YOU DON'T HAVE TO STAY IN A HOTEL...
HOW ABOUT A COMEDY? DO YOU LIKE COMEDIES?

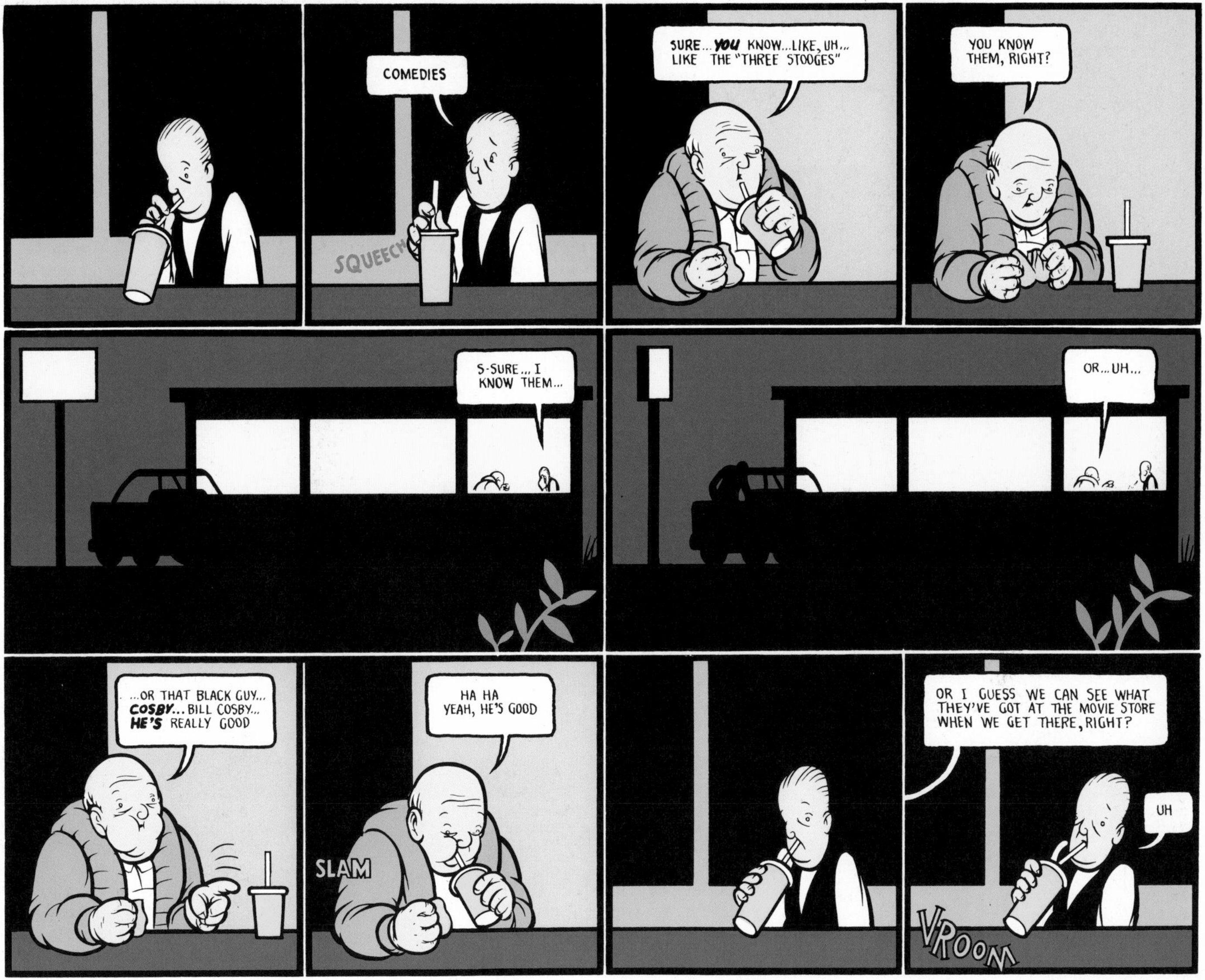
COMEDIES
SQUEECH
SURE... YOU KNOW...LIKE, UH... LIKE THE "THREE STOOGES"
YOU KNOW THEM, RIGHT?
S-SURE... I KNOW THEM...
OR... UH...
...OR THAT BLACK GUY... COSBY... BILL COSBY... HE'S REALLY GOOD
HA HA YEAH, HE'S GOOD
SLAM
OR I GUESS WE CAN SEE WHAT THEY'VE GOT AT THE MOVIE STORE WHEN WE GET THERE, RIGHT?
UH
VROOM

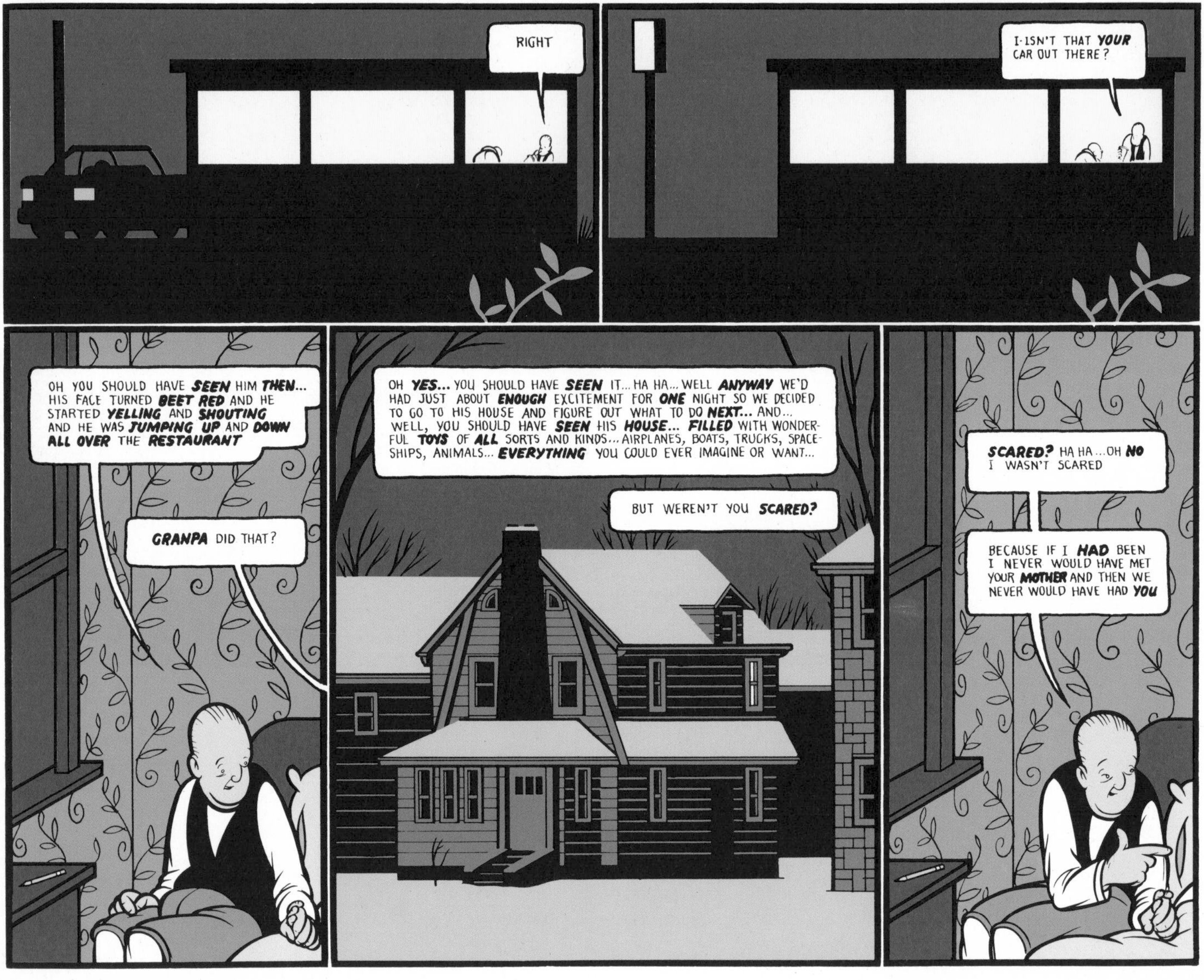
RIGHT
I-ISN'T THAT YOUR CAR OUT THERE?
OH YOU SHOULD HAVE SEEN HIM THEN... HIS FACE TURNED BEET RED AND HE STARTED YELLING AND SHOUTING AND HE WAS JUMPING UP AND DOWN ALL OVER THE RESTAURANT
GRANPA DID THAT?
OH YES... YOU SHOULD HAVE SEEN IT... HA HA... WELL ANYWAY WE'D HAD JUST ABOUT ENOUGH EXCITEMENT FOR ONE NIGHT SO WE DECIDED TO GO TO HIS HOUSE AND FIGURE OUT WHAT TO DO NEXT... AND... WELL, YOU SHOULD HAVE SEEN HIS HOUSE... FILLED WITH WONDERFUL TOYS OF ALL SORTS AND KINDS... AIRPLANES, BOATS, TRUCKS, SPACESHIPS, ANIMALS... EVERYTHING YOU COULD EVER IMAGINE OR WANT...
BUT WEREN'T YOU SCARED?
SCARED? HA HA... OH NO I WASN'T SCARED
BECAUSE IF I HAD BEEN I NEVER WOULD HAVE MET YOUR MOTHER AND THEN WE NEVER WOULD HAVE HAD YOU

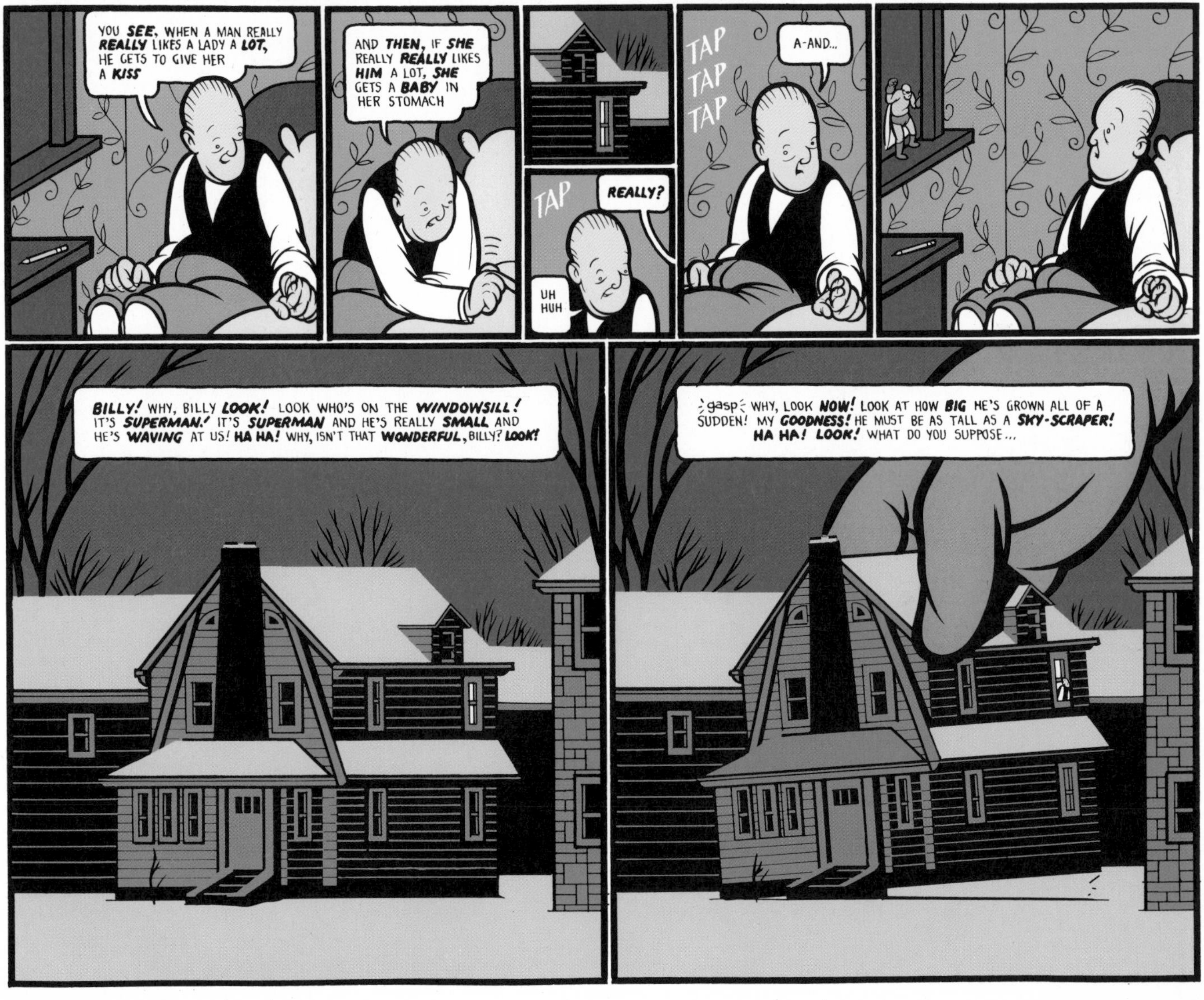
YOU SEE, WHEN A MAN REALLY REALLY LIKES A LADY A LOT, HE GETS TO GIVE HER A KISS
AND THEN, IF SHE REALLY REALLY LIKES HIM A LOT, SHE GETS A BABY IN HER STOMACH
TAP
REALLY?
UH HUH
TAP TAP TAP
A-AND...
BILLY! WHY, BILLY LOOK! LOOK WHO'S ON THE WINDOWSILL! IT'S SUPERMAN! IT'S SUPERMAN AND HE'S REALLY SMALL AND HE'S WAVING AT US! HA HA! WHY, ISN'T THAT WONDERFUL, BILLY? LOOK!
gasp WHY, LOOK NOW! LOOK AT HOW BIG HE'S GROWN ALL OF A SUDDEN! MY GOODNESS! HE MUST BE AS TALL AS A SKY-SCRAPER! HA HA! LOOK! WHAT DO YOU SUPPOSE...

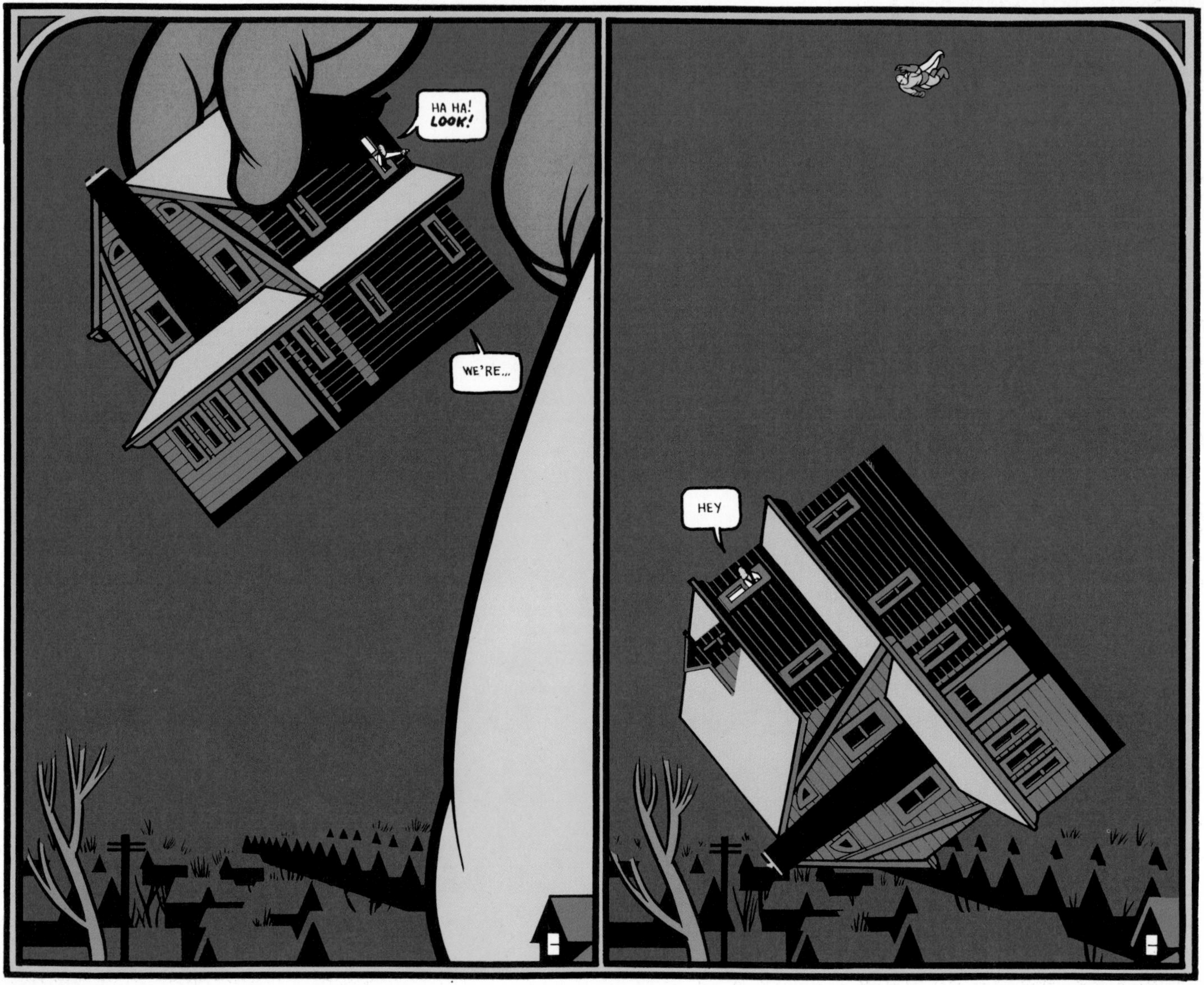
HA HA!
LOOK!
WE'RE...
HEY

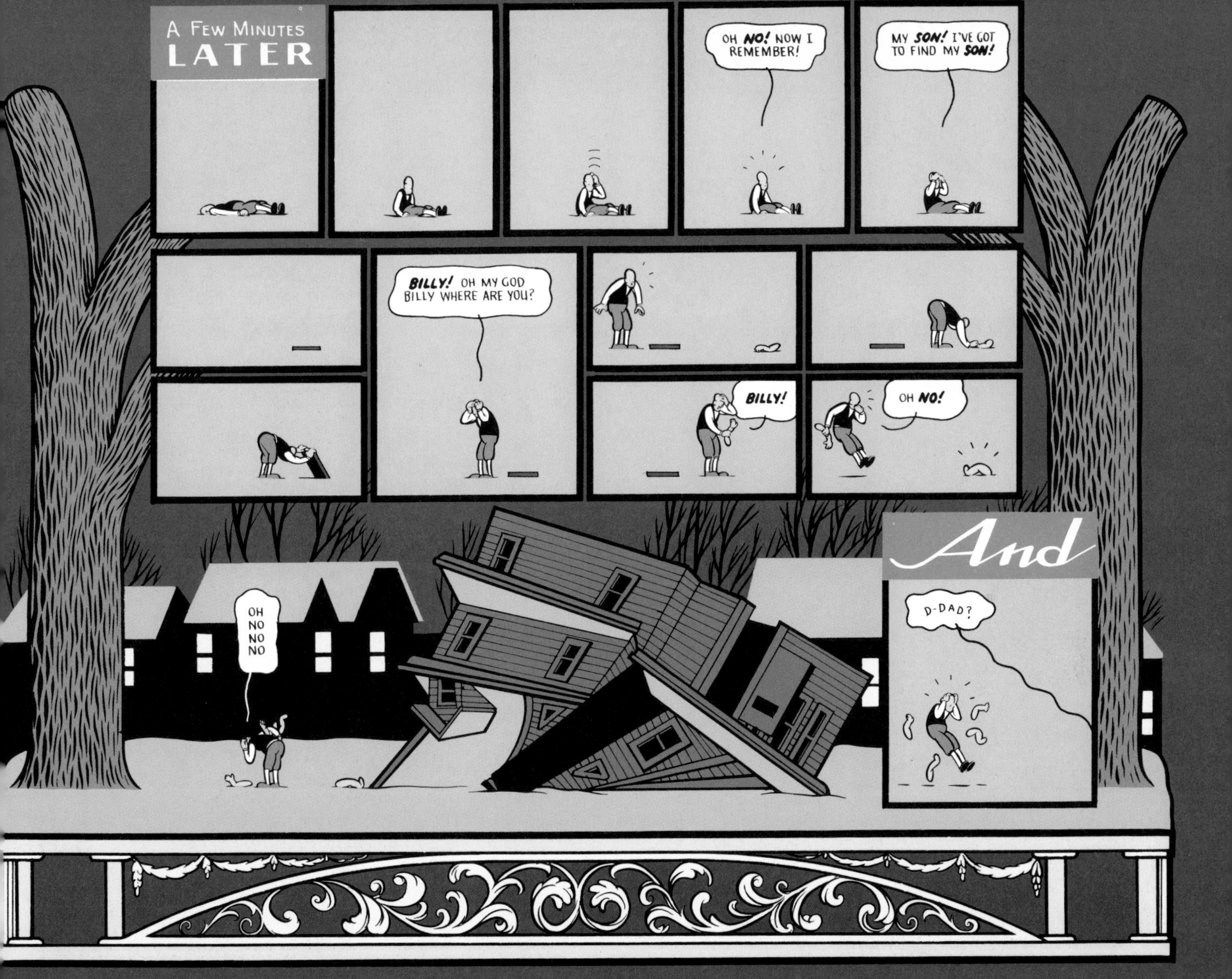
A Few Minutes
LATER
OH NO! NOW I REMEMBER!
MY SON! I'VE GOT TO FIND MY SON!
BILLY! OH MY GOD BILLY WHERE ARE YOU?
BILLY!
OH NO!
OH NO NO NO
And
D-DAD?

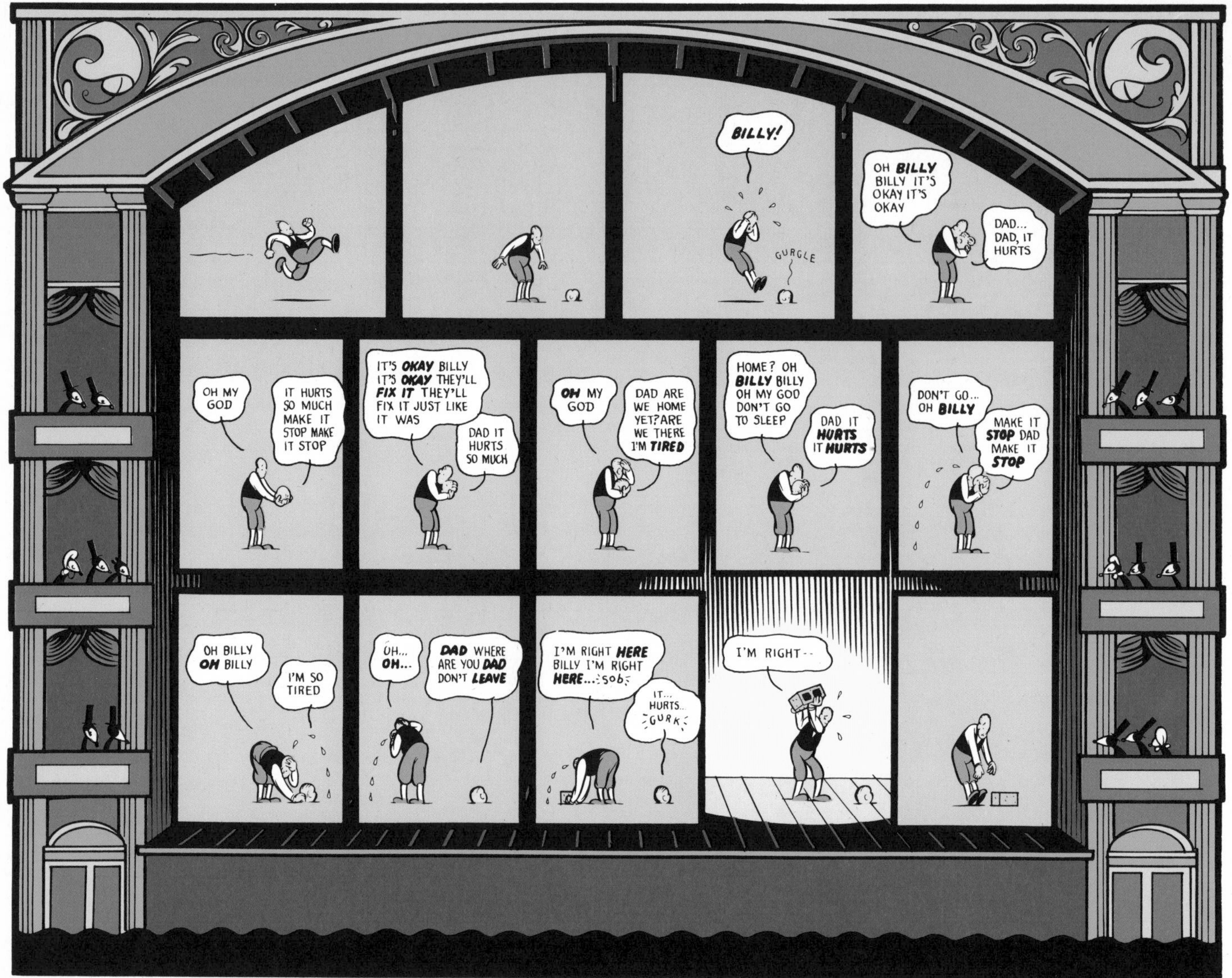

BILLY!
GURGLE
OH BILLY BILLY IT'S OKAY IT'S OKAY
DAD... DAD, IT HURTS
OH MY GOD
IT HURTS SO MUCH MAKE IT STOP MAKE IT STOP
IT'S OKAY BILLY IT'S OKAY THEY'LL FIX IT THEY'LL FIX IT JUST LIKE IT WAS
DAD IT HURTS SO MUCH
OH MY GOD
DAD ARE WE HOME YET? ARE WE THERE I'M TIRED
HOME? OH BILLY BILLY OH MY GOD DON'T GO TO SLEEP
DAD IT HURTS IT HURTS
DON'T GO... OH BILLY
MAKE IT STOP DAD MAKE IT STOP
OH BILLY OH BILLY
I'M SO TIRED
OH... OH...
DAD WHERE ARE YOU DAD DON'T LEAVE
I'M RIGHT HERE BILLY I'M RIGHT HERE... sob
IT... HURTS.. GURK
I'M RIGHT--

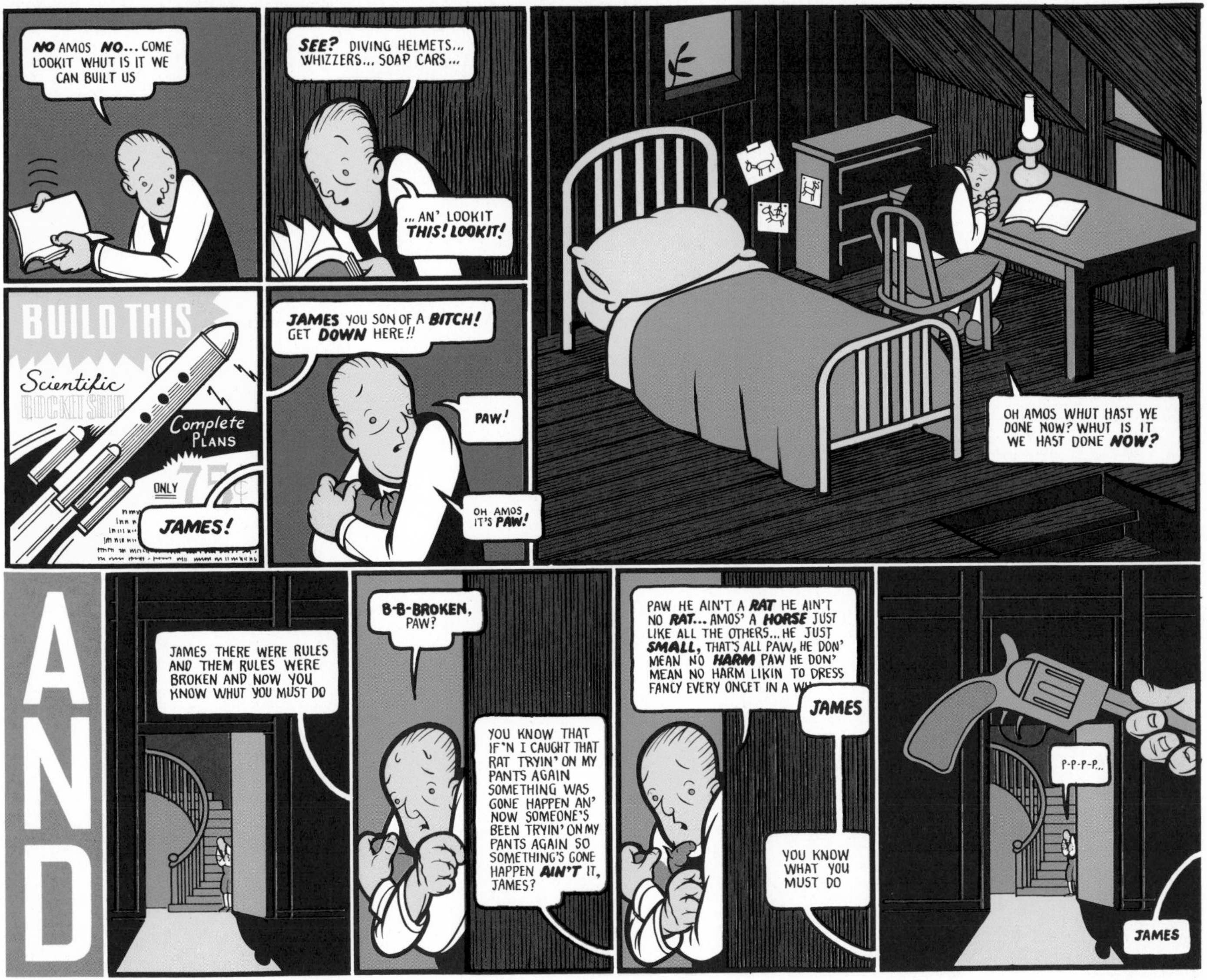
NO AMOS NO... COME LOOKIT WHUT IS IT WE CAN BUILT US
SEE? DIVING HELMETS... WHIZZERS... SOAP CARS...
...AN' LOOKIT THIS! LOOKIT!
BUILD THIS
Scientific
ROCKET SHIP
Complete PLANS
ONLY 75¢
JAMES!
JAMES YOU SON OF A BITCH! GET DOWN HERE!!
PAW!
OH AMOS IT'S PAW!
OH AMOS WHUT HAST WE DONE NOW? WHUT IS IT WE HAST DONE NOW?
AND
JAMES THERE WERE RULES AND THEM RULES WERE BROKEN AND NOW YOU KNOW WHUT YOU MUST DO
B-B-BROKEN, PAW?
YOU KNOW THAT IF'N I CAUGHT THAT RAT TRYIN' ON MY PANTS AGAIN SOMETHING WAS GONE HAPPEN AN' NOW SOMEONE'S BEEN TRYIN' ON MY PANTS AGAIN SO SOMETHING'S GONE HAPPEN AIN'T IT, JAMES?
PAW HE AIN'T A RAT HE AIN'T NO RAT... AMOS' A HORSE JUST LIKE ALL THE OTHERS... HE JUST SMALL, THAT'S ALL PAW, HE DON' MEAN NO HARM PAW HE DON' MEAN NO HARM LIKIN TO DRESS FANCY EVERY ONCET IN A
JAMES
YOU KNOW WHAT YOU MUST DO
P-P-P-P...
JAMES

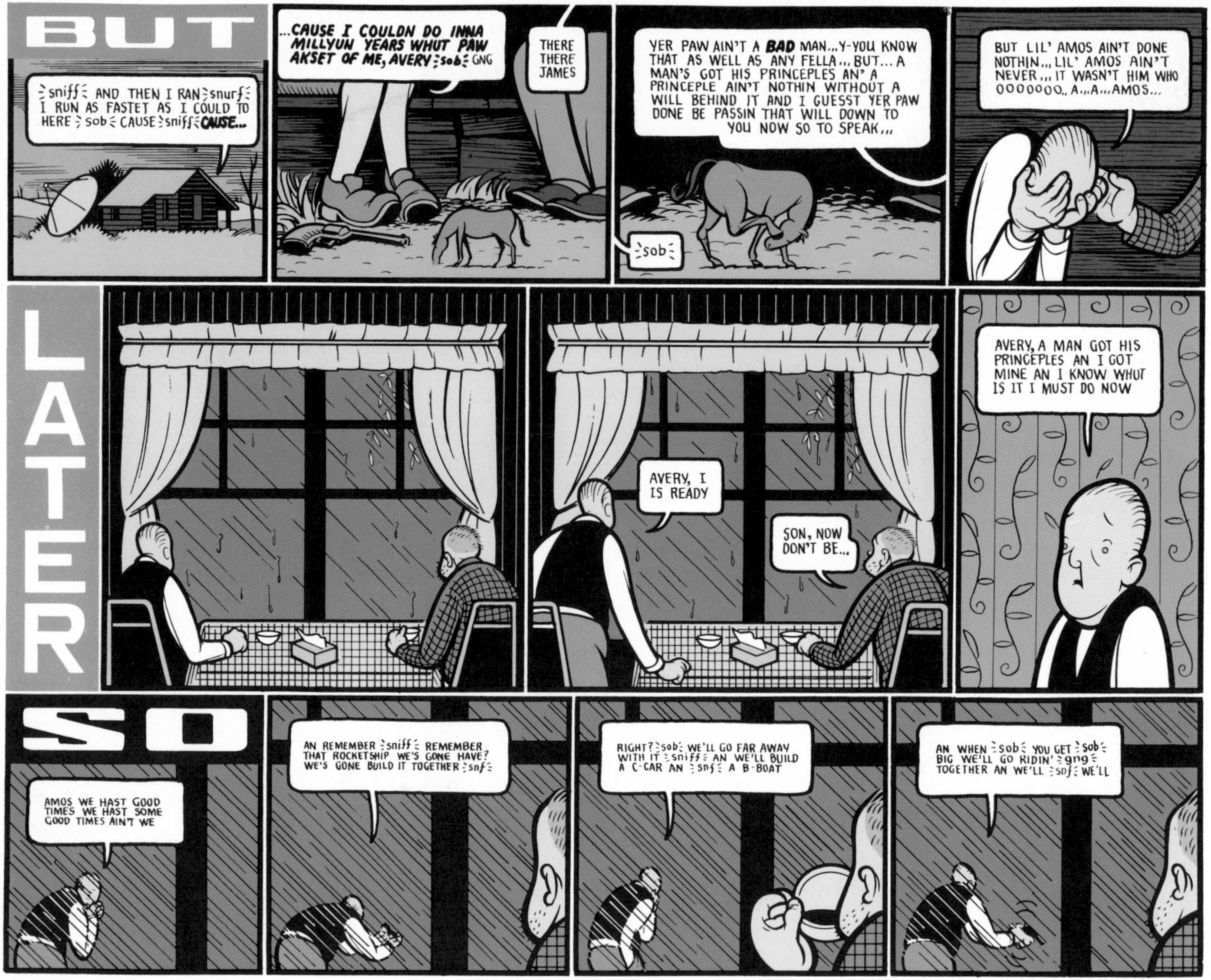
BUT
sniff AND THEN I RAN snurf I RUN AS FASTET AS I COULD TO HERE sob CAUSE sniff CAUSE...
...CAUSE I COULDN DO INNA MILLYUN YEARS WHUT PAW AKSET OF ME, AVERY sob GNG
THERE THERE JAMES
YER PAW AIN'T A BAD MAN...Y-YOU KNOW THAT AS WELL AS ANY FELLA... BUT... A MAN'S GOT HIS PRINCEPLES AN' A PRINCEPLE AIN'T NOTHIN WITHOUT A WILL BEHIND IT AND I GUESST YER PAW DONE BE PASSIN THAT WILL DOWN TO YOU NOW SO TO SPEAK...
sob
BUT LIL' AMOS AIN'T DONE NOTHIN... LIL' AMOS AIN'T NEVER... IT WASN'T HIM WHO OOOOOOO.. A...A...AMOS...
LATER
AVERY, I IS READY
SON, NOW DON'T BE...
AVERY, A MAN GOT HIS PRINCEPLES AN I GOT MINE AN I KNOW WHUT IS IT I MUST DO NOW
SO
AMOS WE HAST GOOD TIMES WE HAST SOME GOOD TIMES AIN'T WE
AN REMEMBER sniff REMEMBER THAT ROCKETSHIP WE'S GONE HAVE? WE'S GONE BUILD IT TOGETHER snf
RIGHT? sob WE'LL GO FAR AWAY WITH IT sniff AN WE'LL BUILD A C-CAR AN snf A B-BOAT
AN WHEN sob YOU GET sob BIG WE'LL GO RIDIN' gng TOGETHER AN WE'LL snf WE'LL

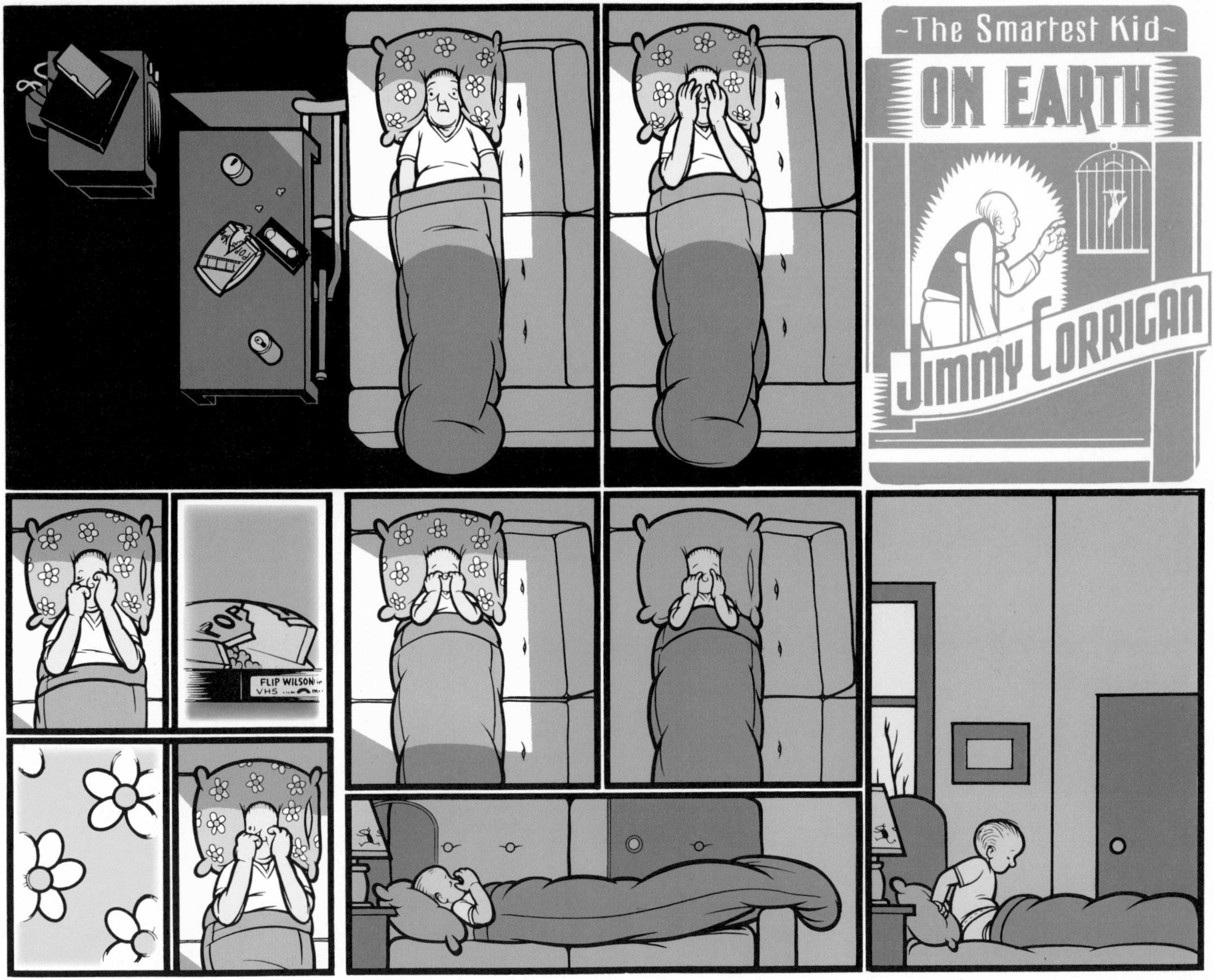
~The Smartest Kid~
ON EARTH
Jimmy Corrigan
POP
FLIP WILSON
VHS

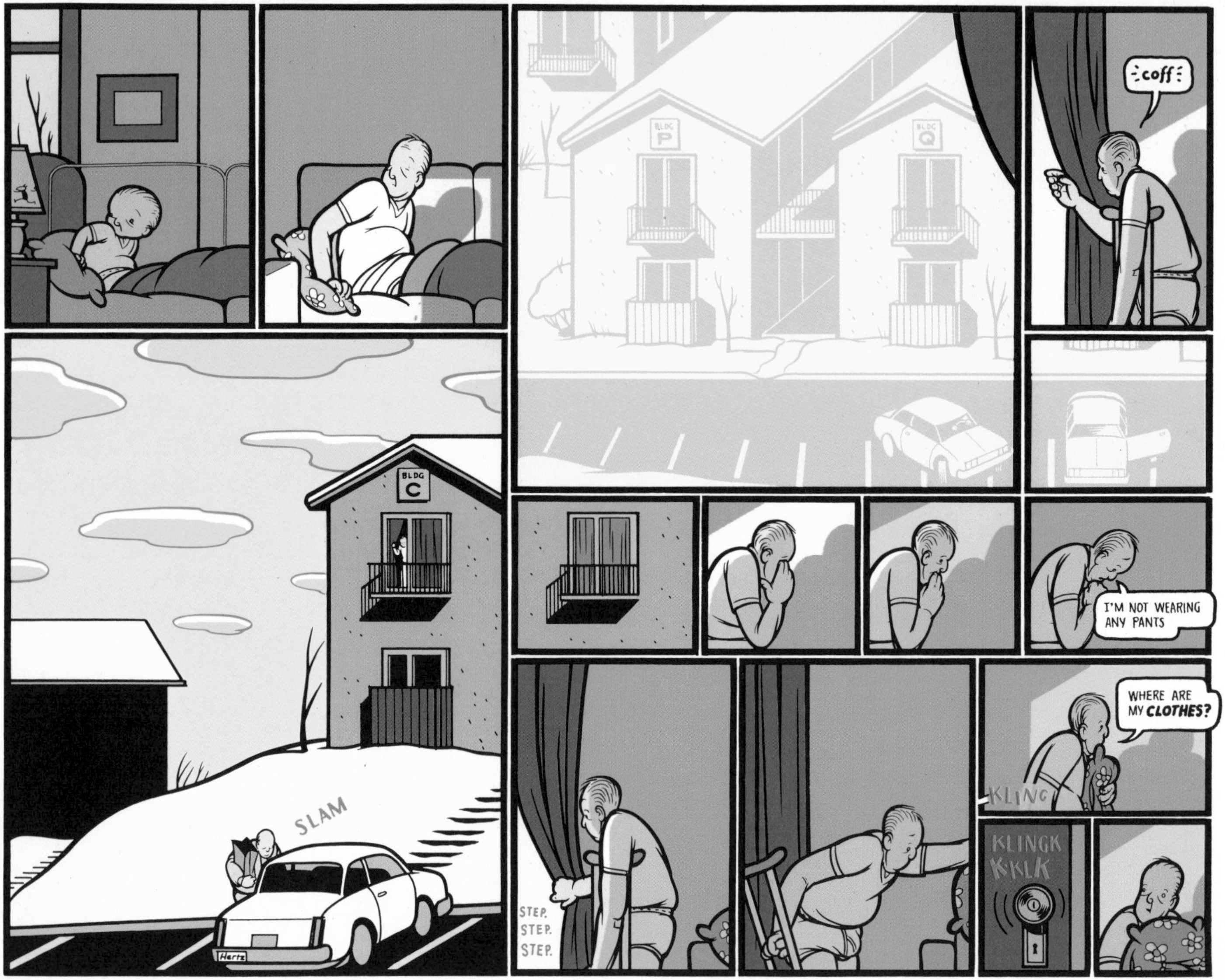
coff
BLDG P
BLDG Q
BLDG C
SLAM
Hertz
I'M NOT WEARING ANY PANTS
STEP. STEP. STEP.
WHERE ARE MY CLOTHES?
KLING
KLINGK K·KLK

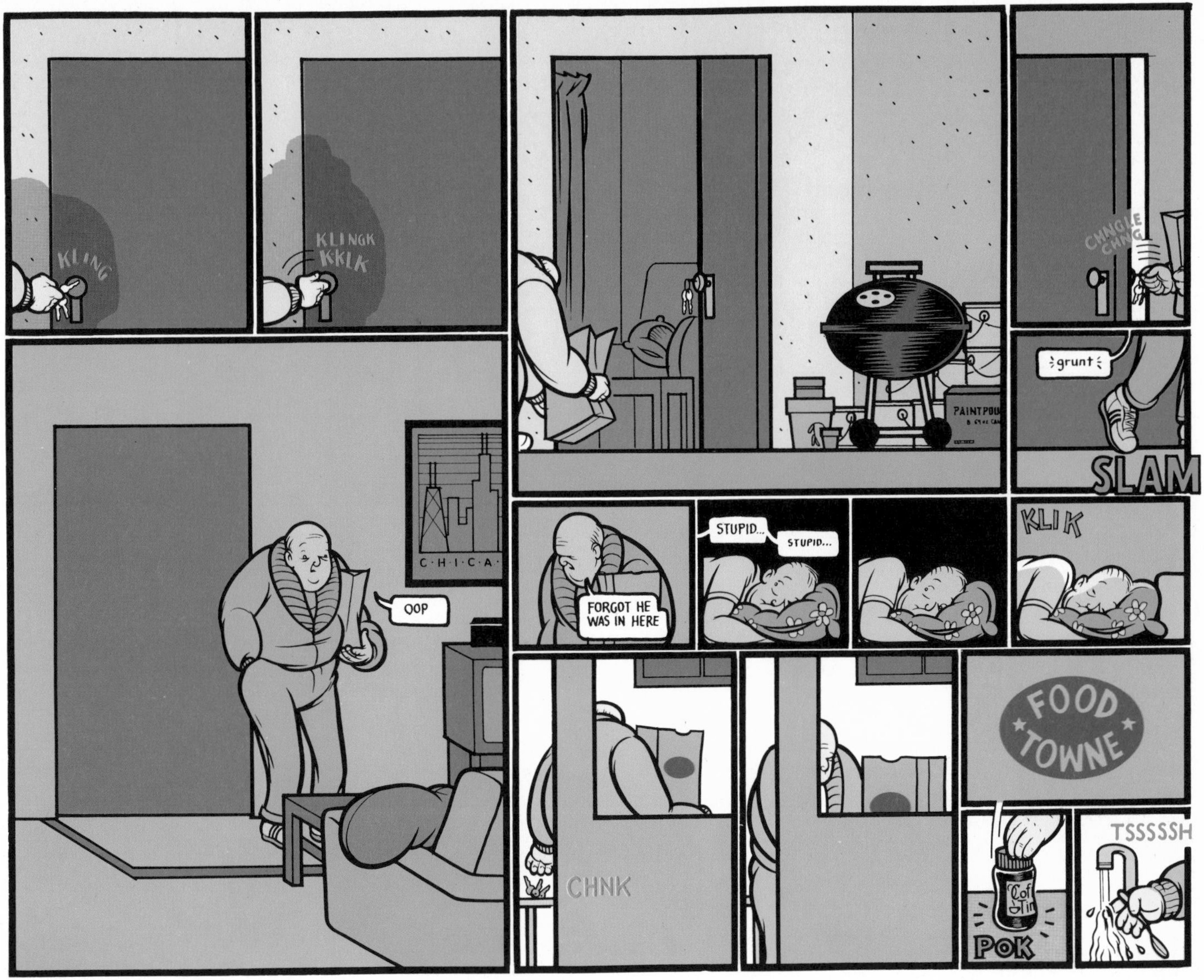
KLING
KLINGK KKLK
CHNGLE CHNG
grunt
SLAM
C·H·I·C·A
OOP
FORGOT HE WAS IN HERE
STUPID...
STUPID...
KLIK
PAINTPOU
CHNK
FOOD TOWNE
Cof Tin
POK
TSSSSSH

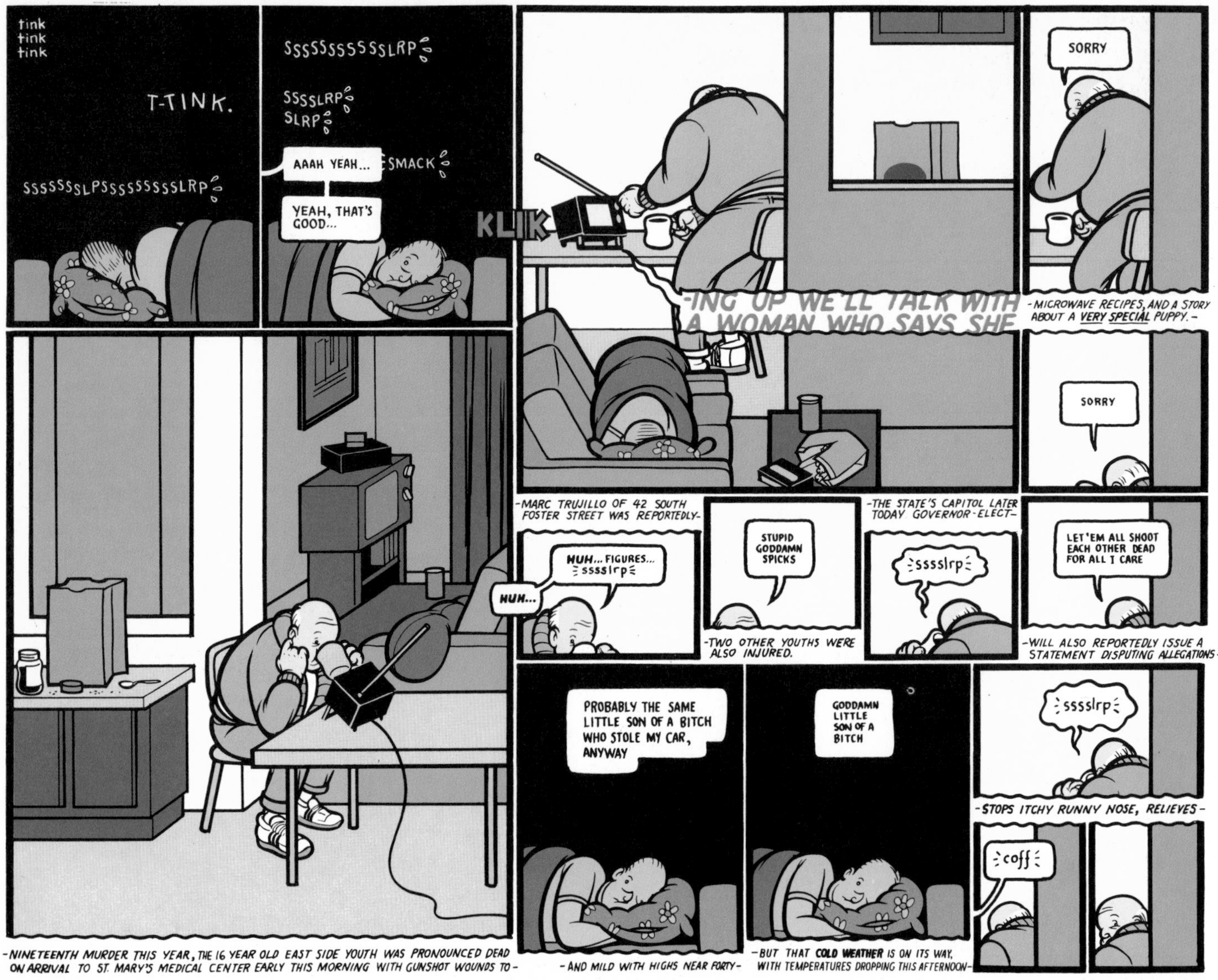

tink
tink
tink
T-TINK.
SSSSSSSLPSSSSSSSSSLRP
SSSSSSSSSSSLRP
SSSSLRP
SLRP
AAAH YEAH...
SMACK
YEAH, THAT'S GOOD...
KLIK
-ING UP WE'LL TALK WITH A WOMAN WHO SAYS SHE
SORRY
-MICROWAVE RECIPES, AND A STORY ABOUT A VERY SPECIAL PUPPY.-
SORRY
-NINETEENTH MURDER THIS YEAR, THE 16 YEAR OLD EAST SIDE YOUTH WAS PRONOUNCED DEAD ON ARRIVAL TO ST. MARY'S MEDICAL CENTER EARLY THIS MORNING WITH GUNSHOT WOUNDS TO-
-MARC TRUJILLO OF 42 SOUTH FOSTER STREET WAS REPORTEDLY-
HUH...
HUH... FIGURES... sssslrp
STUPID GODDAMN SPICKS
-TWO OTHER YOUTHS WERE ALSO INJURED.
-THE STATE'S CAPITOL LATER TODAY GOVERNOR-ELECT-
sssslrp
LET'EM ALL SHOOT EACH OTHER DEAD FOR ALL I CARE
-WILL ALSO REPORTEDLY ISSUE A STATEMENT DISPUTING ALLEGATIONS-
PROBABLY THE SAME LITTLE SON OF A BITCH WHO STOLE MY CAR, ANYWAY
-AND MILD WITH HIGHS NEAR FORTY-
GODDAMN LITTLE SON OF A BITCH
-BUT THAT COLD WEATHER IS ON ITS WAY, WITH TEMPERATURES DROPPING THIS AFTERNOON-
sssslrp
-STOPS ITCHY RUNNY NOSE, RELIEVES-
coff

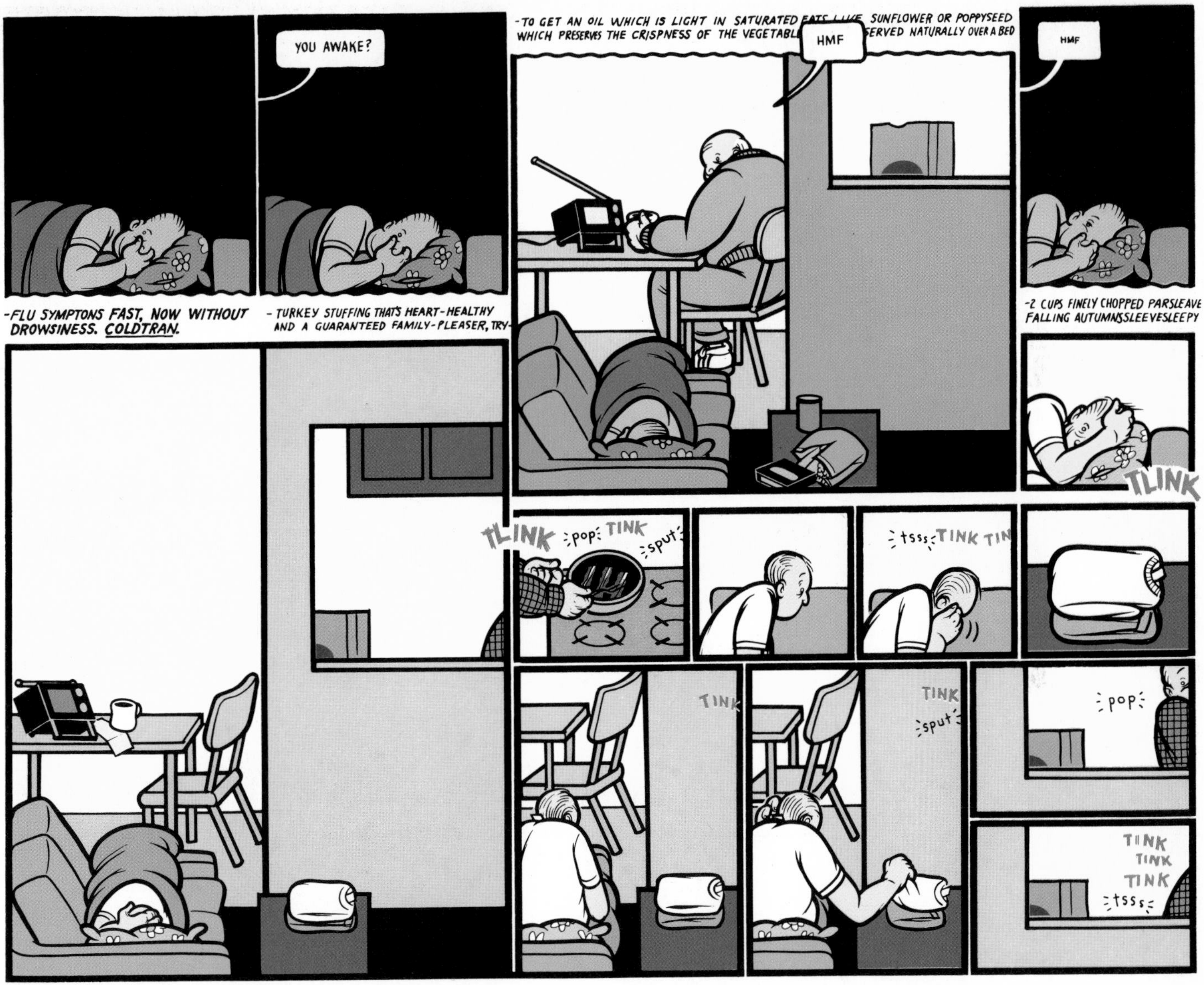
-FLU SYMPTONS FAST, NOW WITHOUT DROWSINESS. COLDTRAN.
YOU AWAKE?
- TURKEY STUFFING THAT'S HEART-HEALTHY AND A GUARANTEED FAMILY-PLEASER, TRY-
-TO GET AN OIL WHICH IS LIGHT IN SATURATED
SUNFLOWER OR POPPYSEED
WHICH PRESERVES THE CRISPNESS OF THE VEGETABL
SERVED NATURALLY OVER A BED
HMF
HMF
-2 CUPS FINELY CHOPPED PARSLEAVE FALLING AUTUMNSSLEEVESLEEPY
TLINK
TLINK
pop
TINK
sput
tsss
TINK TIN
TINK
TINK
sput
pop
TINK
TINK
TINK
tsss

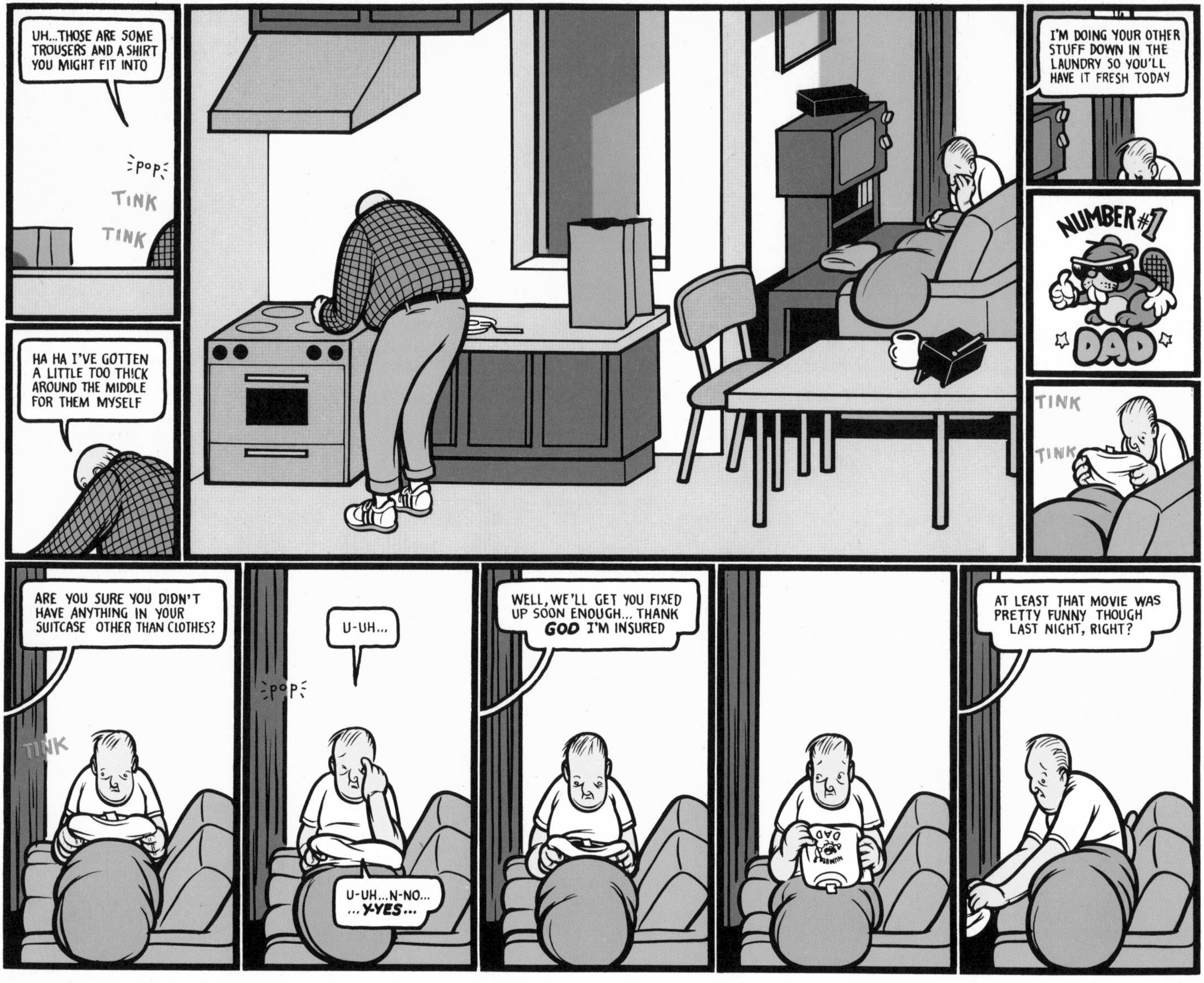

UH...THOSE ARE SOME TROUSERS AND A SHIRT YOU MIGHT FIT INTO
POP
TINK
TINK
HA HA I'VE GOTTEN A LITTLE TOO THICK AROUND THE MIDDLE FOR THEM MYSELF
I'M DOING YOUR OTHER STUFF DOWN IN THE LAUNDRY SO YOU'LL HAVE IT FRESH TODAY
NUMBER #1
DAD
TINK
TINK
ARE YOU SURE YOU DIDN'T HAVE ANYTHING IN YOUR SUITCASE OTHER THAN CLOTHES?
TINK
U-UH...
POP
U-UH...N-NO... ...Y-YES...
WELL, WE'LL GET YOU FIXED UP SOON ENOUGH... THANK GOD I'M INSURED
AT LEAST THAT MOVIE WAS PRETTY FUNNY THOUGH LAST NIGHT, RIGHT?

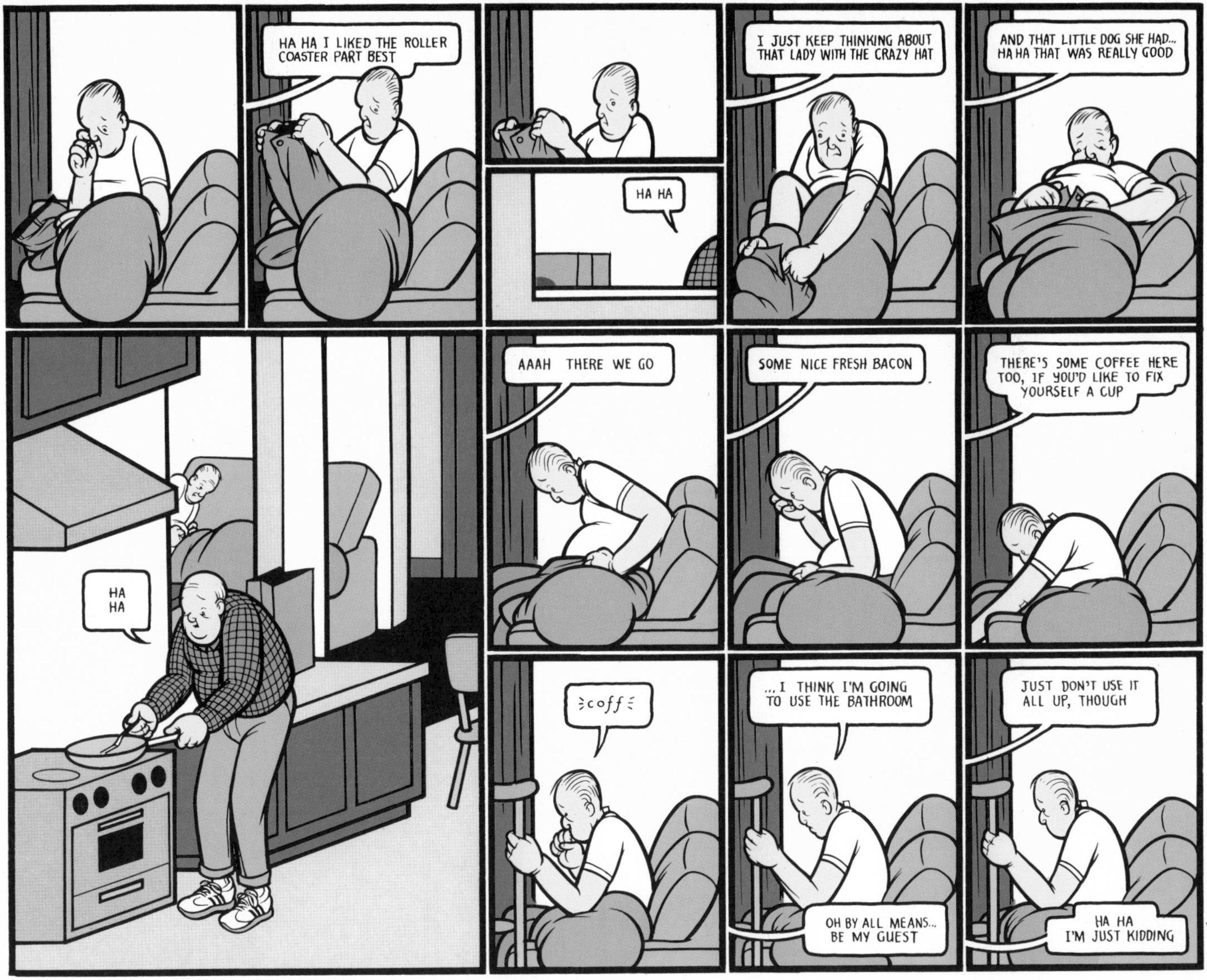
HA HA I LIKED THE ROLLER COASTER PART BEST
HA HA
I JUST KEEP THINKING ABOUT THAT LADY WITH THE CRAZY HAT
AND THAT LITTLE DOG SHE HAD... HA HA THAT WAS REALLY GOOD
HA HA
AAAH THERE WE GO
SOME NICE FRESH BACON
THERE'S SOME COFFEE HERE TOO, IF YOU'D LIKE TO FIX YOURSELF A CUP
coff
...I THINK I'M GOING TO USE THE BATHROOM
OH BY ALL MEANS... BE MY GUEST
JUST DON'T USE IT ALL UP, THOUGH
HA HA I'M JUST KIDDING

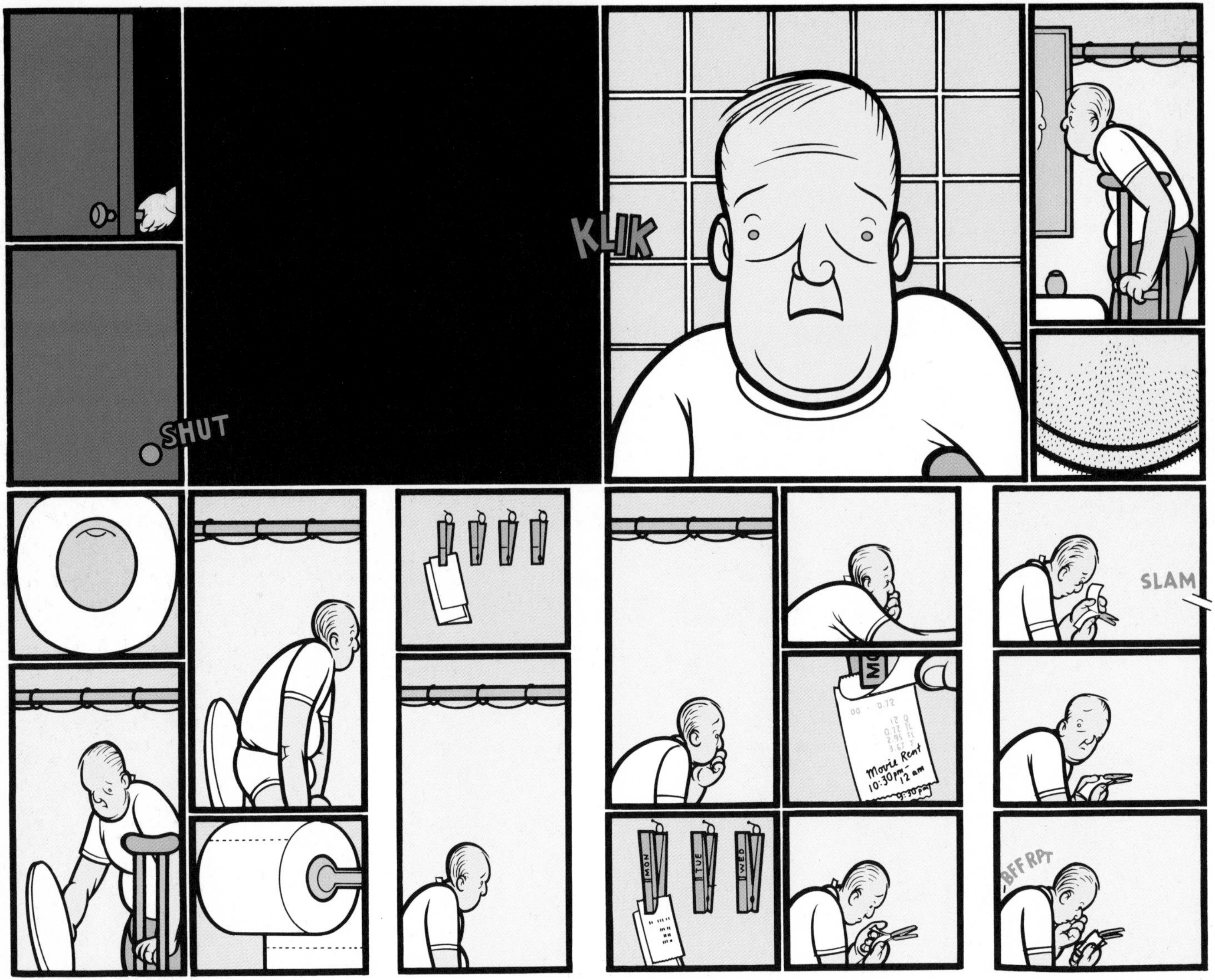
SHUT
KLIK
SLAM
Movie Rent
10:30pm - 12 am
9:30pm
MON
TUE
WED
BFFRPT

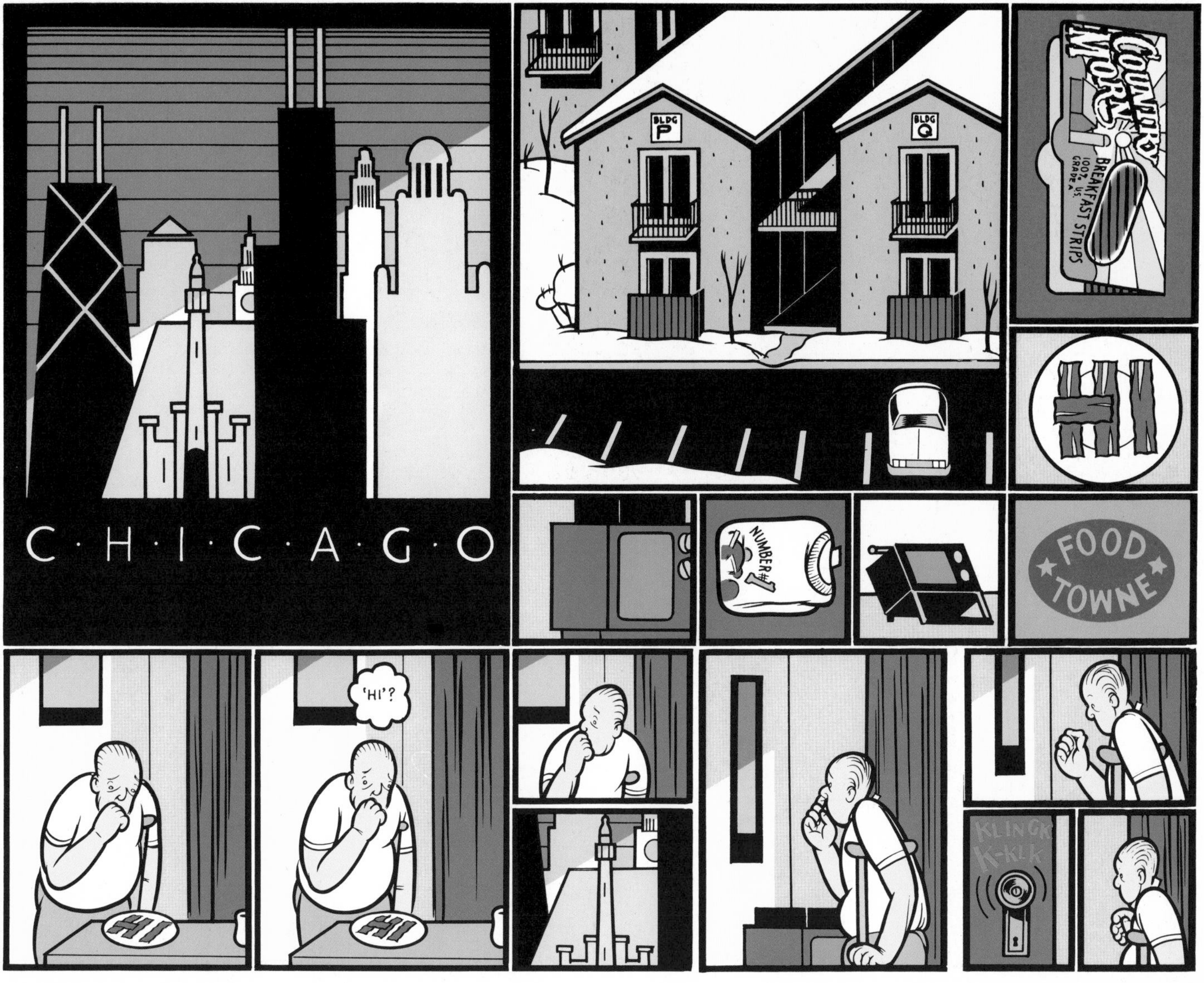
C·H·I·C·A·G·O
BLDG P
BLDG Q
COUNTRY MORN
BREAKFAST STRIPS
100% U.S. GRADE A
NUMBER #1
FOOD TOWNE
HI
'HI'?
HI
KLINGK
K-KLK

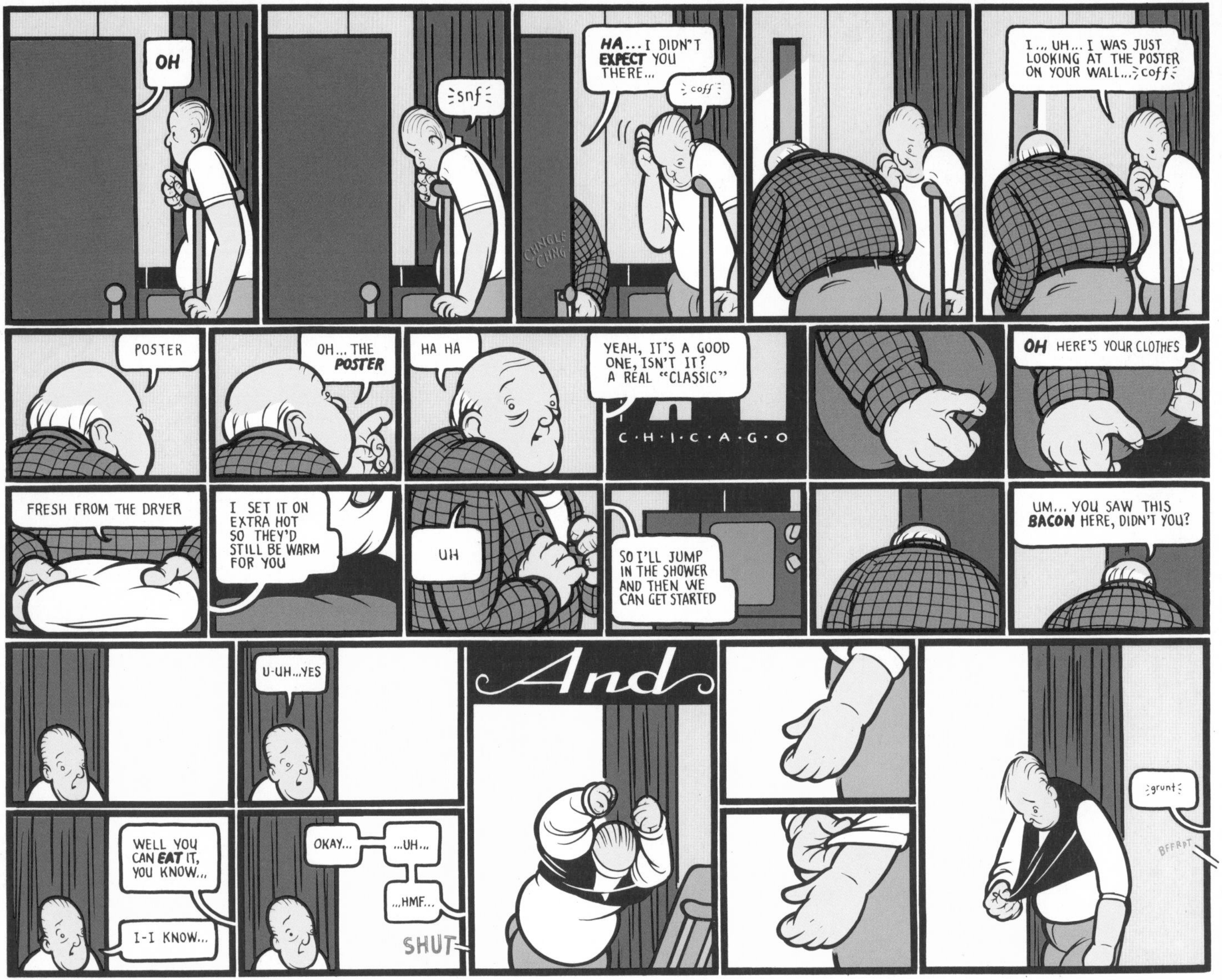
OH
snf
HA... I DIDN'T EXPECT YOU THERE...
coff
I... UH... I WAS JUST LOOKING AT THE POSTER ON YOUR WALL... coff
POSTER
OH... THE POSTER
HA HA
YEAH, IT'S A GOOD ONE, ISN'T IT? A REAL "CLASSIC"
C·H·I·C·A·G·O
OH HERE'S YOUR CLOTHES
FRESH FROM THE DRYER
I SET IT ON EXTRA HOT SO THEY'D STILL BE WARM FOR YOU
UH
SO I'LL JUMP IN THE SHOWER AND THEN WE CAN GET STARTED
UM... YOU SAW THIS BACON HERE, DIDN'T YOU?
U-UH...YES
WELL YOU CAN EAT IT, YOU KNOW...
I-I KNOW...
OKAY...
...UH...
...HMF...
SHUT
And
grunt
BFFRPT

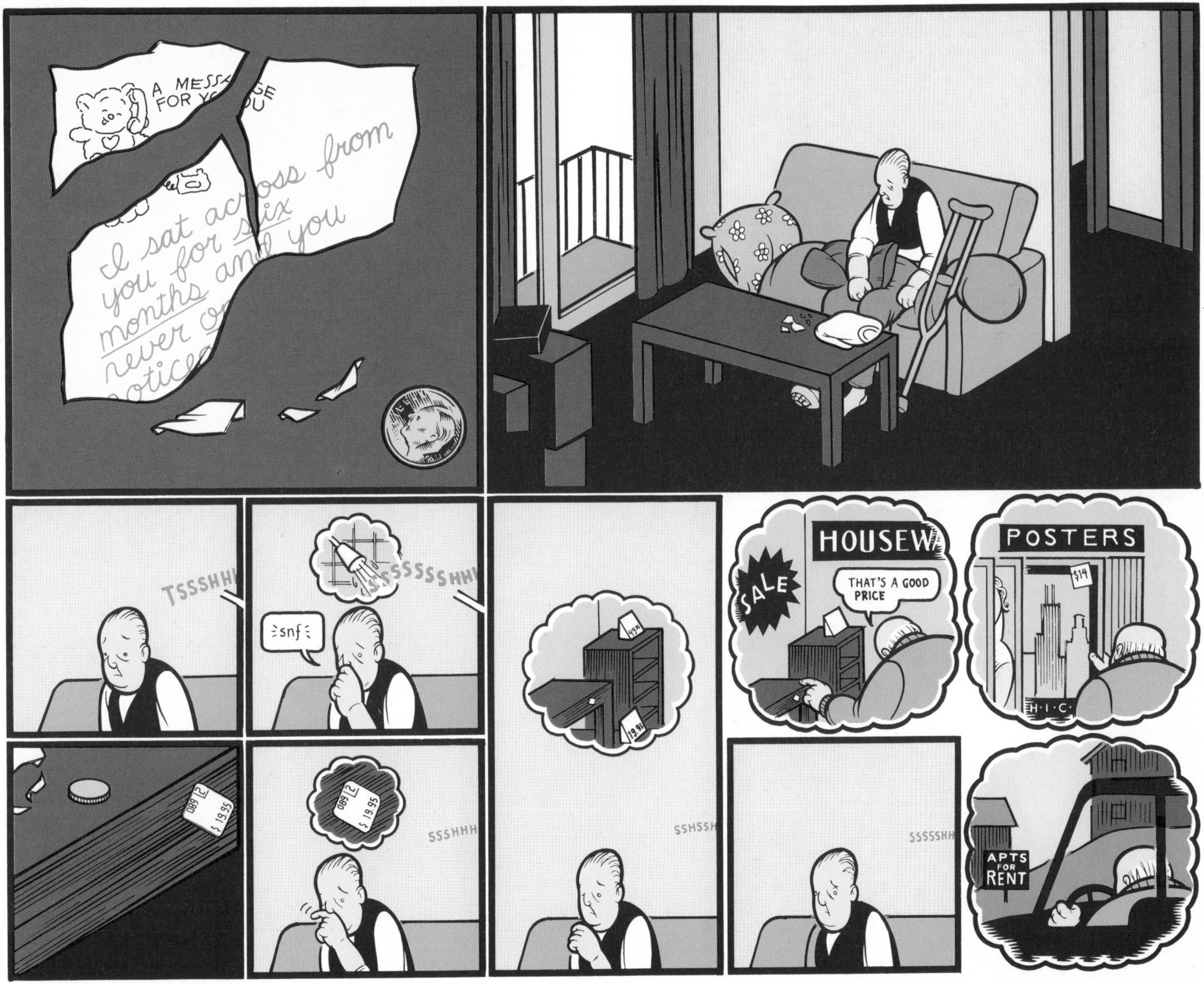

A MESS GE
FOR YO U
I sat ac oss from
you for six
months and you
never o
otice
TSSSHH
snf
SSSSSSSHH
089 12
$ 19.95
SSSHHH
SSHSSH
SALE
HOUSEW
THAT'S A GOOD PRICE
POSTERS
$14
H·I·C·
SSSSSHH
APTS FOR RENT

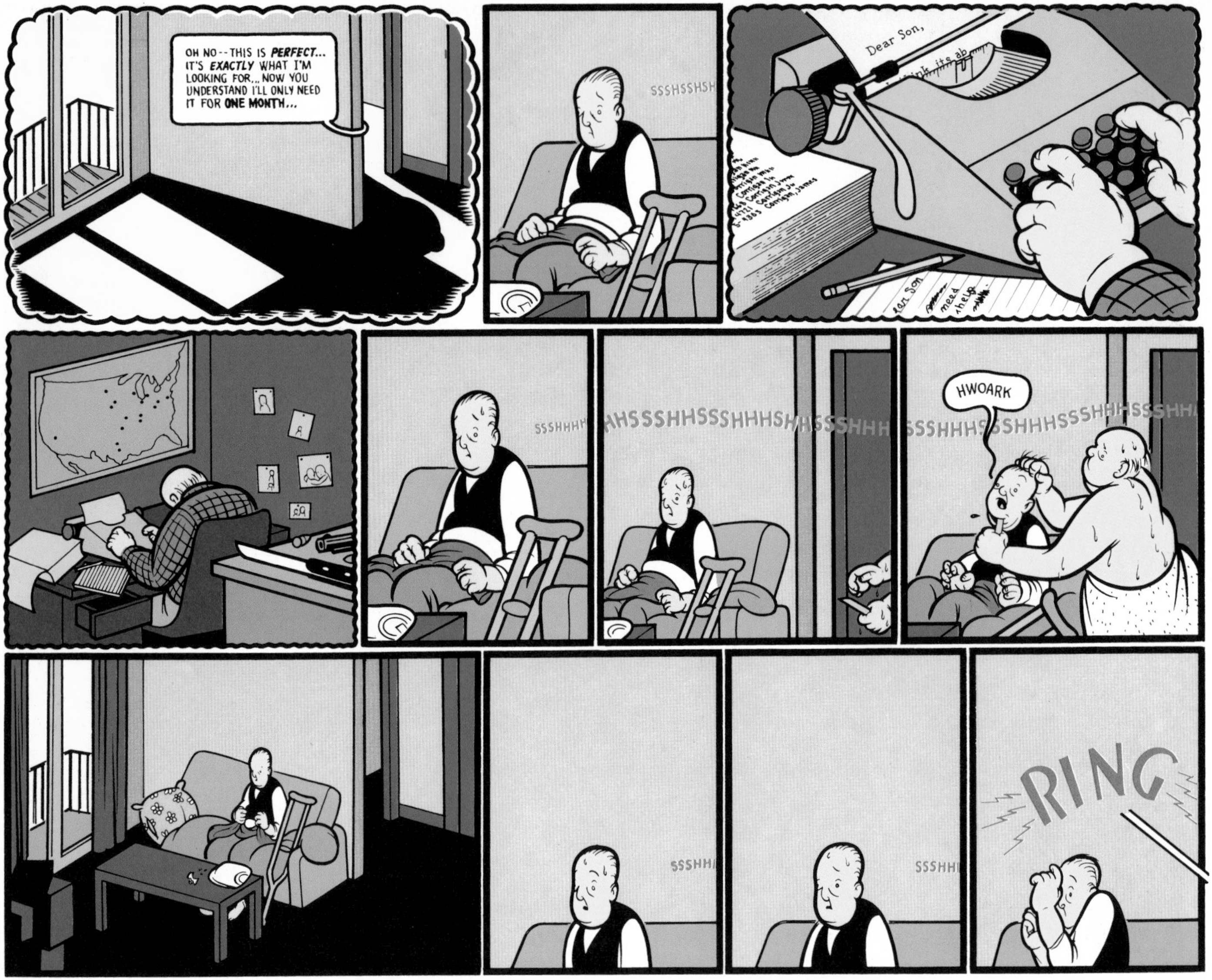
OH NO--THIS IS PERFECT... IT'S EXACTLY WHAT I'M LOOKING FOR... NOW YOU UNDERSTAND I'LL ONLY NEED IT FOR ONE MONTH...
SSSHSSHSH
Dear Son,
SSSHHHH
HWOARK
SSSHH
SSSHH
RING

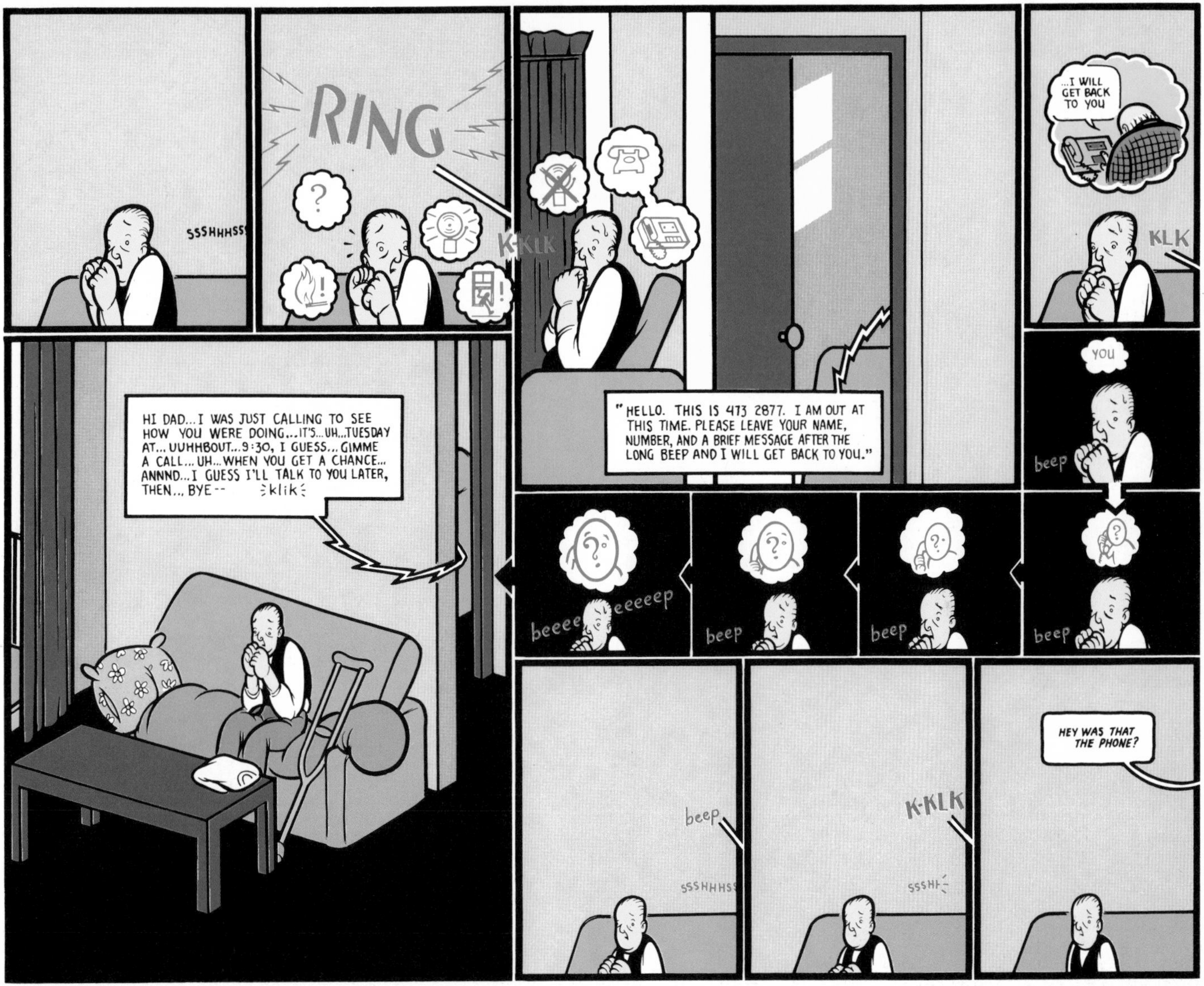
SSSHHHSSS
RING
K-KLK
"HELLO. THIS IS 473 2877. I AM OUT AT THIS TIME. PLEASE LEAVE YOUR NAME, NUMBER, AND A BRIEF MESSAGE AFTER THE LONG BEEP AND I WILL GET BACK TO YOU."
...I WILL GET BACK TO YOU
KLK
YOU
beep
beep
beep
beep
beeee eeeeep
HI DAD... I WAS JUST CALLING TO SEE HOW YOU WERE DOING... IT'S... UH... TUESDAY AT... UUHHBOUT... 9:30, I GUESS... GIMME A CALL... UH... WHEN YOU GET A CHANCE... ANNND... I GUESS I'LL TALK TO YOU LATER, THEN... BYE-- klik
beep
SSSHHHSS
K-KLK
SSSHH
HEY WAS THAT THE PHONE?

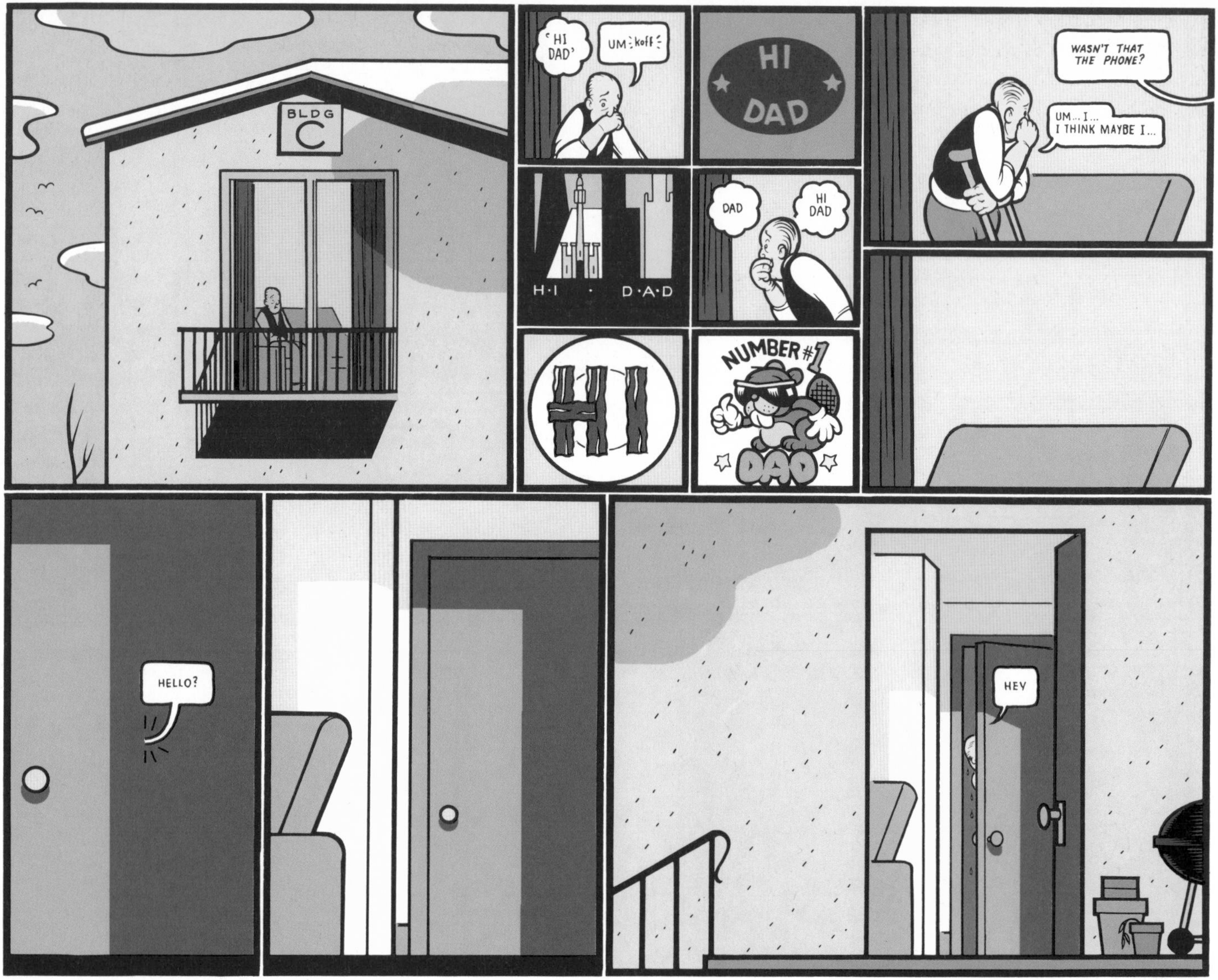
BLDG
C
HI
DAD
UM koff
HI
DAD
H·I · D·A·D
DAD
HI
DAD
HI
NUMBER #1
DAD
WASN'T THAT
THE PHONE?
UM... I...
I THINK MAYBE I...
HELLO?
HEY

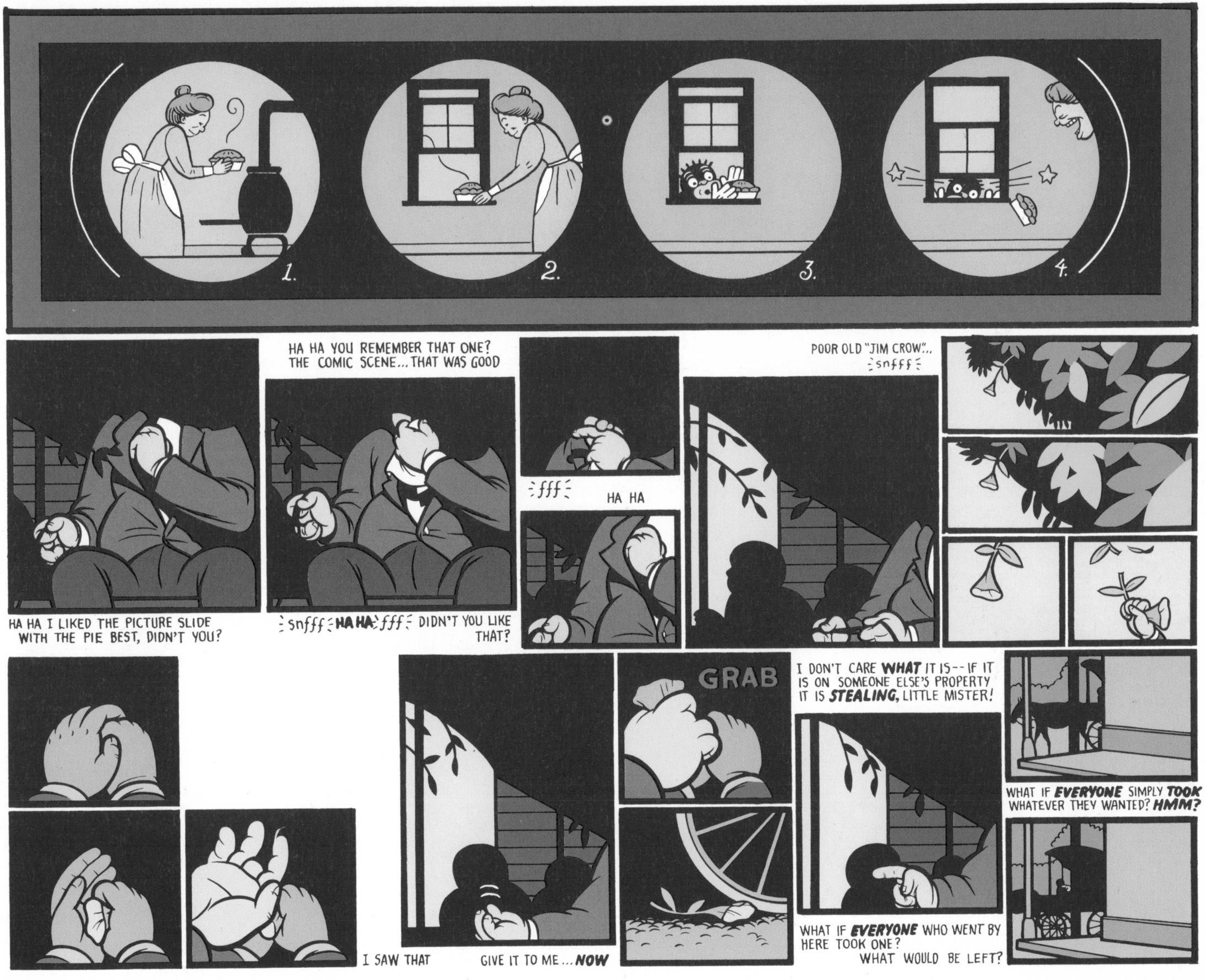
1.
2.
3.
4.
HA HA I LIKED THE PICTURE SLIDE WITH THE PIE BEST, DIDN'T YOU?
HA HA YOU REMEMBER THAT ONE? THE COMIC SCENE... THAT WAS GOOD
snfff HA HA fff DIDN'T YOU LIKE THAT?
fff
HA HA
POOR OLD "JIM CROW"...
snfff
I SAW THAT
GIVE IT TO ME... NOW
GRAB
I DON'T CARE WHAT IT IS-- IF IT IS ON SOMEONE ELSE'S PROPERTY IT IS STEALING, LITTLE MISTER!
WHAT IF EVERYONE WHO WENT BY HERE TOOK ONE? WHAT WOULD BE LEFT?
WHAT IF EVERYONE SIMPLY TOOK WHATEVER THEY WANTED? HMM?

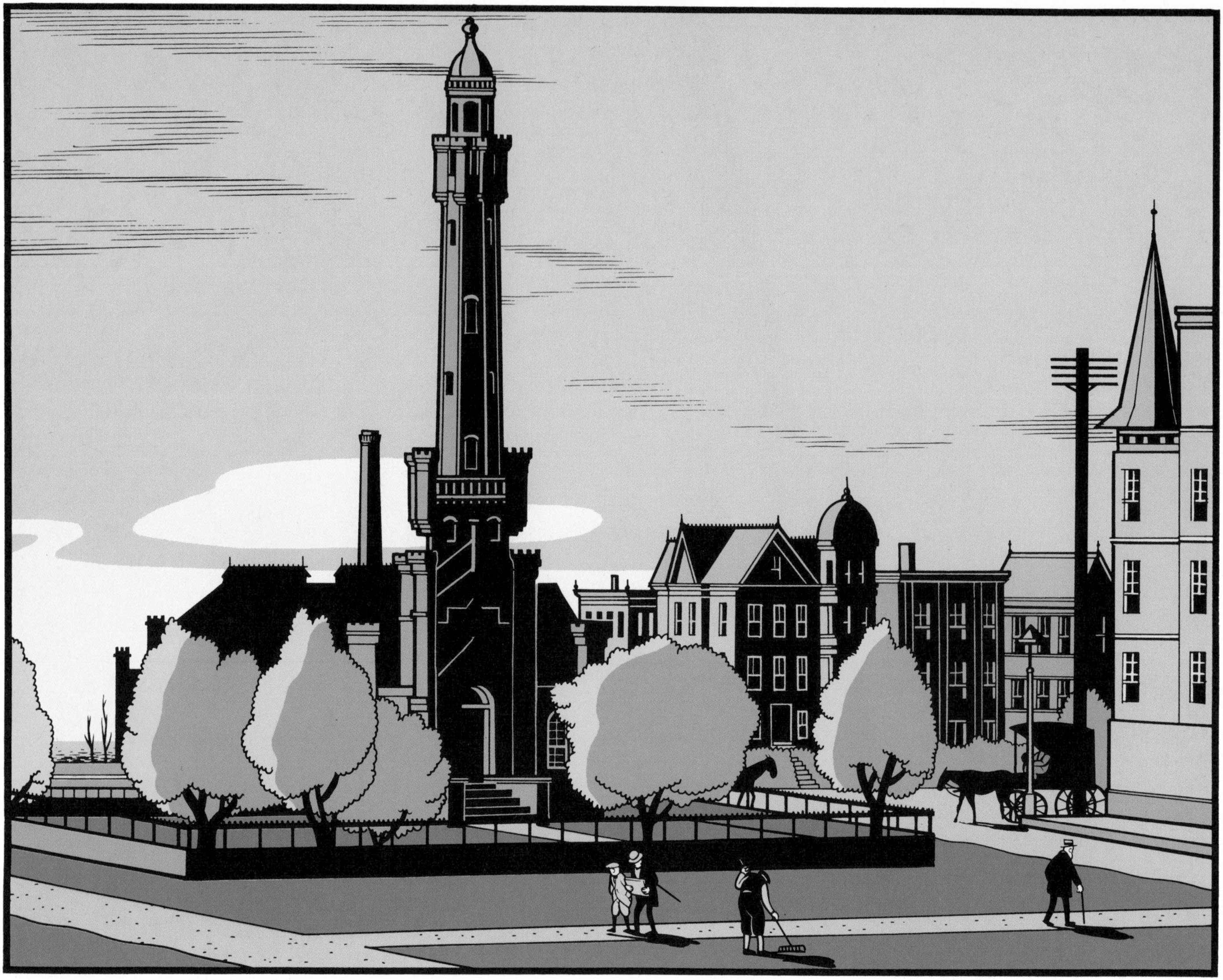

HMM? THEN WHERE WOULD WE BE?

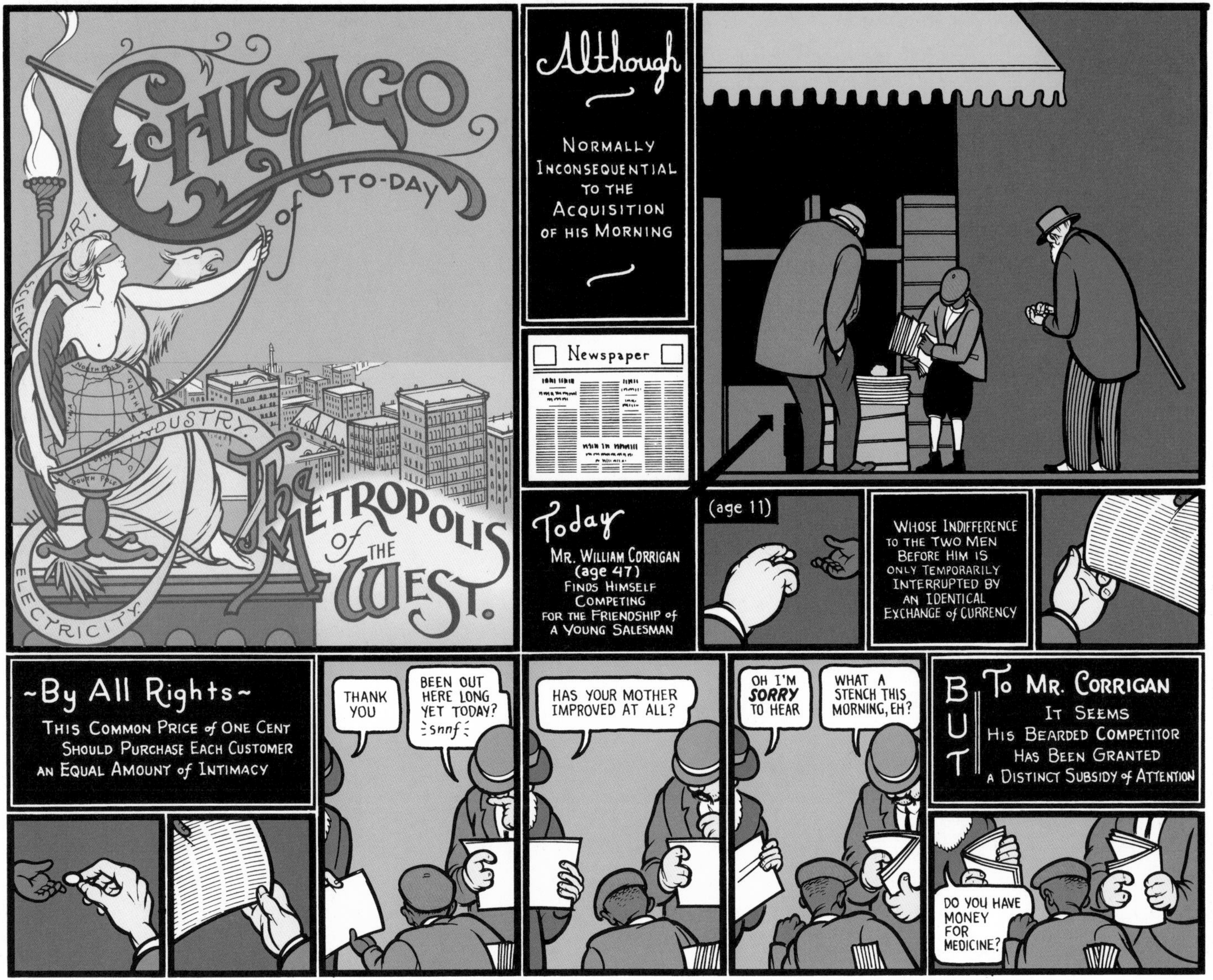

CHICAGO of TO-DAY
ART.
SCIENCE.
INDUSTRY
ELECTRICITY.
The METROPOLIS of THE WEST.
Although
NORMALLY INCONSEQUENTIAL TO THE ACQUISITION OF HIS MORNING
Newspaper
Today
MR. WILLIAM CORRIGAN (age 47) FINDS HIMSELF COMPETING FOR THE FRIENDSHIP of A YOUNG SALESMAN
(age 11)
WHOSE INDIFFERENCE TO THE TWO MEN BEFORE HIM IS ONLY TEMPORARILY INTERRUPTED BY AN IDENTICAL EXCHANGE of CURRENCY
~By All Rights~
THIS COMMON PRICE of ONE CENT SHOULD PURCHASE EACH CUSTOMER AN EQUAL AMOUNT of INTIMACY
THANK YOU
BEEN OUT HERE LONG YET TODAY?
snnf
HAS YOUR MOTHER IMPROVED AT ALL?
OH I'M SORRY TO HEAR
WHAT A STENCH THIS MORNING, EH?
BUT
TO MR. CORRIGAN IT SEEMS HIS BEARDED COMPETITOR HAS BEEN GRANTED A DISTINCT SUBSIDY of ATTENTION
DO YOU HAVE MONEY FOR MEDICINE?

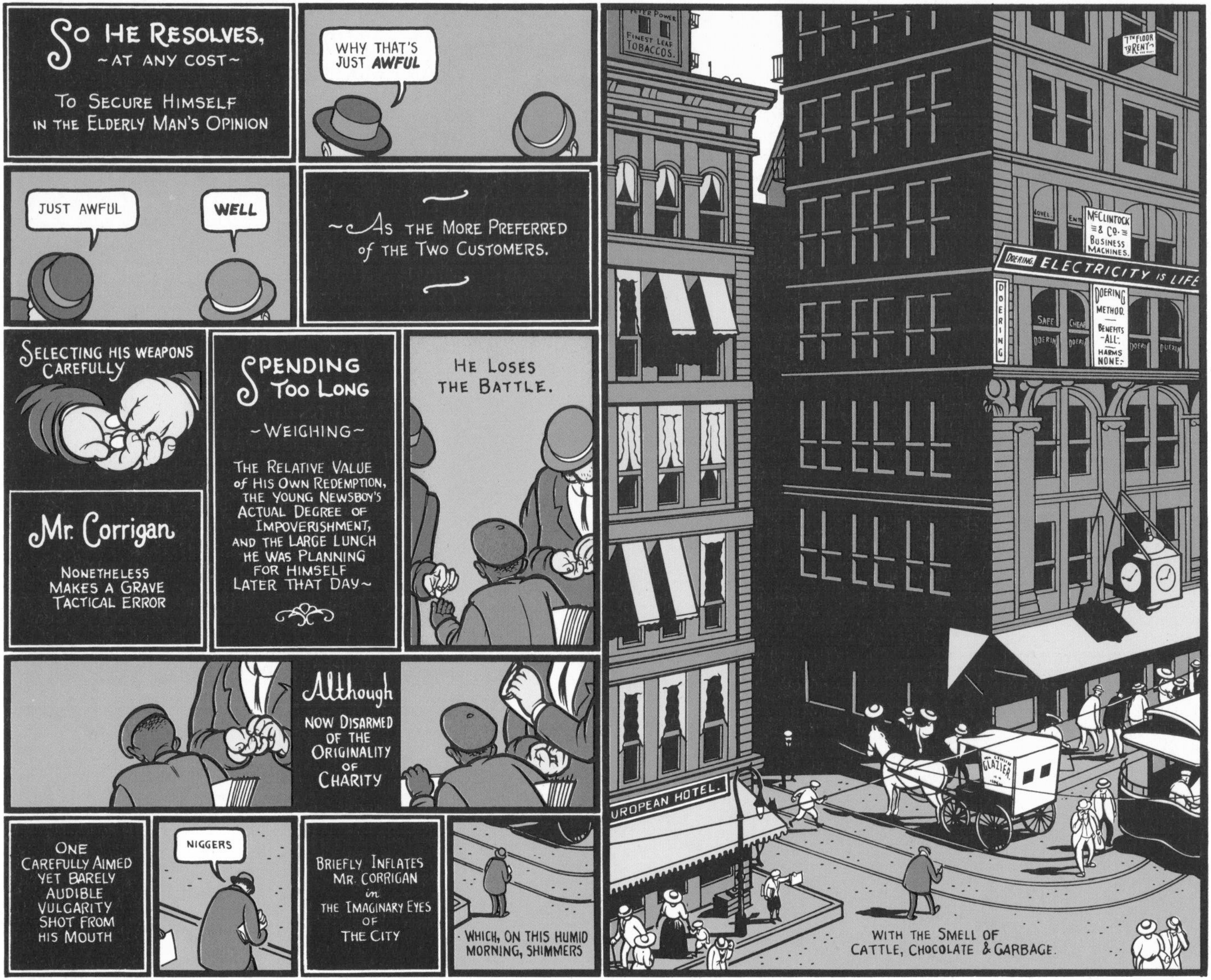

So He Resolves,
~at any cost~
To Secure Himself
in the Elderly Man's Opinion
WHY THAT'S JUST AWFUL
JUST AWFUL
WELL
~As the More Preferred
of the Two Customers.
Selecting his weapons carefully
Spending Too Long
~Weighing~
The Relative Value of His Own Redemption, the Young Newsboy's Actual Degree of Impoverishment, and the Large Lunch He Was Planning for Himself Later That Day~
He Loses the Battle.
Mr. Corrigan
Nonetheless Makes a Grave Tactical Error
Although
Now Disarmed of the Originality of Charity
One Carefully Aimed yet Barely Audible Vulgarity Shot From His Mouth
NIGGERS
Briefly Inflates Mr. Corrigan in the Imaginary Eyes of The City
Which, on this humid morning, shimmers
Finest Leaf Tobaccos.
7th Floor to Rent
McClintock & Co. Business Machines.
Doering Electricity is Life
Doering Method. Benefits All: Harms None:
Safe
Cheap
uropean Hotel.
Glazier
With the Smell of Cattle, Chocolate & Garbage.

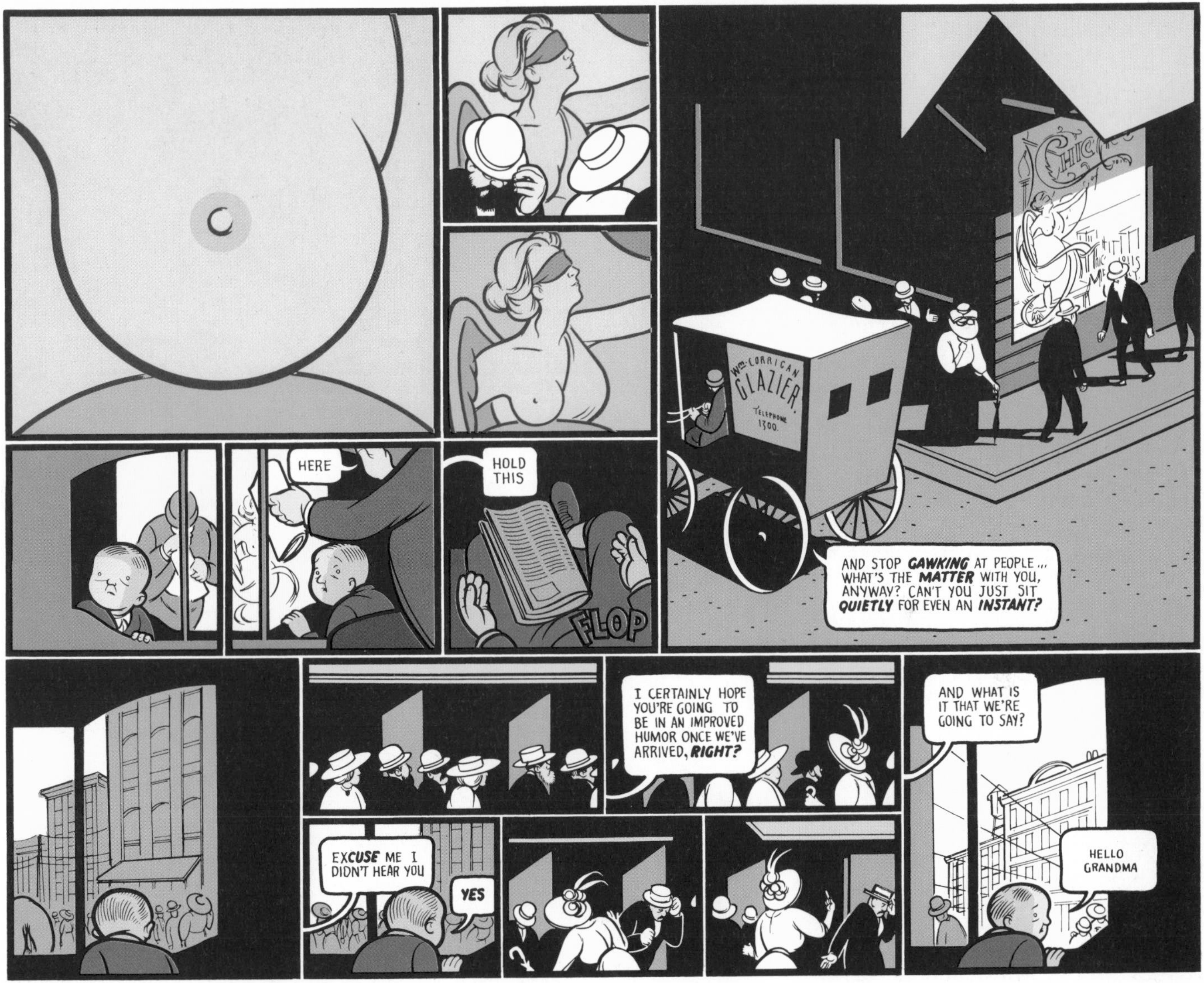

WM. CORRIGAN GLAZIER. TELEPHONE 1300.
HERE
HOLD THIS
FLOP
AND STOP GAWKING AT PEOPLE... WHAT'S THE MATTER WITH YOU, ANYWAY? CAN'T YOU JUST SIT QUIETLY FOR EVEN AN INSTANT?
I CERTAINLY HOPE YOU'RE GOING TO BE IN AN IMPROVED HUMOR ONCE WE'VE ARRIVED, RIGHT?
EXCUSE ME I DIDN'T HEAR YOU
YES
AND WHAT IS IT THAT WE'RE GOING TO SAY?
HELLO GRANDMA

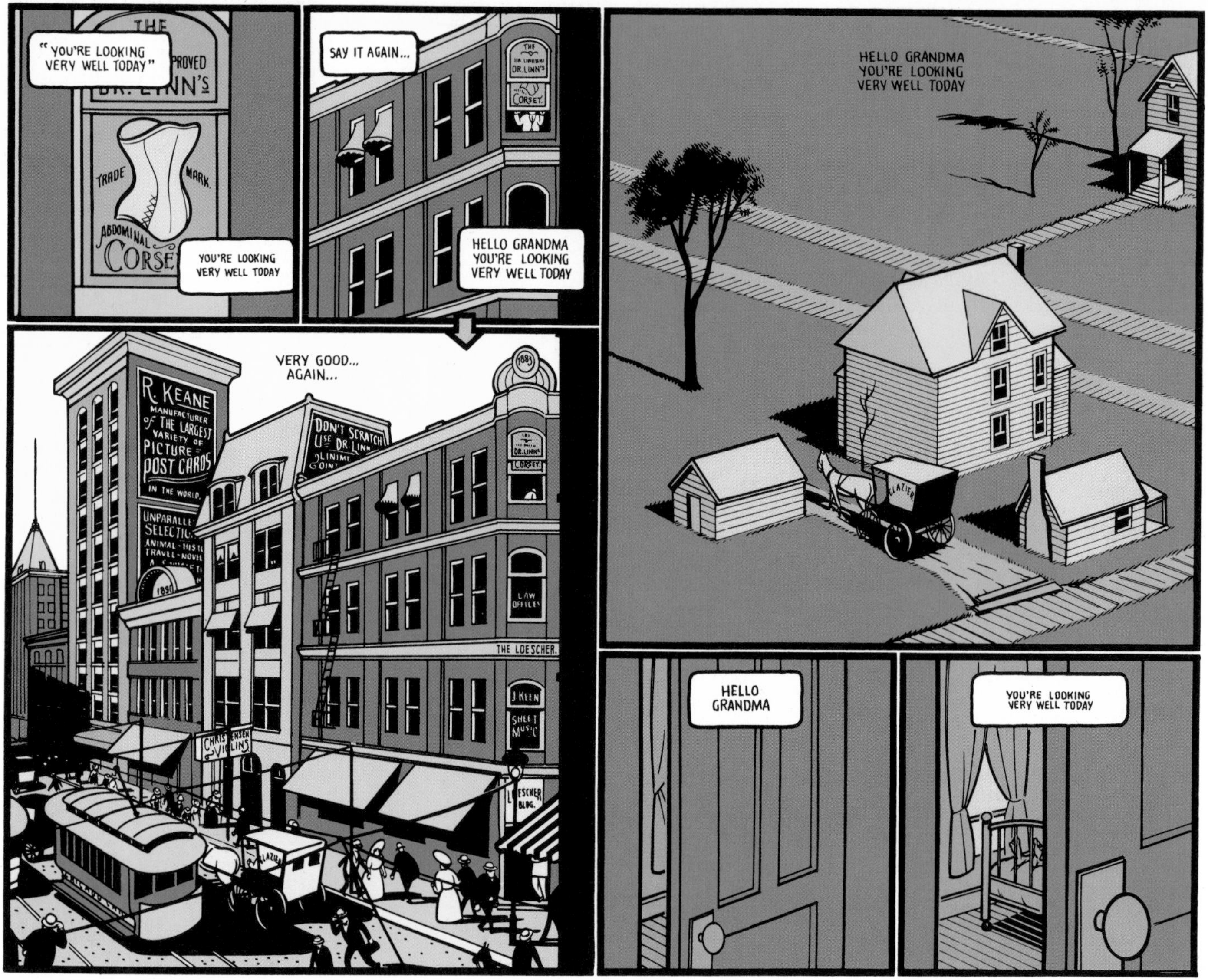

"YOU'RE LOOKING VERY WELL TODAY"
TRADE MARK.
YOU'RE LOOKING VERY WELL TODAY
SAY IT AGAIN...
HELLO GRANDMA YOU'RE LOOKING VERY WELL TODAY
VERY GOOD... AGAIN...
R. KEANE MANUFACTURER OF THE LARGEST VARIETY OF PICTURE POST CARDS IN THE WORLD.
DON'T SCRATCH
CORSET
LAW OFFICES
THE LOESCHER.
J. KEEN
SHEET MUSIC
HELLO GRANDMA YOU'RE LOOKING VERY WELL TODAY
HELLO GRANDMA
YOU'RE LOOKING VERY WELL TODAY

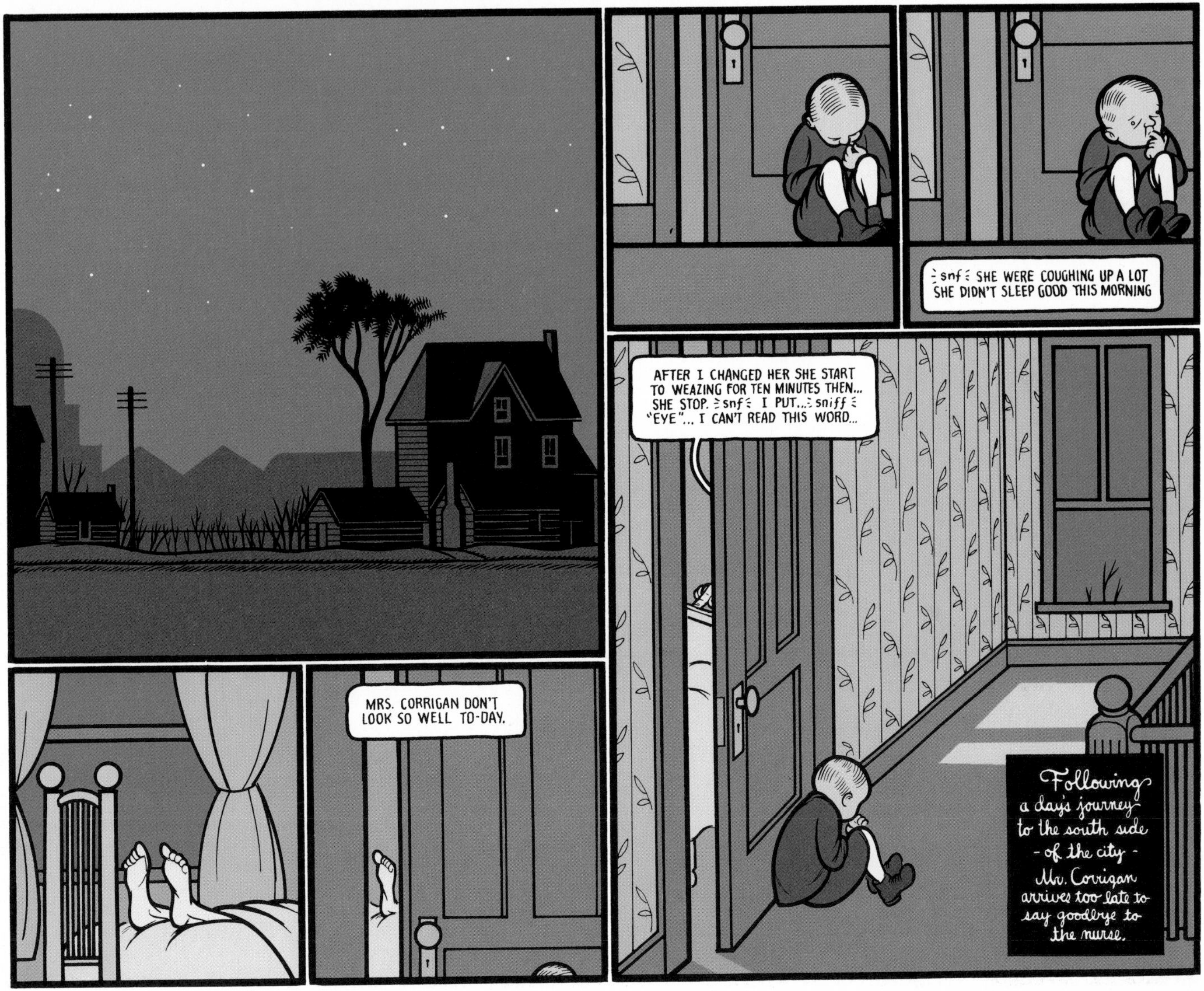
MRS. CORRIGAN DON'T LOOK SO WELL TO-DAY.
snf SHE WERE COUGHING UP A LOT SHE DIDN'T SLEEP GOOD THIS MORNING
AFTER I CHANGED HER SHE START TO WEAZING FOR TEN MINUTES THEN... SHE STOP. snf I PUT... sniff "EYE"... I CAN'T READ THIS WORD...
Following a day's journey to the south side - of the city - Mr. Corrigan arrives too late to say goodbye to the nurse.

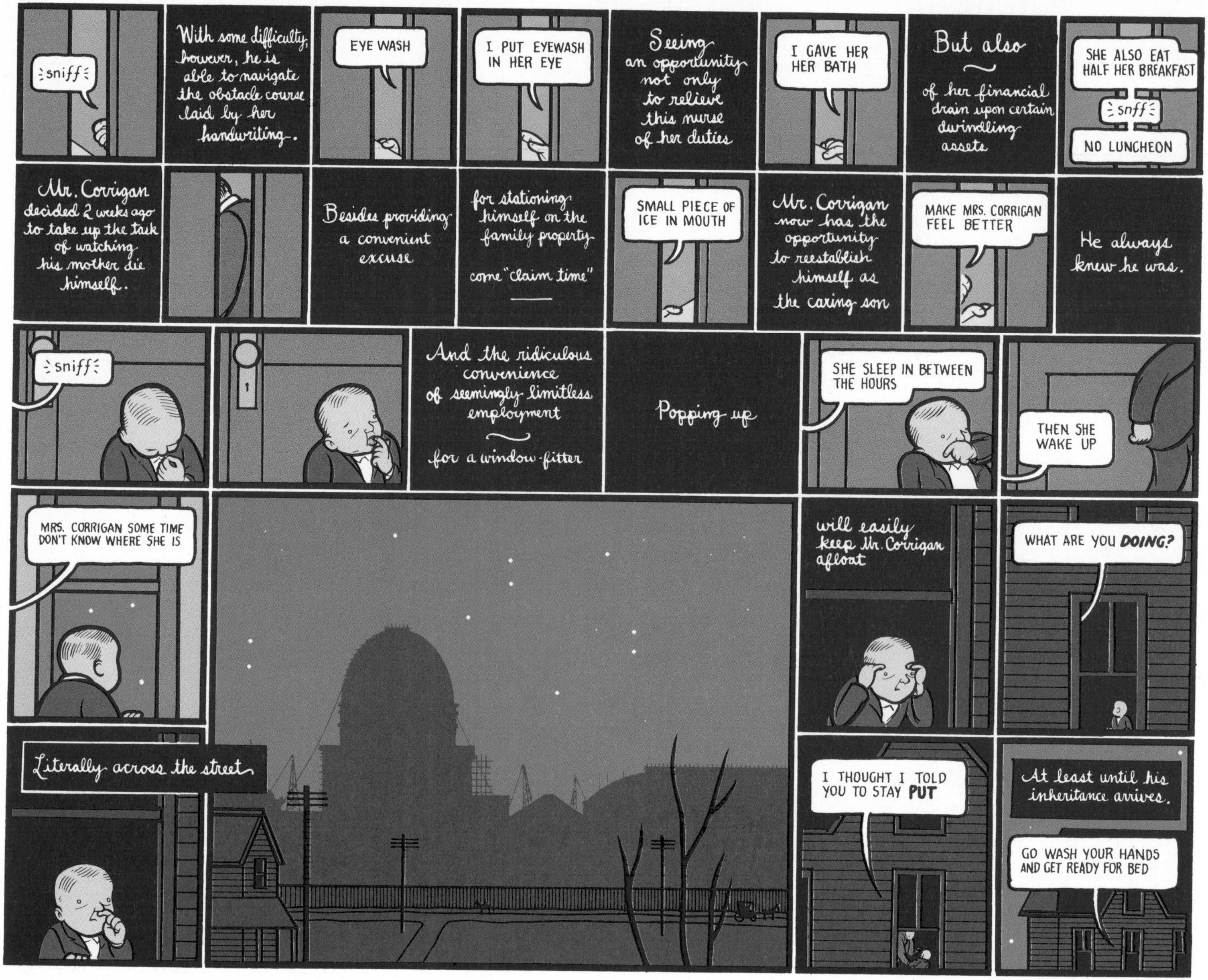
sniff
With some difficulty, however, he is able to navigate the obstacle course laid by her handwriting.
EYE WASH
I PUT EYEWASH IN HER EYE
Seeing an opportunity not only to relieve this nurse of her duties
I GAVE HER HER BATH
But also
of her financial drain upon certain dwindling assets
SHE ALSO EAT HALF HER BREAKFAST
snff
NO LUNCHEON
Mr. Corrigan decided 2 weeks ago to take up the task of watching his mother die himself.
Besides providing a convenient excuse
for stationing himself on the family property
come "claim time"
SMALL PIECE OF ICE IN MOUTH
Mr. Corrigan now has the opportunity to reestablish himself as the caring son
MAKE MRS. CORRIGAN FEEL BETTER
He always knew he was.
sniff
And the ridiculous convenience of seemingly limitless employment
for a window-fitter
Popping up
SHE SLEEP IN BETWEEN THE HOURS
THEN SHE WAKE UP
MRS. CORRIGAN SOME TIME DON'T KNOW WHERE SHE IS
Literally across the street
will easily keep Mr. Corrigan afloat
WHAT ARE YOU DOING?
I THOUGHT I TOLD YOU TO STAY PUT
At least until his inheritance arrives.
GO WASH YOUR HANDS AND GET READY FOR BED

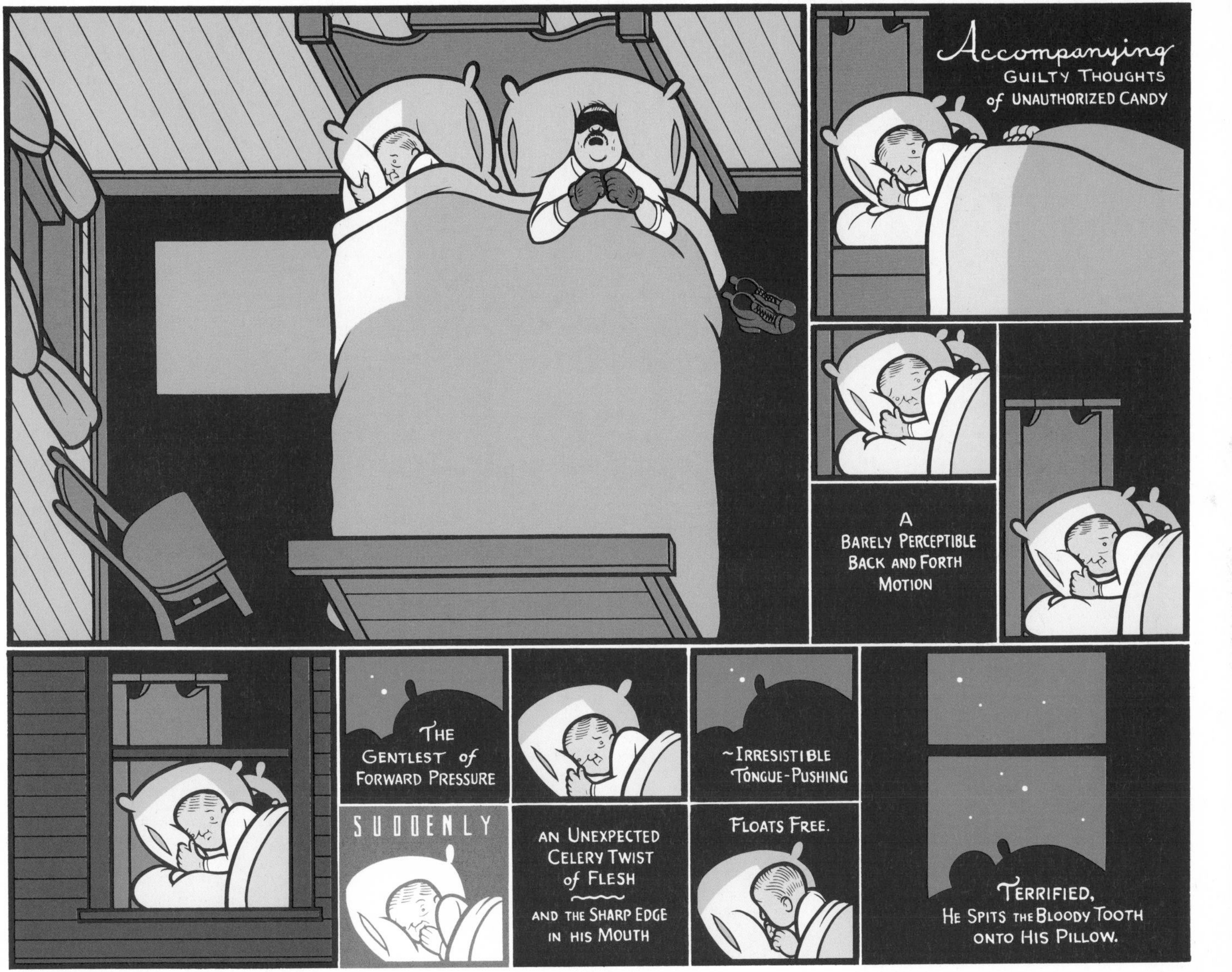
Accompanying
Guilty Thoughts of Unauthorized Candy
A Barely Perceptible Back and Forth Motion
The Gentlest of Forward Pressure
~Irresistible Tongue-Pushing
Suddenly
an Unexpected Celery Twist of Flesh
and the Sharp Edge in his Mouth
Floats Free.
Terrified, He Spits the Bloody Tooth onto His Pillow.

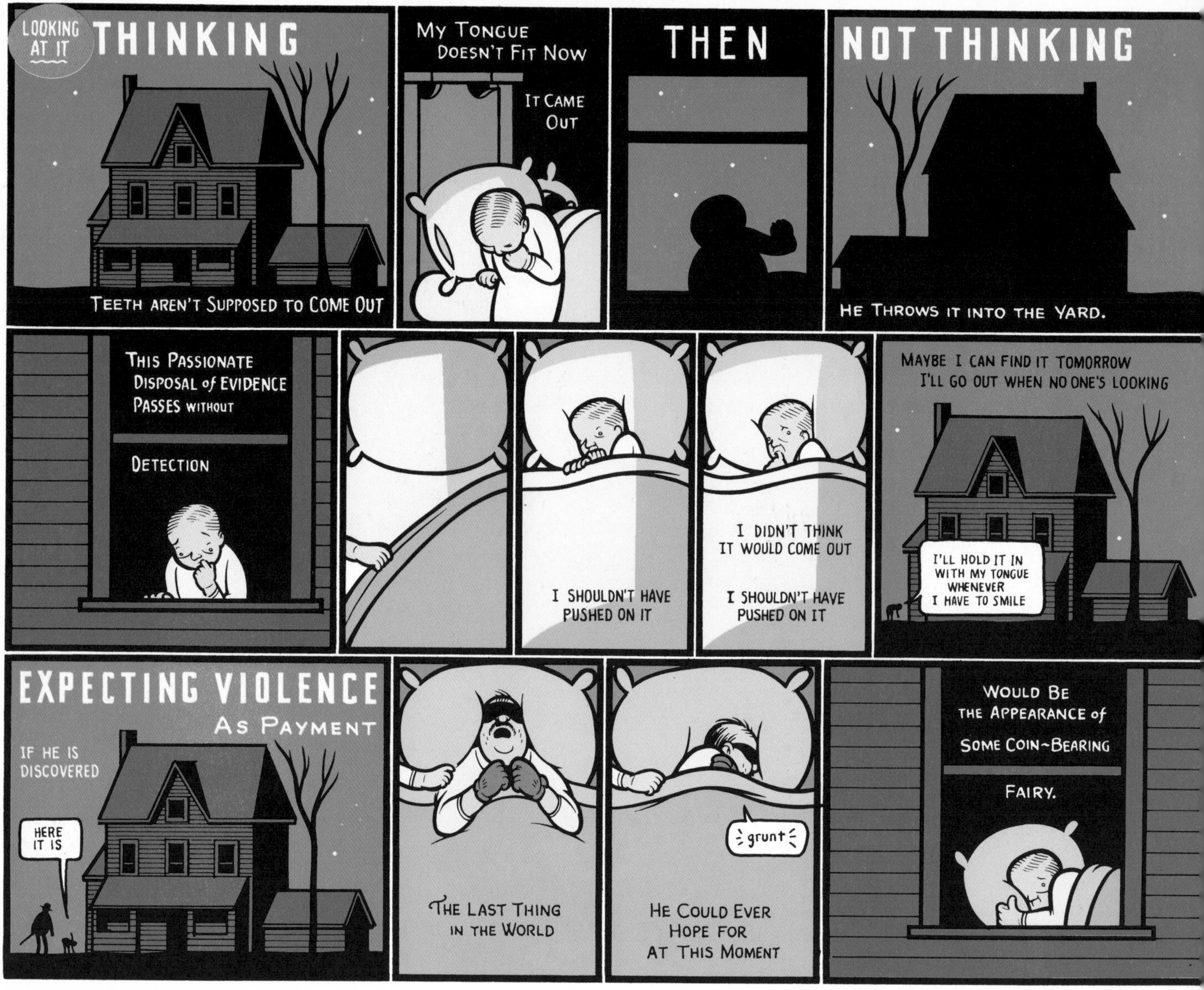
LOOKING AT IT
THINKING
TEETH AREN'T SUPPOSED TO COME OUT
MY TONGUE DOESN'T FIT NOW
IT CAME OUT
THEN
NOT THINKING
HE THROWS IT INTO THE YARD.
THIS PASSIONATE DISPOSAL of EVIDENCE PASSES WITHOUT
DETECTION
I SHOULDN'T HAVE PUSHED ON IT
I DIDN'T THINK IT WOULD COME OUT
I SHOULDN'T HAVE PUSHED ON IT
MAYBE I CAN FIND IT TOMORROW
I'LL GO OUT WHEN NO ONE'S LOOKING
I'LL HOLD IT IN WITH MY TONGUE WHENEVER I HAVE TO SMILE
EXPECTING VIOLENCE
AS PAYMENT
IF HE IS DISCOVERED
HERE IT IS
THE LAST THING IN THE WORLD
grunt
HE COULD EVER HOPE FOR AT THIS MOMENT
WOULD BE THE APPEARANCE of SOME COIN~BEARING
FAIRY.

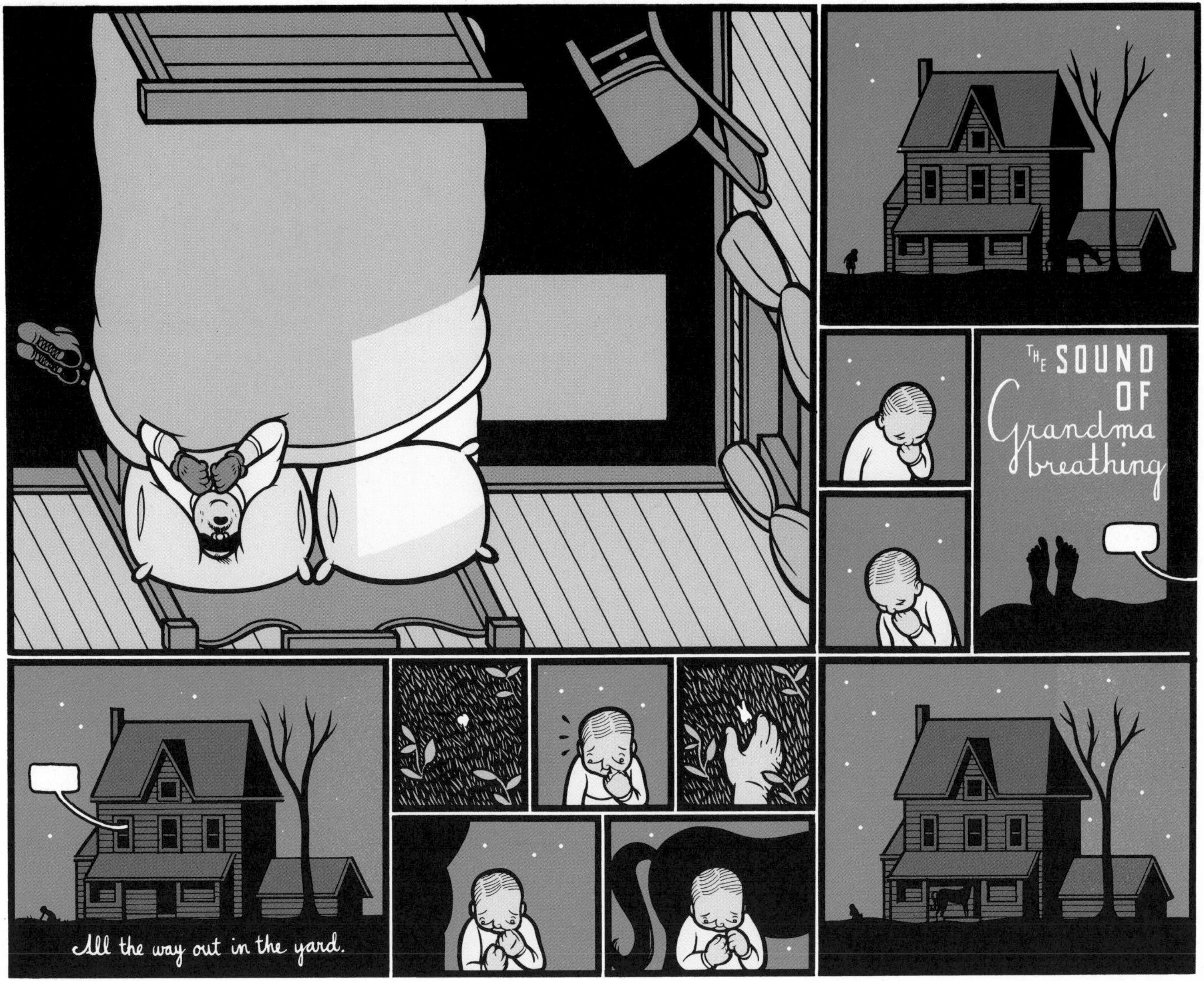
THE SOUND OF Grandma breathing
All the way out in the yard.

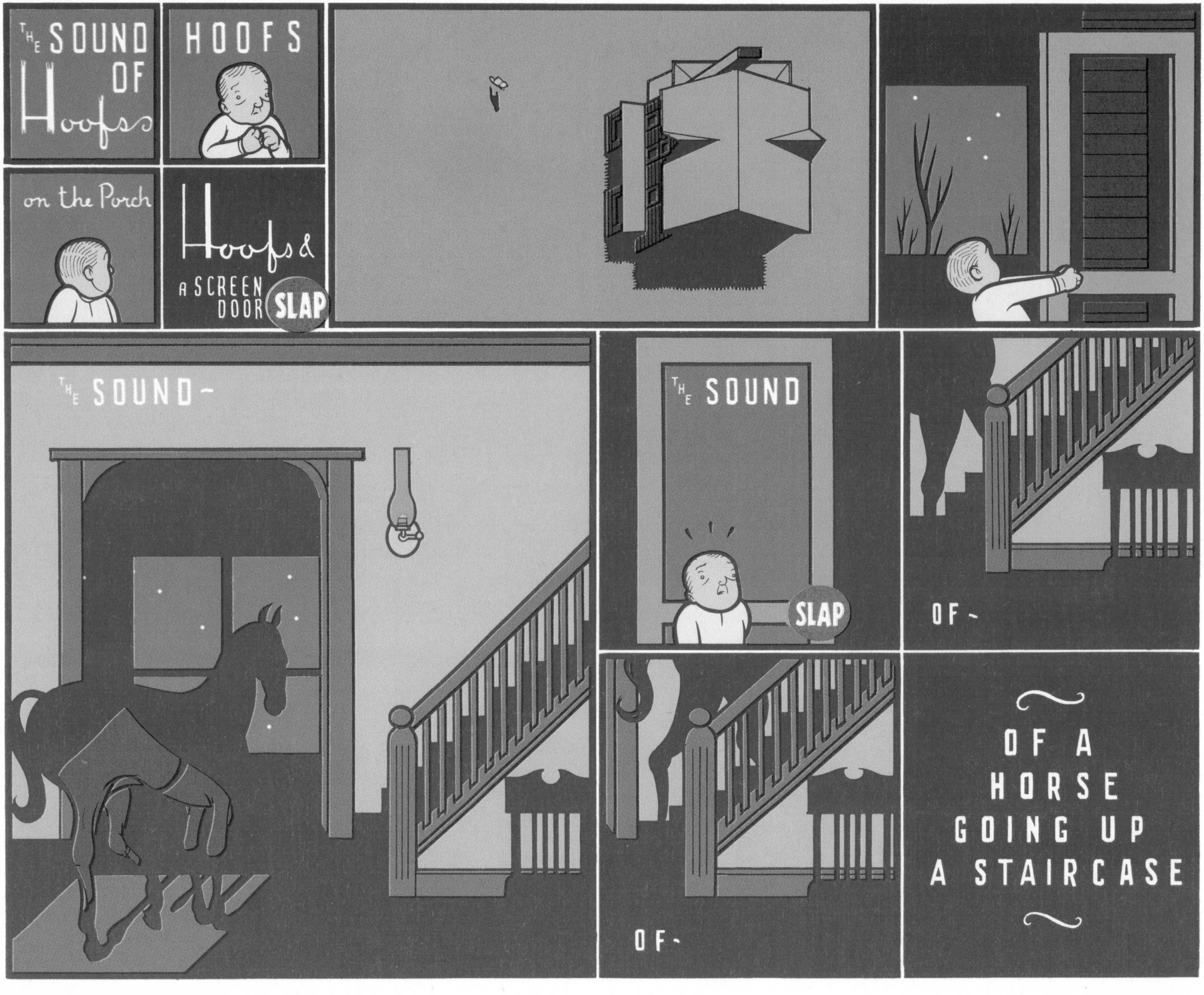
THE SOUND OF Hoofs
HOOFS
on the Porch
Hoofs &
A SCREEN DOOR SLAP
THE SOUND-
THE SOUND
SLAP
OF-
OF-
OF A HORSE GOING UP A STAIRCASE

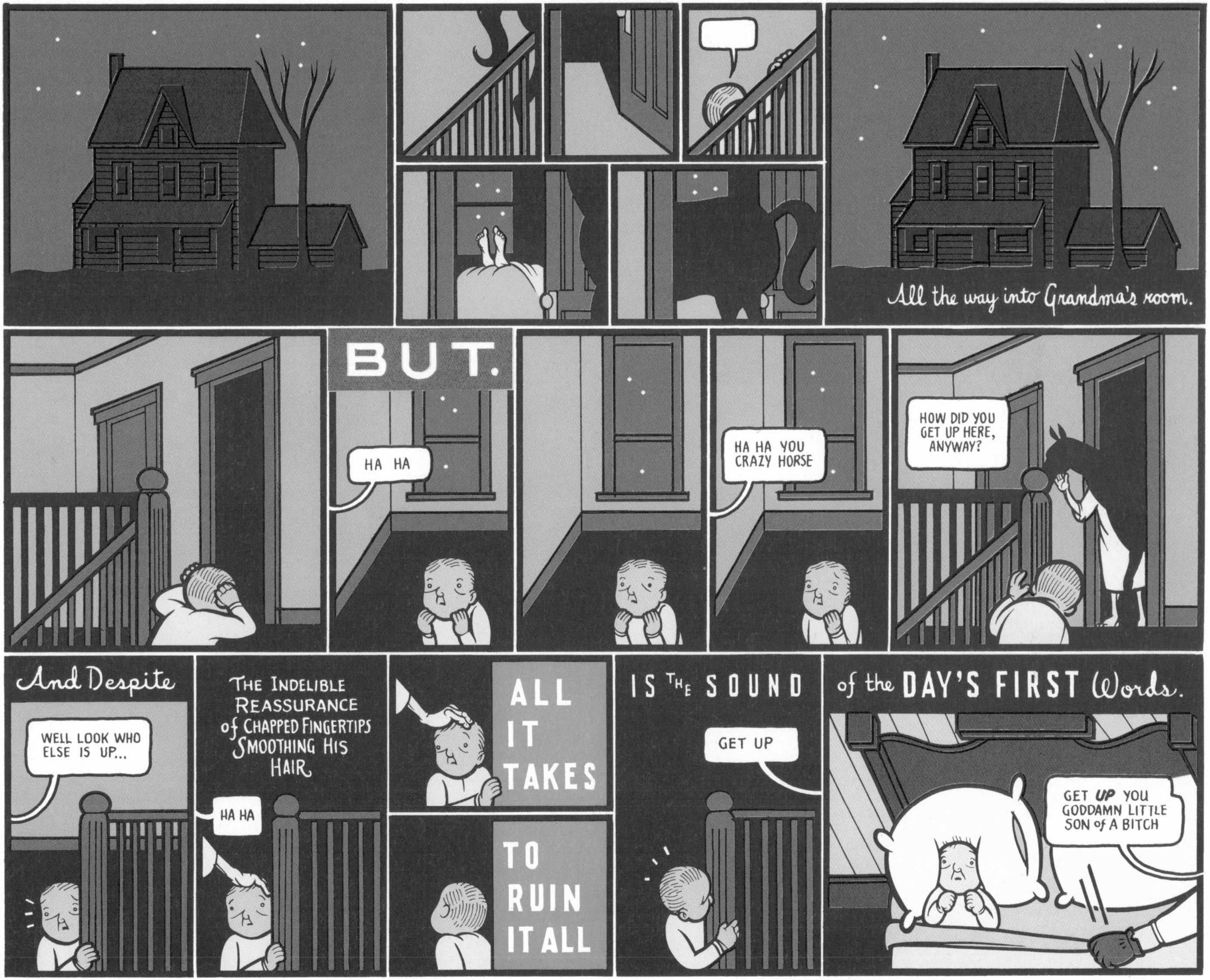
All the way into Grandma's room.
BUT.
HA HA
HA HA YOU CRAZY HORSE
HOW DID YOU GET UP HERE, ANYWAY?
And Despite
WELL LOOK WHO ELSE IS UP...
THE INDELIBLE REASSURANCE of CHAPPED FINGERTIPS SMOOTHING HIS HAIR
HA HA
ALL IT TAKES
TO RUIN IT ALL
IS THE SOUND
GET UP
of the DAY'S FIRST Words.
GET UP YOU GODDAMN LITTLE SON of A BITCH

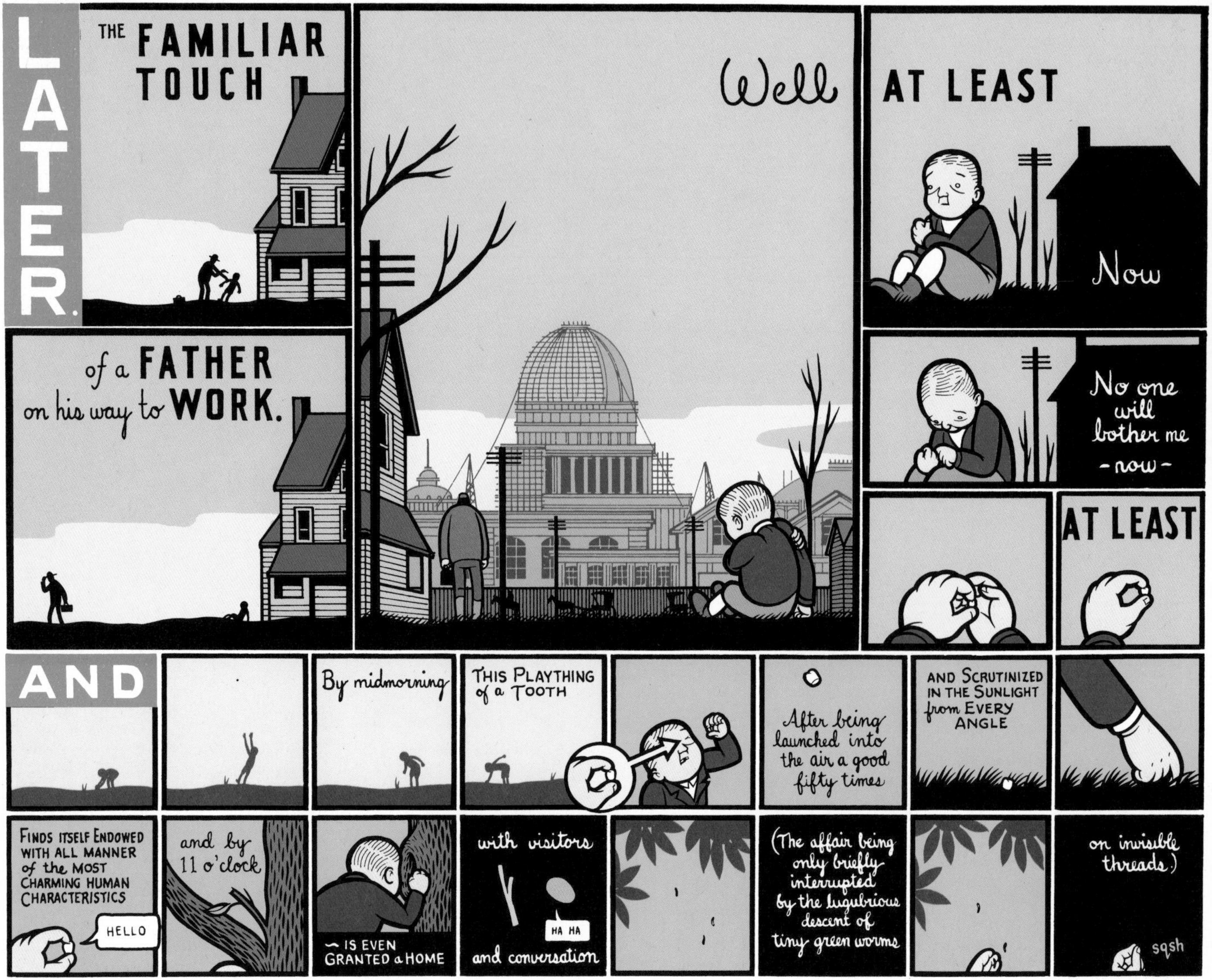
LATER.
THE FAMILIAR TOUCH
of a FATHER on his way to WORK.
Well
AT LEAST
Now
No one will bother me -now-
AT LEAST
AND
By midmorning
THIS PLAYTHING of a TOOTH
After being launched into the air a good fifty times
AND SCRUTINIZED IN THE SUNLIGHT from EVERY ANGLE
FINDS ITSELF ENDOWED WITH ALL MANNER of the MOST CHARMING HUMAN CHARACTERISTICS
HELLO
and by 11 o'clock
– IS EVEN GRANTED a HOME
with visitors
HA HA
and conversation
(The affair being only briefly interrupted by the lugubrious descent of tiny green worms
on invisible threads.)
sqsh

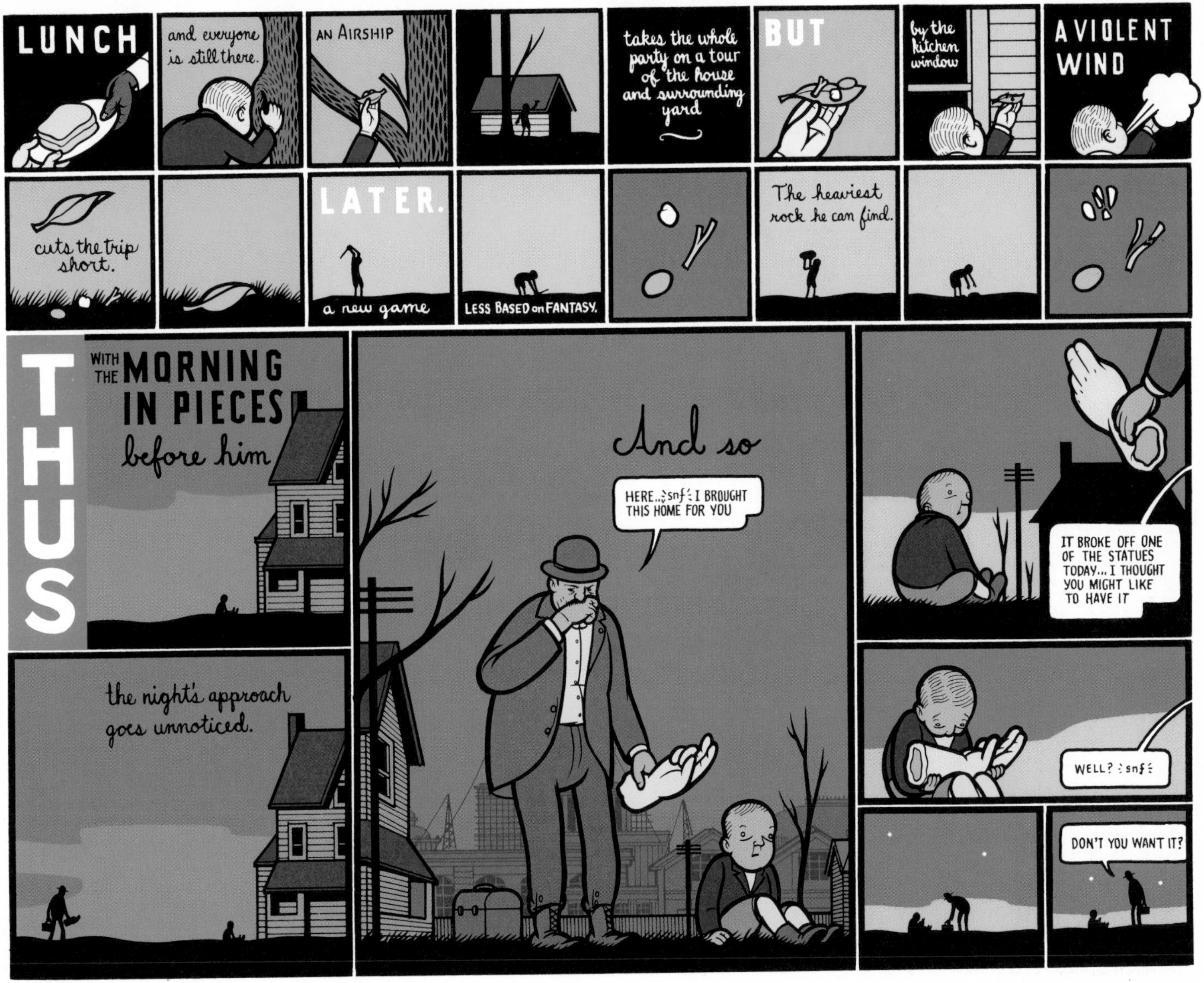
LUNCH
and everyone is still there.
AN AIRSHIP
takes the whole party on a tour of the house and surrounding yard
BUT
by the kitchen window
A VIOLENT WIND
cuts the trip short.
LATER.
a new game
LESS BASED on FANTASY.
The heaviest rock he can find.
THUS
WITH THE MORNING IN PIECES before him
the night's approach goes unnoticed.
And so
HERE.. snf I BROUGHT THIS HOME FOR YOU
IT BROKE OFF ONE OF THE STATUES TODAY... I THOUGHT YOU MIGHT LIKE TO HAVE IT
WELL? snf
DON'T YOU WANT IT?

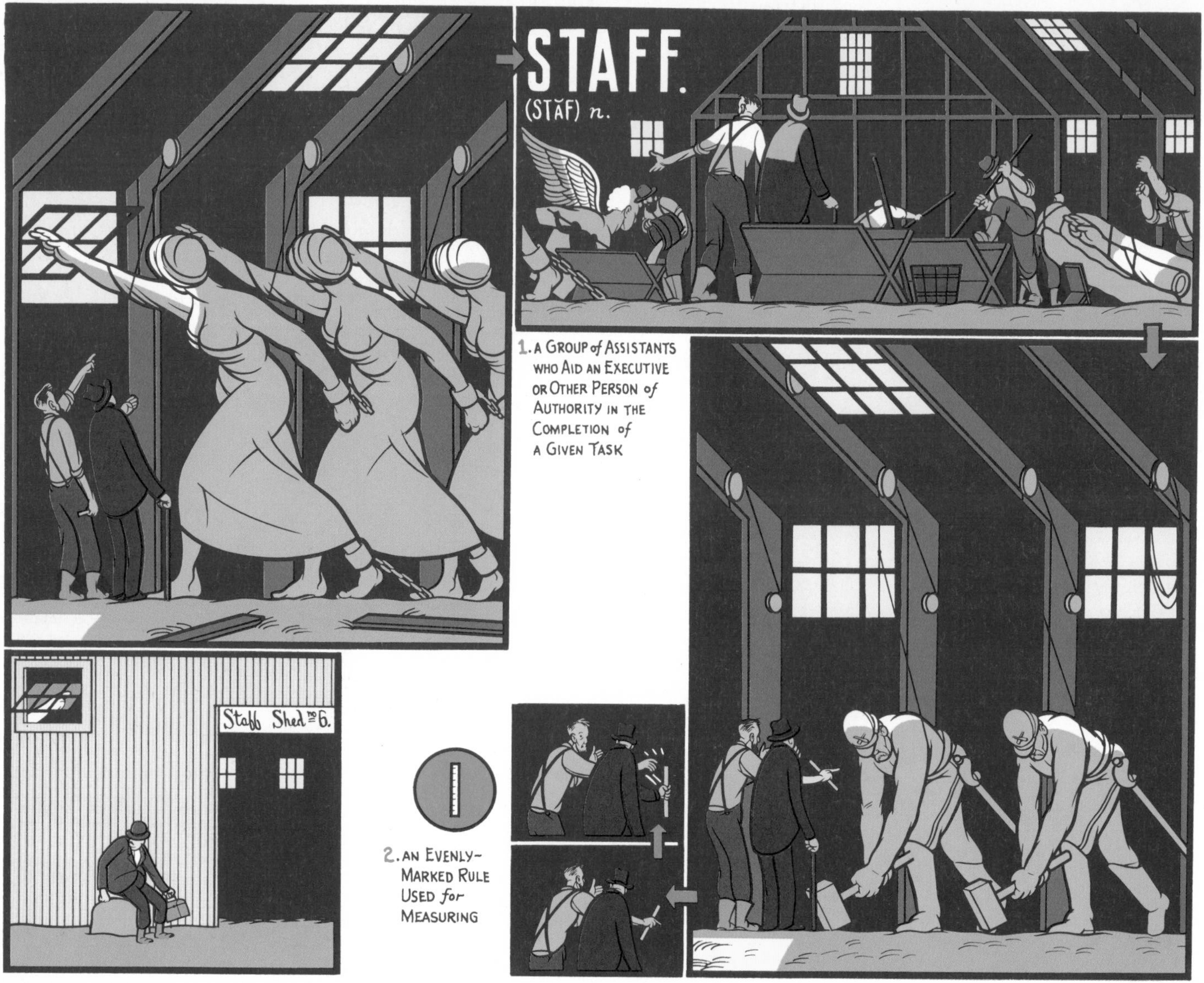
STAFF.
(STĂF) n.
1. A GROUP of ASSISTANTS WHO AID AN EXECUTIVE OR OTHER PERSON of AUTHORITY IN THE COMPLETION of A GIVEN TASK
Staff Shed No 6.
2. AN EVENLY-MARKED RULE USED for MEASURING

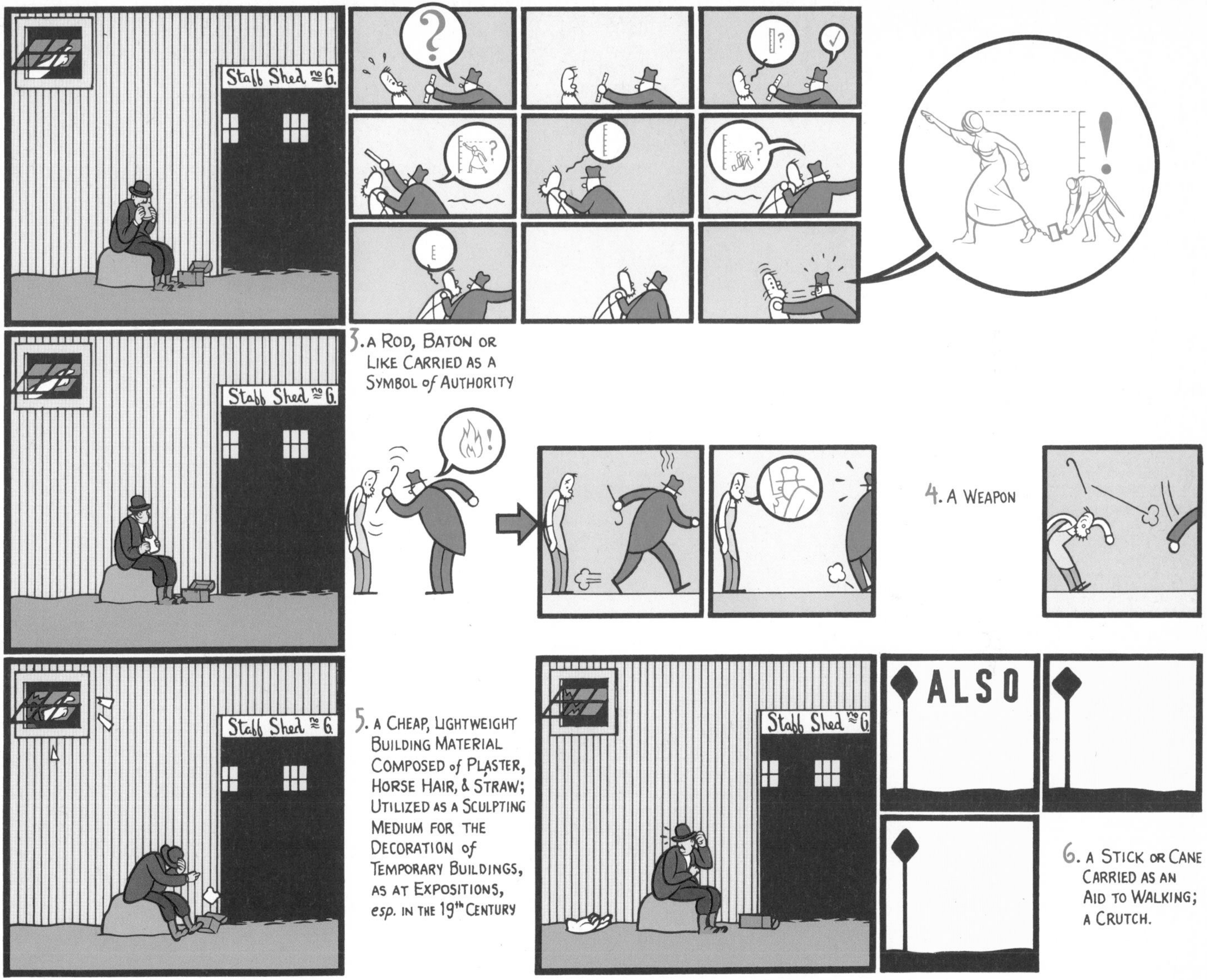

Staff Shed No 6.
?
?
✓
?
?
!
Staff Shed No 6.
3. A Rod, Baton or Like Carried as a Symbol of Authority
!
4. A Weapon
Staff Shed No 6.
5. A Cheap, Lightweight Building Material Composed of Plaster, Horse Hair, & Straw; Utilized as a Sculpting Medium for the Decoration of Temporary Buildings, as at Expositions, esp. in the 19th Century
Staff Shed No 6.
ALSO
6. A Stick or Cane Carried as an Aid to Walking; a Crutch.

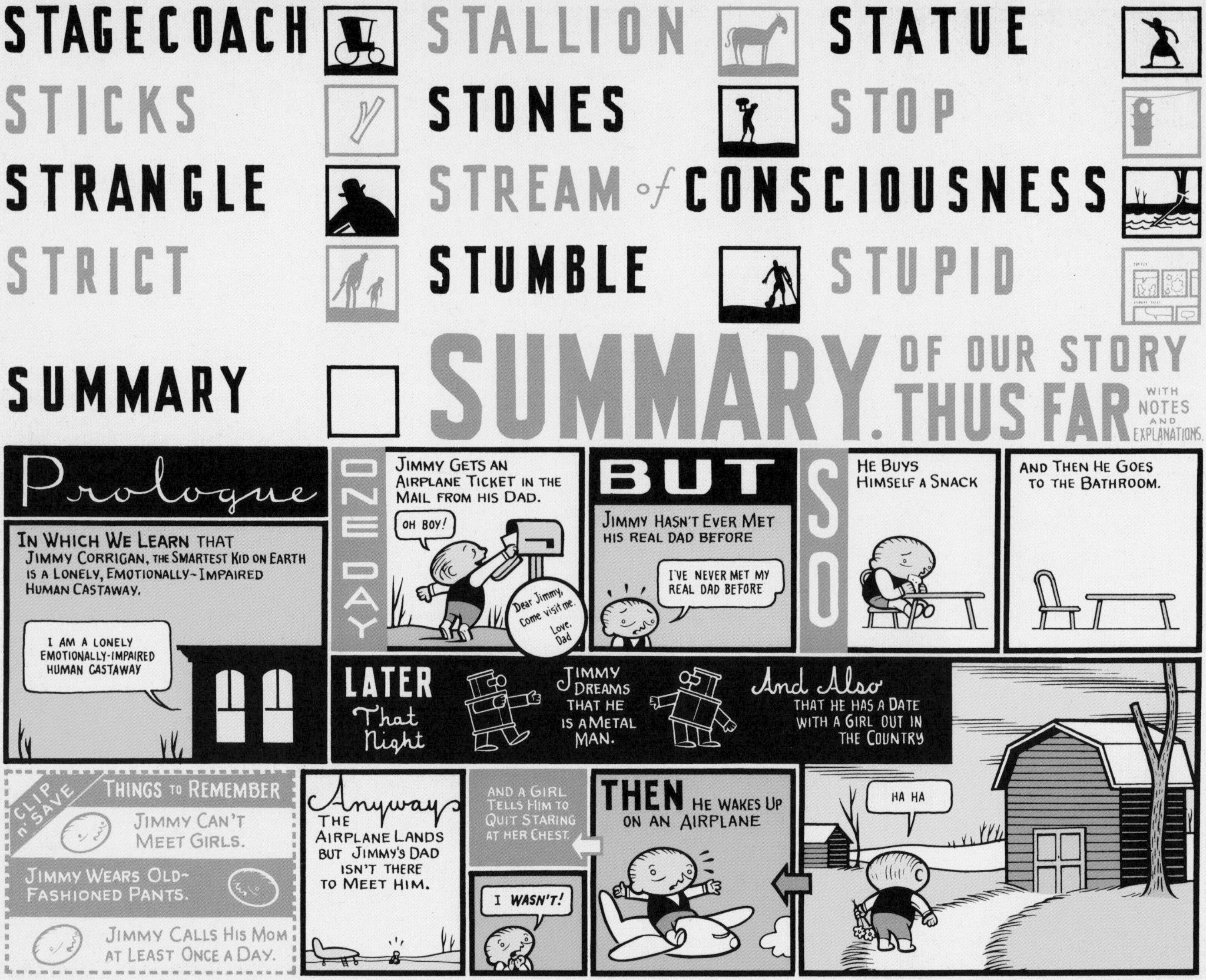
STAGECOACH
STALLION
STATUE
STICKS
STONES
STOP
STRANGLE
STREAM of CONSCIOUSNESS
STRICT
STUMBLE
STUPID
SUMMARY
SUMMARY. OF OUR STORY THUS FAR WITH NOTES AND EXPLANATIONS.
Prologue
IN WHICH WE LEARN THAT JIMMY CORRIGAN, THE SMARTEST KID ON EARTH IS A LONELY, EMOTIONALLY~IMPAIRED HUMAN CASTAWAY.
I AM A LONELY EMOTIONALLY-IMPAIRED HUMAN CASTAWAY
ONE DAY
JIMMY GETS AN AIRPLANE TICKET IN THE MAIL FROM HIS DAD.
OH BOY!
Dear Jimmy, Come visit me. Love, Dad
BUT
JIMMY HASN'T EVER MET HIS REAL DAD BEFORE
I'VE NEVER MET MY REAL DAD BEFORE
SO
HE BUYS HIMSELF A SNACK
AND THEN HE GOES TO THE BATHROOM.
LATER That Night
JIMMY DREAMS THAT HE IS A METAL MAN.
And Also THAT HE HAS A DATE WITH A GIRL OUT IN THE COUNTRY
HA HA
AND A GIRL TELLS HIM TO QUIT STARING AT HER CHEST.
I WASN'T!
THEN HE WAKES UP ON AN AIRPLANE
Anyway THE AIRPLANE LANDS BUT JIMMY'S DAD ISN'T THERE TO MEET HIM.
CLIP n' SAVE
THINGS TO REMEMBER
JIMMY CAN'T MEET GIRLS.
JIMMY WEARS OLD~FASHIONED PANTS.
JIMMY CALLS HIS MOM AT LEAST ONCE A DAY.

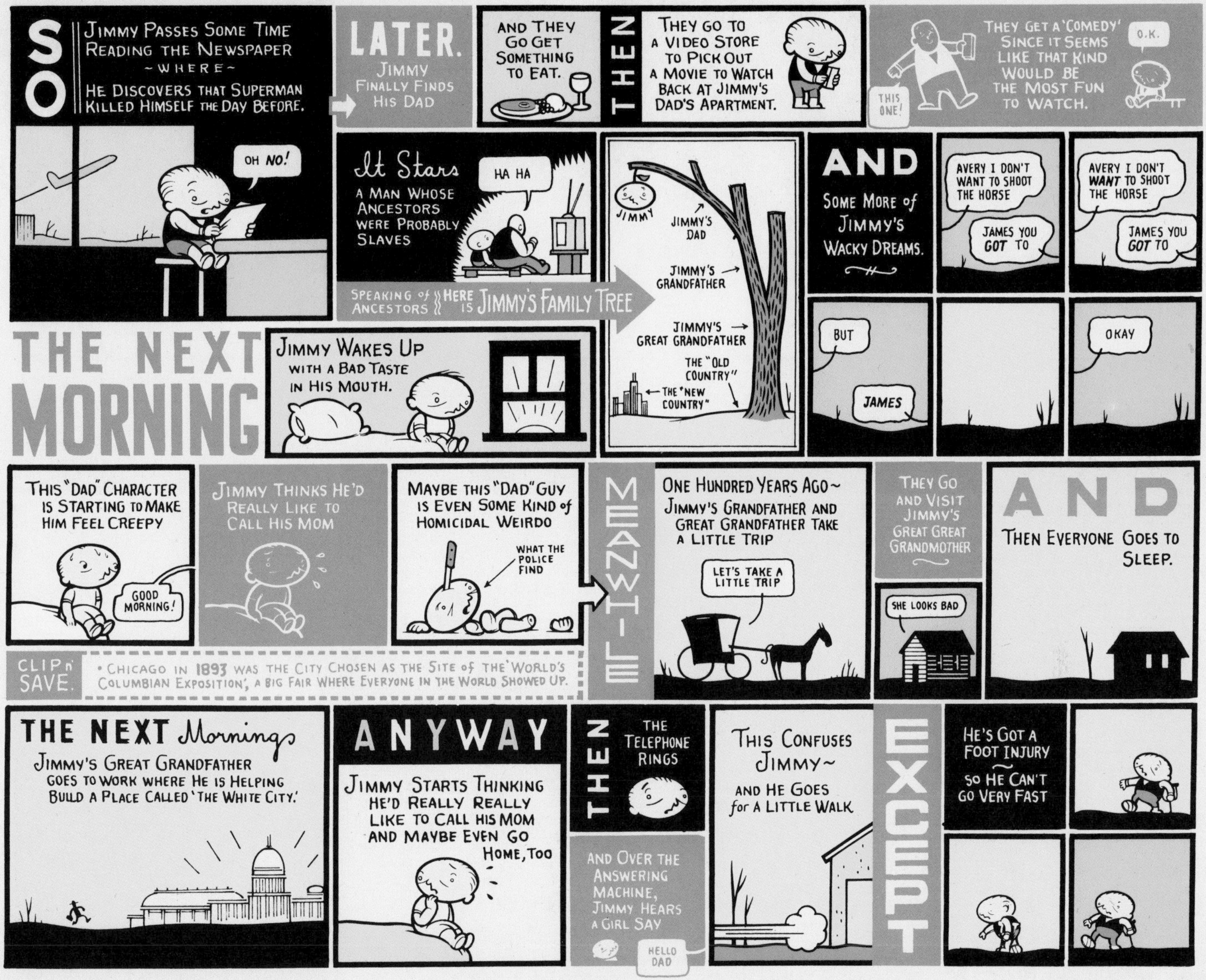
SO
JIMMY PASSES SOME TIME READING THE NEWSPAPER
~WHERE~
HE DISCOVERS THAT SUPERMAN KILLED HIMSELF THE DAY BEFORE.
OH NO!
LATER.
JIMMY FINALLY FINDS HIS DAD
AND THEY GO GET SOMETHING TO EAT.
THEN
THEY GO TO A VIDEO STORE TO PICK OUT A MOVIE TO WATCH BACK AT JIMMY'S DAD'S APARTMENT.
THEY GET A 'COMEDY' SINCE IT SEEMS LIKE THAT KIND WOULD BE THE MOST FUN TO WATCH.
THIS ONE!
O.K.
It Stars
A MAN WHOSE ANCESTORS WERE PROBABLY SLAVES
HA HA
SPEAKING of ANCESTORS
HERE IS JIMMY'S FAMILY TREE
JIMMY
JIMMY'S DAD
JIMMY'S GRANDFATHER
JIMMY'S GREAT GRANDFATHER
THE "OLD COUNTRY"
THE "NEW COUNTRY"
AND
SOME MORE of JIMMY'S WACKY DREAMS.
AVERY I DON'T WANT TO SHOOT THE HORSE
JAMES YOU GOT TO
AVERY I DON'T WANT TO SHOOT THE HORSE
JAMES YOU GOT TO
BUT
JAMES
OKAY
THE NEXT MORNING
JIMMY WAKES UP WITH A BAD TASTE IN HIS MOUTH.
THIS "DAD" CHARACTER IS STARTING TO MAKE HIM FEEL CREEPY
GOOD MORNING!
JIMMY THINKS HE'D REALLY LIKE TO CALL HIS MOM
MAYBE THIS "DAD" GUY IS EVEN SOME KIND of HOMICIDAL WEIRDO
WHAT THE POLICE FIND
MEANWHILE
ONE HUNDRED YEARS AGO~
JIMMY'S GRANDFATHER AND GREAT GRANDFATHER TAKE A LITTLE TRIP
LET'S TAKE A LITTLE TRIP
THEY GO AND VISIT JIMMY'S GREAT GREAT GRANDMOTHER
SHE LOOKS BAD
AND
THEN EVERYONE GOES TO SLEEP.
CLIP n' SAVE.
• CHICAGO IN 1893 WAS THE CITY CHOSEN AS THE SITE of THE 'WORLD'S COLUMBIAN EXPOSITION', A BIG FAIR WHERE EVERYONE IN THE WORLD SHOWED UP.
THE NEXT Mornings
JIMMY'S GREAT GRANDFATHER GOES TO WORK WHERE HE IS HELPING BUILD A PLACE CALLED 'THE WHITE CITY.'
ANYWAY
JIMMY STARTS THINKING HE'D REALLY REALLY LIKE TO CALL HIS MOM AND MAYBE EVEN GO HOME, TOO
THEN
THE TELEPHONE RINGS
AND OVER THE ANSWERING MACHINE, JIMMY HEARS A GIRL SAY
HELLO DAD
THIS CONFUSES JIMMY~
AND HE GOES for A LITTLE WALK
EXCEPT
HE'S GOT A FOOT INJURY
SO HE CAN'T GO VERY FAST

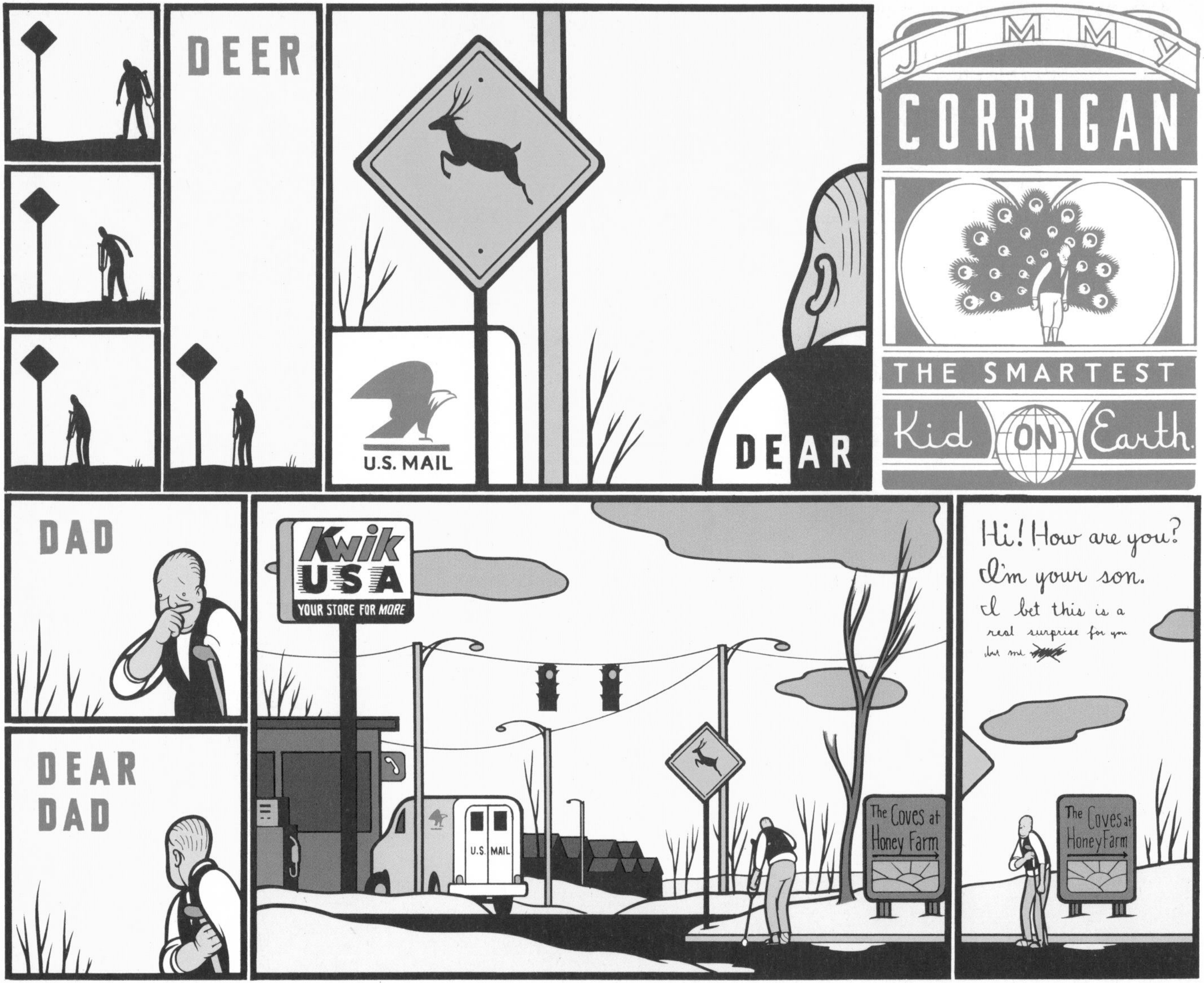
DEER
U.S. MAIL
DEAR
JIMMY
CORRIGAN
THE SMARTEST
Kid ON Earth.
DAD
DEAR
DAD
Kwik
USA
YOUR STORE FOR MORE
U.S. MAIL
The Coves at
Honey Farm
The Coves at
Honey Farm
Hi! How are you?
I'm your son.
I bet this is a
real surprise for you

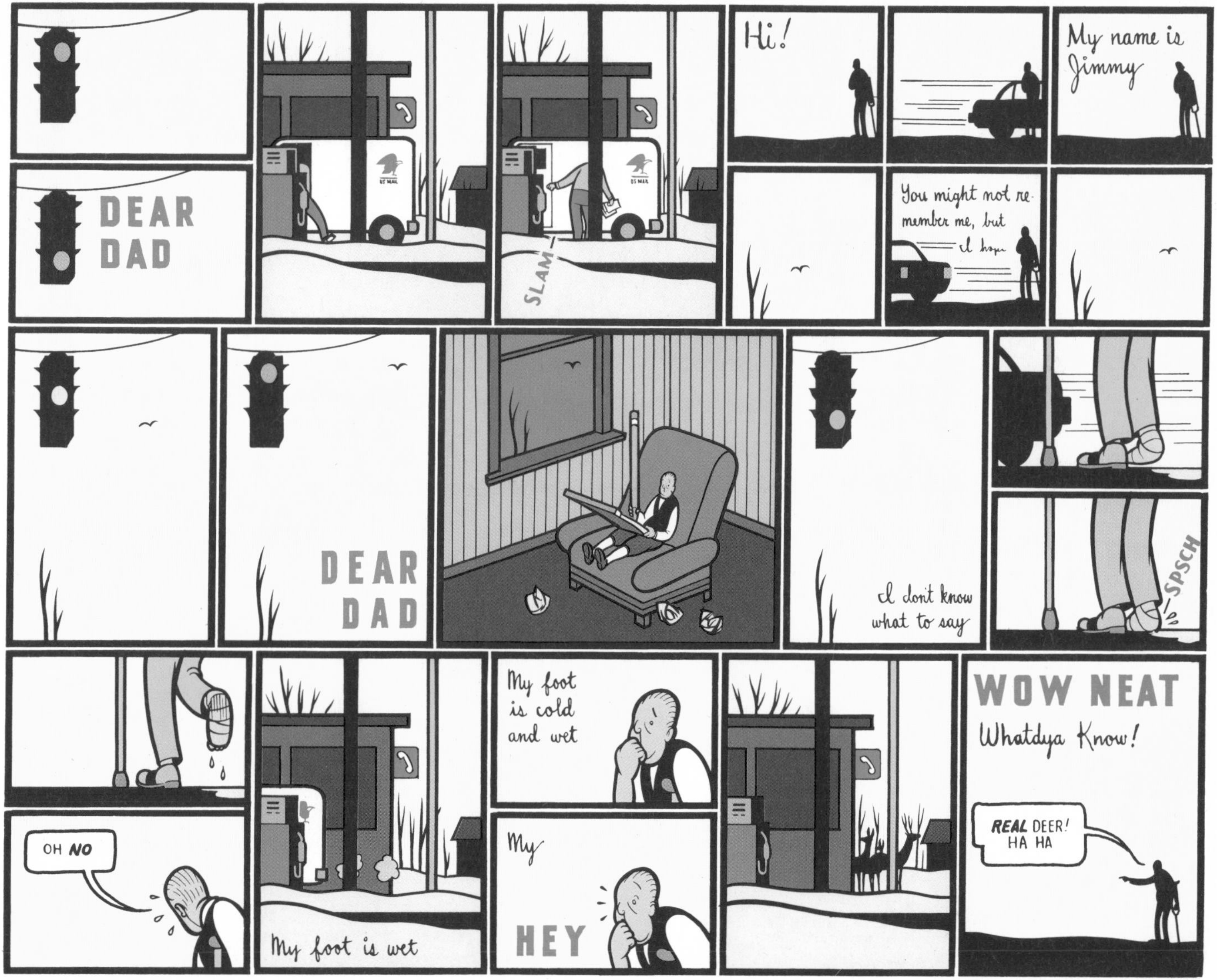
DEAR DAD
SLAM
Hi!
My name is Jimmy
You might not remember me, but
I hope
DEAR DAD
I don't know what to say
SPSCH
OH NO
My foot is wet
My foot is cold and wet
My
HEY
WOW NEAT
Whatdya Know!
REAL DEER! HA HA

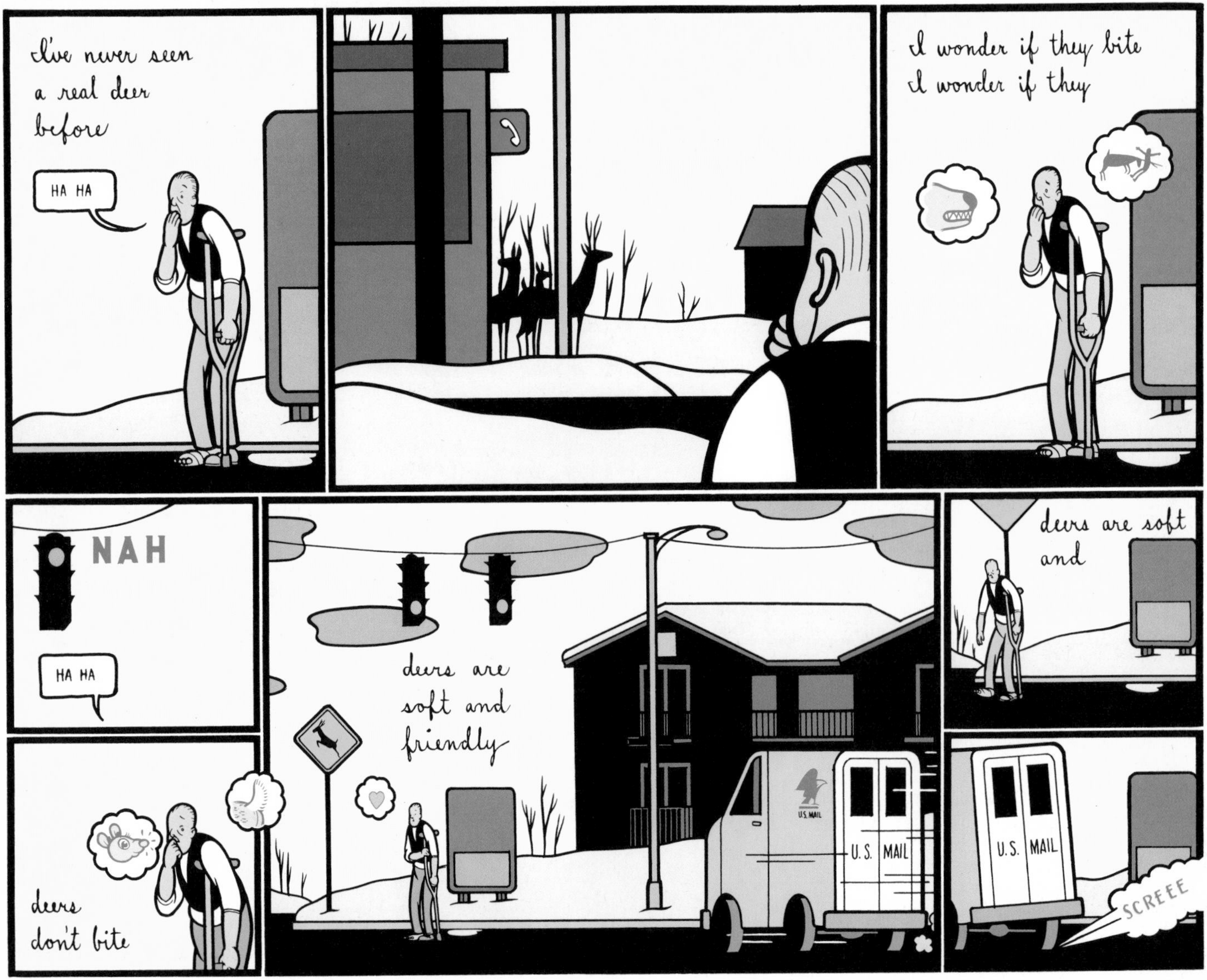
I've never seen
a real deer
before
HA HA
I wonder if they bite
I wonder if they
NAH
HA HA
deers
don't bite
deers are
soft and
friendly
U.S. MAIL
U.S. MAIL
U.S. MAIL
deers are soft
and
U.S. MAIL
SCREEE

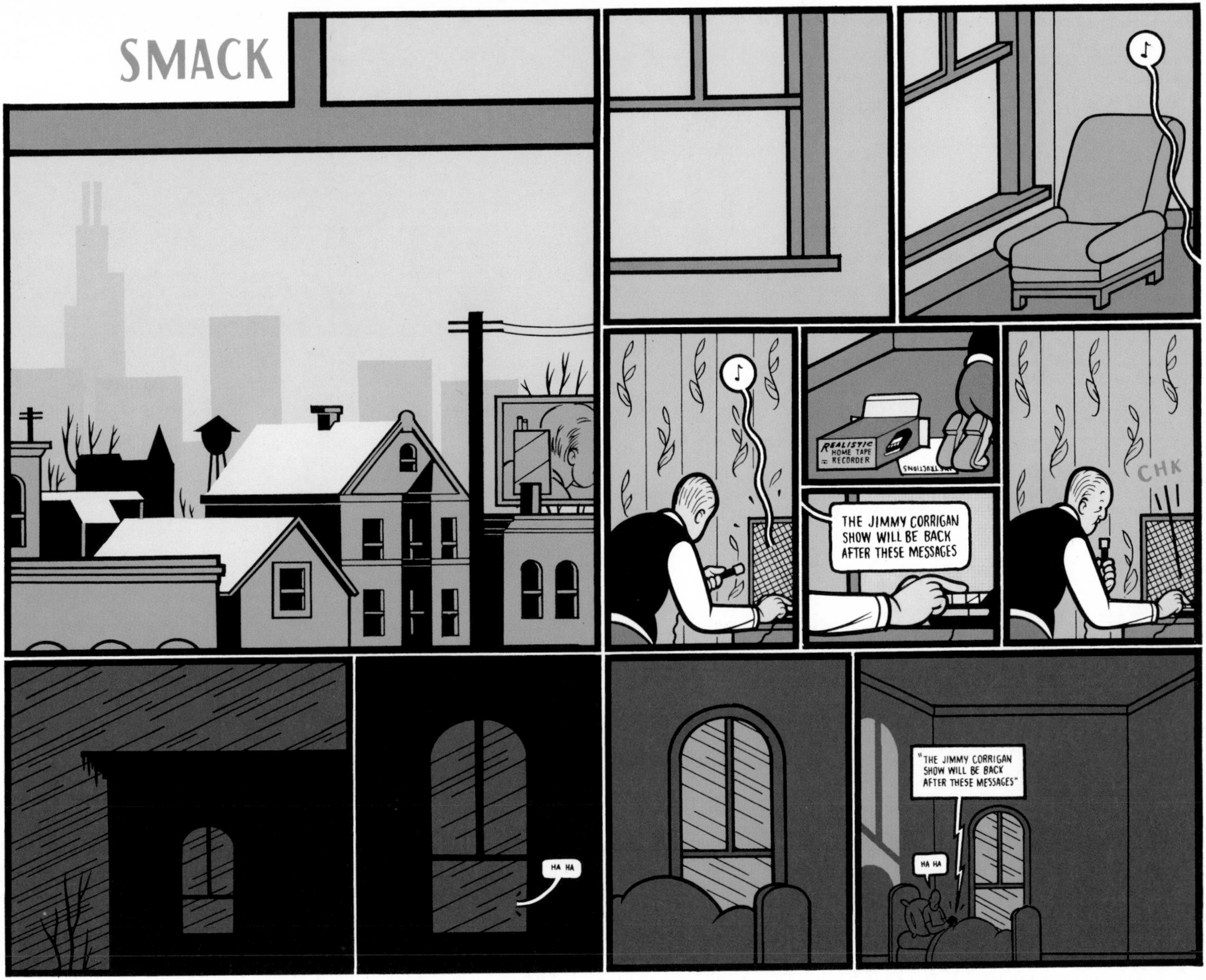
SMACK
REALISTIC
HOME TAPE
RECORDER
THE JIMMY CORRIGAN SHOW WILL BE BACK AFTER THESE MESSAGES
CHK
HA HA
"THE JIMMY CORRIGAN SHOW WILL BE BACK AFTER THESE MESSAGES"
HA HA

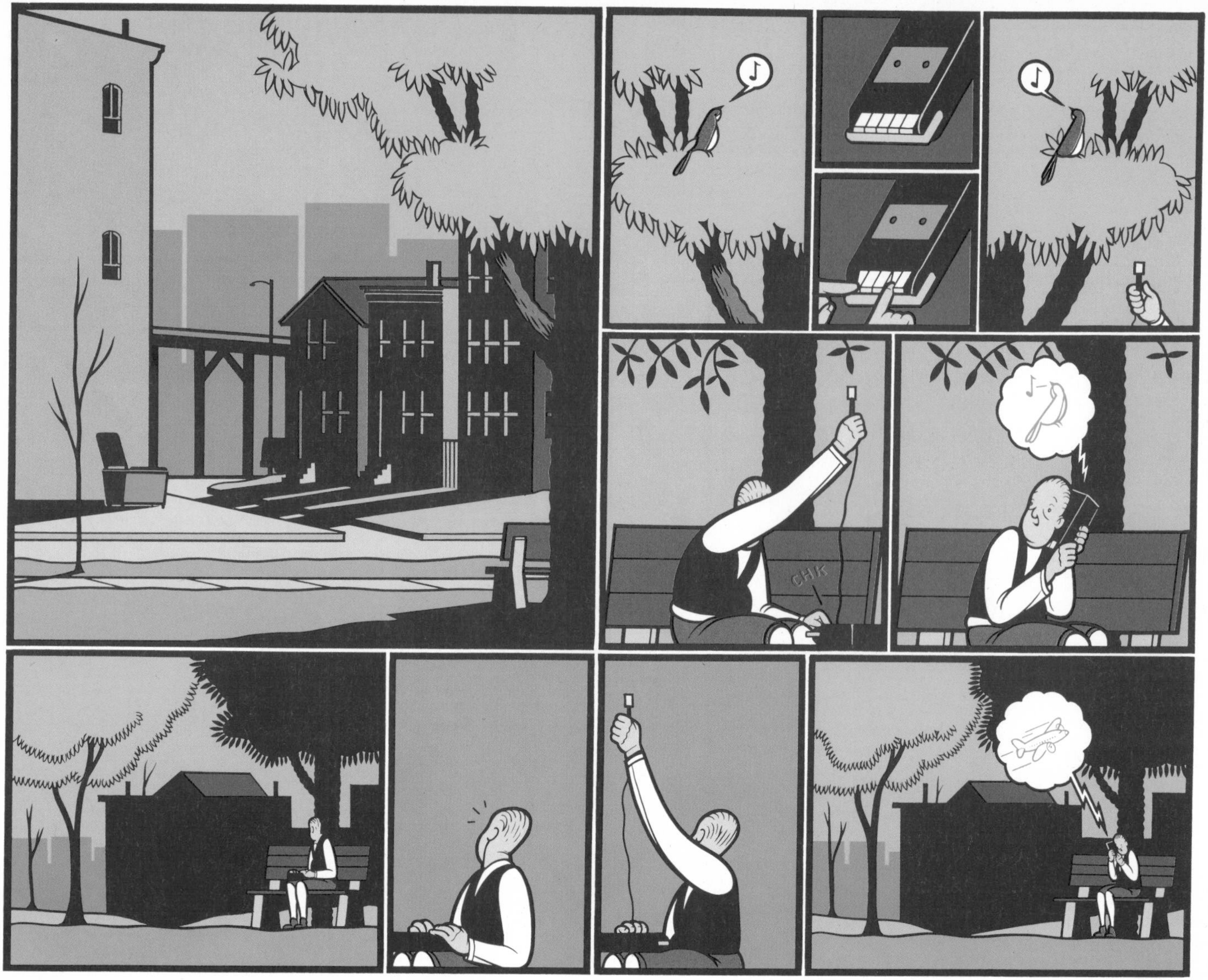
CHK

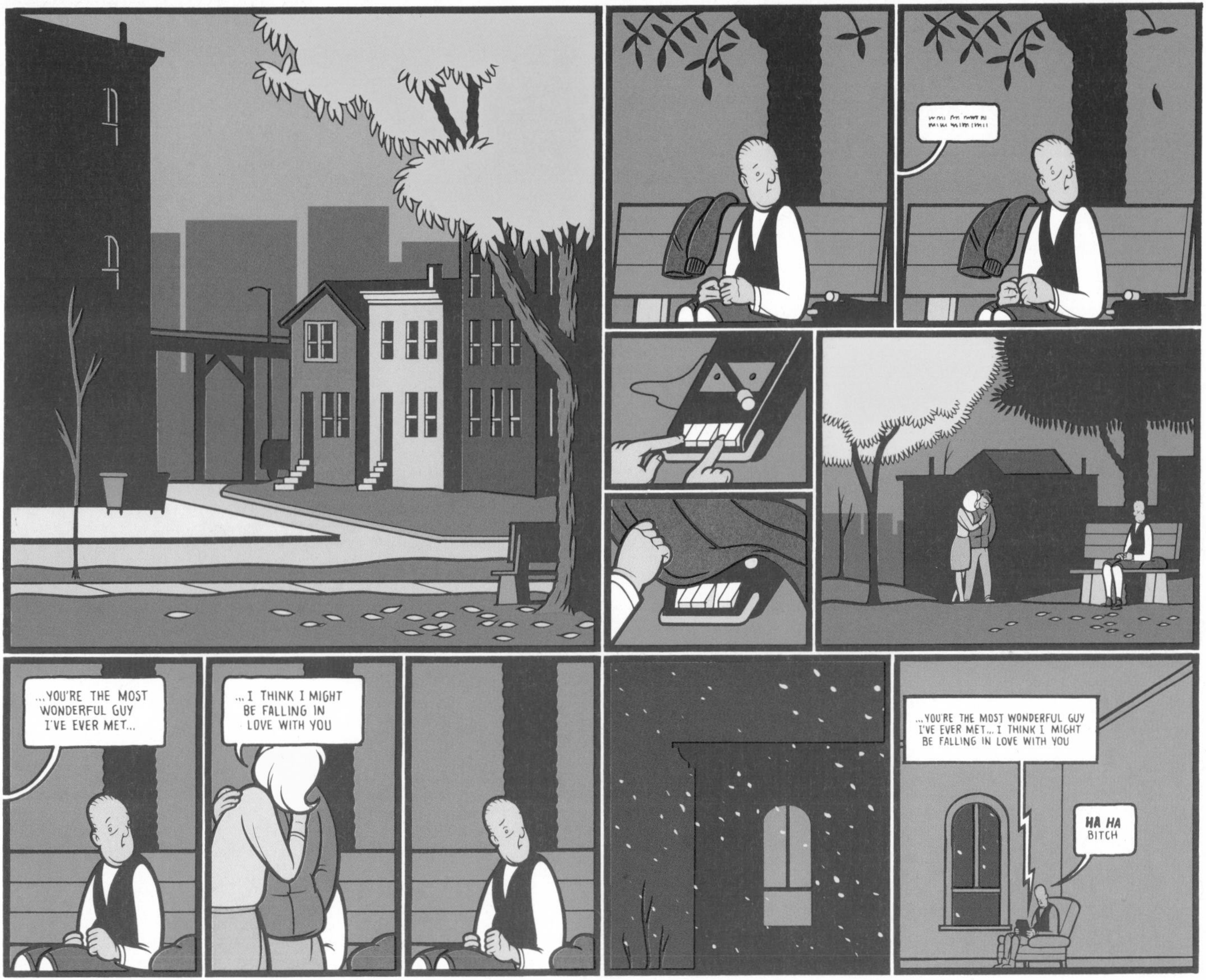
...YOU'RE THE MOST WONDERFUL GUY I'VE EVER MET...
...I THINK I MIGHT BE FALLING IN LOVE WITH YOU
...YOU'RE THE MOST WONDERFUL GUY I'VE EVER MET... I THINK I MIGHT BE FALLING IN LOVE WITH YOU
HA HA BITCH

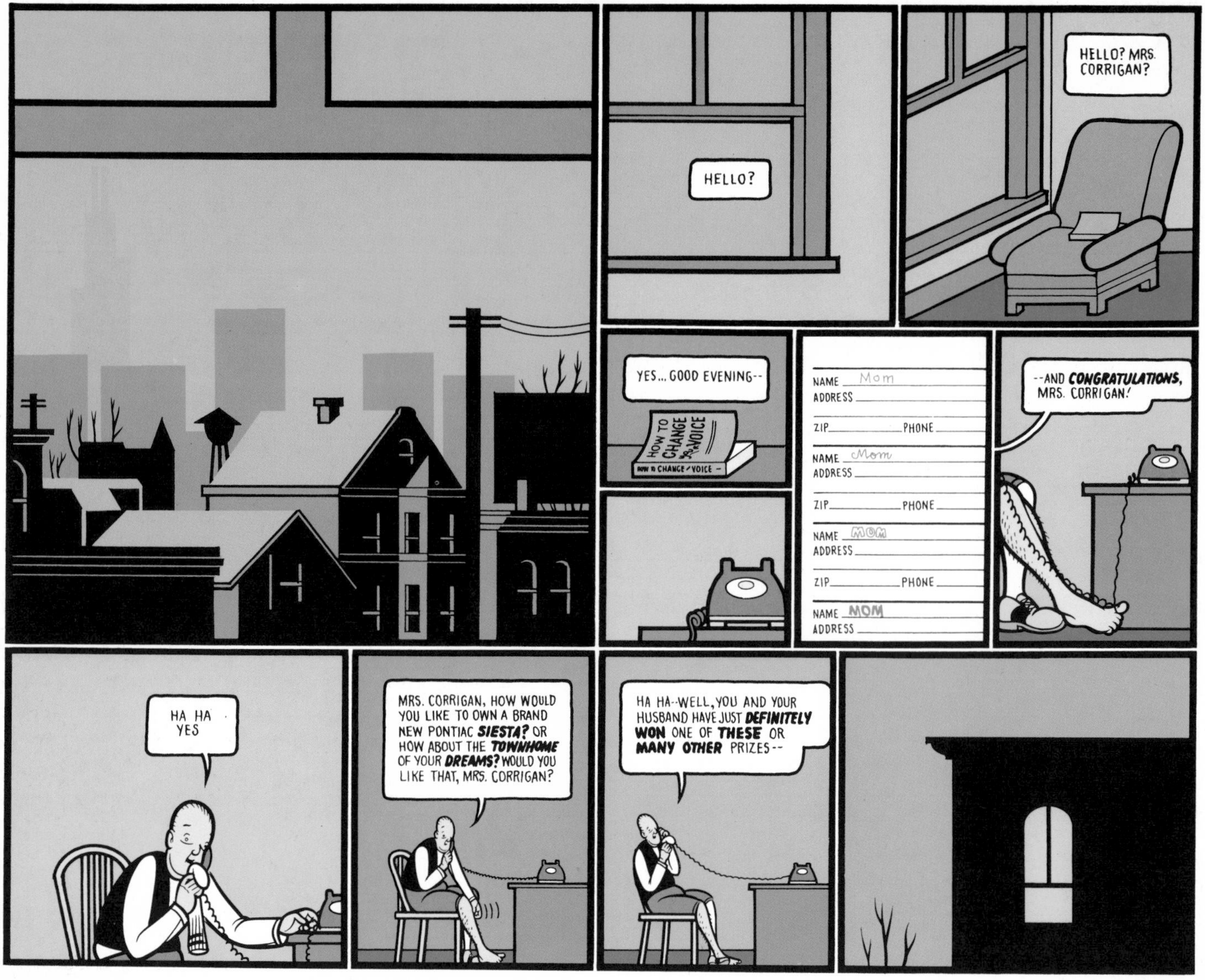
HELLO?
HELLO? MRS. CORRIGAN?
YES... GOOD EVENING--
HOW TO CHANGE YOUR VOICE
NAME Mom
ADDRESS
ZIP PHONE
NAME Mom
ADDRESS
ZIP PHONE
NAME MOM
ADDRESS
ZIP PHONE
NAME MOM
ADDRESS
--AND CONGRATULATIONS, MRS. CORRIGAN!
HA HA YES
MRS. CORRIGAN, HOW WOULD YOU LIKE TO OWN A BRAND NEW PONTIAC SIESTA? OR HOW ABOUT THE TOWNHOME OF YOUR DREAMS? WOULD YOU LIKE THAT, MRS. CORRIGAN?
HA HA--WELL, YOU AND YOUR HUSBAND HAVE JUST DEFINITELY WON ONE OF THESE OR MANY OTHER PRIZES--

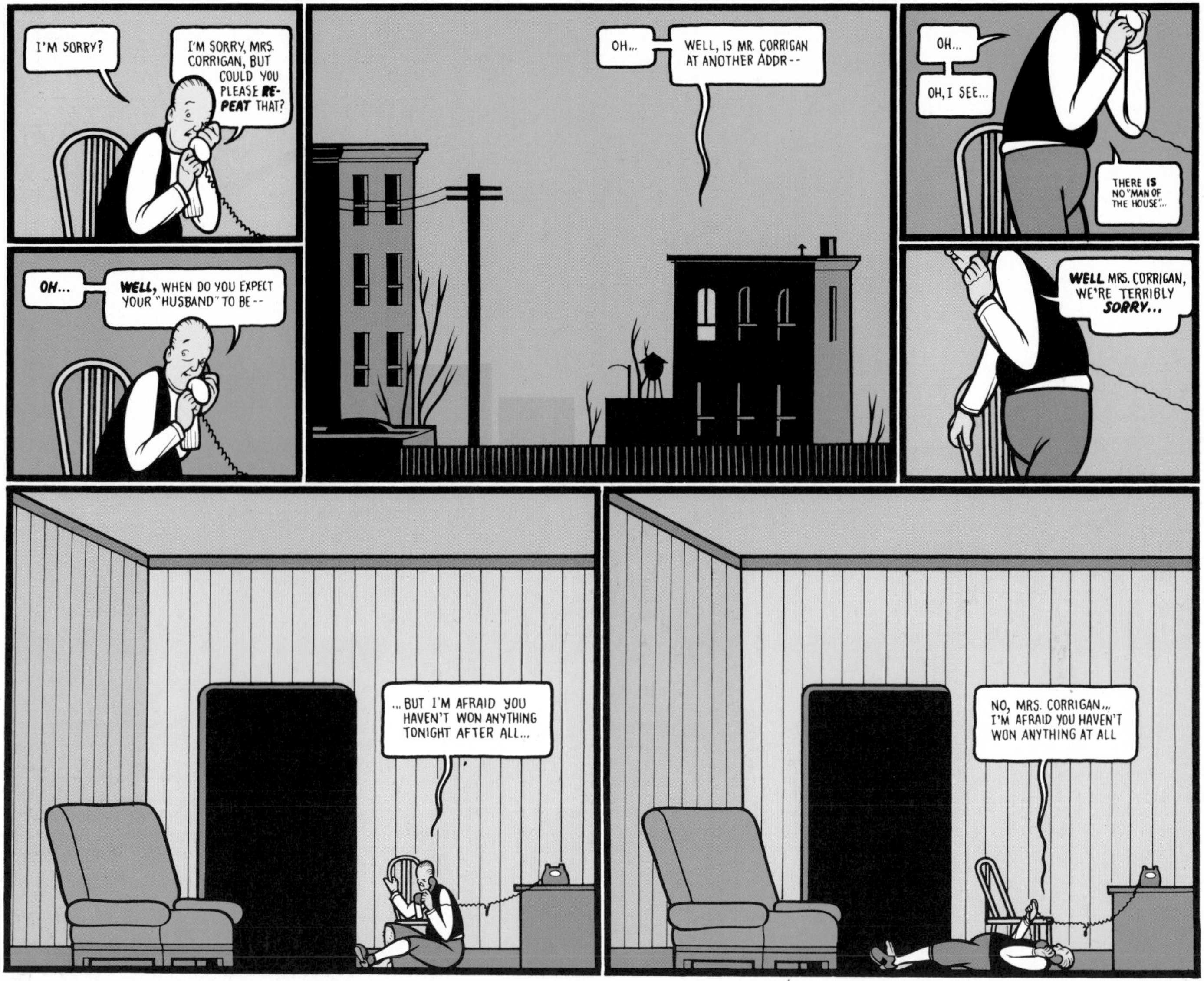
I'M SORRY?
I'M SORRY, MRS. CORRIGAN, BUT COULD YOU PLEASE RE-PEAT THAT?
OH...
WELL, WHEN DO YOU EXPECT YOUR "HUSBAND" TO BE--
OH...
WELL, IS MR. CORRIGAN AT ANOTHER ADDR--
OH...
OH, I SEE...
THERE IS NO "MAN OF THE HOUSE"...
WELL MRS. CORRIGAN, WE'RE TERRIBLY SORRY...
...BUT I'M AFRAID YOU HAVEN'T WON ANYTHING TONIGHT AFTER ALL...
NO, MRS. CORRIGAN... I'M AFRAID YOU HAVEN'T WON ANYTHING AT ALL

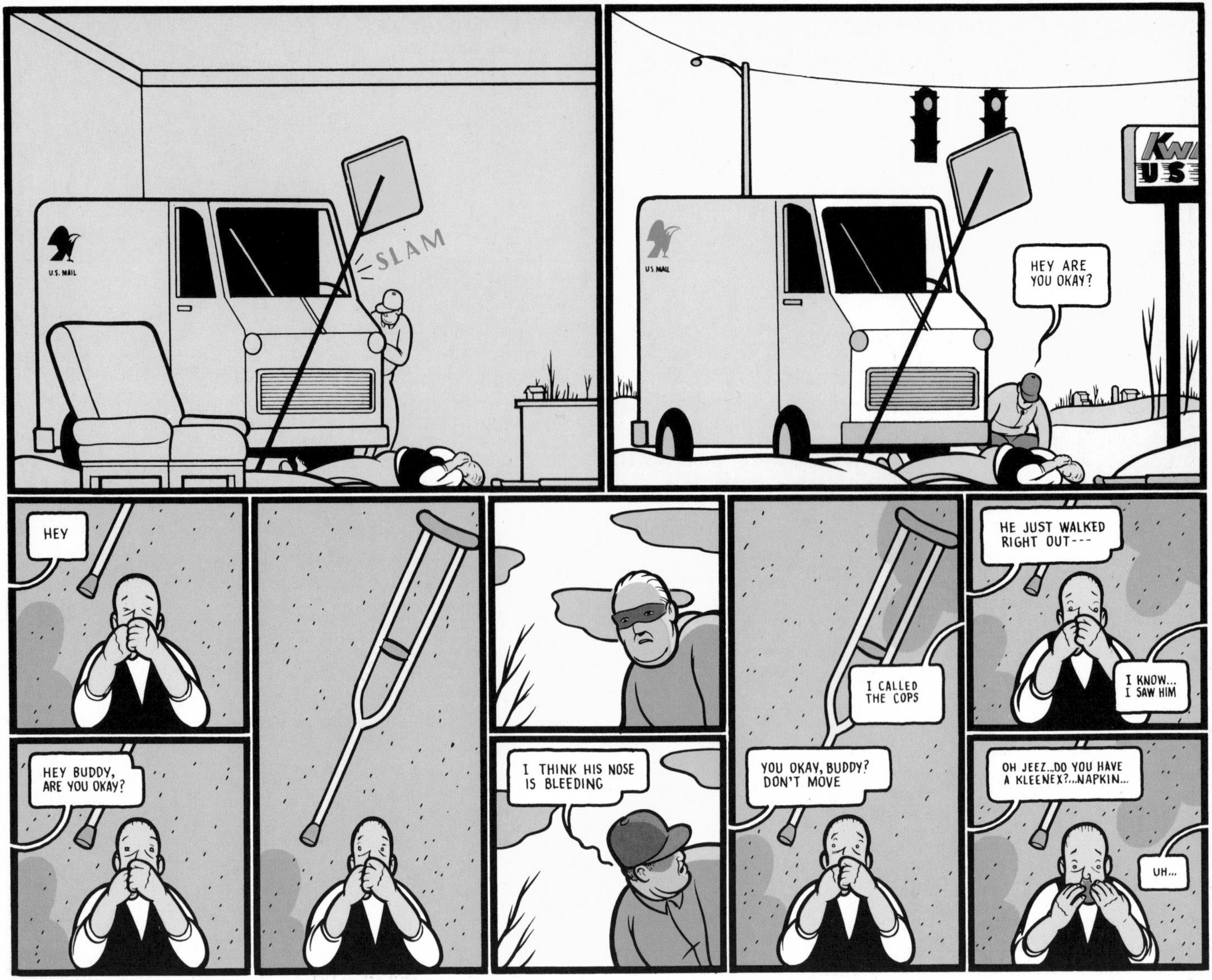
SLAM
U.S. MAIL
U.S. MAIL
HEY ARE YOU OKAY?
HEY
HEY BUDDY, ARE YOU OKAY?
I THINK HIS NOSE IS BLEEDING
I CALLED THE COPS
YOU OKAY, BUDDY? DON'T MOVE
HE JUST WALKED RIGHT OUT---
I KNOW... I SAW HIM
OH JEEZ...DO YOU HAVE A KLEENEX?...NAPKIN...
UH...

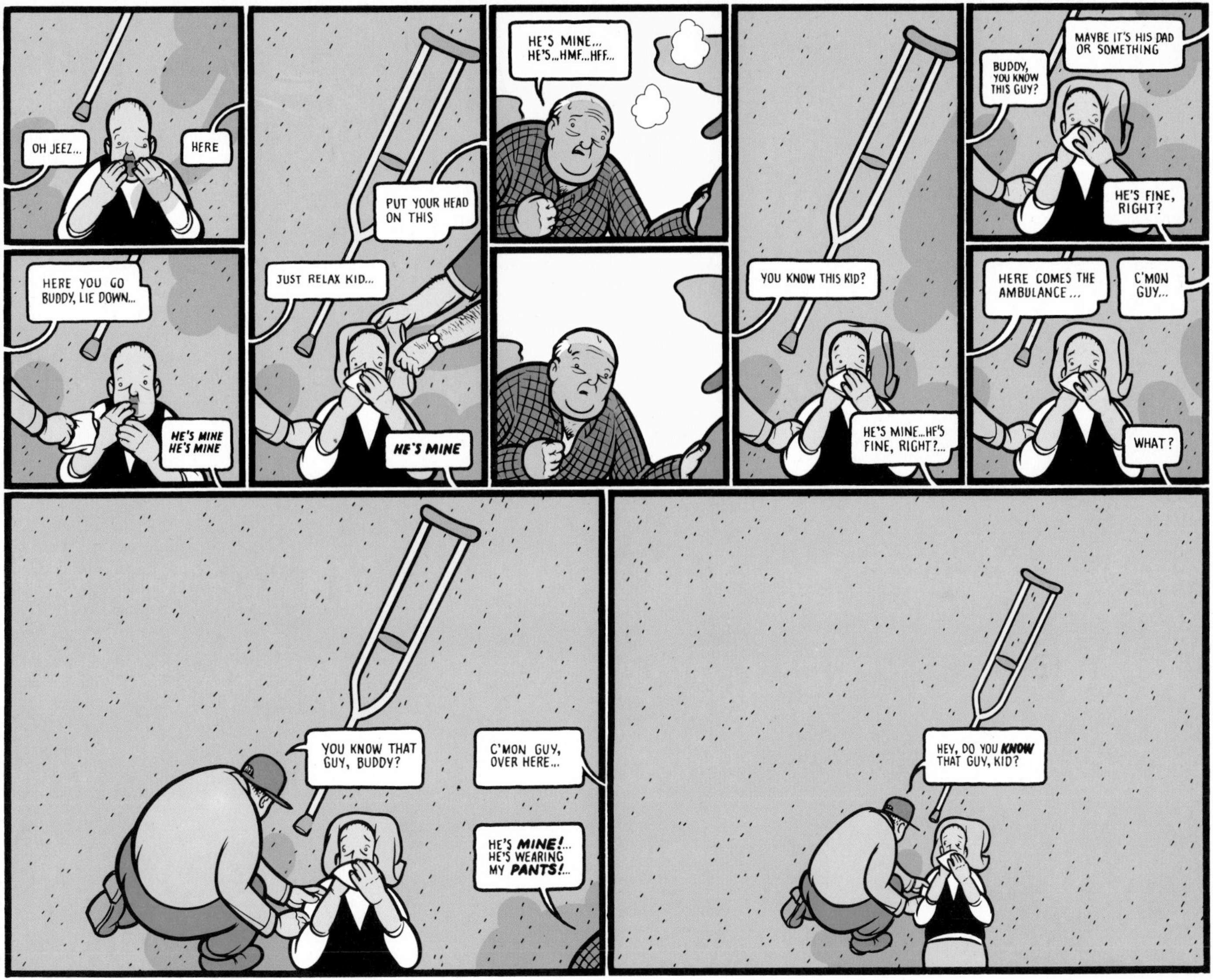
OH JEEZ...
HERE
HERE YOU GO BUDDY, LIE DOWN...
HE'S MINE HE'S MINE
PUT YOUR HEAD ON THIS
JUST RELAX KID...
HE'S MINE
HE'S MINE... HE'S...HMF...HFF...
YOU KNOW THIS KID?
HE'S MINE...HE'S FINE, RIGHT?...
MAYBE IT'S HIS DAD OR SOMETHING
BUDDY, YOU KNOW THIS GUY?
HE'S FINE, RIGHT?
HERE COMES THE AMBULANCE...
C'MON GUY...
WHAT?
YOU KNOW THAT GUY, BUDDY?
C'MON GUY, OVER HERE...
HE'S MINE!... HE'S WEARING MY PANTS!...
HEY, DO YOU KNOW THAT GUY, KID?

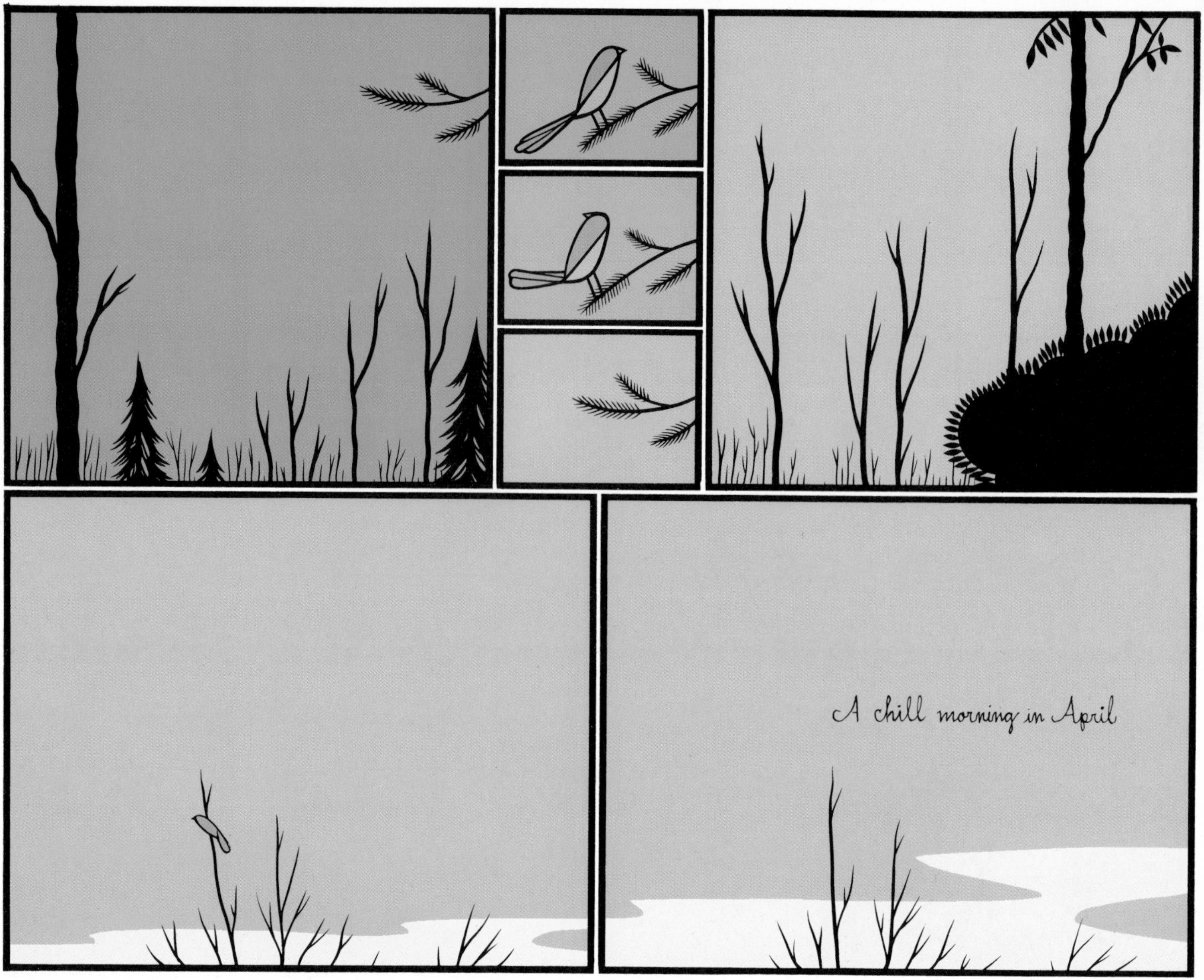
A chill morning in April

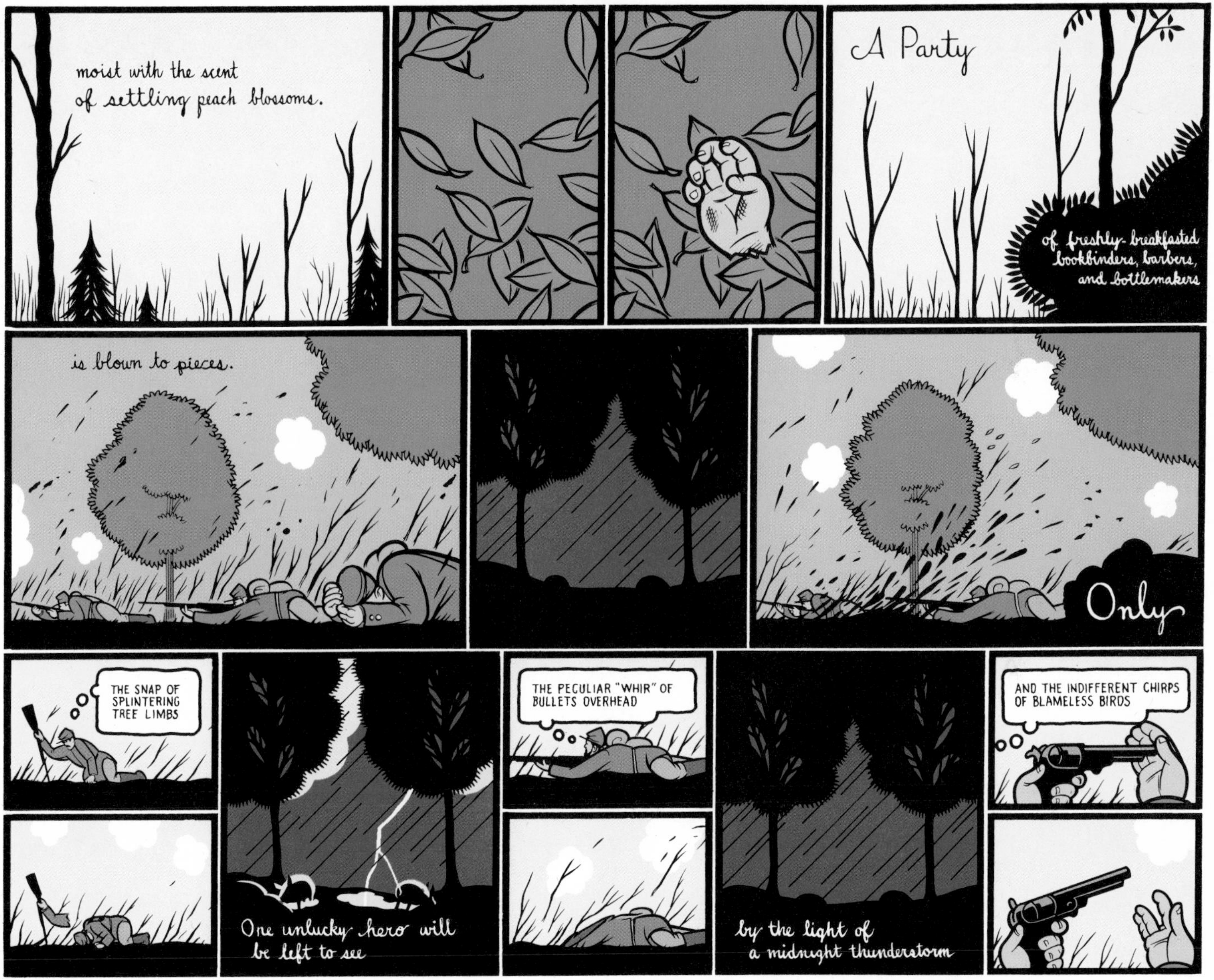
moist with the scent
of settling peach blossoms.
A Party
of freshly-breakfasted bookbinders, barbers, and bottlemakers
is blown to pieces.
Only
THE SNAP OF SPLINTERING TREE LIMBS
One unlucky hero will be left to see
THE PECULIAR "WHIR" OF BULLETS OVERHEAD
by the light of a midnight thunderstorm
AND THE INDIFFERENT CHIRPS OF BLAMELESS BIRDS

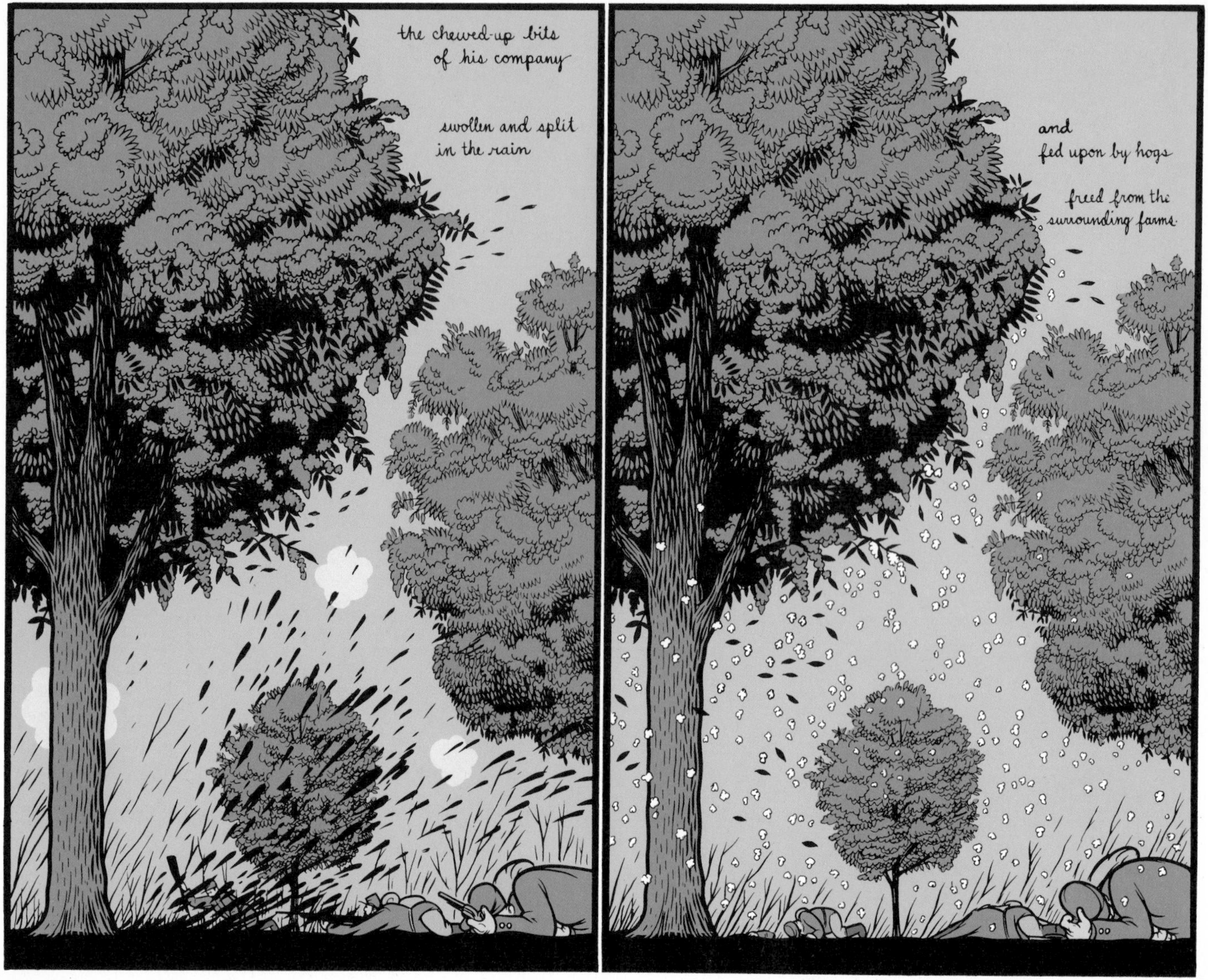
the chewed-up bits of his company
swollen and split in the rain
and fed upon by hogs
freed from the surrounding farms.

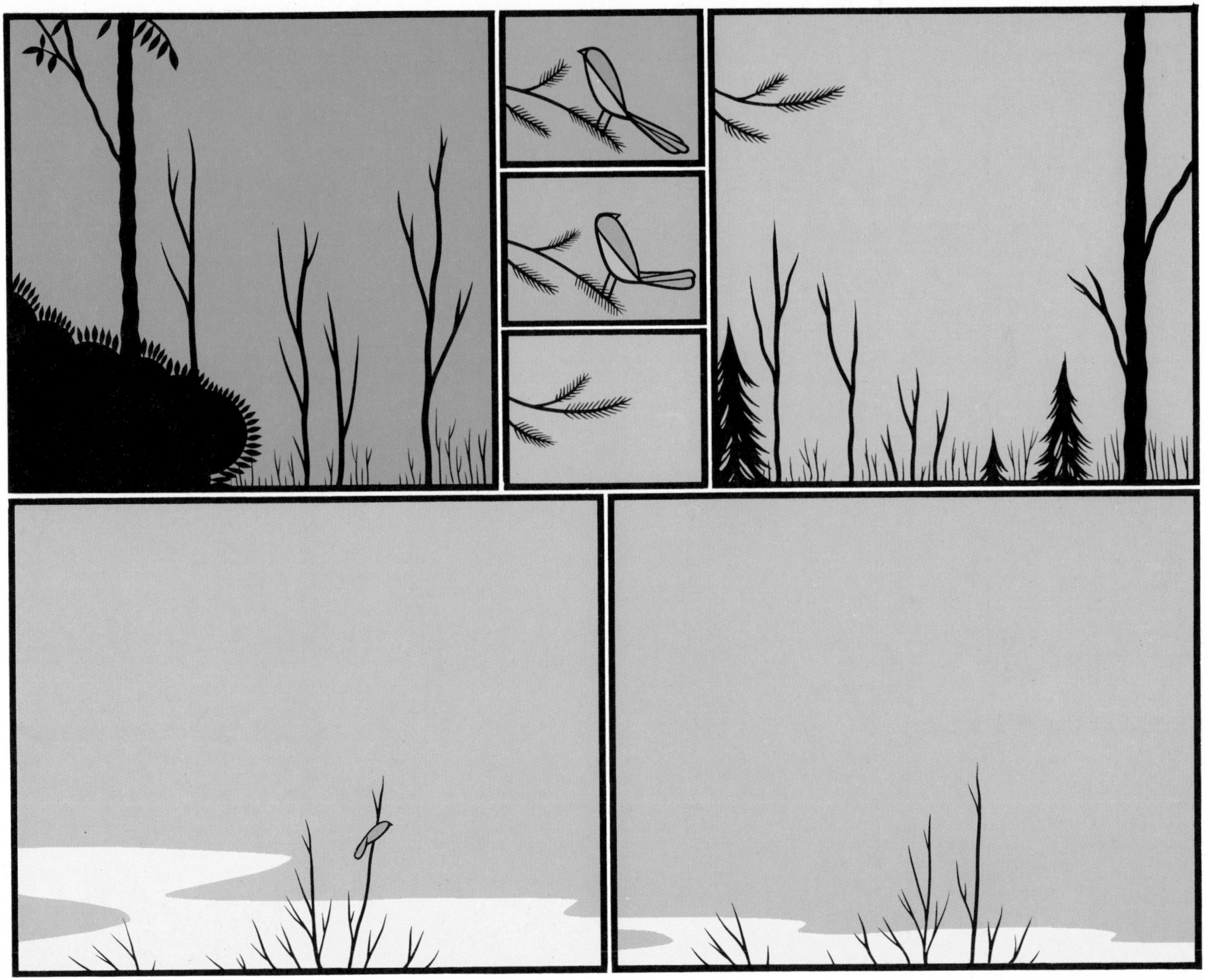

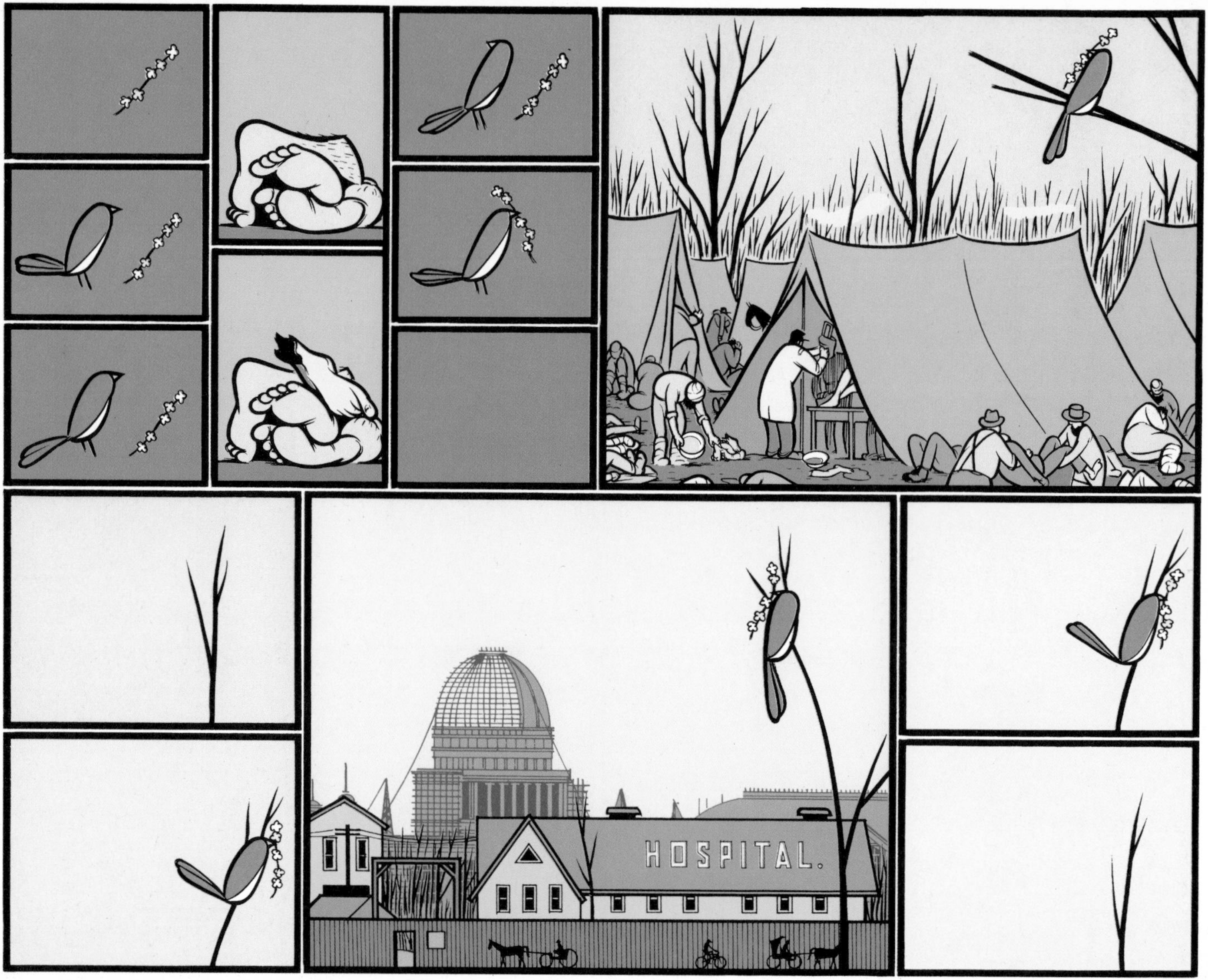
HOSPITAL.

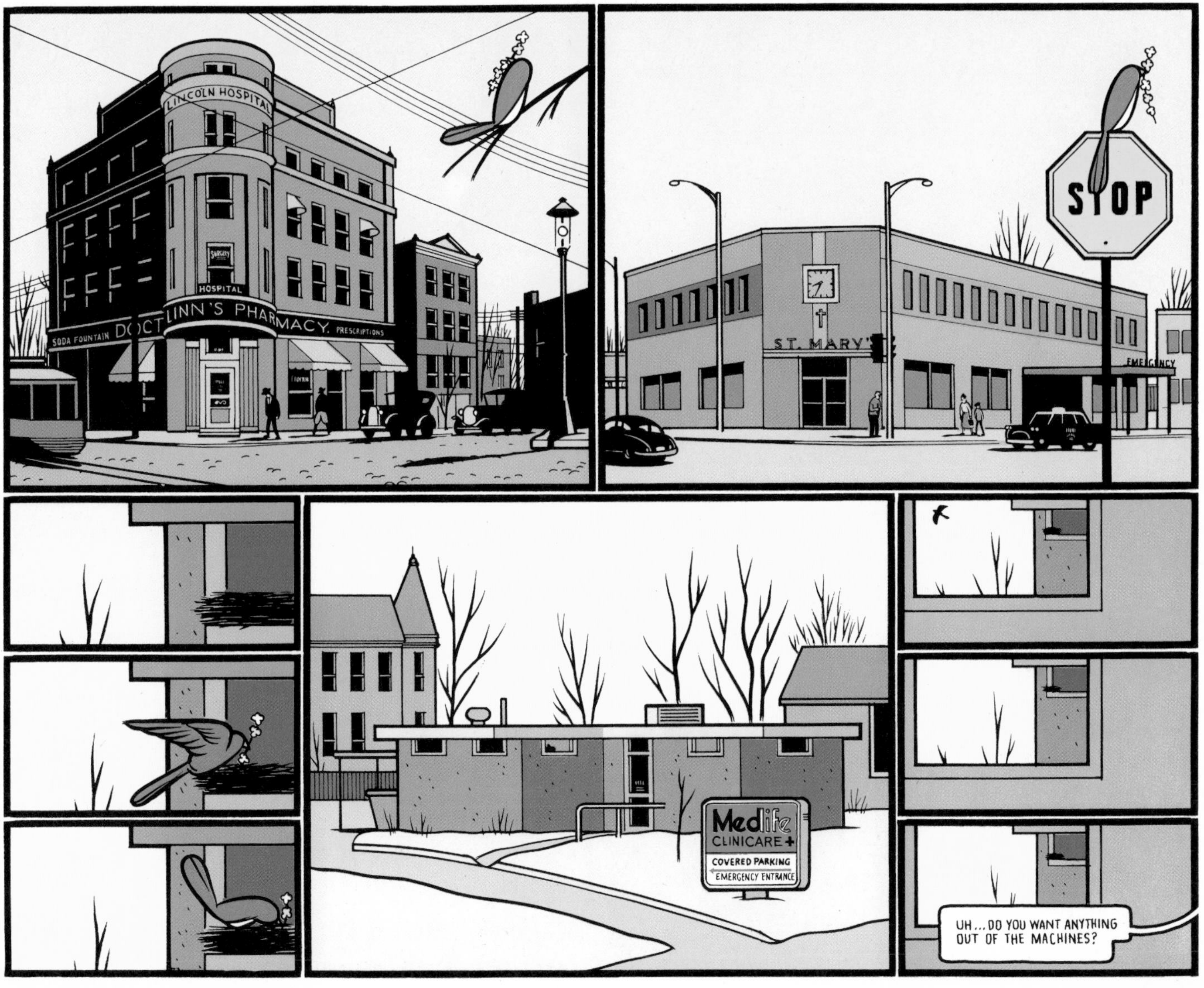
LINCOLN HOSPITAL
SURGERY
HOSPITAL
SODA FOUNTAIN
DOCT
LINN'S PHARMACY.
PRESCRIPTIONS
STOP
ST. MARY'S
EMERGENCY
Medlife
CLINICARE+
COVERED PARKING
EMERGENCY ENTRANCE
UH... DO YOU WANT ANYTHING OUT OF THE MACHINES?

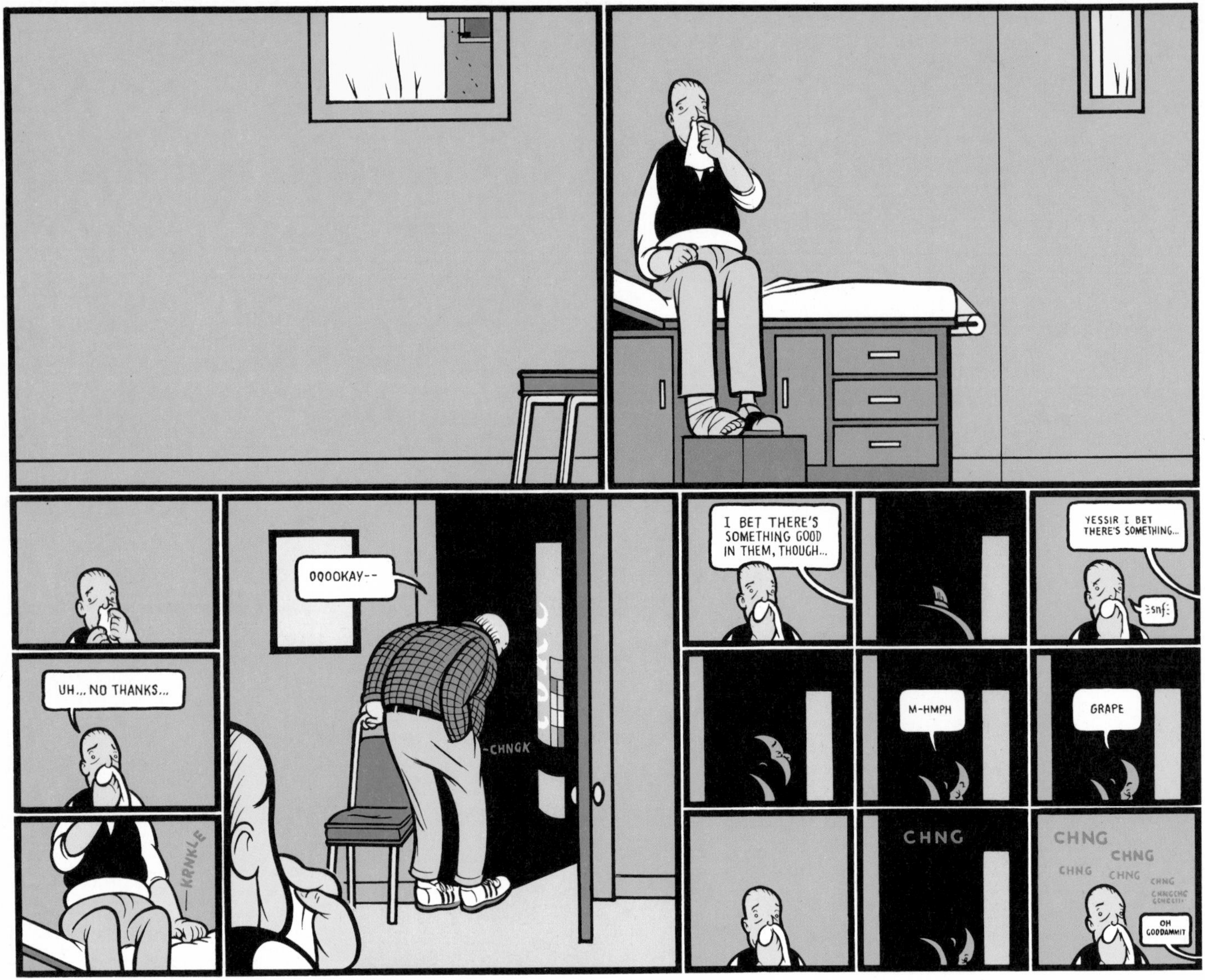
UH... NO THANKS...
KRNKLE
OOOOKAY--
-CHNGK
I BET THERE'S SOMETHING GOOD IN THEM, THOUGH...
YESSIR I BET THERE'S SOMETHING...
snf
M-HMPH
GRAPE
CHNG
CHNG
CHNG
CHNG
CHNG
CHNG
CHNGCHG
OH GODDAMMIT

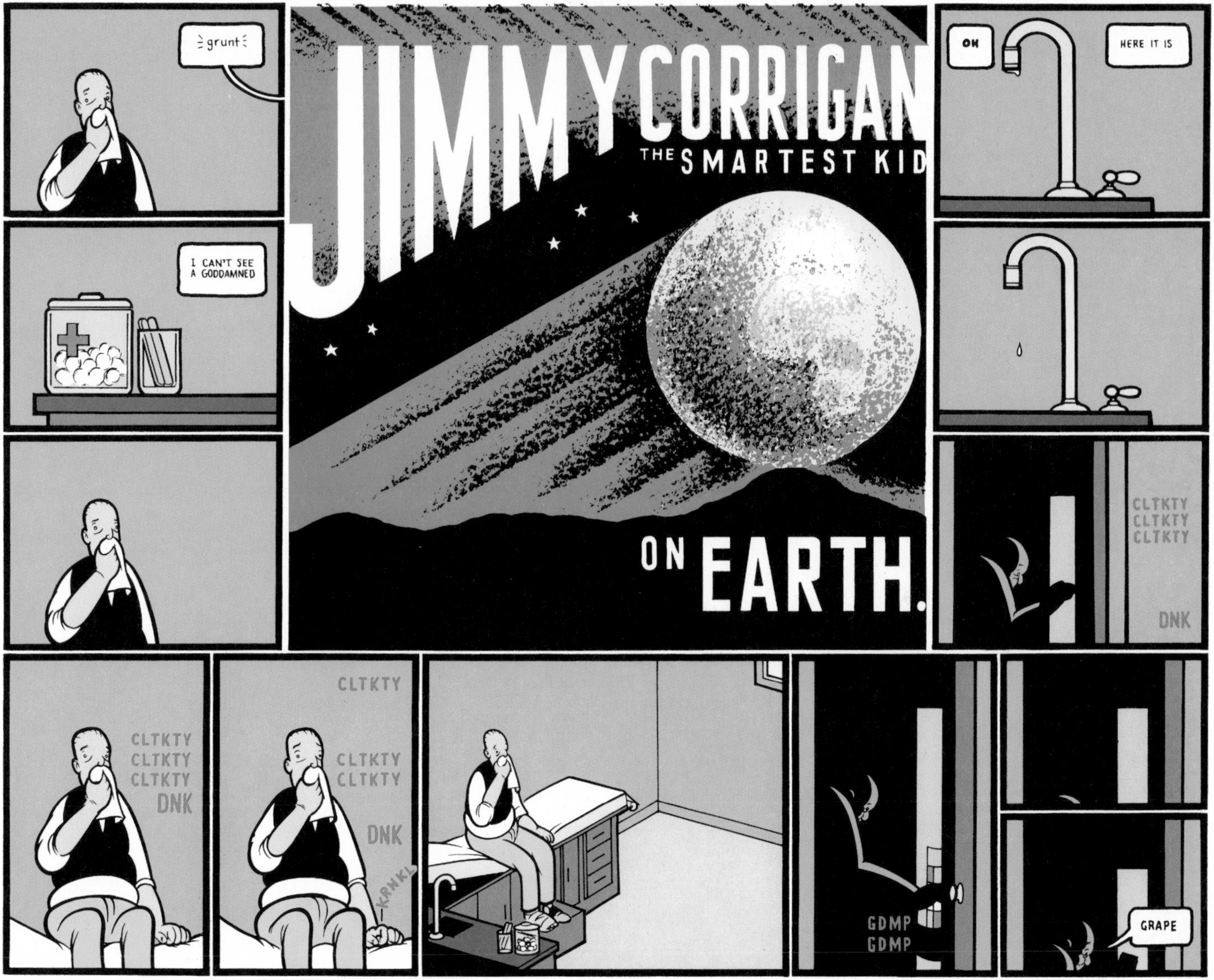

grunt
I CAN'T SEE A GODDAMNED
JIMMY CORRIGAN
THE SMARTEST KID
ON EARTH.
OH
HERE IT IS
CLTKTY CLTKTY CLTKTY
DNK
CLTKTY CLTKTY CLTKTY
DNK
CLTKTY
CLTKTY CLTKTY
DNK
KRNKL
GDMP GDMP
GRAPE

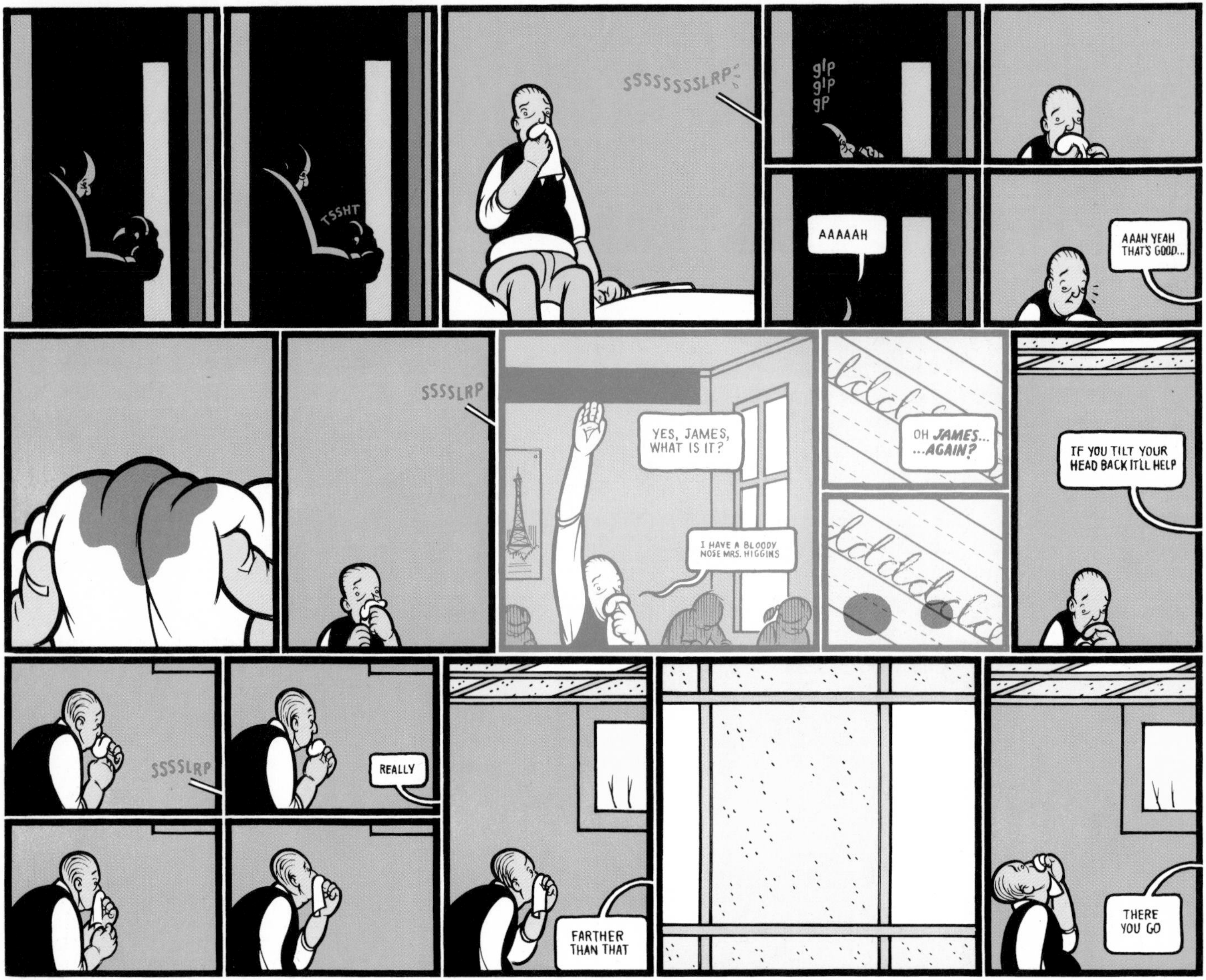
TSSHT
SSSSSSSSLRP
glp
glp
gp
AAAAAH
AAAH YEAH THAT'S GOOD...
SSSSLRP
YES, JAMES, WHAT IS IT?
I HAVE A BLOODY NOSE MRS. HIGGINS
OH JAMES... ...AGAIN?
IF YOU TILT YOUR HEAD BACK IT'LL HELP
SSSSLRP
REALLY
FARTHER THAN THAT
THERE YOU GO

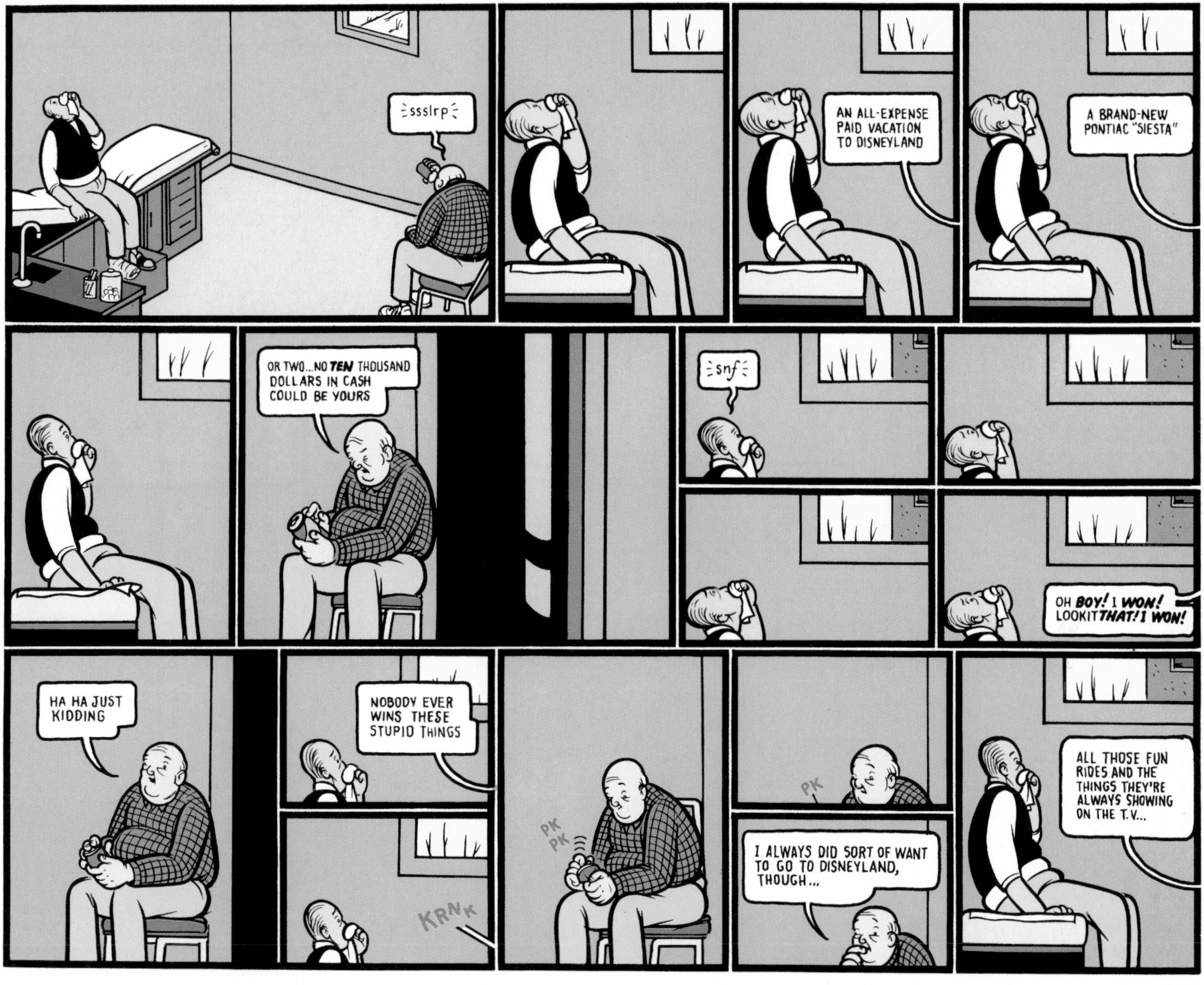
ssslrp
AN ALL-EXPENSE PAID VACATION TO DISNEYLAND
A BRAND-NEW PONTIAC "SIESTA"
OR TWO...NO TEN THOUSAND DOLLARS IN CASH COULD BE YOURS
snf
OH BOY! I WON! LOOKIT THAT! I WON!
HA HA JUST KIDDING
NOBODY EVER WINS THESE STUPID THINGS
KRNK
PK PK
PK
I ALWAYS DID SORT OF WANT TO GO TO DISNEYLAND, THOUGH...
ALL THOSE FUN RIDES AND THE THINGS THEY'RE ALWAYS SHOWING ON THE T.V...

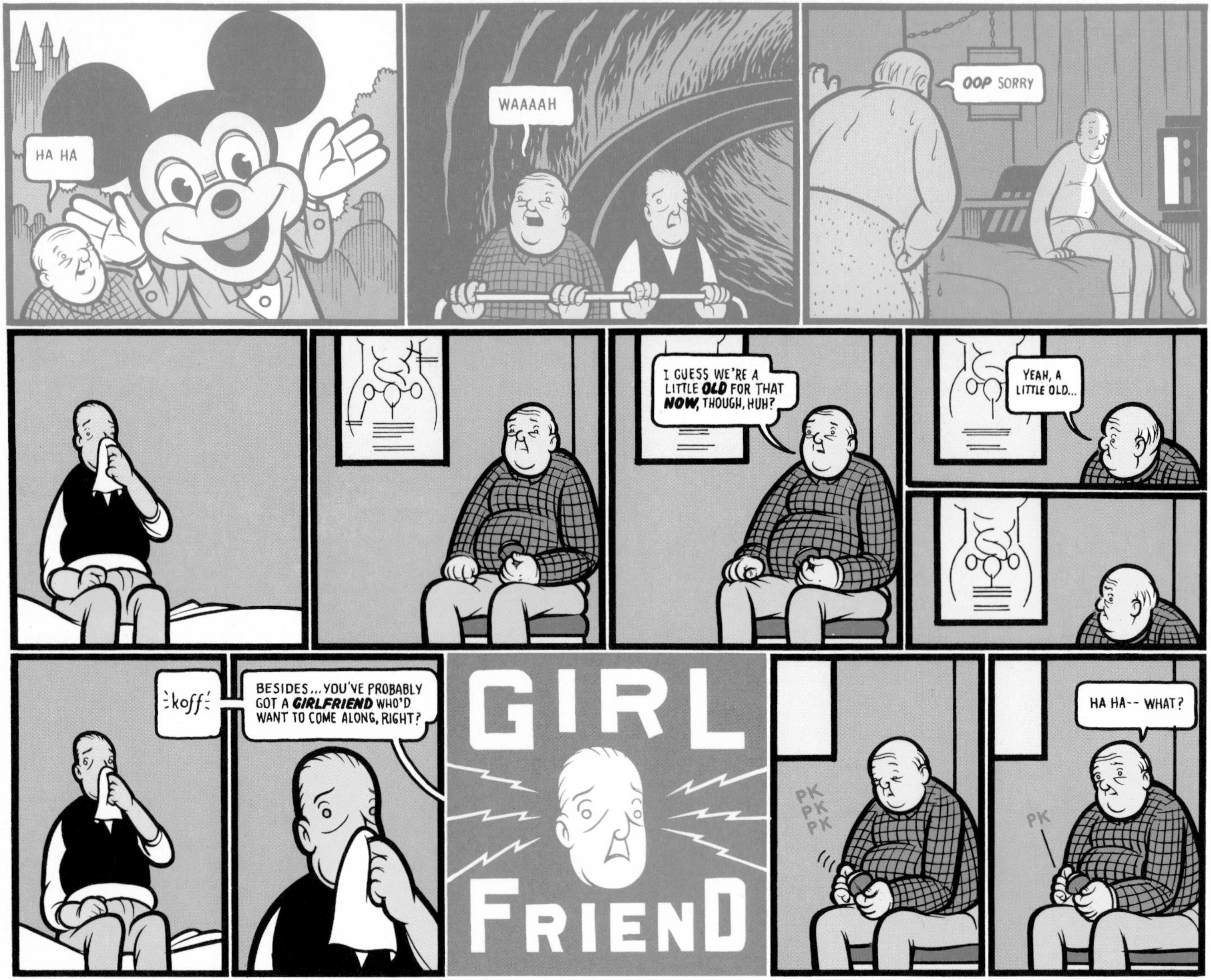
HA HA
WAAAAH
OOP SORRY
I GUESS WE'RE A LITTLE OLD FOR THAT NOW, THOUGH, HUH?
YEAH, A LITTLE OLD...
koff
BESIDES... YOU'VE PROBABLY GOT A GIRLFRIEND WHO'D WANT TO COME ALONG, RIGHT?
GIRL
FRIEND
PK
PK
PK
PK
HA HA-- WHAT?

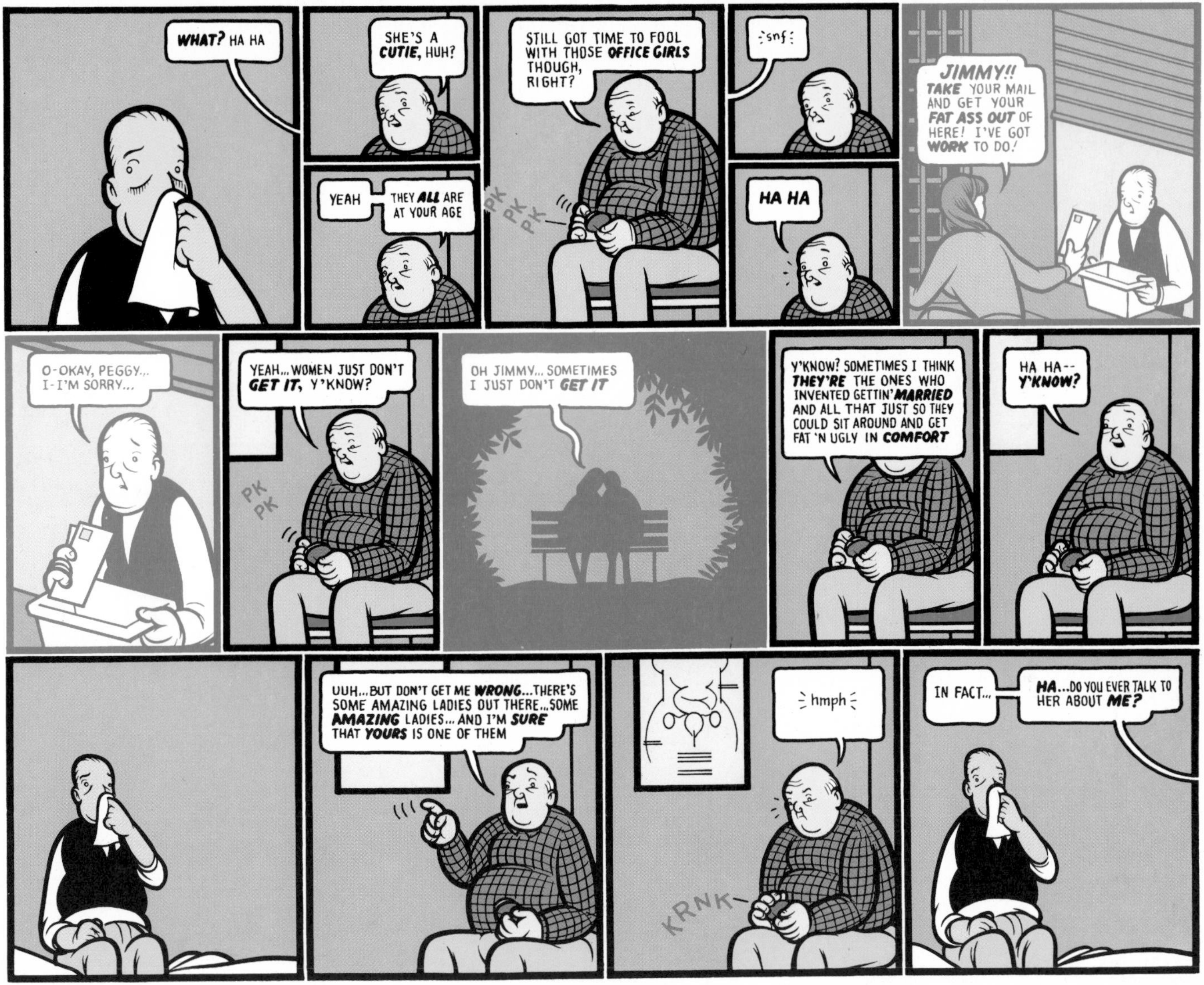
WHAT? HA HA
SHE'S A CUTIE, HUH?
YEAH
THEY ALL ARE AT YOUR AGE
STILL GOT TIME TO FOOL WITH THOSE OFFICE GIRLS THOUGH, RIGHT?
PK PK PK
snf
HA HA
JIMMY!! TAKE YOUR MAIL AND GET YOUR FAT ASS OUT OF HERE! I'VE GOT WORK TO DO!
O-OKAY, PEGGY... I-I'M SORRY...
YEAH... WOMEN JUST DON'T GET IT, Y'KNOW?
PK PK
OH JIMMY... SOMETIMES I JUST DON'T GET IT
Y'KNOW? SOMETIMES I THINK THEY'RE THE ONES WHO INVENTED GETTIN' MARRIED AND ALL THAT JUST SO THEY COULD SIT AROUND AND GET FAT 'N UGLY IN COMFORT
HA HA-- Y'KNOW?
UUH... BUT DON'T GET ME WRONG... THERE'S SOME AMAZING LADIES OUT THERE... SOME AMAZING LADIES... AND I'M SURE THAT YOURS IS ONE OF THEM
hmph
KRNK
IN FACT...
HA... DO YOU EVER TALK TO HER ABOUT ME?

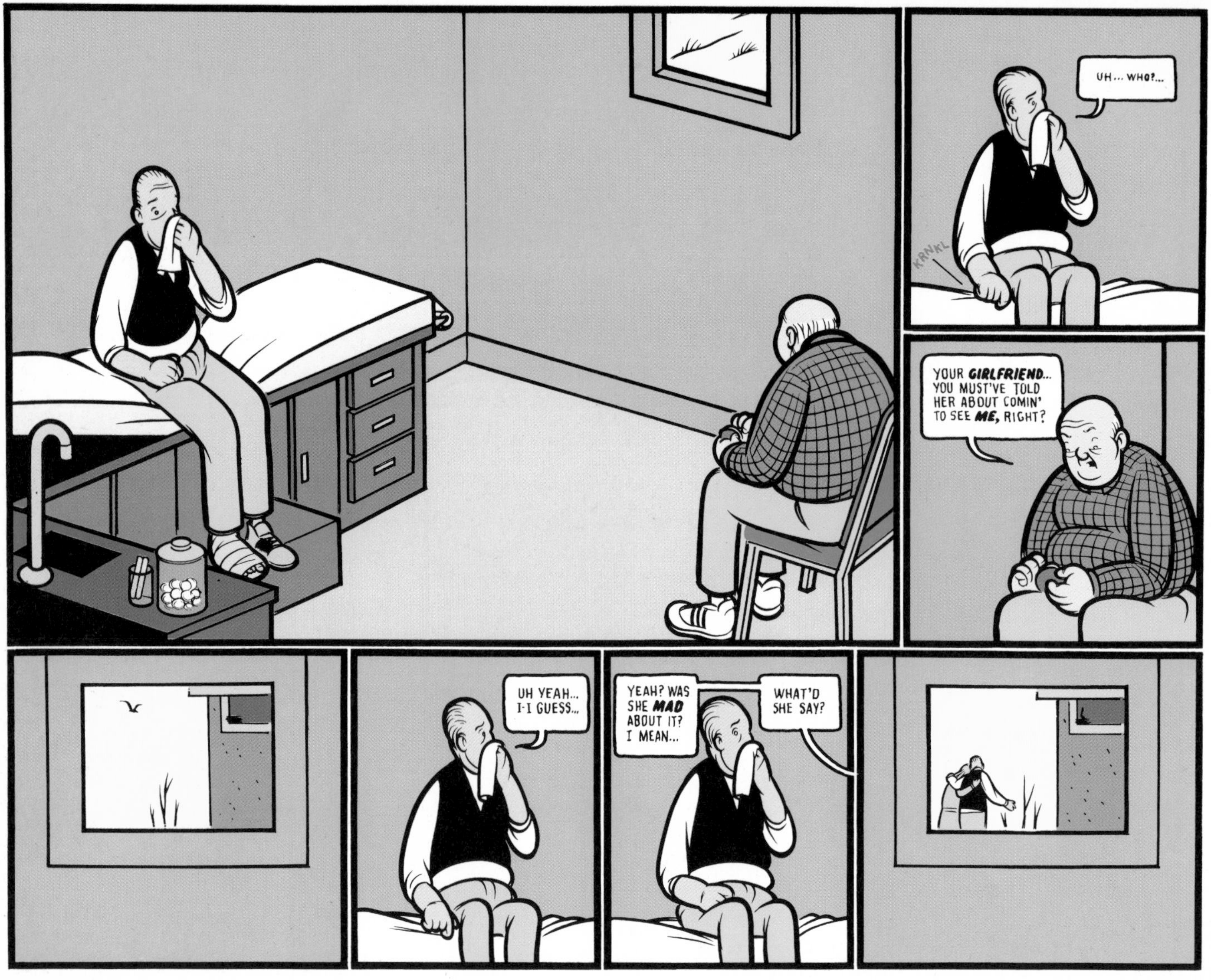
UH... WHO?...
KRNKL
YOUR GIRLFRIEND... YOU MUST'VE TOLD HER ABOUT COMIN' TO SEE ME, RIGHT?
UH YEAH... I-I GUESS...
YEAH? WAS SHE MAD ABOUT IT? I MEAN...
WHAT'D SHE SAY?

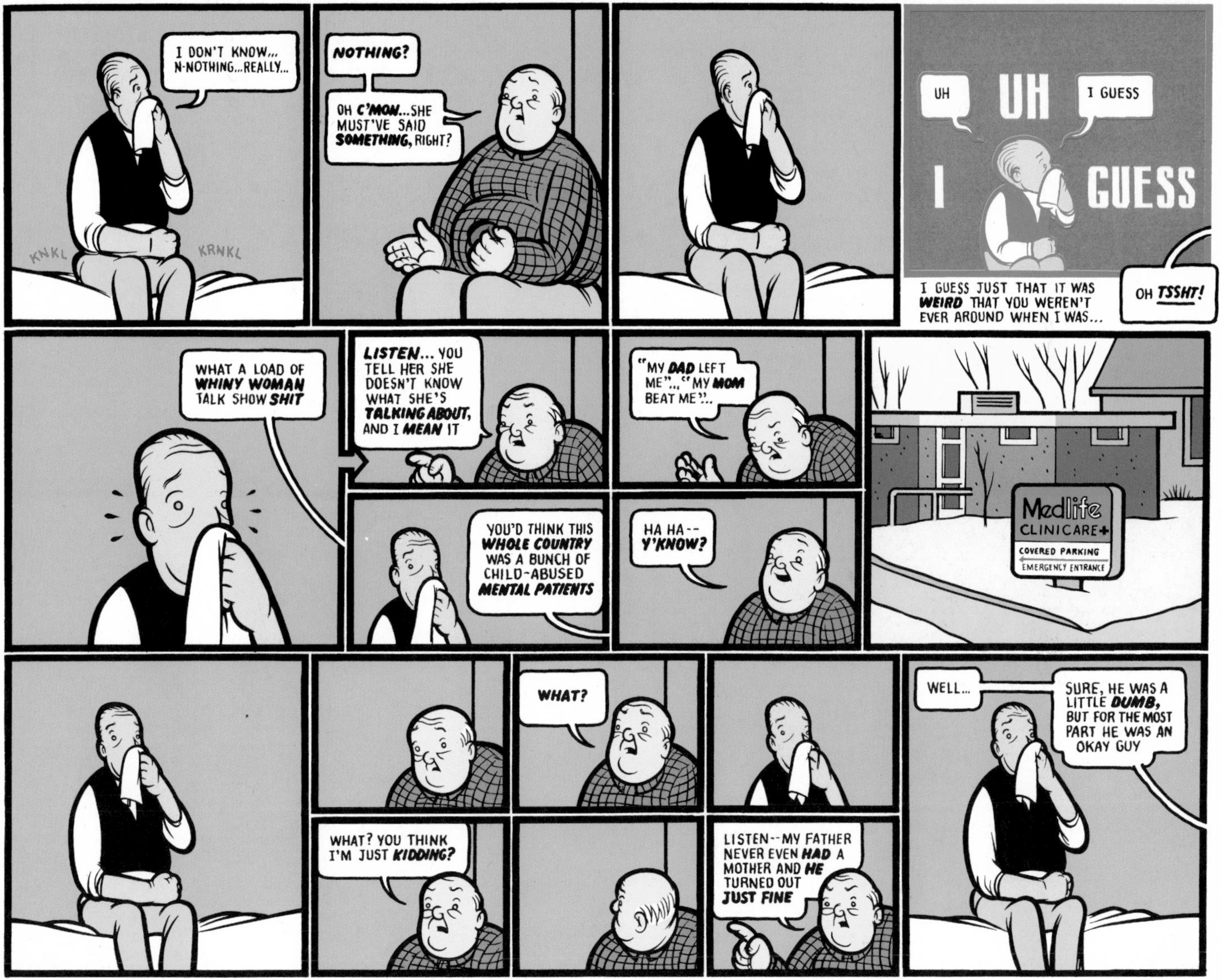
I DON'T KNOW... N-NOTHING...REALLY...
KNKL
KRNKL
NOTHING?
OH C'MON...SHE MUST'VE SAID SOMETHING, RIGHT?
UH
UH
I GUESS
I
GUESS
I GUESS JUST THAT IT WAS WEIRD THAT YOU WEREN'T EVER AROUND WHEN I WAS...
OH TSSHT!
WHAT A LOAD OF WHINY WOMAN TALK SHOW SHIT
LISTEN... YOU TELL HER SHE DOESN'T KNOW WHAT SHE'S TALKING ABOUT, AND I MEAN IT
"MY DAD LEFT ME"... "MY MOM BEAT ME"...
YOU'D THINK THIS WHOLE COUNTRY WAS A BUNCH OF CHILD-ABUSED MENTAL PATIENTS
HA HA-- Y'KNOW?
Medlife
CLINICARE+
COVERED PARKING
EMERGENCY ENTRANCE
WHAT?
WHAT? YOU THINK I'M JUST KIDDING?
LISTEN--MY FATHER NEVER EVEN HAD A MOTHER AND HE TURNED OUT JUST FINE
WELL...
SURE, HE WAS A LITTLE DUMB, BUT FOR THE MOST PART HE WAS AN OKAY GUY

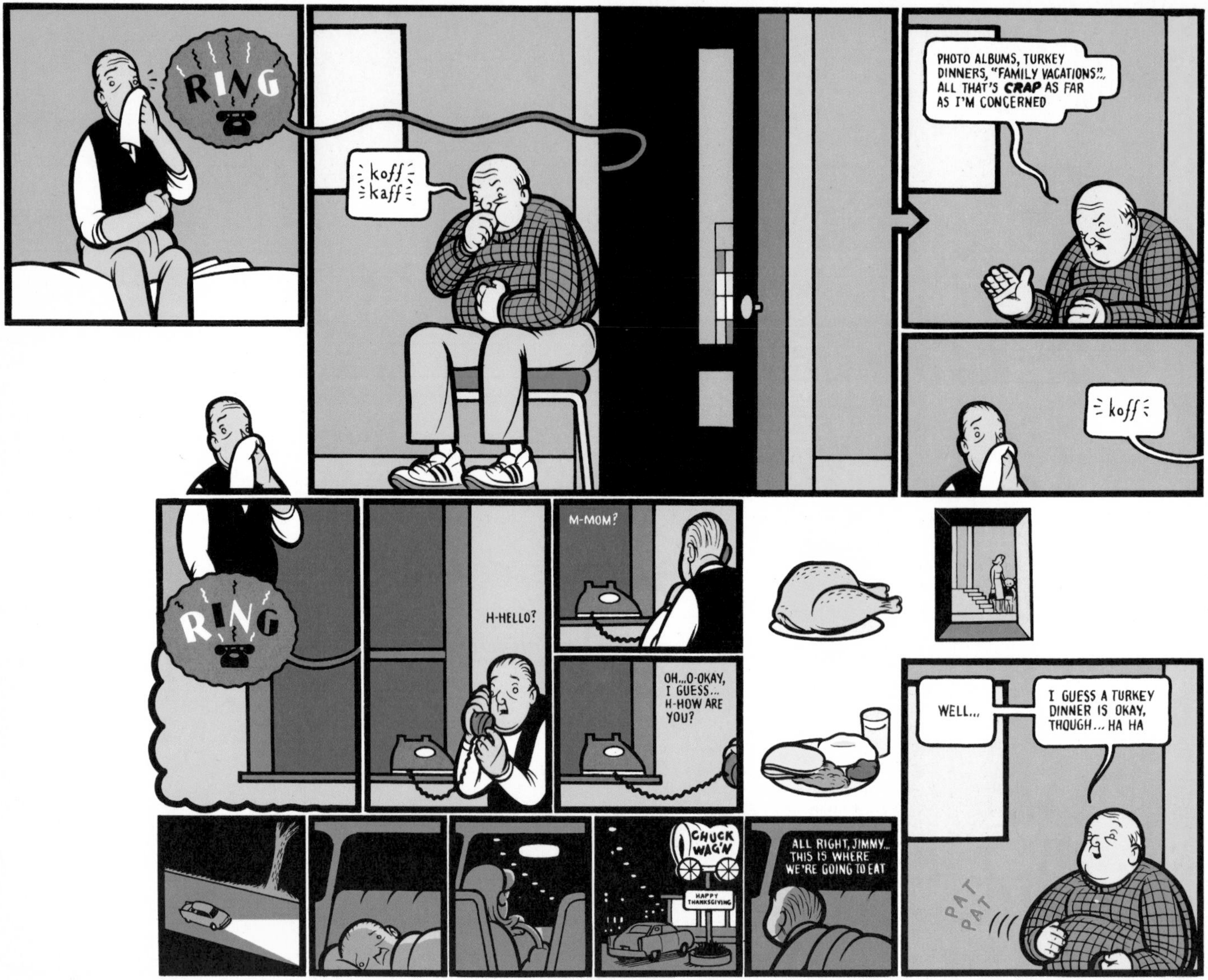
RING
koff kaff
PHOTO ALBUMS, TURKEY DINNERS, "FAMILY VACATIONS"... ALL THAT'S CRAP AS FAR AS I'M CONCERNED
koff
RING
H-HELLO?
M-MOM?
OH...O-OKAY, I GUESS... H-HOW ARE YOU?
WELL...
I GUESS A TURKEY DINNER IS OKAY, THOUGH... HA HA
PAT PAT
CHUCK WAG'N
HAPPY THANKSGIVING
ALL RIGHT, JIMMY... THIS IS WHERE WE'RE GOING TO EAT

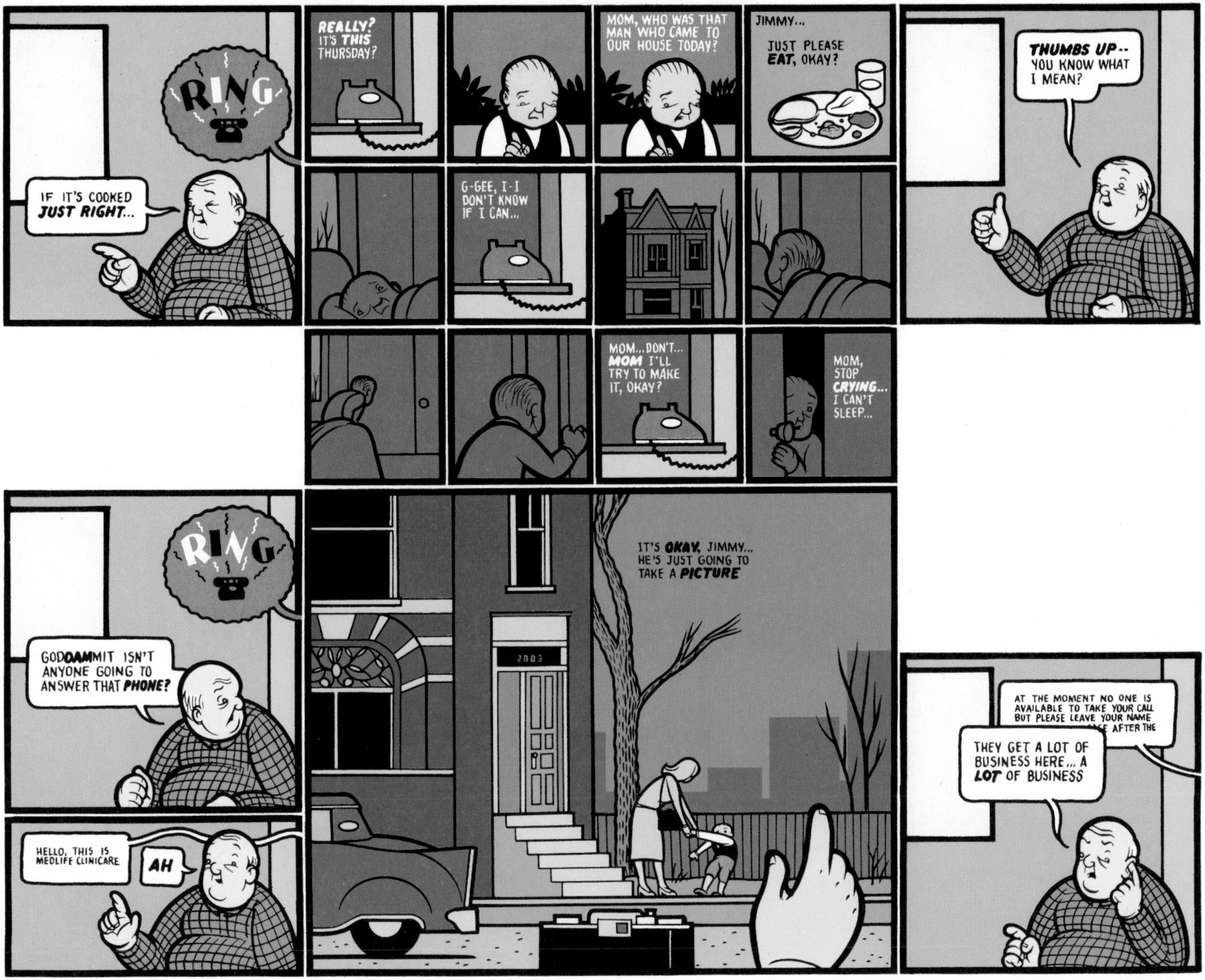
RING
IF IT'S COOKED JUST RIGHT...
REALLY? IT'S THIS THURSDAY?
MOM, WHO WAS THAT MAN WHO CAME TO OUR HOUSE TODAY?
JIMMY...
JUST PLEASE EAT, OKAY?
THUMBS UP.. YOU KNOW WHAT I MEAN?
G-GEE, I-I DON'T KNOW IF I CAN...
MOM...DON'T... MOM I'LL TRY TO MAKE IT, OKAY?
MOM, STOP CRYING... I CAN'T SLEEP...
RING
GODDAMMIT ISN'T ANYONE GOING TO ANSWER THAT PHONE?
HELLO, THIS IS MEDLIFE CLINICARE
AH
IT'S OKAY, JIMMY... HE'S JUST GOING TO TAKE A PICTURE
2003
AT THE MOMENT NO ONE IS AVAILABLE TO TAKE YOUR CALL BUT PLEASE LEAVE YOUR NAME
AFTER THE
THEY GET A LOT OF BUSINESS HERE... A LOT OF BUSINESS

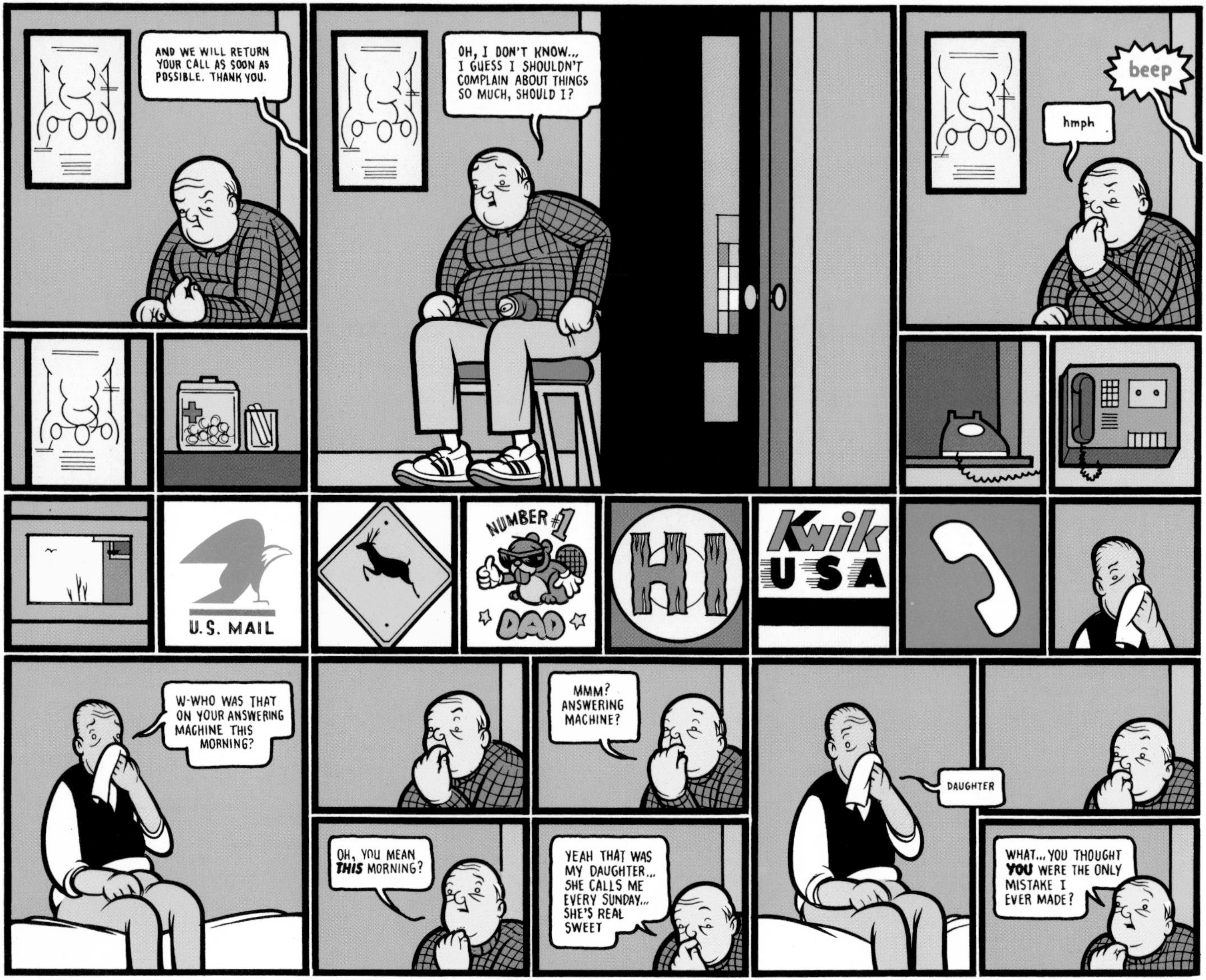
AND WE WILL RETURN YOUR CALL AS SOON AS POSSIBLE. THANK YOU.
OH, I DON'T KNOW.., I GUESS I SHOULDN'T COMPLAIN ABOUT THINGS SO MUCH, SHOULD I?
beep
hmph
U.S. MAIL
NUMBER #1
DAD
HI
Kwik
USA
W-WHO WAS THAT ON YOUR ANSWERING MACHINE THIS MORNING?
MMM? ANSWERING MACHINE?
OH, YOU MEAN THIS MORNING?
YEAH THAT WAS MY DAUGHTER... SHE CALLS ME EVERY SUNDAY... SHE'S REAL SWEET
DAUGHTER
WHAT... YOU THOUGHT YOU WERE THE ONLY MISTAKE I EVER MADE?

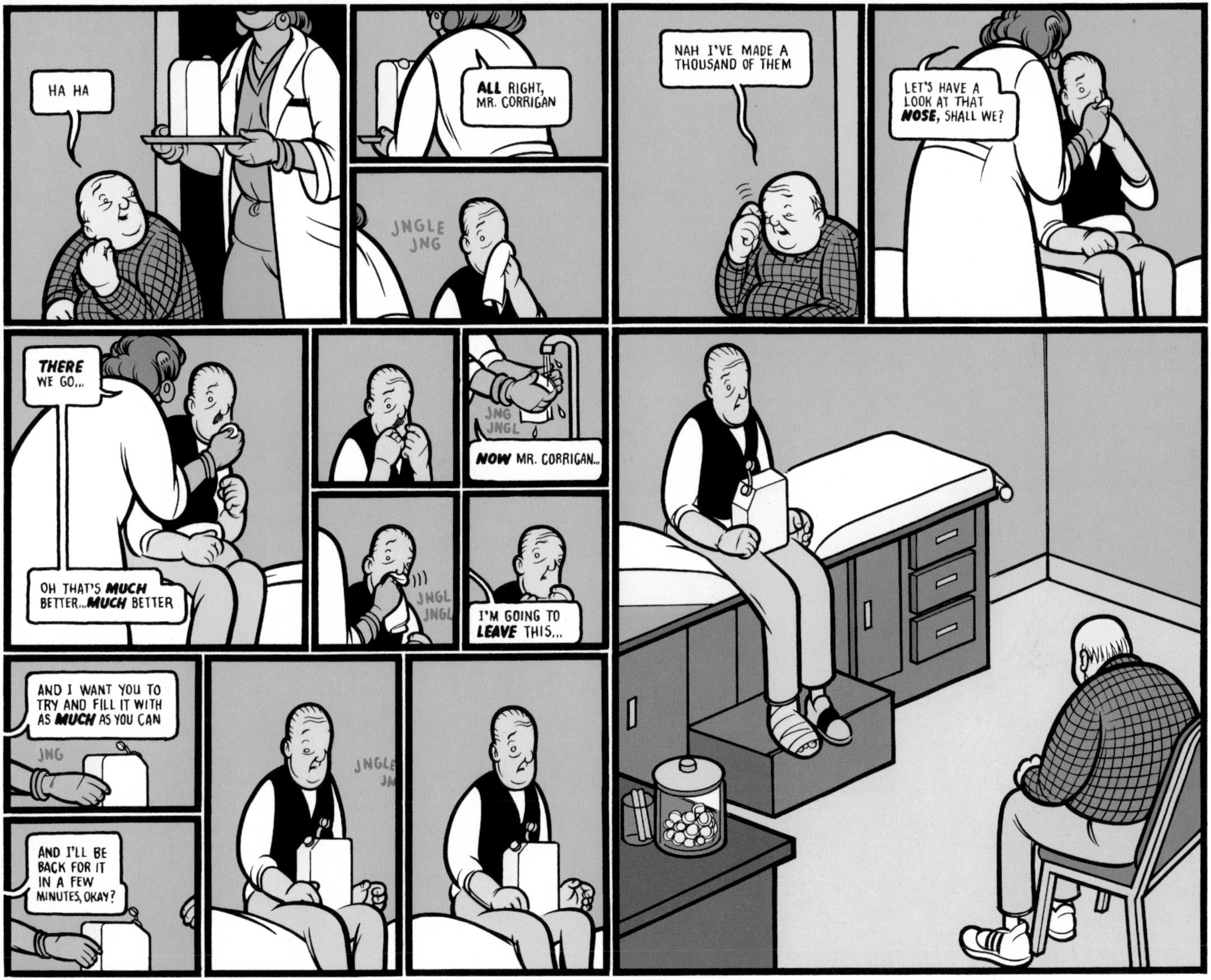

HA HA
ALL RIGHT, MR. CORRIGAN
JNGLE JNG
NAH I'VE MADE A THOUSAND OF THEM
LET'S HAVE A LOOK AT THAT NOSE, SHALL WE?
THERE WE GO...
OH THAT'S MUCH BETTER...MUCH BETTER
JNG JNGL
NOW MR. CORRIGAN...
JNGL JNGL
I'M GOING TO LEAVE THIS...
AND I WANT YOU TO TRY AND FILL IT WITH AS MUCH AS YOU CAN
JNG
AND I'LL BE BACK FOR IT IN A FEW MINUTES, OKAY?

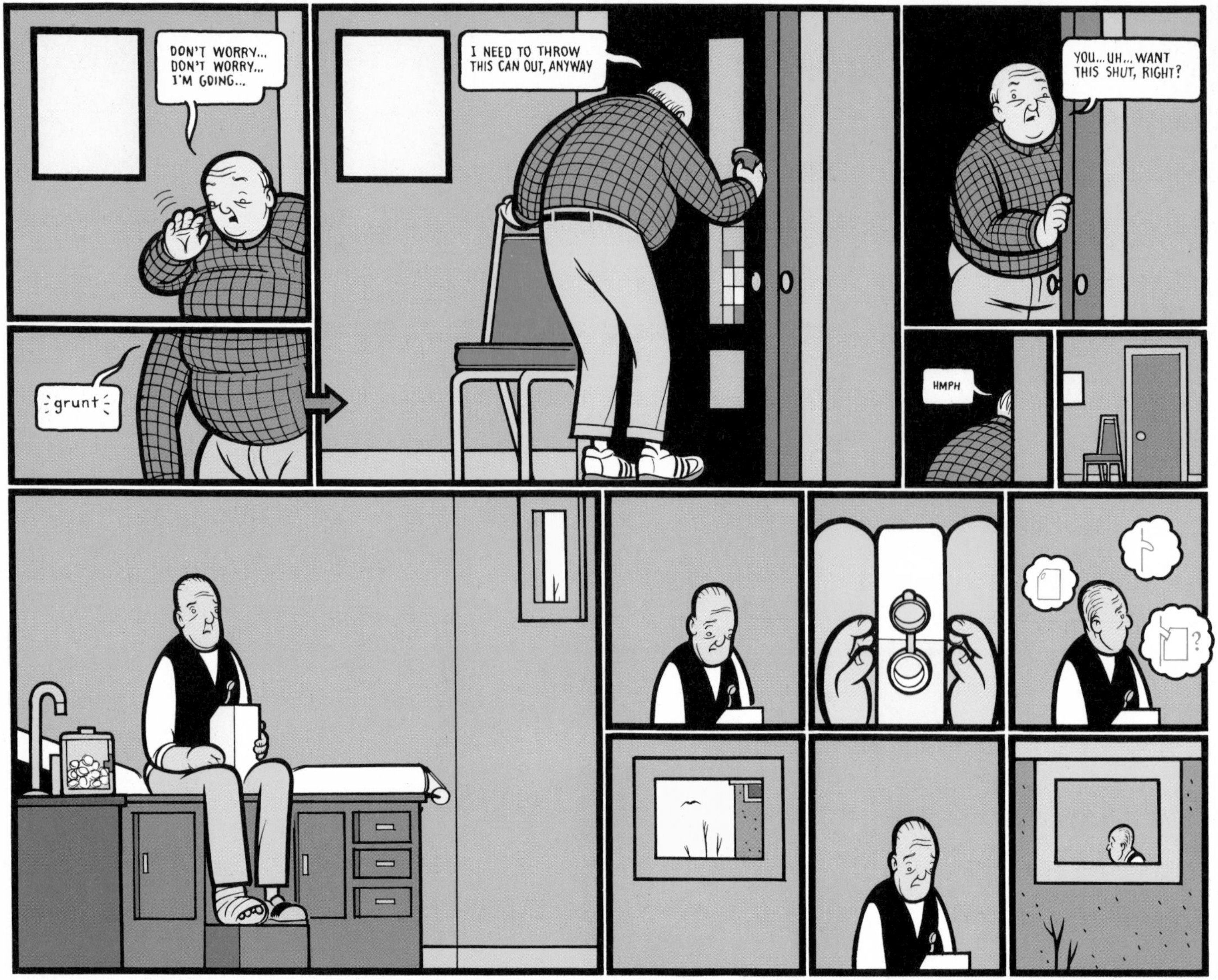
DON'T WORRY...
DON'T WORRY...
I'M GOING...
grunt
I NEED TO THROW
THIS CAN OUT, ANYWAY
YOU... UH... WANT
THIS SHUT, RIGHT?
HMPH

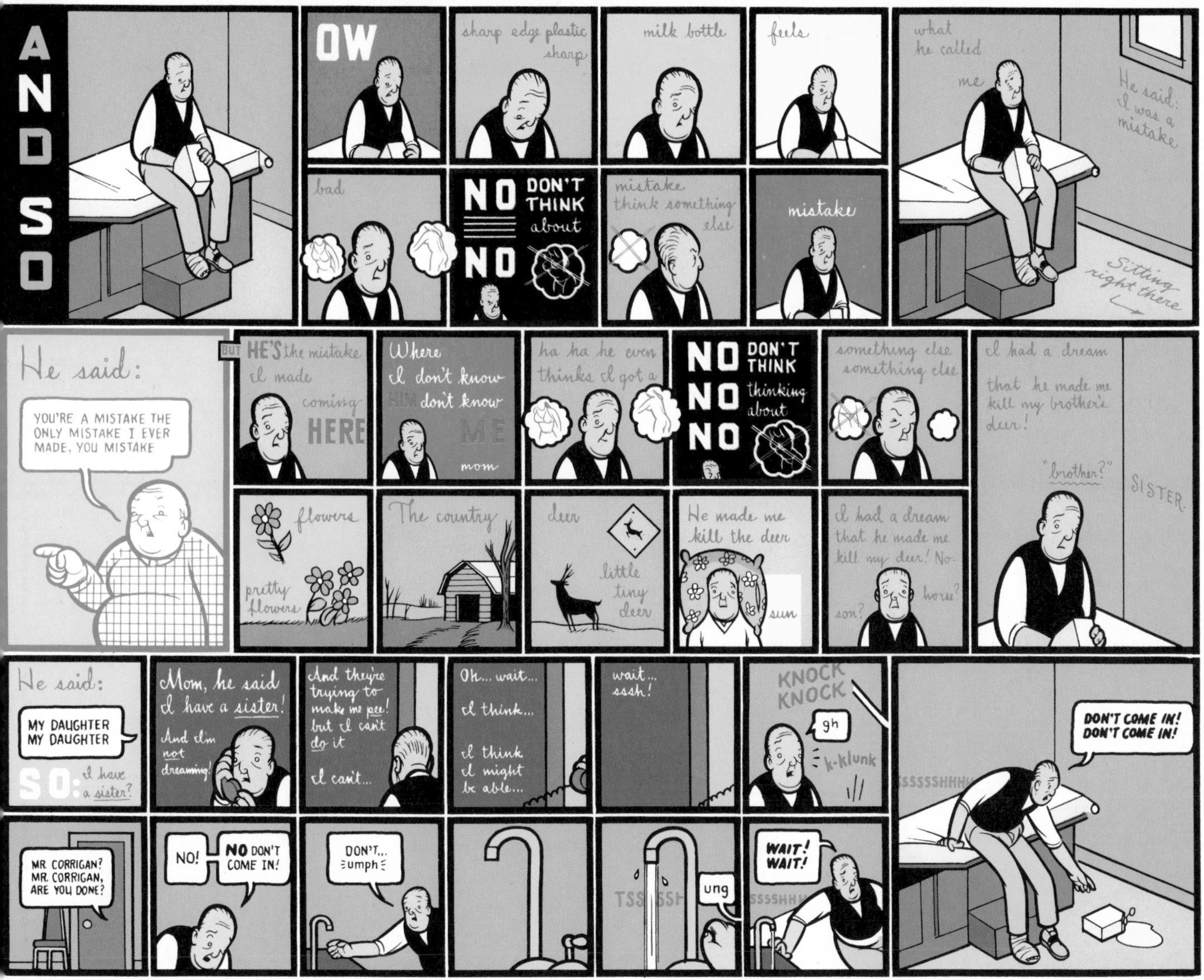
AND SO
OW
sharp edge plastic sharp
milk bottle
feels
what he called me
He said: I was a mistake
Sitting right there
bad
NO DON'T THINK about NO
mistake think something else
mistake
He said:
YOU'RE A MISTAKE THE ONLY MISTAKE I EVER MADE, YOU MISTAKE
BUT HE'S the mistake I made coming HERE
Where I don't know HIM don't know ME
mom
ha ha he even thinks I got a
NO DON'T THINK NO thinking NO about
something else something else
I had a dream that he made me kill my brother's deer!
"brother?"
SISTER.
flowers
pretty flowers
The country
deer
little tiny deer
He made me kill the deer
sun
I had a dream that he made me kill my deer! No-
son?
horse?
He said:
MY DAUGHTER MY DAUGHTER
SO: I have a sister?
Mom, he said I have a sister!
And I'm not dreaming!
And they're trying to make me pee! but I can't do it
I can't...
Oh... wait...
I think...
I think I might be able...
wait... sssh!
KNOCK KNOCK
gh
k-klunk
DON'T COME IN! DON'T COME IN!
MR. CORRIGAN? MR. CORRIGAN, ARE YOU DONE?
NO!
NO DON'T COME IN!
DON'T,... umph
ung
WAIT! WAIT!

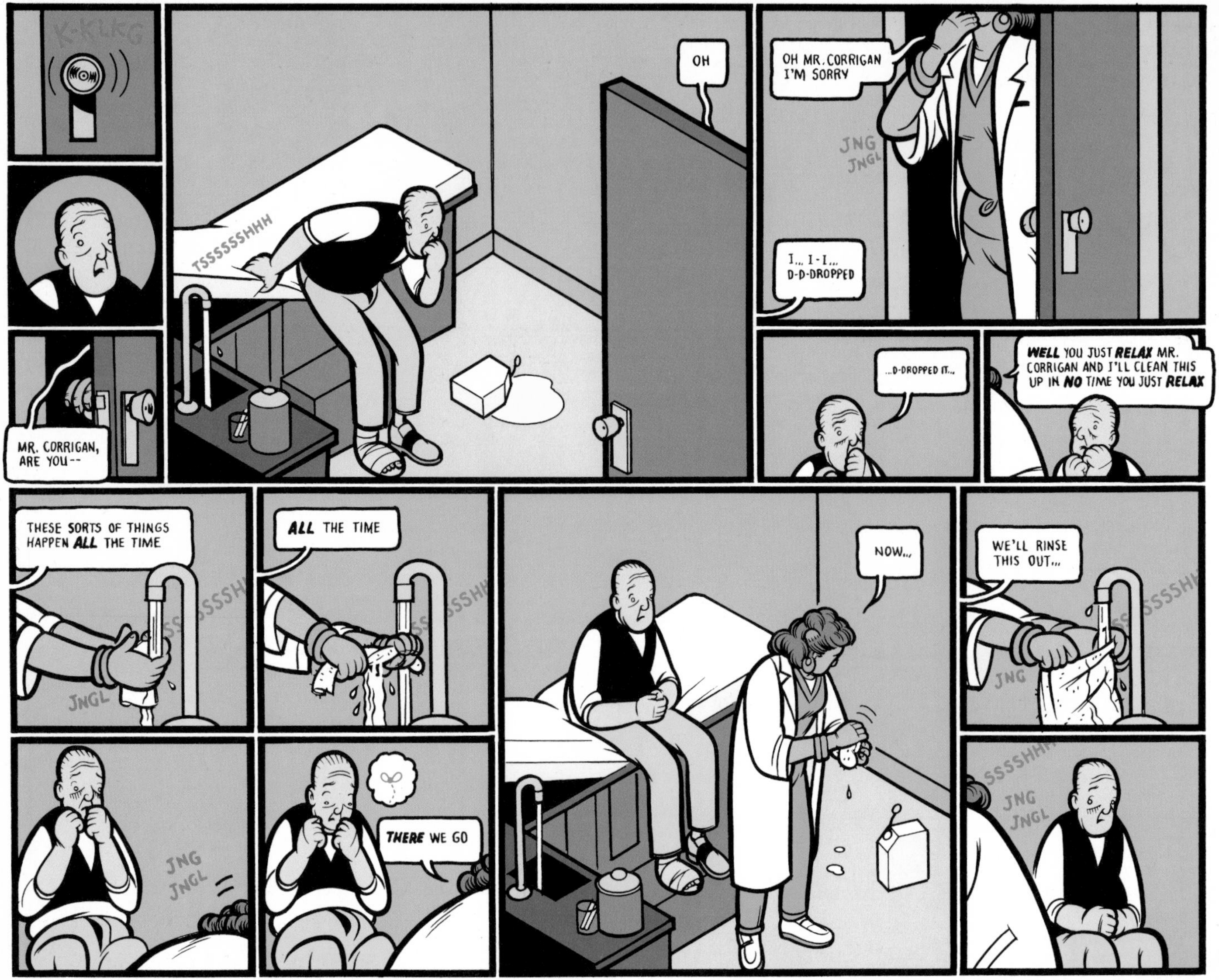

K-KLKG
TSSSSSSHHH
MR. CORRIGAN, ARE YOU--
OH
OH MR. CORRIGAN I'M SORRY
JNG JNGL
I... I-I... D-D-DROPPED
...D-DROPPED IT...
WELL YOU JUST RELAX MR. CORRIGAN AND I'LL CLEAN THIS UP IN NO TIME YOU JUST RELAX
THESE SORTS OF THINGS HAPPEN ALL THE TIME
JNGL
ALL THE TIME
NOW...
WE'LL RINSE THIS OUT...
JNG
JNG JNGL
THERE WE GO
JNG JNGL

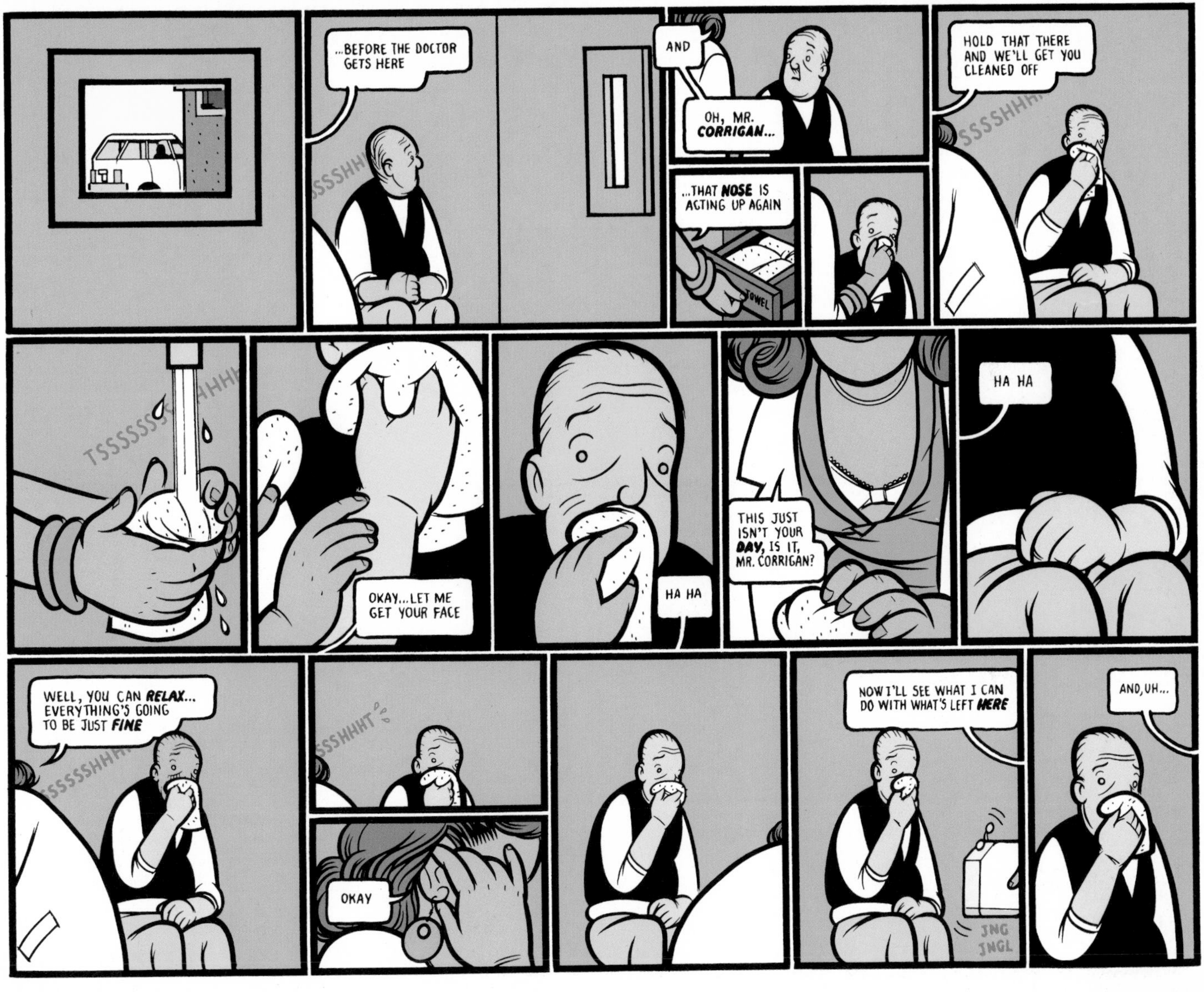

...BEFORE THE DOCTOR GETS HERE
SSSSHH
AND
OH, MR. CORRIGAN...
HOLD THAT THERE AND WE'LL GET YOU CLEANED OFF
SSSSHHH
...THAT NOSE IS ACTING UP AGAIN
TOWEL
TSSSSSSSHHHH
OKAY...LET ME GET YOUR FACE
HA HA
THIS JUST ISN'T YOUR DAY, IS IT, MR. CORRIGAN?
HA HA
WELL, YOU CAN RELAX... EVERYTHING'S GOING TO BE JUST FINE
TSSSSSHHH
SSSHHHT
OKAY
NOW I'LL SEE WHAT I CAN DO WITH WHAT'S LEFT HERE
JNG JNGL
AND, UH...

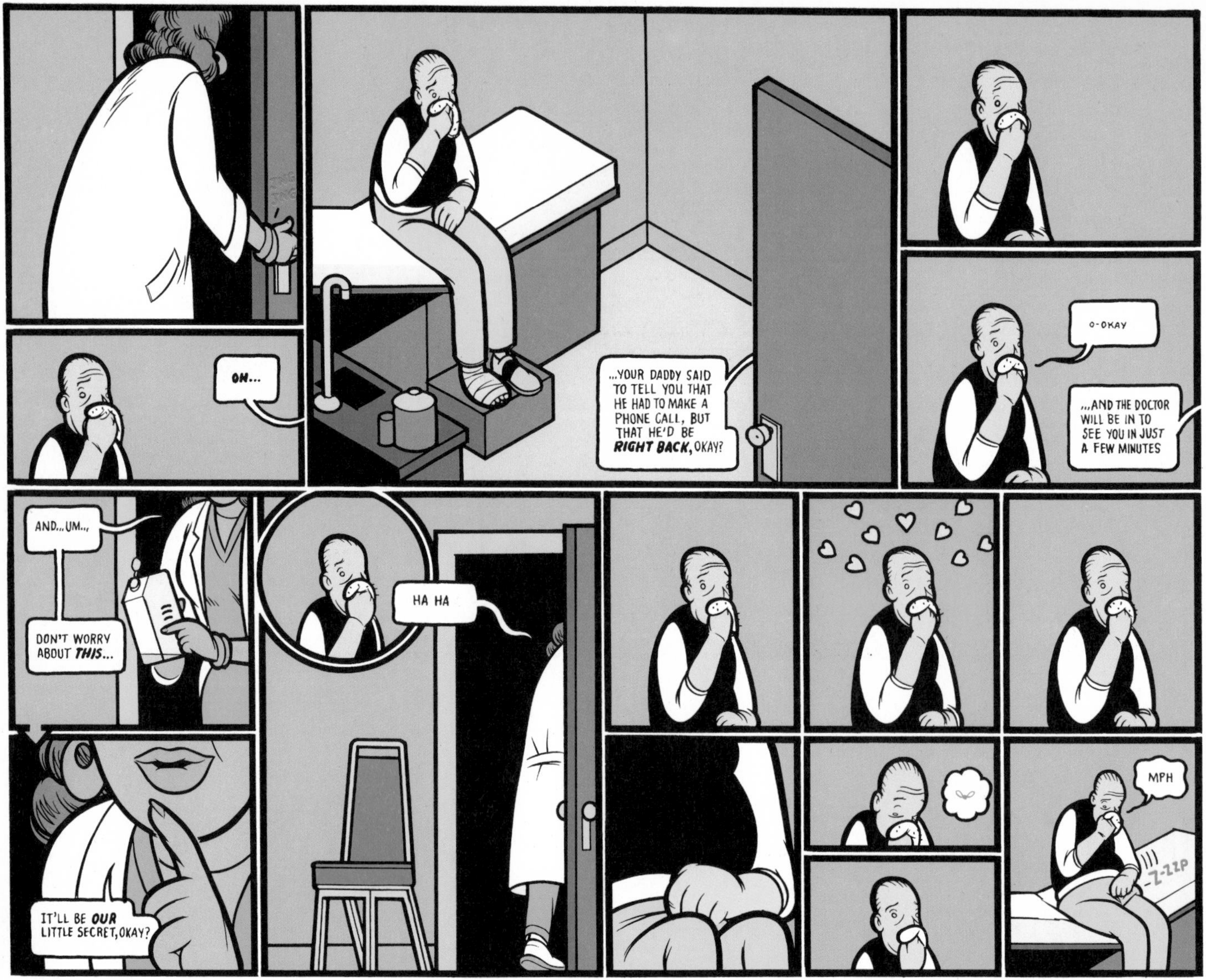

...YOUR DADDY SAID TO TELL YOU THAT HE HAD TO MAKE A PHONE CALL, BUT THAT HE'D BE **RIGHT BACK,** OKAY?
OH...
...AND THE DOCTOR WILL BE IN TO SEE YOU IN JUST A FEW MINUTES
O-OKAY
AND... UM...,
DON'T WORRY ABOUT **THIS**...
IT'LL BE **OUR** LITTLE SECRET, OKAY?
HA HA
MPH
-Z-ZZP

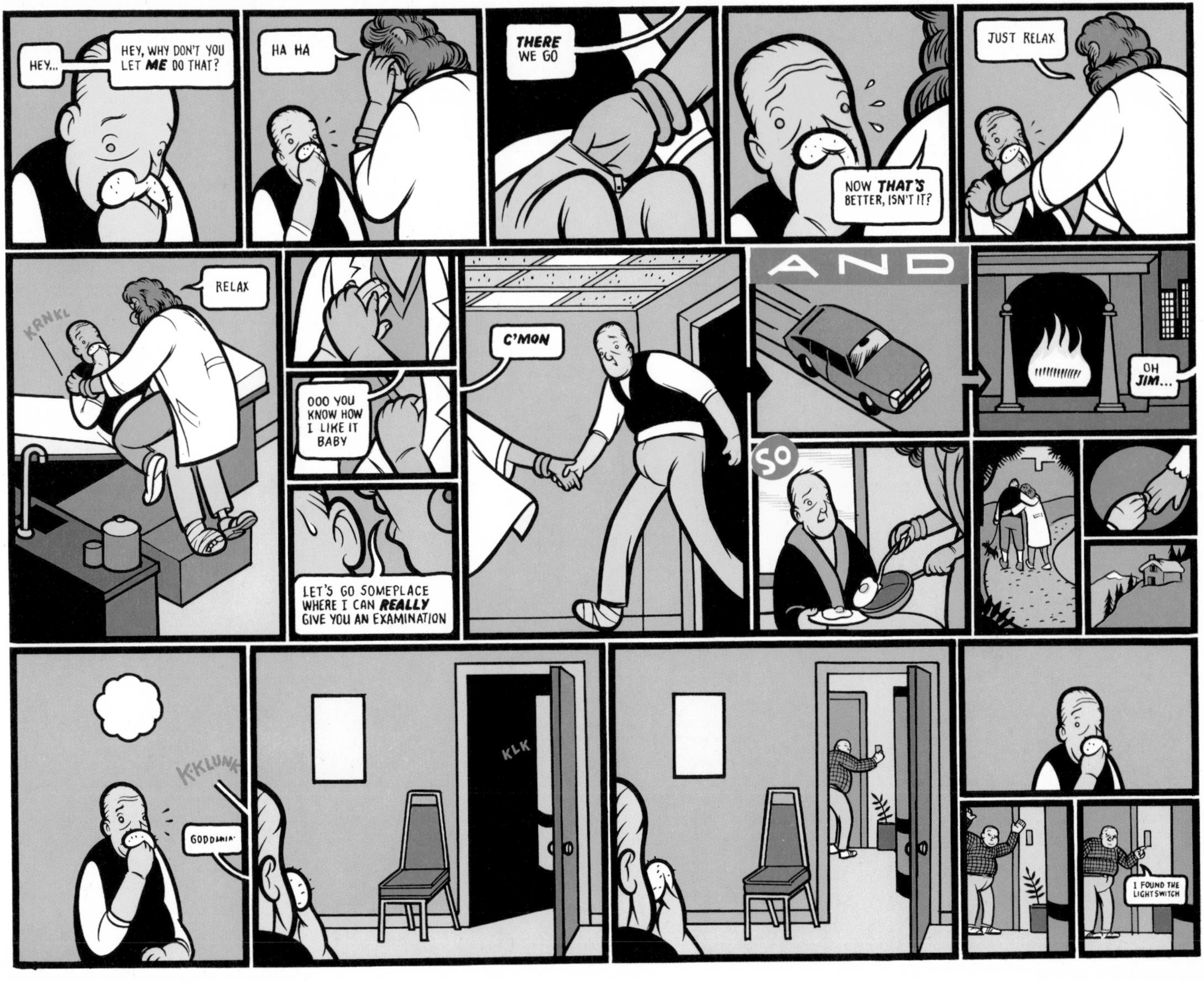

HEY...
HEY, WHY DON'T YOU LET **ME** DO THAT?
HA HA
THERE WE GO
NOW **THAT'S** BETTER, ISN'T IT?
JUST RELAX
KRNKL
RELAX
OOO YOU KNOW HOW I LIKE IT BABY
LET'S GO SOMEPLACE WHERE I CAN **REALLY** GIVE YOU AN EXAMINATION
C'MON
AND
OH **JIM...**
SO
K-KLUNK
GODDAMN
KLK
I FOUND THE LIGHTSWITCH

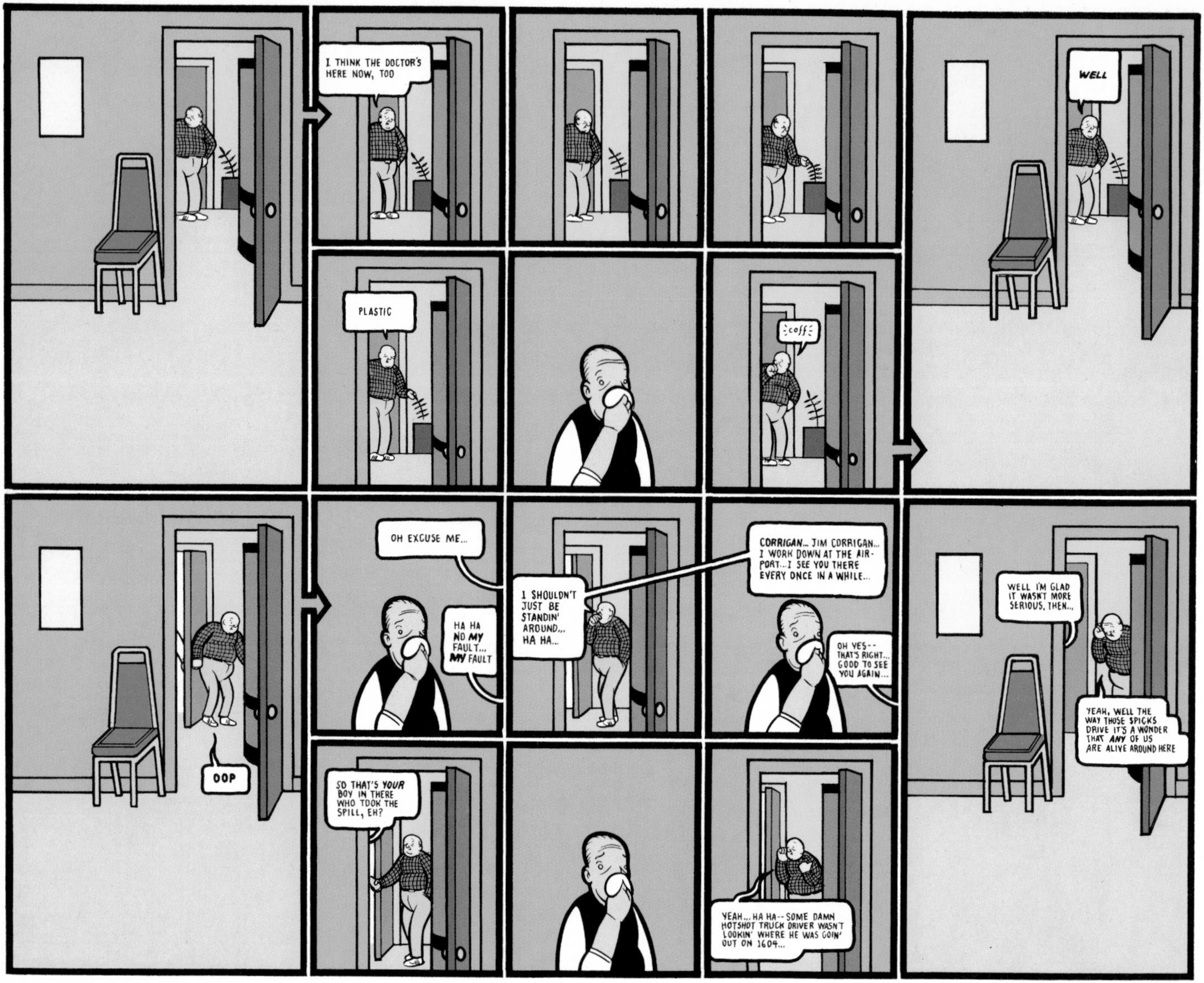
I THINK THE DOCTOR'S HERE NOW, TOO
PLASTIC
coff
WELL
OOP
OH EXCUSE ME...
HA HA NO MY FAULT... MY FAULT
I SHOULDN'T JUST BE STANDIN' AROUND,,, HA HA...
CORRIGAN... JIM CORRIGAN... I WORK DOWN AT THE AIR-PORT... I SEE YOU THERE EVERY ONCE IN A WHILE...
OH YES-- THAT'S RIGHT... GOOD TO SEE YOU AGAIN...
SO THAT'S YOUR BOY IN THERE WHO TOOK THE SPILL, EH?
YEAH... HA HA-- SOME DAMN HOTSHOT TRUCK DRIVER WASN'T LOOKIN' WHERE HE WAS GOIN' OUT ON 1604...
WELL I'M GLAD IT WASN'T MORE SERIOUS, THEN...
YEAH, WELL THE WAY THOSE SPICKS DRIVE IT'S A WONDER THAT ANY OF US ARE ALIVE AROUND HERE

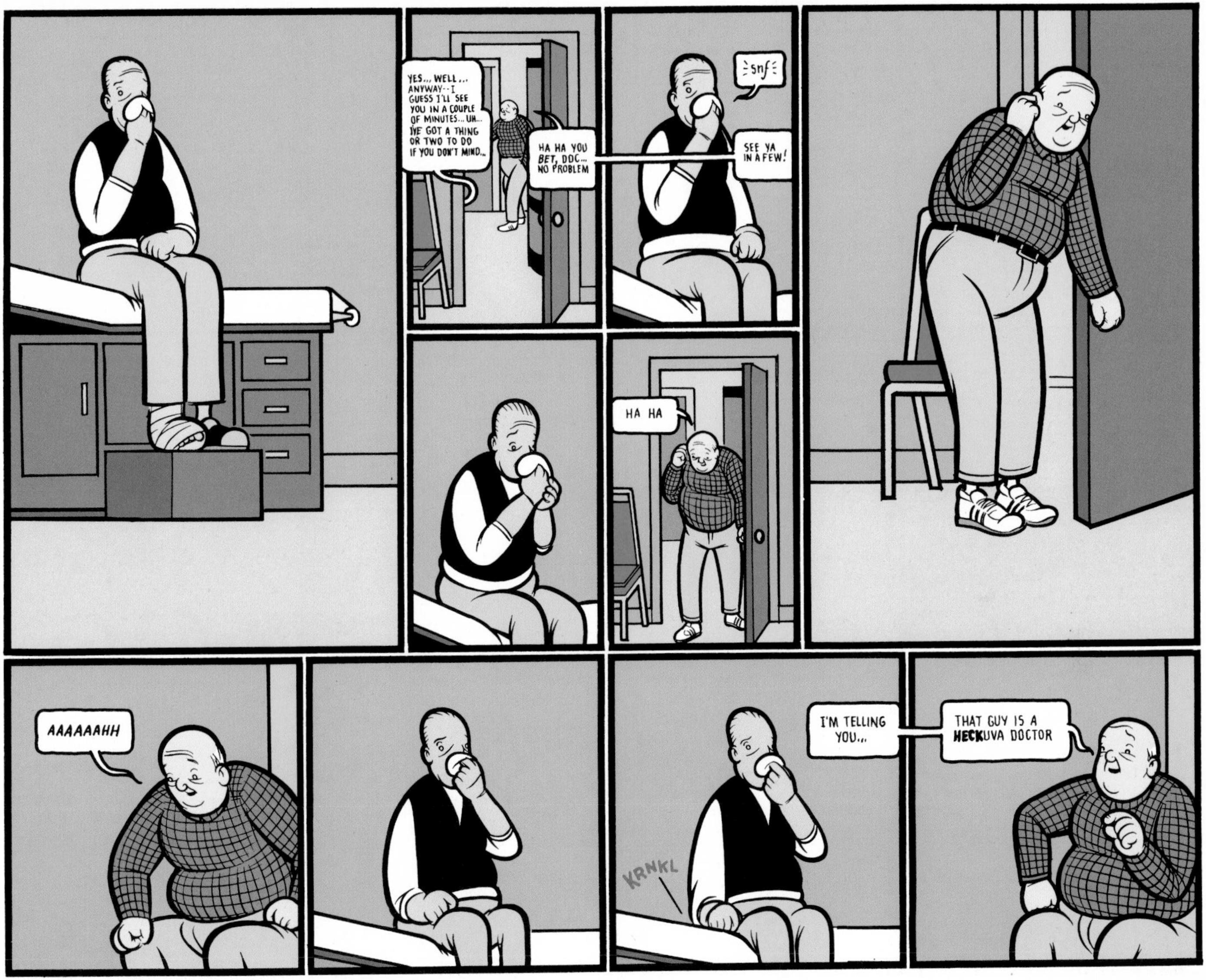

YES... WELL... ANYWAY--I GUESS I'LL SEE YOU IN A COUPLE OF MINUTES... UH... I'VE GOT A THING OR TWO TO DO IF YOU DON'T MIND...
HA HA YOU BET, DOC... NO PROBLEM
snf
SEE YA IN A FEW!
HA HA
AAAAAAHH
KRNKL
I'M TELLING YOU...
THAT GUY IS A HECKUVA DOCTOR

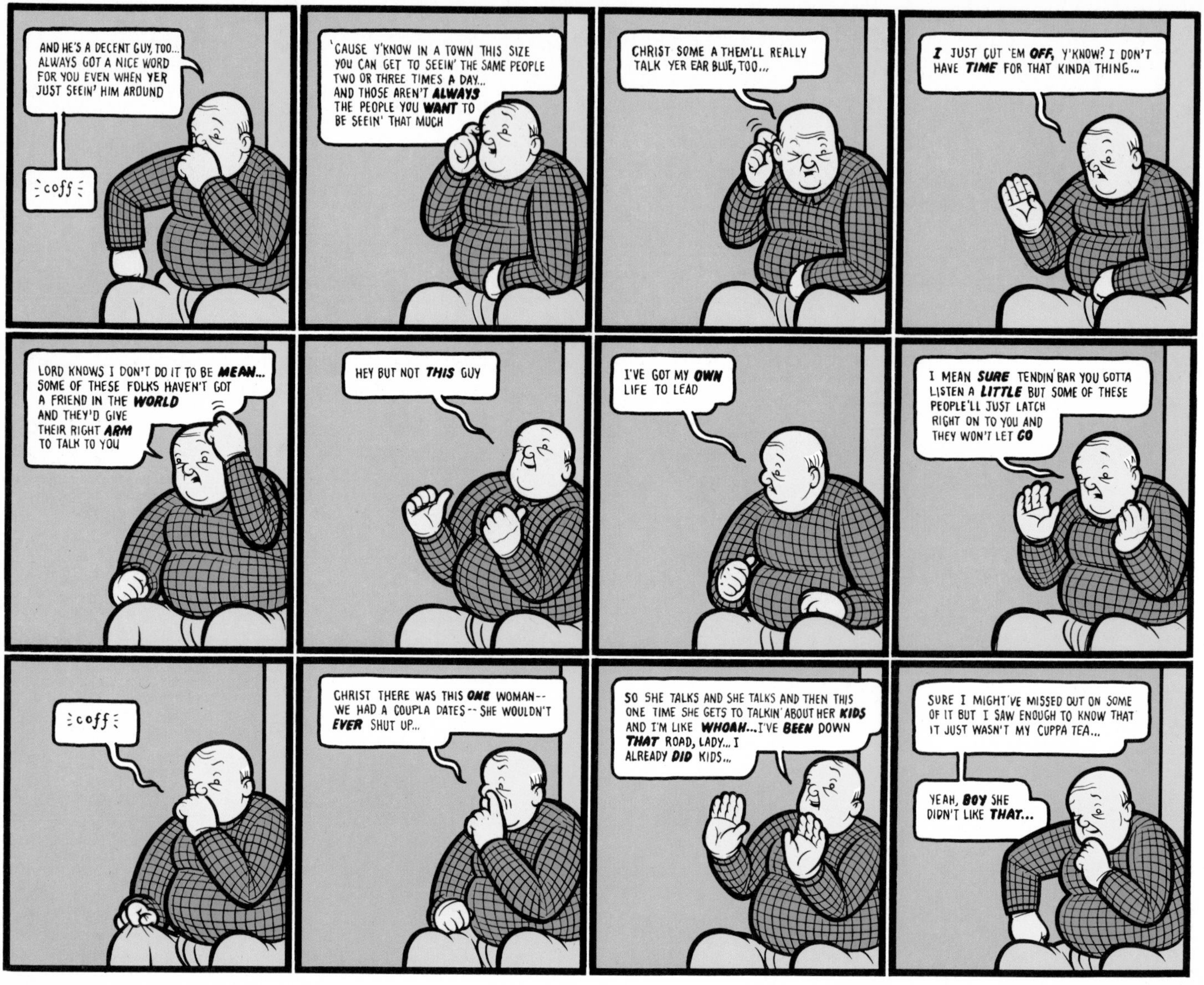
AND HE'S A DECENT GUY, TOO... ALWAYS GOT A NICE WORD FOR YOU EVEN WHEN YER JUST SEEIN' HIM AROUND
coff
'CAUSE Y'KNOW IN A TOWN THIS SIZE YOU CAN GET TO SEEIN' THE SAME PEOPLE TWO OR THREE TIMES A DAY... AND THOSE AREN'T ALWAYS THE PEOPLE YOU WANT TO BE SEEIN' THAT MUCH
CHRIST SOME A THEM'LL REALLY TALK YER EAR BLUE, TOO...
I JUST CUT 'EM OFF, Y'KNOW? I DON'T HAVE TIME FOR THAT KINDA THING...
LORD KNOWS I DON'T DO IT TO BE MEAN... SOME OF THESE FOLKS HAVEN'T GOT A FRIEND IN THE WORLD AND THEY'D GIVE THEIR RIGHT ARM TO TALK TO YOU
HEY BUT NOT THIS GUY
I'VE GOT MY OWN LIFE TO LEAD
I MEAN SURE TENDIN' BAR YOU GOTTA LISTEN A LITTLE BUT SOME OF THESE PEOPLE'LL JUST LATCH RIGHT ON TO YOU AND THEY WON'T LET GO
coff
CHRIST THERE WAS THIS ONE WOMAN-- WE HAD A COUPLA DATES -- SHE WOULDN'T EVER SHUT UP...
SO SHE TALKS AND SHE TALKS AND THEN THIS ONE TIME SHE GETS TO TALKIN' ABOUT HER KIDS AND I'M LIKE WHOAH... I'VE BEEN DOWN THAT ROAD, LADY... I ALREADY DID KIDS...
SURE I MIGHT'VE MISSED OUT ON SOME OF IT BUT I SAW ENOUGH TO KNOW THAT IT JUST WASN'T MY CUPPA TEA...
YEAH, BOY SHE DIDN'T LIKE THAT...

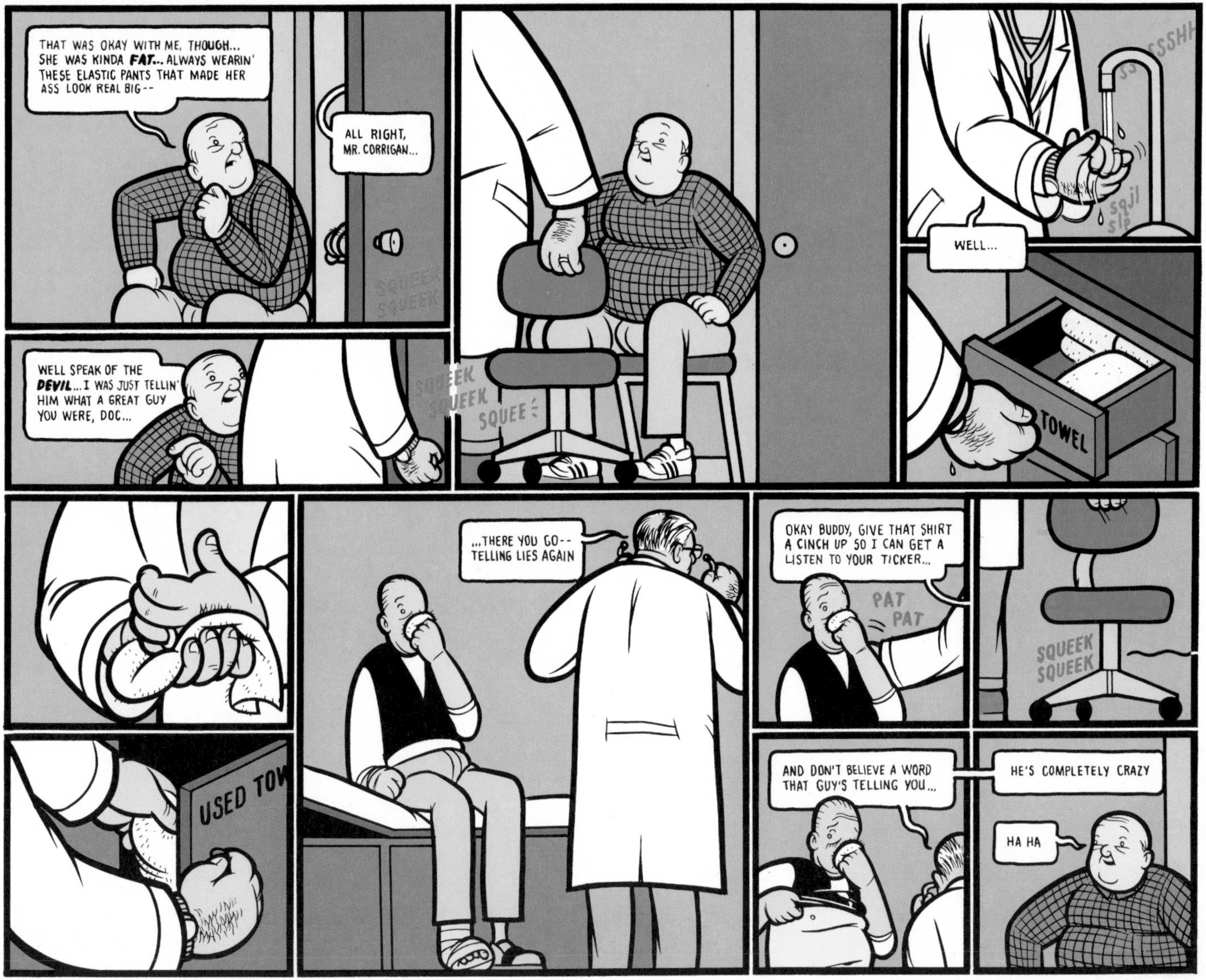
THAT WAS OKAY WITH ME, THOUGH... SHE WAS KINDA FAT... ALWAYS WEARIN' THESE ELASTIC PANTS THAT MADE HER ASS LOOK REAL BIG--
ALL RIGHT, MR. CORRIGAN...
SQUEEK SQUEEK
WELL SPEAK OF THE DEVIL... I WAS JUST TELLIN' HIM WHAT A GREAT GUY YOU WERE, DOC...
SQUEEK SQUEEK SQUEE
SSSSSHH
WELL...
TOWEL
USED TOW
...THERE YOU GO-- TELLING LIES AGAIN
OKAY BUDDY, GIVE THAT SHIRT A CINCH UP SO I CAN GET A LISTEN TO YOUR TICKER...
PAT PAT
SQUEEK SQUEEK
AND DON'T BELIEVE A WORD THAT GUY'S TELLING YOU...
HE'S COMPLETELY CRAZY
HA HA

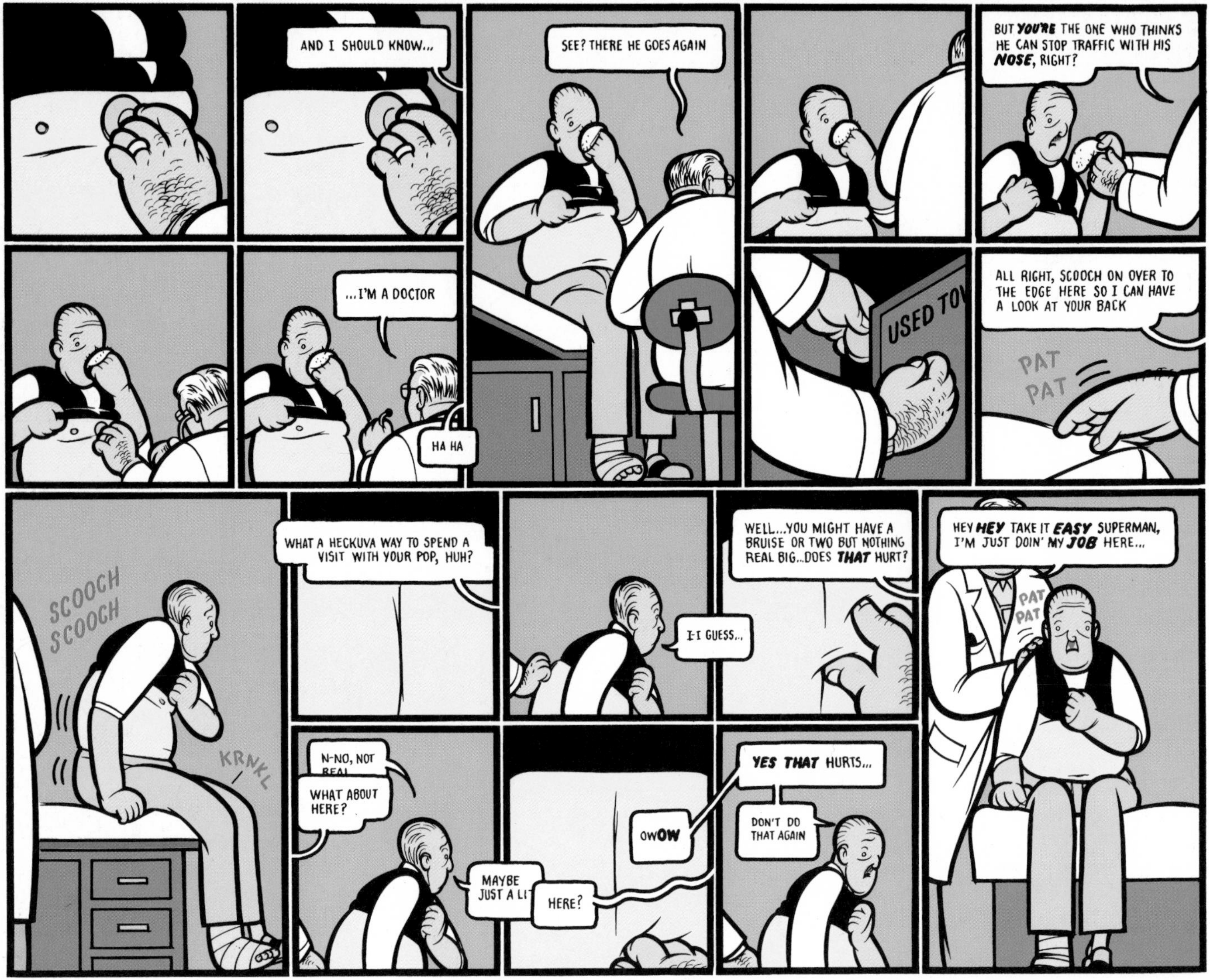
AND I SHOULD KNOW...
SEE? THERE HE GOES AGAIN
BUT YOU'RE THE ONE WHO THINKS HE CAN STOP TRAFFIC WITH HIS NOSE, RIGHT?
...I'M A DOCTOR
HA HA
USED TO
ALL RIGHT, SCOOCH ON OVER TO THE EDGE HERE SO I CAN HAVE A LOOK AT YOUR BACK
PAT PAT
SCOOCH SCOOCH
KRNKL
WHAT A HECKUVA WAY TO SPEND A VISIT WITH YOUR POP, HUH?
I-I GUESS...
WELL...YOU MIGHT HAVE A BRUISE OR TWO BUT NOTHING REAL BIG...DOES THAT HURT?
N-NO, NOT REAL
WHAT ABOUT HERE?
MAYBE JUST A LI
HERE?
OWOW
YES THAT HURTS...
DON'T DO THAT AGAIN
HEY HEY TAKE IT EASY SUPERMAN, I'M JUST DOIN' MY JOB HERE...
PAT PAT

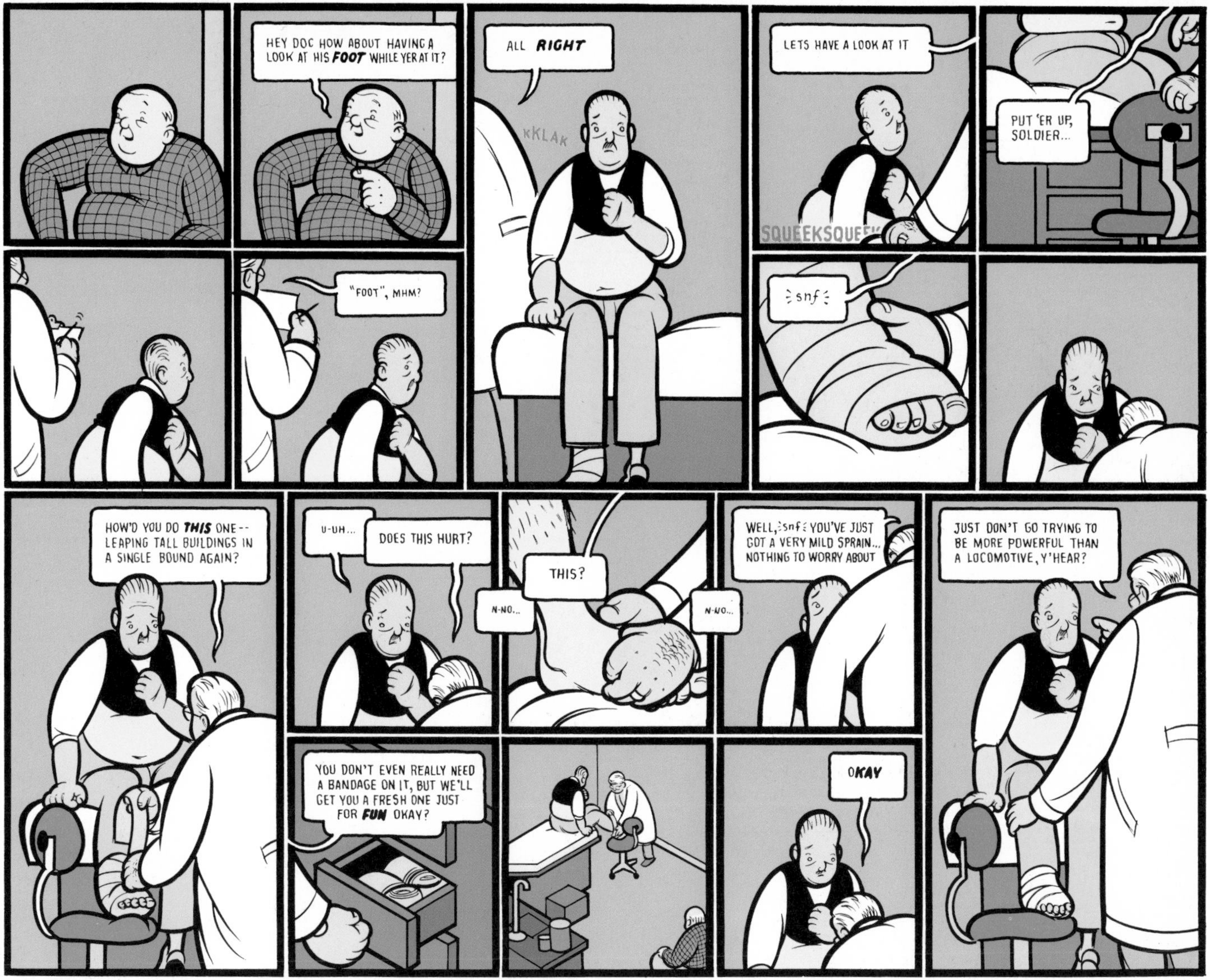

HEY DOC HOW ABOUT HAVING A LOOK AT HIS FOOT WHILE YER AT IT?
ALL RIGHT
KKLAK
LETS HAVE A LOOK AT IT
SQUEEKSQUEE
PUT 'ER UP, SOLDIER...
"FOOT", MHM?
snf
HOW'D YOU DO THIS ONE-- LEAPING TALL BUILDINGS IN A SINGLE BOUND AGAIN?
U-UH...
DOES THIS HURT?
THIS?
N-NO...
N-NO...
WELL, snf YOU'VE JUST GOT A VERY MILD SPRAIN... NOTHING TO WORRY ABOUT
JUST DON'T GO TRYING TO BE MORE POWERFUL THAN A LOCOMOTIVE, Y'HEAR?
YOU DON'T EVEN REALLY NEED A BANDAGE ON IT, BUT WE'LL GET YOU A FRESH ONE JUST FOR FUN OKAY?
OKAY

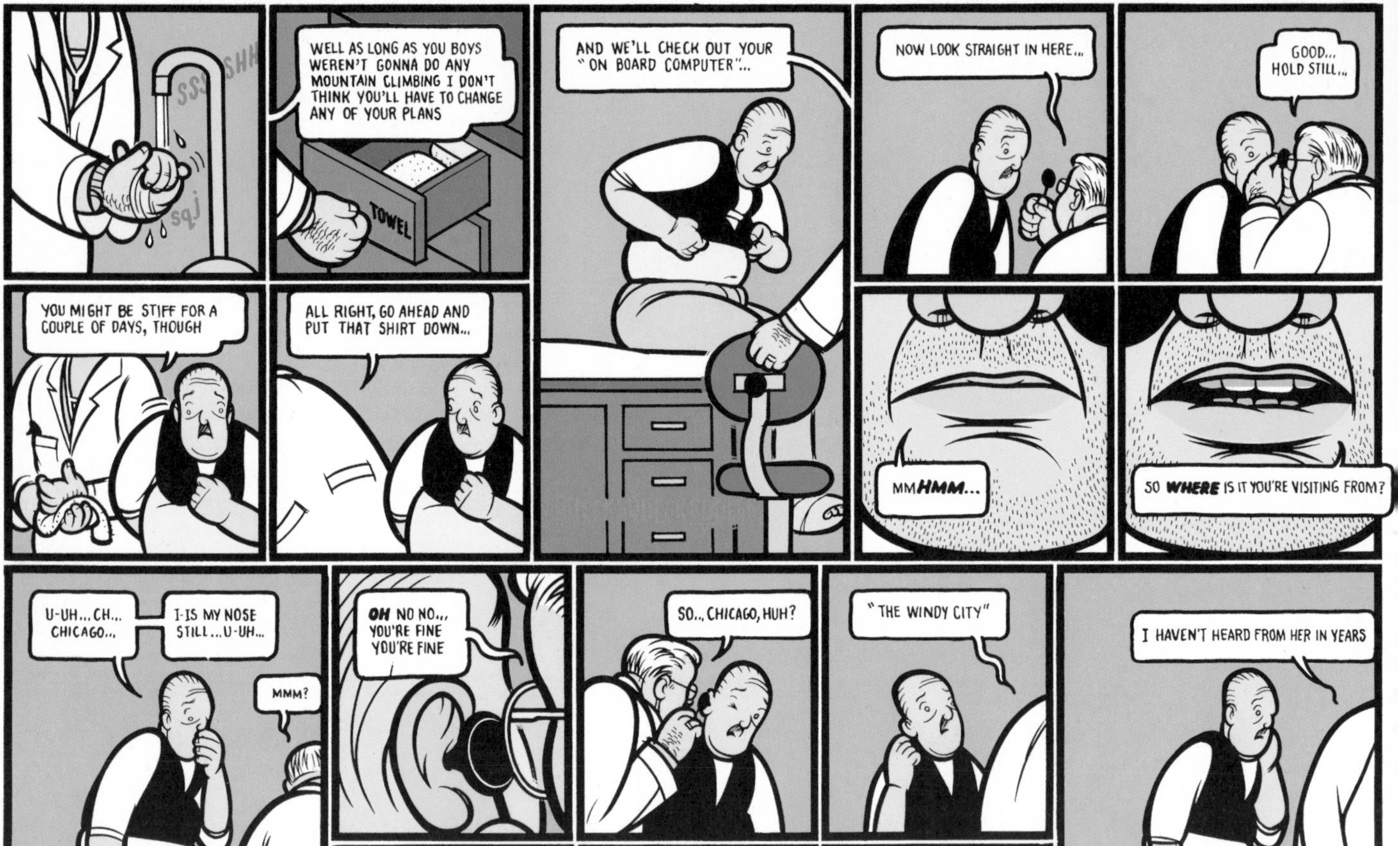
SSSSHH
sqj
WELL AS LONG AS YOU BOYS WEREN'T GONNA DO ANY MOUNTAIN CLIMBING I DON'T THINK YOU'LL HAVE TO CHANGE ANY OF YOUR PLANS
TOWEL
AND WE'LL CHECK OUT YOUR "ON BOARD COMPUTER"...
NOW LOOK STRAIGHT IN HERE...
GOOD... HOLD STILL...
YOU MIGHT BE STIFF FOR A COUPLE OF DAYS, THOUGH
ALL RIGHT, GO AHEAD AND PUT THAT SHIRT DOWN...
MMHMM...
SO WHERE IS IT YOU'RE VISITING FROM?
U-UH... CH... CHICAGO...
I-IS MY NOSE STILL... U-UH...
MMM?
OH NO NO... YOU'RE FINE YOU'RE FINE
SO... CHICAGO, HUH?
"THE WINDY CITY"
I USED TO HAVE A DAUGHTER IN CHICAGO
HEY DOC--HAHA I DIDN'T KNOW YOU HAD A DAUGHTER
WELL TO TELL YOU THE TRUTH, I SOMETIMES SORT OF FORGET MYSELF...
koff
I HAVEN'T HEARD FROM HER IN YEARS
SQUEEK

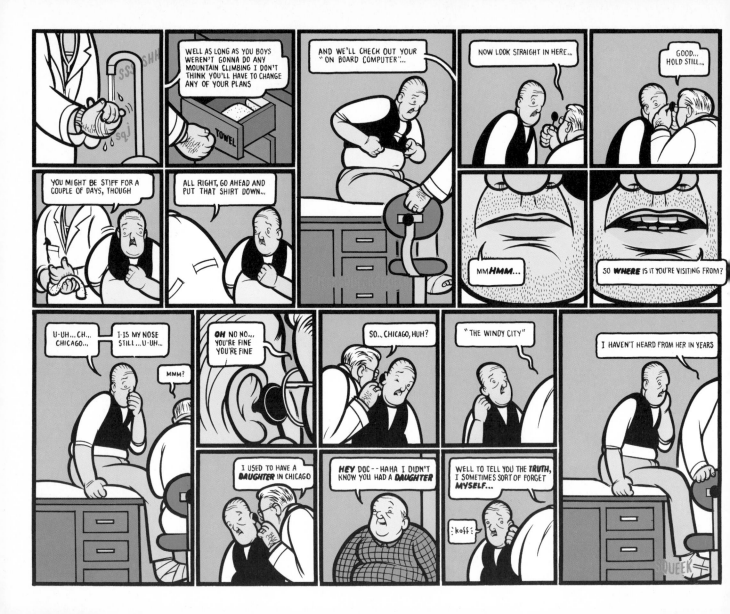

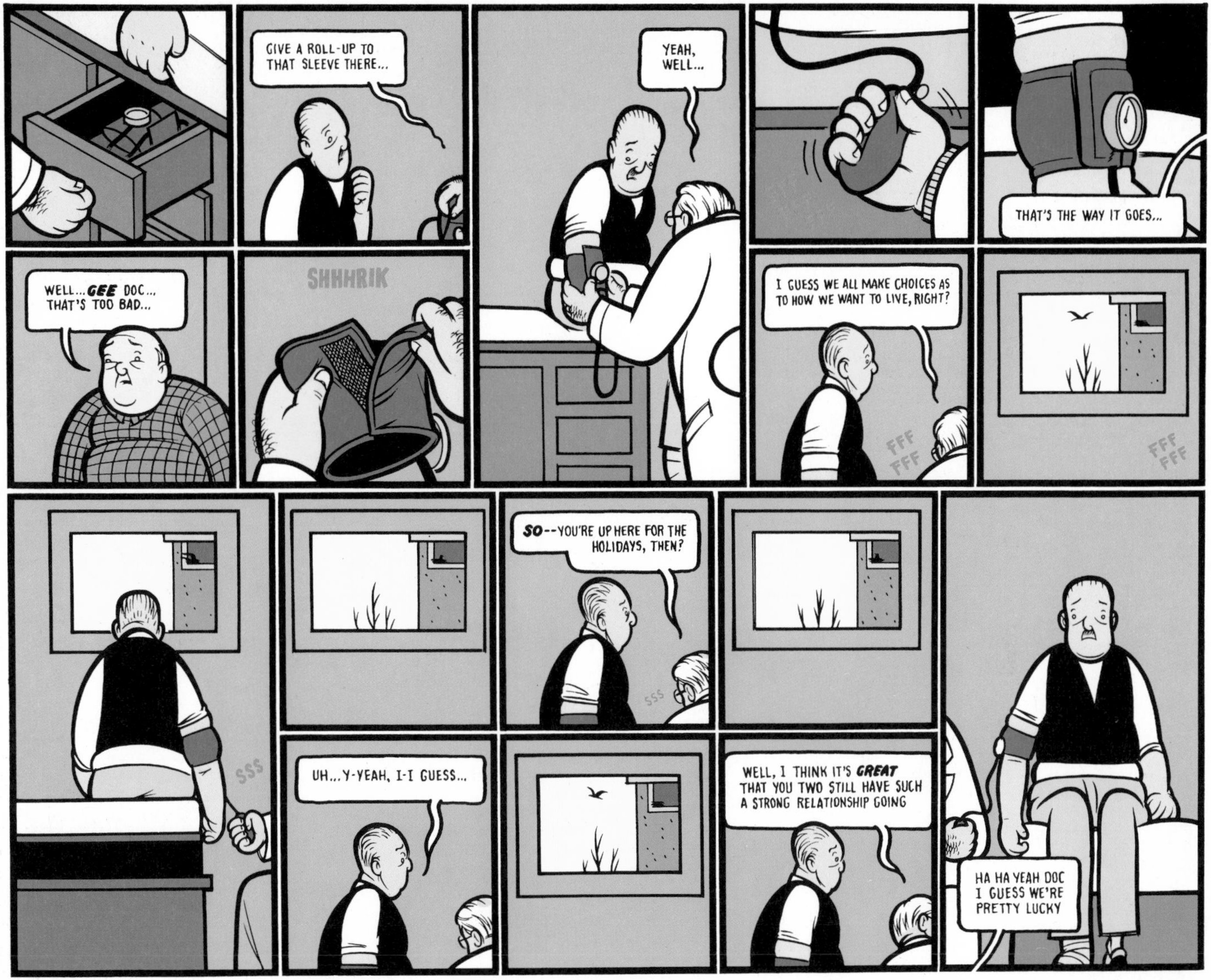
GIVE A ROLL-UP TO THAT SLEEVE THERE...
YEAH, WELL...
THAT'S THE WAY IT GOES...
WELL... **GEE** DOC... THAT'S TOO BAD...
SHHHRIK
I GUESS WE ALL MAKE CHOICES AS TO HOW WE WANT TO LIVE, RIGHT?
FFF FFF
FFF FFF
SSS
SO--YOU'RE UP HERE FOR THE HOLIDAYS, THEN?
SSS
UH... Y-YEAH, I-I GUESS...
WELL, I THINK IT'S **GREAT** THAT YOU TWO STILL HAVE SUCH A STRONG RELATIONSHIP GOING
HA HA YEAH DOC I GUESS WE'RE PRETTY LUCKY

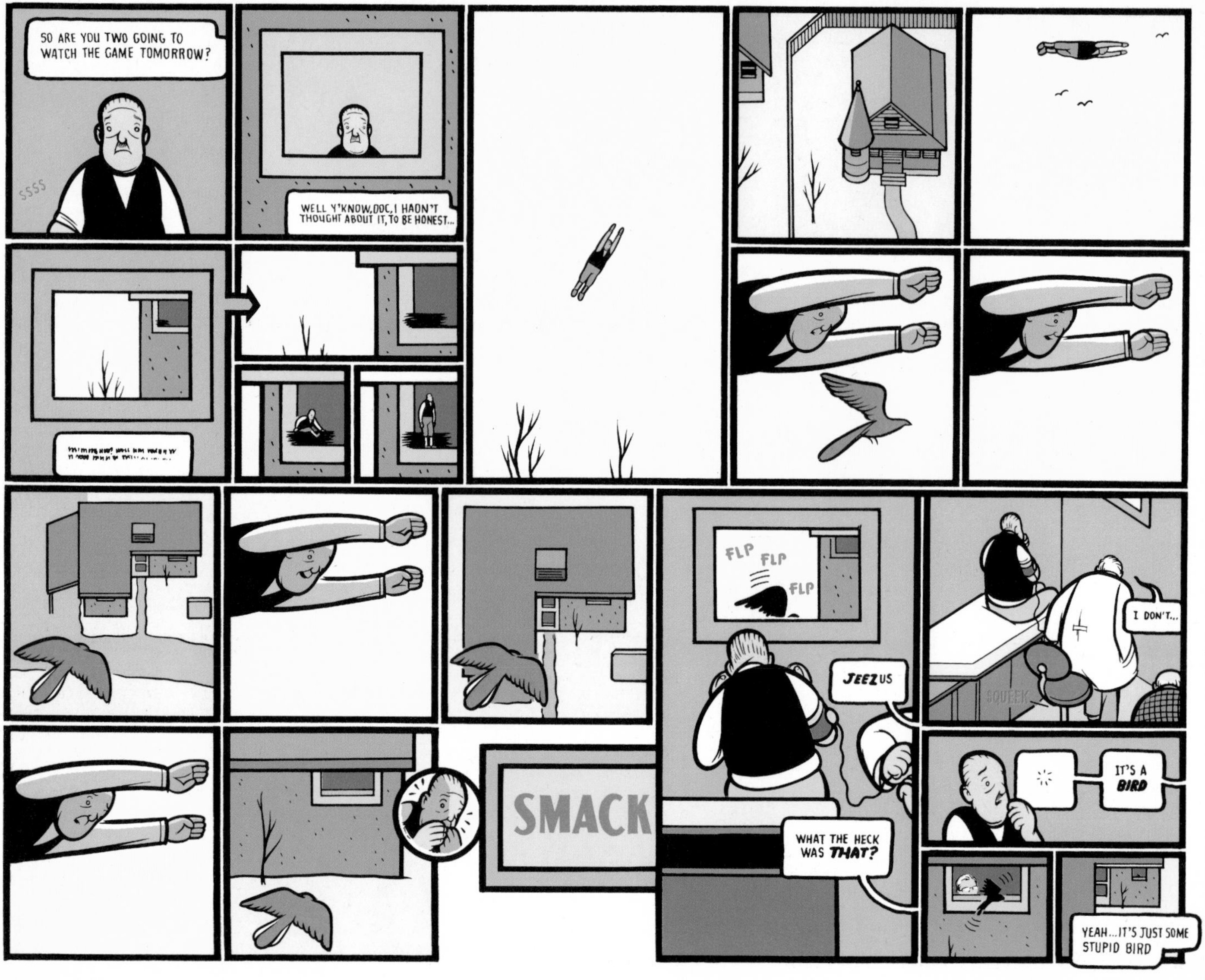

SO ARE YOU TWO GOING TO WATCH THE GAME TOMORROW?
SSSS
WELL Y'KNOW, DOC, I HADN'T THOUGHT ABOUT IT, TO BE HONEST...
SMACK
FLP
FLP
FLP
JEEZUS
WHAT THE HECK WAS THAT?
I DON'T...
SQUEEK
IT'S A BIRD
YEAH...IT'S JUST SOME STUPID BIRD

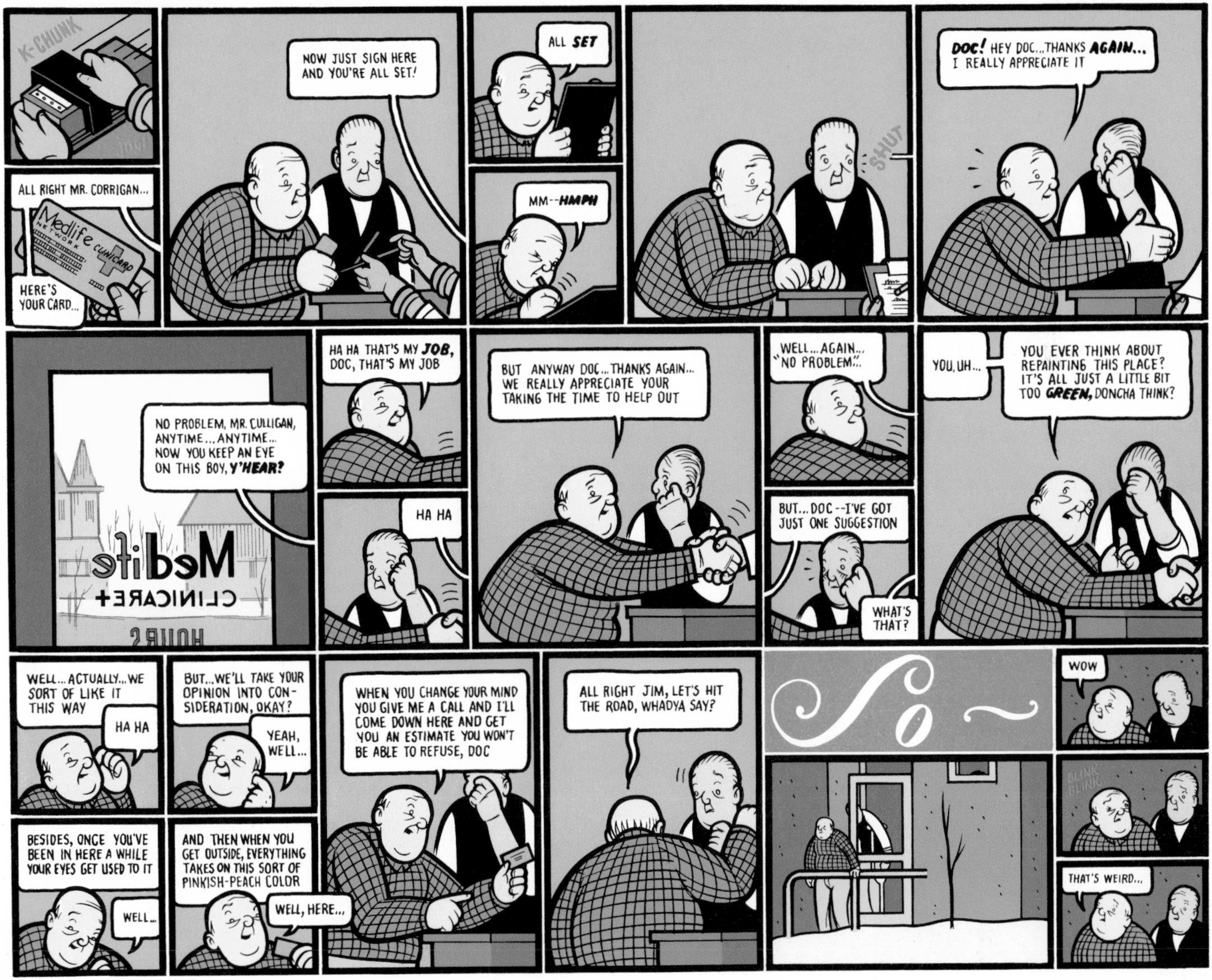
K-CHUNK
ALL RIGHT MR. CORRIGAN...
Medlife NETWORK CLINICARD
HERE'S YOUR CARD...
NOW JUST SIGN HERE AND YOU'RE ALL SET!
ALL SET
MM--HMPH
SHUT
DOC! HEY DOC...THANKS AGAIN... I REALLY APPRECIATE IT
NO PROBLEM, MR. CULLIGAN, ANYTIME... ANYTIME... NOW YOU KEEP AN EYE ON THIS BOY, Y'HEAR?
Medlife CLINICARE+
HA HA THAT'S MY JOB, DOC, THAT'S MY JOB
HA HA
BUT ANYWAY DOC... THANKS AGAIN... WE REALLY APPRECIATE YOUR TAKING THE TIME TO HELP OUT
WELL... AGAIN... "NO PROBLEM."
BUT... DOC --I'VE GOT JUST ONE SUGGESTION
WHAT'S THAT?
YOU, UH...
YOU EVER THINK ABOUT REPAINTING THIS PLACE? IT'S ALL JUST A LITTLE BIT TOO GREEN, DONCHA THINK?
WELL... ACTUALLY... WE SORT OF LIKE IT THIS WAY
HA HA
BESIDES, ONCE YOU'VE BEEN IN HERE A WHILE YOUR EYES GET USED TO IT
WELL...
BUT... WE'LL TAKE YOUR OPINION INTO CON-SIDERATION, OKAY?
YEAH, WELL...
AND THEN WHEN YOU GET OUTSIDE, EVERYTHING TAKES ON THIS SORT OF PINKISH-PEACH COLOR
WELL, HERE...
WHEN YOU CHANGE YOUR MIND YOU GIVE ME A CALL AND I'LL COME DOWN HERE AND GET YOU AN ESTIMATE YOU WON'T BE ABLE TO REFUSE, DOC
ALL RIGHT JIM, LET'S HIT THE ROAD, WHADYA SAY?
WOW
BLINK BLINK
THAT'S WEIRD...

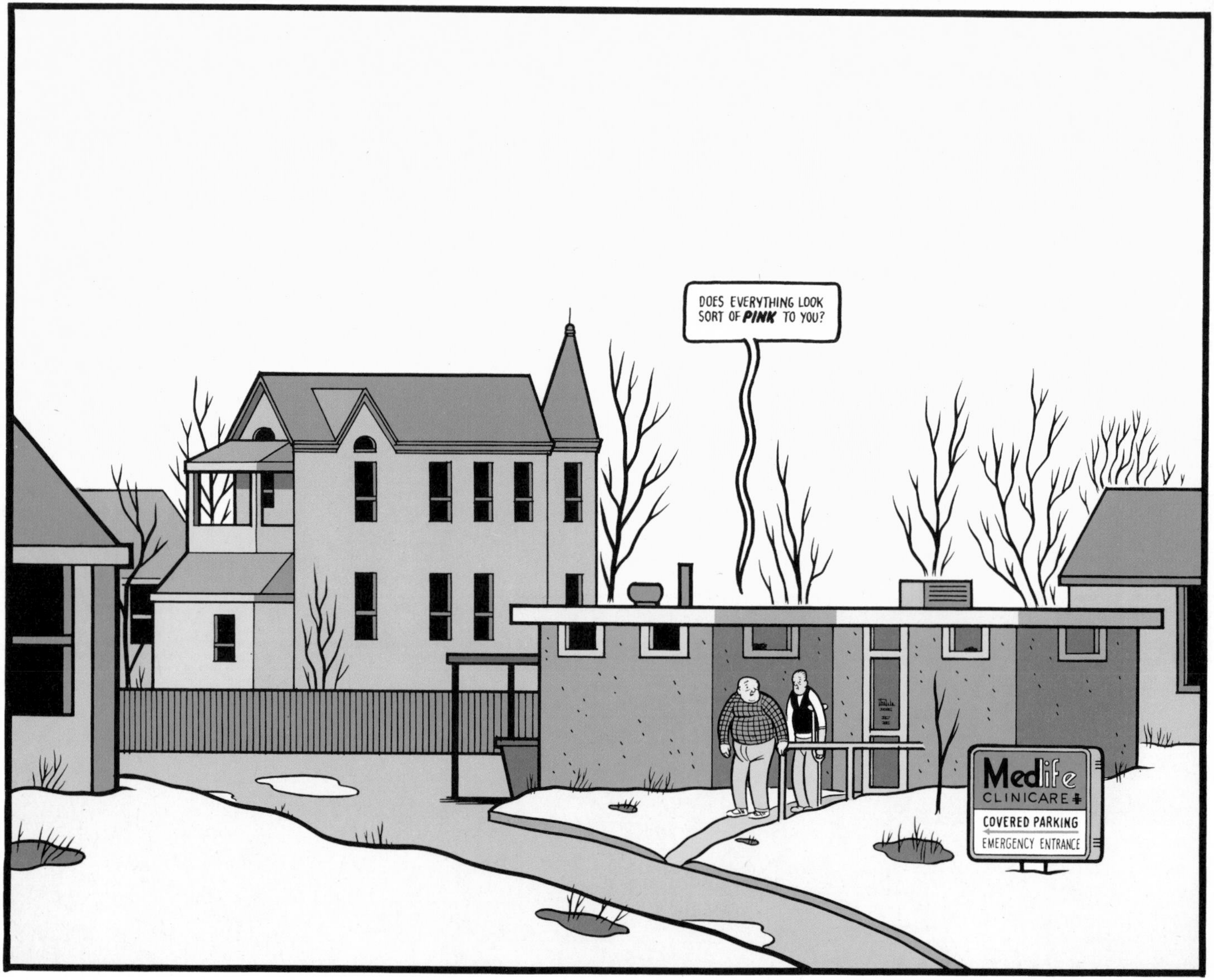
DOES EVERYTHING LOOK SORT OF PINK TO YOU?
Medlife CLINICARE
COVERED PARKING
EMERGENCY ENTRANCE

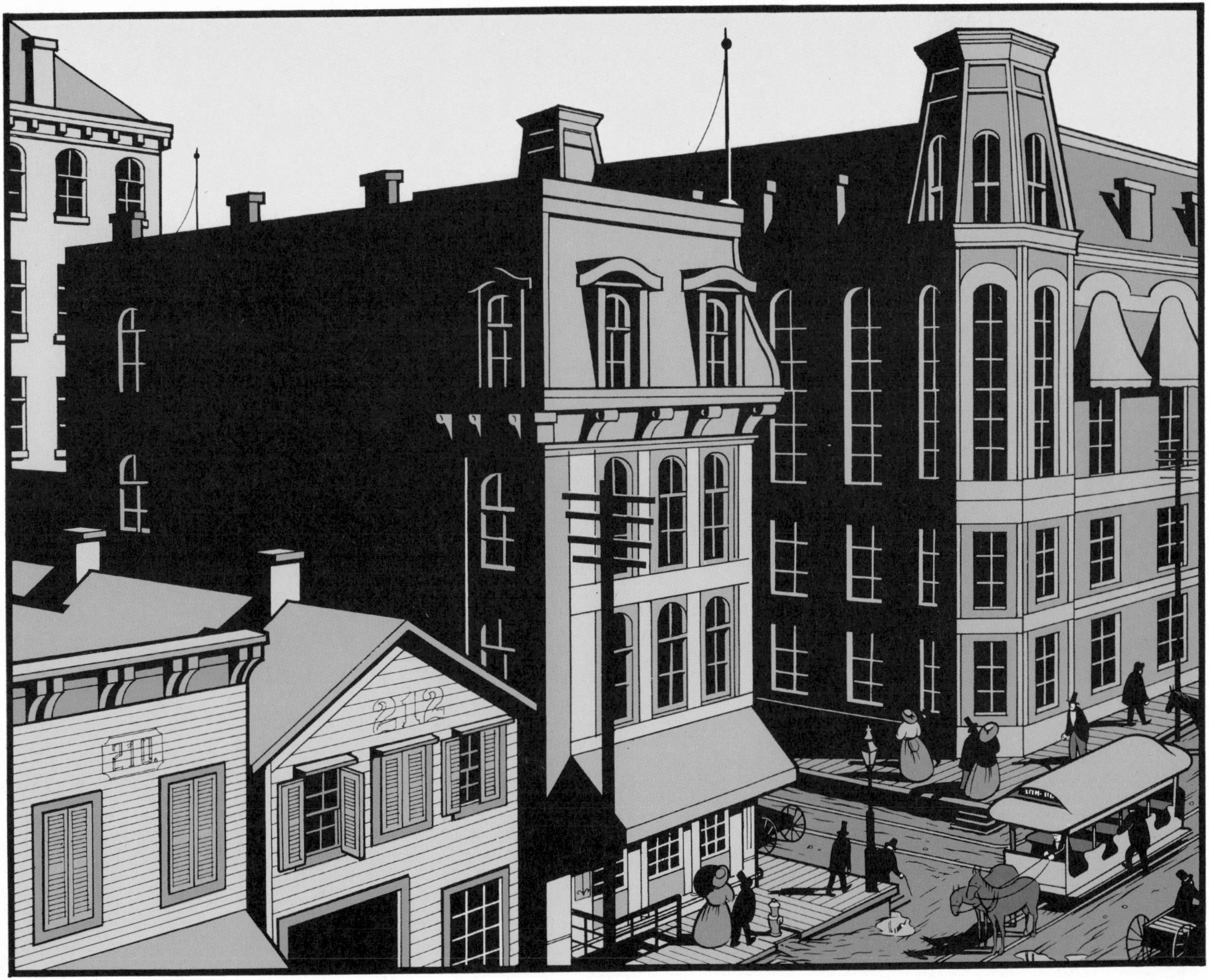
210
212

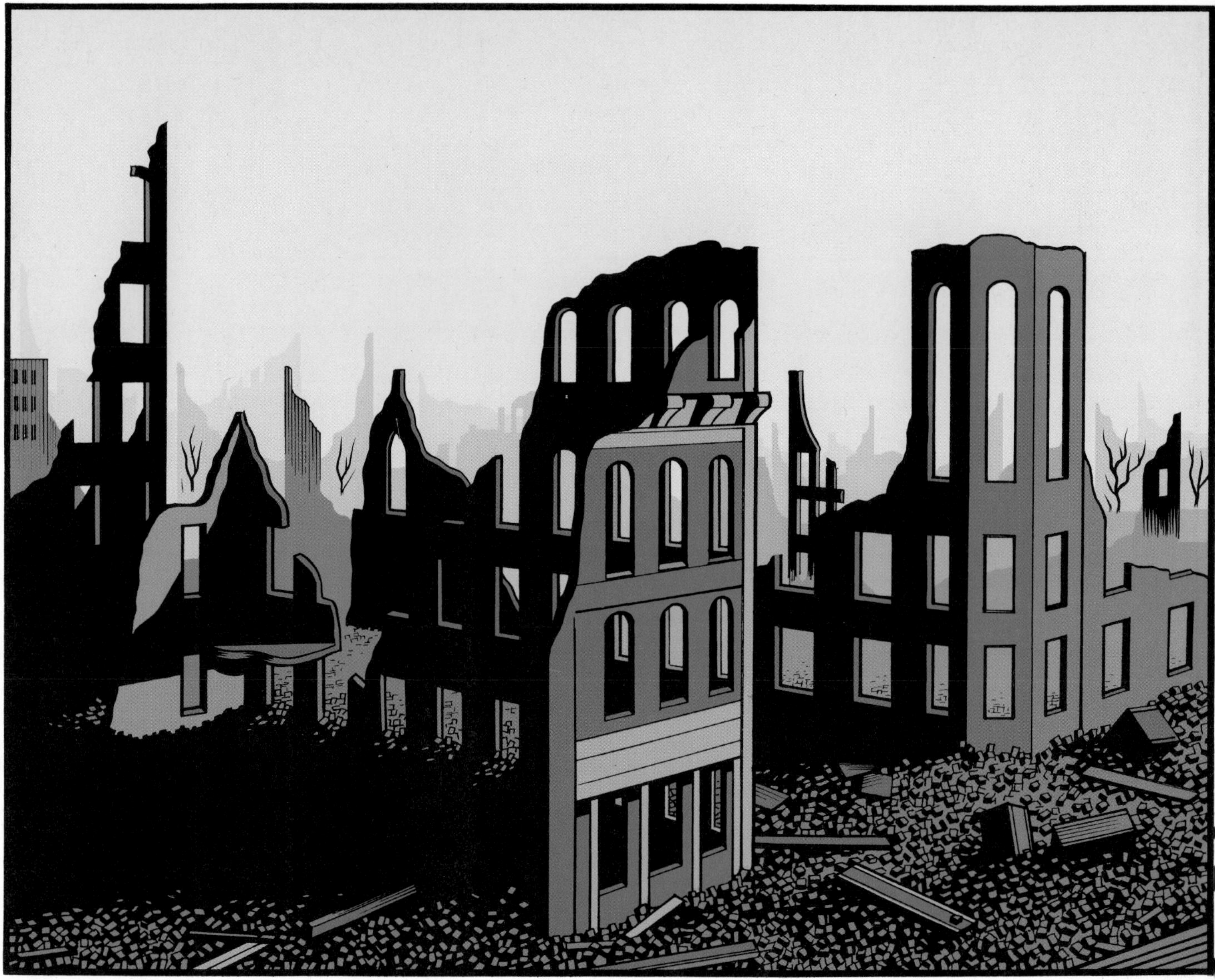

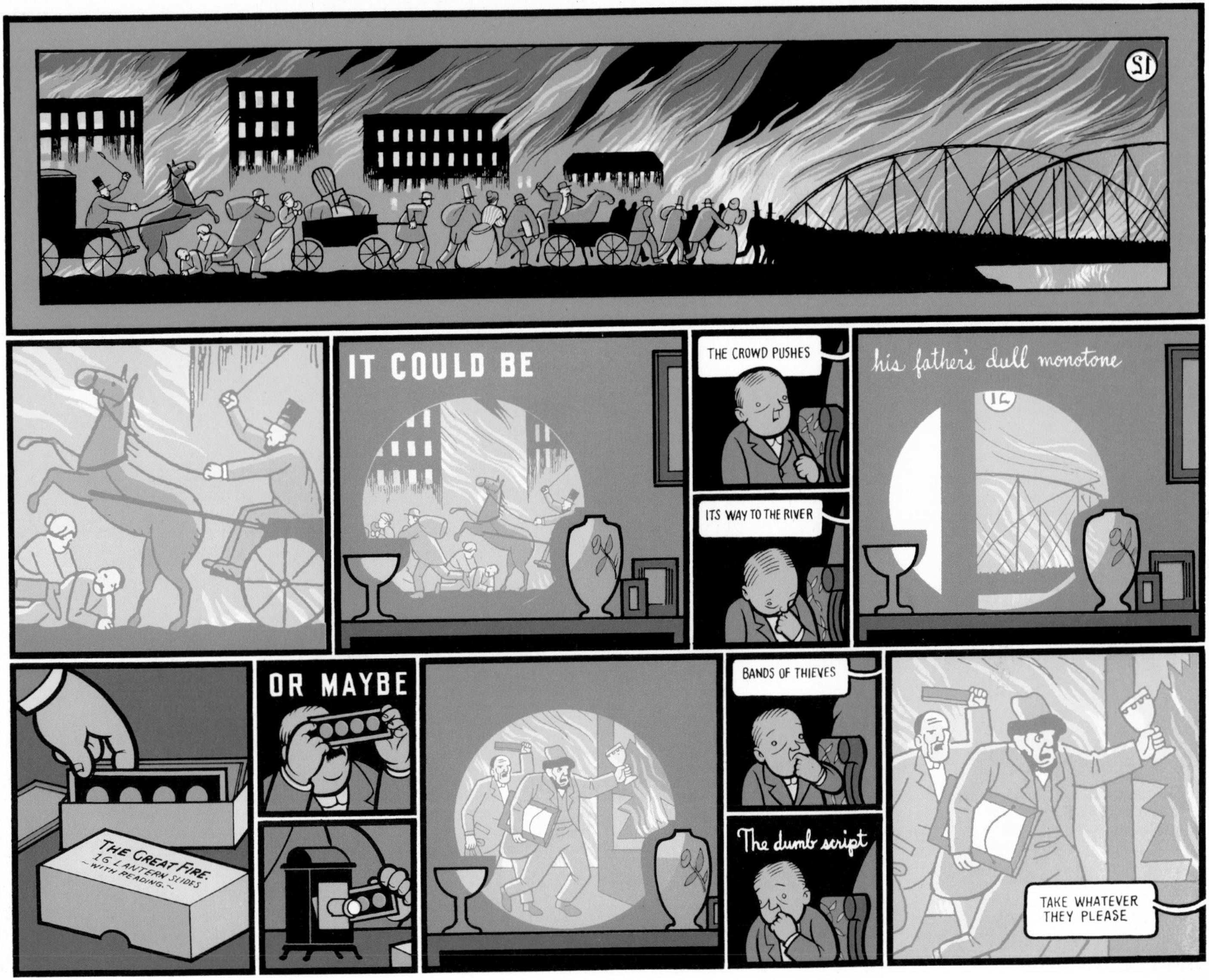

IT COULD BE
THE CROWD PUSHES
ITS WAY TO THE RIVER
his father's dull monotone
OR MAYBE
THE GREAT FIRE.
16 LANTERN SLIDES
~WITH READING.~
BANDS OF THIEVES
The dumb script
TAKE WHATEVER THEY PLEASE

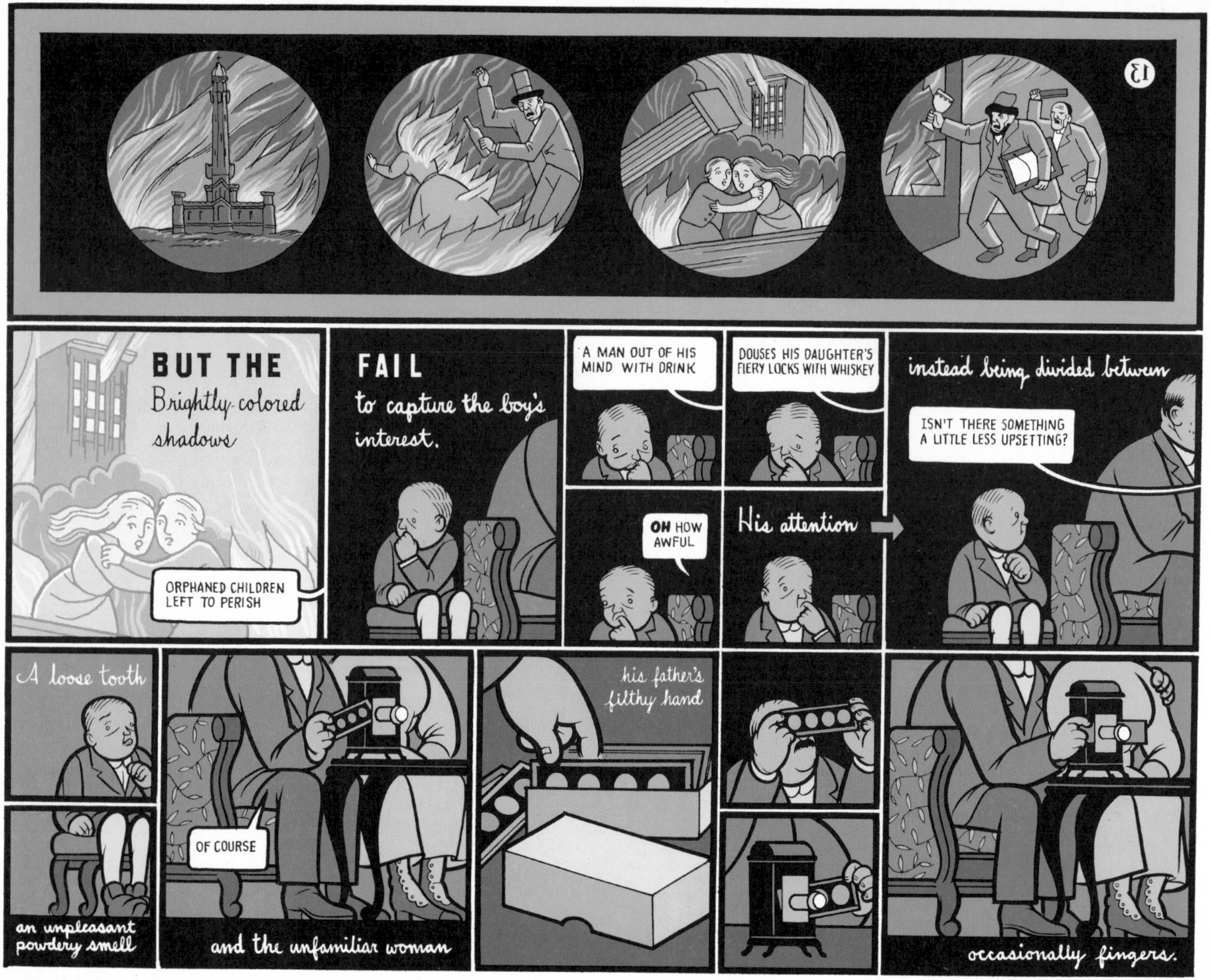
BUT THE
Brightly-colored shadows
ORPHANED CHILDREN LEFT TO PERISH
FAIL
to capture the boy's interest.
A MAN OUT OF HIS MIND WITH DRINK
DOUSES HIS DAUGHTER'S FIERY LOCKS WITH WHISKEY
OH HOW AWFUL
His attention
instead being divided between
ISN'T THERE SOMETHING A LITTLE LESS UPSETTING?
A loose tooth
an unpleasant powdery smell
OF COURSE
and the unfamiliar woman
his father's filthy hand
occasionally fingers.

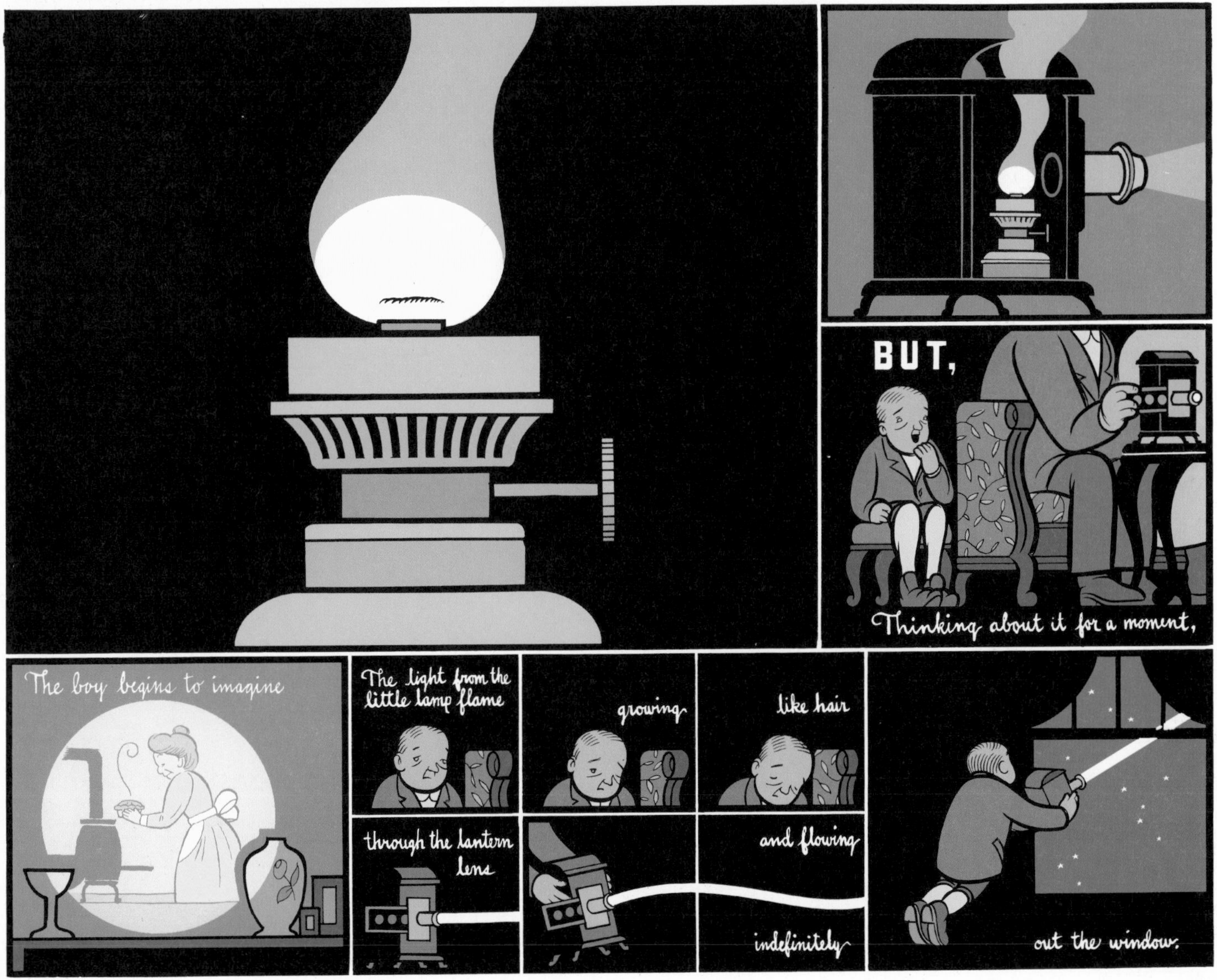
BUT,
Thinking about it for a moment,
The boy begins to imagine
The light from the little lamp flame
growing
like hair
through the lantern lens
and flowing
indefinitely
out the window.

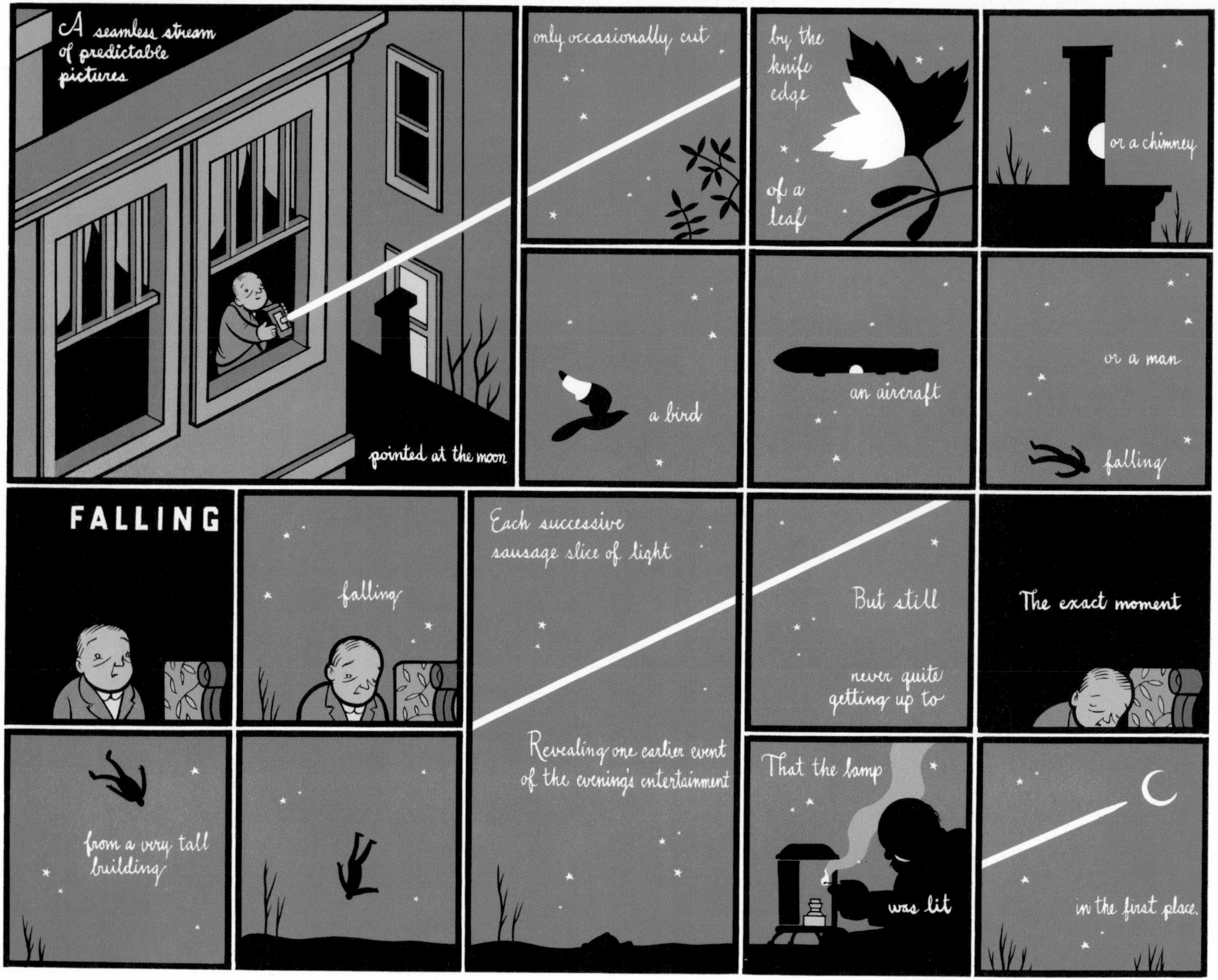

A seamless stream of predictable pictures
pointed at the moon
only occasionally cut
by the knife edge
of a leaf
or a chimney
a bird
an aircraft
or a man
falling
FALLING
falling
from a very tall building
Each successive sausage slice of light
Revealing one earlier event of the evening's entertainment
But still
never quite getting up to
That the lamp
was lit
The exact moment
in the first place.

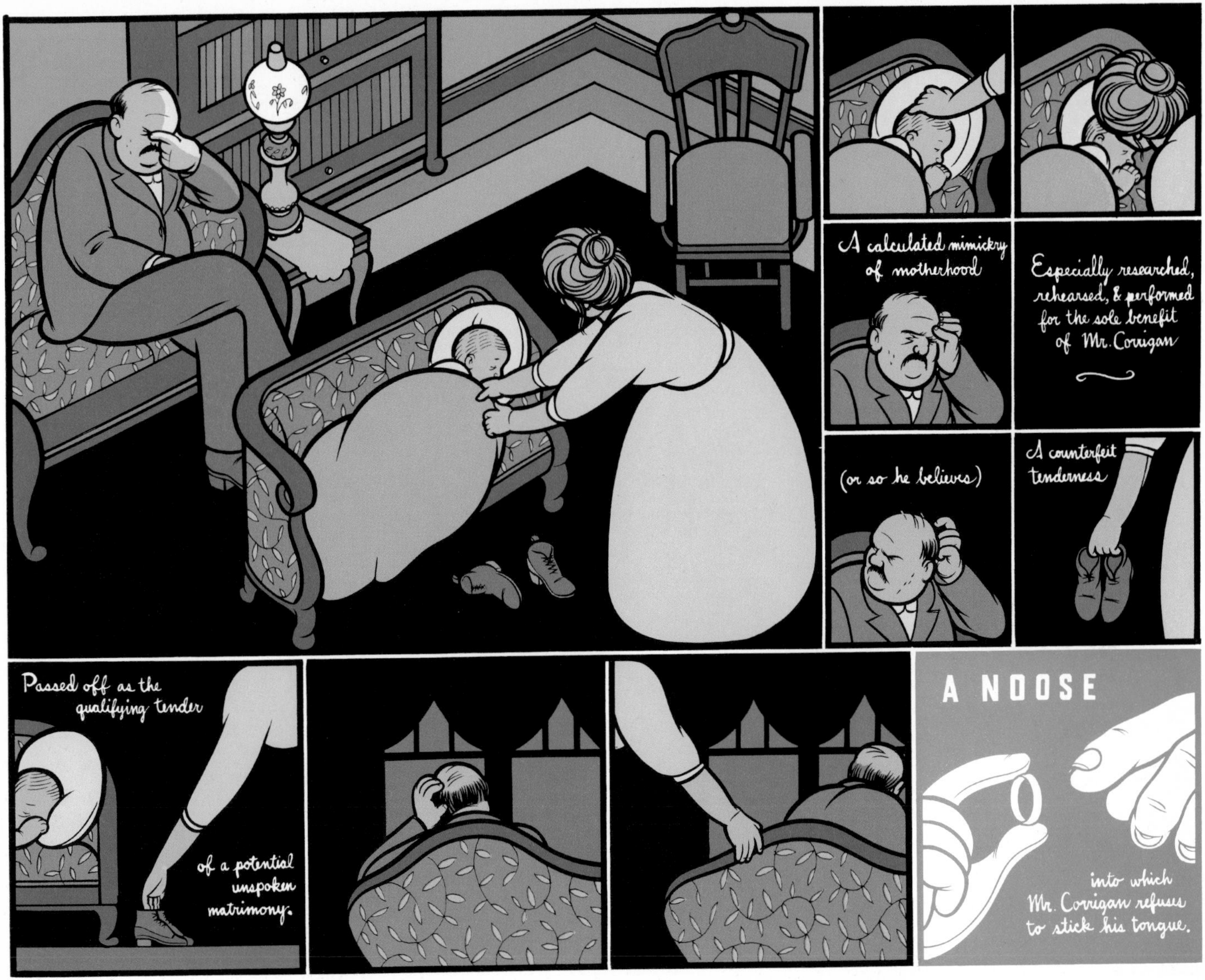
A calculated mimicry of motherhood
Especially researched, rehearsed, & performed for the sole benefit of Mr. Corrigan
(or so he believes)
A counterfeit tenderness
Passed off as the qualifying tender
of a potential unspoken matrimony.
A NOOSE
into which Mr. Corrigan refuses to stick his tongue.

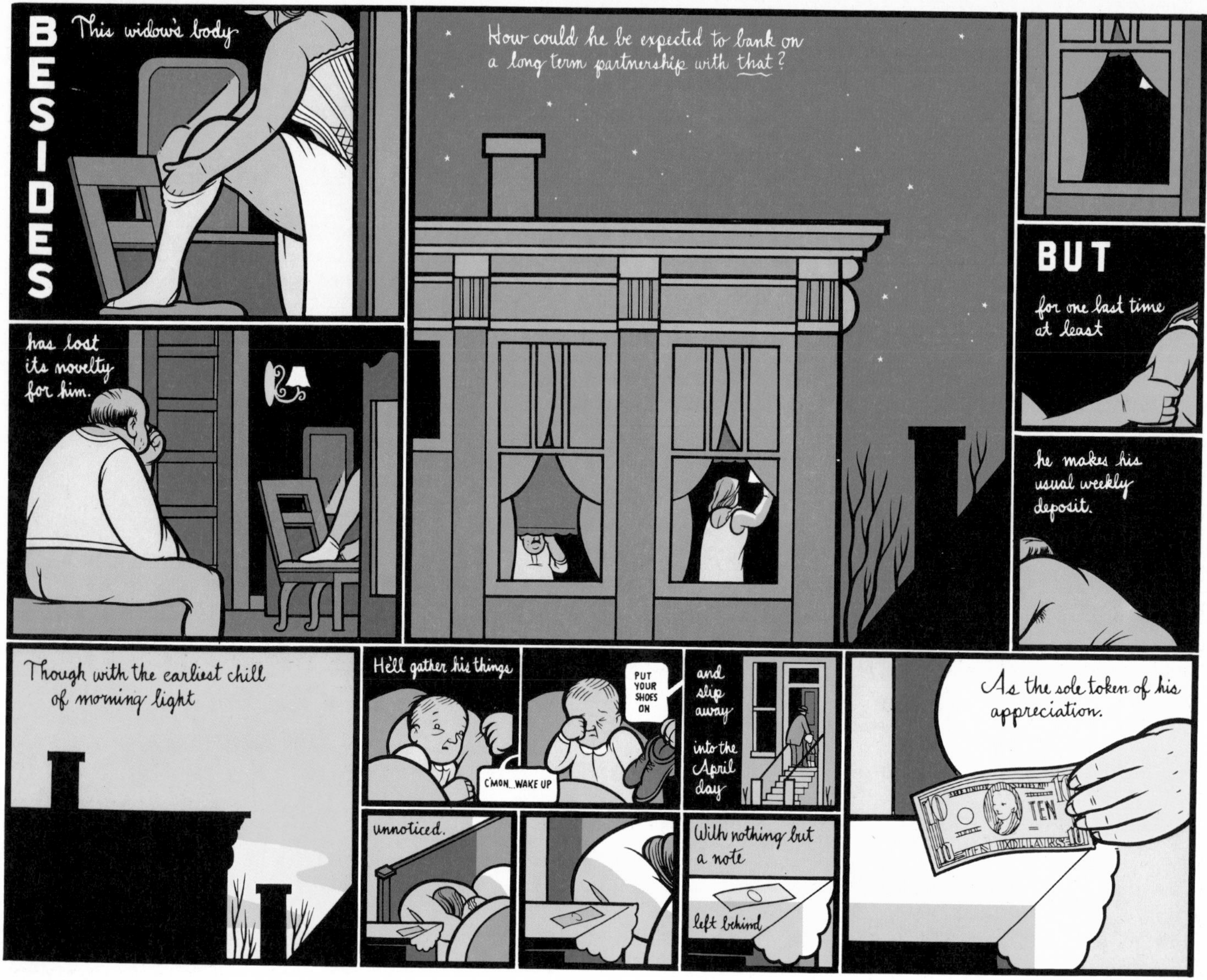
BESIDES
This widow's body
has lost its novelty for him.
How could he be expected to bank on a long term partnership with that?
BUT
for one last time at least
he makes his usual weekly deposit.
Though with the earliest chill of morning light
He'll gather his things
C'MON...WAKE UP
PUT YOUR SHOES ON
and slip away into the April day
unnoticed.
With nothing but a note
left behind
As the sole token of his appreciation.
TEN

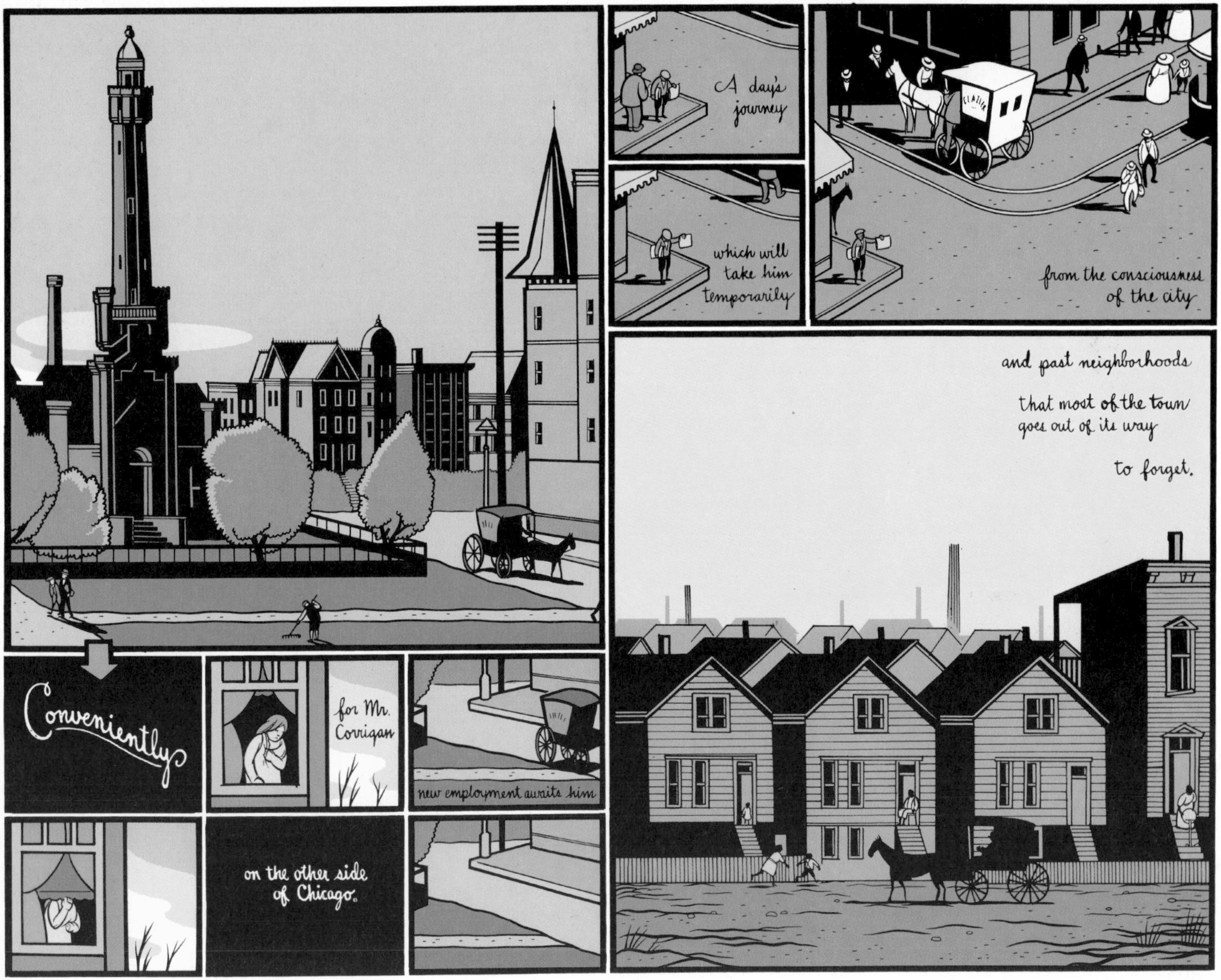
Conveniently
for Mr. Corrigan
new employment awaits him
on the other side of Chicago.
A day's journey
which will take him temporarily
from the consciousness of the city
and past neighborhoods
that most of the town goes out of its way
to forget.

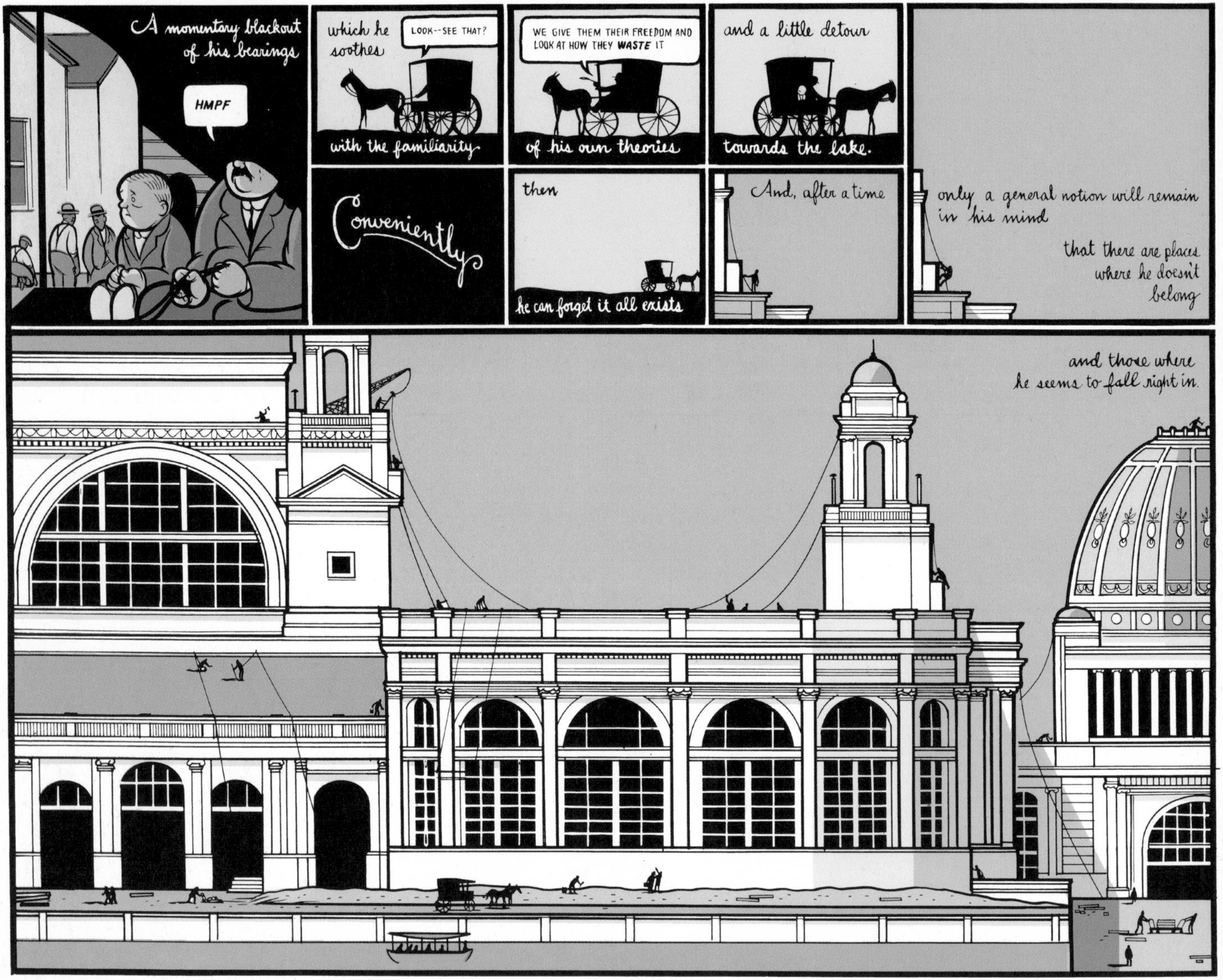
A momentary blackout of his bearings
HMPF
which he soothes
LOOK--SEE THAT?
with the familiarity
WE GIVE THEM THEIR FREEDOM AND LOOK AT HOW THEY WASTE IT
of his own theories
and a little detour
towards the lake.
Conveniently
then
he can forget it all exists
And, after a time
only a general notion will remain in his mind
that there are places where he doesn't belong
and those where he seems to fall right in.

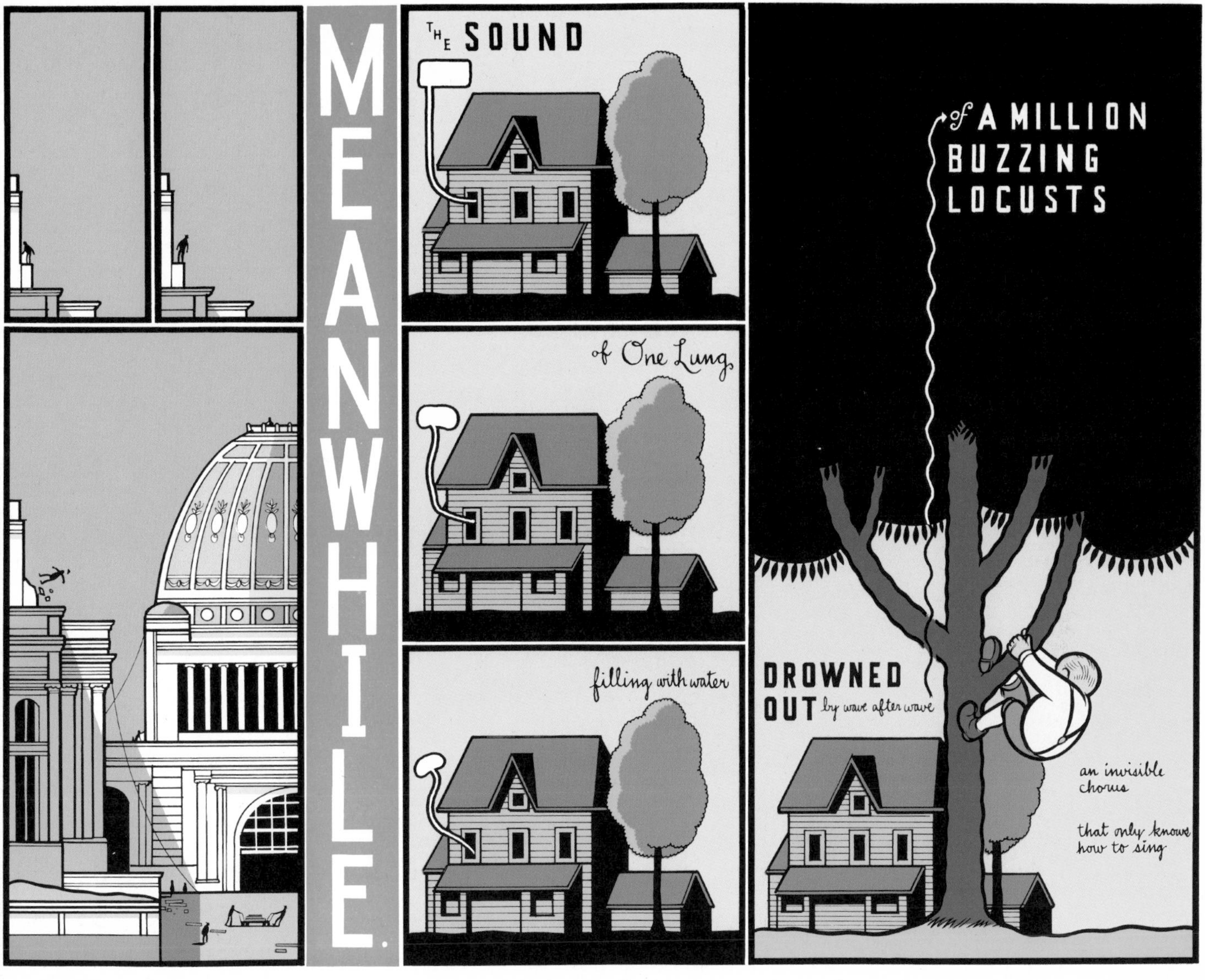
MEANWHILE.
THE SOUND
of One Lung
filling with water
of A MILLION BUZZING LOCUSTS
DROWNED OUT by wave after wave
an invisible chorus
that only knows how to sing

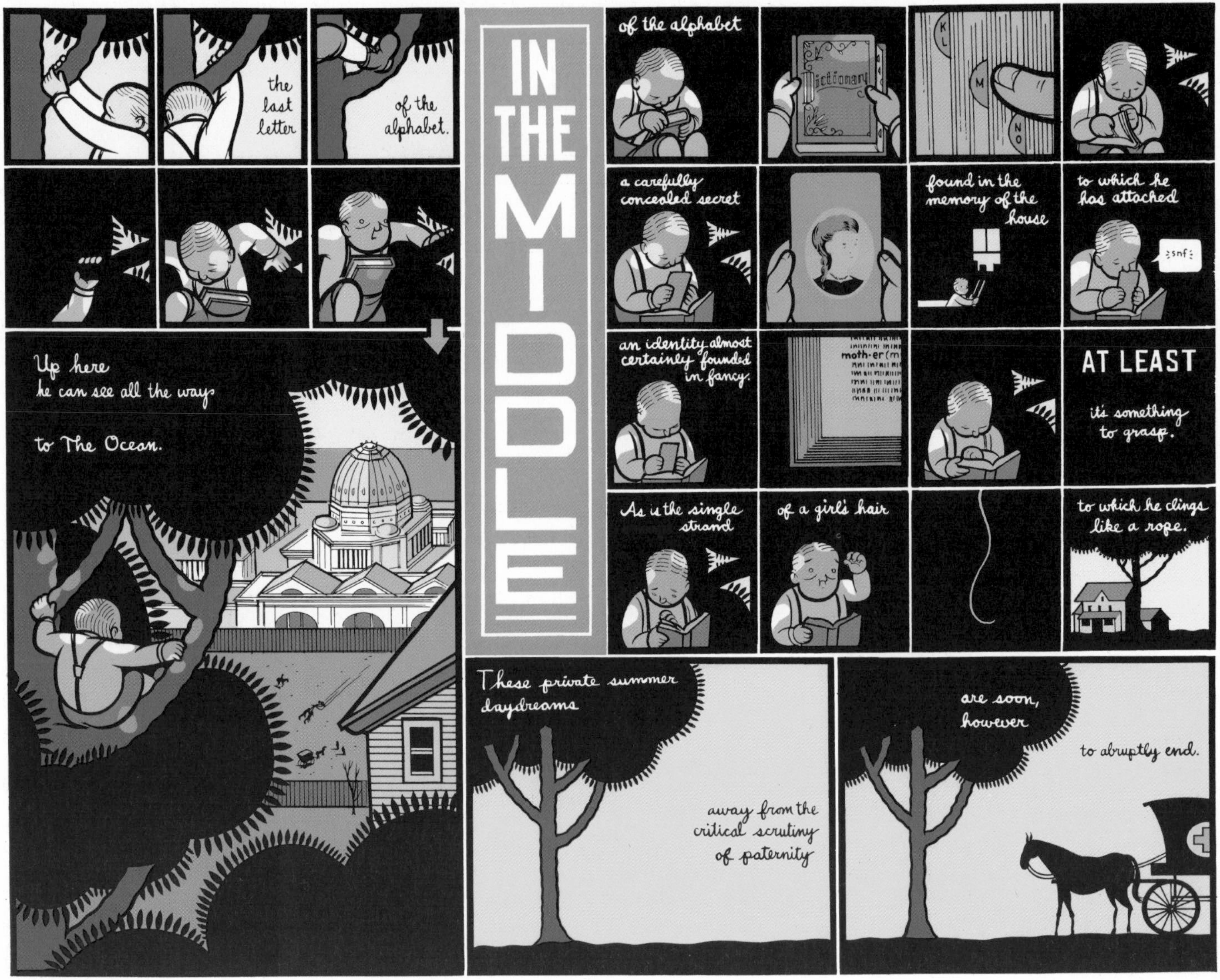

the last letter
of the alphabet.
IN THE MIDDLE
of the alphabet
Dictionary
K L
M
N O
a carefully concealed secret
found in the memory of the house
to which he has attached
snf
an identity almost certainly founded in fancy.
moth-er (m
AT LEAST
it's something to grasp.
As is the single strand
of a girl's hair
to which he clings like a rope.
Up here he can see all the ways
to The Ocean.
These private summer daydreams
away from the critical scrutiny of paternity
are soon, however
to abruptly end.

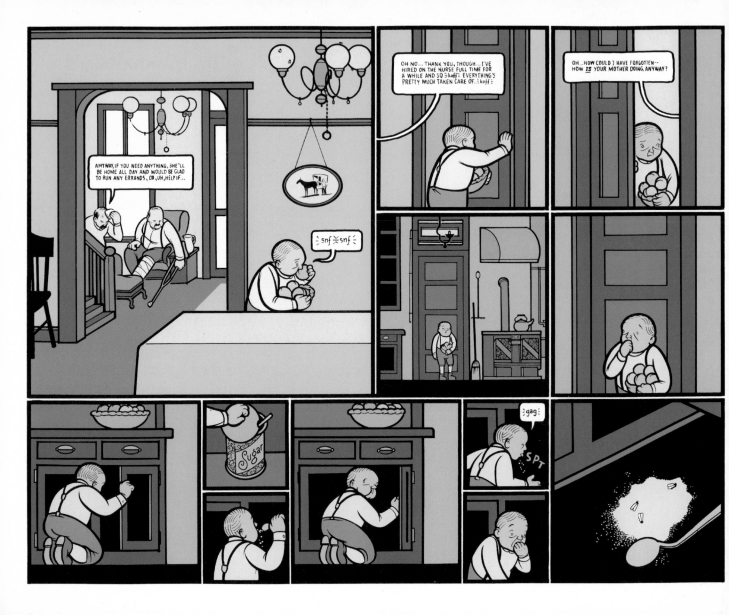

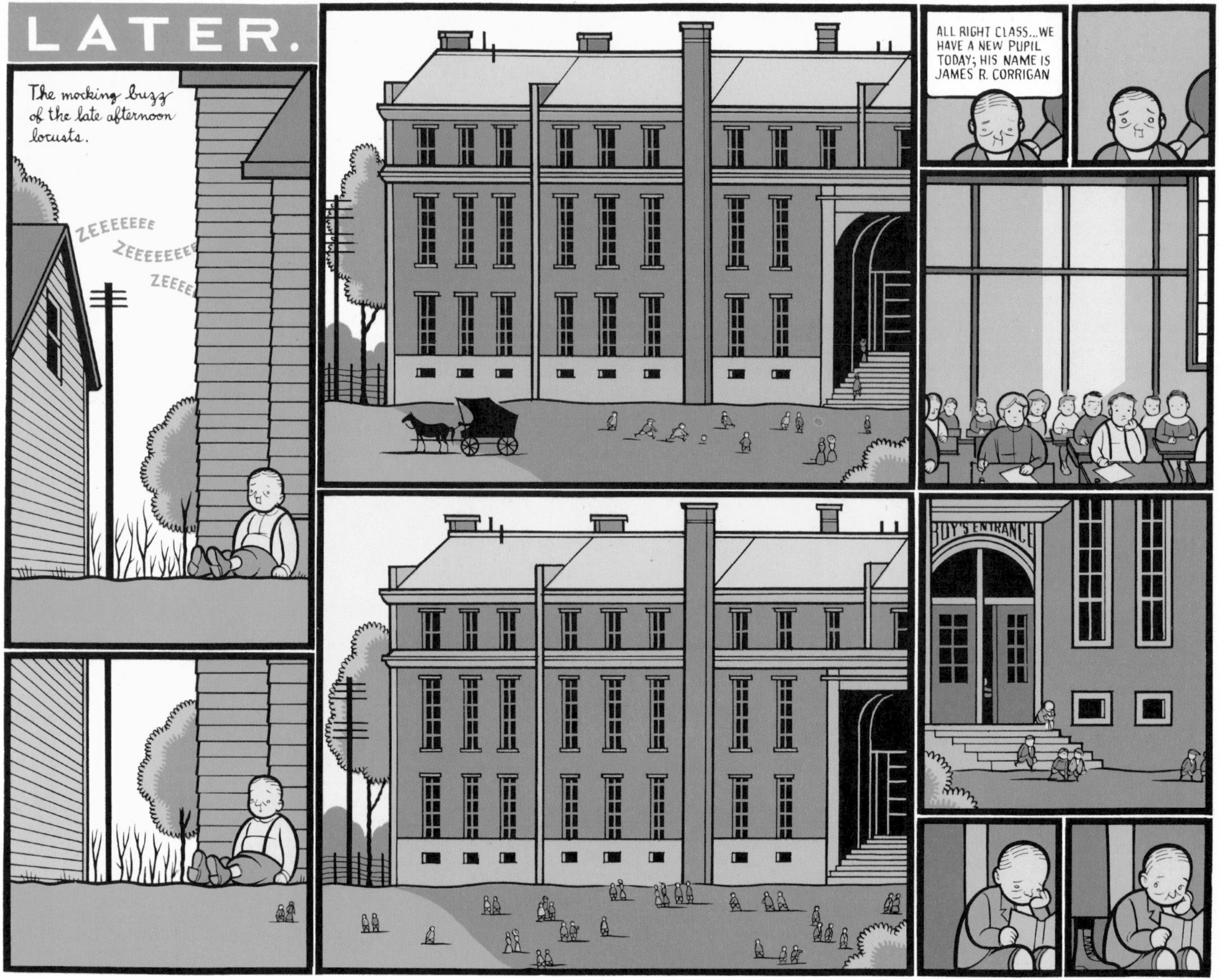

LATER.
The mocking buzz of the late afternoon locusts.
ZEEEEEEE
ZEEEEEEEE
ZEEEE
ALL RIGHT CLASS...WE HAVE A NEW PUPIL TODAY; HIS NAME IS JAMES R. CORRIGAN
BOY'S ENTRANCE

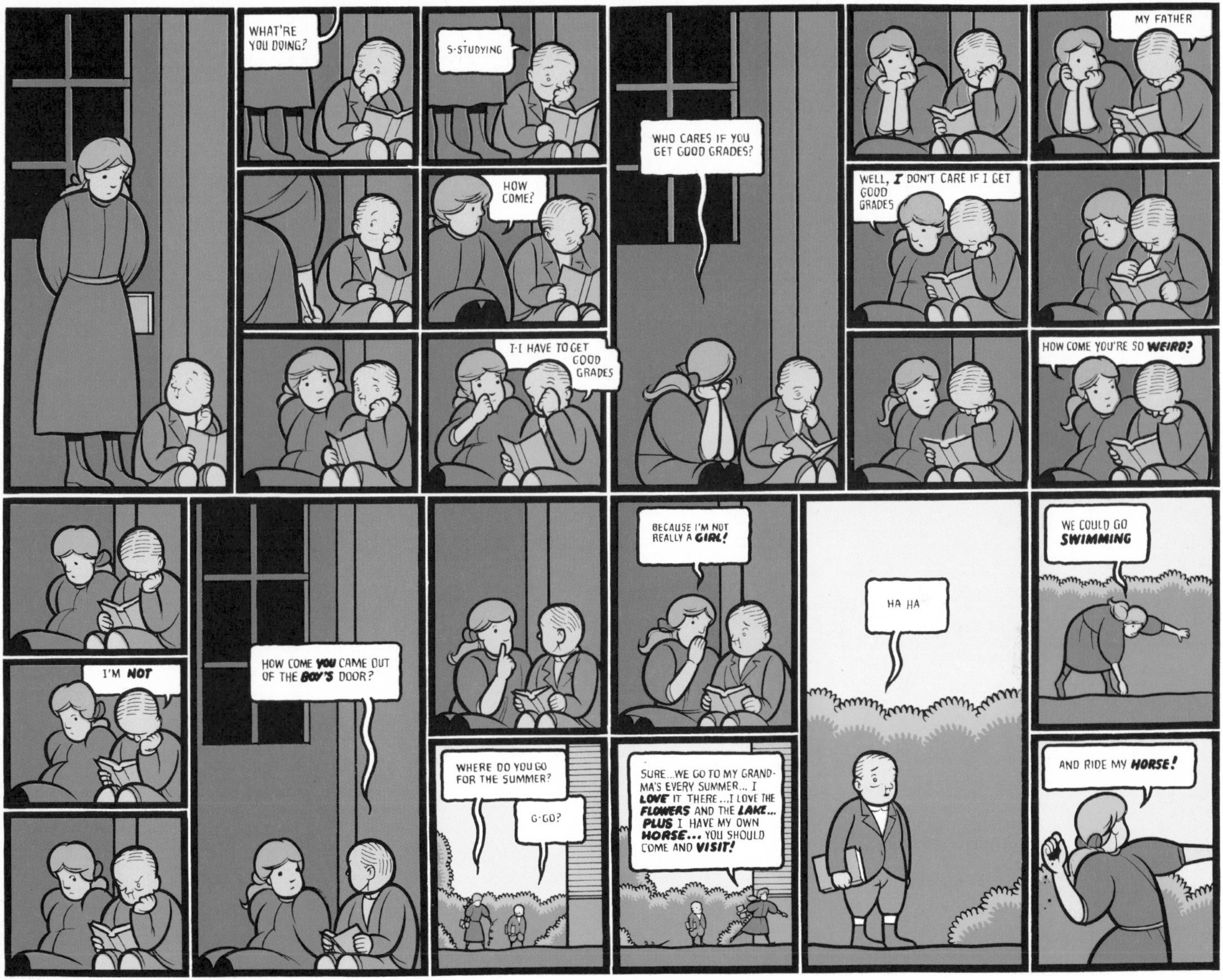
WHAT'RE YOU DOING?
S-STUDYING
HOW COME?
I-I HAVE TO GET GOOD GRADES
WHO CARES IF YOU GET GOOD GRADES?
MY FATHER
WELL, I DON'T CARE IF I GET GOOD GRADES
HOW COME YOU'RE SO WEIRD?
I'M NOT
HOW COME YOU CAME OUT OF THE BOY'S DOOR?
BECAUSE I'M NOT REALLY A GIRL!
WHERE DO YOU GO FOR THE SUMMER?
G-GO?
SURE...WE GO TO MY GRANDMA'S EVERY SUMMER... I LOVE IT THERE...I LOVE THE FLOWERS AND THE LAKE... PLUS I HAVE MY OWN HORSE... YOU SHOULD COME AND VISIT!
HA HA
WE COULD GO SWIMMING
AND RIDE MY HORSE!

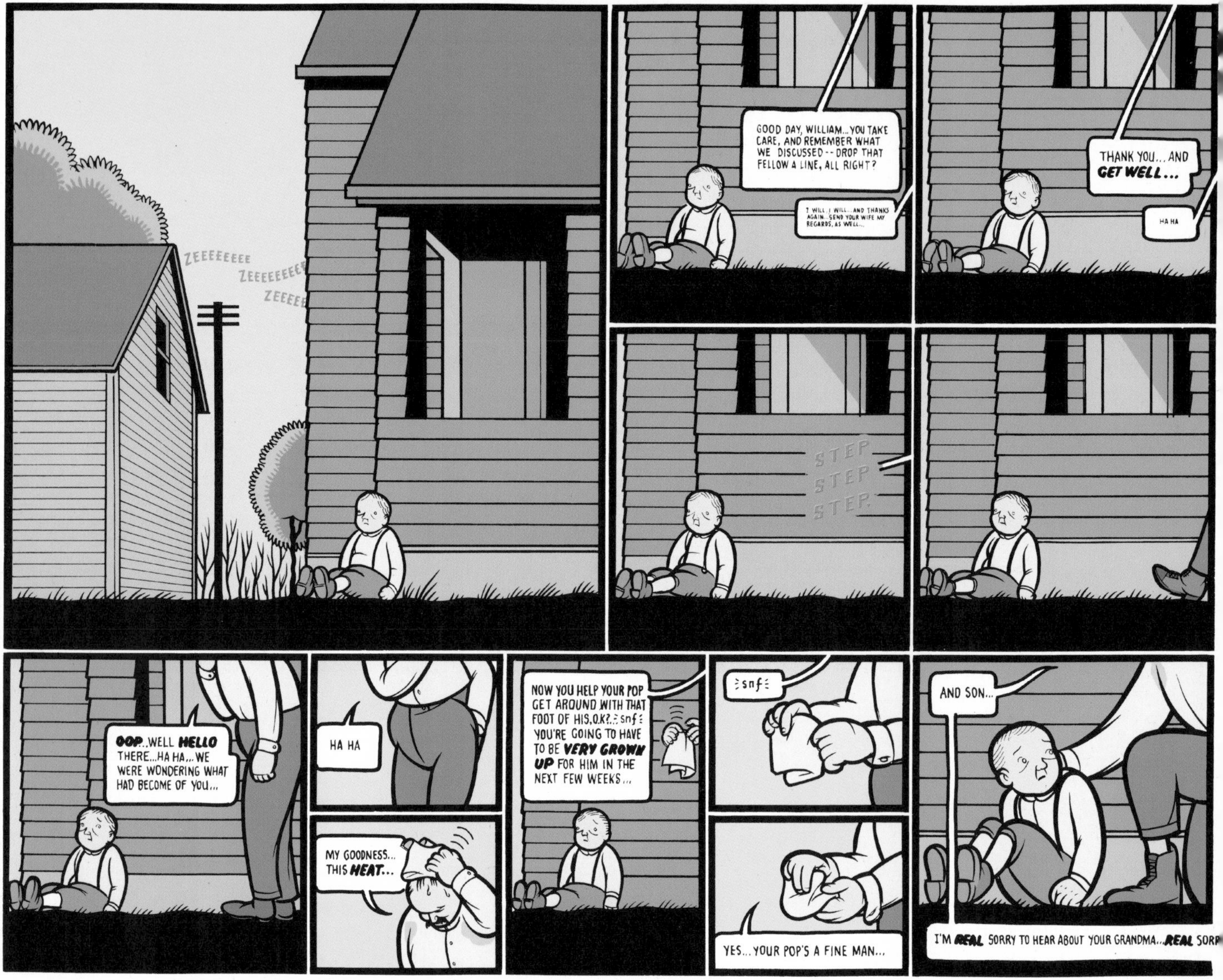
ZEEEEEEEE
ZEEEEEEEEE
ZEEEEE
GOOD DAY, WILLIAM... YOU TAKE CARE, AND REMEMBER WHAT WE DISCUSSED -- DROP THAT FELLOW A LINE, ALL RIGHT?
I WILL, I WILL... AND THANKS AGAIN... SEND YOUR WIFE MY REGARDS, AS WELL...
THANK YOU... AND **GET WELL...**
HA HA
STEP STEP STEP
OOP..WELL **HELLO** THERE...HA HA,.. WE WERE WONDERING WHAT HAD BECOME OF YOU...
HA HA
MY GOODNESS... THIS **HEAT...**
NOW YOU HELP YOUR POP GET AROUND WITH THAT FOOT OF HIS, O.K?.. snf YOU'RE GOING TO HAVE TO BE **VERY GROWN UP** FOR HIM IN THE NEXT FEW WEEKS...
snf
YES... YOUR POP'S A FINE MAN...
AND SON...
I'M **REAL** SORRY TO HEAR ABOUT YOUR GRANDMA... **REAL** SORR

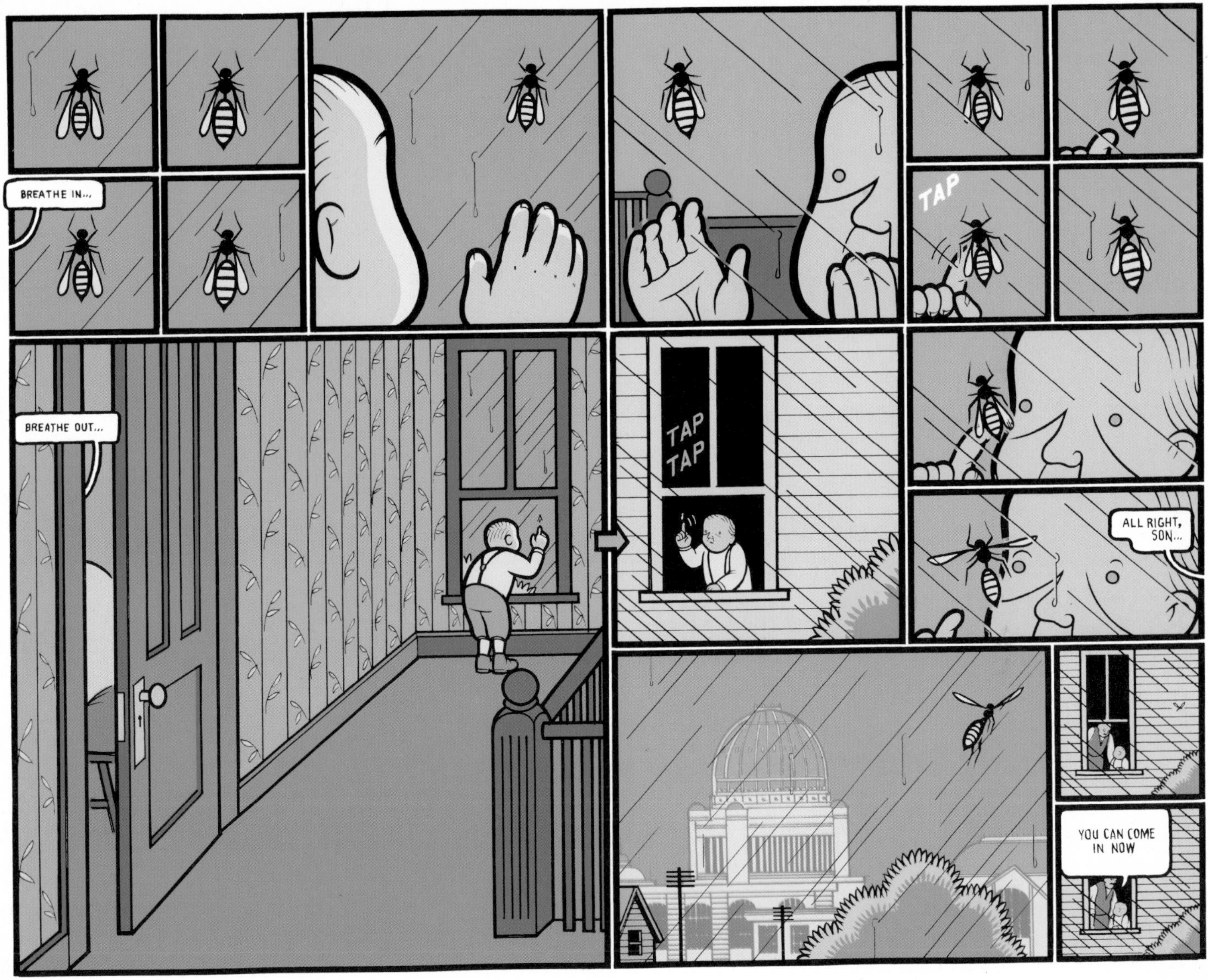
BREATHE IN...
BREATHE OUT...
TAP
TAP
TAP
ALL RIGHT, SON...
YOU CAN COME IN NOW

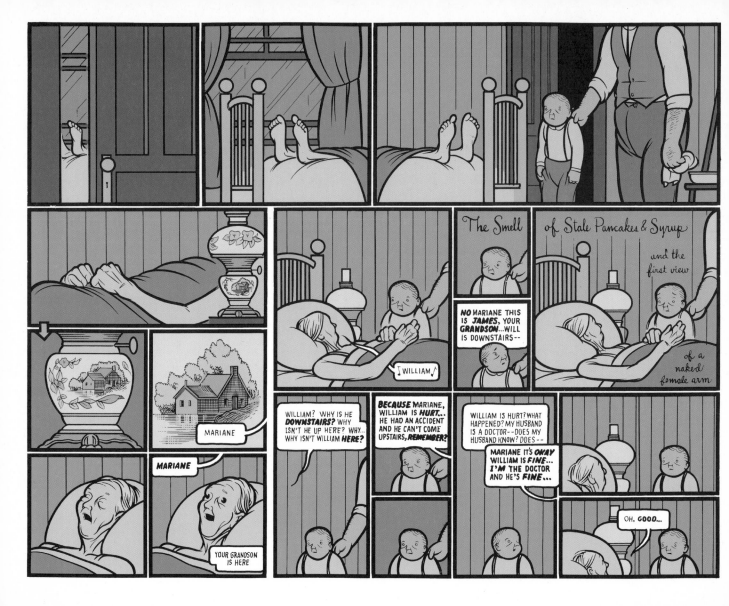

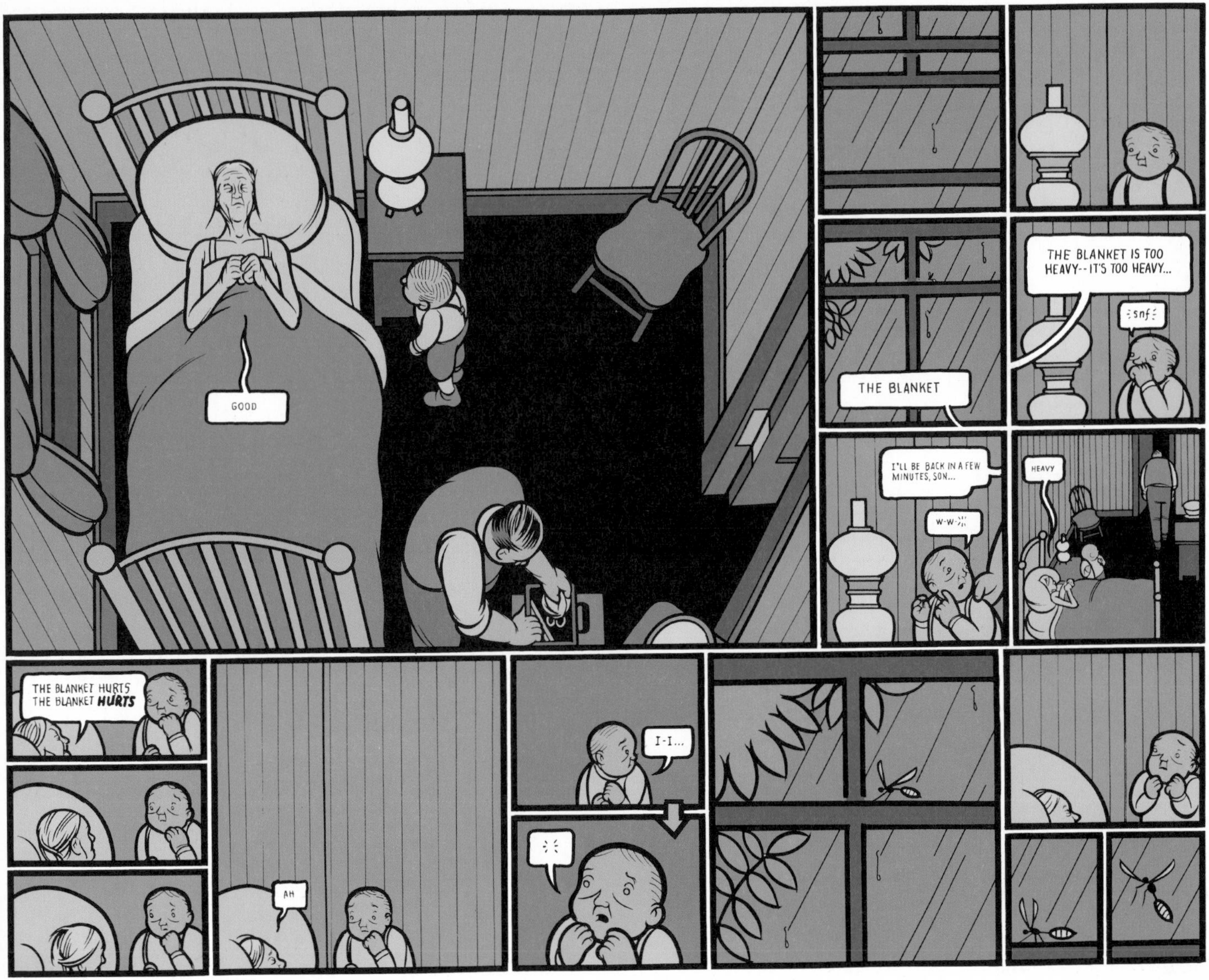
GOOD
THE BLANKET
THE BLANKET IS TOO HEAVY-- IT'S TOO HEAVY...
snf
I'LL BE BACK IN A FEW MINUTES, SON...
W-W-
HEAVY
THE BLANKET HURTS THE BLANKET **HURTS**
AH
I-I...

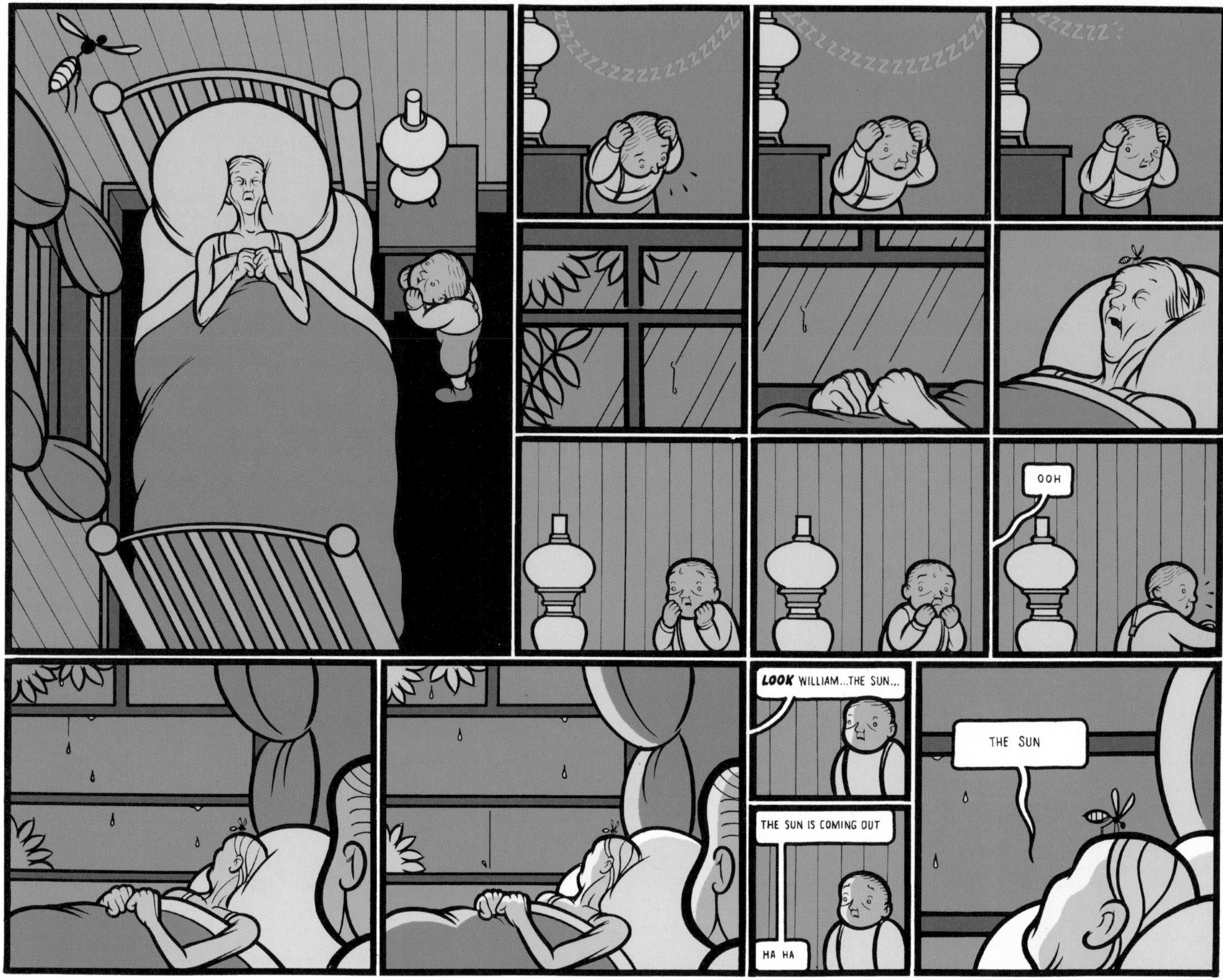

ZZZZZZZZZZZZZZZZZ
ZZZZZZZZZZZZZZZZZ
ZZZZZZ
OOH
LOOK WILLIAM...THE SUN...
THE SUN IS COMING OUT
HA HA
THE SUN

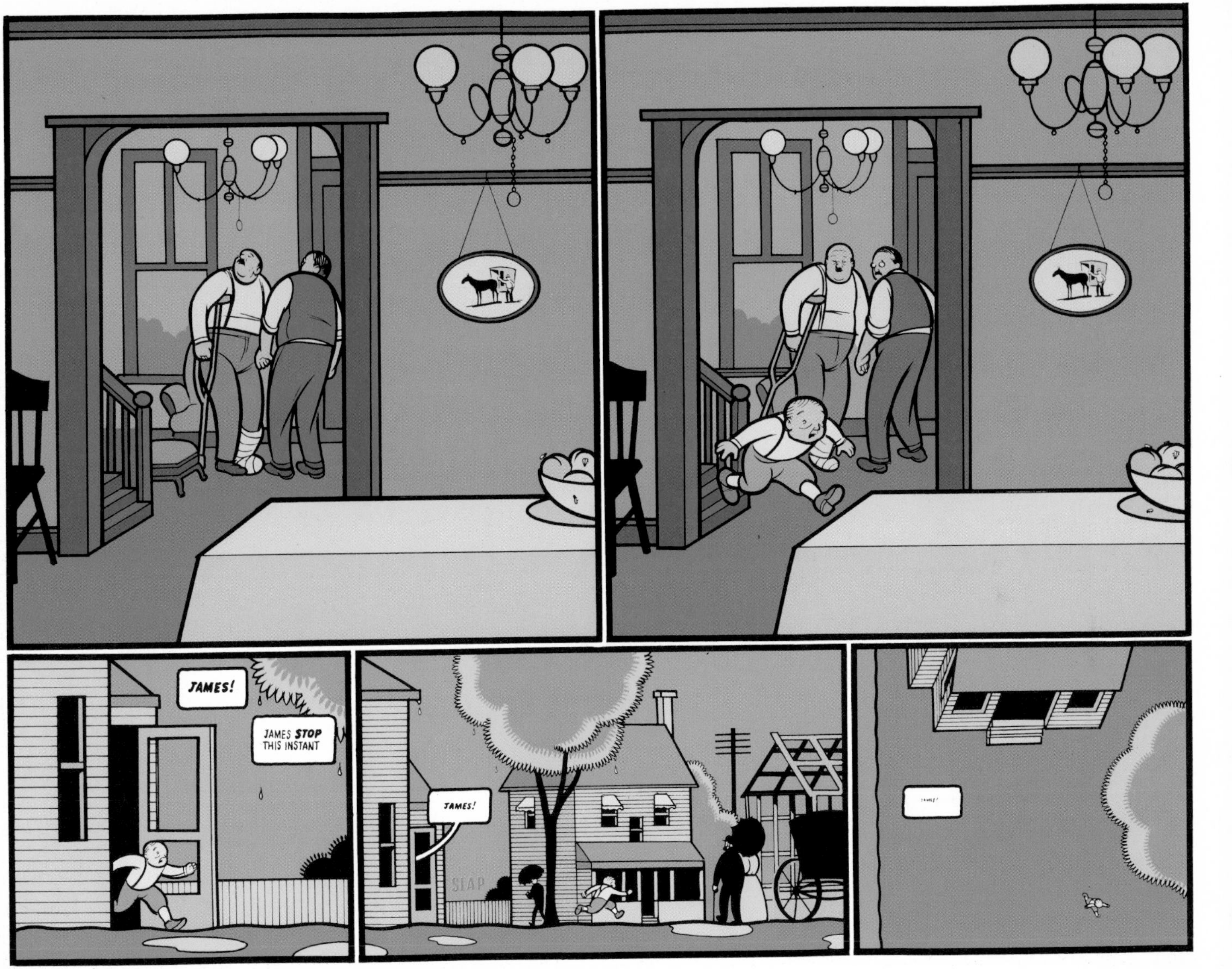
JAMES!
JAMES STOP THIS INSTANT
JAMES!
SLAP

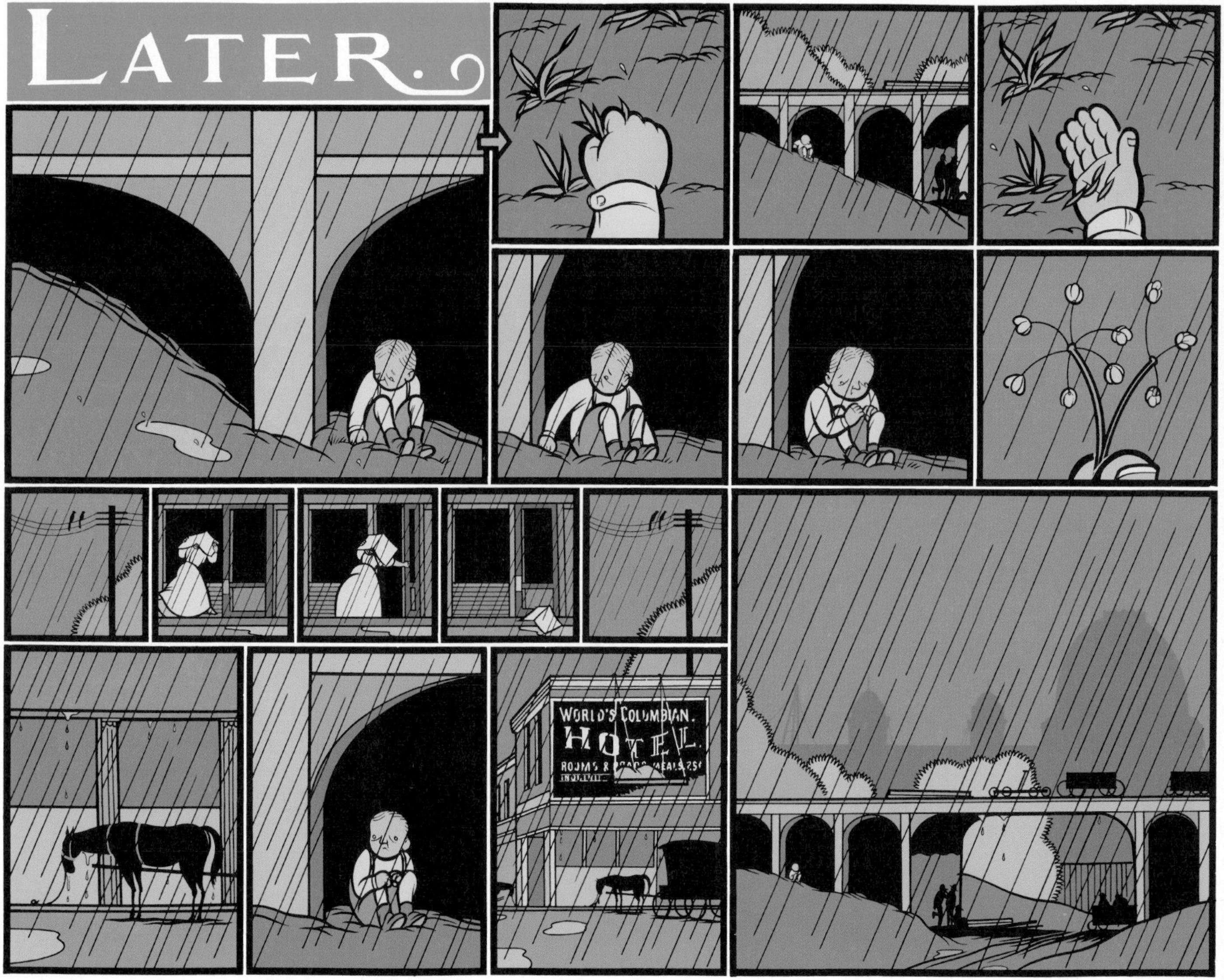
LATER.
WORLD'S COLUMBIAN.
HOTEL.
ROOMS &
MEALS 25¢

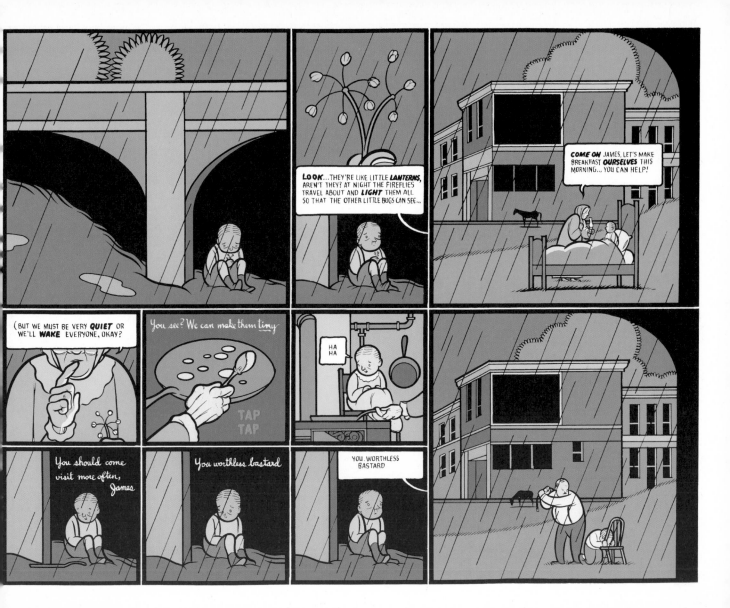

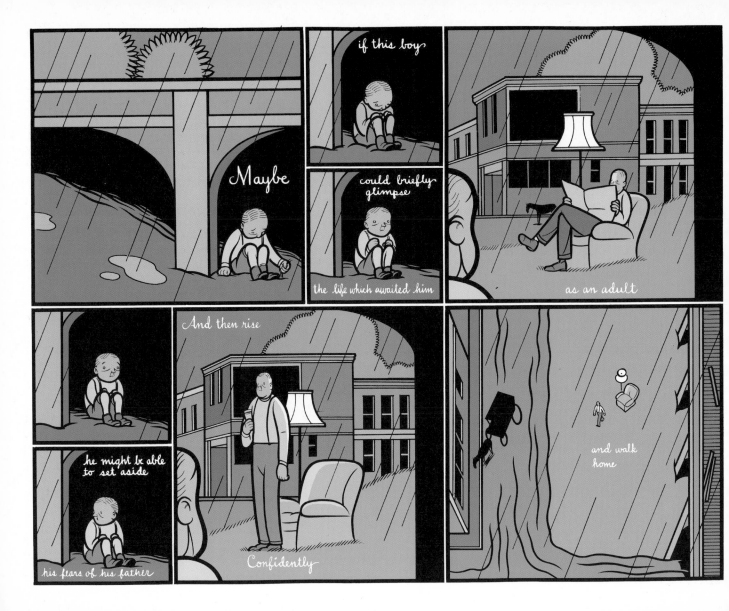

A distant roll of thunder

and A cooling breeze

Crickets, fireflies...

...bearing the slur of neighborhood voices emerging from the stale house heat

All ruined

by a stomach-turning sense of dread,

It makes his toes hurt.

(and the familiar sniff of his own kneecaps

which always precedes any punishment.)

SOMETIMES if he pushes on his eyeballs hard enough

he sees pictures

Red splotches and patterns of purple green sparkles, silvery smears

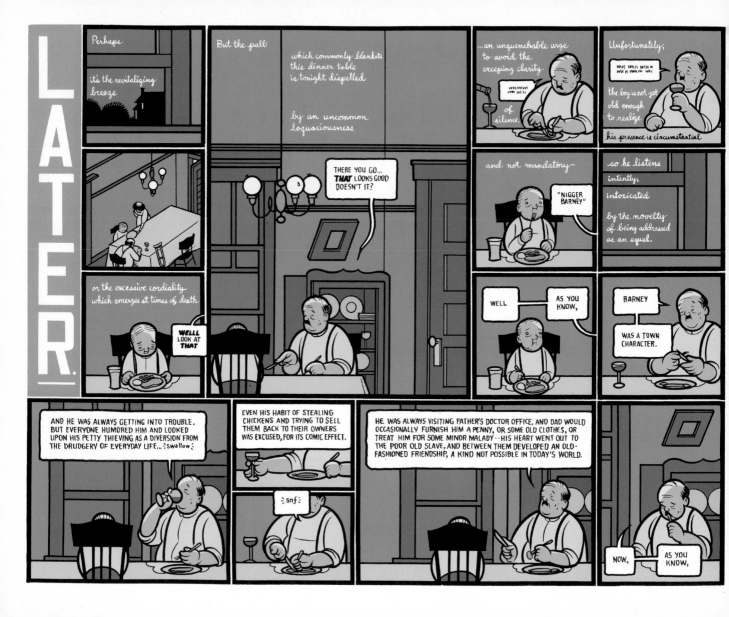

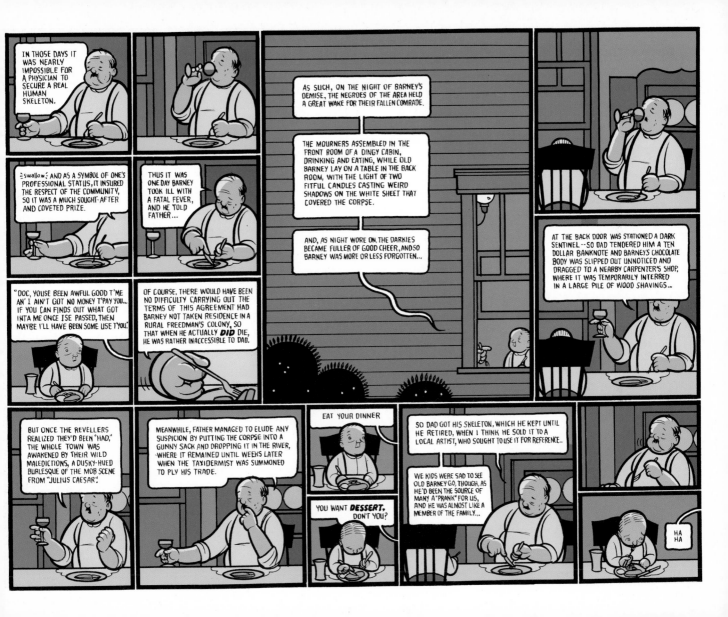

IN THOSE DAYS IT WAS NEARLY IMPOSSIBLE FOR A PHYSICIAN TO SECURE A REAL HUMAN SKELETON.

≈swallow≈ AND AS A SYMBOL OF ONE'S PROFESSIONAL STATUS, IT INSURED THE RESPECT OF THE COMMUNITY, SO IT WAS A MUCH SOUGHT-AFTER AND COVETED PRIZE.

THUS IT WAS ONE DAY BARNEY TOOK ILL WITH A FATAL FEVER, AND HE TOLD FATHER...

"DOC, YOUSE BEEN AWFUL GOOD T'ME AN' I AIN'T GOT NO MONEY T'PAY YOU... IF YOU CAN FINDS OUT WHAT GOT INTA ME ONCE ISE PASSED, THEN MAYBE I'LL HAVE BEEN SOME USE T'YOU."

OF COURSE, THERE WOULD HAVE BEEN NO DIFFICULTY CARRYING OUT THE TERMS OF THIS AGREEMENT HAD BARNEY NOT TAKEN RESIDENCE IN A RURAL FREEDMAN'S COLONY, SO THAT WHEN HE ACTUALLY **DID** DIE, HE WAS RATHER INACCESSIBLE TO DAD.

AS SUCH, ON THE NIGHT OF BARNEY'S DEMISE, THE NEGROES OF THE AREA HELD A GREAT WAKE FOR THEIR FALLEN COMRADE.

THE MOURNERS ASSEMBLED IN THE FRONT ROOM OF A DINGY CABIN, DRINKING AND EATING, WHILE OLD BARNEY LAY ON A TABLE IN THE BACK ROOM, WITH THE LIGHT OF TWO FITFUL CANDLES CASTING WEIRD SHADOWS ON THE WHITE SHEET THAT COVERED THE CORPSE.

AND, AS NIGHT WORE ON, THE DARKIES BECAME FULLER OF GOOD CHEER, AND SO BARNEY WAS MORE OR LESS FORGOTTEN...

AT THE BACK DOOR WAS STATIONED A DARK SENTINEL -- SO DAD TENDERED HIM A TEN DOLLAR BANKNOTE AND BARNEY'S CHOCOLATE BODY WAS SLIPPED OUT UNNOTICED AND DRAGGED TO A NEARBY CARPENTER'S SHOP, WHERE IT WAS TEMPORARILY INTERRED IN A LARGE PILE OF WOOD SHAVINGS...

BUT ONCE THE REVELLERS REALIZED THEY'D BEEN "HAD," THE WHOLE TOWN WAS AWAKENED BY THEIR WILD MALEDICTIONS, A DUSKY-HUED BURLESQUE OF THE MOB SCENE FROM "JULIUS CAESAR."

MEANWHILE, FATHER MANAGED TO ELUDE ANY SUSPICION BY PUTTING THE CORPSE INTO A GUNNY SACK AND DROPPING IT IN THE RIVER, WHERE IT REMAINED UNTIL WEEKS LATER WHEN THE TAXIDERMIST WAS SUMMONED TO PLY HIS TRADE.

EAT YOUR DINNER

YOU WANT **DESSERT**, DON'T YOU?

SO DAD GOT HIS SKELETON, WHICH HE KEPT UNTIL HE RETIRED, WHEN I THINK HE SOLD IT TO A LOCAL ARTIST, WHO SOUGHT TO USE IT FOR REFERENCE...

WE KIDS WERE SAD TO SEE OLD BARNEY GO, THOUGH, AS HE'D BEEN THE SOURCE OF MANY A "PRANK" FOR US, AND HE WAS ALMOST LIKE A MEMBER OF THE FAMILY...

HA HA

BUS
STOP
BARGAIN
FOR SALE
Dairy Queen
OPEN 24 HOURS
Buyalot
LIQUOR TOWN
CLUB MEGA
STOP 'N SPEND
Pam's
WAGON WHEEL
Restaurant
COUNTRY
wash
The Supper Club
COCKTAILS
FOOD
EMERGENCY

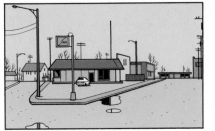

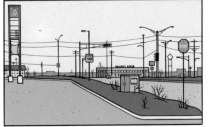

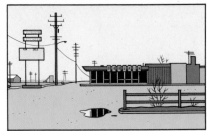

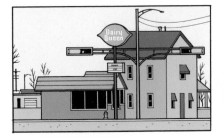

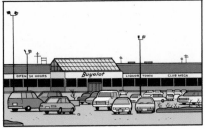

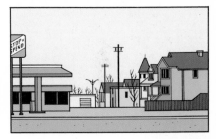

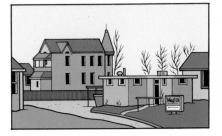

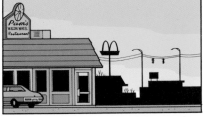

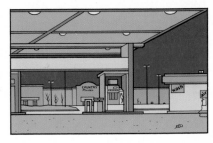

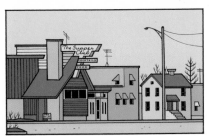

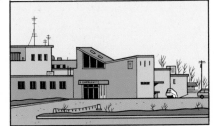

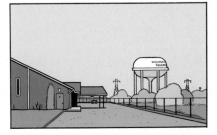

A DECLARATION OF GLORY.

Left to itself, this unpretentious scene of commercial beauty might garner ne'er a second glance from the casual passer-by, but in it may be found a striking model of modern elegance, form, and convenience. The "Bargain Showcase" (one of the most successful mercantiles in the history of the city of Waukosha) was established in 1964 as a means of providing quality goods at an affordable price to citizens of modest means, and it always went to great lengths and distant lands to procure such wares, often at risk of financial jeopardy and civic certification. Many of the younger residents of Waukosha also enjoyed gainful employment at this fine outlet, and, in some cases, founded a whole new generation of customers in the passenger seats of automobiles in the parking lot after closing time. While the lean honesty of the signage and the sleek, enthusiastic slope of the entryway invited thousands of local townspeople during its reign, it temporarily sits awaiting restoration; one hopes that the doors may once again swing open with the familiar strains of continuously playing popular ballads, and that the waft of polyester carpet binding may once again fill the nostrils with its promising allure and mystery.

VISTA.

No pine thicket, no birch grove, and no apple orchard could hope to compete with the the visual complexity of any scene selected from our contemporary interstate system, especially those cospes situated nearby the highway's many entries and exits, wherein the fagged voyager might seek sustenance and succor in the various eateries and refueling stations. The broad sweep of power lines, the delicate articulation of poles, signs, and warning lights, and the deep forest of advertisements all conspire to occasion countless views of complicated beauty, conceiving wonder in the curious onlooker at man's great achievement, however ductile. Great expanses of asphalt (here at the intersection of I-90 and highway 334) reflect the sun's blinding rays into the eyes of travellers, and provide an unconscious waste receptacle for items dropped overboard in haste to return to the comfort of the personal vehicle or land rover. Much history may be witnessed: the dinner wrappers, the emptied tins of flavored waters, and the frying pools of saliva all whispering a tale to those who might listen over the roar of the passing traffic. Such a fecund landscape! Such a rich heritage – oh! but it only could be frozen in time, for future generations to cherish.

GRAND PORT OF ENTRY.

Here's where it all begins for many sightseers and tourists, the Travel Bureau of the city of Waukosha, built in 1974 at the behest of the city's populace as a common meeting point for travellers seeking aid and advice. Note the rustic shingling, the modest porch, the way that the parking lot just seems to invite you -- all design concerns carefully incorporated by one of the city's leading contractors when designing the space. As well, the building is purposefully "open" on three sides, allowing sunlight to traverse its shallow carpeting in the course of an 8-hour workday, and to remind the visitor that this truly is a "port of all calls". Once a service for passengers of most major modes of transport, the Travel Bureau now focuses exclusively upon that of the public luxury coach, or bus system, as all railroad traffic was diverted from Waukosha in the early 1980s, and the airline which flies to Waukosha chose to handle such reservations itself. This more flexible, personal mode of transportation offers the citizens of Waukosha more than just a way to travel – it's a way to see the world. The new County Court House may be seen in the distance on the right, yet another testament to Waukosha's forward-looking spirit.

WINDSWEPT.

In 1878, when Siptus T. Bluntzer arrived at the arid plain which was to become the city of Concupiscence (renamed "Waukosha" in 1893 in honor of the Indians who once inhabited its dank promontory) little would he have guessed the variety of architecture, commerce, and culture which would one day populate the mild hills and rolling humps of his home. Sitting at the step of his grim little cabin, powder musket in hand, peering out from under the sticky edge of the muslin cheeseboard which he favored as a hat, how could he have known that little over eighty years hence he might simply rise from his perch and walk a few yards to the Stop n' Spend and purchase a sack of Corn Chips or a bottle of Orange spritzer, or perhaps a photo-magazine? Just imagine the lonely life that Mr. Bluntzer must have endured, the hardships he, his wife, and his thirteen children suffered. Their struggles simply to find food, to enjoy the gift of life on this Earth, the many times that he must have relieved himself of ardor against the wall of a barn, or behind a tree, or simply out in a field, and what grand edifice rises from his seed today. Such are the ways of history, and the grand scheme of the world, about which we shall always marvel.

MURMURING PINES.

Once an intraversable field of white pine and blue spruce forestland, this centrally-located plot of real estate was transformed by the City of Waukosha Planning Commission into an multi-purpose shopping facility for its suburban residents in 1987 – and well, the city has just never looked back. Created with ease of access and maximum parking potential (MPP) in mind, the striking simplicity of the majestic compound bespeaks a highly complex internetworking of æsthetic choices and intellectual theory, paired with a sharp sense of economy and surreptitious favors. Note the exciting pattern of windows, regularly spaced and only once interrupted by the main entryway, all harmonizing with the nettle of light-towers, evenly spaced as to provide the most efficient and convenient illumination under any conditions. Concomitantly, as an "open design" it tries to account for the fact that the visual field would be under constant flux, with the myriad automobiles and delivery trucks all coming and going; thus, the edifice remains stolid, stern – yet receptive – a beneficent reminder of the commercial bloodlines which bind us all together.

SILHOUETTE OF HISTORY.

Here's one of the most famous spots in all of Waukosha: "Treaty Rock", or "The Blood Stone" as old-timers like to call it. The site of one of the most potentially violent and fierce Indian uprisings in the city's history, it was the fearsomeness and pluck of one man which quelled a potential war upon the good people of "Concupiscence". Though many details of the event have been lost, the essential drama remains: our proud ancestors' families and livelihoods were threatened in 1881 by a small tribe of Indians who seemed to come from nowhere, with no regard at all for the society which was firmly established in God's name on the hallowed ground. The townspeople, of course, tried to reason with the unruly invaders, offering them sustenance and aid, but no words would seem to quell their fierce intent; none until Mr. Viscus Flatula, a local merchant, was able to speak with them. It is here that the details are sketchy, but the town was eventually renamed at the time of the Great Chicago Exposition in honor of these noble savages who saw the Christian reasoning of Mr. Flatula; votes to name the town after the great man himself were narrowly missed by two in the town council. *Note: rock is behind building, out of photo.*

CITY OF PERPETUAL MOONLIGHT.

One of the most novel and forward-looking features of the spritely city of Waukosha was its sophisticated illumination system established at the turn of the century, an ever-expanding array of tungsten, fluorescent, and halogen gas-burning glass globules which bathed the metropolis in a heavenly glow of dusty pinks, ambers, and icy blues – thus prompting the nickname "The City of Perpetual Moonlight". Almost entirely eliminating all ambient starlight, this *aurora artificialis* now allows for the continuance of commerce well into the wee hours, a whole new "segment" of the working-class population operating under an entrancing "færie sparkle". As well, this wonderful invention has engendered an exciting "night culture" of local meeting places and "after hours" supply depots all over Waukosha, some families even choosing to do their marketing at midnight, or to visit restaurants in their bedclothes when things get too emotionally stressful at home. Greatly expanding the possibilities for one's enjoyment of life, the "City of Perpetual Moonlight" was a bold step forward for the modest burgh of Waukosha, a path soon to be followed by cites all over this great land.

SUN'S FAREWELL KISS.

What could be better than a patty melt with curly fries, or a milkshake, or a good old-fashioned square of frozen mayonnaise? You bet. And Pam's "Wagon Wheel" has been serving up good, hearty fare like this for generations, ever since 1977. A favorite of young and old alike, the stories of its patrons are everywhere to be found: welded underneath table seventeen is a piece of gum stuck October 8th, 1981 at 8:24 AM by a heartbroken girl whose adoptive mother had just died of lung cancer in the city hospital the night before; crushed into the carpet by the southernmost window is a fragment of lettuce dislodged from the plate of an elderly man who for sixteen years was kept alive by a salad and a cup of coffee served in more or less that same spot; still adhering to the artificial leaves of the plant by the end of the center counter is the residue of a sneeze deposited by a widow whose most beloved feature of her college-aged body by her husband was the small dimple at the base of her skull into which his pinky would naturally rest when embracing her; and tucked away into the space between the ceiling tiles and the concrete above is a darkened space equal to the collective volume of a small church congregation, which no one ever thinks or cares about.

SIMPLICITY, SIMPLICITY.

What an easy blend of utility and domesticity may be glimpsed in this, a truly modern, yet nostalgic scene of midwestern modesty and efficiency. One of the many lovely "apothecary clinics" which conveniently dot the landscape of Waukosha – contrasted with the majesty and gentility of the ideal home world behind; see how these two sides of life complement and enrich each other; see how the bright blue sign and the trash removal receptacle counterpoint the quiet rhythms of the picket fence. Such "minor injury centers" cater to those citizens who have suffered only light complaints: common cuts and abrasions, sour stomach, and other "ow-ies" are well-served by the "on call" staff of specialists, while more major personal damage is attended to by physicians at the larger *hospital* down the street (from the Greek *hospes*, receiver of guests, and *tal*, meaning large, or tall) such as loss of limb, violent seizure, and unstoppable bleeding. No screams are to be heard sneaking through the walls of this happy little building, only the soft buzz of the central air conditioner, or the click and hum of the cozy heating unit switching on in the soft silence of a snowy November afternoon.

SERENE PANORAMA.

As one leaves or enters Waukosha, one cannot help but be struck by the majesty and dignity of the great aqueous tower which dominates the horizon, a common point of reference for all inhabitants of the happy hamlet, easily visible from most locales, especially from the periphery of the town. Painted with the name of the High School's 1992 State Champion Watersquad, the "Squaws", it is a solemn reminder of the great men and women who established themselves years ago on the lonely plain, and the noble savages they faced, befriended, and slaughtered. Many intoxicated teenagers have fallen to their deaths from the peripheral railing of this great monument, and many have attempted to inscribe their names in its marbly skin, not to mention the countless numbers who have chosen it as a "challenge destination" for trysting, the many discarded liquor bottles and crusted prophylactics clinging to its surface bespeaking the rich chronicle of loves won and lost. Tanking 85 thousand gallons of water to all inhabitants of Waukosha, each citizen should be grateful for the service it provides, bring the fresh elixir of life into every home, and providing a means for whisking away urine and feces at the pull of a lever.

SHARP TRUTH.

One of the finest medical facilities available to inhabitants of the Waukosha area, the Saint Mary Foundation was established in 1893 as the "Saint Mary Mother of God Sanitorium and Foundlings Infirmary or Beneficent Society", renamed "The College of Saint Mary Hospital" in 1928 (shortened to "Saint Mary's Hospital" in 1943 when the University lost accreditation), and finally renamed "Saint Mary: The Care Center" in 1989 when it was purchased by a service organization with "diversified interests in patient wellness". Note the striking angles and interesting spaces created by the unusual assemblage of buildings -- not the result of one architect's vision, but a by-product of necessity as the parent corporation grew. The original building – a neo-classical edifice interlaced with touches of "chinoiserie" and the motifs of ancient Egypt – was razed in 1943, and the newer structure, elements of which are still visible in the left of this image, was installed. Over the years, a modern entryway has been added, the parking lot expanded, and a helipad provided to allow for the removal of critical care patients to more specialized facilities in nearby Grand Loam or the Quad cities, insurance policy providing.

A SYMPHONY OF COLORS.

Probably one of the greatest creations of present times is the modern miracle known as *vinyl siding*. Available in a veritable nature's palette of bold and challenging hues, these brightly-toned sheathings are responsible for some of the most magical landscapes of contemporary life. Old, crumbling buildings are miraculously transformed in an autumn afternoon from cruel reminders of mortality into brightly-pigmented examples of hope and clarity, refreshed and renewed for a vernal generation of citizens to infest. A casement of chromatic complexion armoring rotting wood and weeping plaster, this delicate "second skin" can even conceal out-of-style doors, windows, and frivolous decoration; no need to rebuild or repaint when one can simply slather. Plus, with a texture of top-quality birchwood impressed into the plastic, who's the wiser? One watches as the lovely colors fade to a dusty tincture, and crack and pull away and sag as the structure underneath falls to its knees -- what greater metaphor could there be for our time on Earth than vinyl siding? Here, at the intersection of Dry and Futtock Streets in Waukosha such sublimity is readily apparent – and readily available – contact the realtors for particulars.

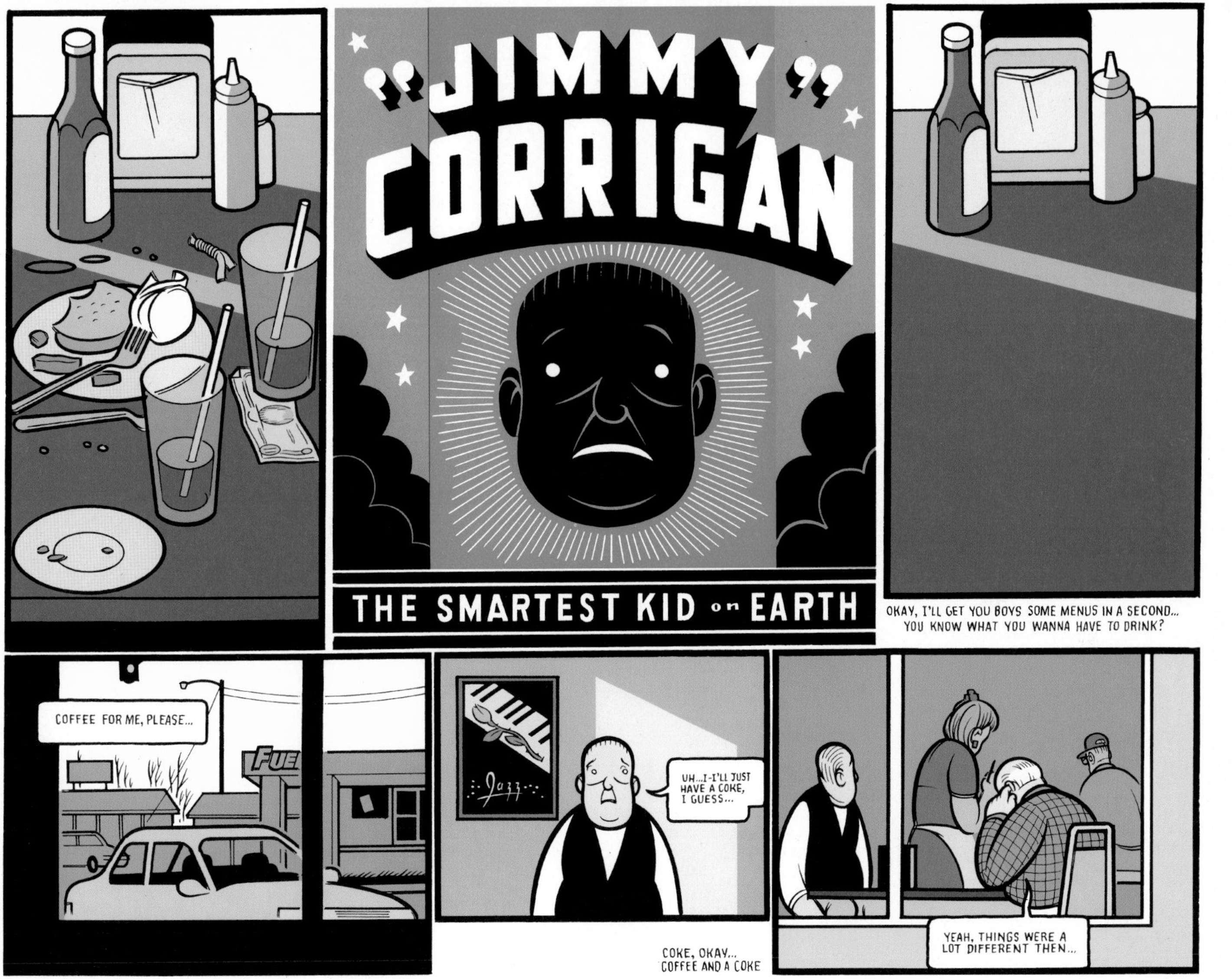
"JIMMY" CORRIGAN
THE SMARTEST KID on EARTH
OKAY, I'LL GET YOU BOYS SOME MENUS IN A SECOND... YOU KNOW WHAT YOU WANNA HAVE TO DRINK?
COFFEE FOR ME, PLEASE...
FUE
Jazz
UH...I-I'LL JUST HAVE A COKE, I GUESS...
COKE, OKAY... COFFEE AND A COKE
YEAH, THINGS WERE A LOT DIFFERENT THEN...

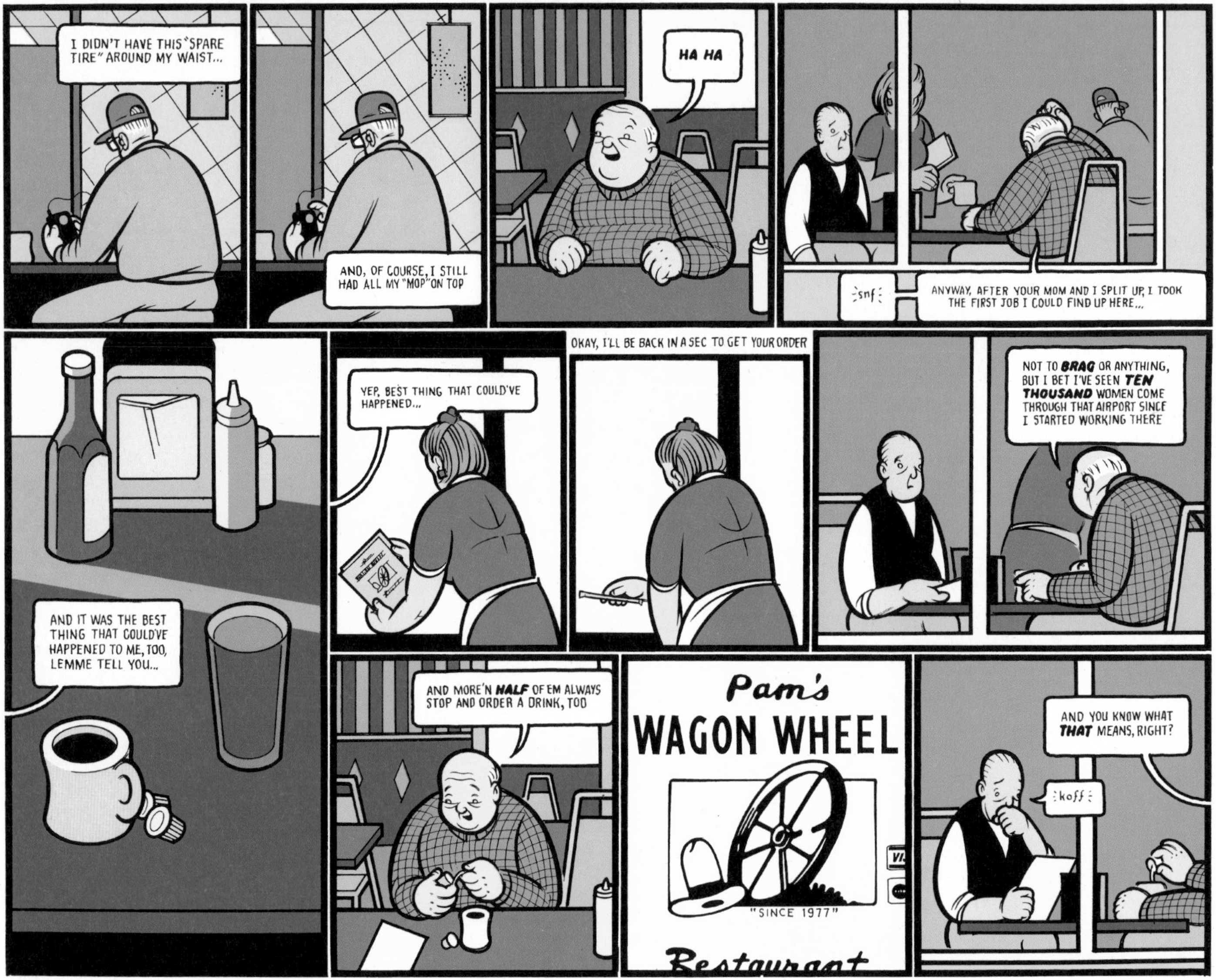

I DIDN'T HAVE THIS "SPARE TIRE" AROUND MY WAIST...
AND, OF COURSE, I STILL HAD ALL MY "MOP" ON TOP
HA HA
snf
ANYWAY, AFTER YOUR MOM AND I SPLIT UP, I TOOK THE FIRST JOB I COULD FIND UP HERE...
AND IT WAS THE BEST THING THAT COULD'VE HAPPENED TO ME, TOO, LEMME TELL YOU...
YEP, BEST THING THAT COULD'VE HAPPENED...
OKAY, I'LL BE BACK IN A SEC TO GET YOUR ORDER
NOT TO BRAG OR ANYTHING, BUT I BET I'VE SEEN TEN THOUSAND WOMEN COME THROUGH THAT AIRPORT SINCE I STARTED WORKING THERE
AND MORE'N HALF OF EM ALWAYS STOP AND ORDER A DRINK, TOO
Pam's
WAGON WHEEL
"SINCE 1977"
Restaurant
AND YOU KNOW WHAT THAT MEANS, RIGHT?
koff

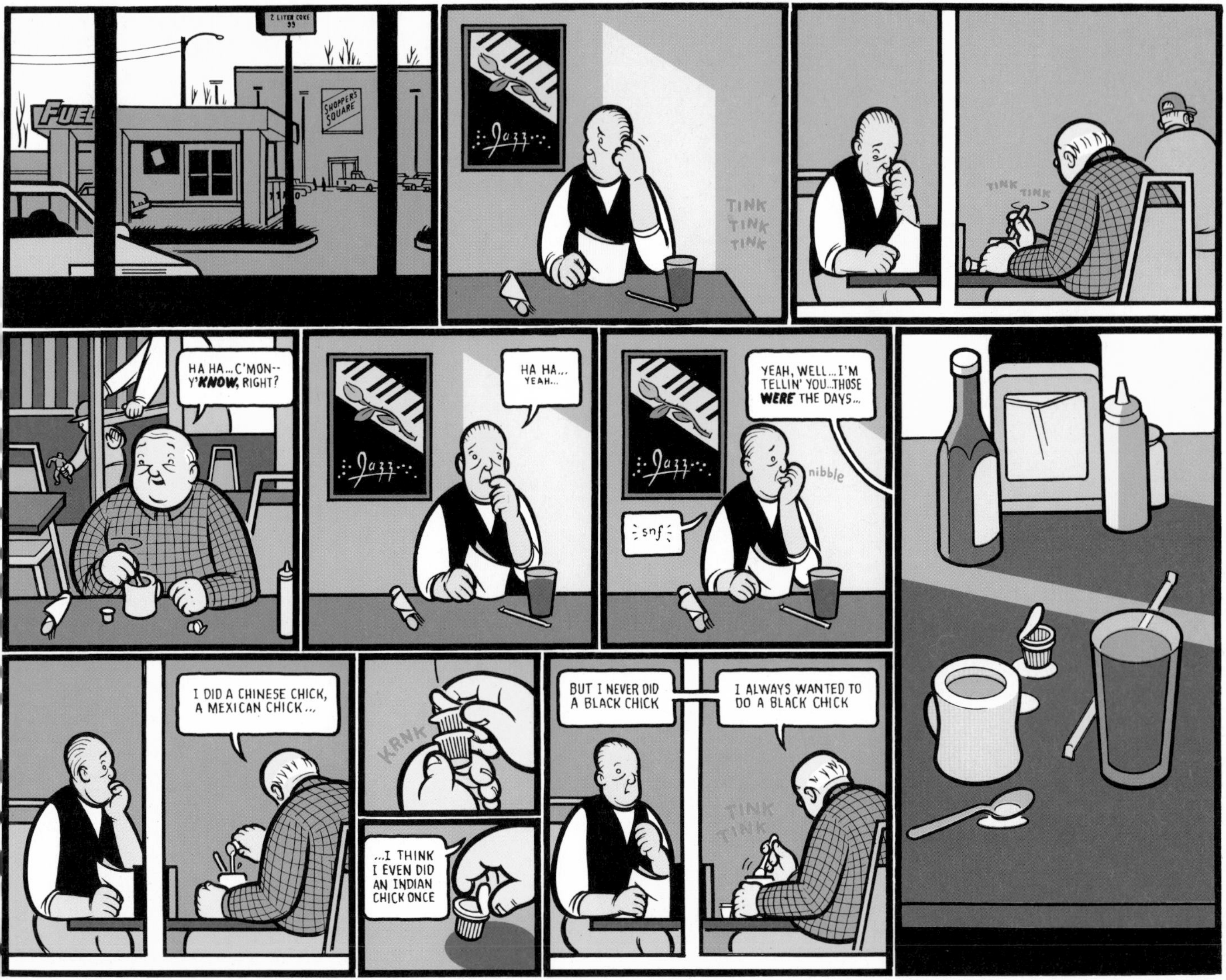
2 LITER COKE 99
FUEL
SHOPPER'S SQUARE
Jazz
TINK TINK TINK
TINK TINK
HA HA... C'MON-- Y'KNOW, RIGHT?
HA HA... YEAH...
YEAH, WELL... I'M TELLIN' YOU...THOSE WERE THE DAYS...
nibble
snf
I DID A CHINESE CHICK, A MEXICAN CHICK...
KRNK
...I THINK I EVEN DID AN INDIAN CHICK ONCE
BUT I NEVER DID A BLACK CHICK
I ALWAYS WANTED TO DO A BLACK CHICK
TINK TINK

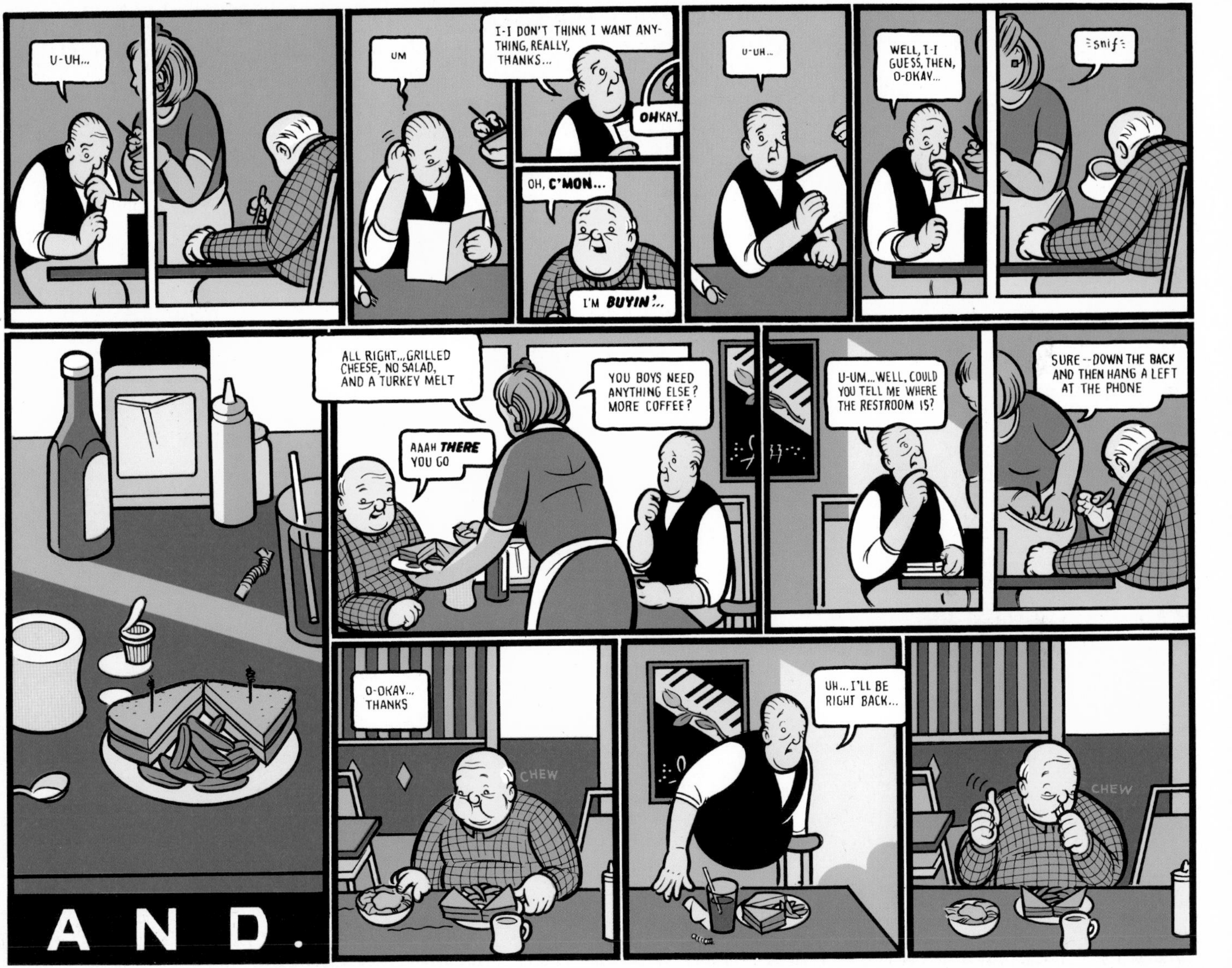
U-UH...
UM
I-I DON'T THINK I WANT ANYTHING, REALLY, THANKS...
OHKAY...
OH, C'MON...
I'M BUYIN'...
U-UH...
WELL, I-I GUESS, THEN, O-OKAY...
snif
ALL RIGHT... GRILLED CHEESE, NO SALAD, AND A TURKEY MELT
AAAH THERE YOU GO
YOU BOYS NEED ANYTHING ELSE? MORE COFFEE?
U-UM... WELL, COULD YOU TELL ME WHERE THE RESTROOM IS?
SURE--DOWN THE BACK AND THEN HANG A LEFT AT THE PHONE
AND.
O-OKAY... THANKS
CHEW
UH... I'LL BE RIGHT BACK...
CHEW

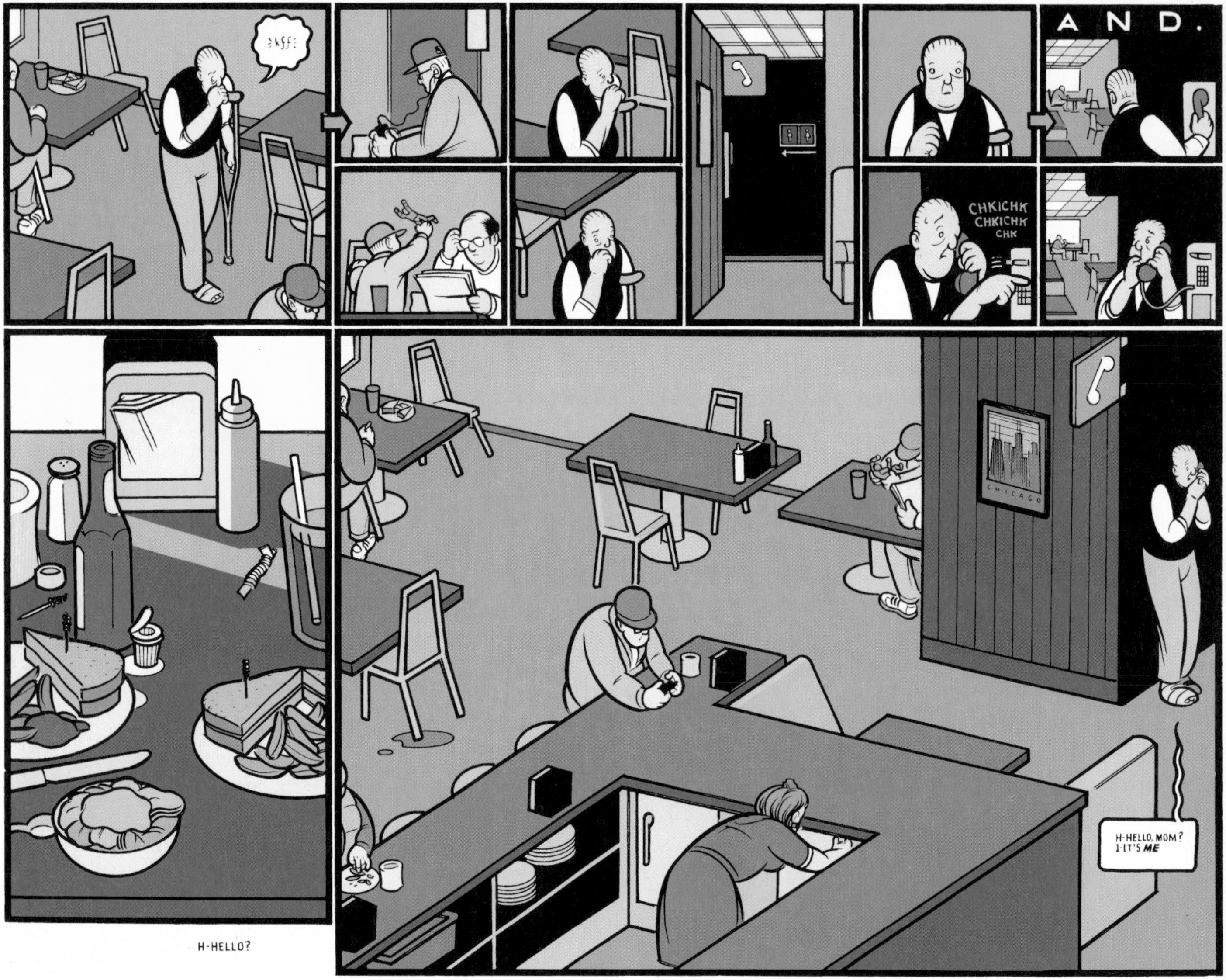
kff
AND.
CHKICHK
CHKICHK
CHK
CHICAGO
H-HELLO?
H-HELLO, MOM? I-IT'S ME

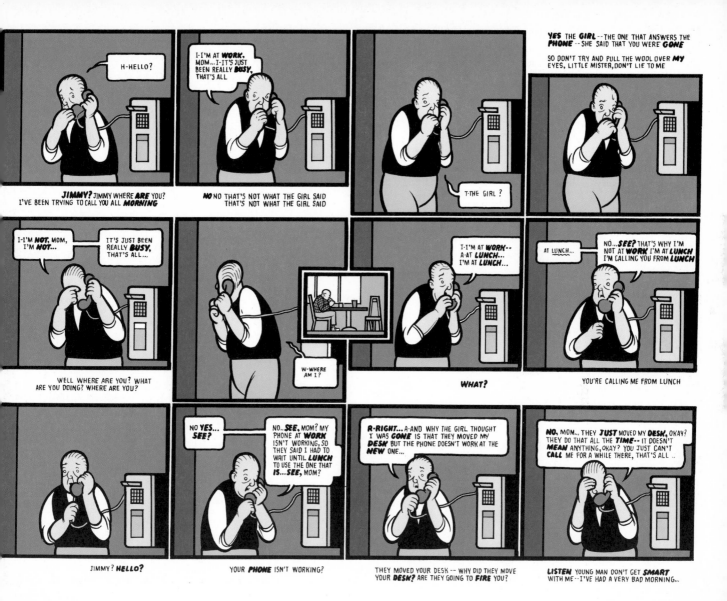

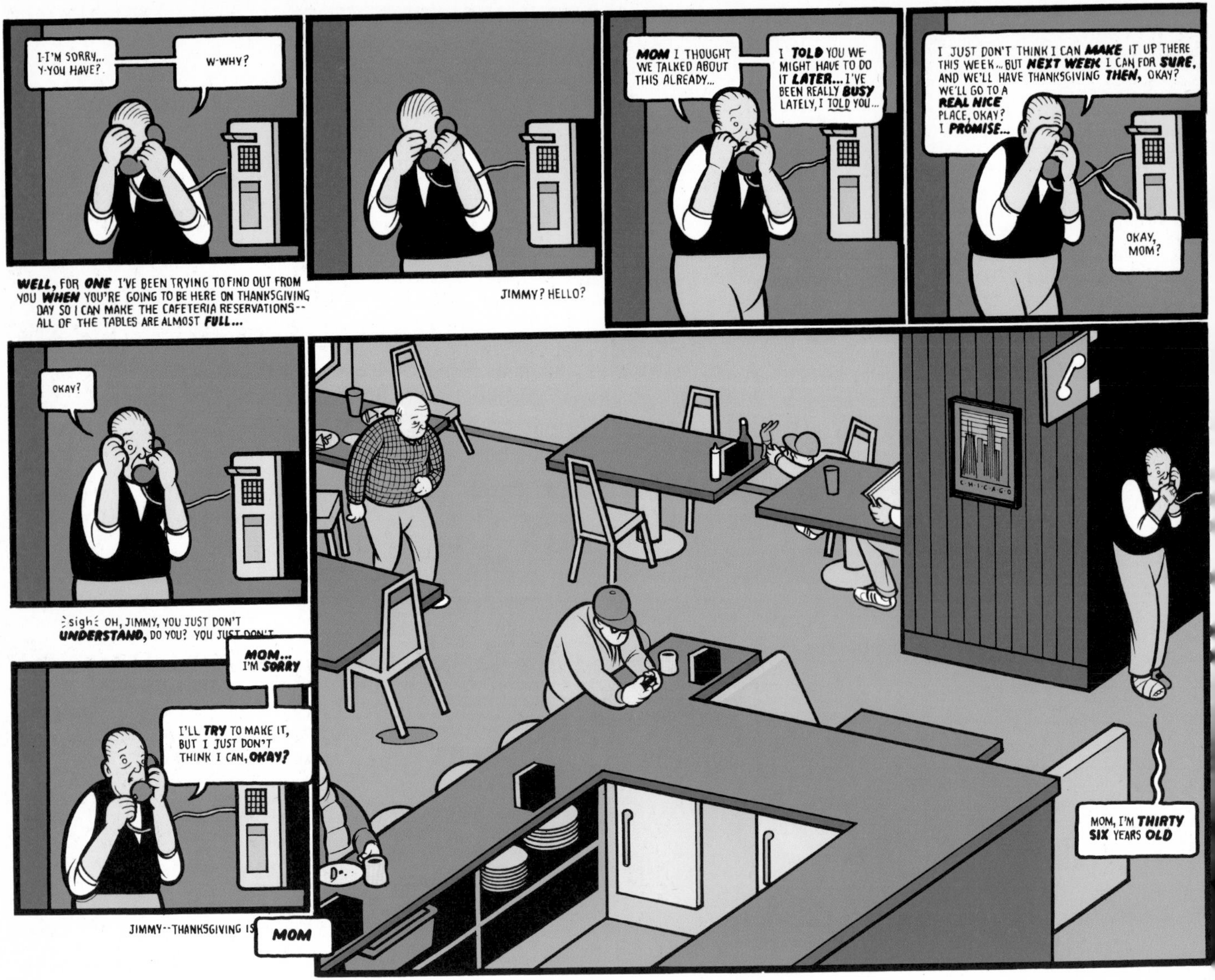

I-I'M SORRY... Y-YOU HAVE?
W-WHY?
WELL, FOR ONE I'VE BEEN TRYING TO FIND OUT FROM YOU WHEN YOU'RE GOING TO BE HERE ON THANKSGIVING DAY SO I CAN MAKE THE CAFETERIA RESERVATIONS -- ALL OF THE TABLES ARE ALMOST FULL...
JIMMY? HELLO?
MOM I THOUGHT WE TALKED ABOUT THIS ALREADY...
I TOLD YOU WE MIGHT HAVE TO DO IT LATER... I'VE BEEN REALLY BUSY LATELY, I TOLD YOU...
I JUST DON'T THINK I CAN MAKE IT UP THERE THIS WEEK... BUT NEXT WEEK I CAN FOR SURE, AND WE'LL HAVE THANKSGIVING THEN, OKAY? WE'LL GO TO A REAL NICE PLACE, OKAY? I PROMISE...
OKAY, MOM?
OKAY?
sigh OH, JIMMY, YOU JUST DON'T UNDERSTAND, DO YOU? YOU JUST DON'T
MOM... I'M SORRY
I'LL TRY TO MAKE IT, BUT I JUST DON'T THINK I CAN, OKAY?
JIMMY--THANKSGIVING IS
MOM
C·H·I·C·A·G·O
MOM, I'M THIRTY SIX YEARS OLD

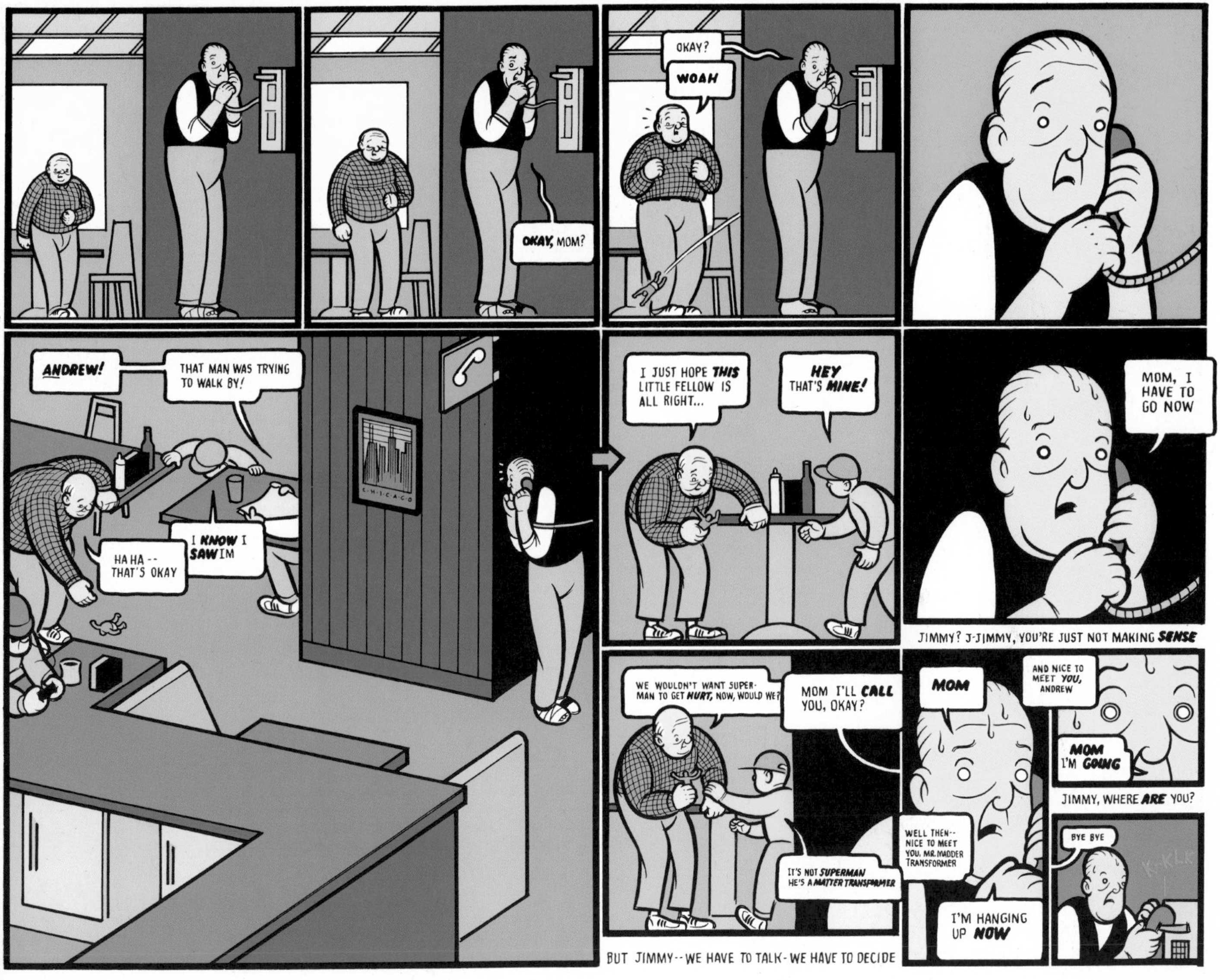
OKAY, MOM?
OKAY?
WOAH
ANDREW!
THAT MAN WAS TRYING TO WALK BY!
I KNOW I SAW IM
HA HA -- THAT'S OKAY
C-H-I-C-A-G-O
I JUST HOPE THIS LITTLE FELLOW IS ALL RIGHT...
HEY THAT'S MINE!
MOM, I HAVE TO GO NOW
JIMMY? J-JIMMY, YOU'RE JUST NOT MAKING SENSE
WE WOULDN'T WANT SUPER-MAN TO GET HURT, NOW, WOULD WE?
MOM I'LL CALL YOU, OKAY?
IT'S NOT SUPERMAN HE'S A MATTER TRANSFORMER
BUT JIMMY-- WE HAVE TO TALK- WE HAVE TO DECIDE
MOM
WELL THEN-- NICE TO MEET YOU, MR. MADDER TRANSFORMER
I'M HANGING UP NOW
AND NICE TO MEET YOU, ANDREW
MOM I'M GOING
JIMMY, WHERE ARE YOU?
BYE BYE
K-KLK

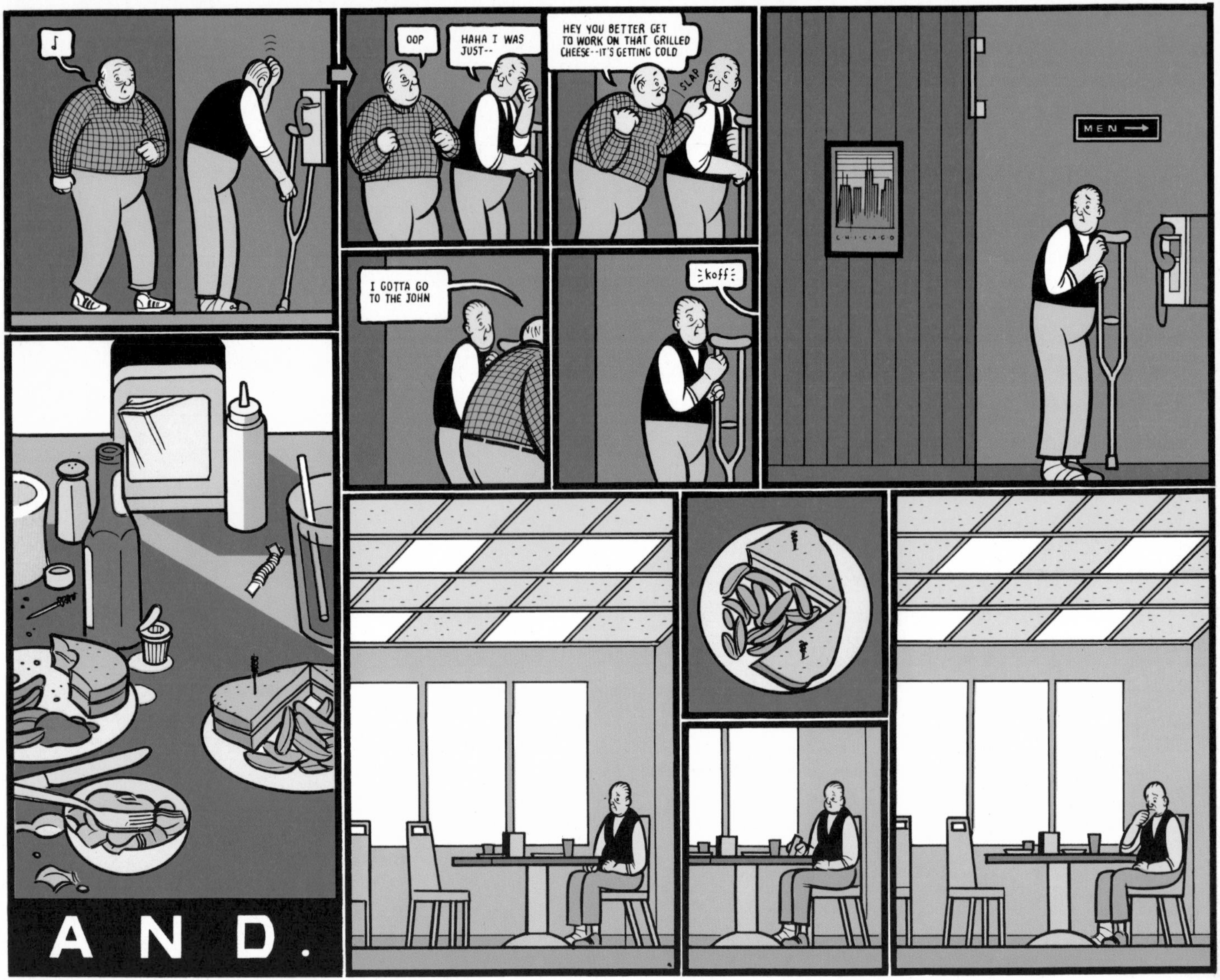

♪
OOP
HAHA I WAS JUST--
HEY YOU BETTER GET TO WORK ON THAT GRILLED CHEESE--IT'S GETTING COLD
SLAP
MEN →
CHICAGO
I GOTTA GO TO THE JOHN
koff
AND.

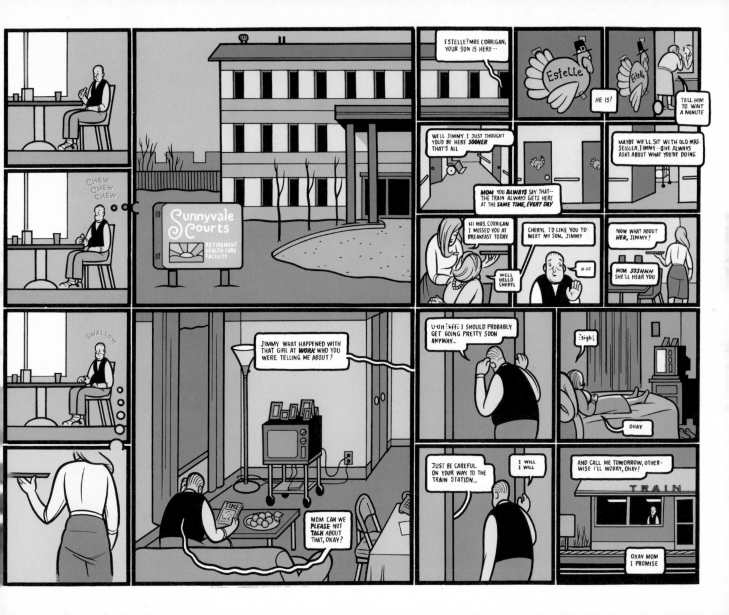

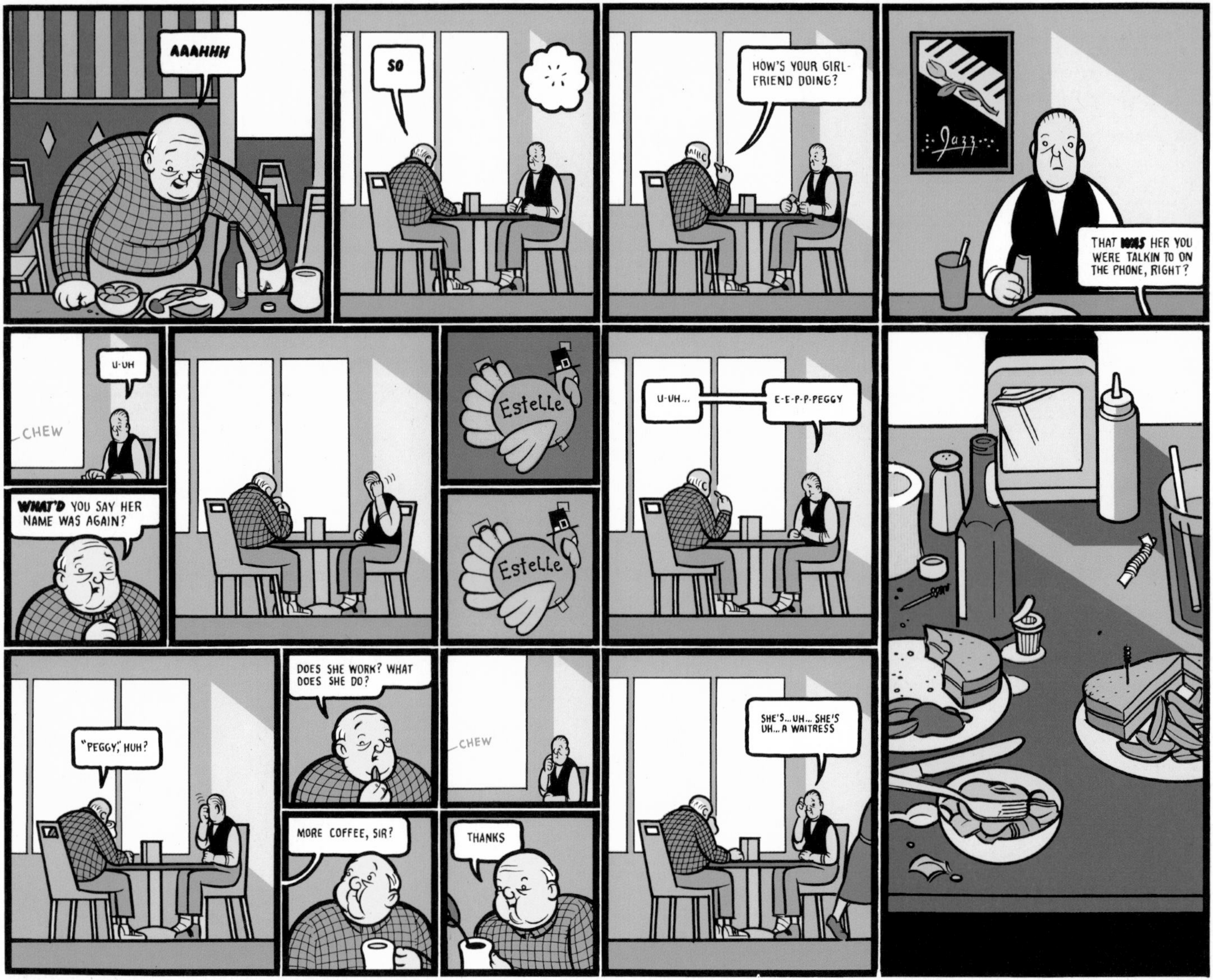
AAAHHH
SO
HOW'S YOUR GIRL-FRIEND DOING?
THAT WAS HER YOU WERE TALKIN TO ON THE PHONE, RIGHT?
U-UH
CHEW
WHAT'D YOU SAY HER NAME WAS AGAIN?
Estelle
Estelle
U-UH...
E-E-P-P-PEGGY
"PEGGY," HUH?
DOES SHE WORK? WHAT DOES SHE DO?
CHEW
MORE COFFEE, SIR?
THANKS
SHE'S...UH... SHE'S UH... A WAITRESS
Jazz

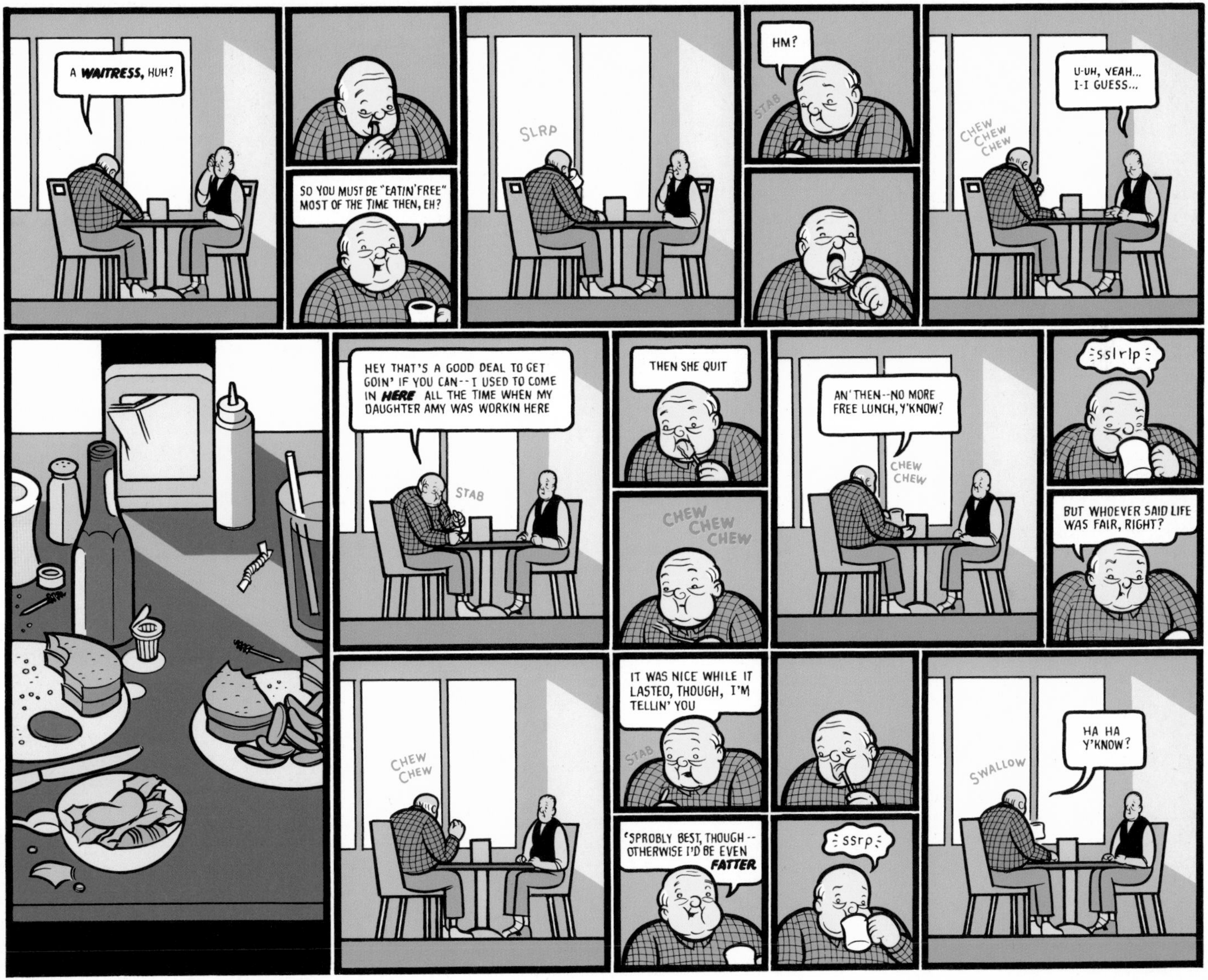
A WAITRESS, HUH?
SO YOU MUST BE "EATIN' FREE" MOST OF THE TIME THEN, EH?
SLRP
HM?
STAB
CHEW CHEW CHEW
U-UH, YEAH... I-I GUESS...
HEY THAT'S A GOOD DEAL TO GET GOIN' IF YOU CAN--I USED TO COME IN HERE ALL THE TIME WHEN MY DAUGHTER AMY WAS WORKIN HERE
STAB
THEN SHE QUIT
CHEW CHEW CHEW
AN' THEN--NO MORE FREE LUNCH, Y'KNOW?
CHEW CHEW
sslrlp
BUT WHOEVER SAID LIFE WAS FAIR, RIGHT?
CHEW CHEW
IT WAS NICE WHILE IT LASTED, THOUGH, I'M TELLIN' YOU
STAB
'SPROBLY BEST, THOUGH--OTHERWISE I'D BE EVEN FATTER
ssrp
SWALLOW
HA HA Y'KNOW?

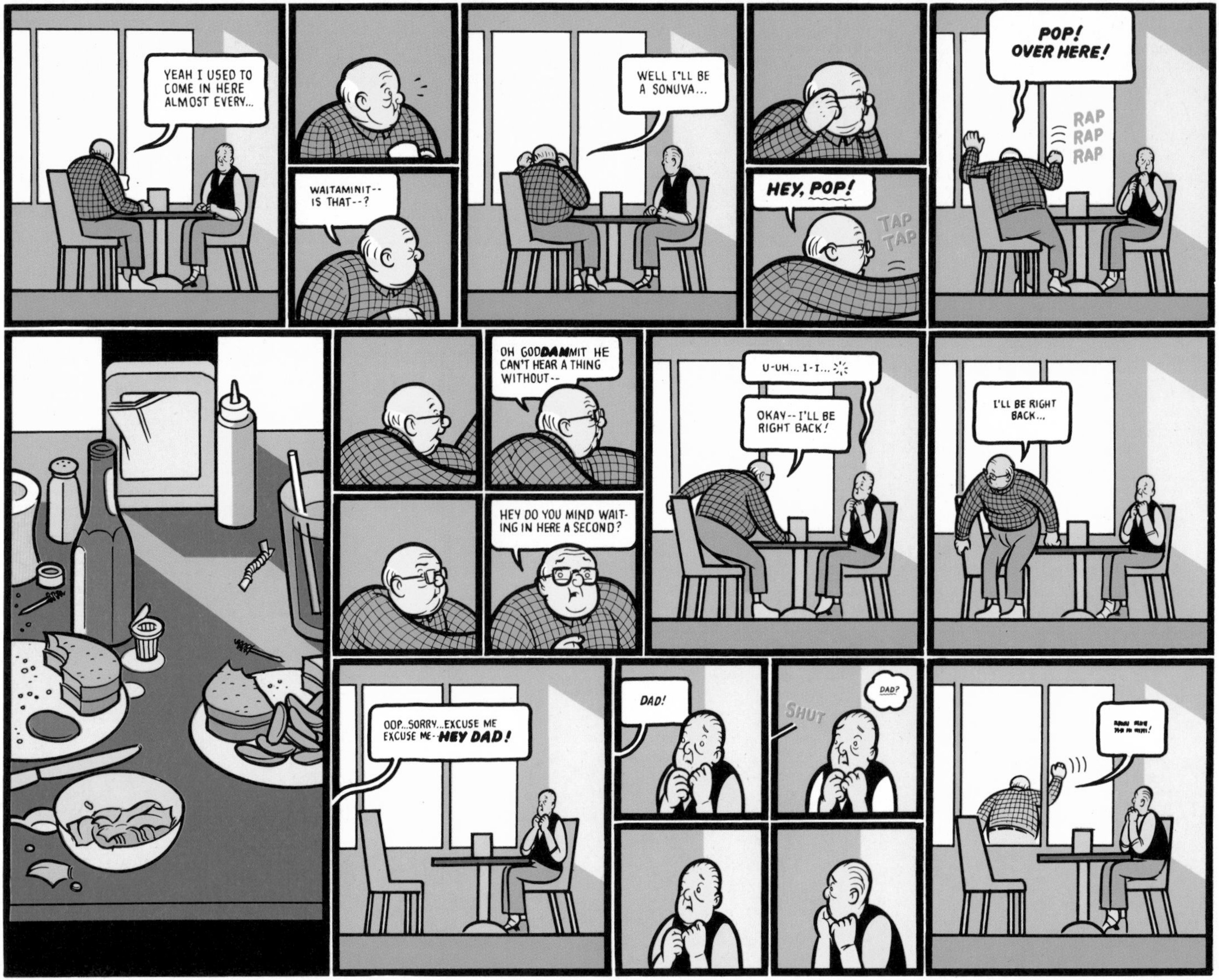
YEAH I USED TO COME IN HERE ALMOST EVERY...
WAITAMINIT-- IS THAT--?
WELL I'LL BE A SONUVA...
HEY, POP!
TAP TAP
POP! OVER HERE!
RAP RAP RAP
OH GODDAMMIT HE CAN'T HEAR A THING WITHOUT--
HEY DO YOU MIND WAITING IN HERE A SECOND?
U-UH... I-I...
OKAY--I'LL BE RIGHT BACK!
I'LL BE RIGHT BACK...
OOP...SORRY...EXCUSE ME EXCUSE ME--HEY DAD!
DAD!
SHUT
DAD?

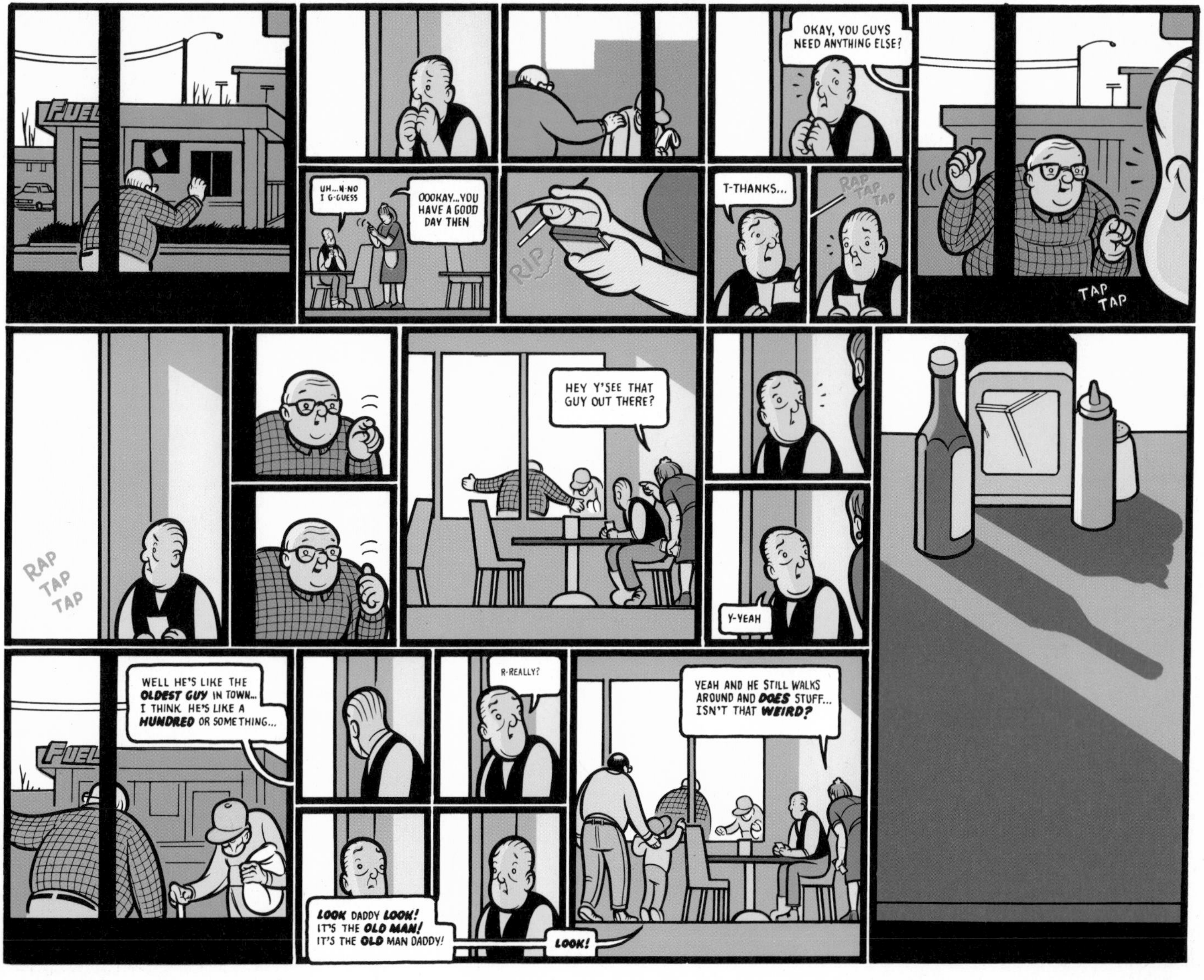
UH...N-NO I G-GUESS
OOOKAY...YOU HAVE A GOOD DAY THEN
RIP
OKAY, YOU GUYS NEED ANYTHING ELSE?
T-THANKS...
RAP TAP TAP
TAP TAP
RAP TAP TAP
HEY Y'SEE THAT GUY OUT THERE?
Y-YEAH
WELL HE'S LIKE THE OLDEST GUY IN TOWN... I THINK HE'S LIKE A HUNDRED OR SOMETHING...
R-REALLY?
YEAH AND HE STILL WALKS AROUND AND DOES STUFF... ISN'T THAT WEIRD?
LOOK DADDY LOOK! IT'S THE OLD MAN! IT'S THE OLD MAN DADDY!
LOOK!

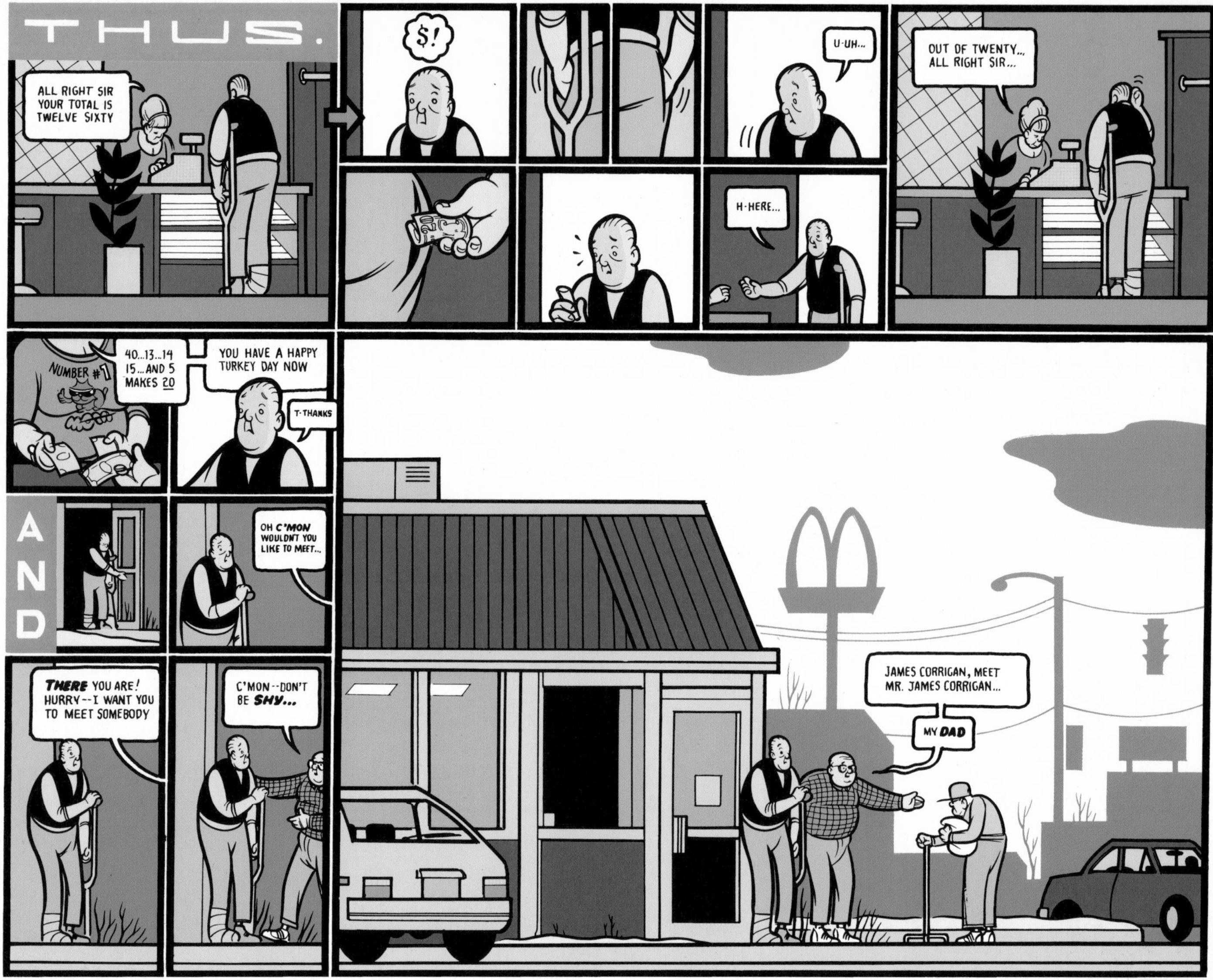
THUS.
ALL RIGHT SIR YOUR TOTAL IS TWELVE SIXTY
$!
U-UH...
OUT OF TWENTY... ALL RIGHT SIR...
H-HERE...
NUMBER #1
40...13...14 15...AND 5 MAKES 20
YOU HAVE A HAPPY TURKEY DAY NOW
T-THANKS
AND
OH C'MON WOULDN'T YOU LIKE TO MEET...
THERE YOU ARE! HURRY--I WANT YOU TO MEET SOMEBODY
C'MON--DON'T BE SHY...
JAMES CORRIGAN, MEET MR. JAMES CORRIGAN...
MY DAD

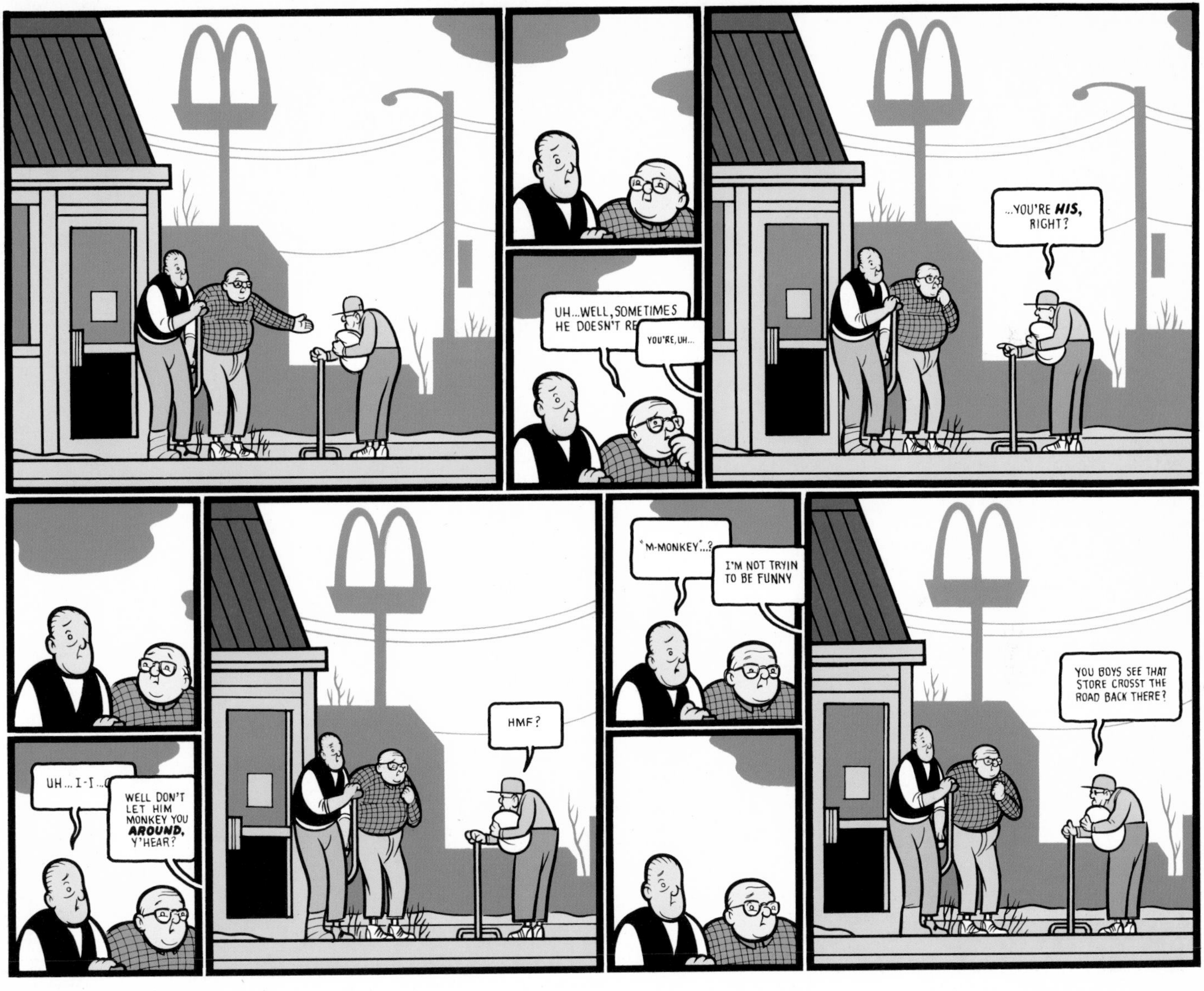
UH...WELL, SOMETIMES HE DOESN'T RE
YOU'RE, UH...
...YOU'RE **HIS,** RIGHT?
UH... I-I...
WELL DON'T LET HIM MONKEY YOU **AROUND,** Y'HEAR?
HMF?
"M-MONKEY"...?
I'M NOT TRYIN TO BE FUNNY
YOU BOYS SEE THAT STORE CROSST THE ROAD BACK THERE?

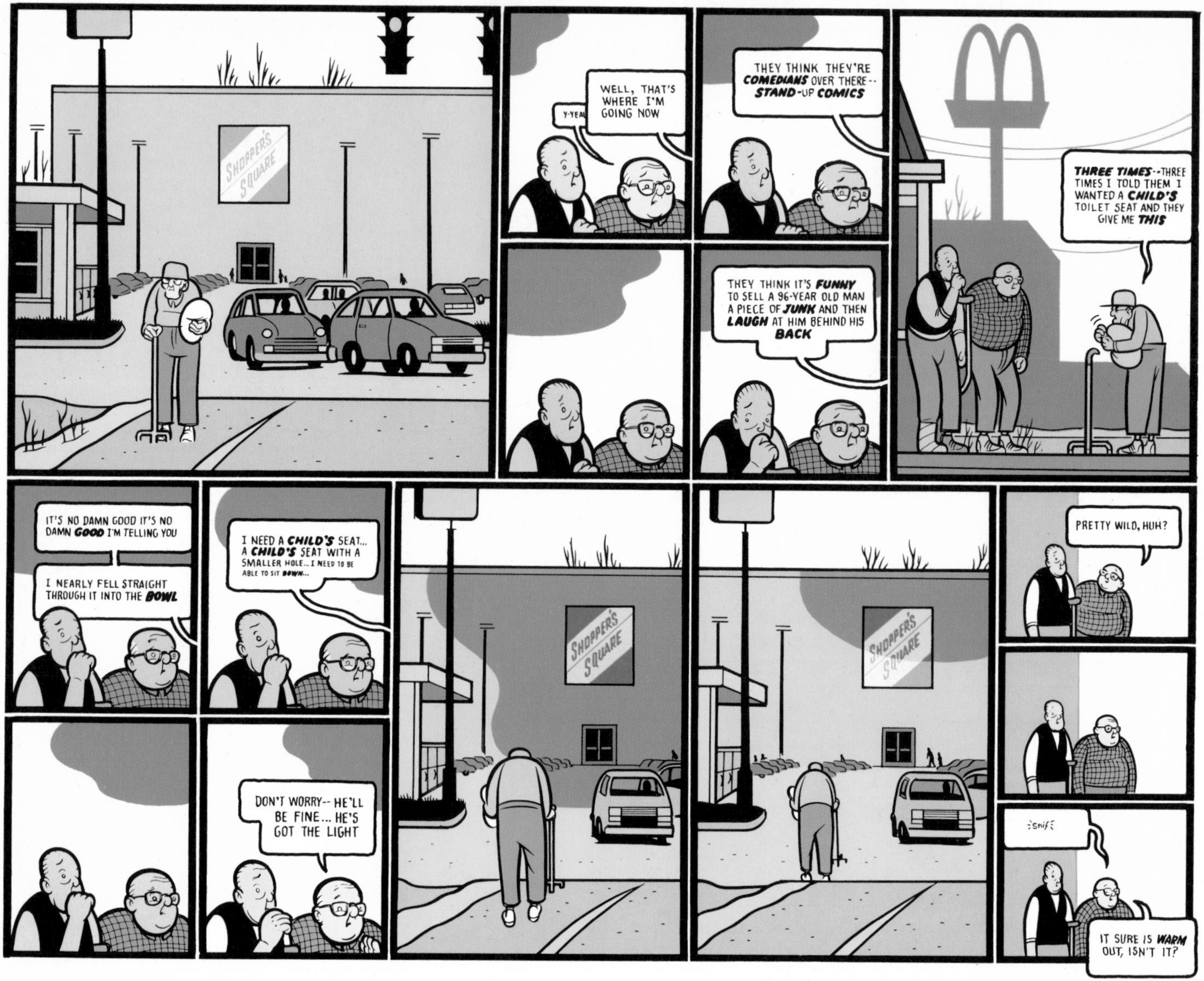

Y-YEAH
WELL, THAT'S WHERE I'M GOING NOW
THEY THINK THEY'RE COMEDIANS OVER THERE -- STAND-UP COMICS
THEY THINK IT'S FUNNY TO SELL A 96-YEAR OLD MAN A PIECE OF JUNK AND THEN LAUGH AT HIM BEHIND HIS BACK
THREE TIMES -- THREE TIMES I TOLD THEM I WANTED A CHILD'S TOILET SEAT AND THEY GIVE ME THIS
IT'S NO DAMN GOOD IT'S NO DAMN GOOD I'M TELLING YOU
I NEARLY FELL STRAIGHT THROUGH IT INTO THE BOWL
I NEED A CHILD'S SEAT... A CHILD'S SEAT WITH A SMALLER HOLE... I NEED TO BE ABLE TO SIT DOWN...
DON'T WORRY-- HE'LL BE FINE... HE'S GOT THE LIGHT
PRETTY WILD, HUH?
snif
IT SURE IS WARM OUT, ISN'T IT?

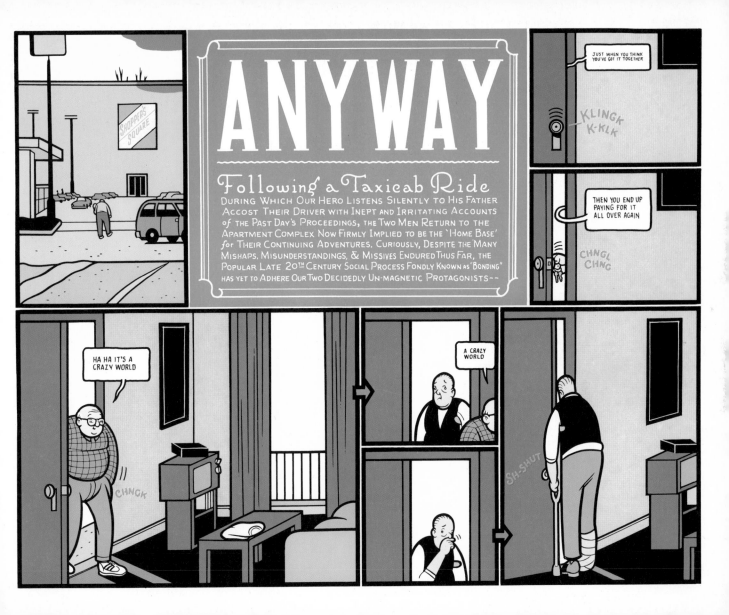

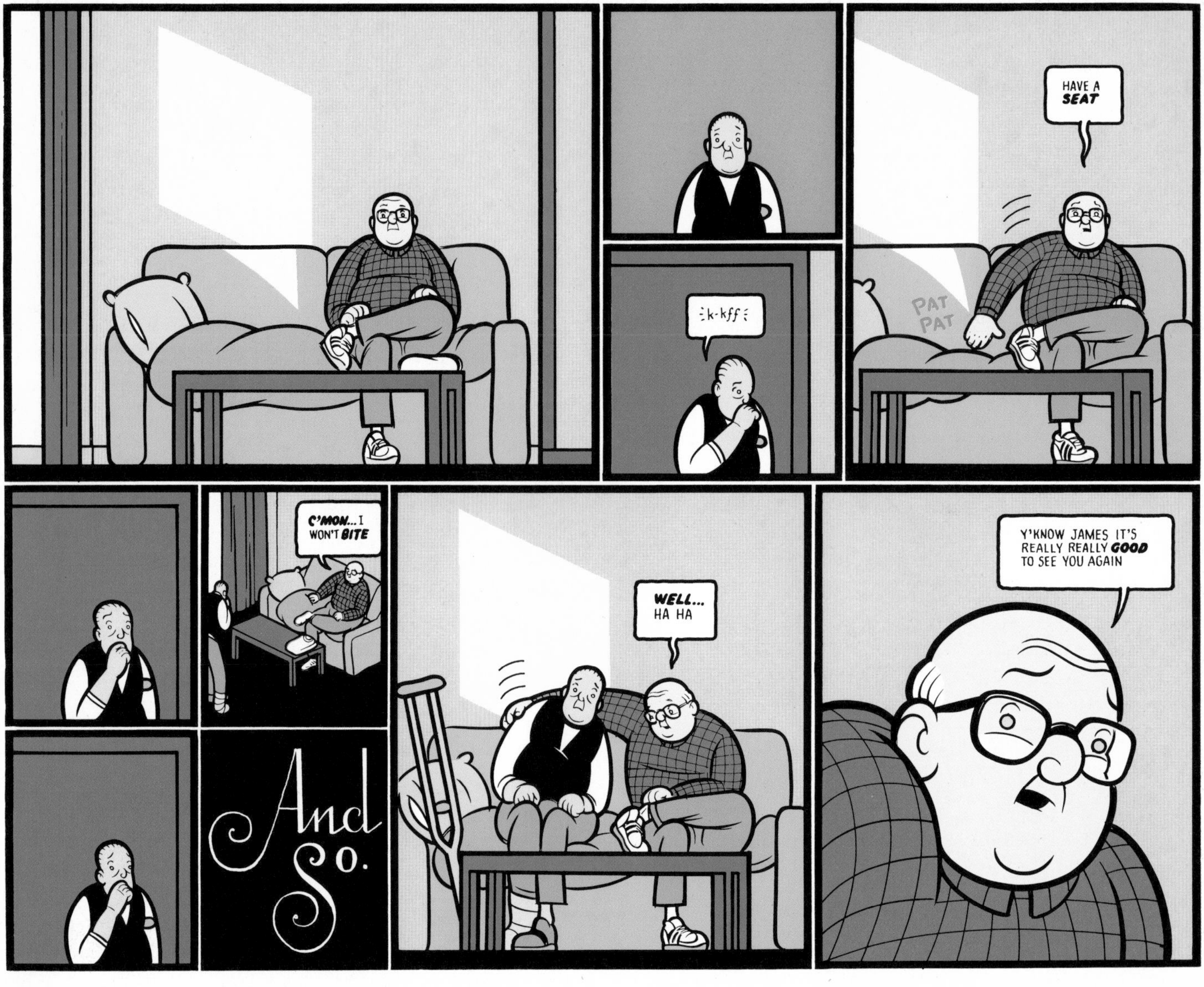

k-kff
HAVE A SEAT
PAT PAT
C'MON... I WON'T BITE
And So.
WELL... HA HA
Y'KNOW JAMES IT'S REALLY REALLY GOOD TO SEE YOU AGAIN

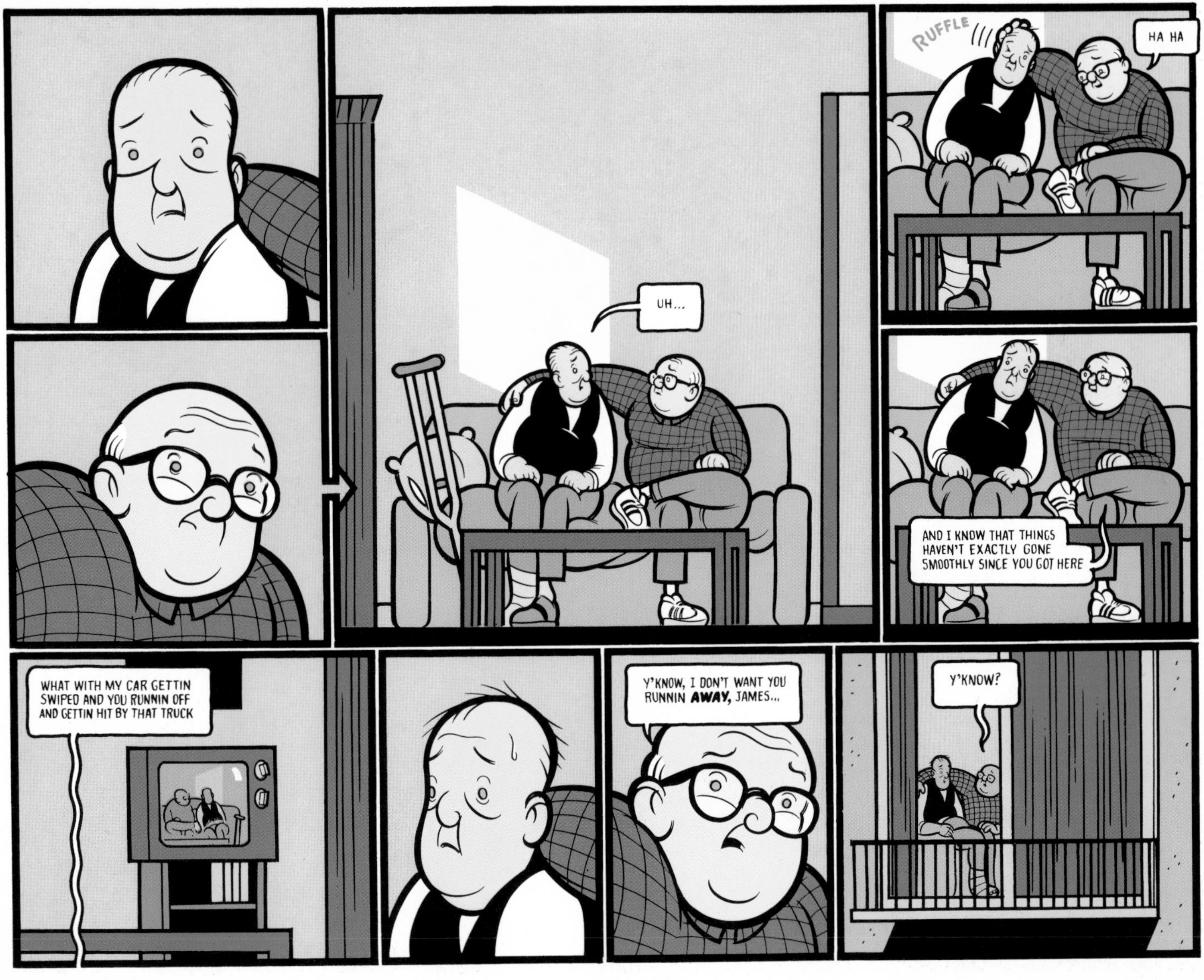
UH...
RUFFLE
HA HA
AND I KNOW THAT THINGS HAVEN'T EXACTLY GONE SMOOTHLY SINCE YOU GOT HERE
WHAT WITH MY CAR GETTIN SWIPED AND YOU RUNNIN OFF AND GETTIN HIT BY THAT TRUCK
Y'KNOW, I DON'T WANT YOU RUNNIN **AWAY,** JAMES...
Y'KNOW?

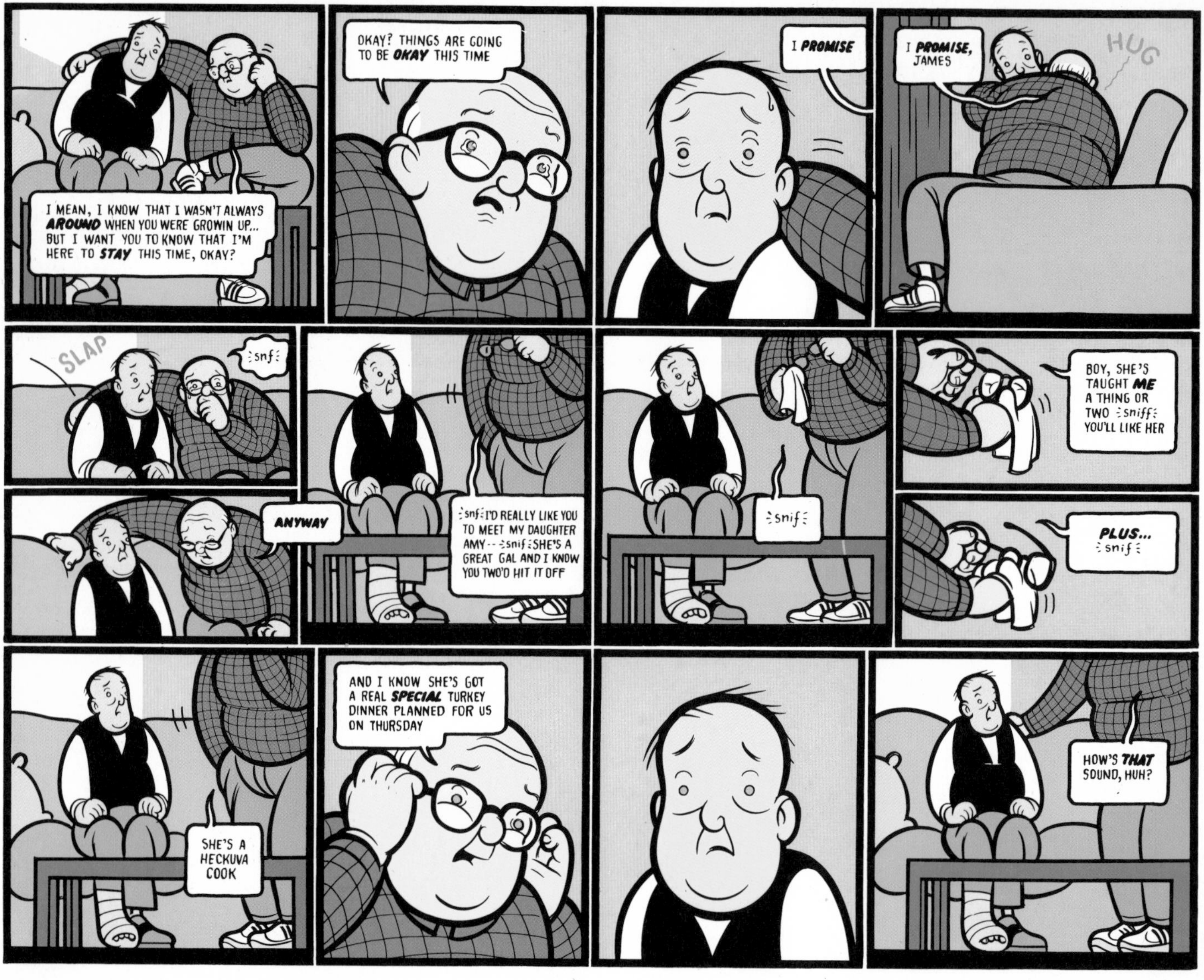
I MEAN, I KNOW THAT I WASN'T ALWAYS AROUND WHEN YOU WERE GROWIN UP... BUT I WANT YOU TO KNOW THAT I'M HERE TO STAY THIS TIME, OKAY?
OKAY? THINGS ARE GOING TO BE OKAY THIS TIME
I PROMISE
I PROMISE, JAMES
HUG
SLAP
snf
ANYWAY
snf I'D REALLY LIKE YOU TO MEET MY DAUGHTER AMY -- snif SHE'S A GREAT GAL AND I KNOW YOU TWO'D HIT IT OFF
snif
BOY, SHE'S TAUGHT ME A THING OR TWO sniff YOU'LL LIKE HER
PLUS... snif
SHE'S A HECKUVA COOK
AND I KNOW SHE'S GOT A REAL SPECIAL TURKEY DINNER PLANNED FOR US ON THURSDAY
HOW'S THAT SOUND, HUH?

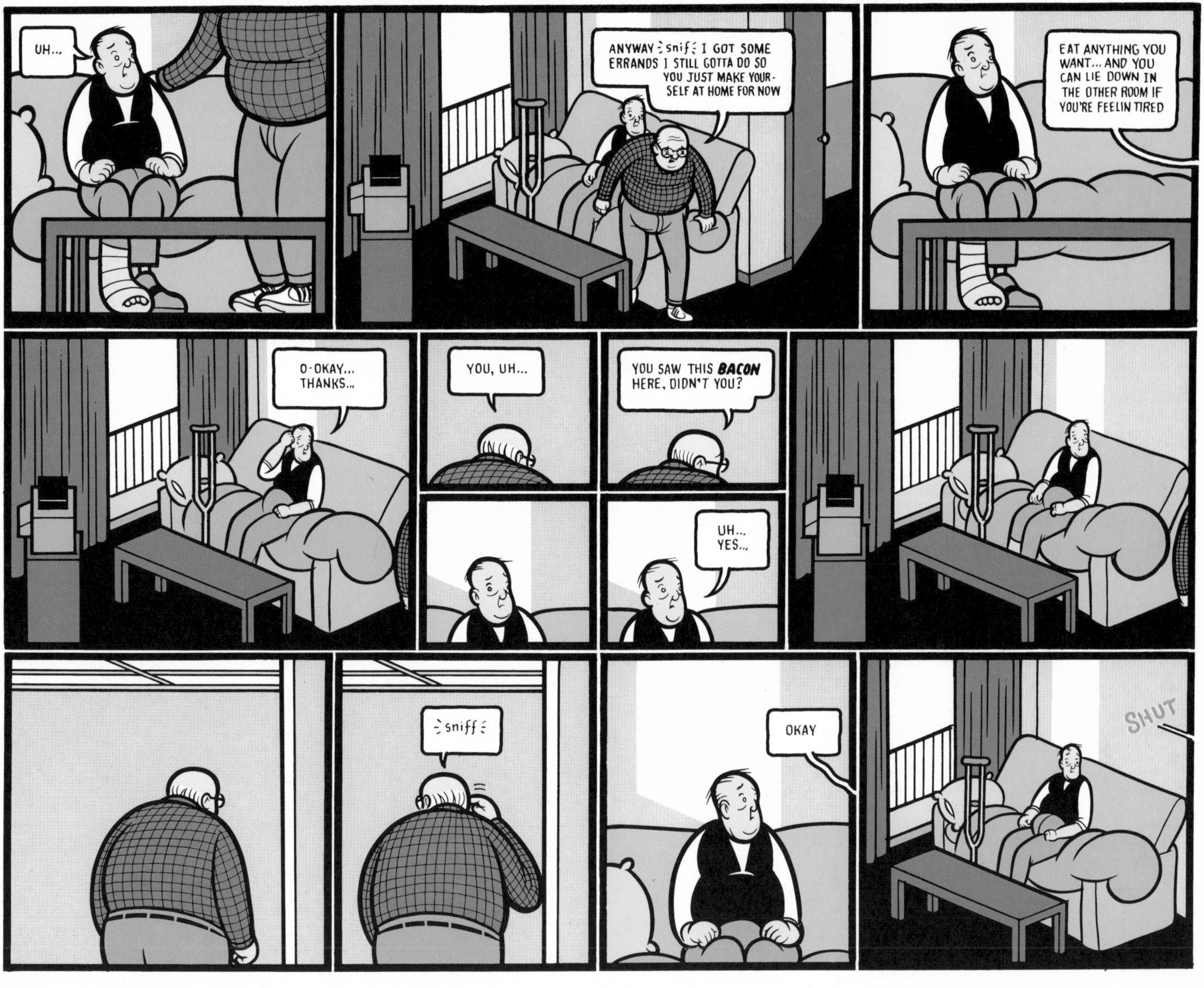
UH...
ANYWAY snif I GOT SOME ERRANDS I STILL GOTTA DO SO YOU JUST MAKE YOURSELF AT HOME FOR NOW
EAT ANYTHING YOU WANT... AND YOU CAN LIE DOWN IN THE OTHER ROOM IF YOU'RE FEELIN TIRED
O-OKAY... THANKS...
YOU, UH...
YOU SAW THIS BACON HERE, DIDN'T YOU?
UH... YES...
sniff
OKAY
SHUT

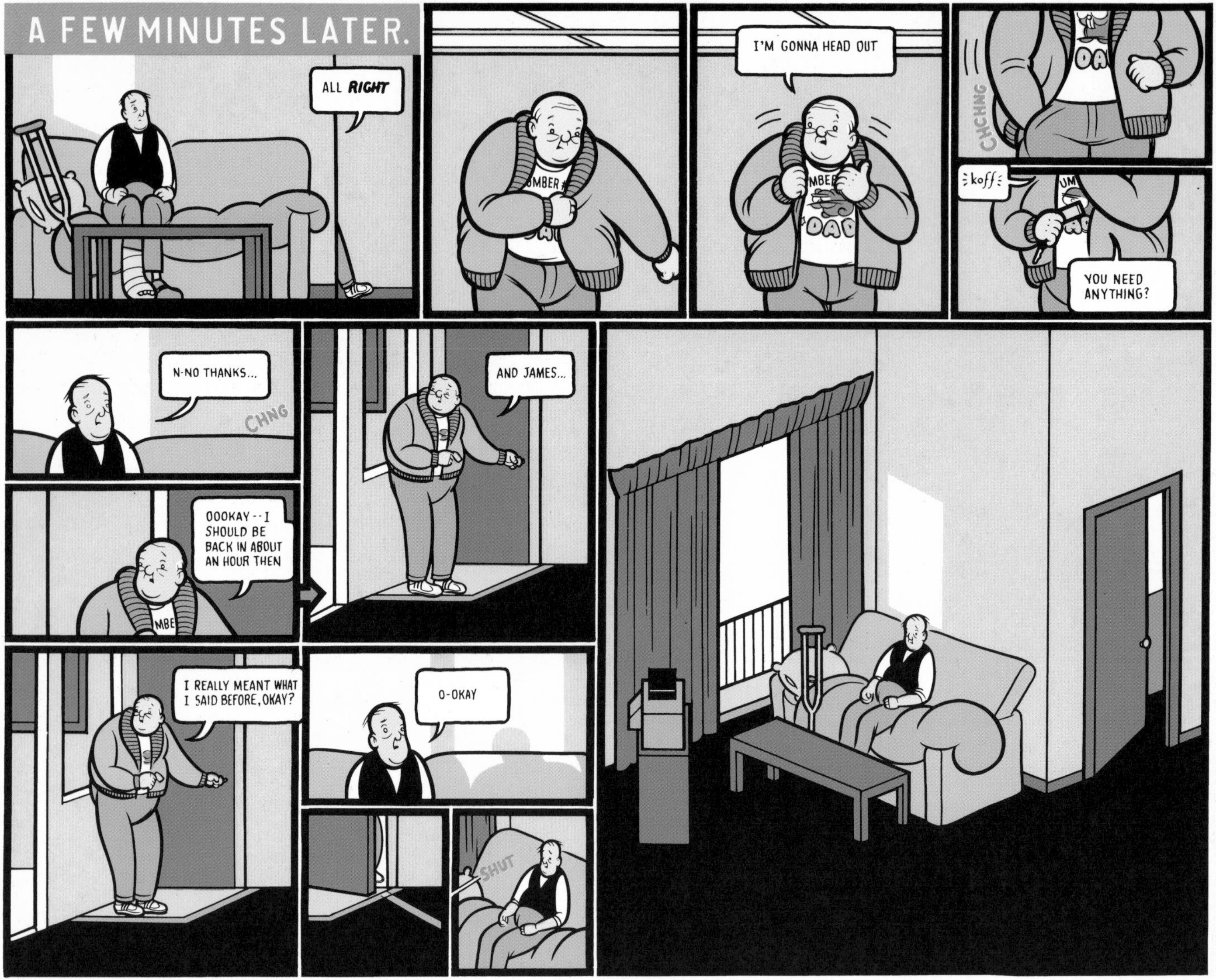

A FEW MINUTES LATER.
ALL RIGHT
I'M GONNA HEAD OUT
CHCHNG
koff
YOU NEED ANYTHING?
N-NO THANKS...
CHNG
OOOKAY--I SHOULD BE BACK IN ABOUT AN HOUR THEN
AND JAMES...
I REALLY MEANT WHAT I SAID BEFORE, OKAY?
O-OKAY
SHUT

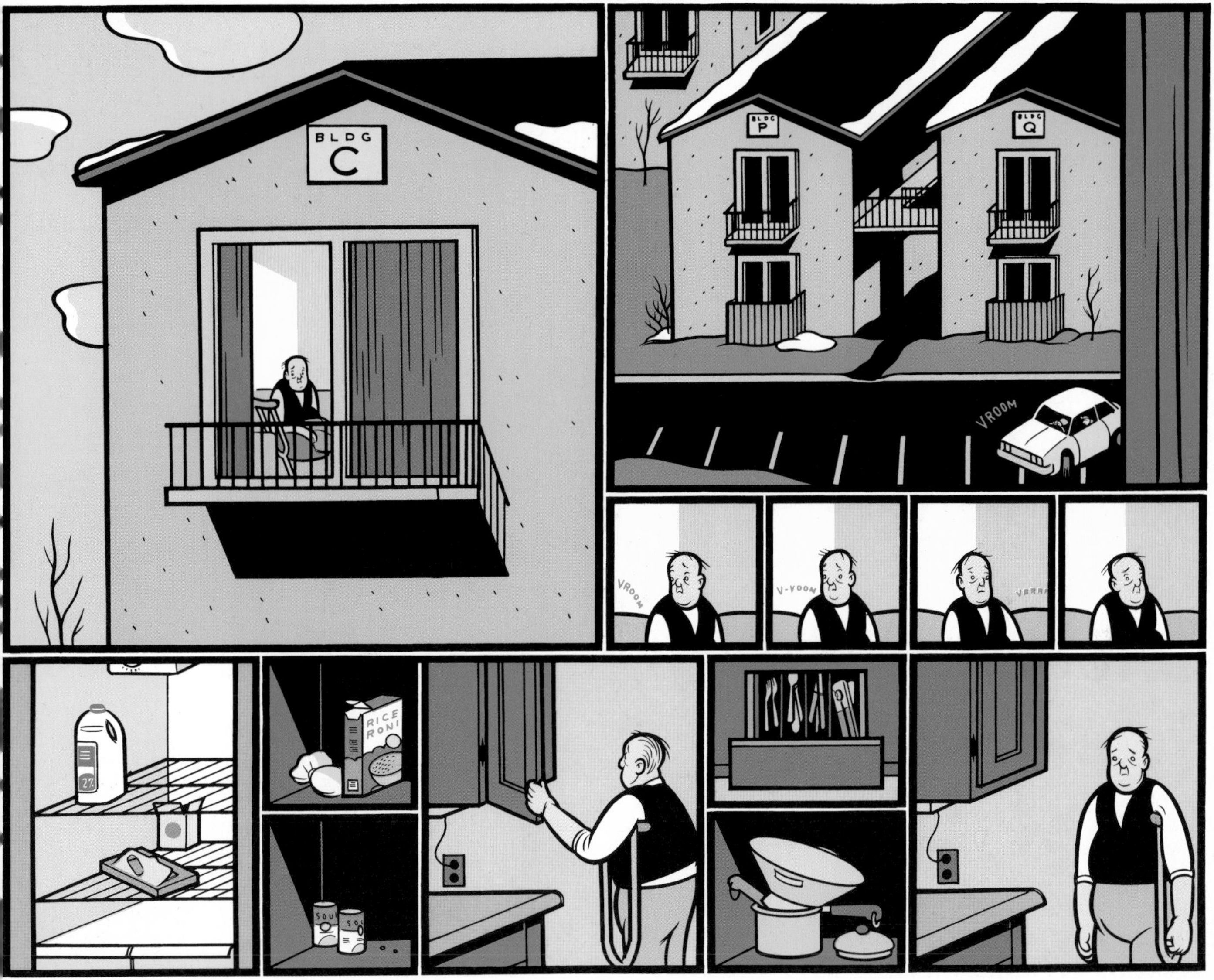
BLDG C
BLDG P
BLDG Q
VROOM
VROOM
V-VOOM
RICE RONI

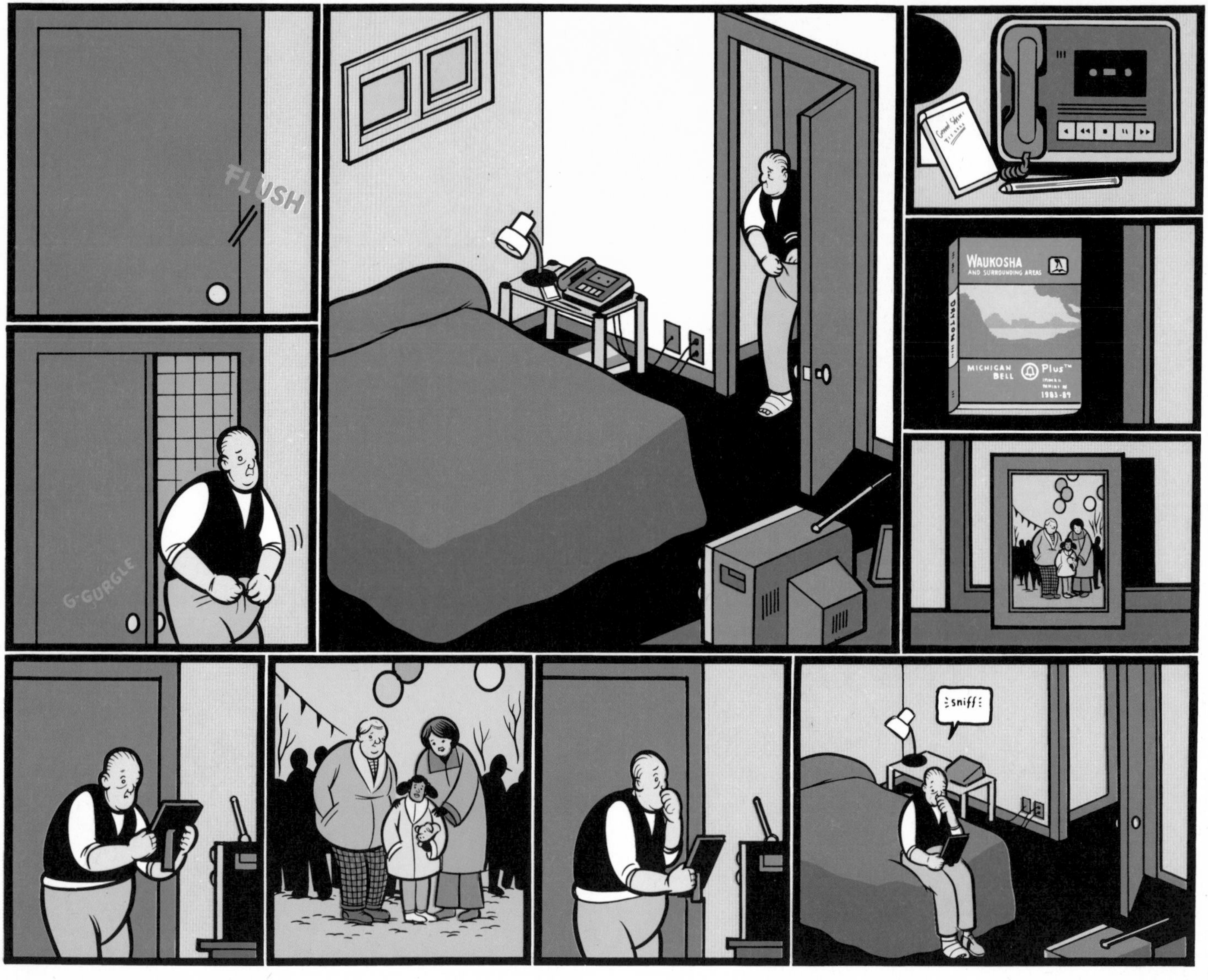
FLUSH
G-GURGLE
WAUKOSHA
AND SURROUNDING AREAS
DAYTON
MICHIGAN BELL
Plus™
1983-84
sniff

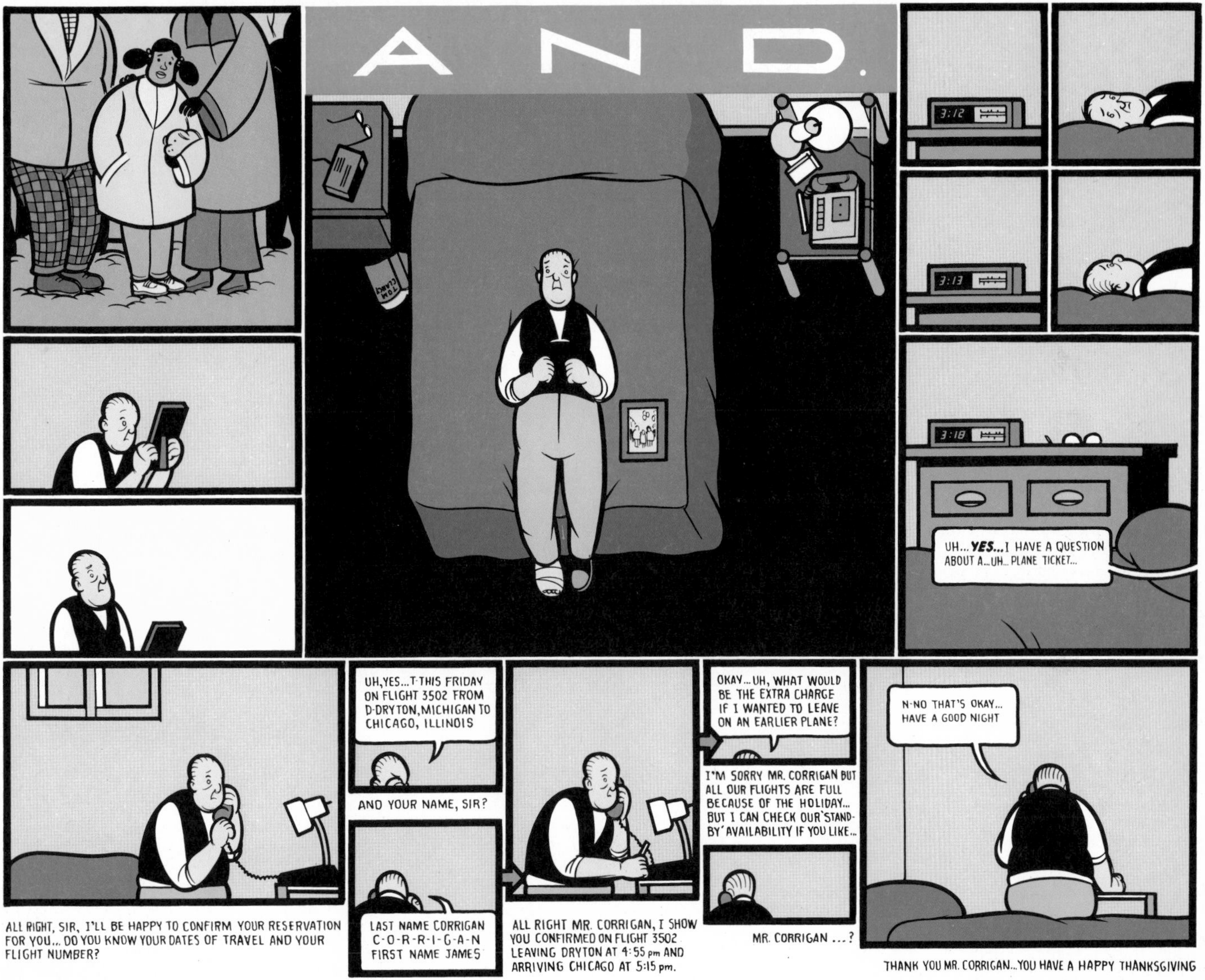
AND.
TOM CLANCY
3:12
3:13
3:18
UH... YES... I HAVE A QUESTION ABOUT A...UH... PLANE TICKET...
ALL RIGHT, SIR, I'LL BE HAPPY TO CONFIRM YOUR RESERVATION FOR YOU... DO YOU KNOW YOUR DATES OF TRAVEL AND YOUR FLIGHT NUMBER?
UH, YES... T-THIS FRIDAY ON FLIGHT 3502 FROM D-DRYTON, MICHIGAN TO CHICAGO, ILLINOIS
AND YOUR NAME, SIR?
LAST NAME CORRIGAN C-O-R-R-I-G-A-N FIRST NAME JAMES
ALL RIGHT MR. CORRIGAN, I SHOW YOU CONFIRMED ON FLIGHT 3502 LEAVING DRYTON AT 4:55 pm AND ARRIVING CHICAGO AT 5:15 pm.
OKAY... UH, WHAT WOULD BE THE EXTRA CHARGE IF I WANTED TO LEAVE ON AN EARLIER PLANE?
I'M SORRY MR. CORRIGAN BUT ALL OUR FLIGHTS ARE FULL BECAUSE OF THE HOLIDAY... BUT I CAN CHECK OUR 'STAND-BY' AVAILABILITY IF YOU LIKE...
MR. CORRIGAN ...?
N-NO THAT'S OKAY... HAVE A GOOD NIGHT
THANK YOU MR. CORRIGAN... YOU HAVE A HAPPY THANKSGIVING

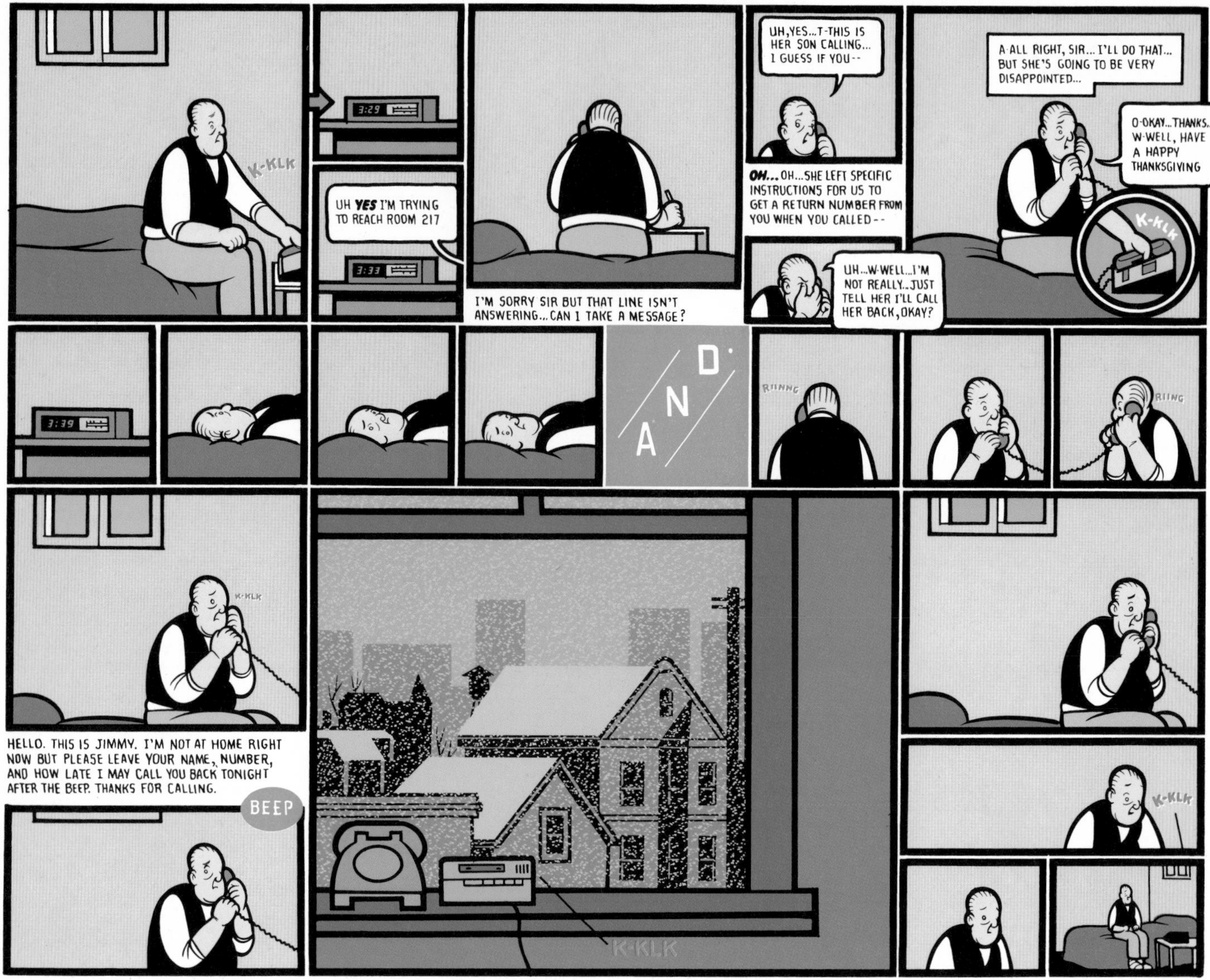
K-KLK
3:29
UH YES I'M TRYING TO REACH ROOM 217
3:33
I'M SORRY SIR BUT THAT LINE ISN'T ANSWERING... CAN I TAKE A MESSAGE?
UH, YES... T-THIS IS HER SON CALLING... I GUESS IF YOU--
OH... OH... SHE LEFT SPECIFIC INSTRUCTIONS FOR US TO GET A RETURN NUMBER FROM YOU WHEN YOU CALLED--
UH... W-WELL... I'M NOT REALLY... JUST TELL HER I'LL CALL HER BACK, OKAY?
A-ALL RIGHT, SIR... I'LL DO THAT... BUT SHE'S GOING TO BE VERY DISAPPOINTED...
O-OKAY... THANKS... W-WELL, HAVE A HAPPY THANKSGIVING
K-KLK
3:39
AND
RIINNG
RIING
K-KLK
HELLO. THIS IS JIMMY. I'M NOT AT HOME RIGHT NOW BUT PLEASE LEAVE YOUR NAME, NUMBER, AND HOW LATE I MAY CALL YOU BACK TONIGHT AFTER THE BEEP. THANKS FOR CALLING.
BEEP
K-KLK
K-KLK

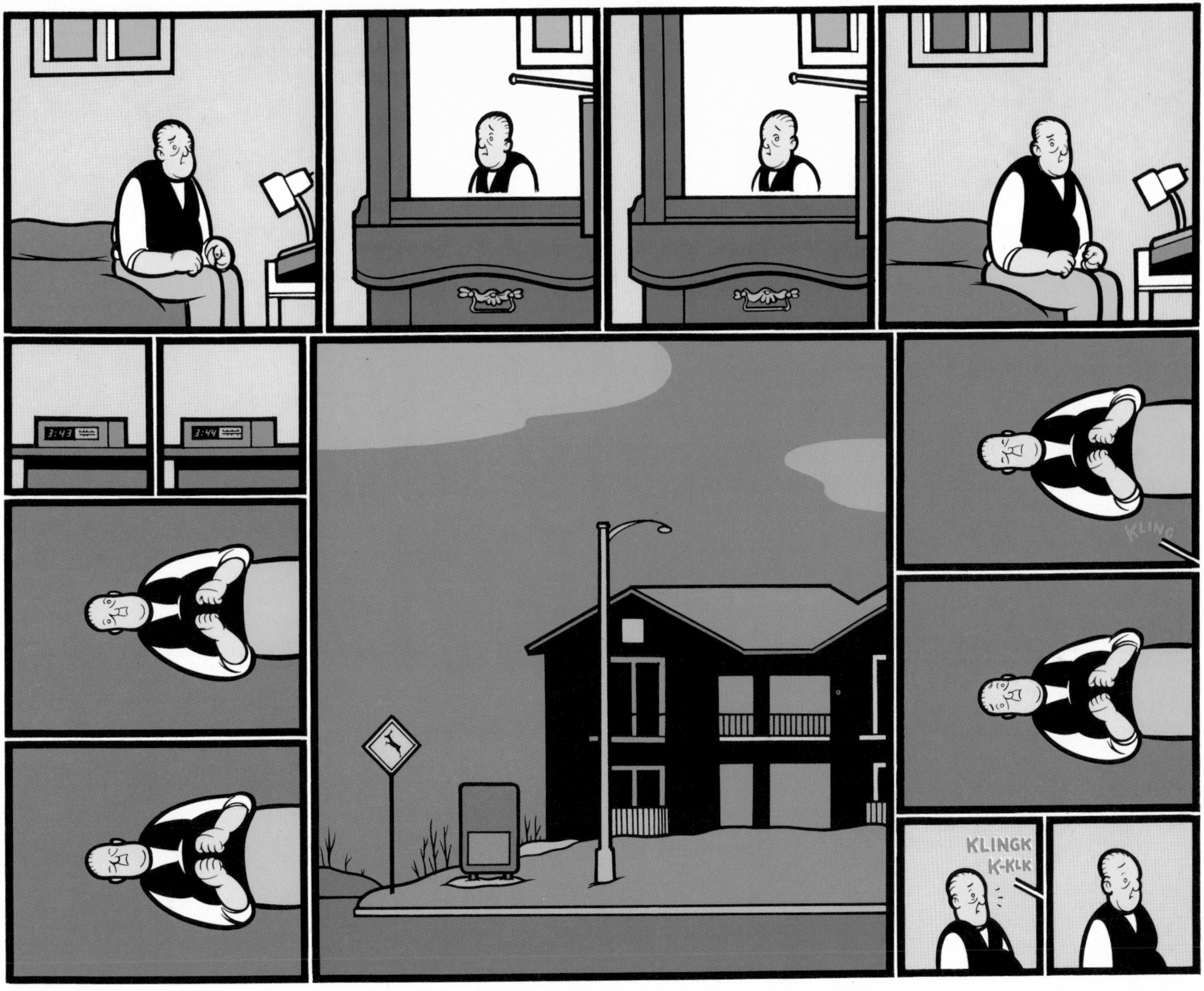
3:43
3:44
KLING
KLINGK
K-KLK

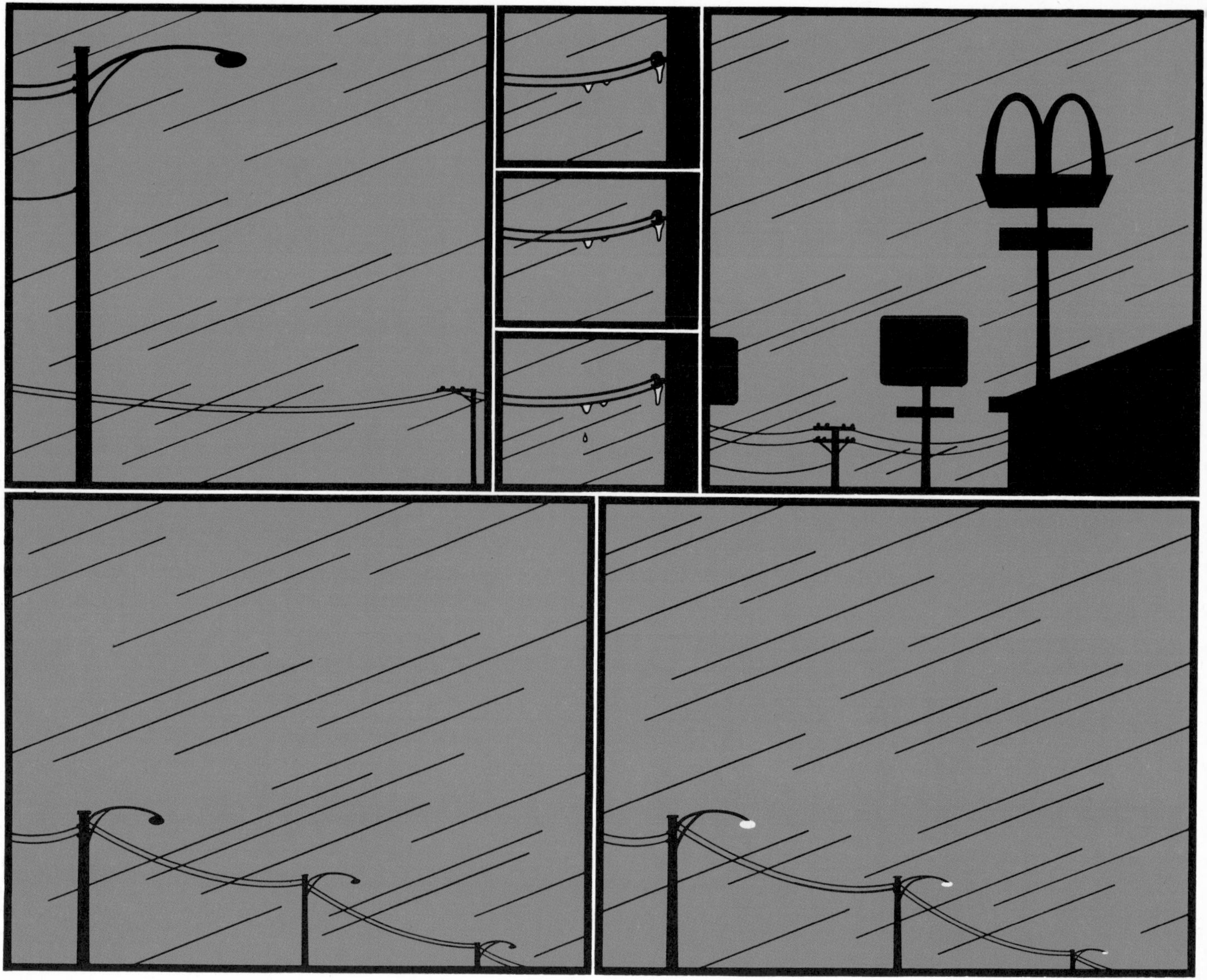

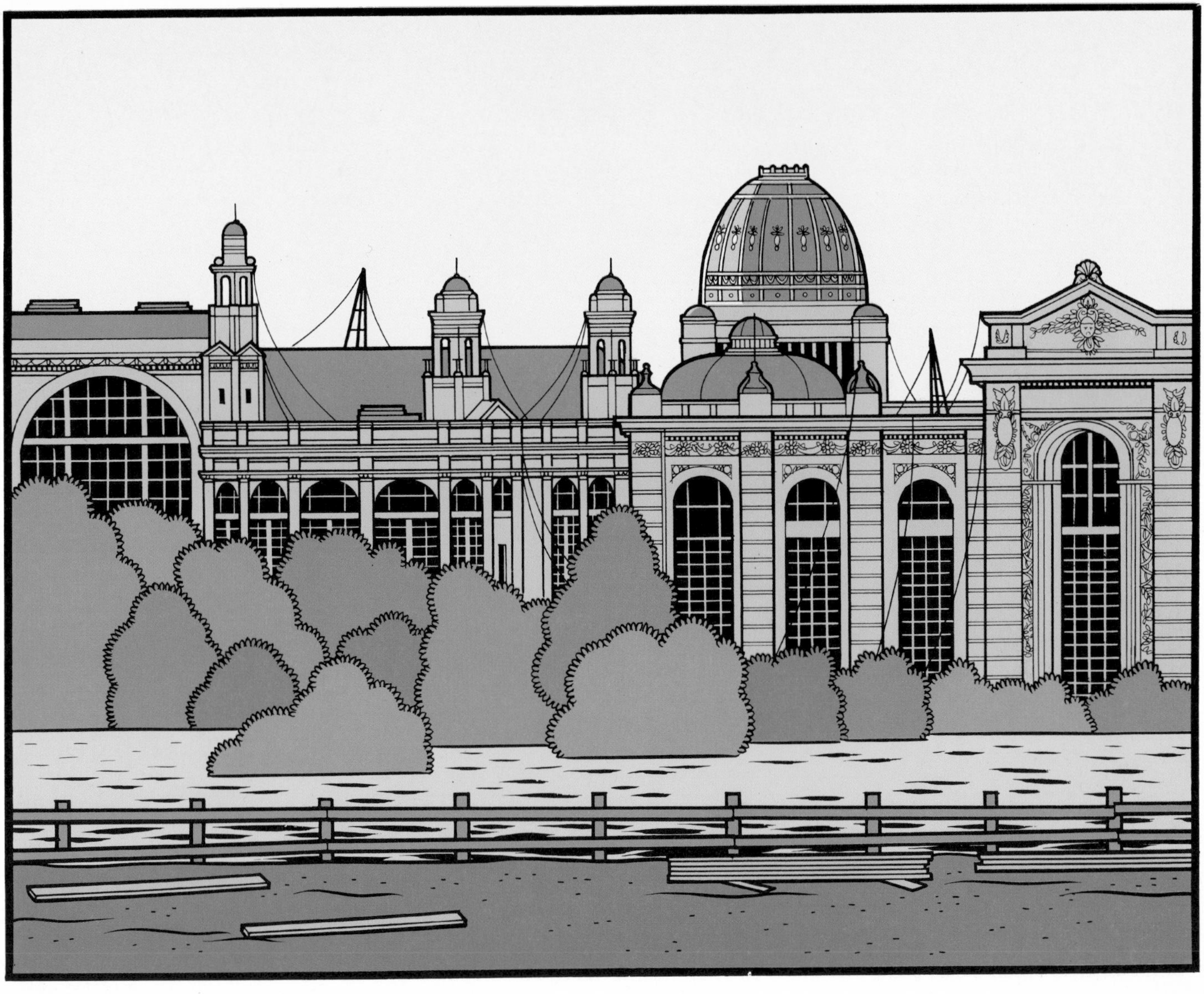

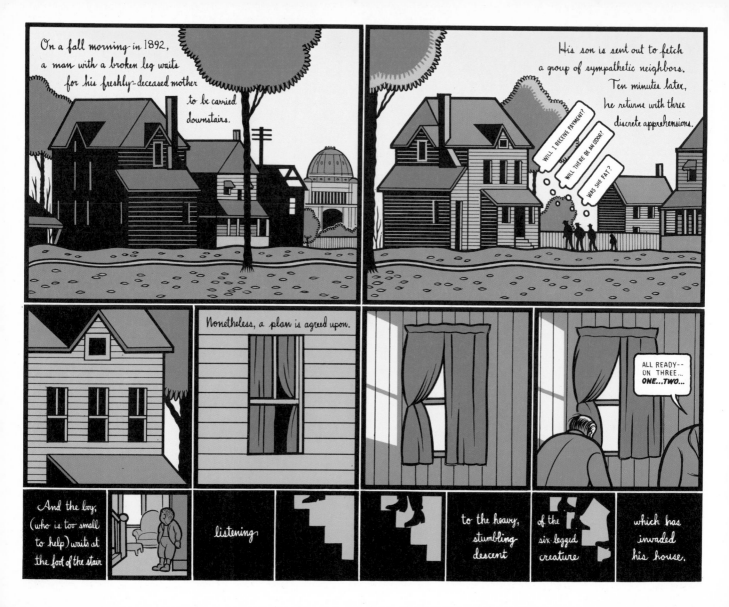

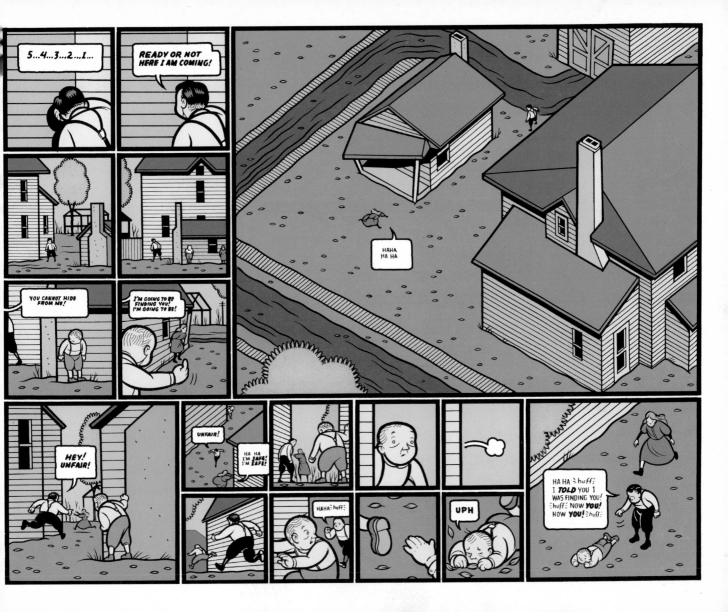

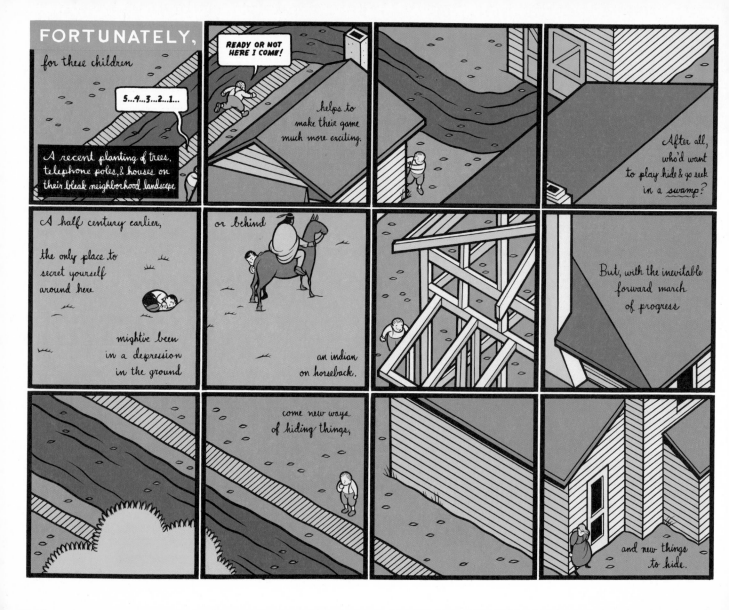

PAGES 206-207. – It should be readily apparent to even the most casual reader of this novella that supplied with it are a handful of piquant and diverting "cut out" reference guides; though such "paper activities" are sometimes dismissed as "child's play" or frivolous "hokum," of no value to the serious student of literature, it is hoped that these uncultured negative preconceptions – which really do serve no other purpose than to truncate one's experience of an evocative work – shall be disspelt by the dainties' masterful esthetic and artistic qualities. Besides, the increasing commonplace of such "paper toys" in respectable books, plays, and corporate presentations is enough to muzzle even the most vocal detractor towards the cause. Though admittedly printed too small to be constructed with any degree of satisfaction or pluck, pantographic or electrostatic enlargement of all primary shapes and careful study of the construction principia will potentially reward the concerted craftsman with models of relative usefulness. An outfit of water-color paints, a sharp knife, and limited background in human romantic contact are, of course, key.

It is, needless to say, not entirely necessary to complete these tasks to fully appreciate the story in question, though those who do attempt the feat will find themselves more acquainted with the rivulets and tributaries of its grander scope, and will besides have nice little miniatures to display to friends and family once the fantasy is nothing more than a swamp of misremembered trifles. However, given the relative intelligence and mathematical skills of this textbook's author, all culpability regarding measurement of parts, tabs, and joinery is hereby forfeit, and no submitted claims to the contrary shall be honored.

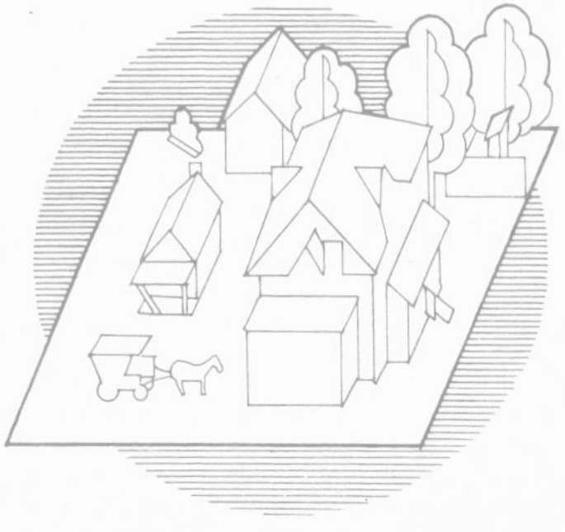

NOTE. – Any student of the history of the neighborhood in question will note that the reconstruction presented here is not without its inconsistencies; based, as it is, upon reminiscence and fragmentary recollection, some details reproduced may possibly contradict and/or overlap one another. Additionally, care should be taken when projecting any of this aid's details temporally forward or backward, as some street names have changed, vegetation has developed, and those personalities concerned with the area have either moved away, perished, or their relative sense of the scale of the world has changed. Regardless, and as elucidated above, those wishing a more fully-developed sense of the events related within these pages may find some diversion by crafting the attached, as it allows a simulated maneuverability about the spaces described, and may, at the very least, prove a lightening influence upon a Sunday afternoon's weakened heart.

INSTRUCTIONS. – Given the generally intuitive level of the task, no detailed directions are provided; it is believed that the matching numerals, letters, and diagrams will be guidance enough to carry the intelligent reader through to completion of the chore. Follow all folds and outlines carefully, and avoid spreading of excess adhesive on exposed elements, as it will spoil the model and prevent attainment of the desired "finished" quality. As well, please take time to allow independent elements to thoroughly dry before committing final assembly; do not "test" parts, as this may compromise sensitive joinery. Those who suffer difficulty should abandon the enterprise immediately.

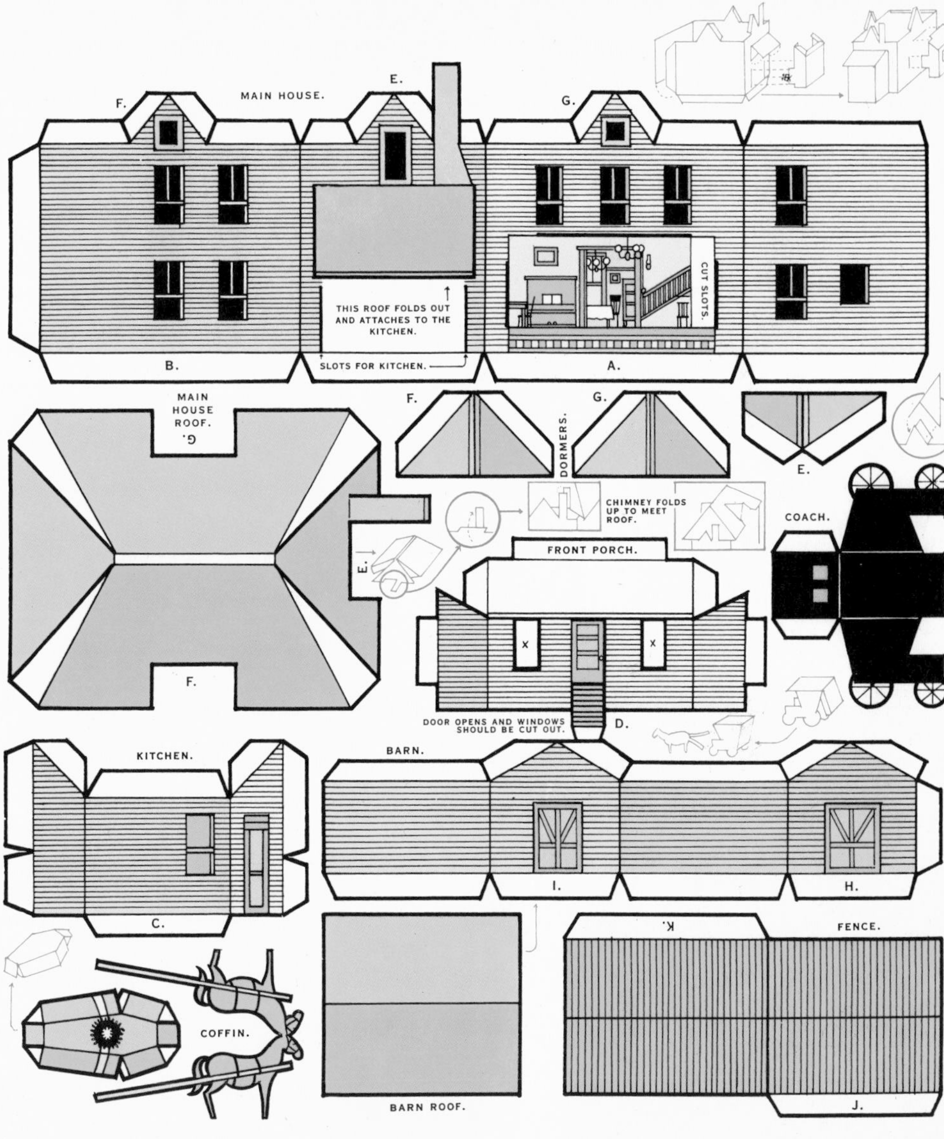
MAIN HOUSE.
F.
E.
G.
THIS ROOF FOLDS OUT AND ATTACHES TO THE KITCHEN.
CUT SLOTS.
B.
SLOTS FOR KITCHEN.
A.
MAIN HOUSE ROOF.
G.
F.
F.
DORMERS.
G.
E.
E.
CHIMNEY FOLDS UP TO MEET ROOF.
COACH.
FRONT PORCH.
DOOR OPENS AND WINDOWS SHOULD BE CUT OUT.
D.
KITCHEN.
C.
BARN.
I.
H.
FENCE.
K.
J.
COFFIN.
BARN ROOF.

CONTINUED ON INSIDE BACK COVER.

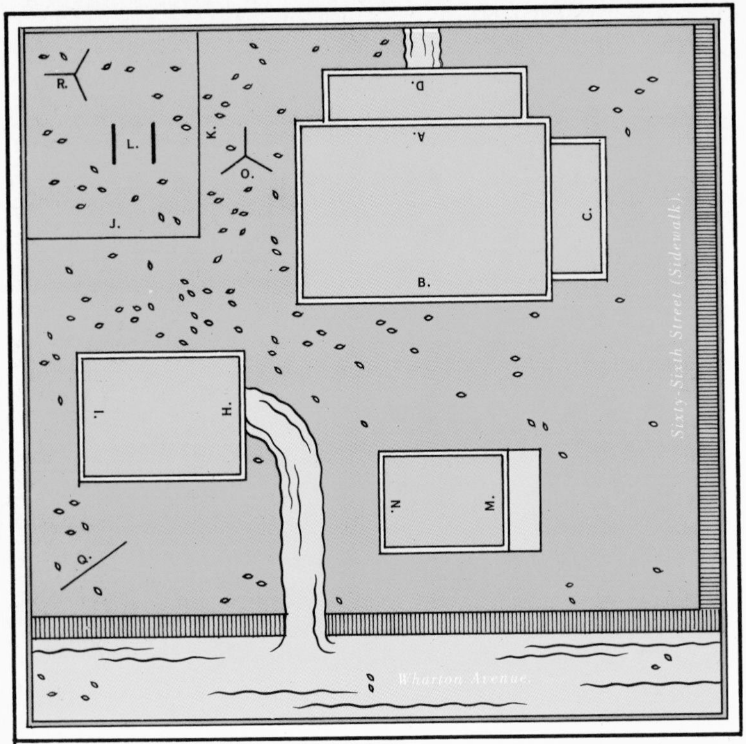
R.
L.
K.
O.
J.
D.
A.
C.
B.
I.
H.
N.
M.
Q.
Sixty-Sixth Street (Sidewalk).
Wharton Avenue.

BASE.

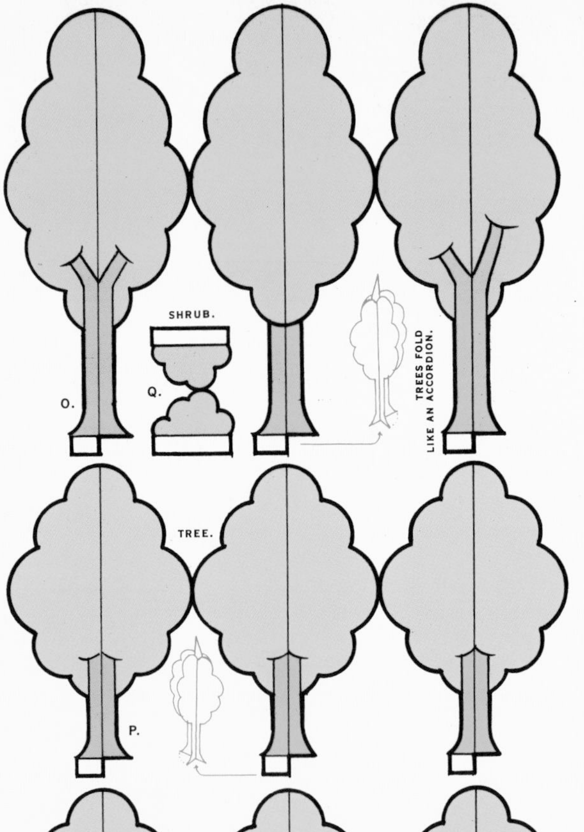
SHRUB.
O.
Q.
TREES FOLD LIKE AN ACCORDION.
TREE.
P.
TREE.
R.

HOMESTEAD.

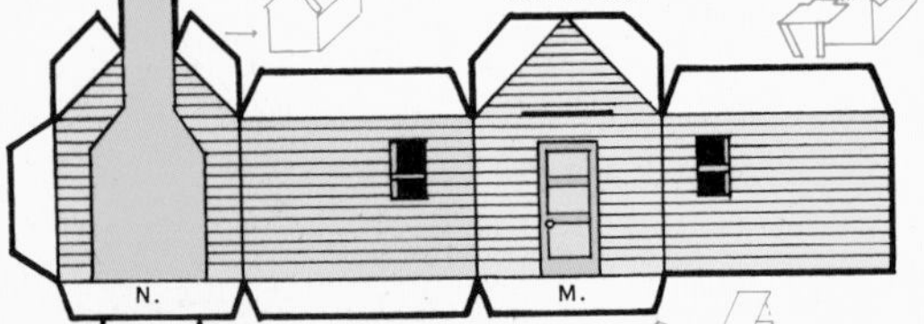
N.
M.

HOMESTEAD ROOF.

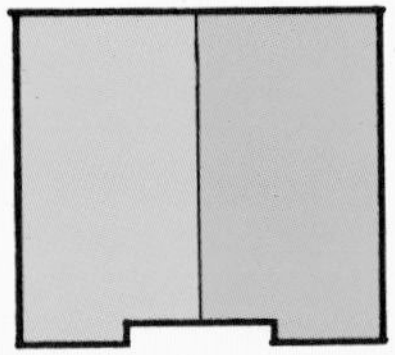

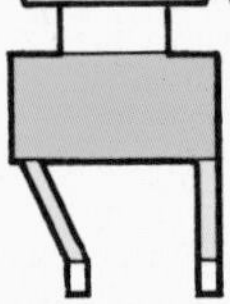

HOMESTEAD PORCH.

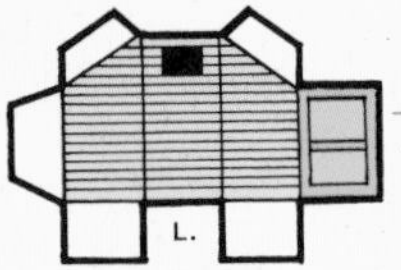
L.

OUTHOUSE.

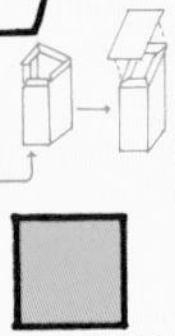

OUTHOUSE ROOF.

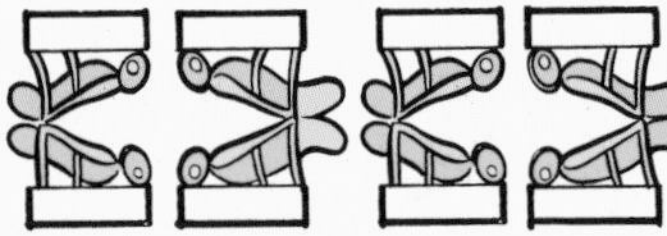

IMAGINARY GIANT GRASSHOPPERS.

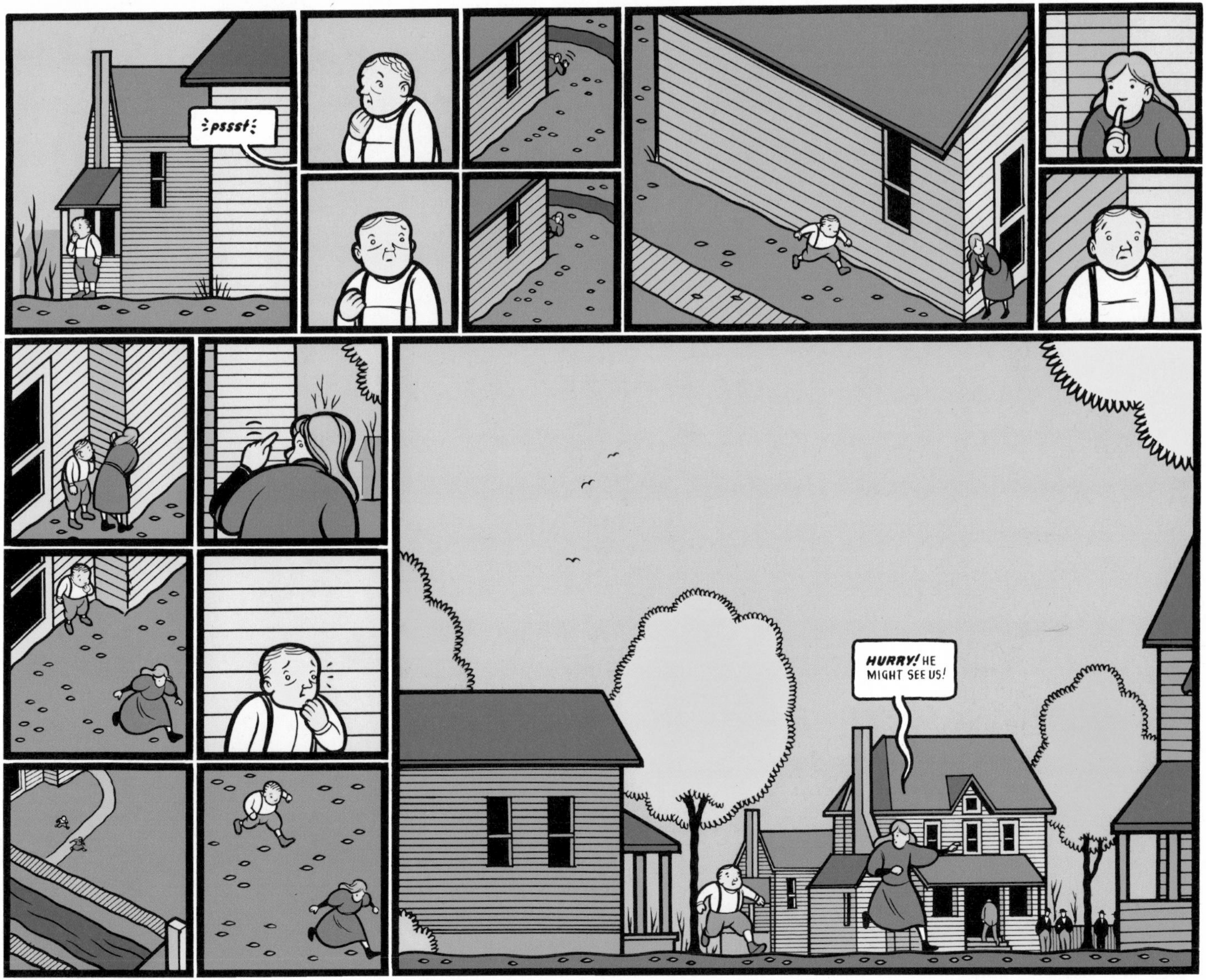
pssst
HURRY! HE MIGHT SEE US!

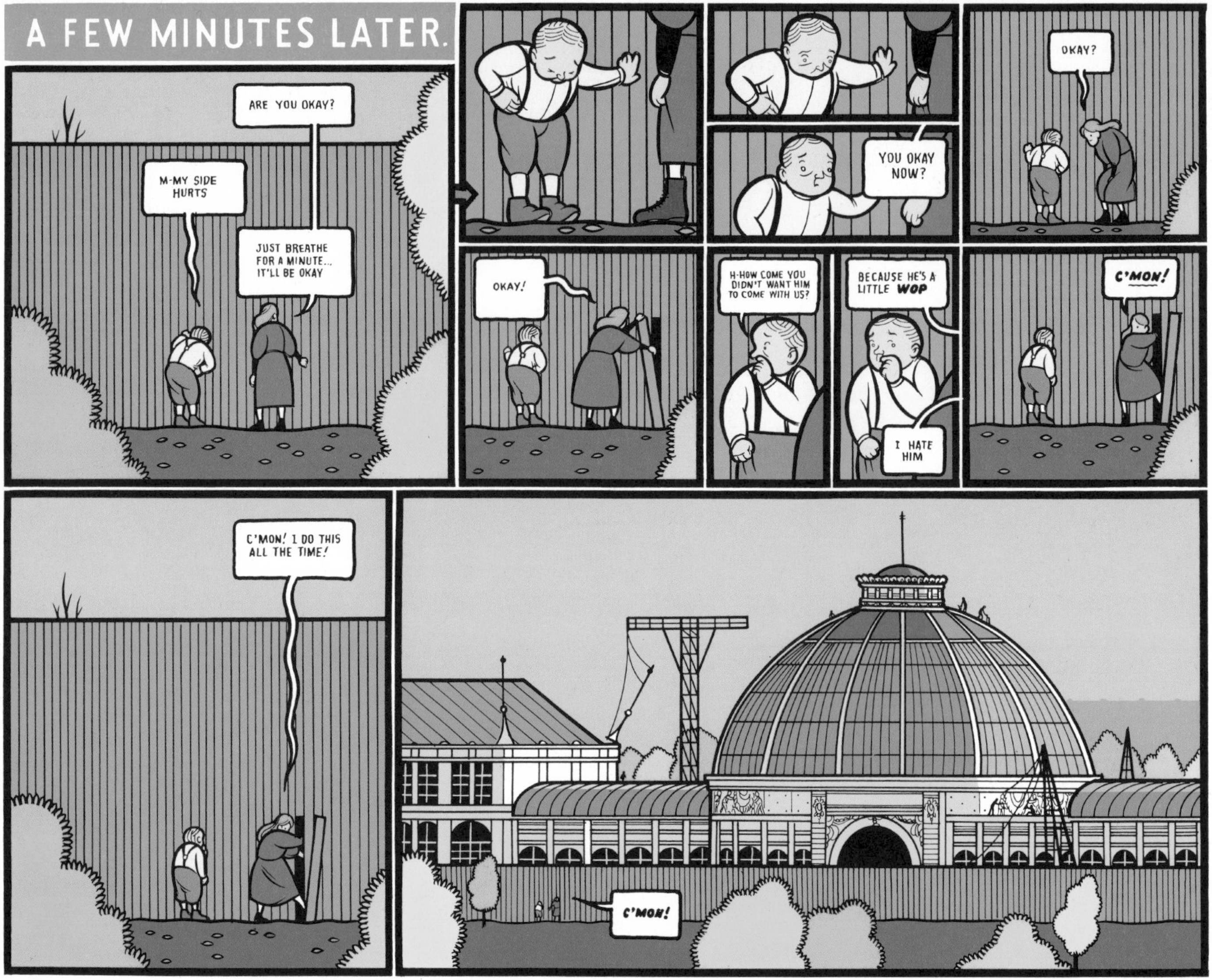
A FEW MINUTES LATER.
ARE YOU OKAY?
M-MY SIDE HURTS
JUST BREATHE FOR A MINUTE... IT'LL BE OKAY
YOU OKAY NOW?
OKAY?
OKAY!
H-HOW COME YOU DIDN'T WANT HIM TO COME WITH US?
BECAUSE HE'S A LITTLE WOP
I HATE HIM
C'MON!
C'MON! I DO THIS ALL THE TIME!
C'MON!

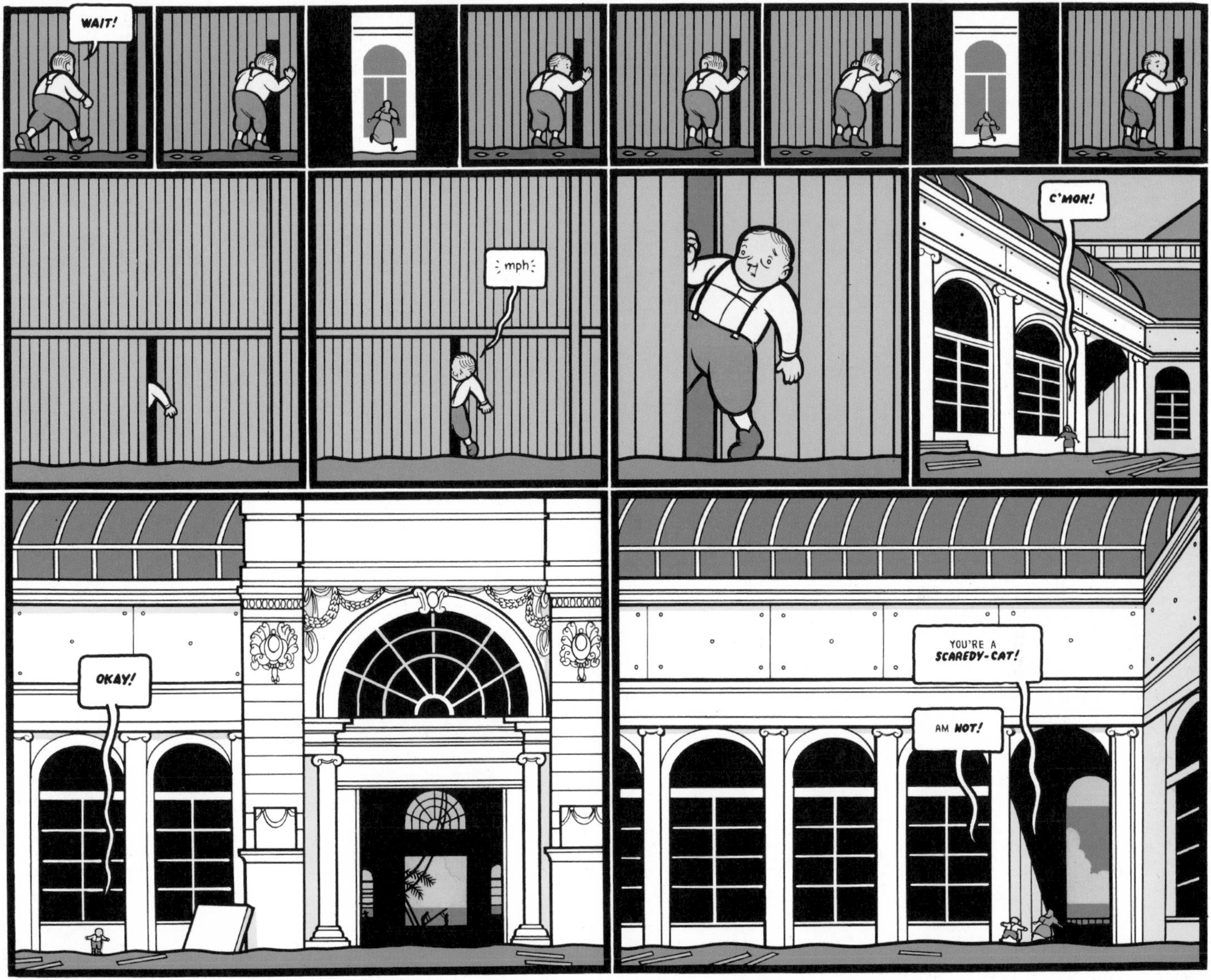
WAIT!
mph
C'MON!
OKAY!
YOU'RE A SCAREDY-CAT!
AM NOT!

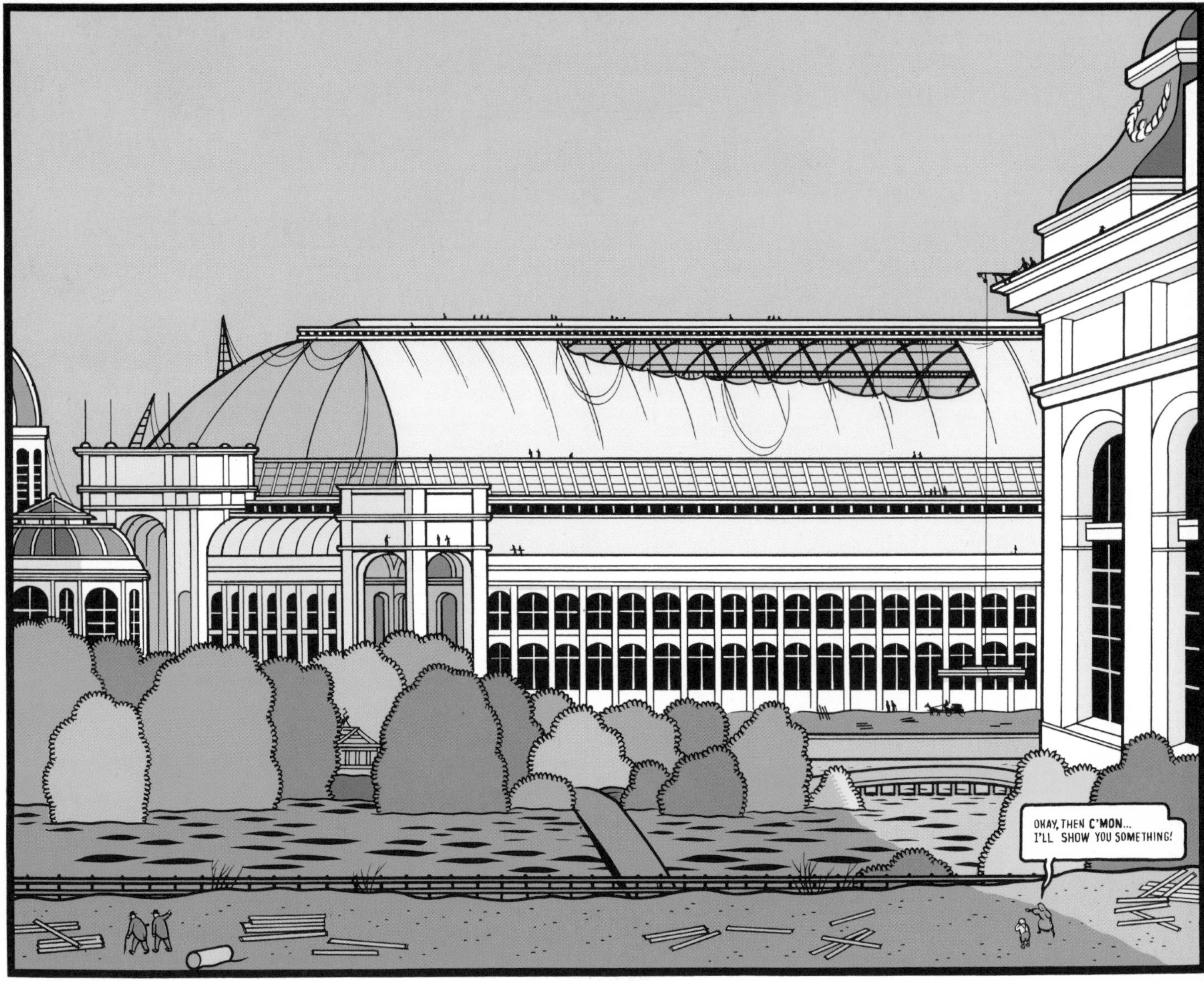
OKAY, THEN C'MON...
I'LL SHOW YOU SOMETHING!

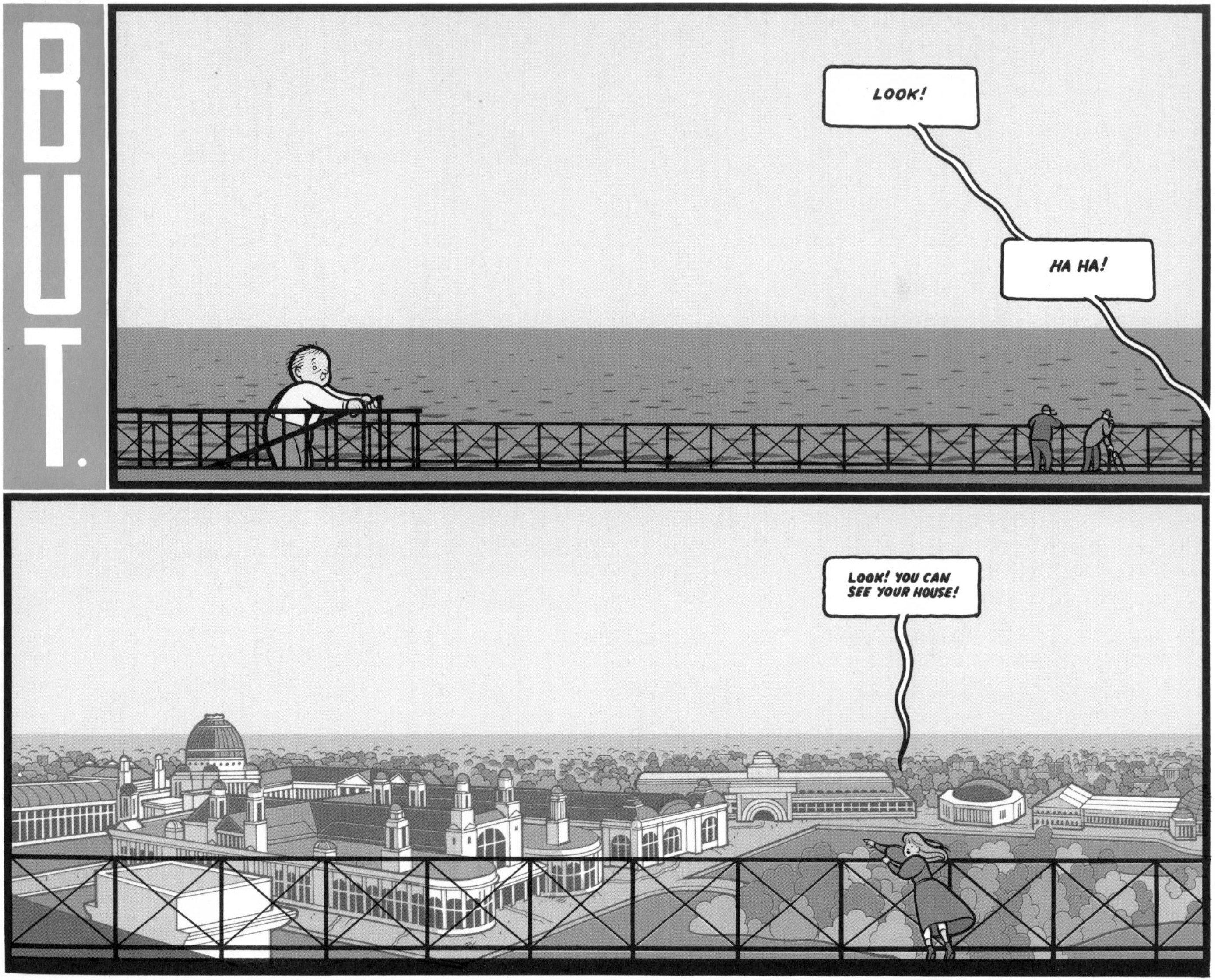
BUT.
LOOK!
HA HA!
LOOK! YOU CAN SEE YOUR HOUSE!

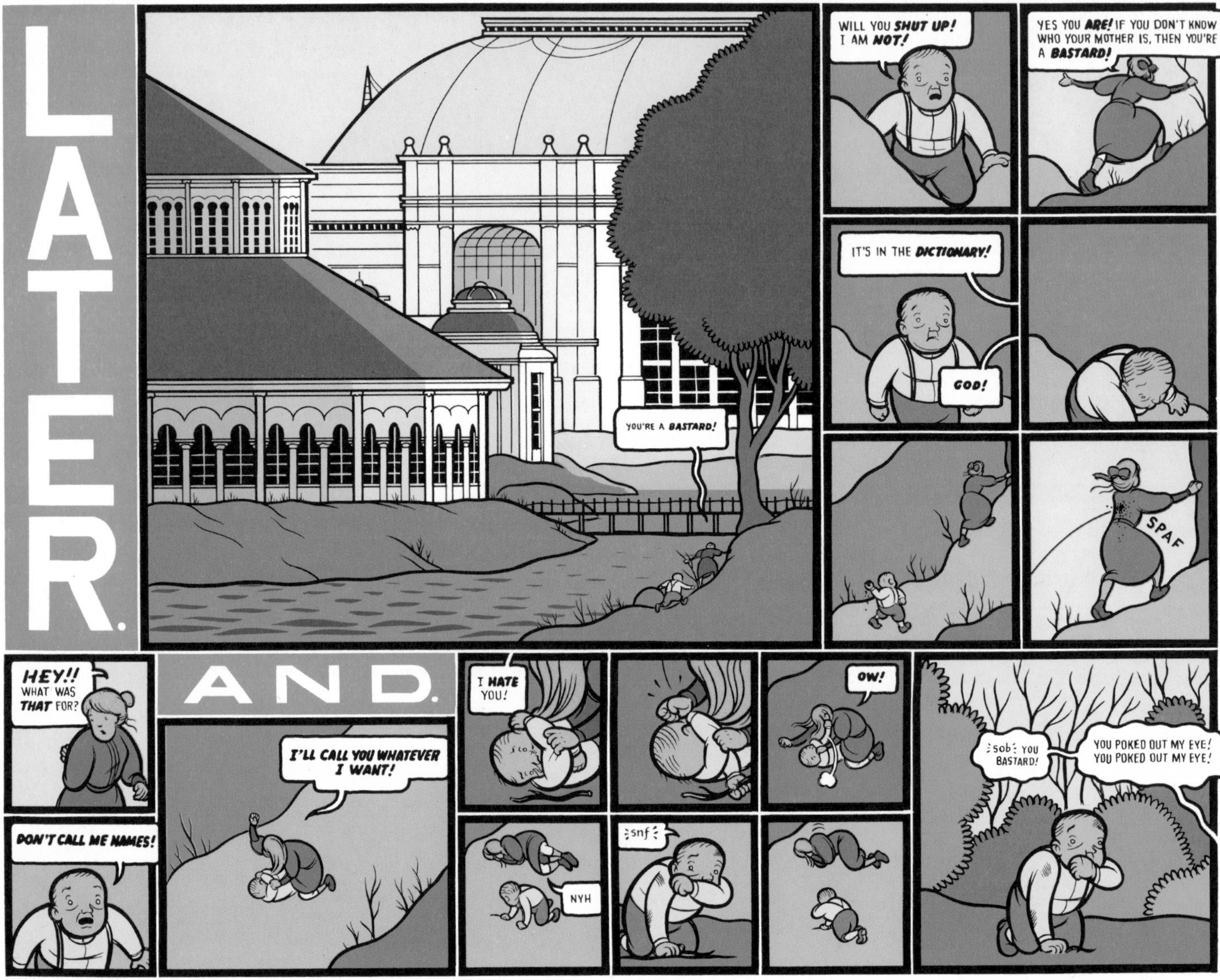

LATER.
YOU'RE A BASTARD!
WILL YOU SHUT UP! I AM NOT!
YES YOU ARE! IF YOU DON'T KNOW WHO YOUR MOTHER IS, THEN YOU'RE A BASTARD!
IT'S IN THE DICTIONARY!
GOD!
SPAF
HEY!! WHAT WAS THAT FOR?
DON'T CALL ME NAMES!
AND.
I'LL CALL YOU WHATEVER I WANT!
I HATE YOU!
OW!
NYH
snf
sob YOU BASTARD!
YOU POKED OUT MY EYE! YOU POKED OUT MY EYE!

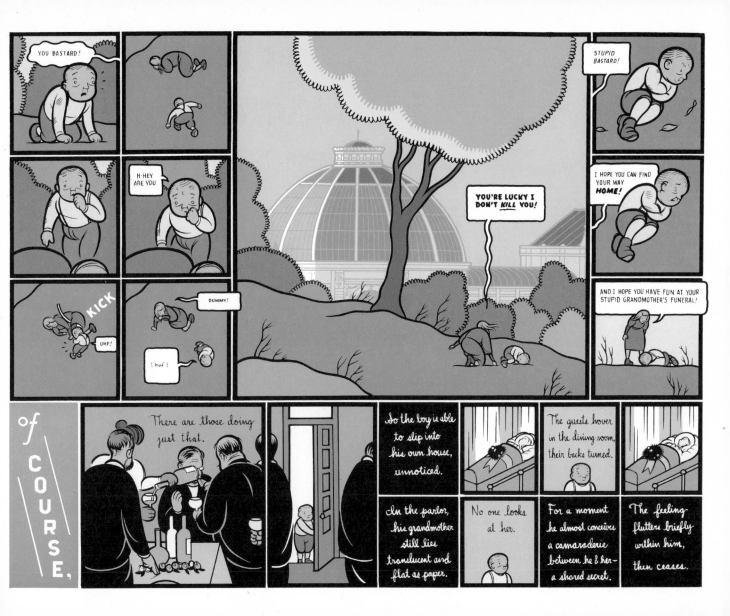

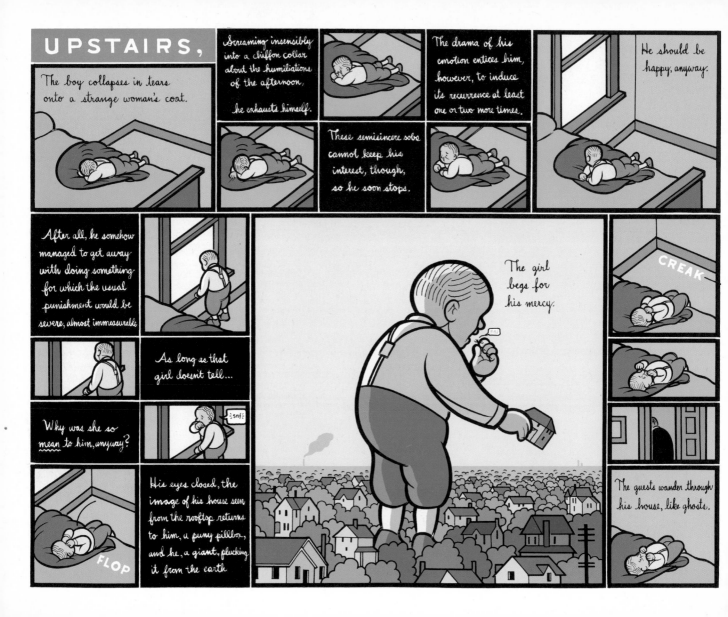

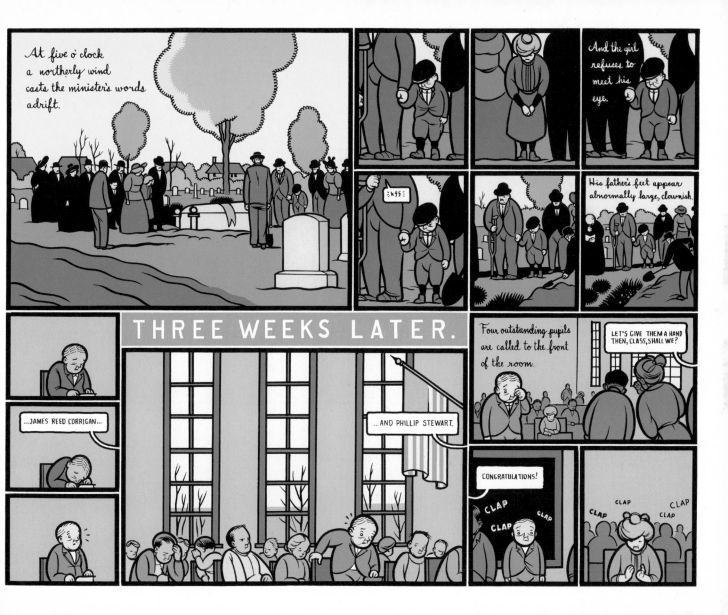

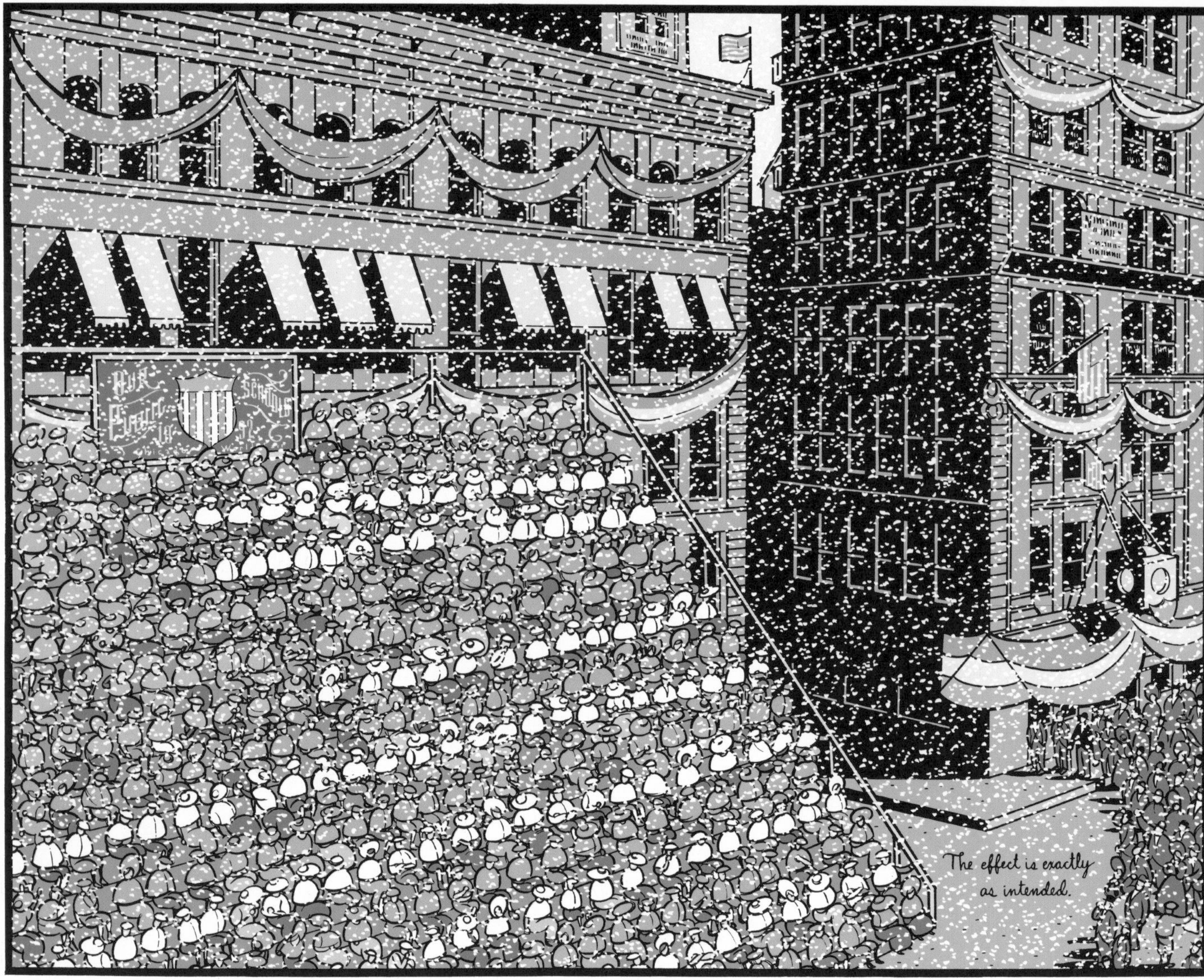
The effect is exactly
as intended.

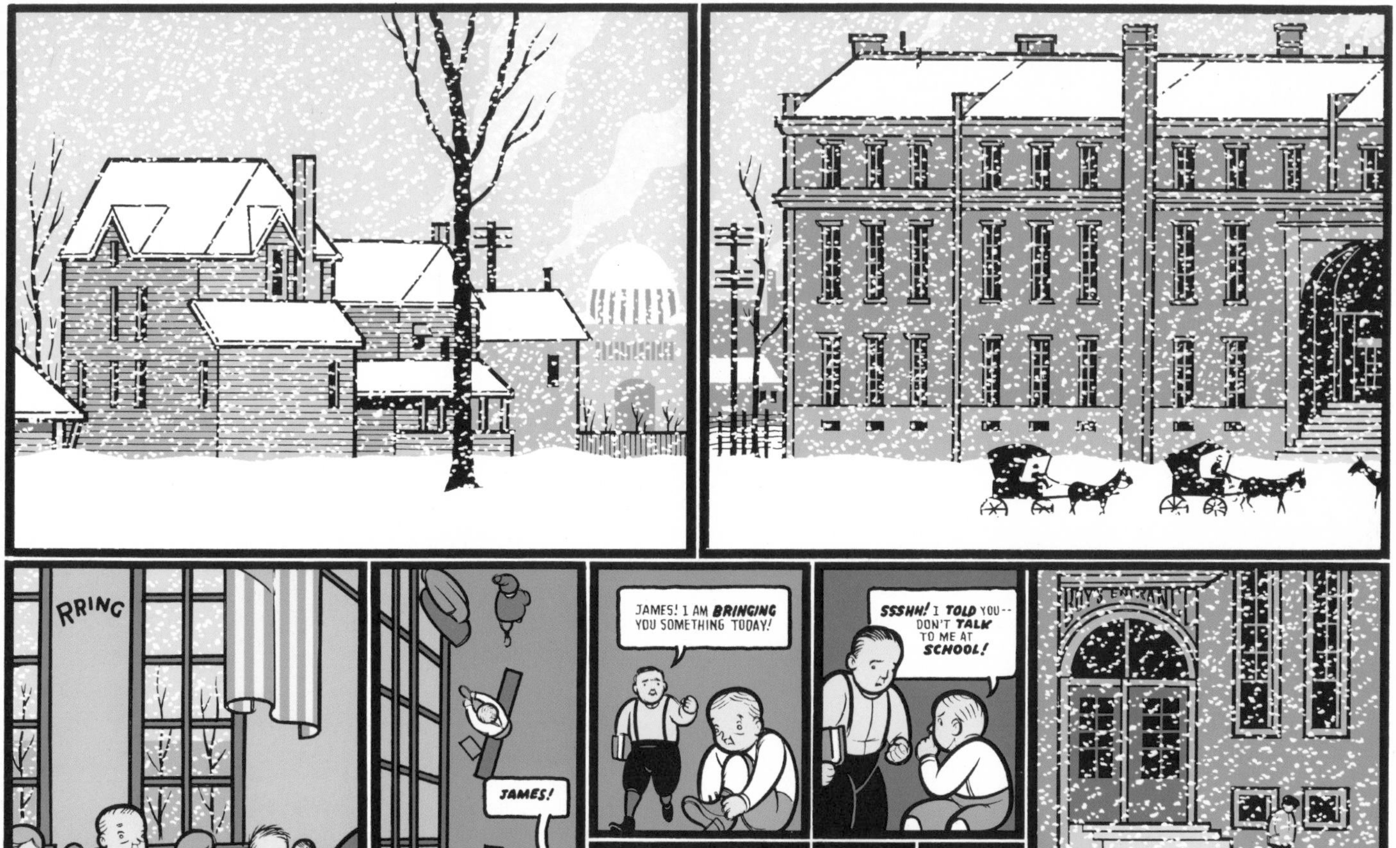
RRING
JAMES!
JAMES! I AM BRINGING YOU SOMETHING TODAY!
SSSHH! I TOLD YOU-- DON'T TALK TO ME AT SCHOOL!
I-I KNOW... I-I JUST AM THINKING THAT SINCE I
SHUT UP OR I WON'T WALK HOME WITH YOU! MEET ME OUTSIDE!
BUT I AM ONLY THIN
SSH!
GOD!

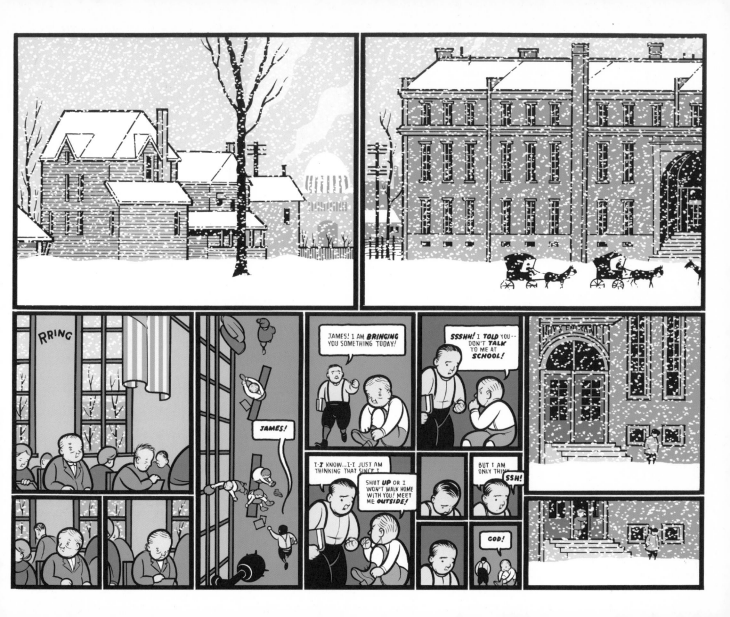

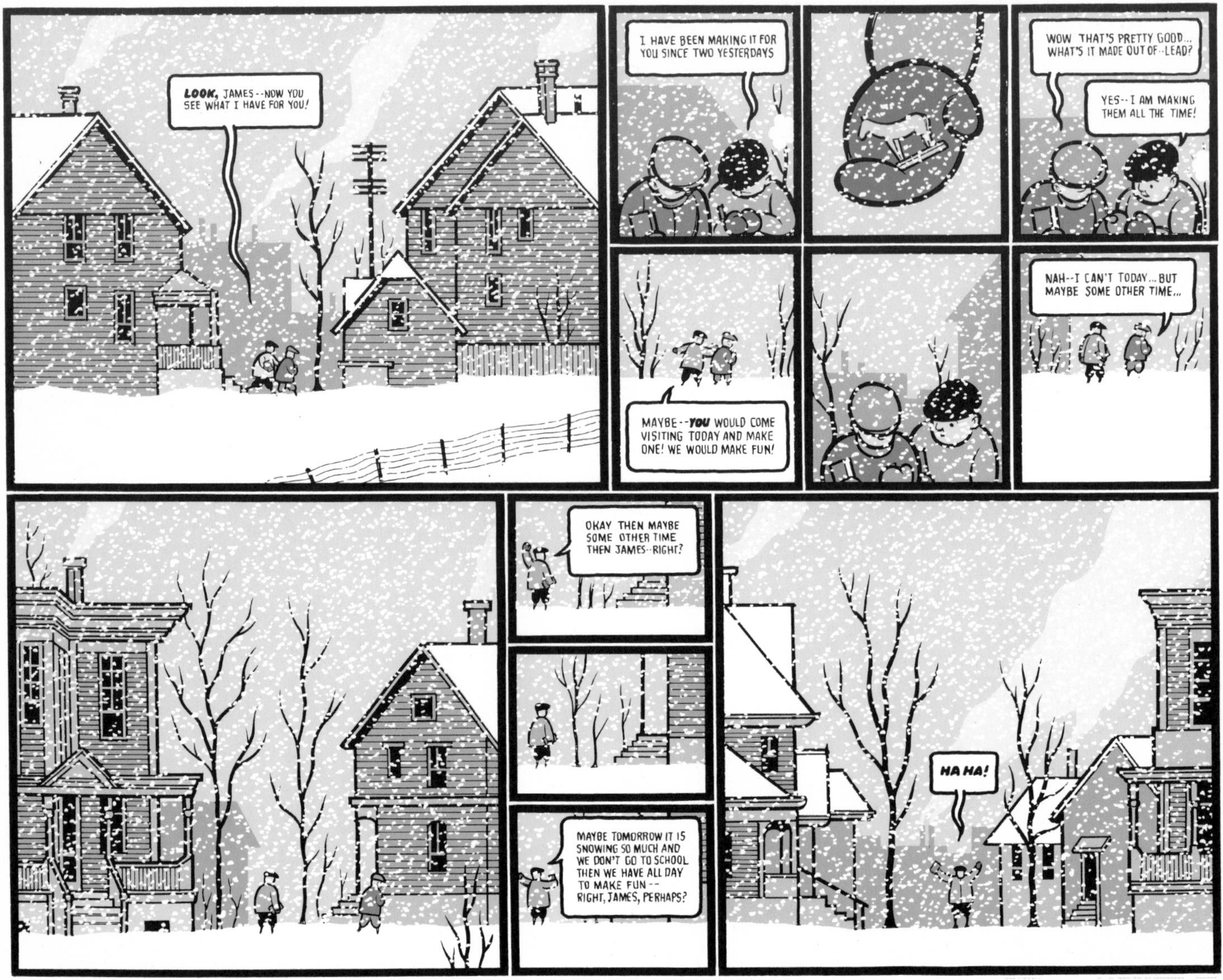
LOOK, JAMES--NOW YOU SEE WHAT I HAVE FOR YOU!
I HAVE BEEN MAKING IT FOR YOU SINCE TWO YESTERDAYS
WOW THAT'S PRETTY GOOD... WHAT'S IT MADE OUT OF--LEAD?
YES--I AM MAKING THEM ALL THE TIME!
MAYBE--YOU WOULD COME VISITING TODAY AND MAKE ONE! WE WOULD MAKE FUN!
NAH--I CAN'T TODAY...BUT MAYBE SOME OTHER TIME...
OKAY THEN MAYBE SOME OTHER TIME THEN JAMES--RIGHT?
MAYBE TOMORROW IT IS SNOWING SO MUCH AND WE DON'T GO TO SCHOOL THEN WE HAVE ALL DAY TO MAKE FUN--RIGHT, JAMES, PERHAPS?
HA HA!

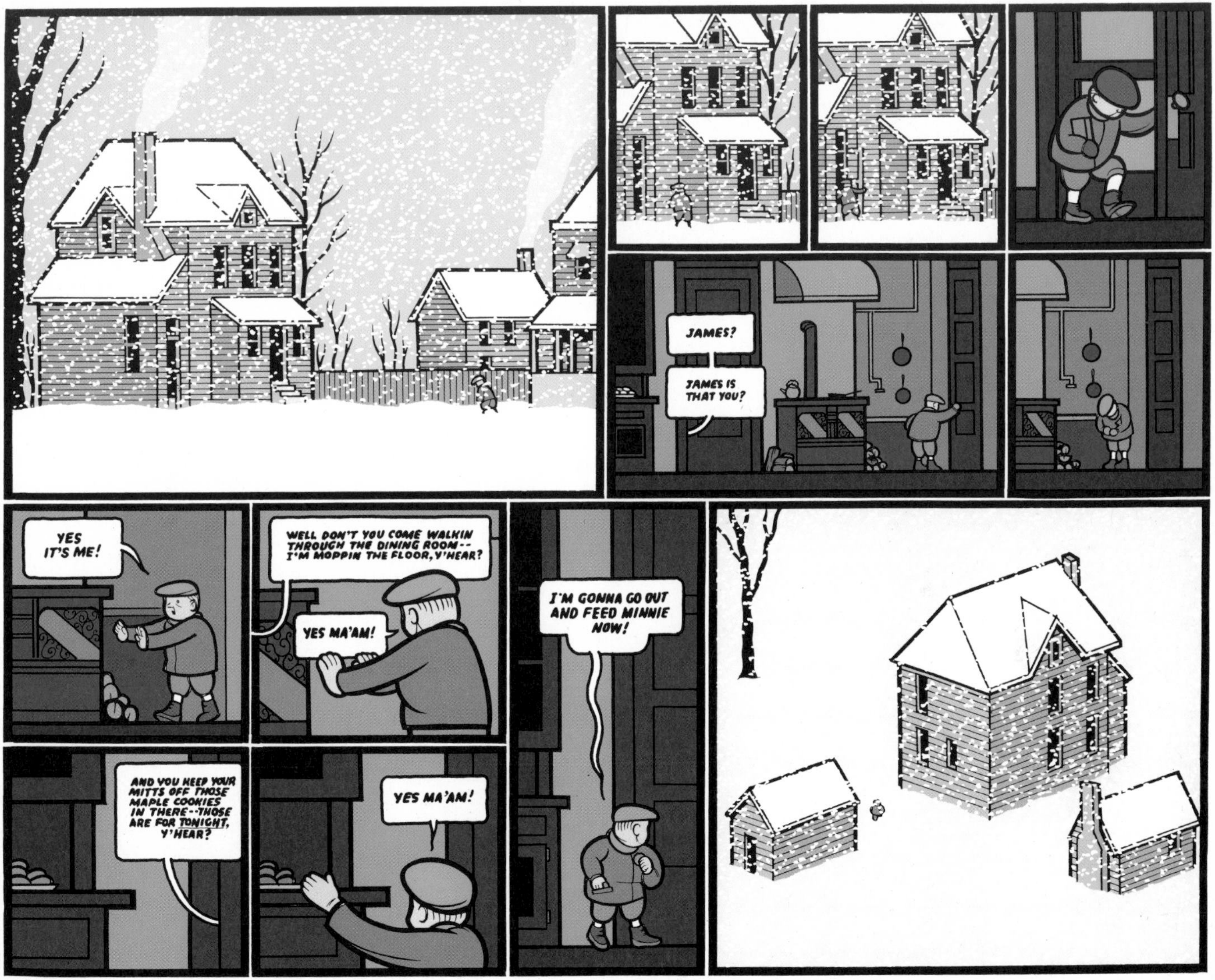
JAMES?
JAMES IS THAT YOU?
YES IT'S ME!
WELL DON'T YOU COME WALKIN THROUGH THE DINING ROOM-- I'M MOPPIN THE FLOOR, Y'HEAR?
YES MA'AM!
AND YOU KEEP YOUR MITTS OFF THOSE MAPLE COOKIES IN THERE--THOSE ARE FOR TONIGHT, Y'HEAR?
YES MA'AM!
I'M GONNA GO OUT AND FEED MINNIE NOW!

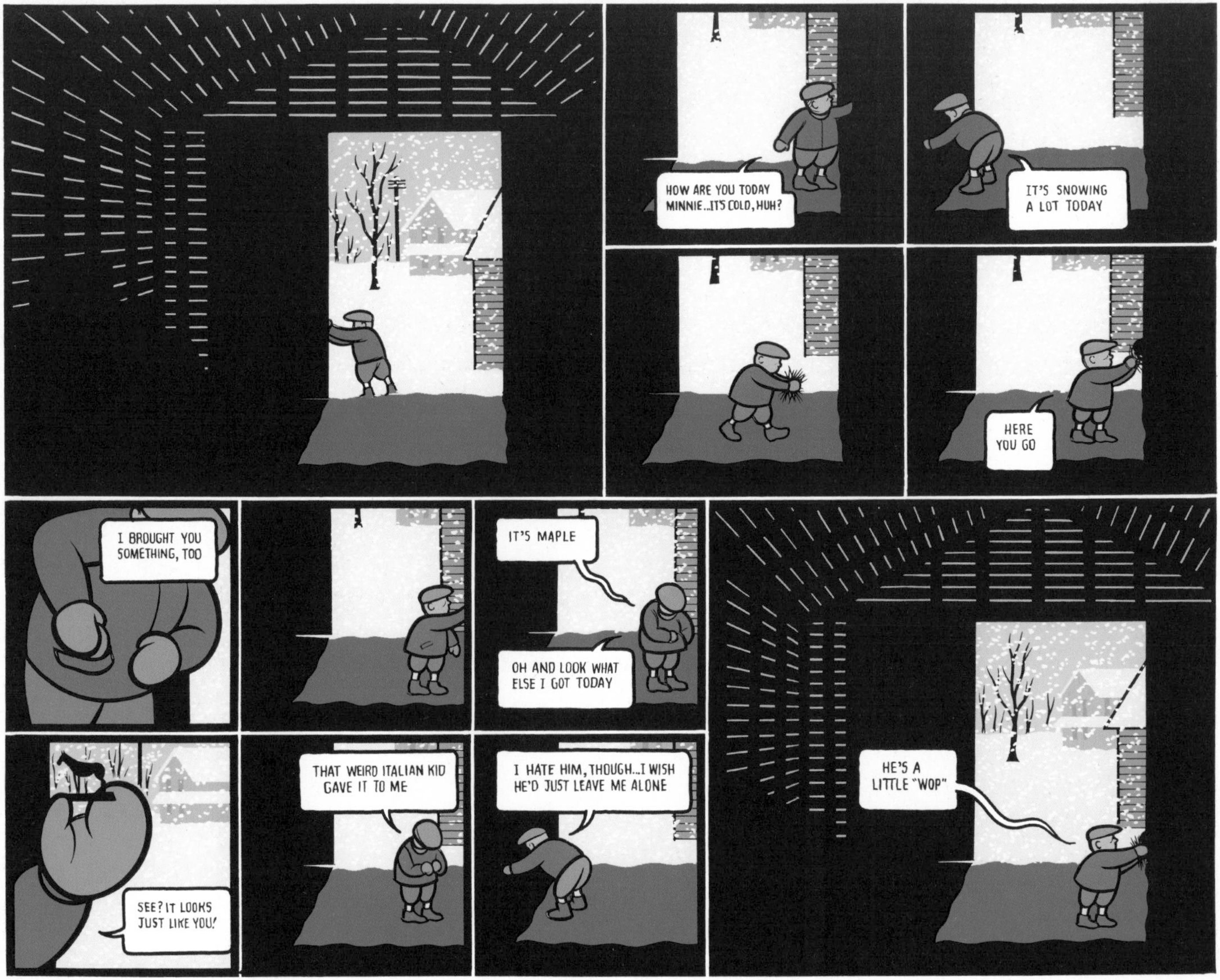
HOW ARE YOU TODAY MINNIE...IT'S COLD, HUH?
IT'S SNOWING A LOT TODAY
HERE YOU GO
I BROUGHT YOU SOMETHING, TOO
IT'S MAPLE
OH AND LOOK WHAT ELSE I GOT TODAY
SEE? IT LOOKS JUST LIKE YOU!
THAT WEIRD ITALIAN KID GAVE IT TO ME
I HATE HIM, THOUGH...I WISH HE'D JUST LEAVE ME ALONE
HE'S A LITTLE "WOP"

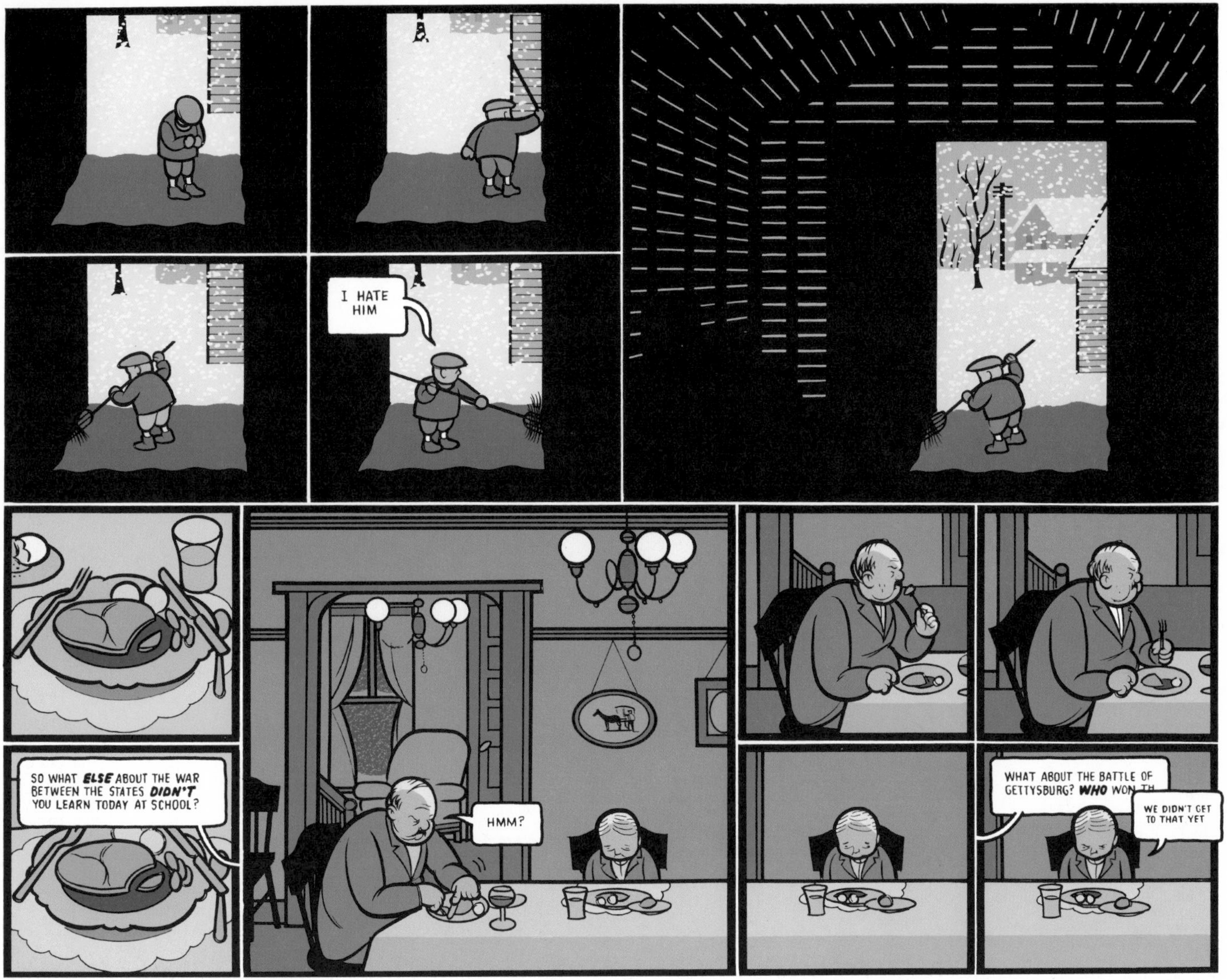
I HATE HIM
SO WHAT **ELSE** ABOUT THE WAR BETWEEN THE STATES **DIDN'T** YOU LEARN TODAY AT SCHOOL?
HMM?
WHAT ABOUT THE BATTLE OF GETTYSBURG? **WHO** WON
WE DIDN'T GET TO THAT YET

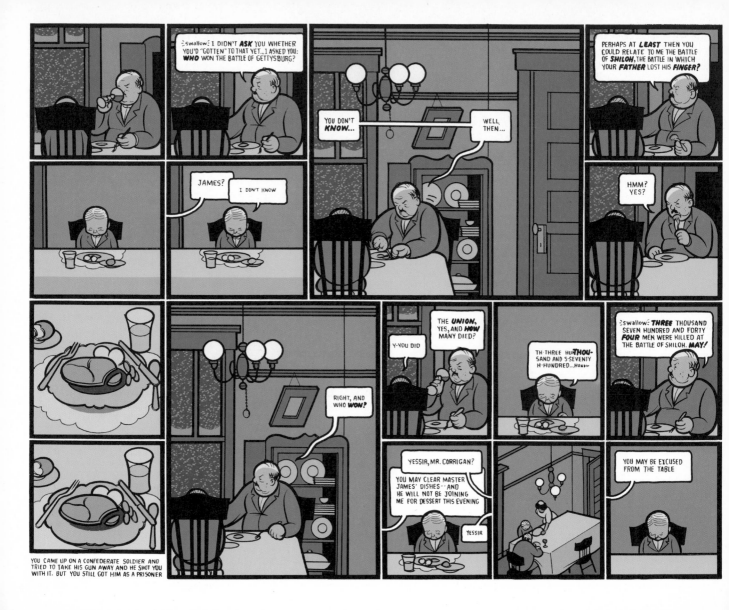

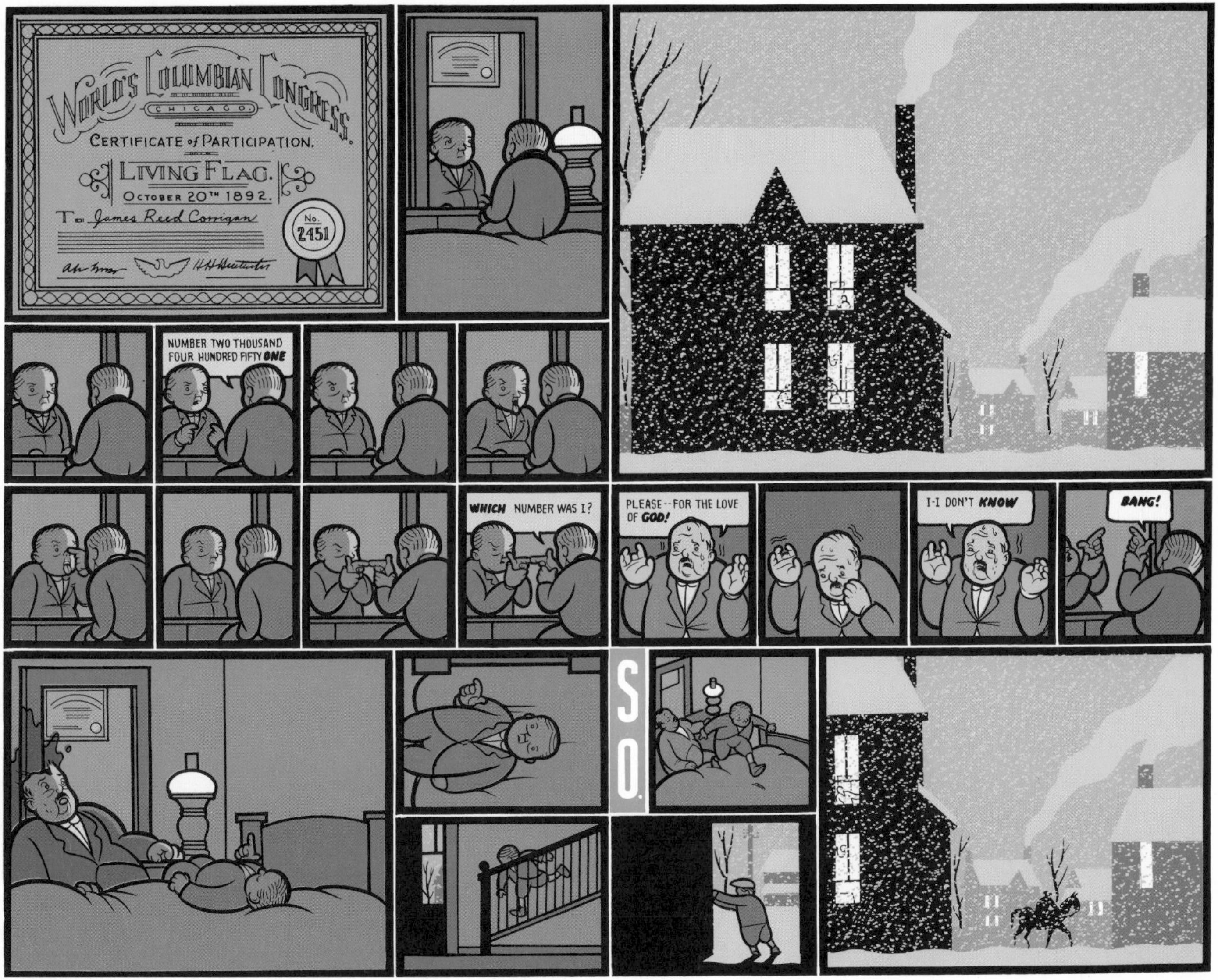

WORLD'S COLUMBIAN CONGRESS.
CHICAGO
CERTIFICATE of PARTICIPATION.
LIVING FLAG.
OCTOBER 20TH 1892.
To: James Reed Corrigan
No. 2451
NUMBER TWO THOUSAND FOUR HUNDRED FIFTY ONE
WHICH NUMBER WAS I?
PLEASE--FOR THE LOVE OF GOD!
I-I DON'T KNOW
BANG!
SO.

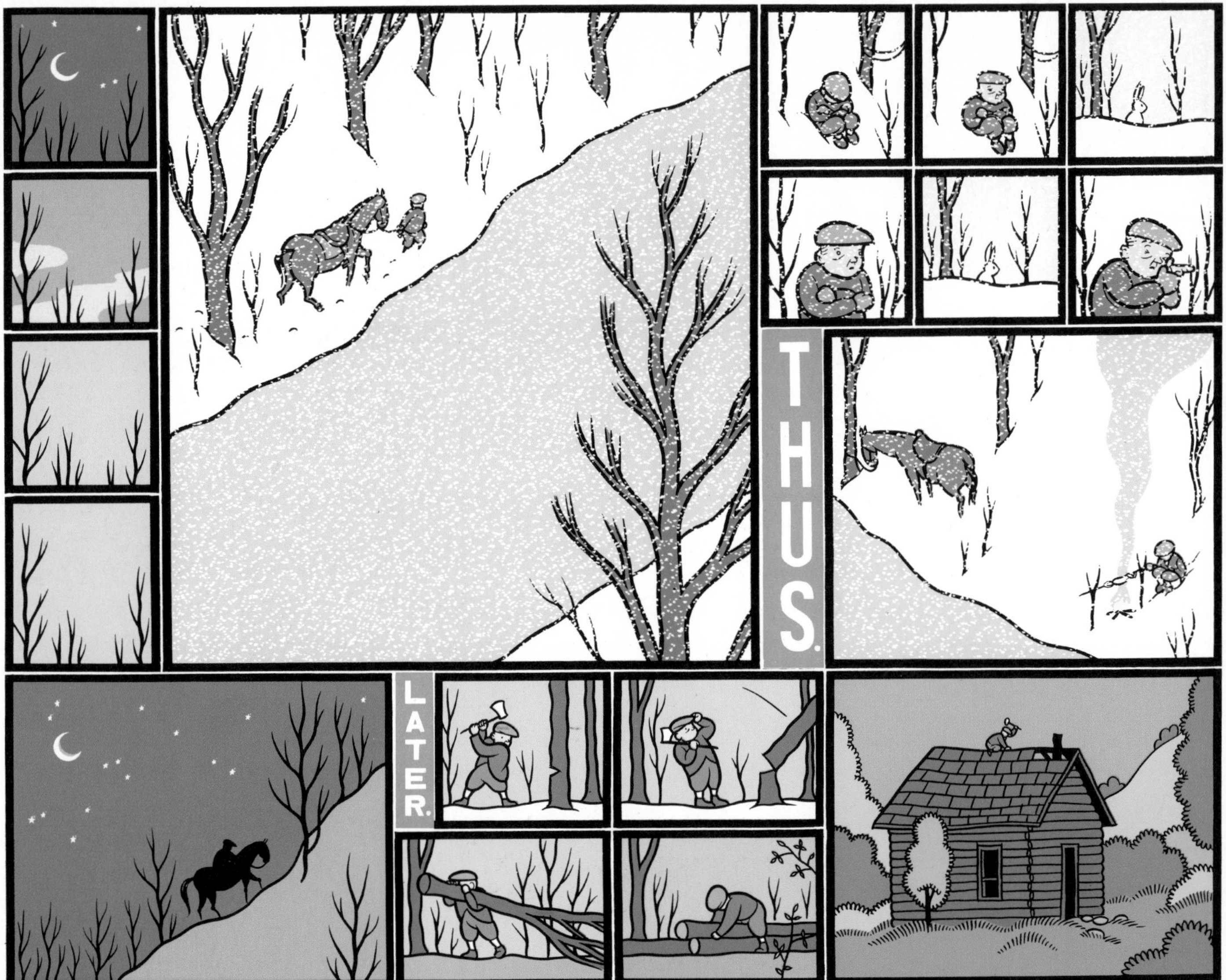
THUS.
LATER.

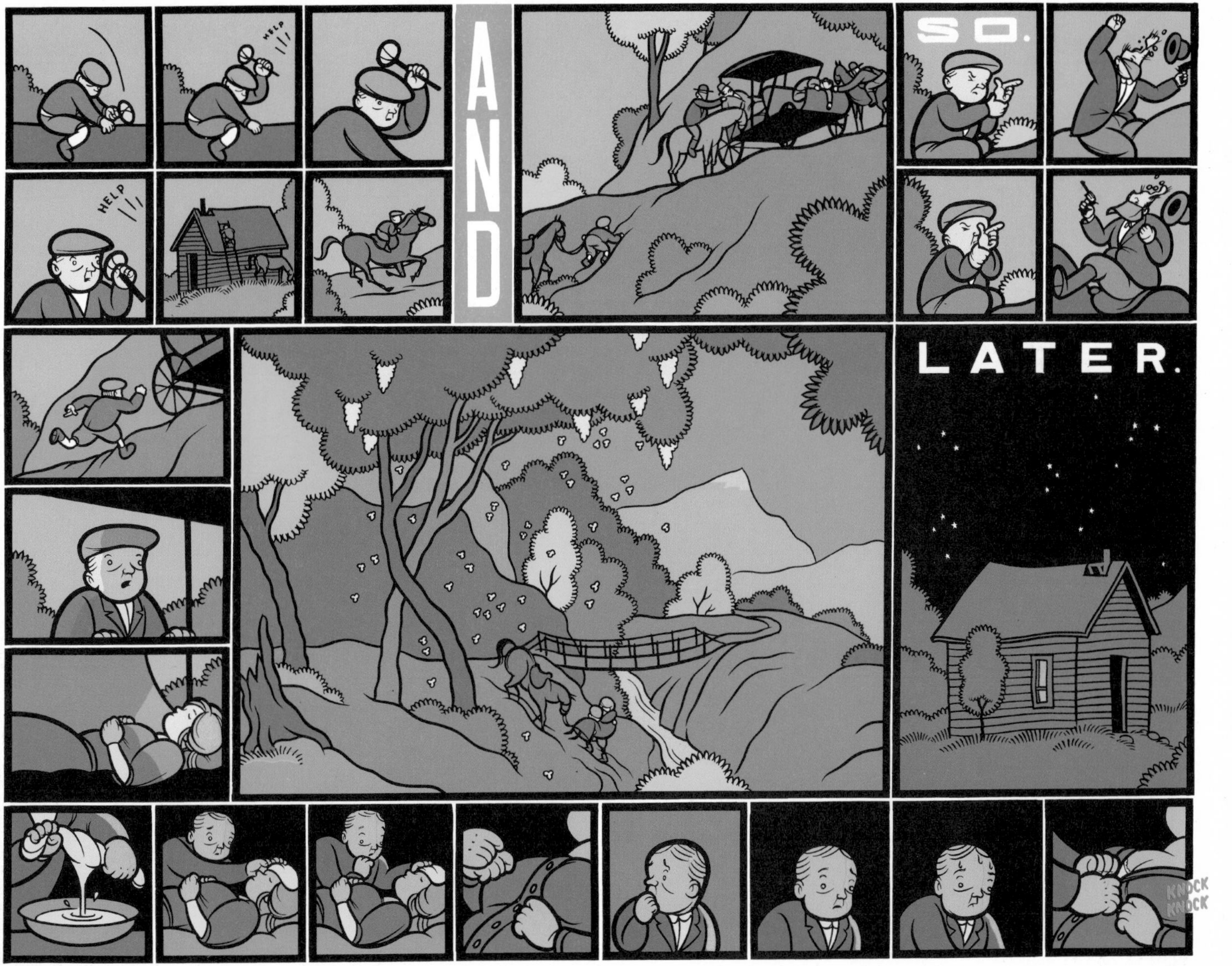

HELP
HELP
AND
SO.
LATER.
KNOCK KNOCK

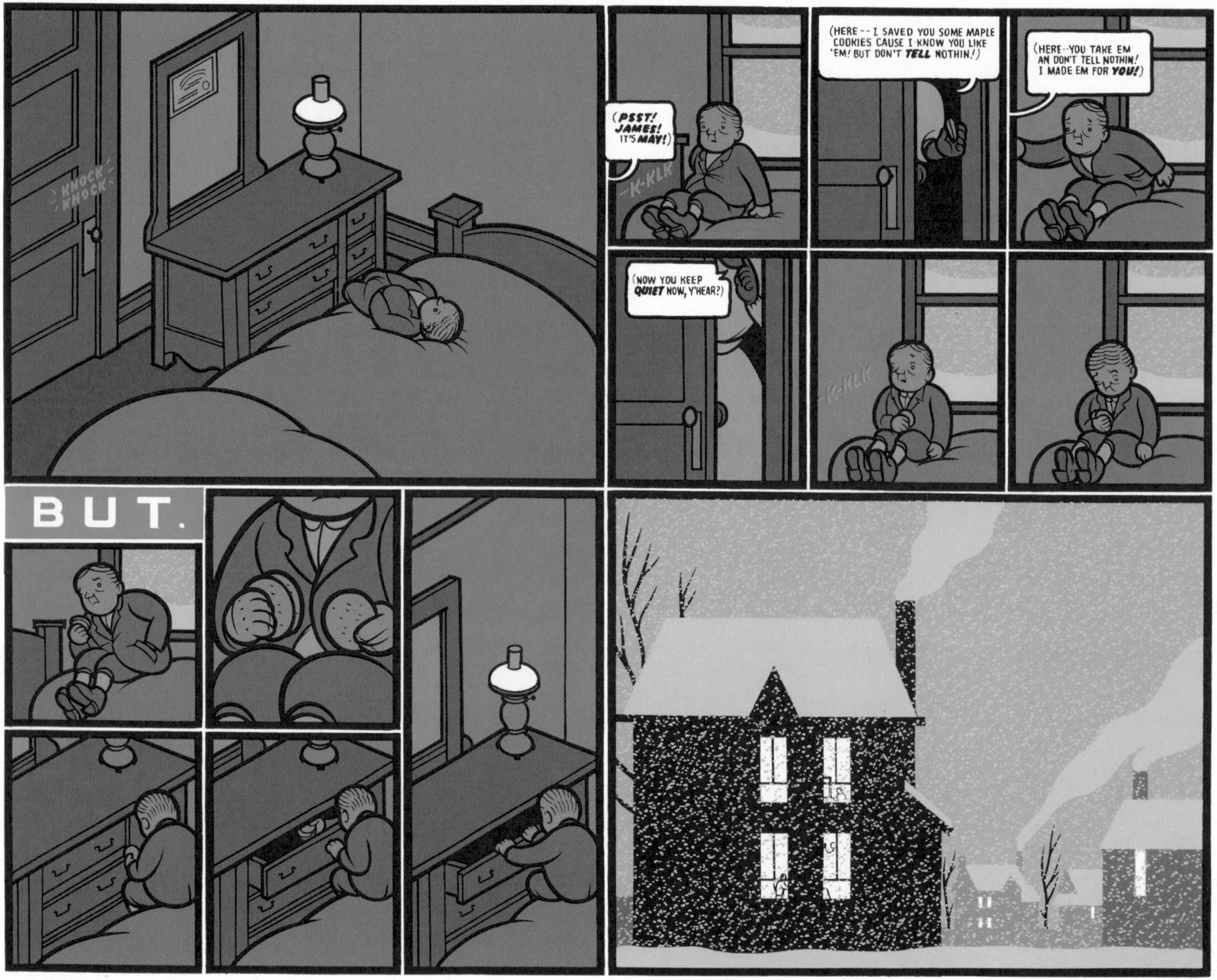
KNOCK KNOCK
(PSST! JAMES! IT'S MAY!)
K-KLK
(HERE -- I SAVED YOU SOME MAPLE COOKIES CAUSE I KNOW YOU LIKE 'EM! BUT DON'T TELL NOTHIN!)
(HERE--YOU TAKE EM AN DON'T TELL NOTHIN! I MADE EM FOR YOU!)
(NOW YOU KEEP QUIET NOW, Y'HEAR?)
K-KLK
BUT.

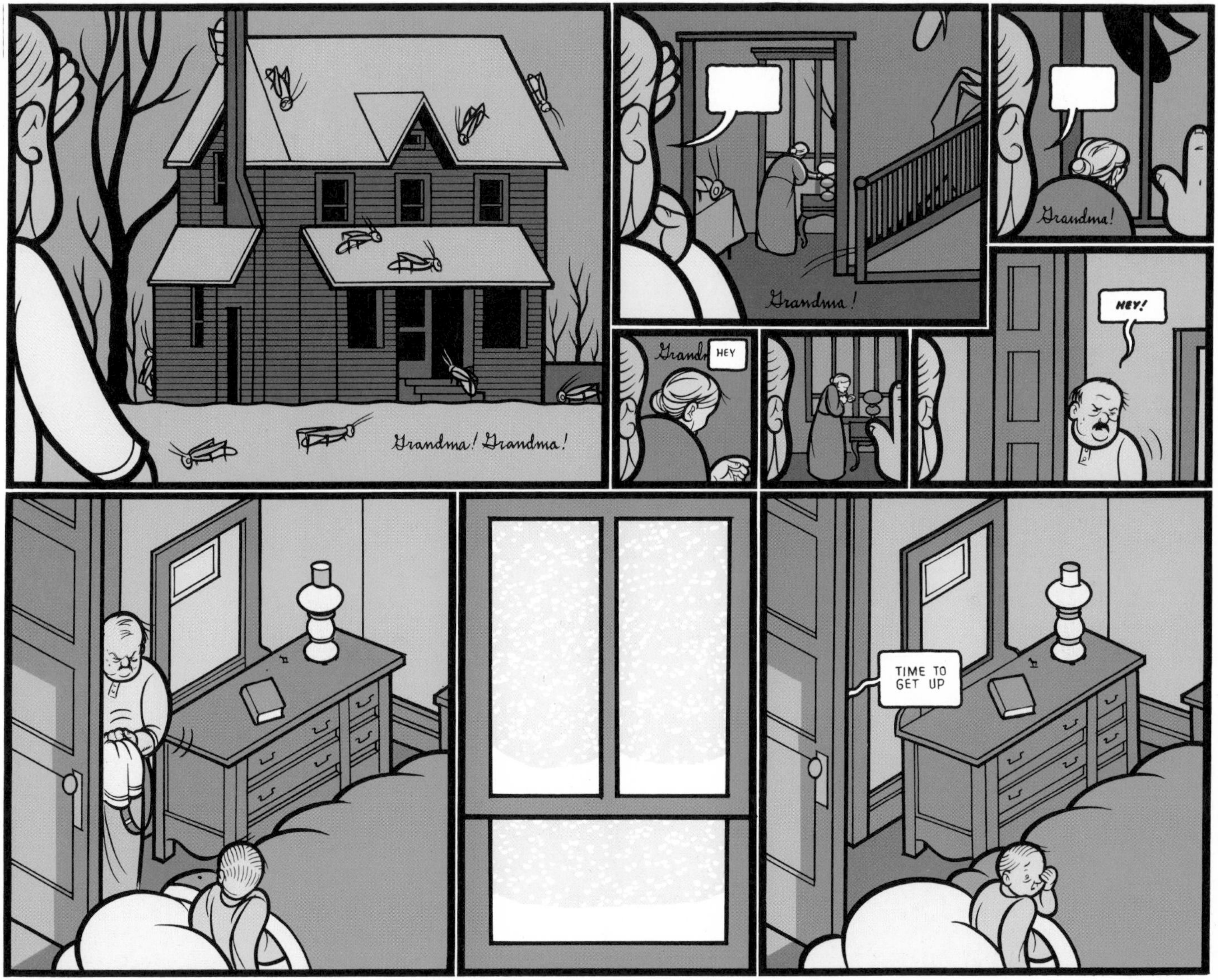

Grandma! Grandma!
Grandma!
Grandma!
Grandm
HEY
HEY!
TIME TO GET UP

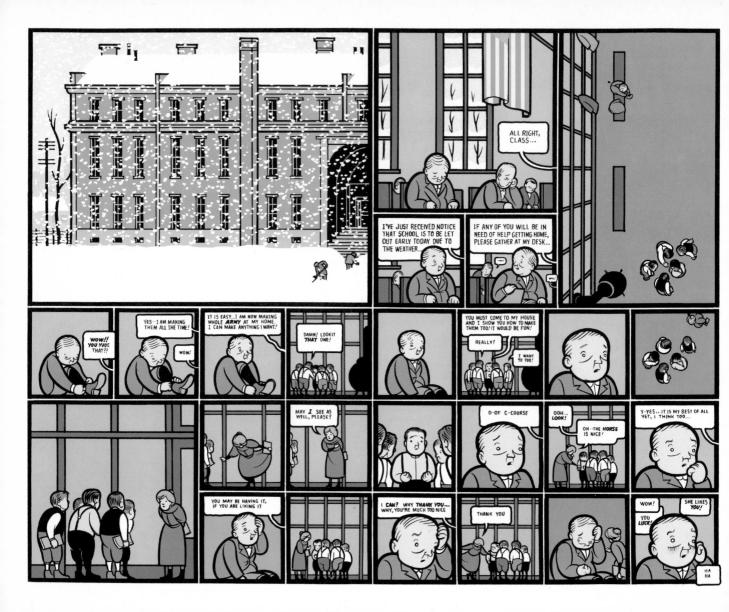

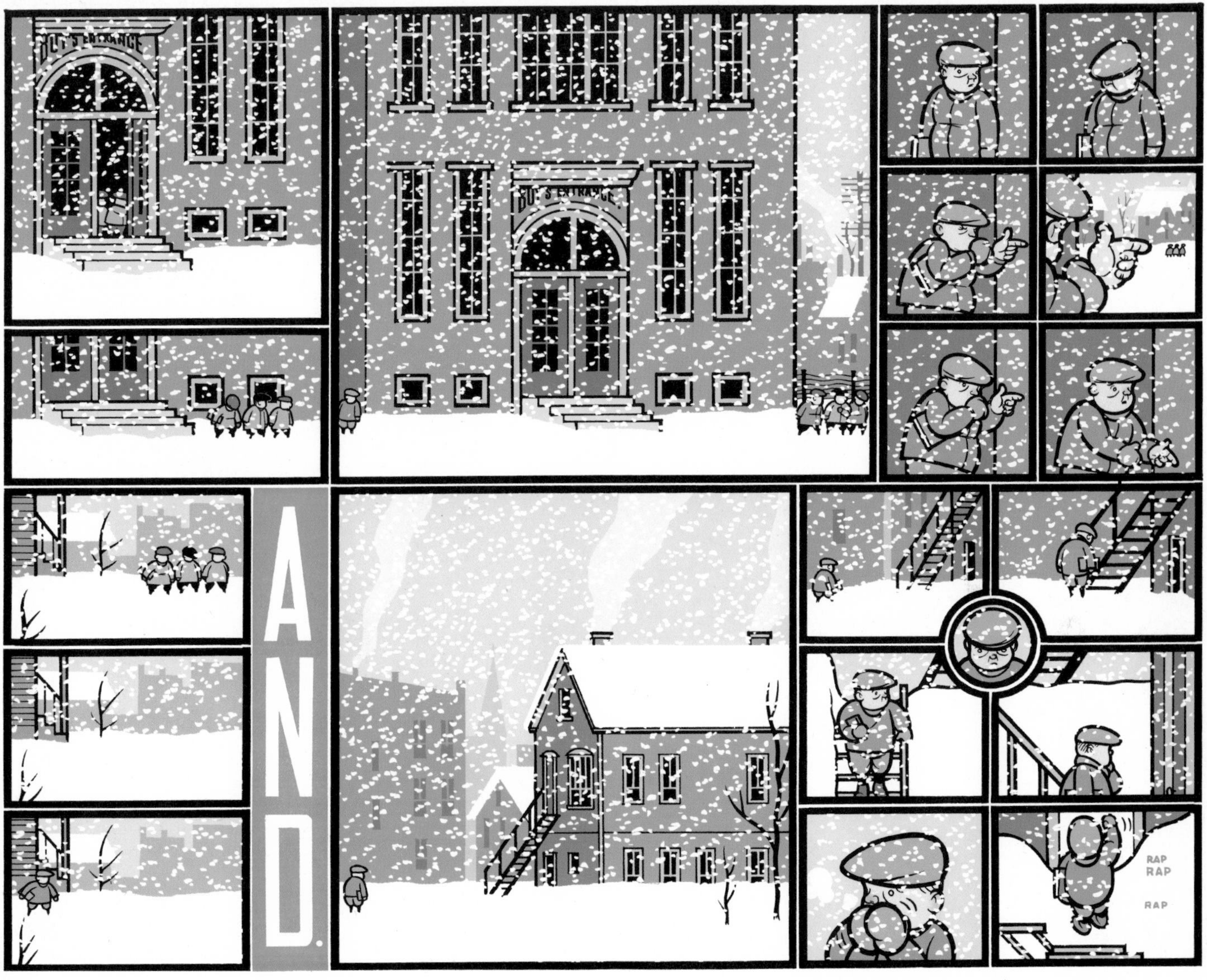
BOY'S ENTRANCE
BOY'S ENTRANCE
AND.
RAP
RAP
RAP

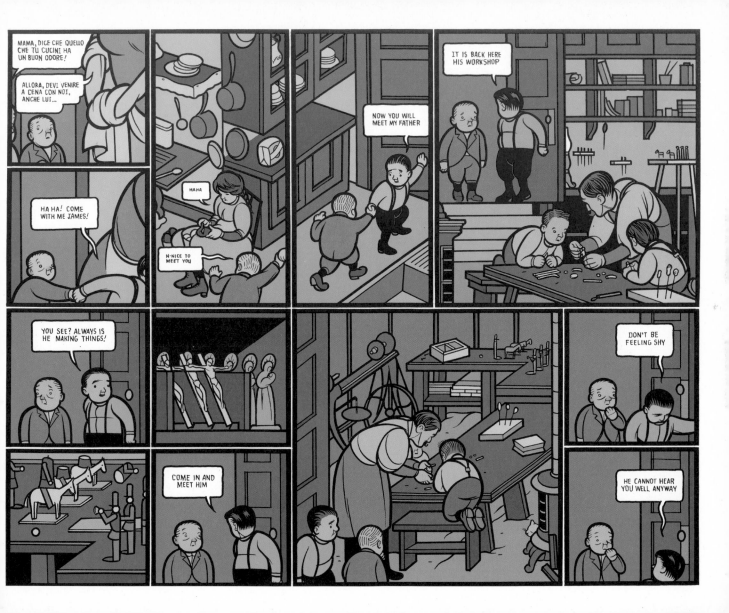

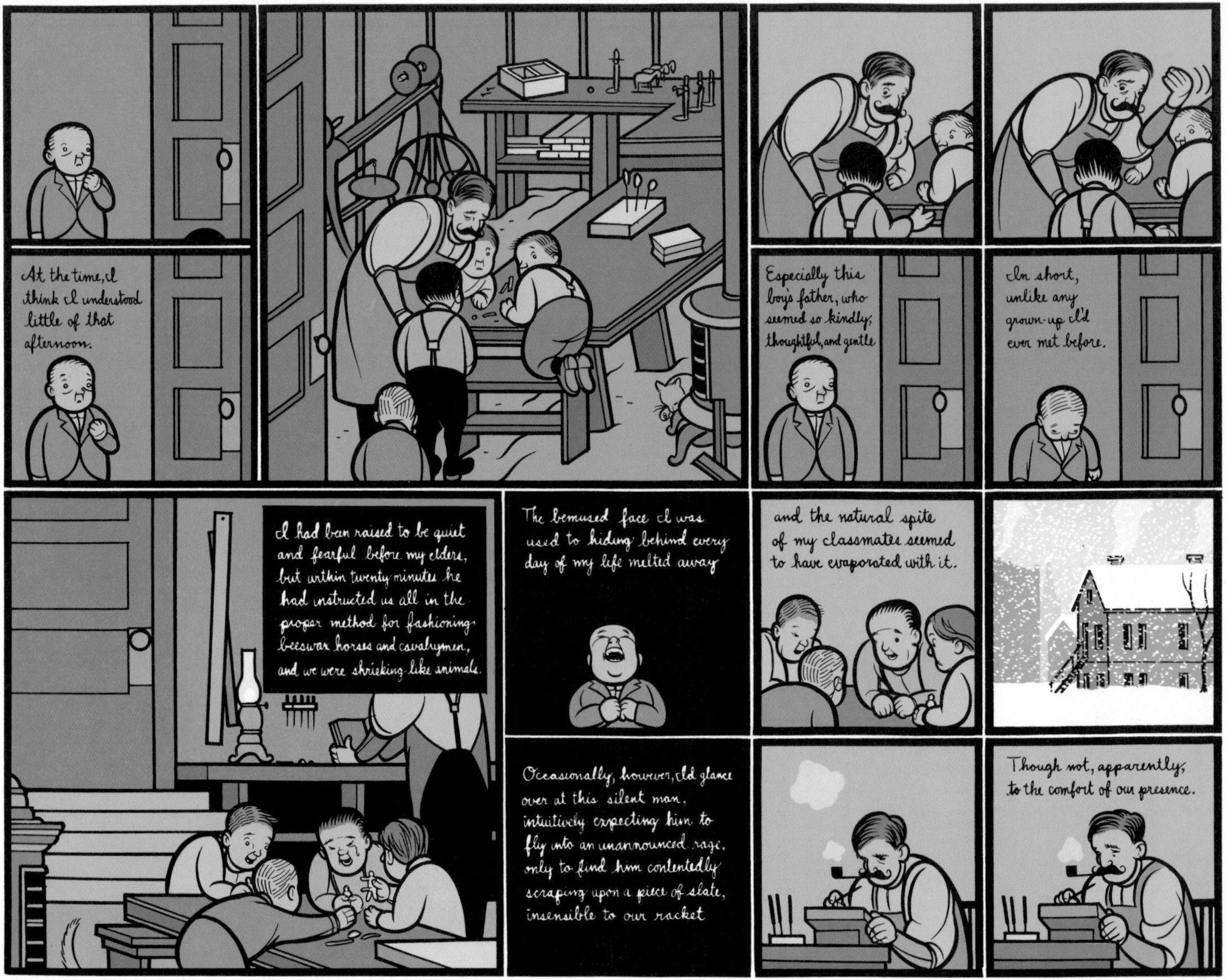

At the time, I think I understood little of that afternoon.
Especially this boy's father, who seemed so kindly, thoughtful, and gentle
In short, unlike any grown-up I'd ever met before.
I had been raised to be quiet and fearful before my elders, but within twenty minutes he had instructed us all in the proper method for fashioning beeswax horses and cavalrymen, and we were shrieking like animals.
The bemused face I was used to hiding behind every day of my life melted away
and the natural spite of my classmates seemed to have evaporated with it.
Occasionally, however, I'd glance over at this silent man, intuitively expecting him to fly into an unannounced rage, only to find him contentedly scraping upon a piece of slate, insensible to our racket
Though not, apparently, to the comfort of our presence.

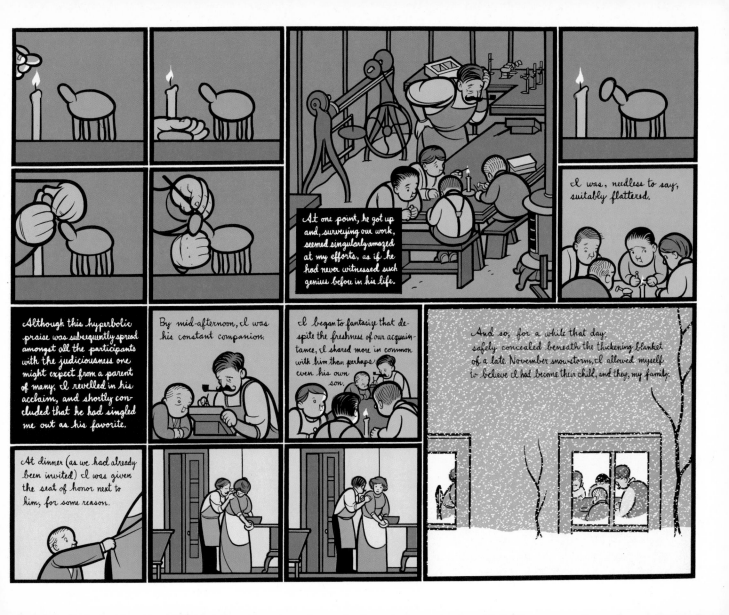

At one point, he got up and, surveying our work, seemed singularly amazed at my efforts, as if he had never witnessed such genius before in his life.

I was, needless to say, suitably flattered.

Although this hyperbolic praise was subsequently spread amongst all the participants with the judiciousness one might expect from a parent of many, I revelled in his acclaim, and shortly concluded that he had singled me out as his favorite.

By mid-afternoon, I was his constant companion.

I began to fantasize that despite the freshness of our acquaintance, I shared more in common with him than perhaps even his own son.

And so, for a while that day, safely concealed beneath the thickening blanket of a late November snowstorm, I allowed myself to believe I had become their child, and they, my family.

At dinner (as we had already been invited) I was given the seat of honor next to him, for some reason.

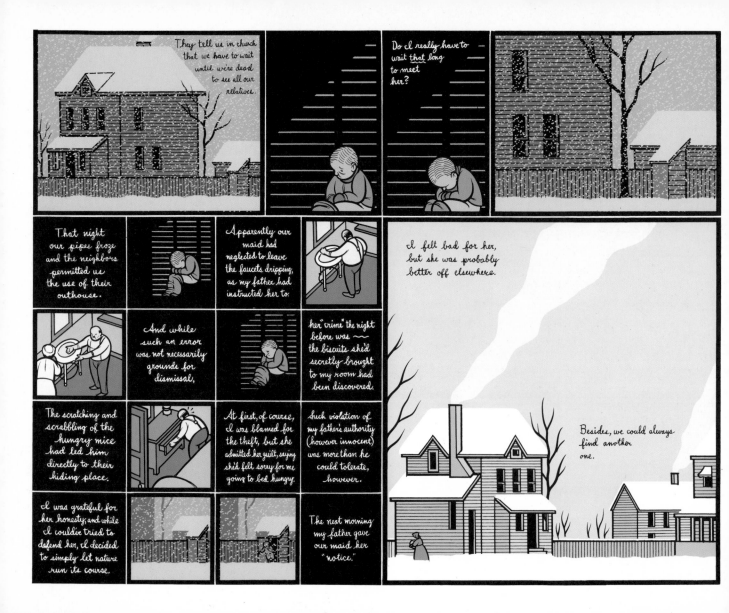

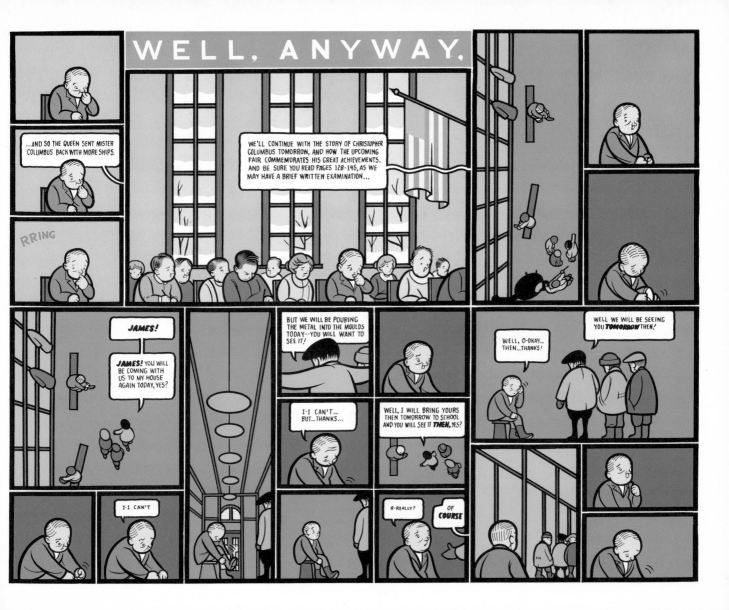

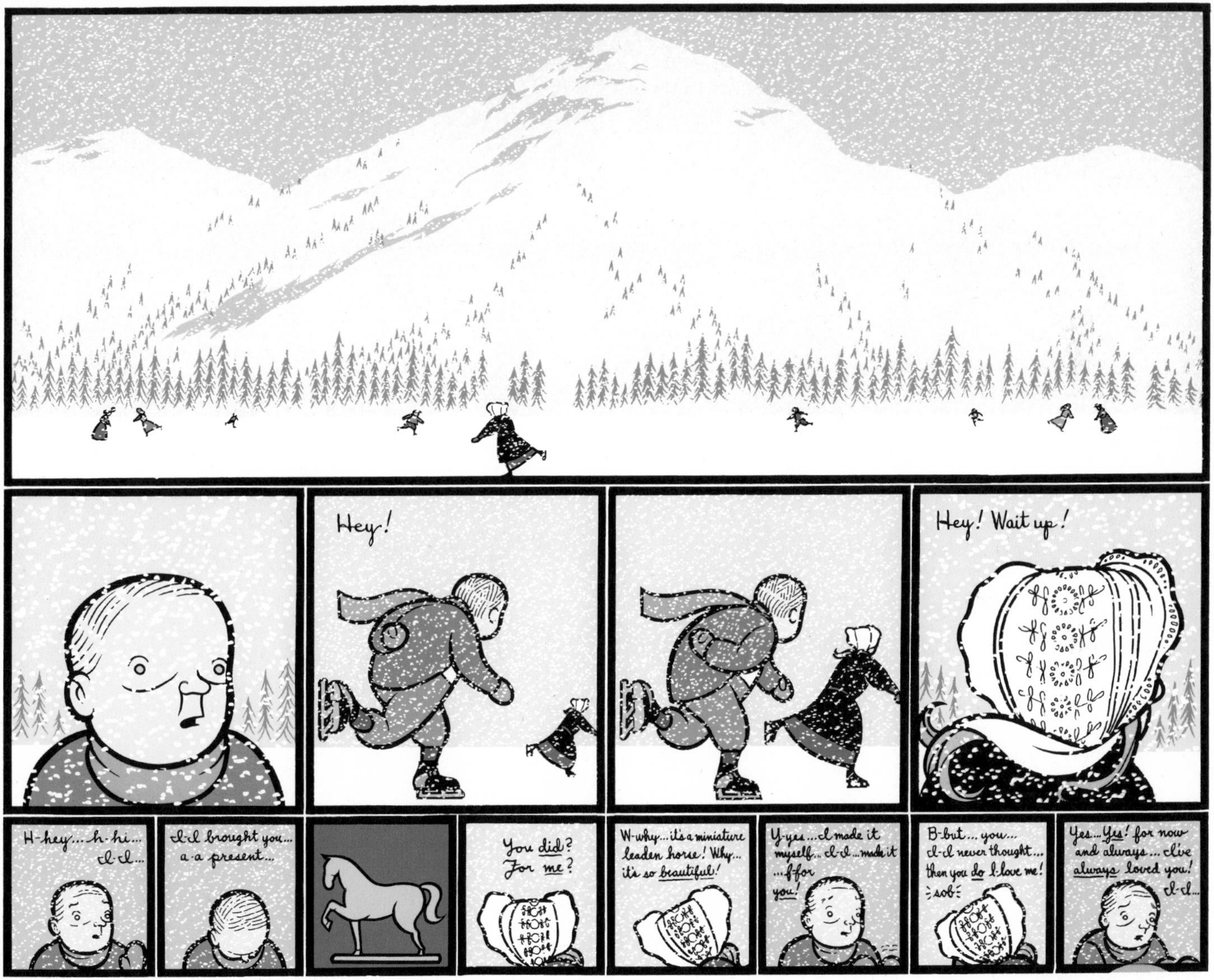
Hey!
Hey! Wait up!
H-hey... h-hi... I-I...
I-I brought you... a-a present...
You did? For me?
W-why... it's a miniature leaden horse! Why... it's so beautiful!
Y-yes... I made it myself... I-I... made it ...f-for you!
B-but... you... I-I never thought... then you do l-love me!
sob
Yes... Yes! for now and always... I've always loved you!
I-I...

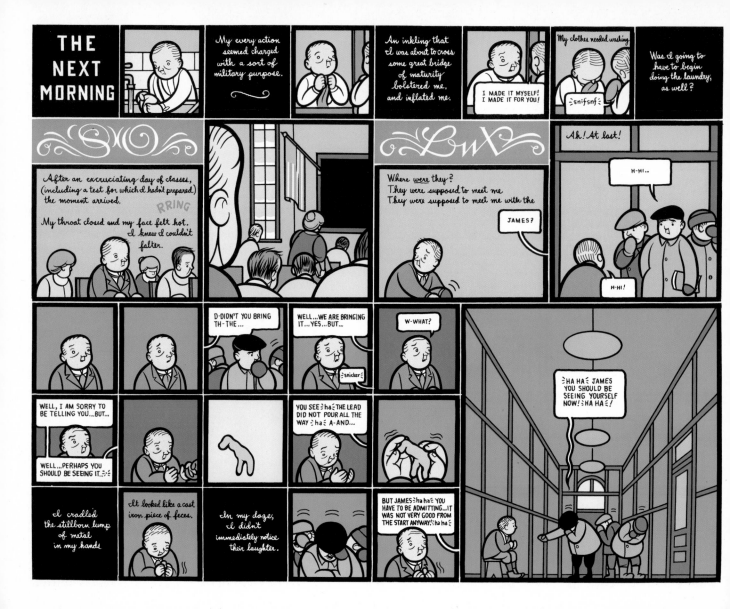

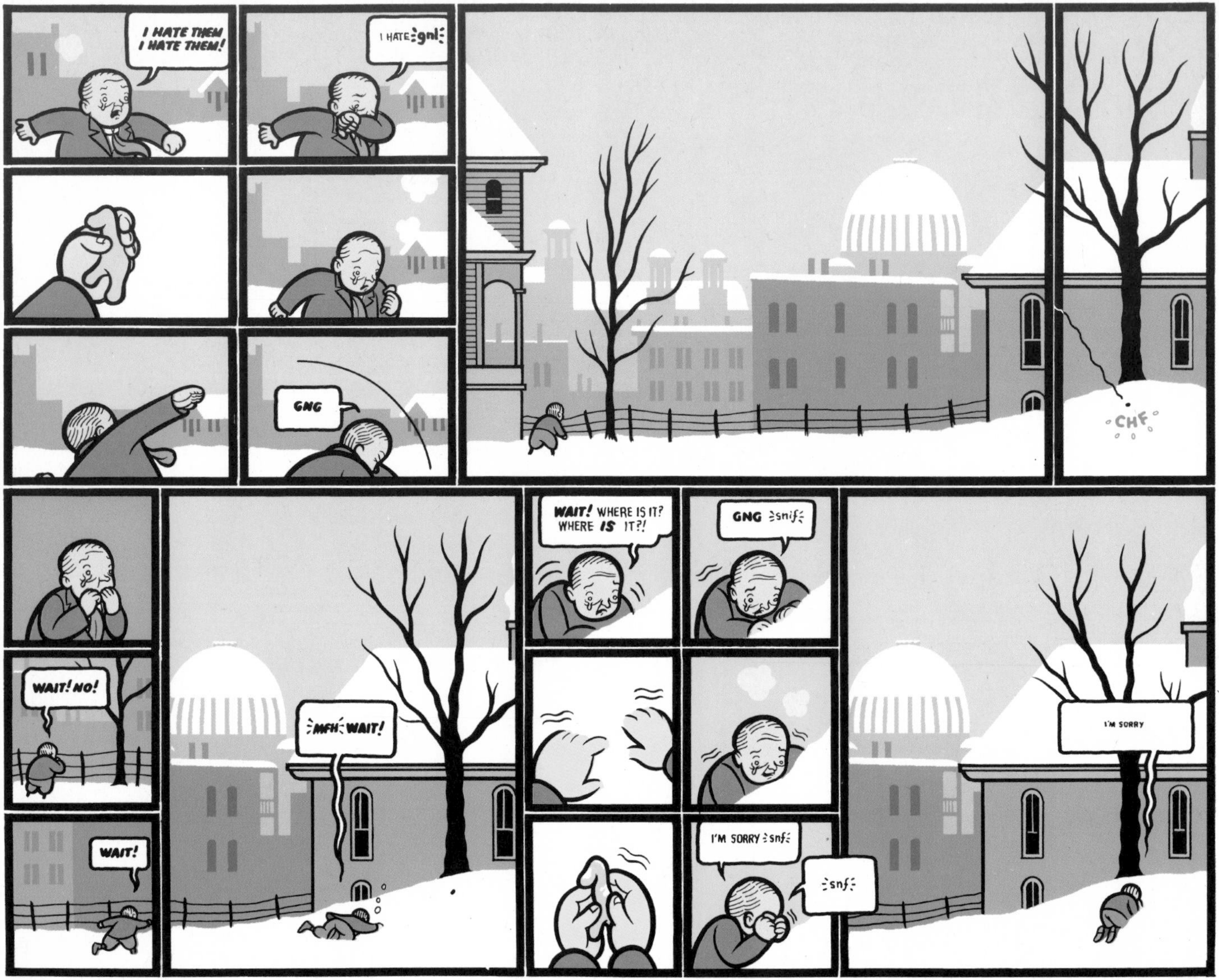

I HATE THEM I HATE THEM!
I HATE gnl
GNG
CHF
WAIT! NO!
WAIT!
MFH WAIT!
WAIT! WHERE IS IT? WHERE IS IT?!
GNG snif
I'M SORRY snf
snf
I'M SORRY

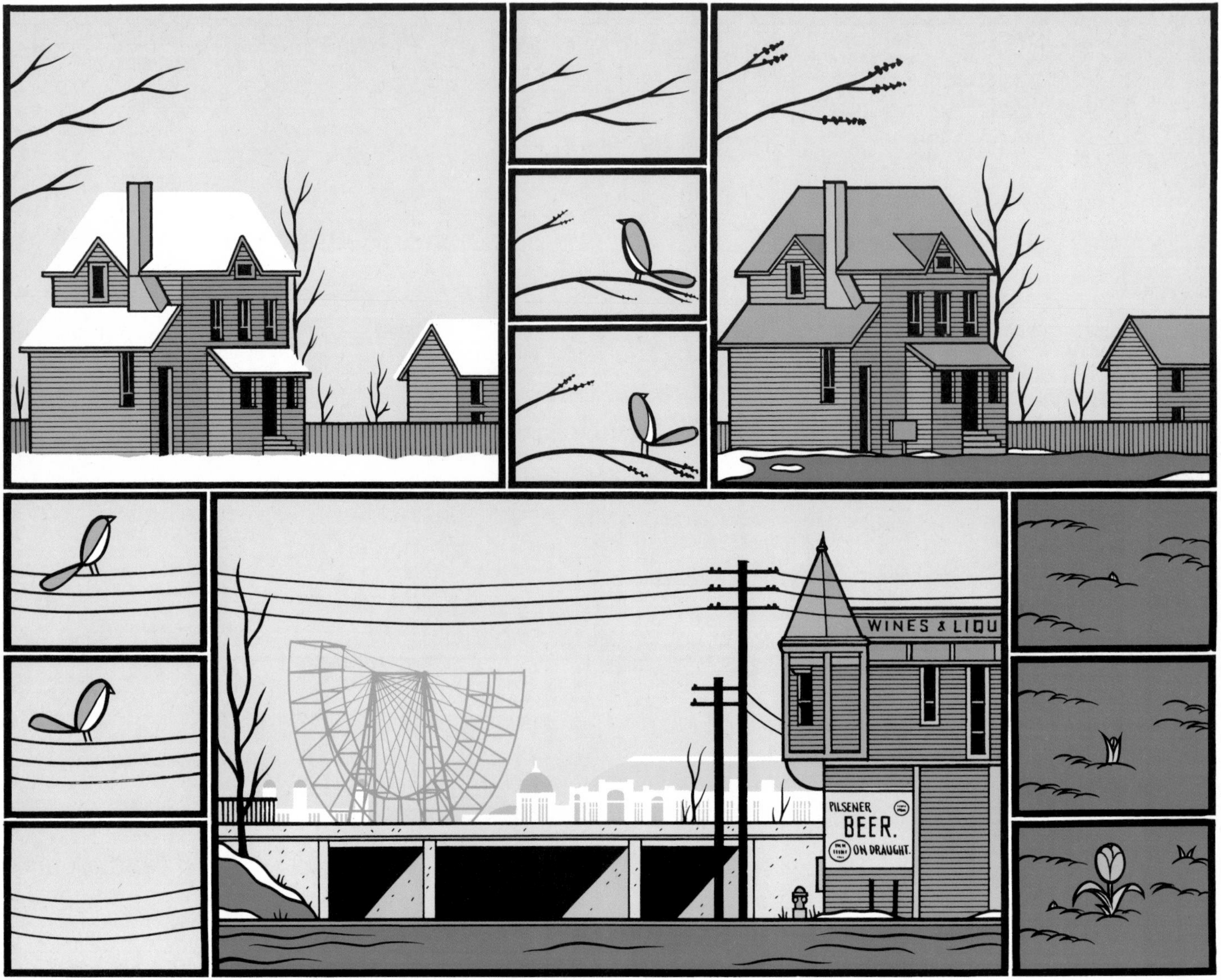
WINES & LIQU
PILSENER
BEER.
ON DRAUGHT.

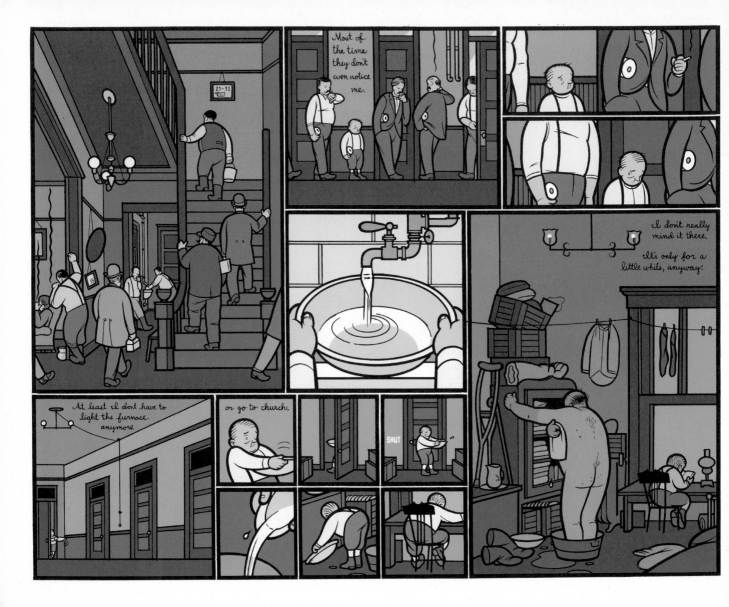

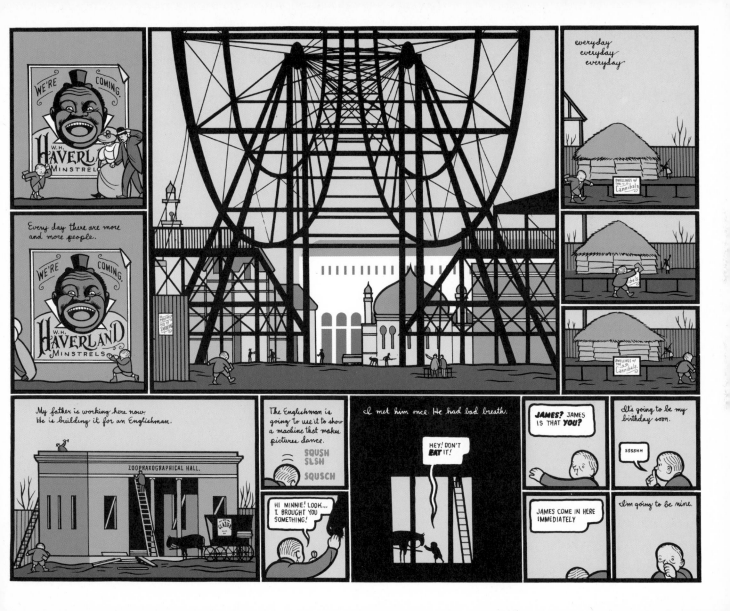

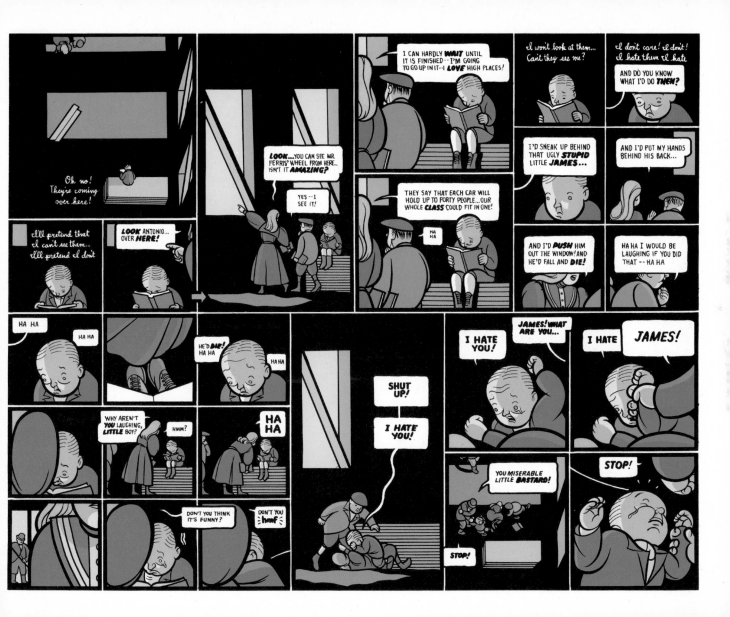

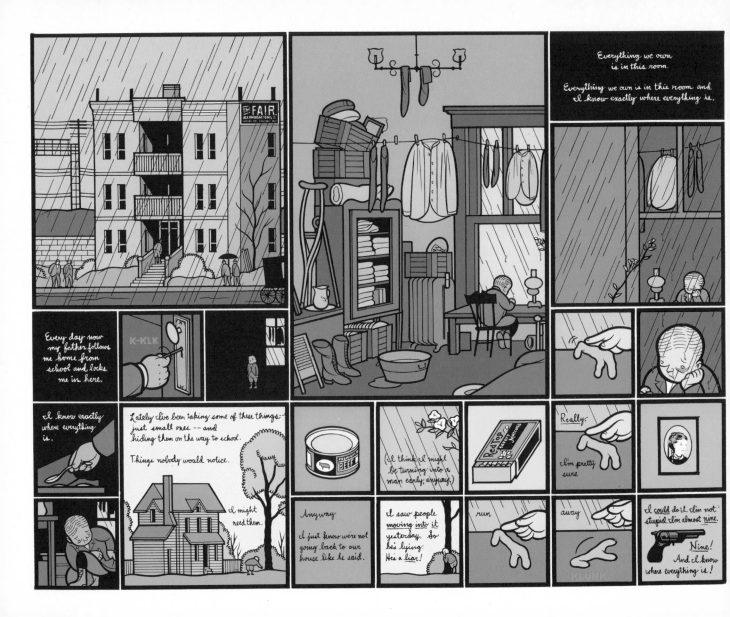

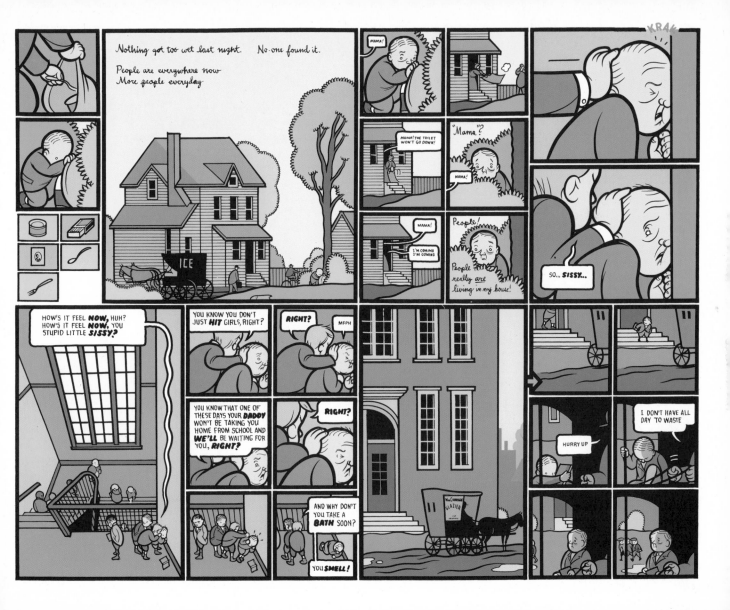

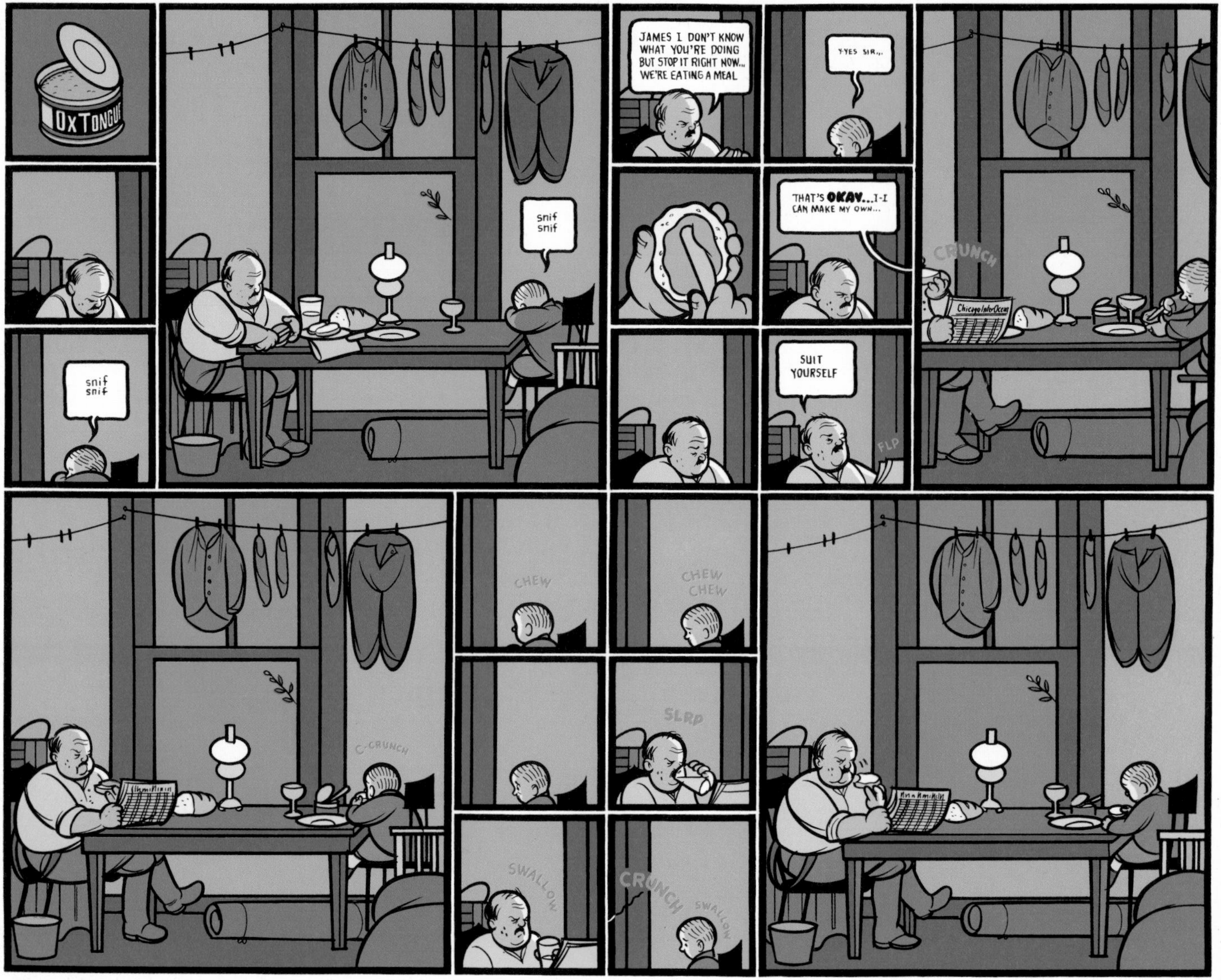
OxTongue
snif
snif
snif
snif
JAMES I DON'T KNOW WHAT YOU'RE DOING BUT STOP IT RIGHT NOW... WE'RE EATING A MEAL
Y-YES SIR...
THAT'S OKAY... I-I CAN MAKE MY OWN...
SUIT YOURSELF
FLP
CRUNCH
Chicago InterOcean
C-CRUNCH
CHEW
SWALLOW
CHEW
CHEW
SLRP
CRUNCH
SWALLOW

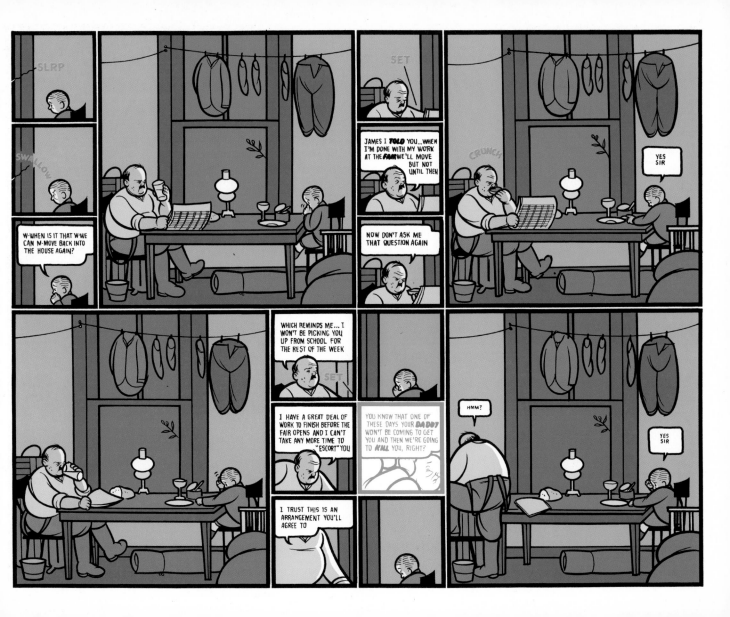

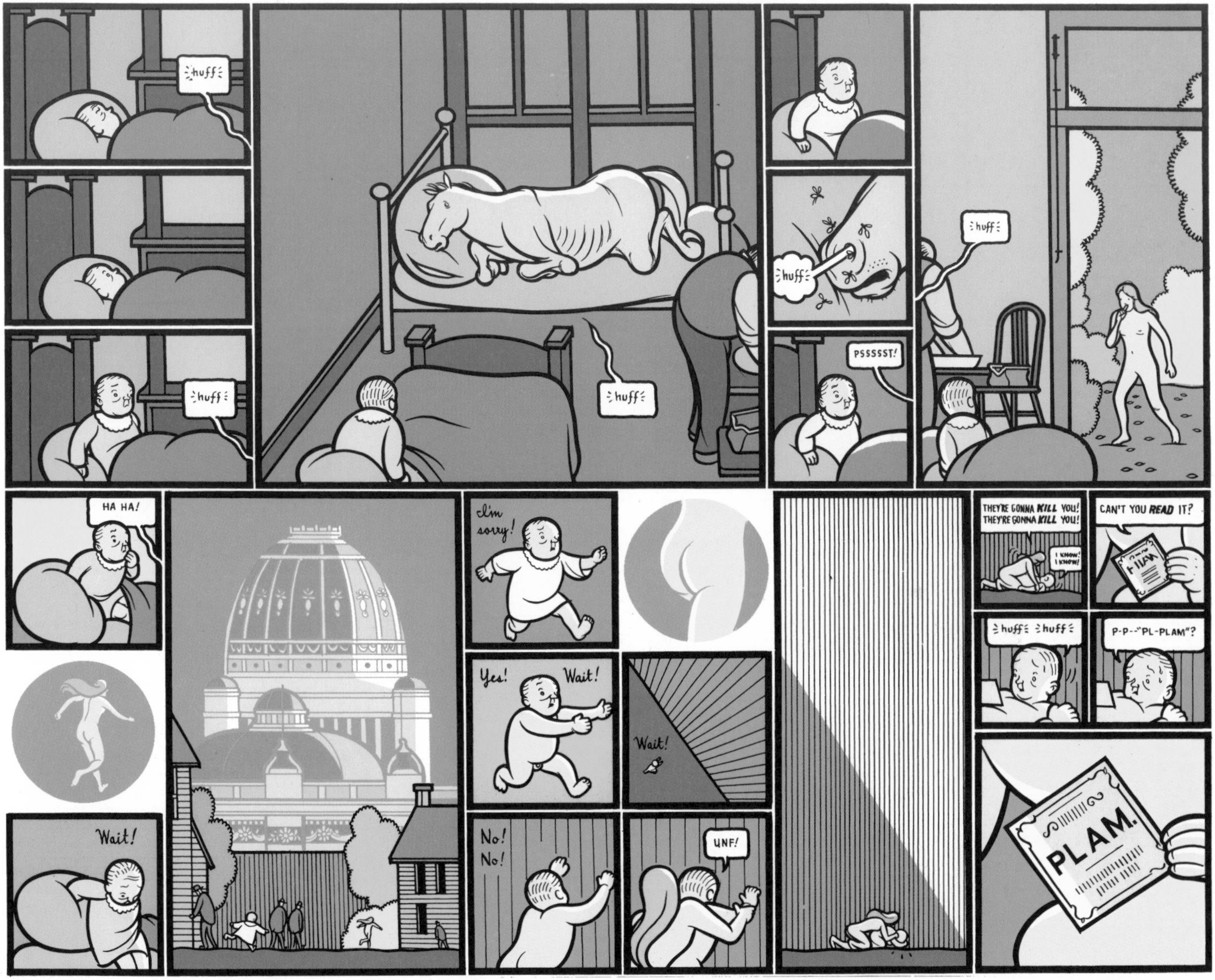
huff
huff
huff
huff
huff
PSSSSST!
huff
HA HA!
Wait!
I'm sorry!
Yes!
Wait!
No! No!
Wait!
UNF!
THEY'RE GONNA KILL YOU! THEY'RE GONNA KILL YOU!
I KNOW! I KNOW!
CAN'T YOU READ IT?
huff huff
P-P--"PL-PLAM"?
PLAM.

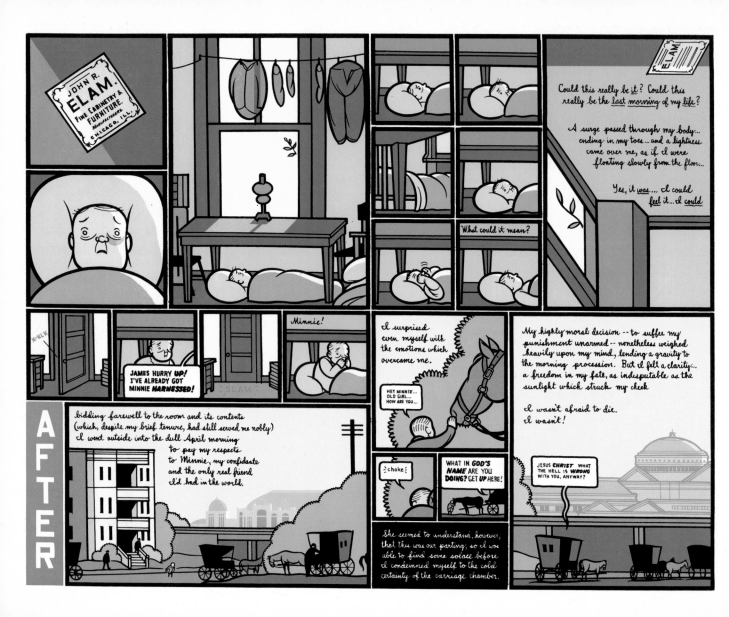

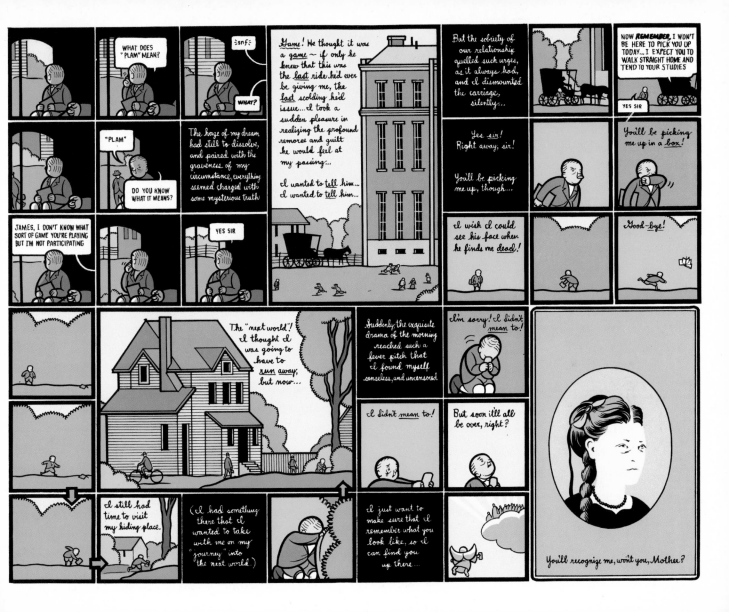

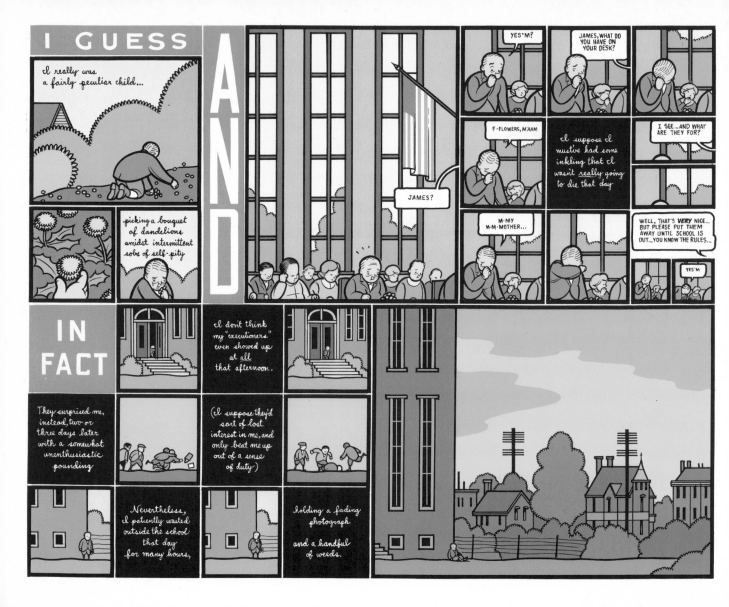

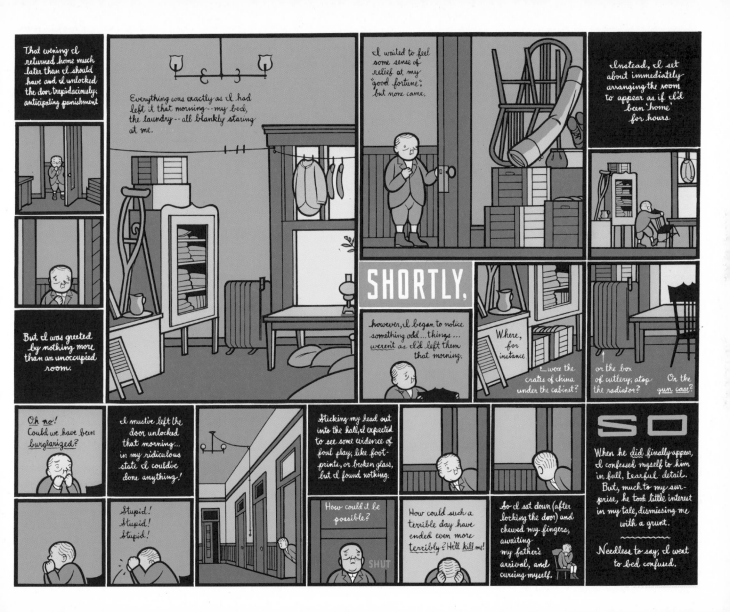

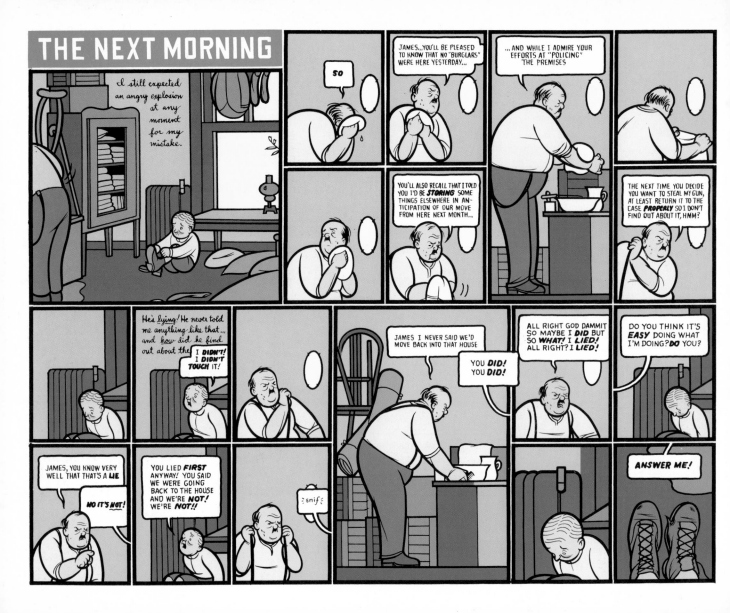

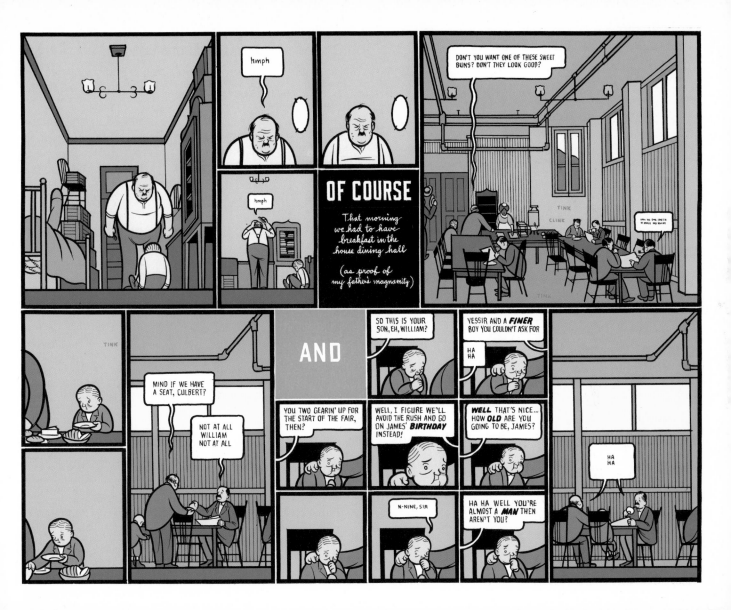

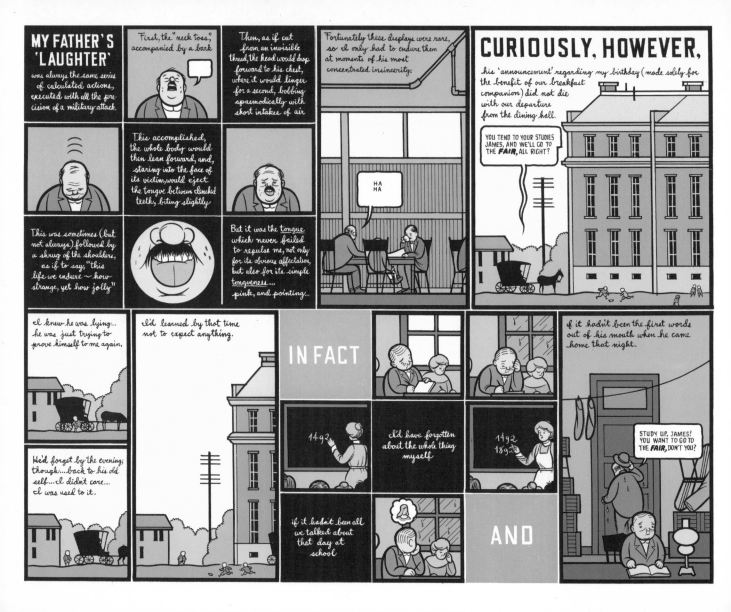

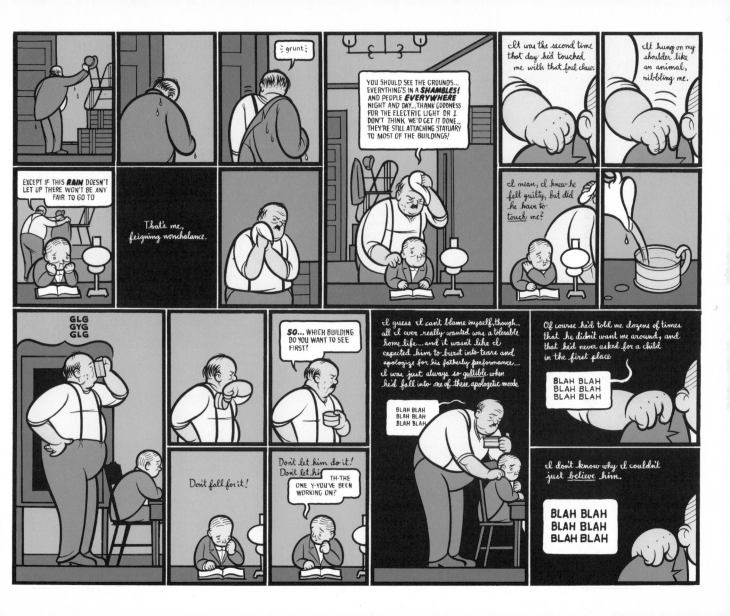

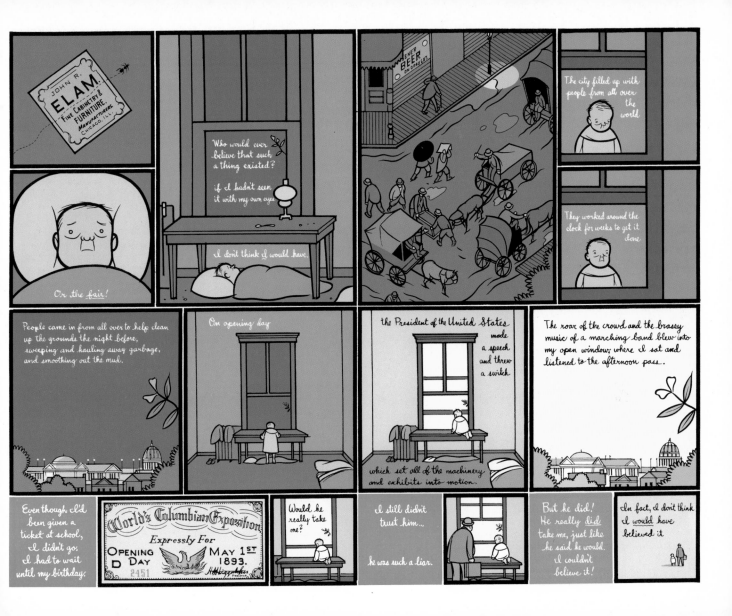

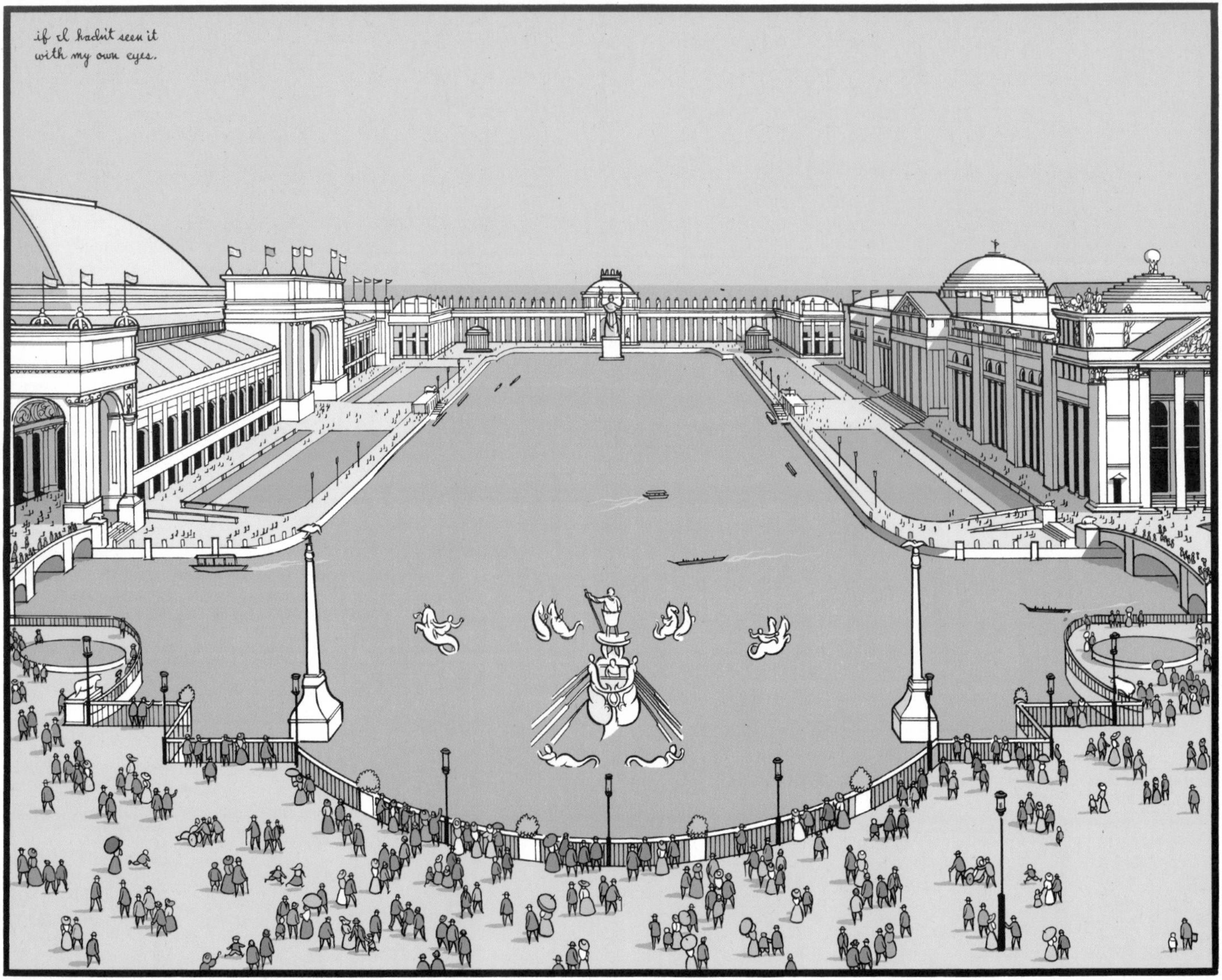
if I hadn't seen it
with my own eyes.

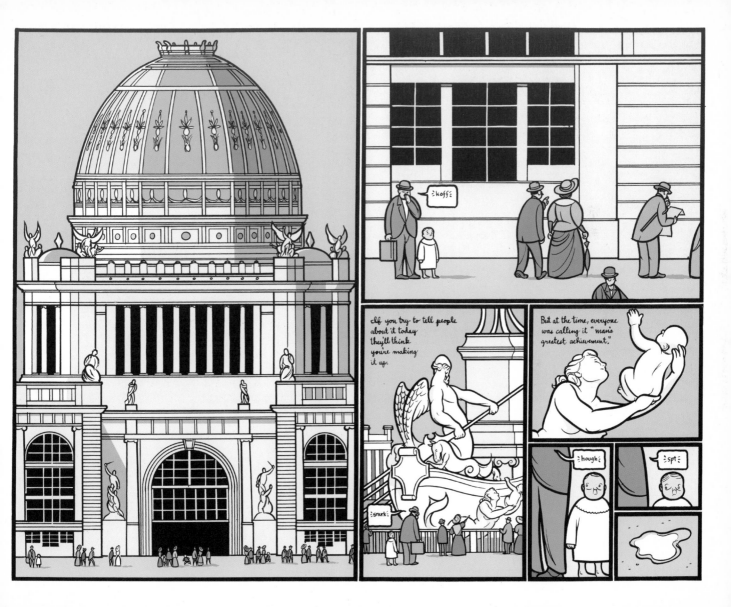

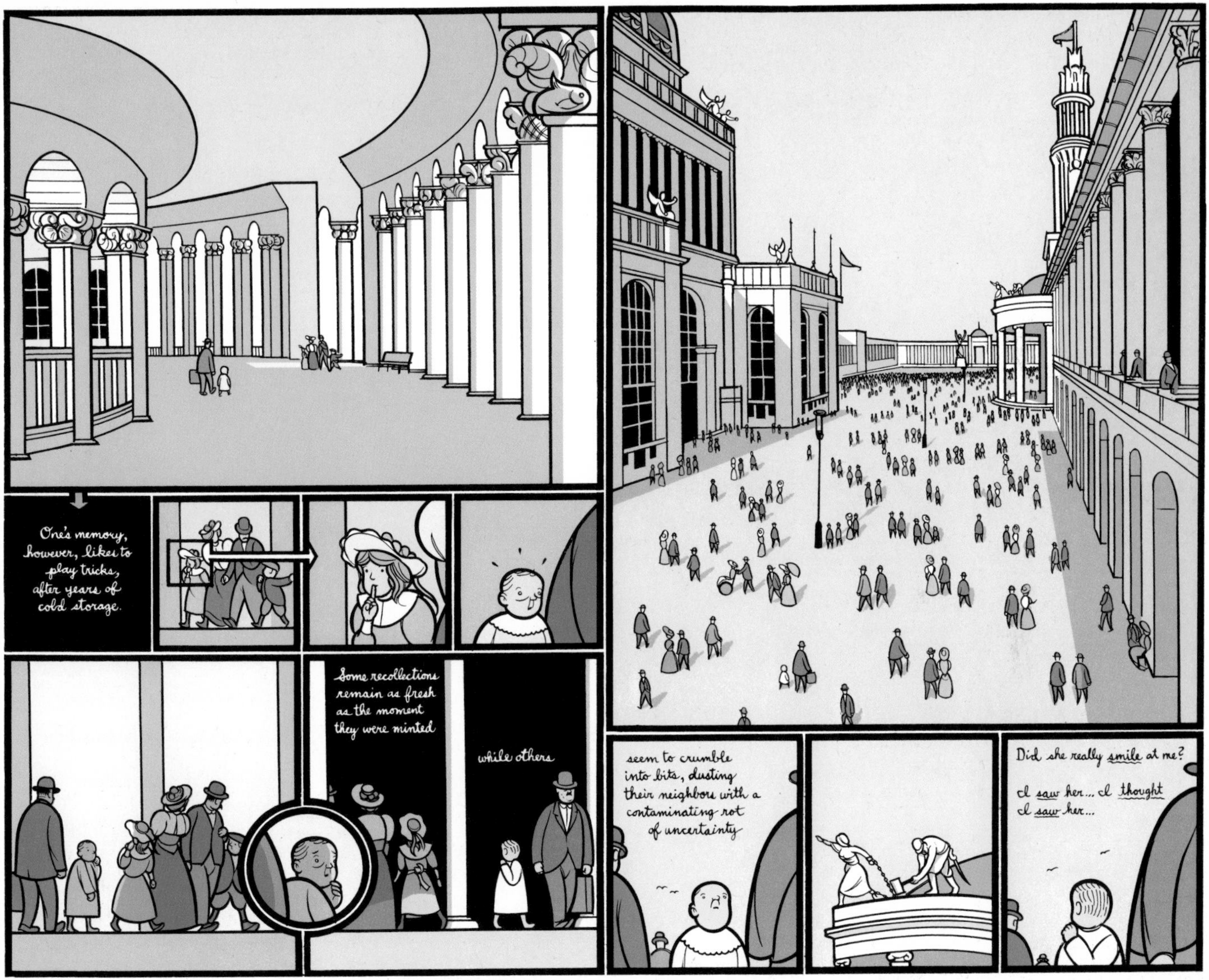
One's memory, however, likes to play tricks, after years of cold storage.
Some recollections remain as fresh as the moment they were minted
while others
seem to crumble into bits, dusting their neighbors with a contaminating rot of uncertainty
Did she really smile at me?
I saw her... I thought I saw her...

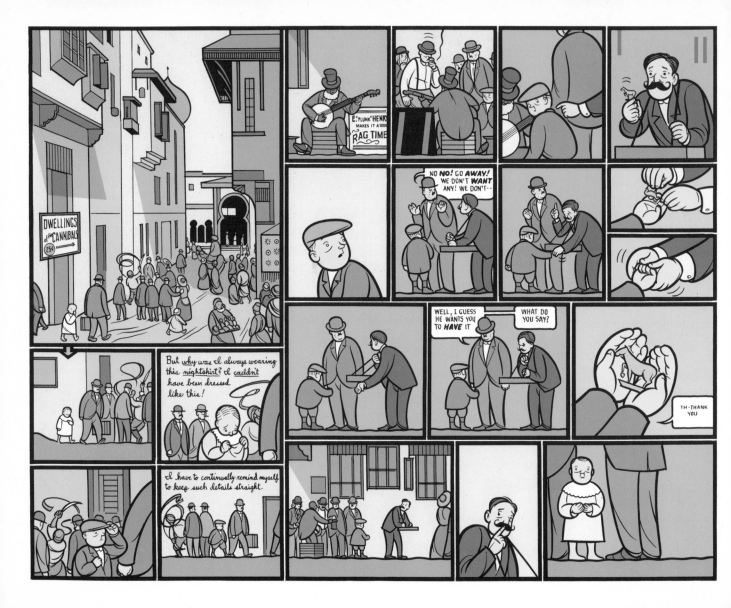

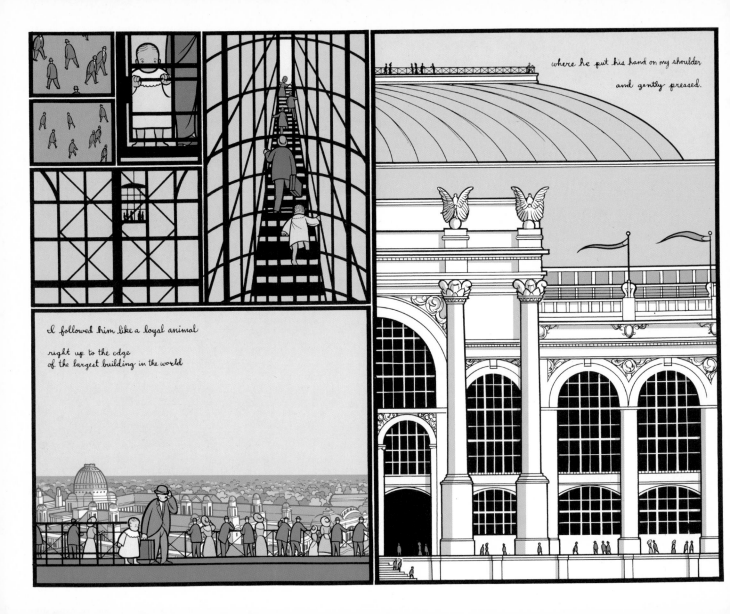

where he put his hand on my shoulder
and gently pressed.

I followed him like a loyal animal

right up to the edge
of the largest building in the world

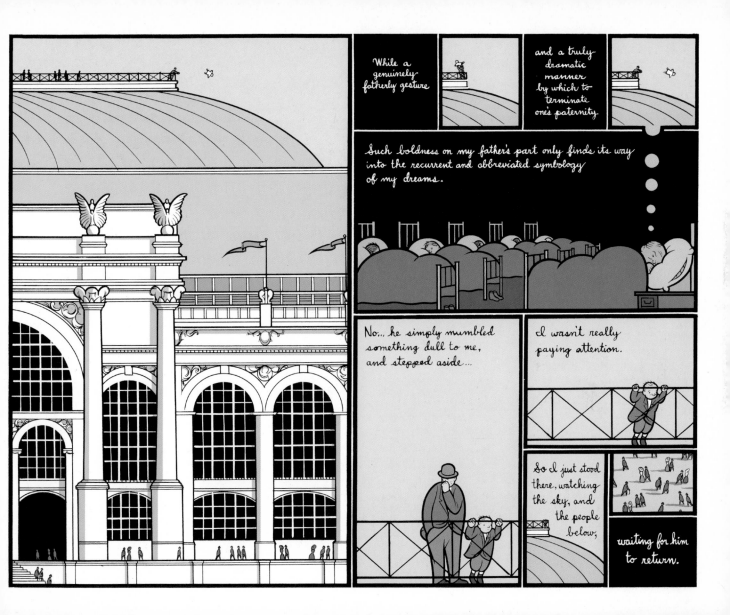

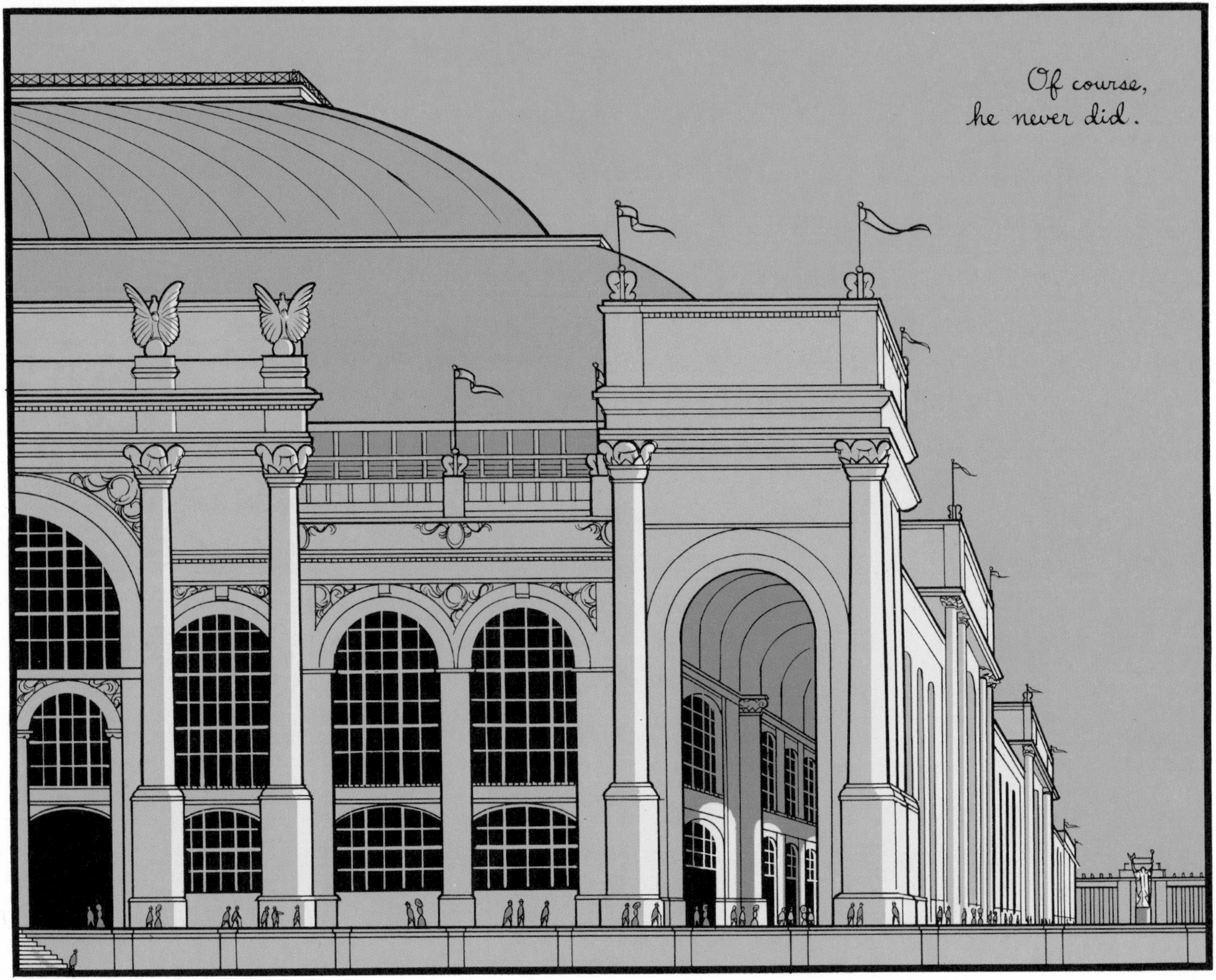
Of course,
he never did.

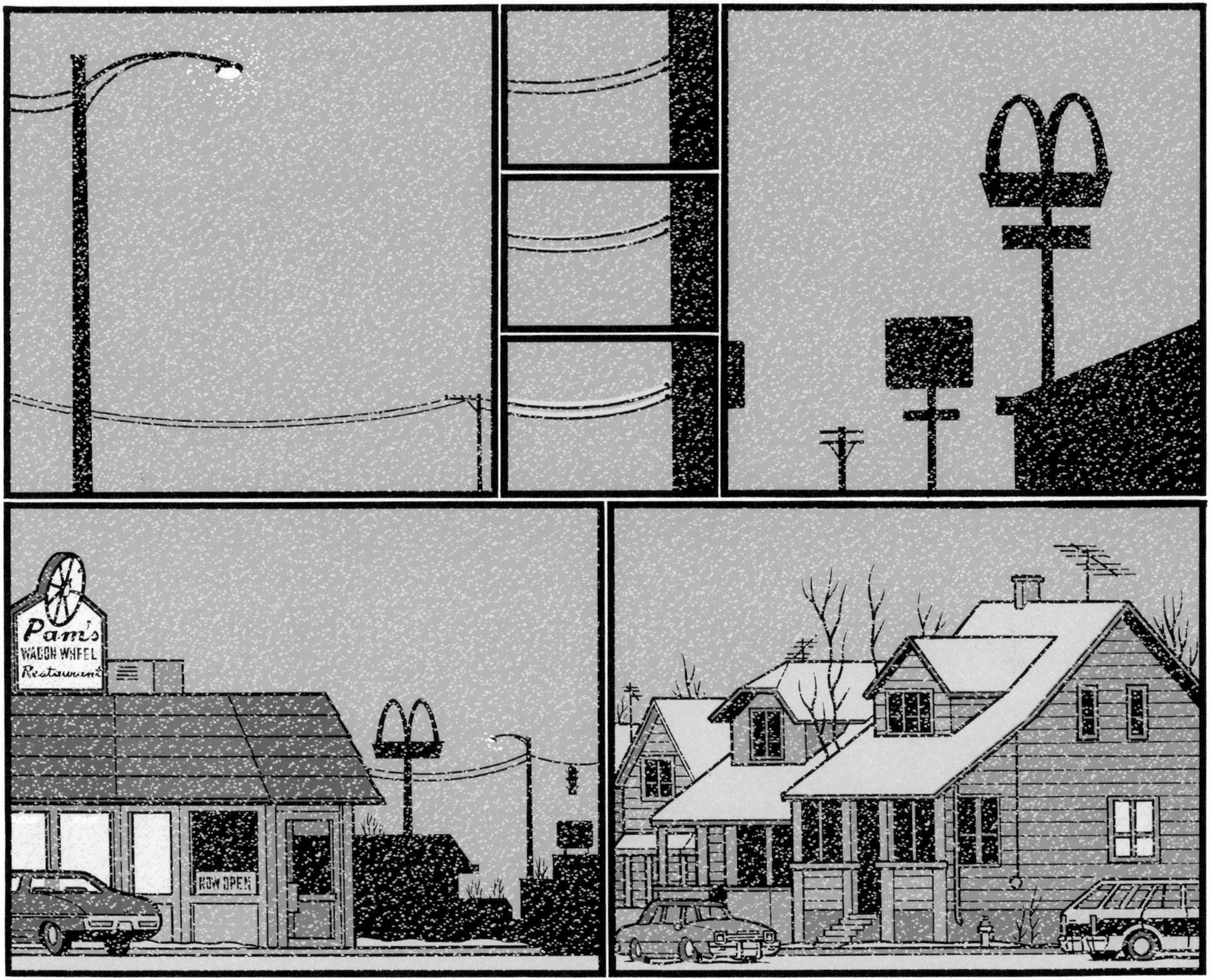

Pam's
WAGON WHEEL
Restaurant
NOW OPEN

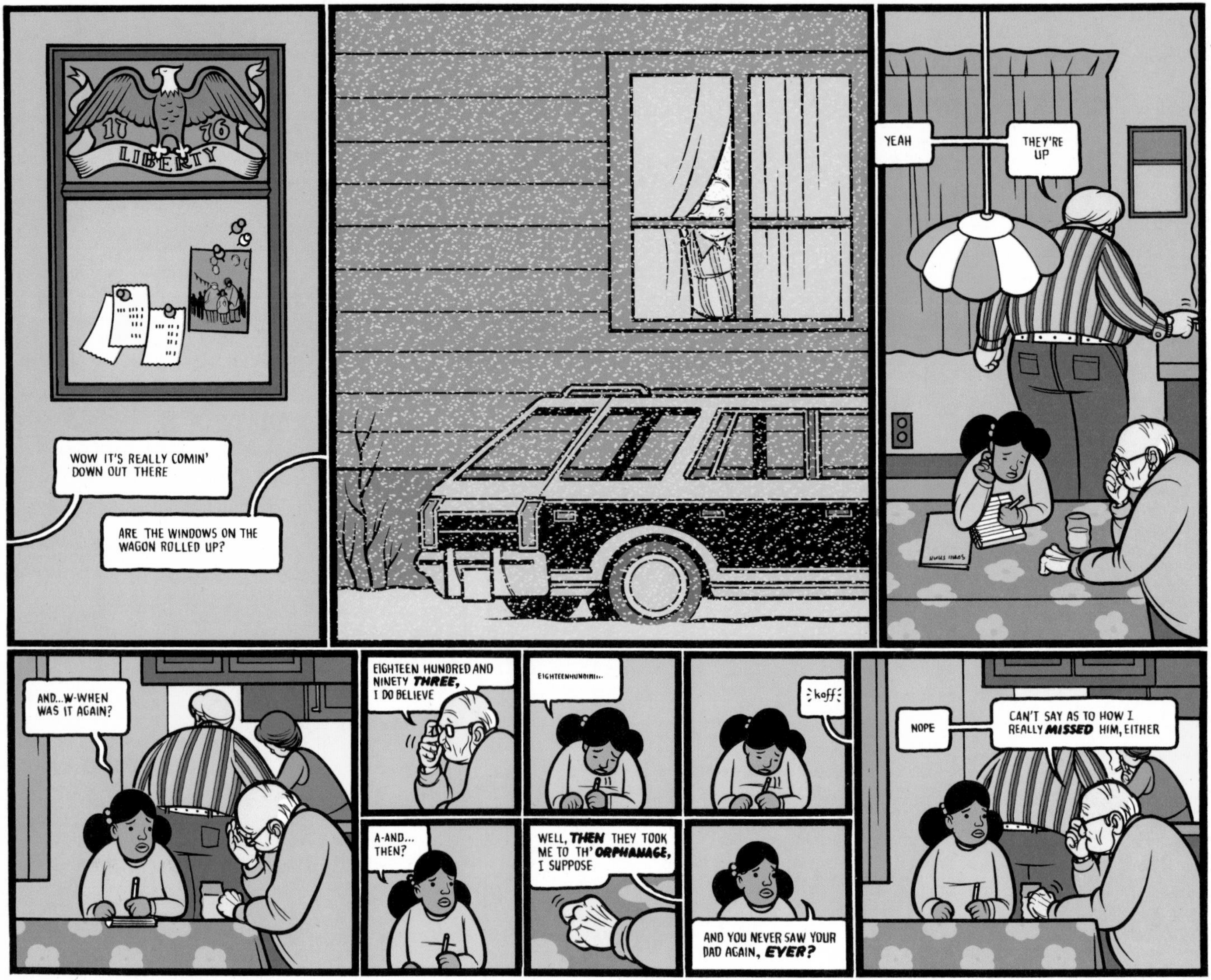
1776
LIBERTY
WOW IT'S REALLY COMIN' DOWN OUT THERE
ARE THE WINDOWS ON THE WAGON ROLLED UP?
YEAH
THEY'RE UP
AND...W-WHEN WAS IT AGAIN?
EIGHTEEN HUNDRED AND NINETY **THREE,** I DO BELIEVE
EIGHTEENHUNDINI...
koff
A-AND... THEN?
WELL, **THEN** THEY TOOK ME TO TH' **ORPHANAGE,** I SUPPOSE
AND YOU NEVER SAW YOUR DAD AGAIN, **EVER?**
NOPE
CAN'T SAY AS TO HOW I REALLY **MISSED** HIM, EITHER

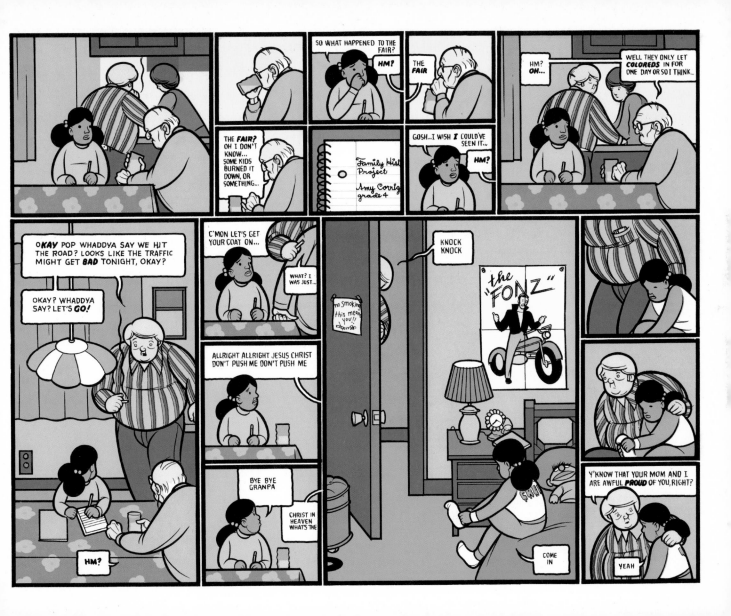

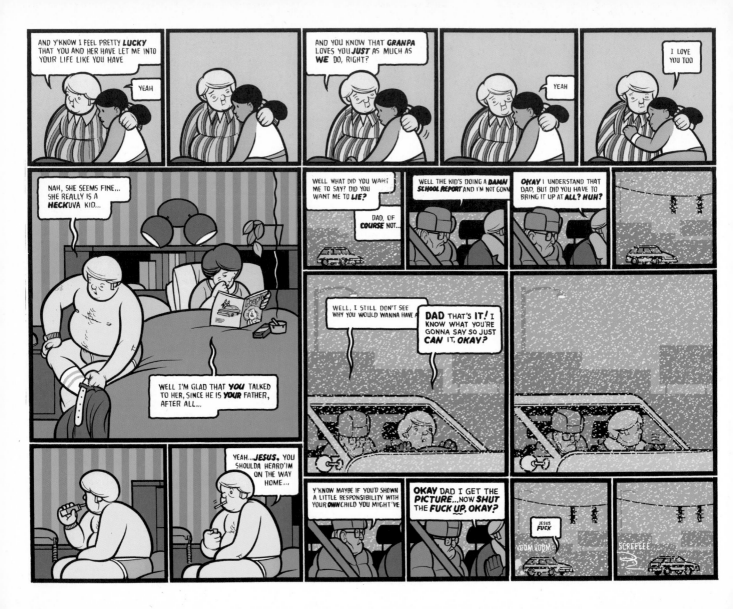

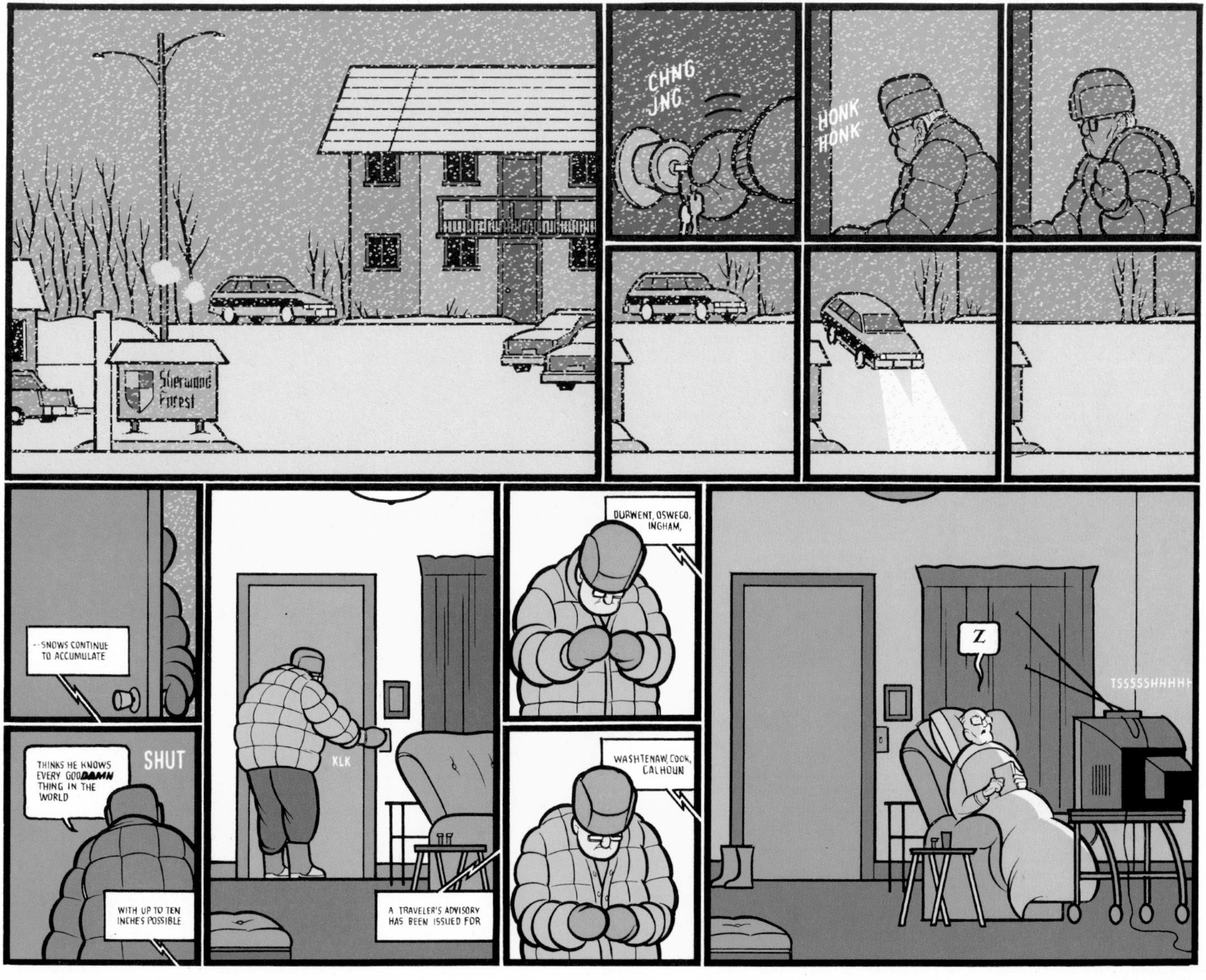

Sherwood Forest
CHNG JNG
HONK HONK
--SNOWS CONTINUE TO ACCUMULATE
THINKS HE KNOWS EVERY GODDAMN THING IN THE WORLD
SHUT
WITH UP TO TEN INCHES POSSIBLE
KLK
A TRAVELER'S ADVISORY HAS BEEN ISSUED FOR
DURWENT, OSWEGO, INGHAM,
WASHTENAW, COOK, CALHOUN
Z
TSSSSSHHHHH

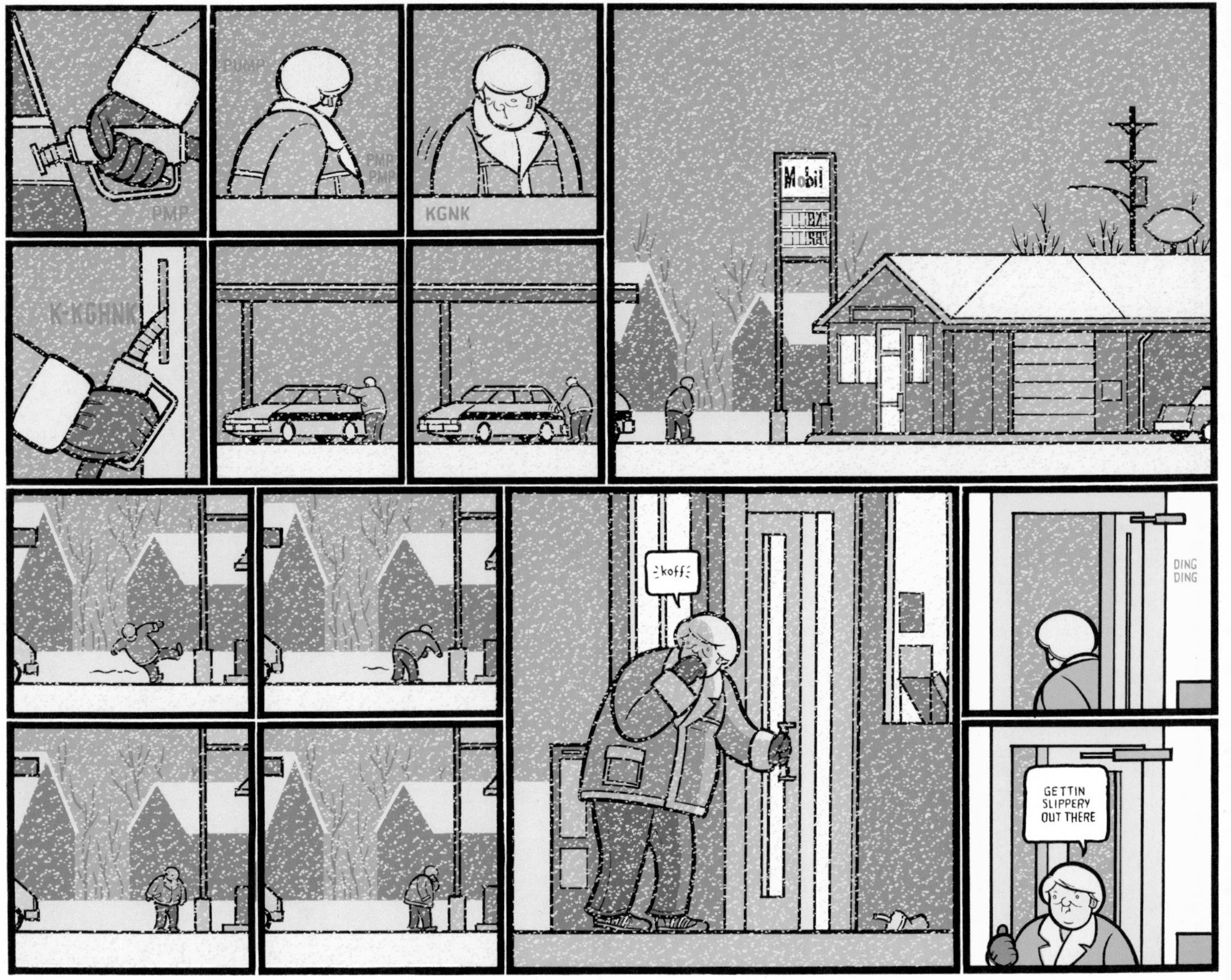
PMP
PUMP
PMP
PMP
KGNK
K-KGHNK
koff
DING
DING
GETTIN SLIPPERY OUT THERE

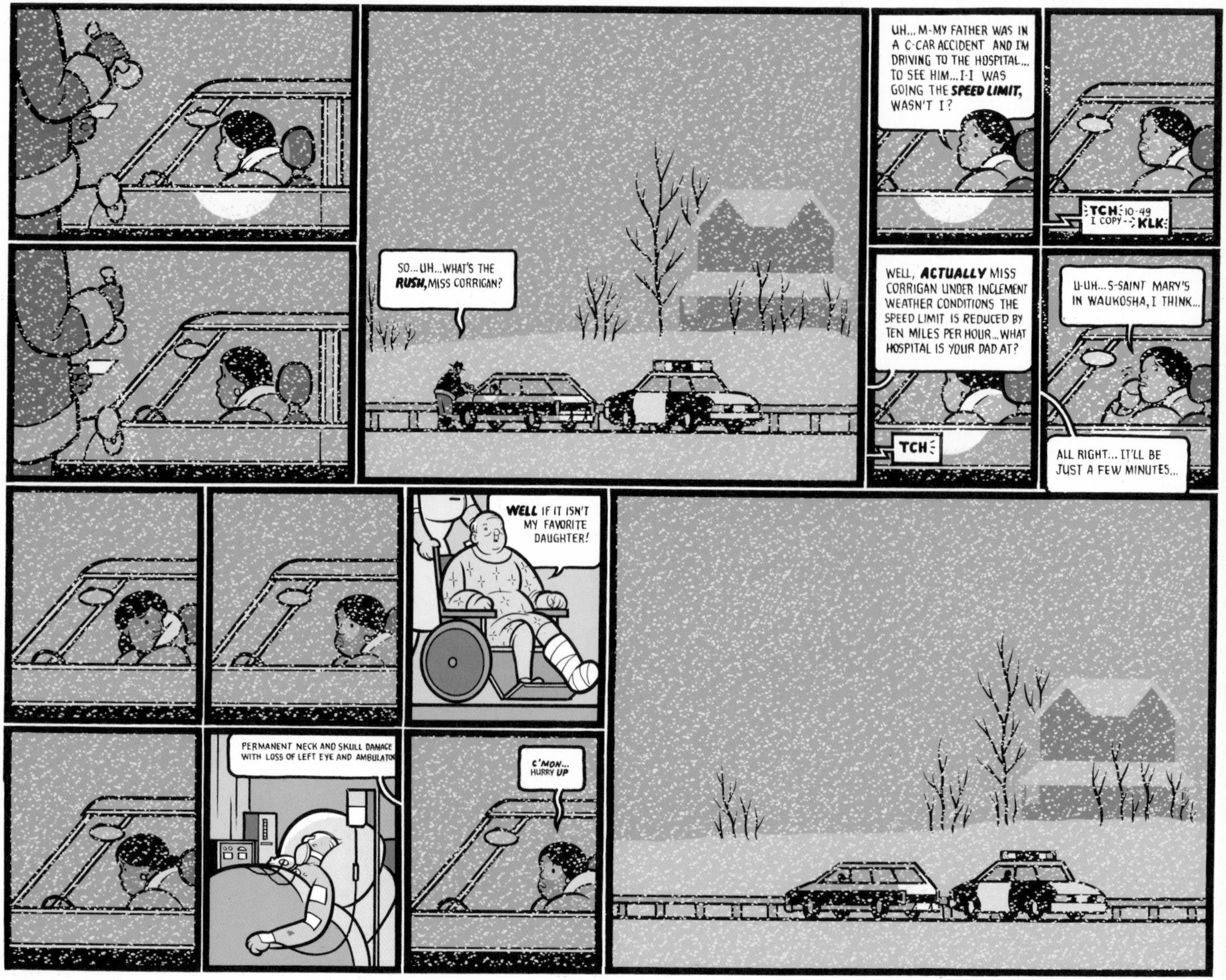
SO... UH... WHAT'S THE **RUSH**, MISS CORRIGAN?
UH... M-MY FATHER WAS IN A C-CAR ACCIDENT AND I'M DRIVING TO THE HOSPITAL... TO SEE HIM... I-I WAS GOING THE **SPEED LIMIT**, WASN'T I?
TCH 10-49
I COPY KLK
WELL, **ACTUALLY** MISS CORRIGAN UNDER INCLEMENT WEATHER CONDITIONS THE SPEED LIMIT IS REDUCED BY TEN MILES PER HOUR... WHAT HOSPITAL IS YOUR DAD AT?
TCH
U-UH... S-SAINT MARY'S IN WAUKOSHA, I THINK...
ALL RIGHT... IT'LL BE JUST A FEW MINUTES...
WELL IF IT ISN'T MY FAVORITE DAUGHTER!
PERMANENT NECK AND SKULL DAMAGE WITH LOSS OF LEFT EYE AND AMBULATO
C'MON... HURRY **UP**

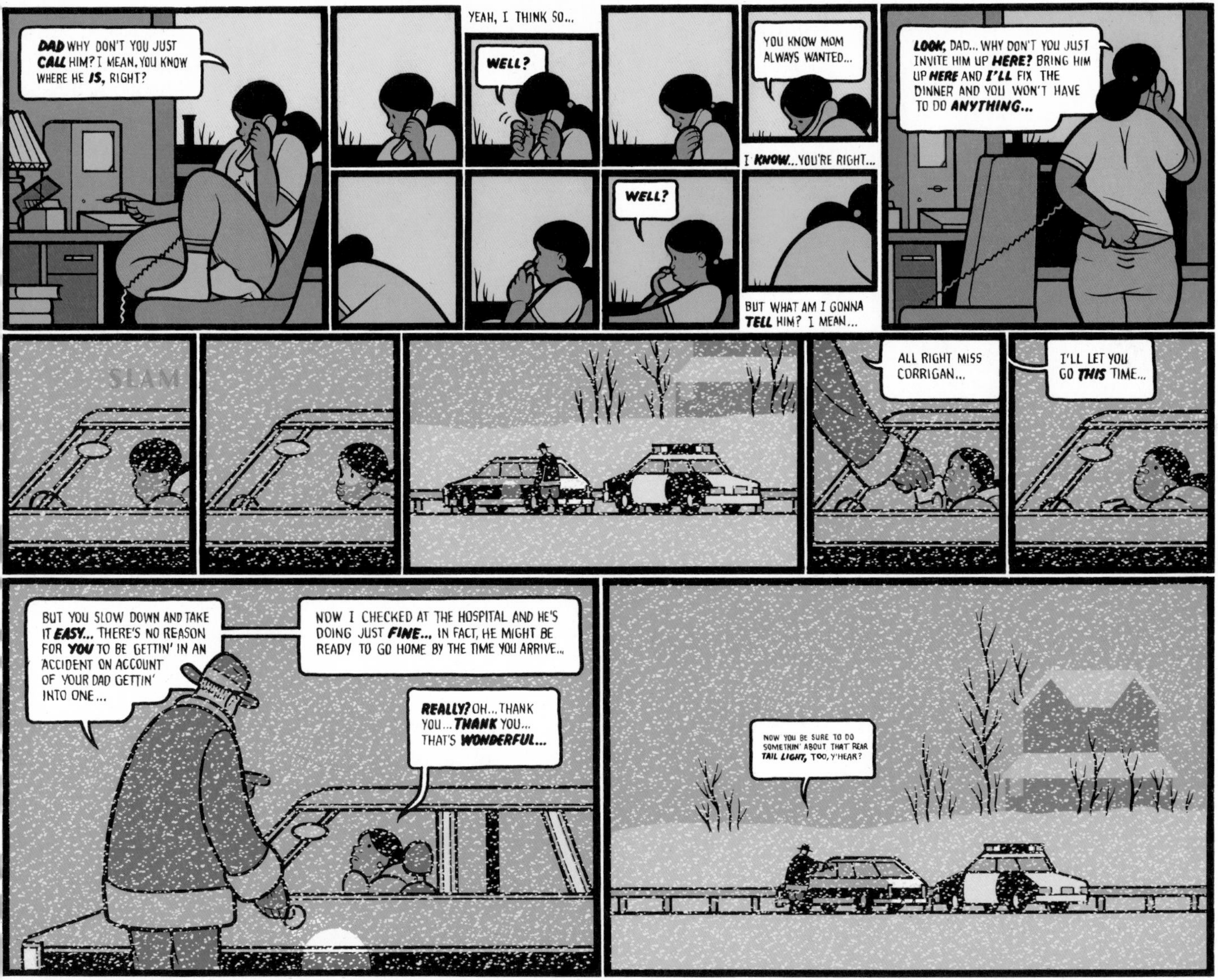

DAD WHY DON'T YOU JUST **CALL** HIM? I MEAN, YOU KNOW WHERE HE **IS**, RIGHT?
YEAH, I THINK SO...
WELL?
WELL?
YOU KNOW MOM ALWAYS WANTED...
I **KNOW**... YOU'RE RIGHT...
BUT WHAT AM I GONNA **TELL** HIM? I MEAN...
LOOK, DAD... WHY DON'T YOU JUST INVITE HIM UP **HERE?** BRING HIM UP **HERE** AND **I'LL** FIX THE DINNER AND YOU WON'T HAVE TO DO **ANYTHING...**
SLAM
ALL RIGHT MISS CORRIGAN...
I'LL LET YOU GO **THIS** TIME...
BUT YOU SLOW DOWN AND TAKE IT **EASY...** THERE'S NO REASON FOR **YOU** TO BE GETTIN' IN AN ACCIDENT ON ACCOUNT OF YOUR DAD GETTIN' INTO ONE...
NOW I CHECKED AT THE HOSPITAL AND HE'S DOING JUST **FINE...** IN FACT, HE MIGHT BE READY TO GO HOME BY THE TIME YOU ARRIVE...
REALLY? OH... THANK YOU... **THANK** YOU... THAT'S **WONDERFUL...**
NOW YOU BE SURE TO DO SOMETHIN' ABOUT THAT REAR **TAIL LIGHT,** TOO, Y'HEAR?

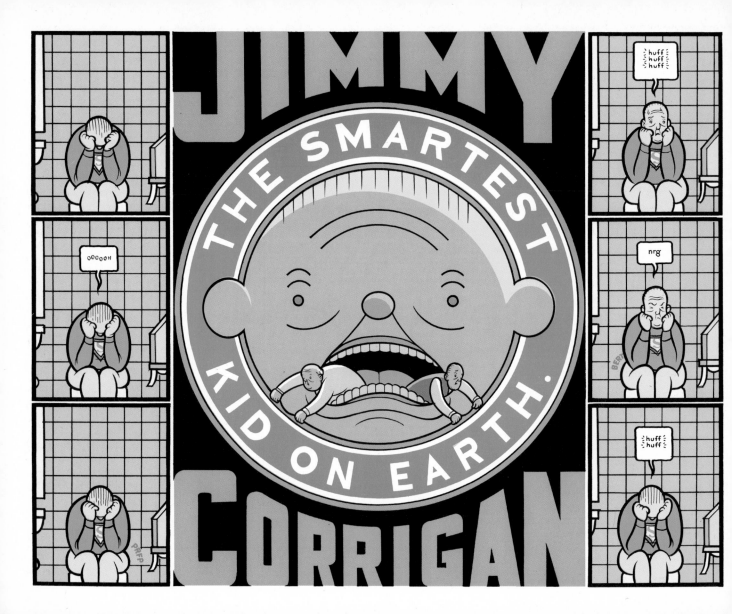

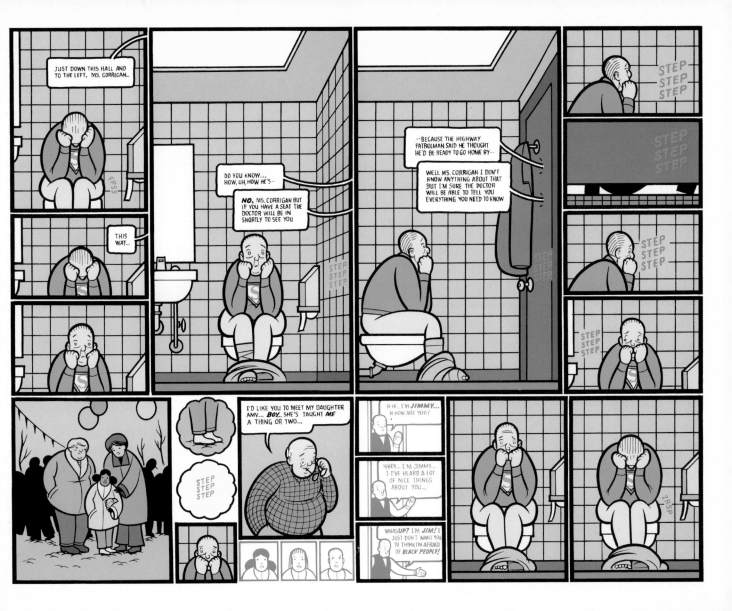

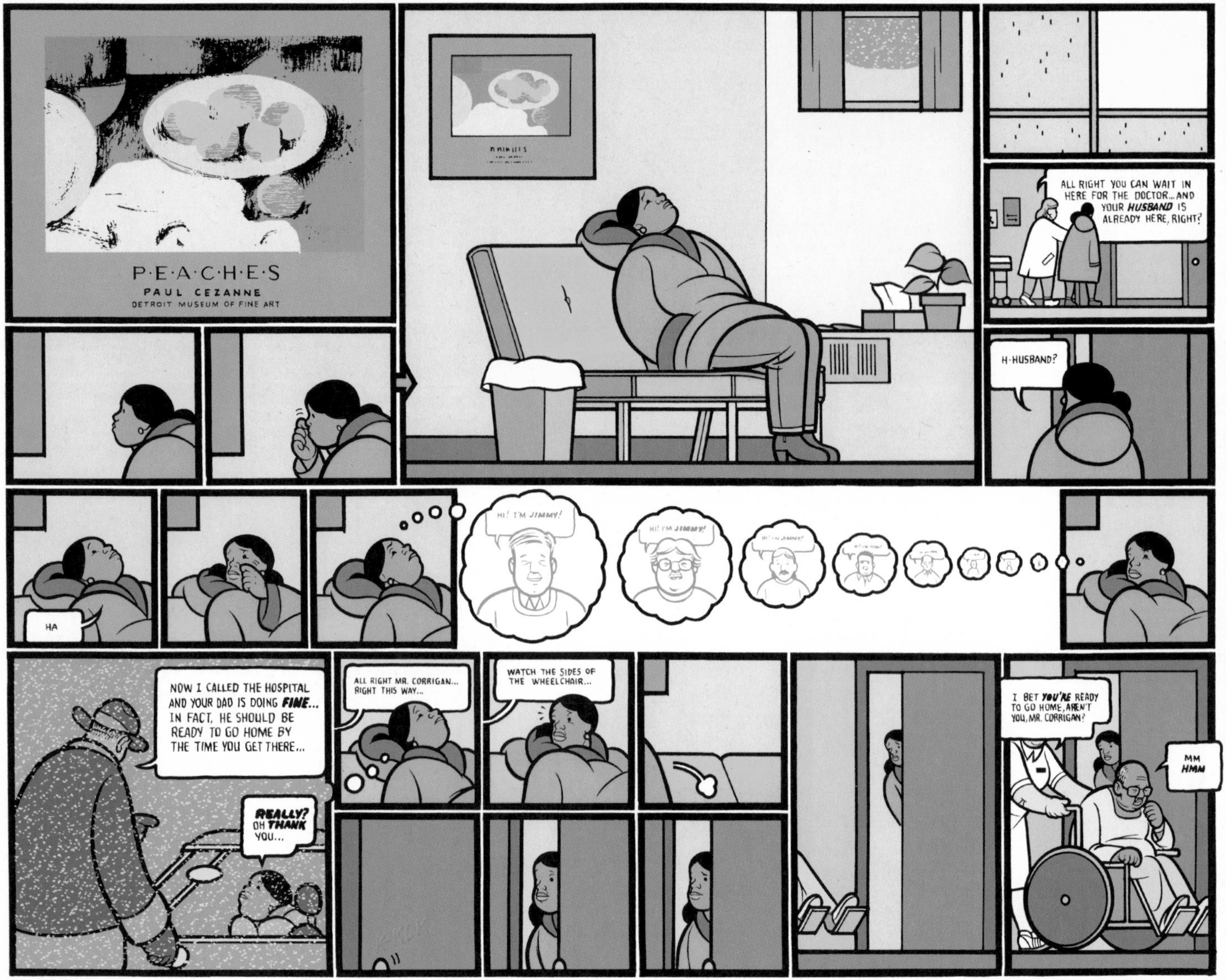
P·E·A·C·H·E·S
PAUL CEZANNE
DETROIT MUSEUM OF FINE ART
ALL RIGHT YOU CAN WAIT IN HERE FOR THE DOCTOR... AND YOUR **HUSBAND** IS ALREADY HERE, RIGHT?
H-HUSBAND?
HA
HI! I'M *JIMMY!*
HI! I'M *JIMMY!*
NOW I CALLED THE HOSPITAL AND YOUR DAD IS DOING **FINE**... IN FACT, HE SHOULD BE READY TO GO HOME BY THE TIME YOU GET THERE...
REALLY? OH **THANK** YOU...
ALL RIGHT MR. CORRIGAN... RIGHT THIS WAY...
WATCH THE SIDES OF THE WHEELCHAIR...
I BET **YOU'RE** READY TO GO HOME, AREN'T YOU, MR. CORRIGAN?
MM HMM

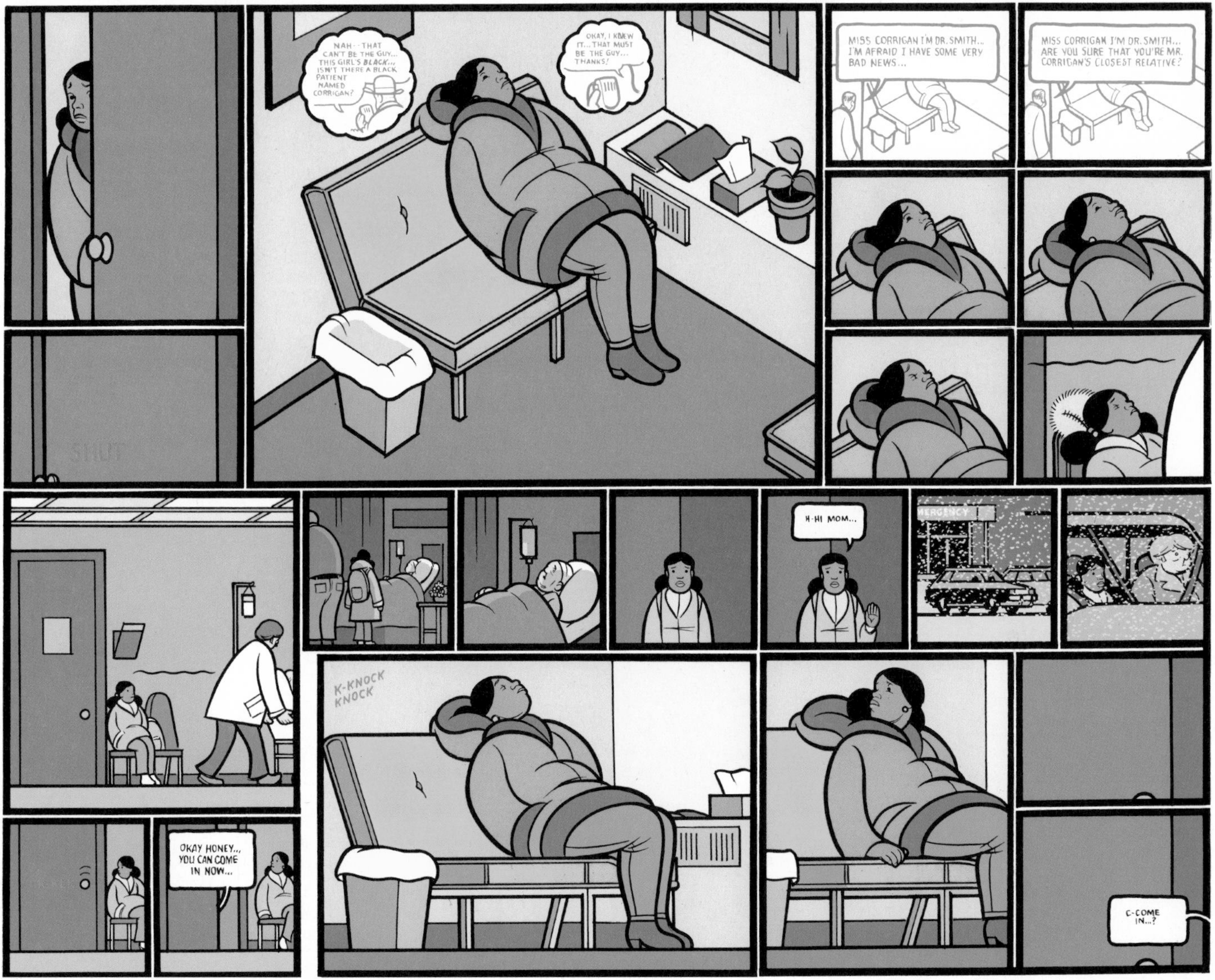
SHUT
NAH-- THAT CAN'T BE THE GUY... THIS GIRL'S BLACK... ISN'T THERE A BLACK PATIENT NAMED CORRIGAN?
OKAY, I KNEW IT... THAT MUST BE THE GUY... THANKS!
MISS CORRIGAN I'M DR. SMITH.. I'M AFRAID I HAVE SOME VERY BAD NEWS...
MISS CORRIGAN I'M DR. SMITH... ARE YOU SURE THAT YOU'RE MR. CORRIGAN'S CLOSEST RELATIVE?
H-HI MOM...
OKAY HONEY... YOU CAN COME IN NOW...
K-KNOCK KNOCK
C-COME IN...?

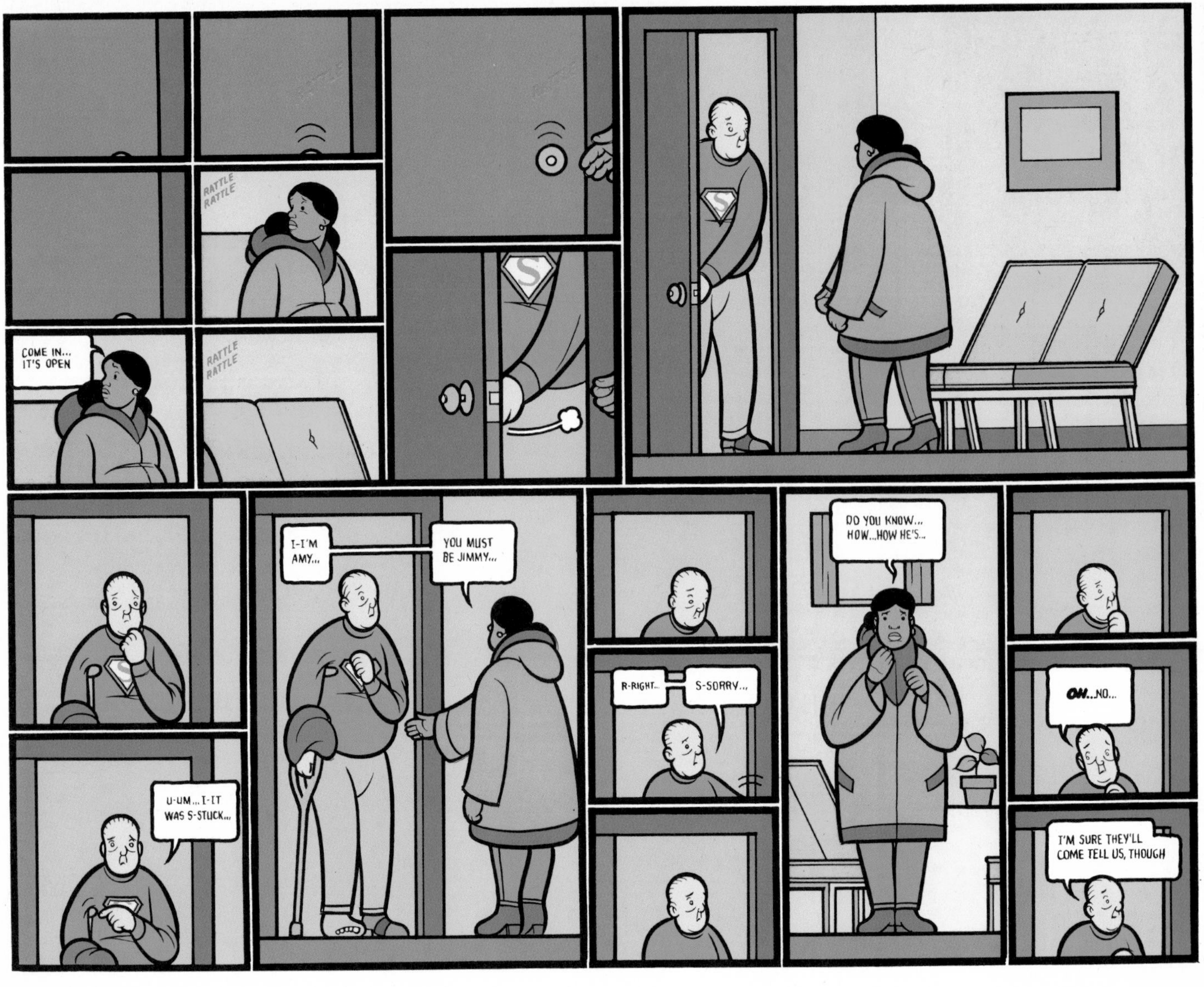
RATTLE
RATTLE
RATTLE
RATTLE
RATTLE
RATTLE
COME IN... IT'S OPEN
U-UM... I-IT WAS S-STUCK...
I-I'M AMY...
YOU MUST BE JIMMY...
R-RIGHT...
S-SORRY...
DO YOU KNOW... HOW...HOW HE'S...
OH...NO...
I'M SURE THEY'LL COME TELL US, THOUGH

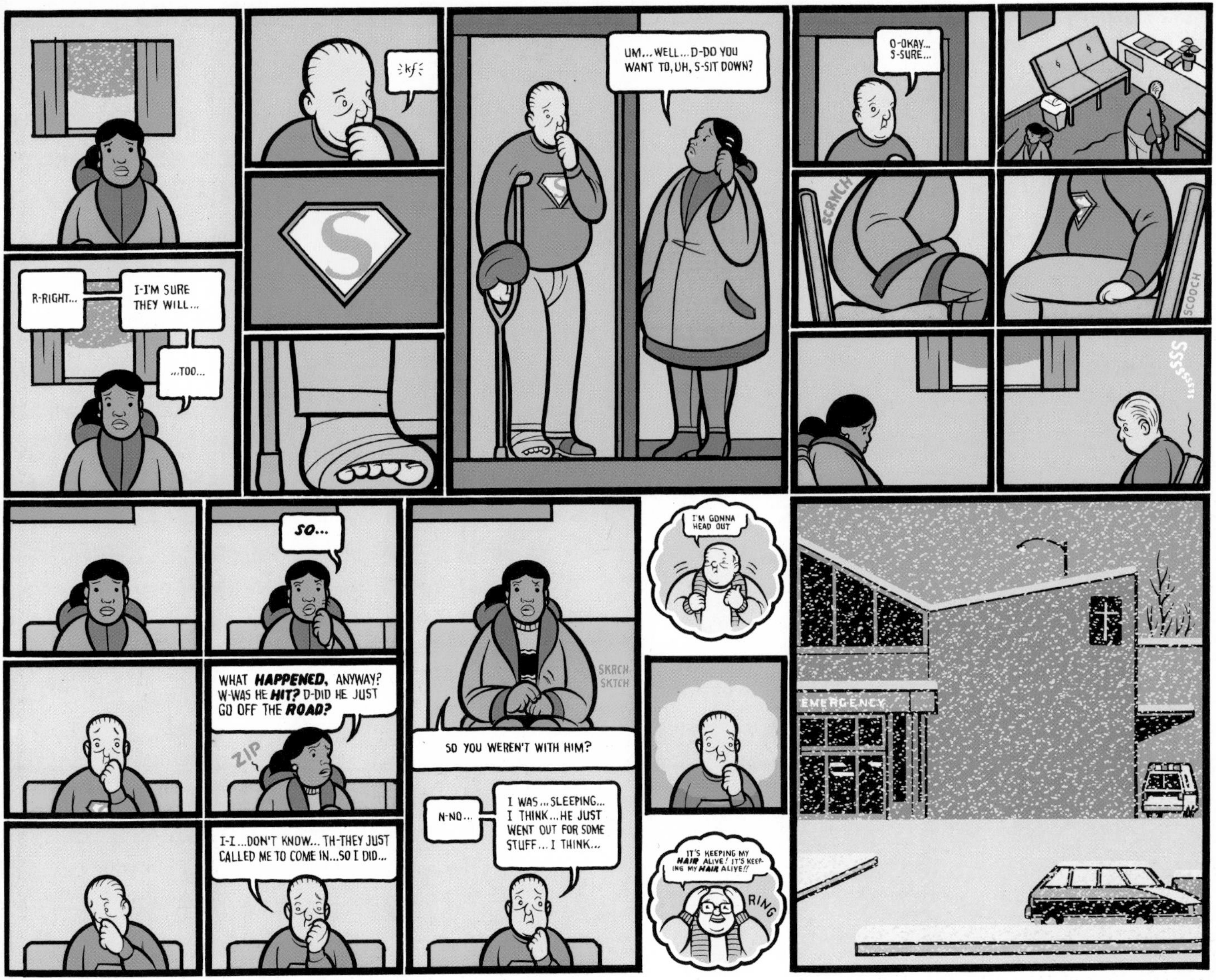
R-RIGHT...
I-I'M SURE THEY WILL...
...TOO...
kf
UM... WELL... D-DO YOU WANT TO, UH, S-SIT DOWN?
O-OKAY... S-SURE...
SCRNCH
SCOOCH
Sssssss
SO...
WHAT HAPPENED, ANYWAY? W-WAS HE HIT? D-DID HE JUST GO OFF THE ROAD?
ZIP
I-I...DON'T KNOW... TH-THEY JUST CALLED ME TO COME IN...SO I DID...
SKRCH
SKTCH
SO YOU WEREN'T WITH HIM?
N-NO...
I WAS...SLEEPING... I THINK...HE JUST WENT OUT FOR SOME STUFF... I THINK...
I'M GONNA HEAD OUT
IT'S KEEPING MY HAIR ALIVE! IT'S KEEPING MY HAIR ALIVE!!
RING
EMERGENCY

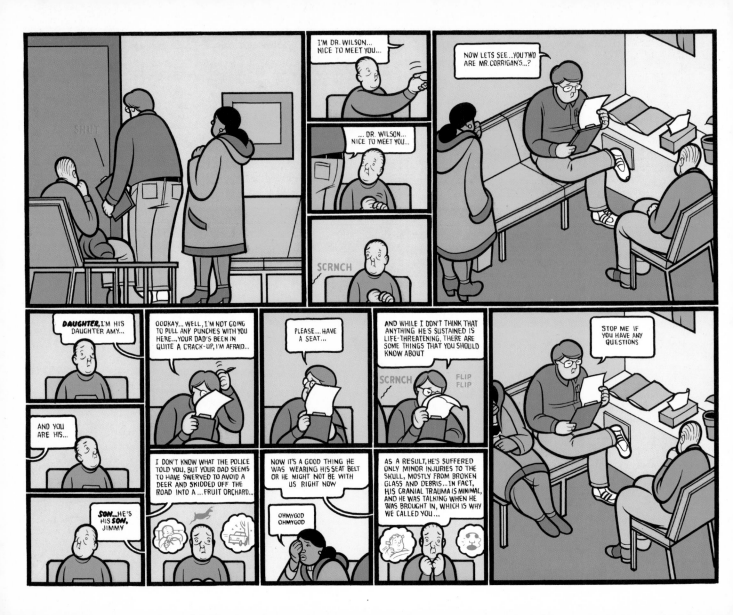

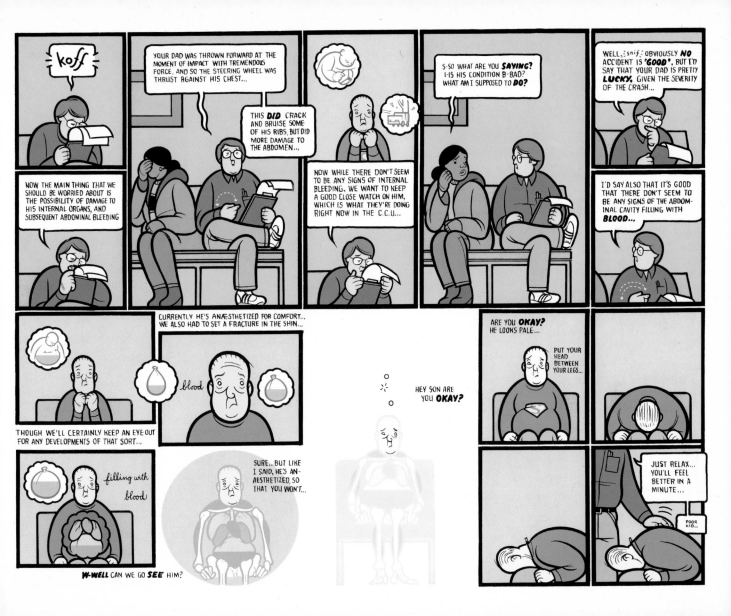

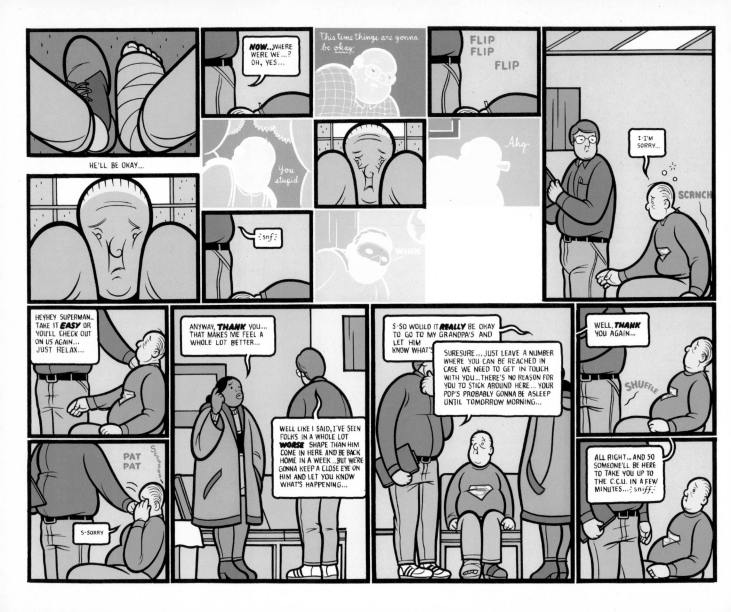

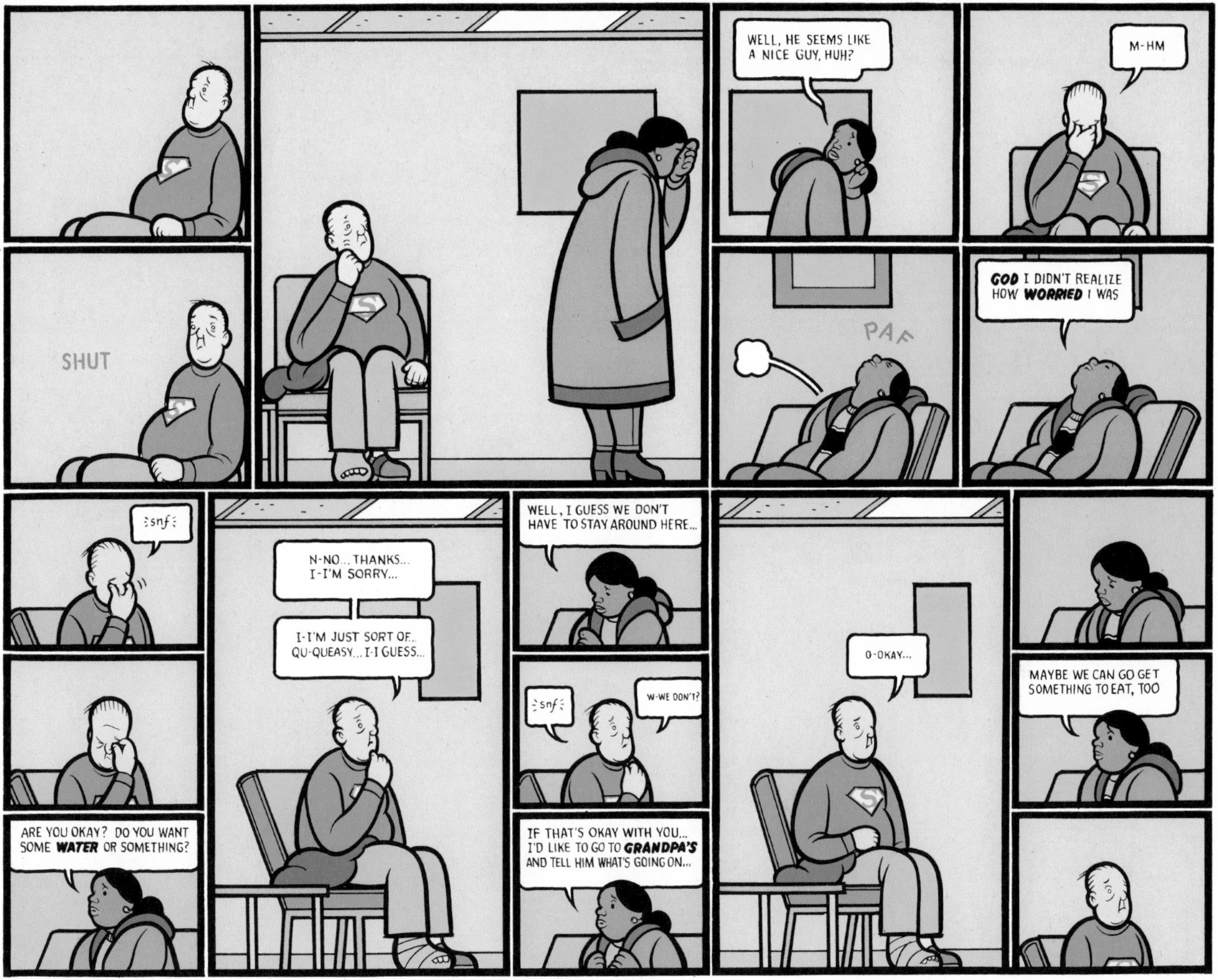
SHUT
WELL, HE SEEMS LIKE A NICE GUY, HUH?
M-HM
PAF
GOD I DIDN'T REALIZE HOW WORRIED I WAS
snf
ARE YOU OKAY? DO YOU WANT SOME WATER OR SOMETHING?
N-NO... THANKS... I-I'M SORRY...
I-I'M JUST SORT OF.. QU-QUEASY... I-I GUESS...
WELL, I GUESS WE DON'T HAVE TO STAY AROUND HERE...
snf
W-WE DON'T?
IF THAT'S OKAY WITH YOU... I'D LIKE TO GO TO GRANDPA'S AND TELL HIM WHAT'S GOING ON...
O-OKAY...
MAYBE WE CAN GO GET SOMETHING TO EAT, TOO

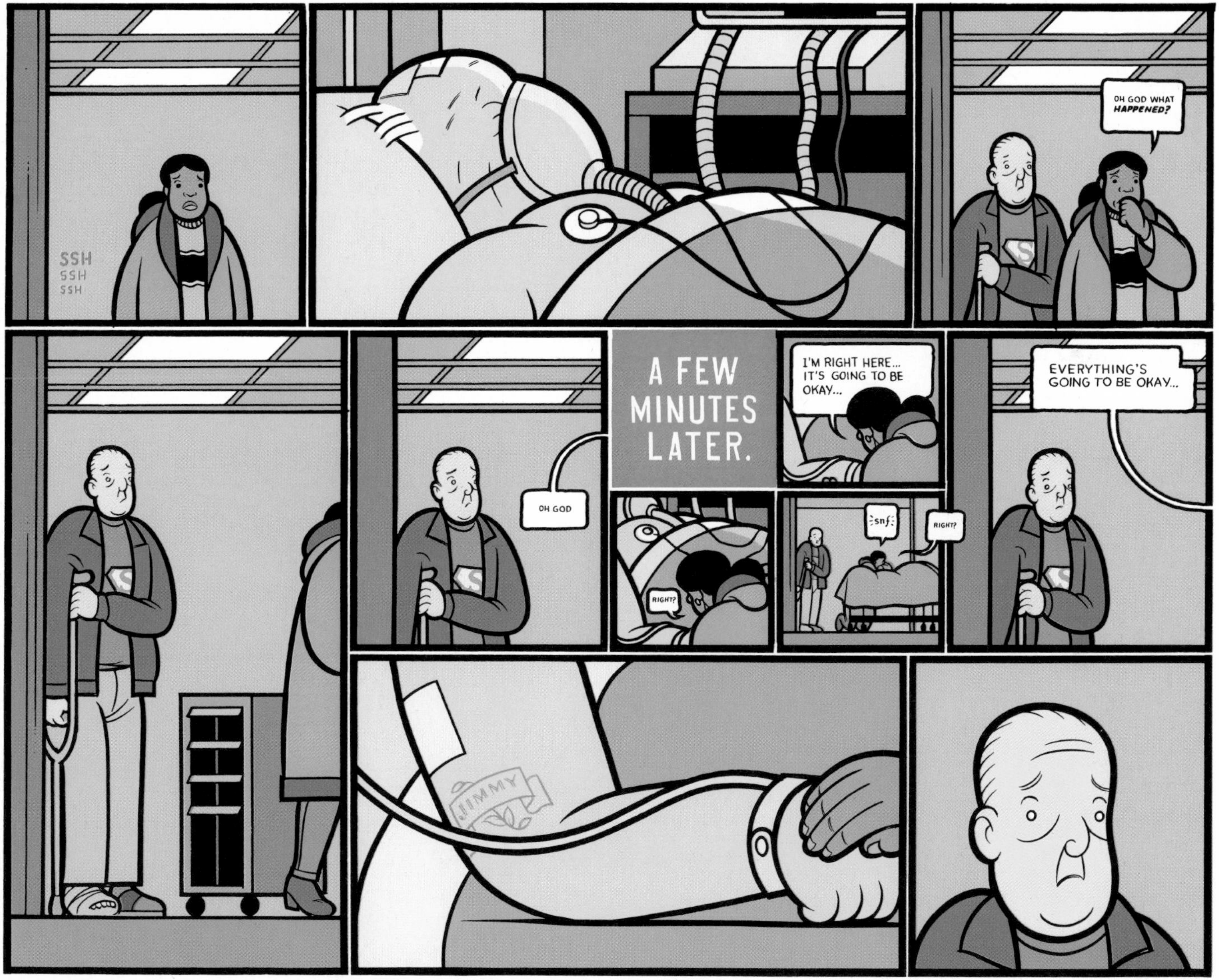
SSH
SSH
SSH
OH GOD WHAT HAPPENED?
OH GOD
A FEW MINUTES LATER.
I'M RIGHT HERE... IT'S GOING TO BE OKAY...
RIGHT?
snf
RIGHT?
EVERYTHING'S GOING TO BE OKAY...
JIMMY

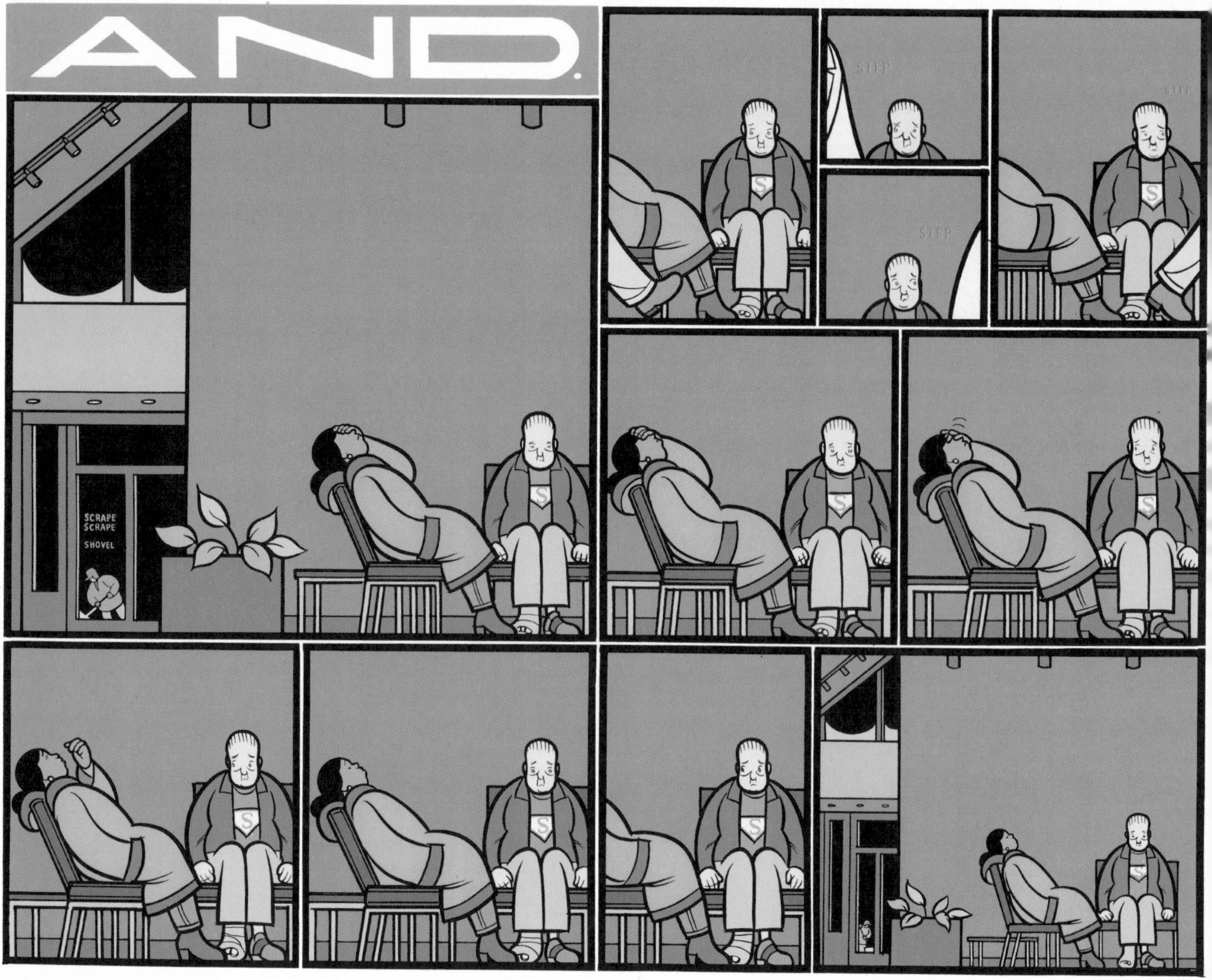
AND.
SCRAPE
SCRAPE
SHOVEL
STEP
STEP
STEP

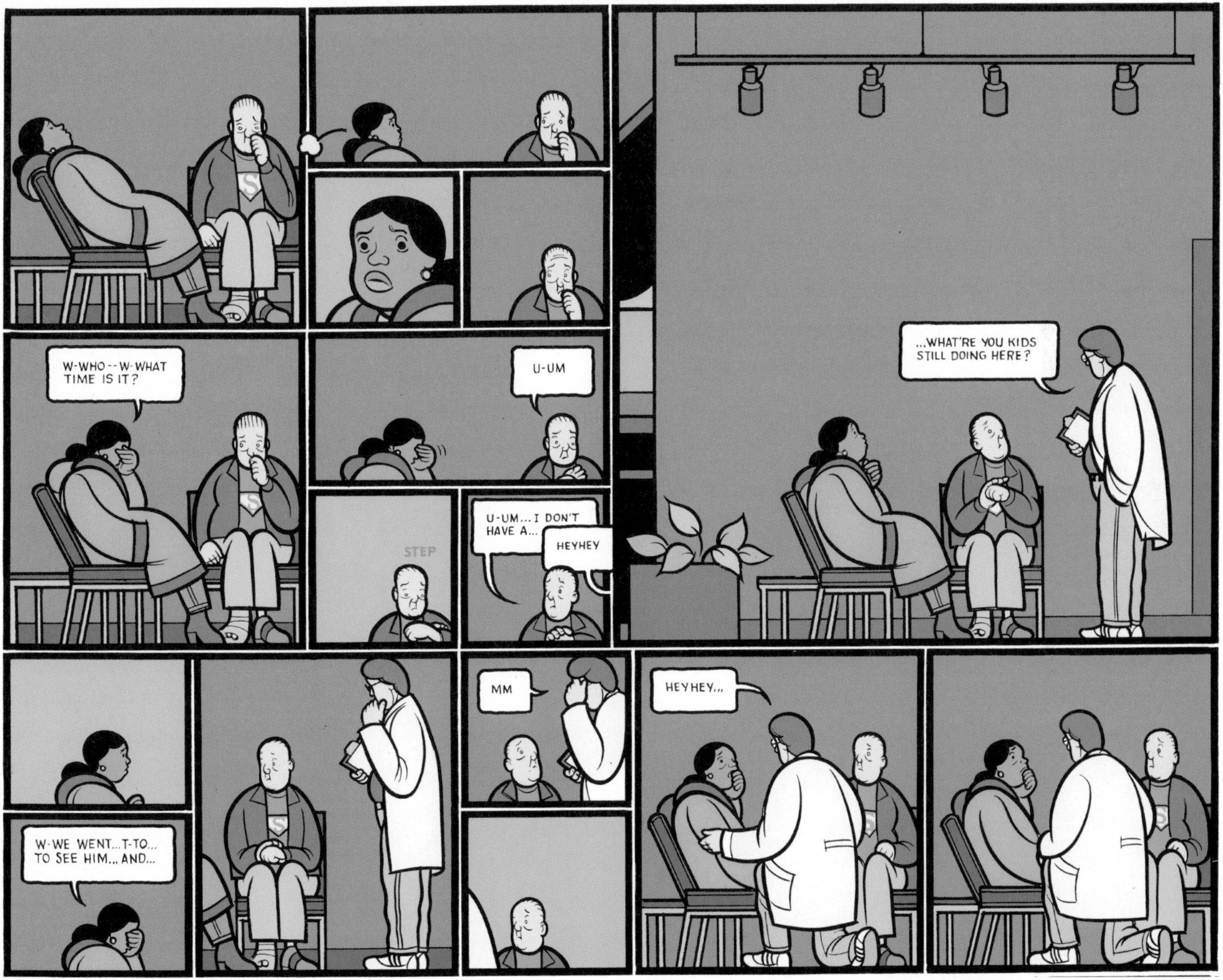
W-WHO--W-WHAT TIME IS IT?
U-UM
STEP
U-UM... I DON'T HAVE A...
HEYHEY
...WHAT'RE YOU KIDS STILL DOING HERE?
W-WE WENT...T-TO... TO SEE HIM... AND...
MM
HEYHEY...

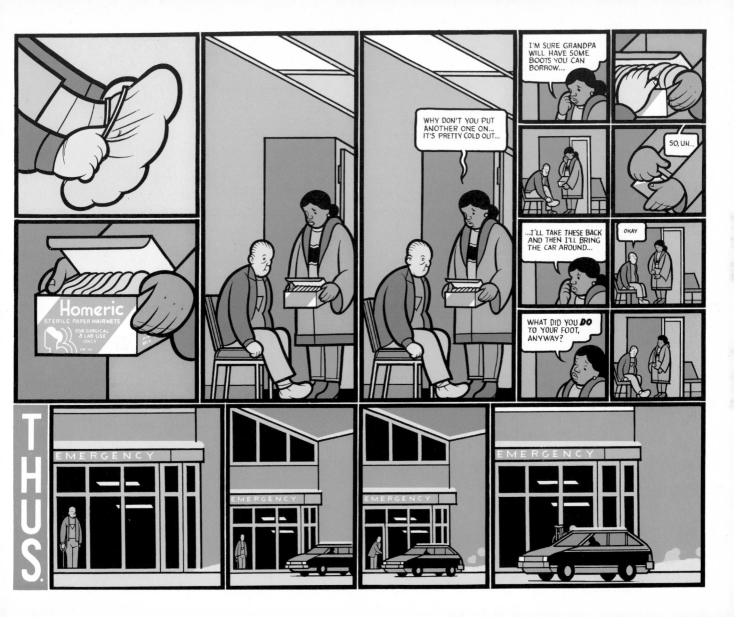

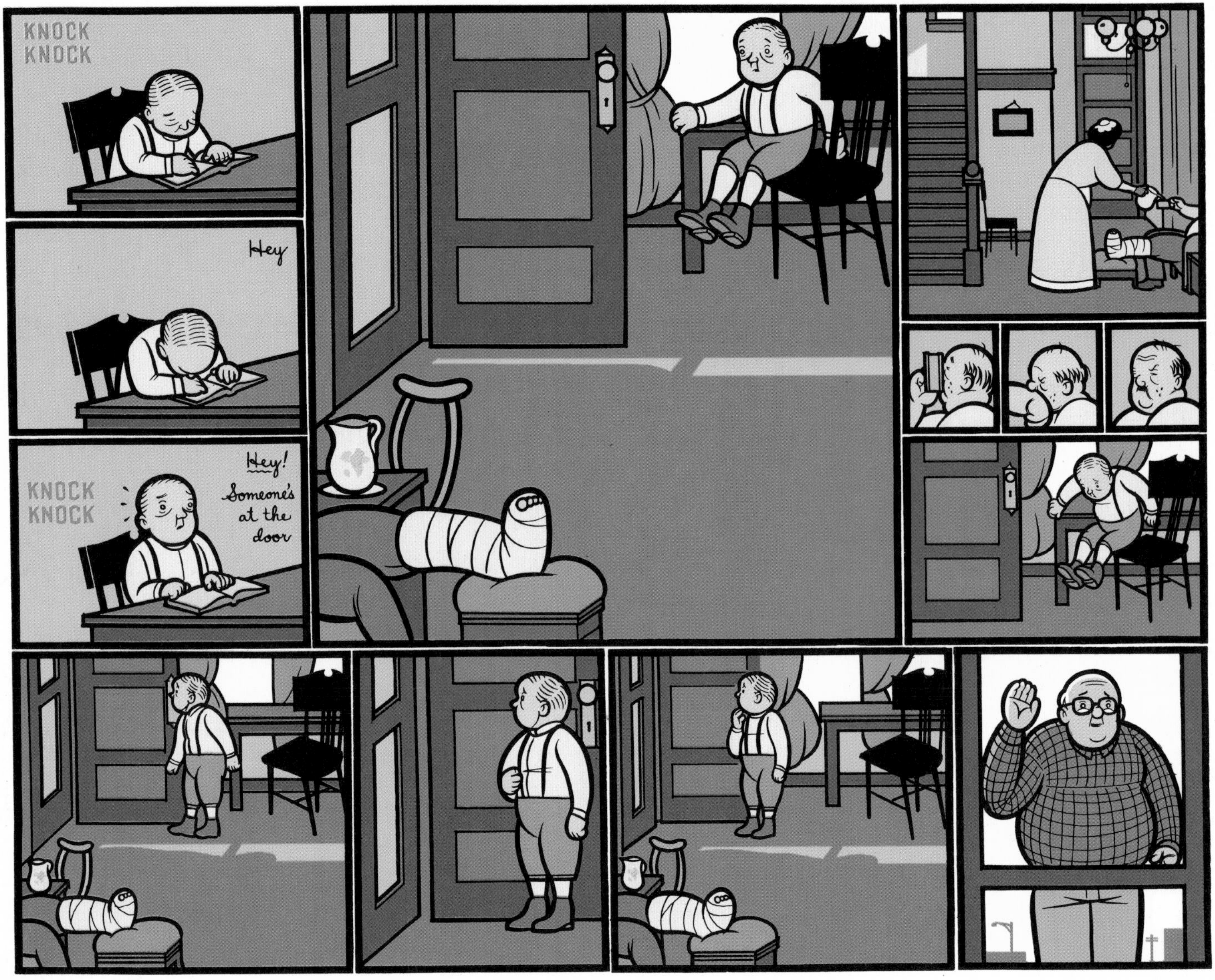
KNOCK
KNOCK
Hey
KNOCK
KNOCK
Hey!
Someone's at the door

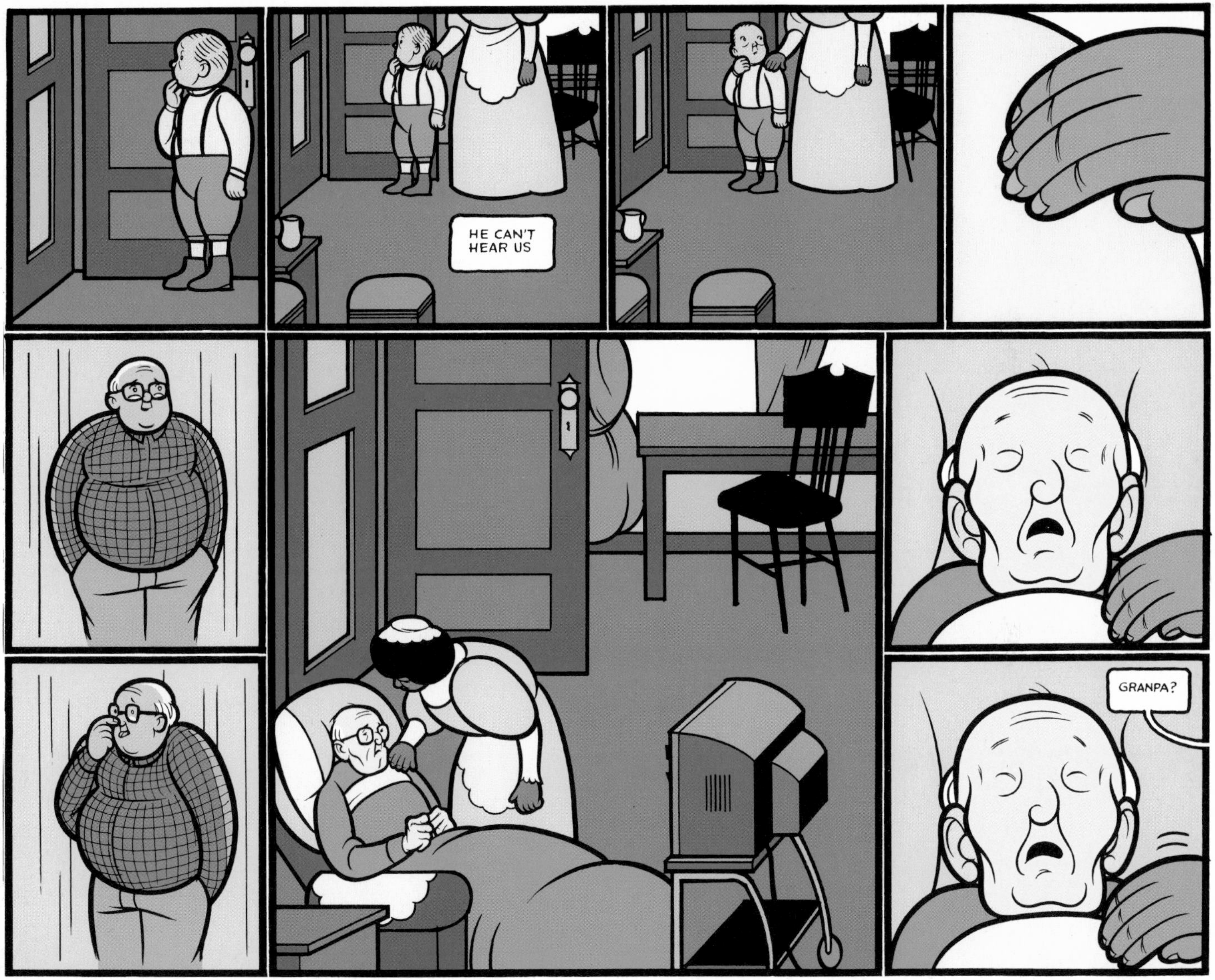
HE CAN'T HEAR US
GRANPA?

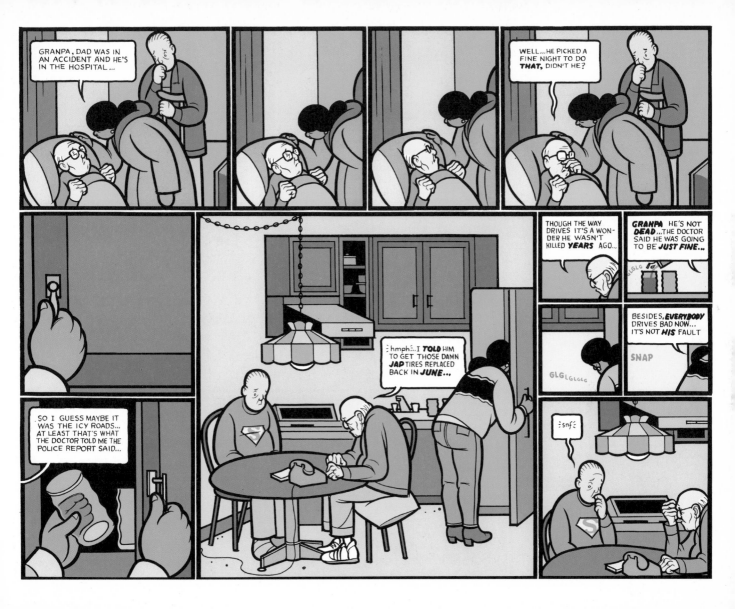

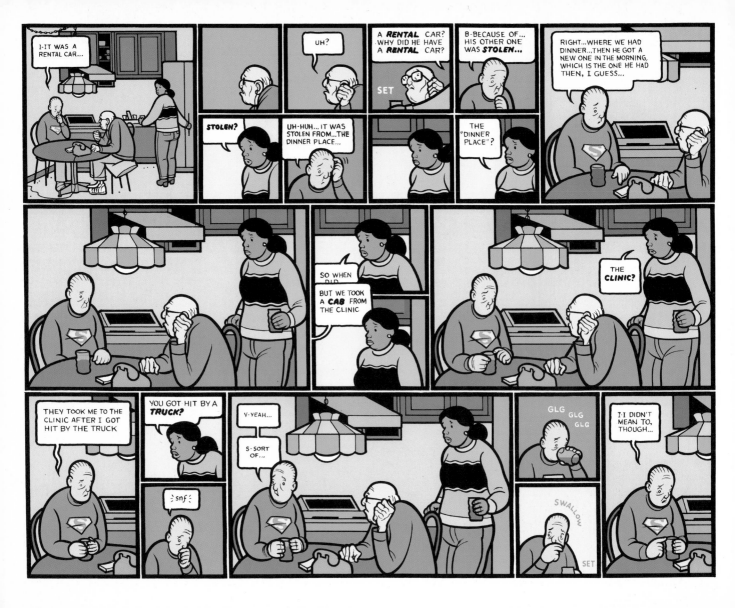

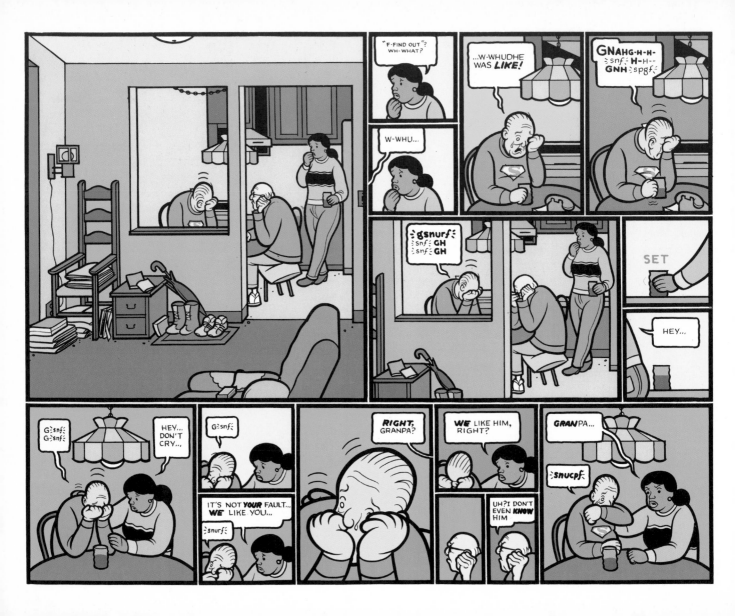

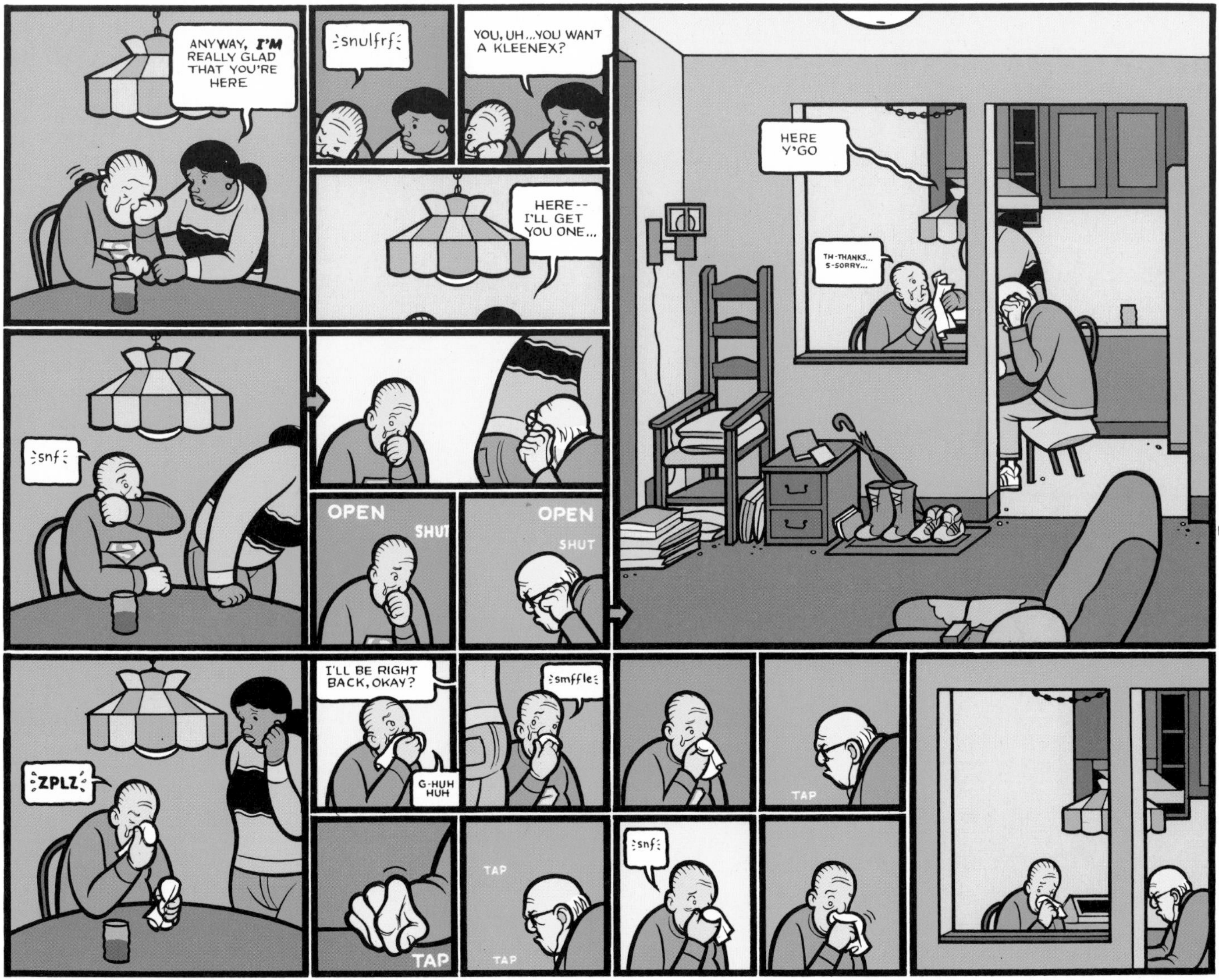
ANYWAY, I'M REALLY GLAD THAT YOU'RE HERE
snulfrf
YOU, UH...YOU WANT A KLEENEX?
HERE-- I'LL GET YOU ONE...
snf
OPEN
SHUT
OPEN
SHUT
HERE Y'GO
TH-THANKS... S-SORRY...
ZPLZ
I'LL BE RIGHT BACK, OKAY?
G-HUH HUH
smffle
TAP
TAP
TAP
TAP
snf

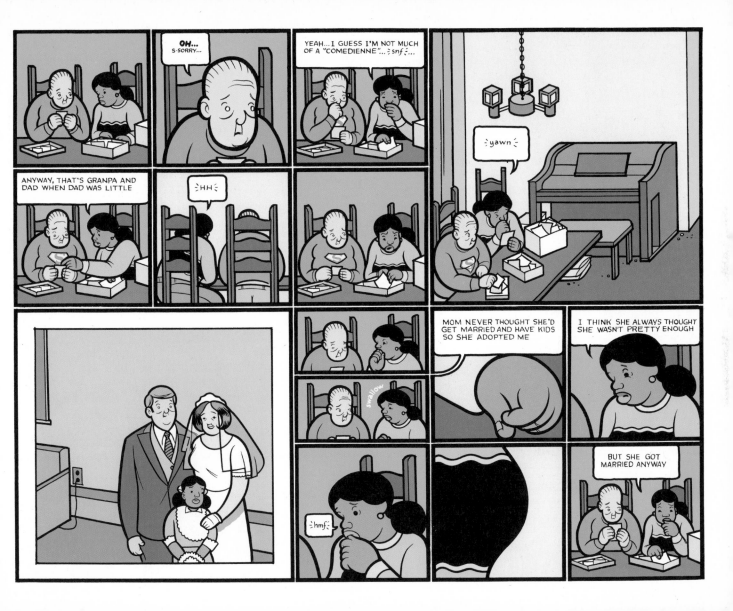

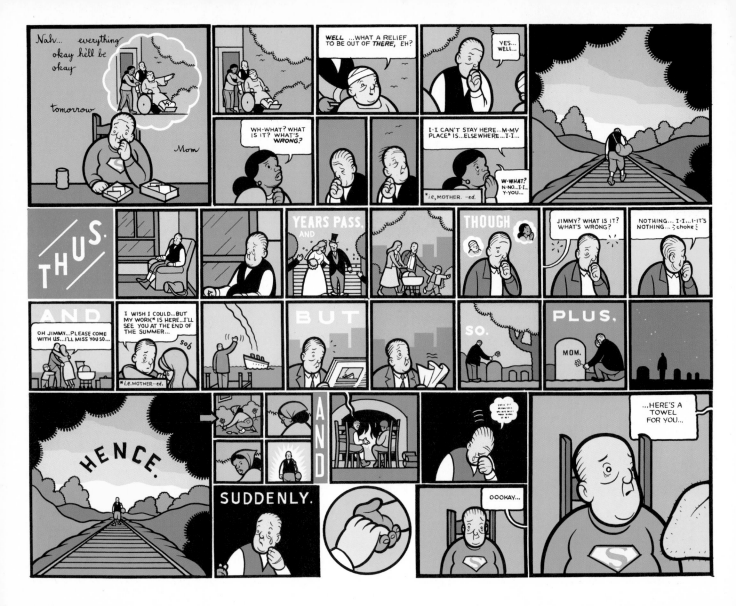

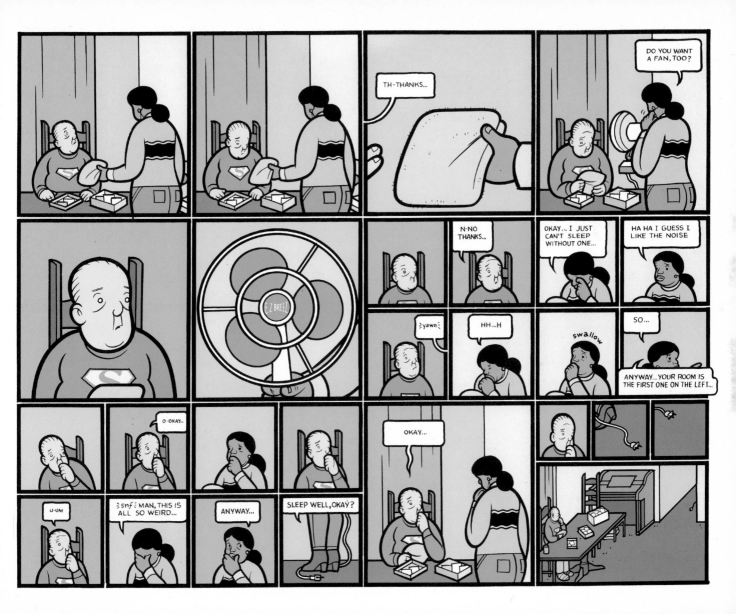

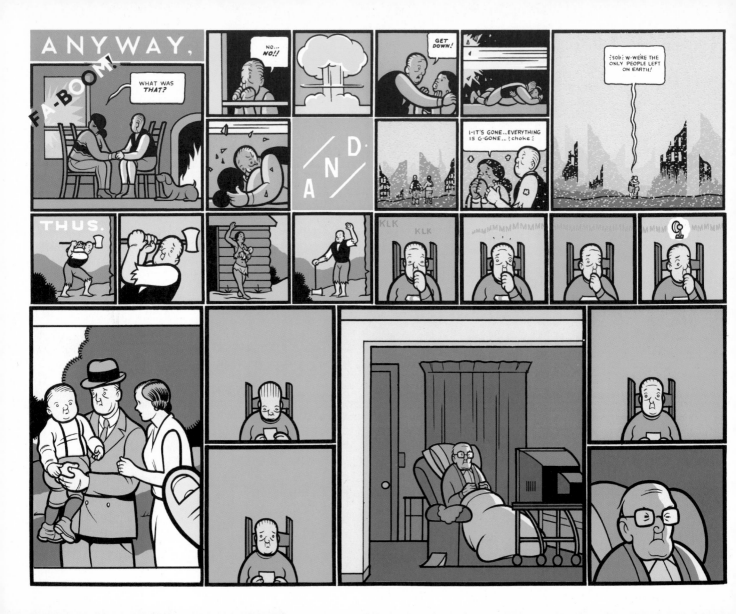

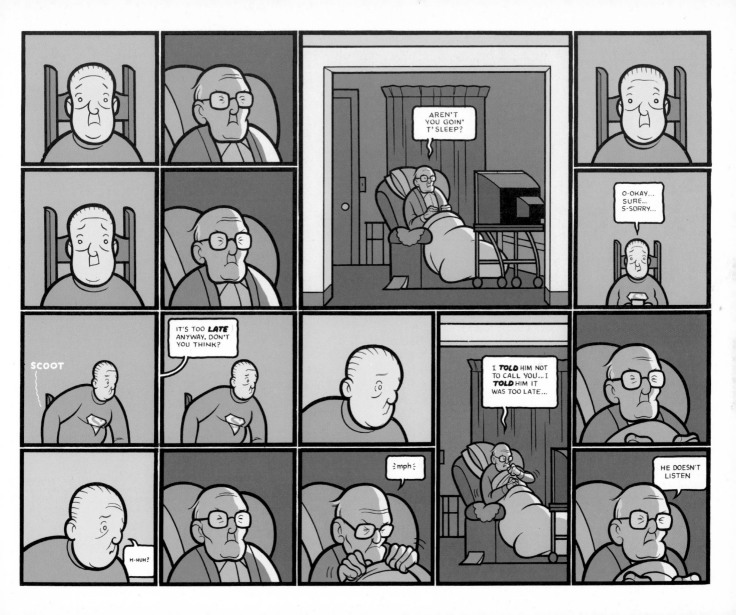

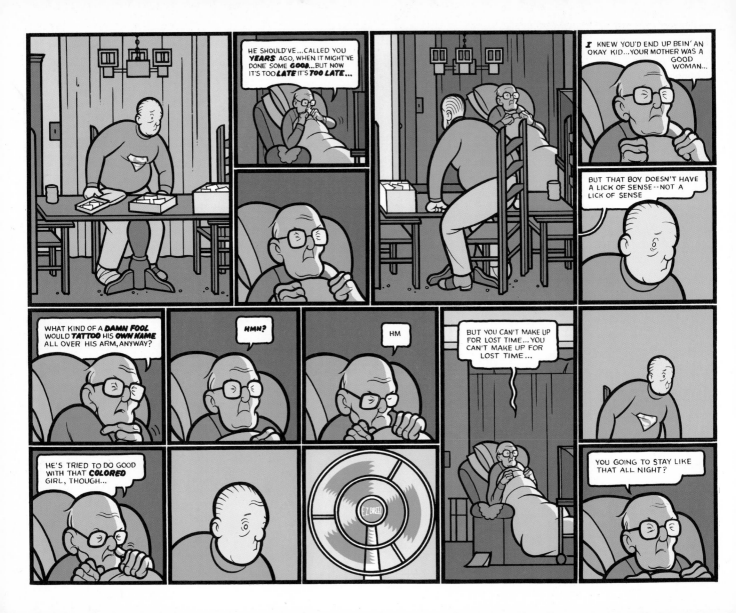

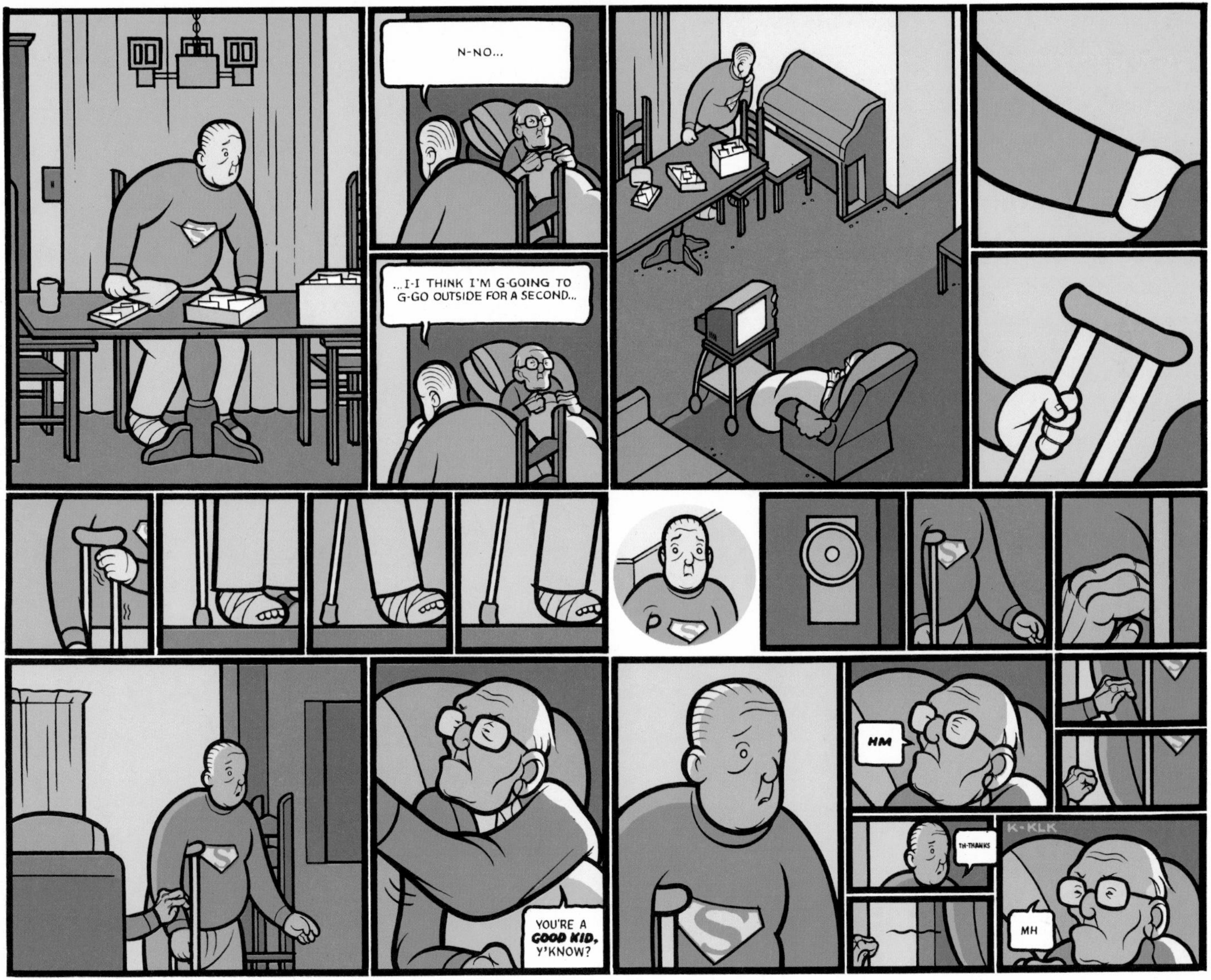

N-NO...
...I-I THINK I'M G-GOING TO G-GO OUTSIDE FOR A SECOND...
YOU'RE A GOOD KID, Y'KNOW?
HM
TH-THANKS
K-KLK
MH

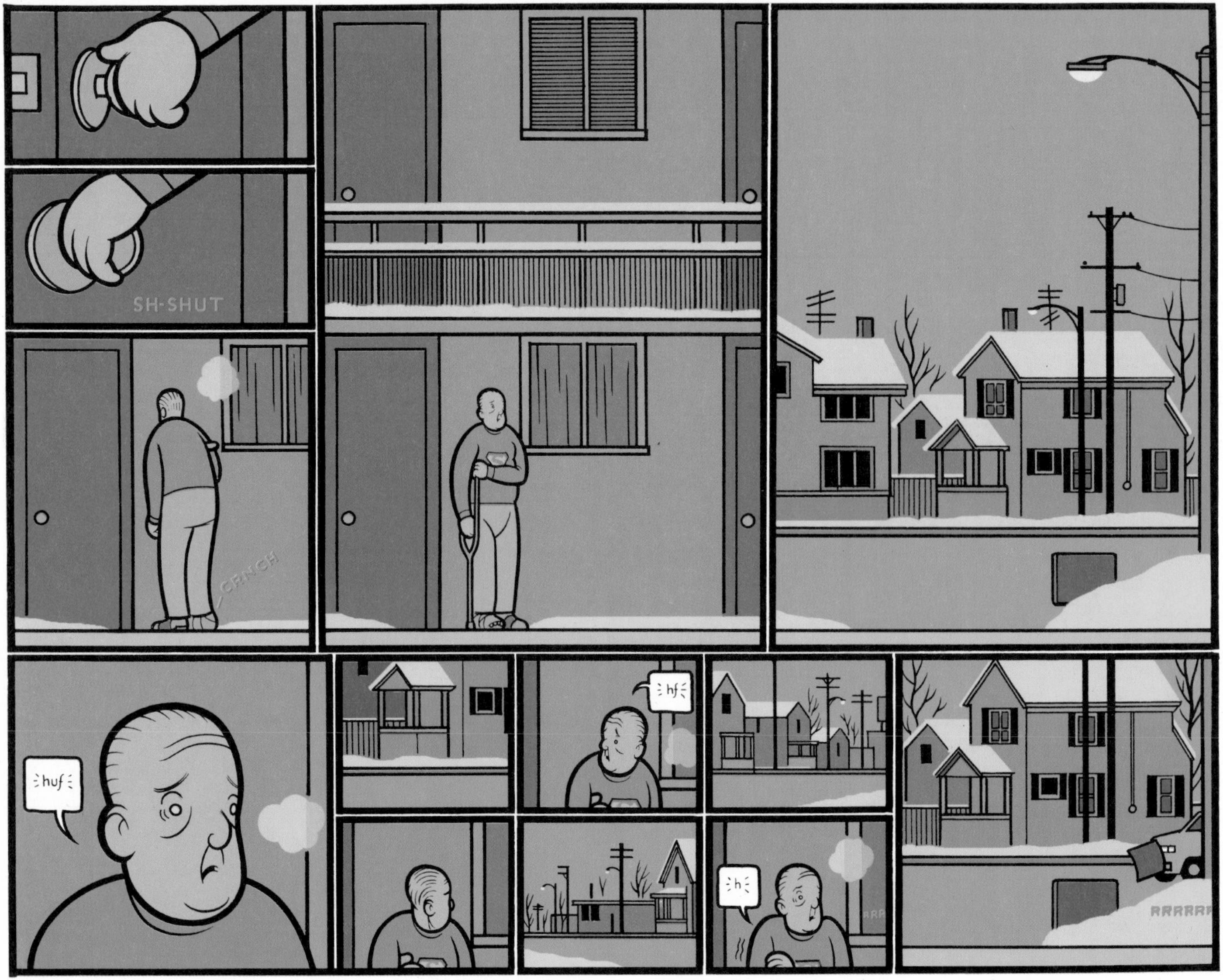
SH-SHUT
CRNCH
huf
hf
h
RRRRRR

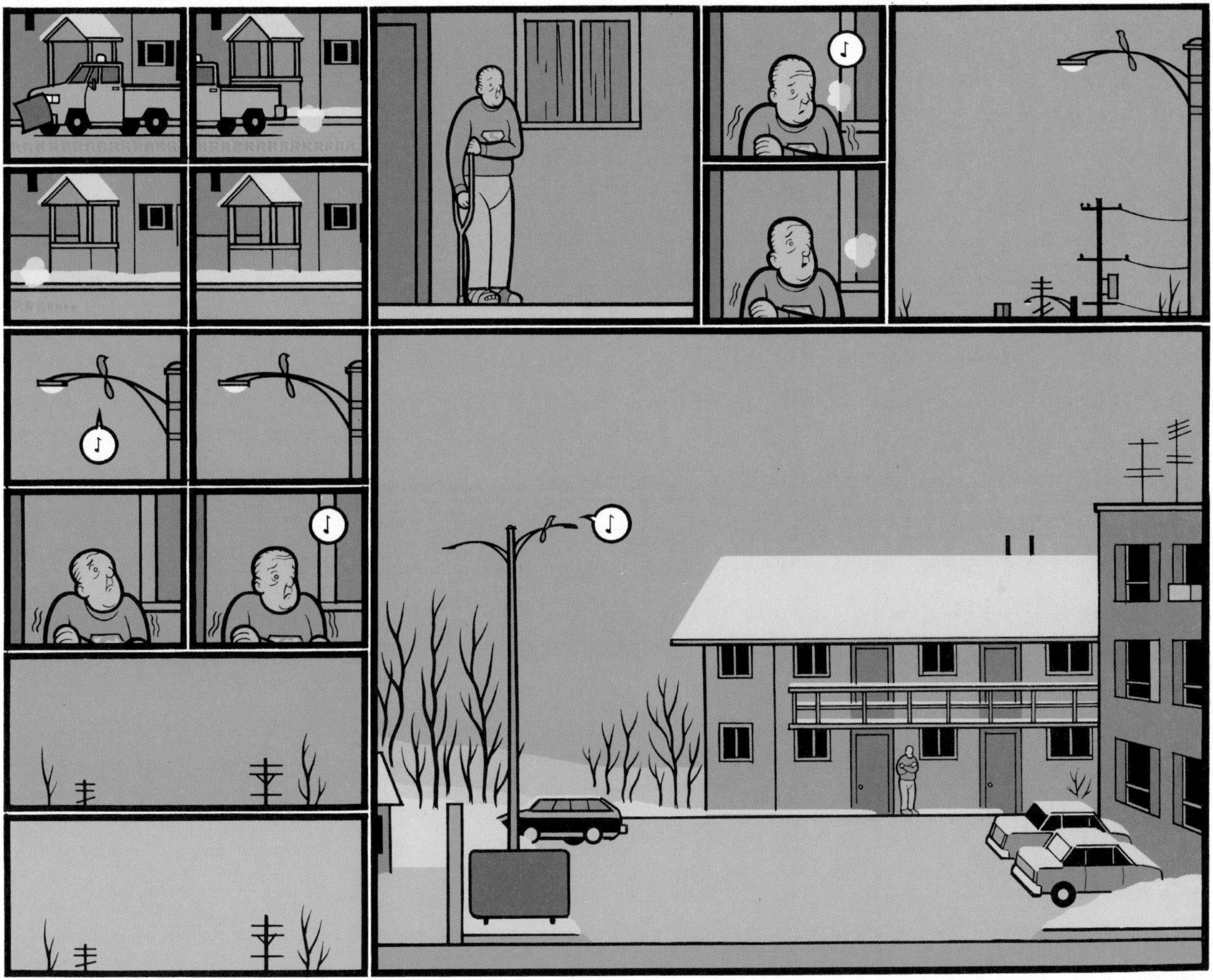

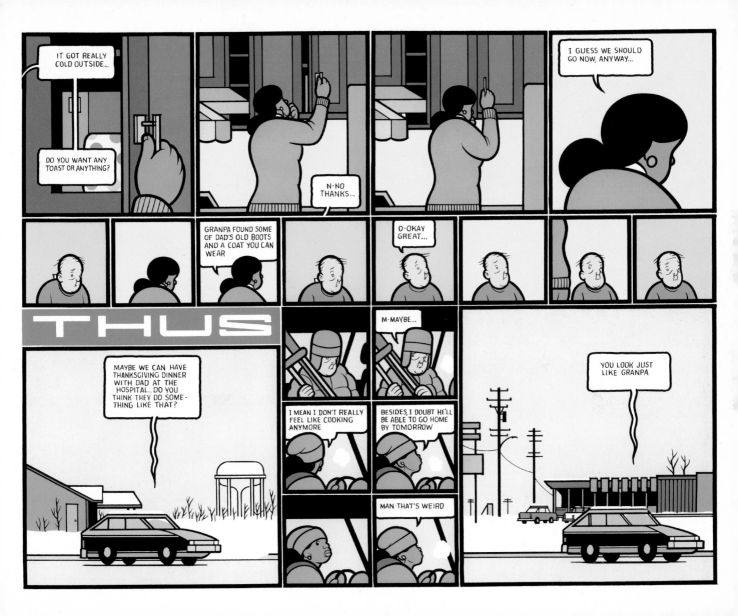

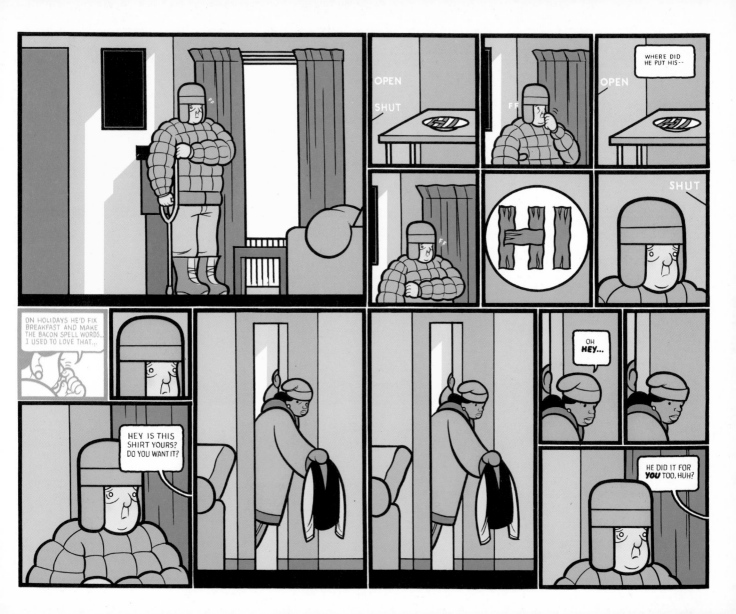

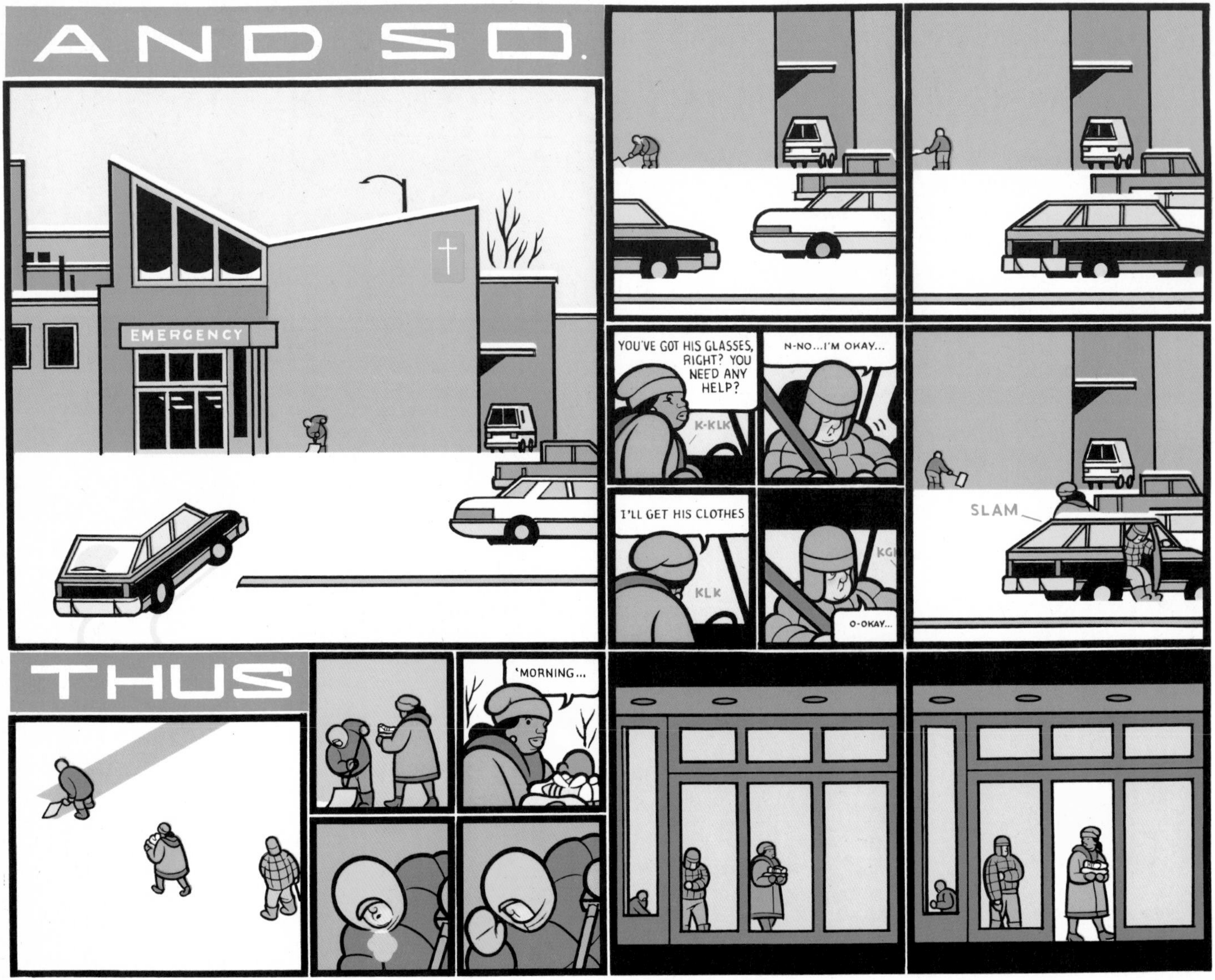
AND SO.
EMERGENCY
YOU'VE GOT HIS GLASSES, RIGHT? YOU NEED ANY HELP?
K-KLK
N-NO...I'M OKAY...
I'LL GET HIS CLOTHES
KLK
O-OKAY...
SLAM
THUS
'MORNING...

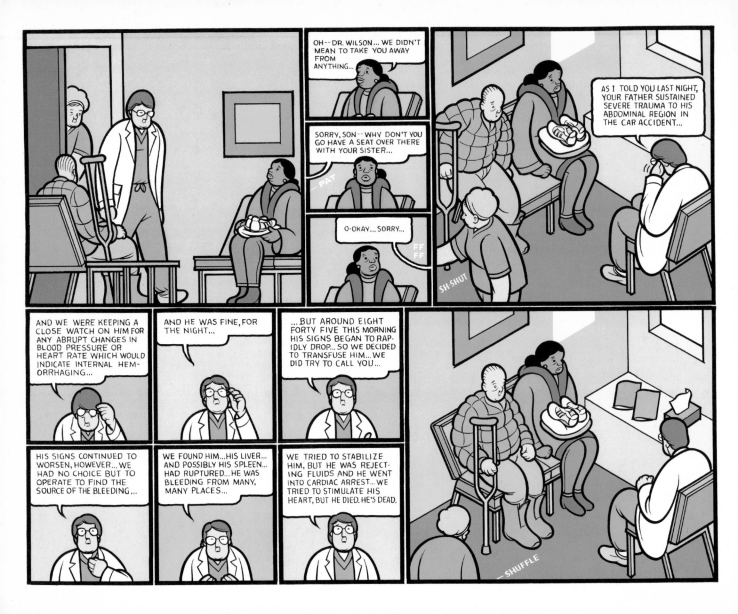

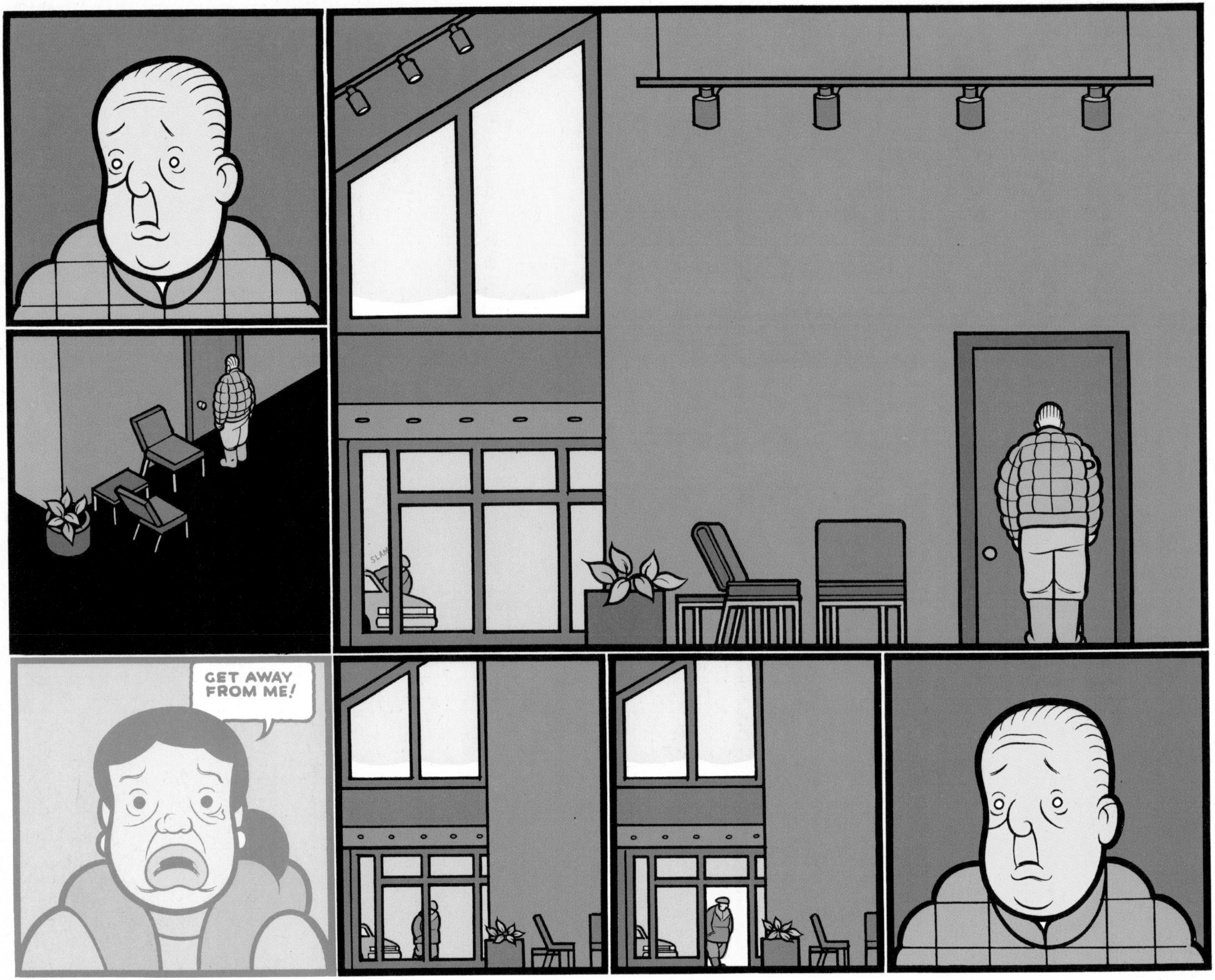
SLAM
GET AWAY FROM ME!

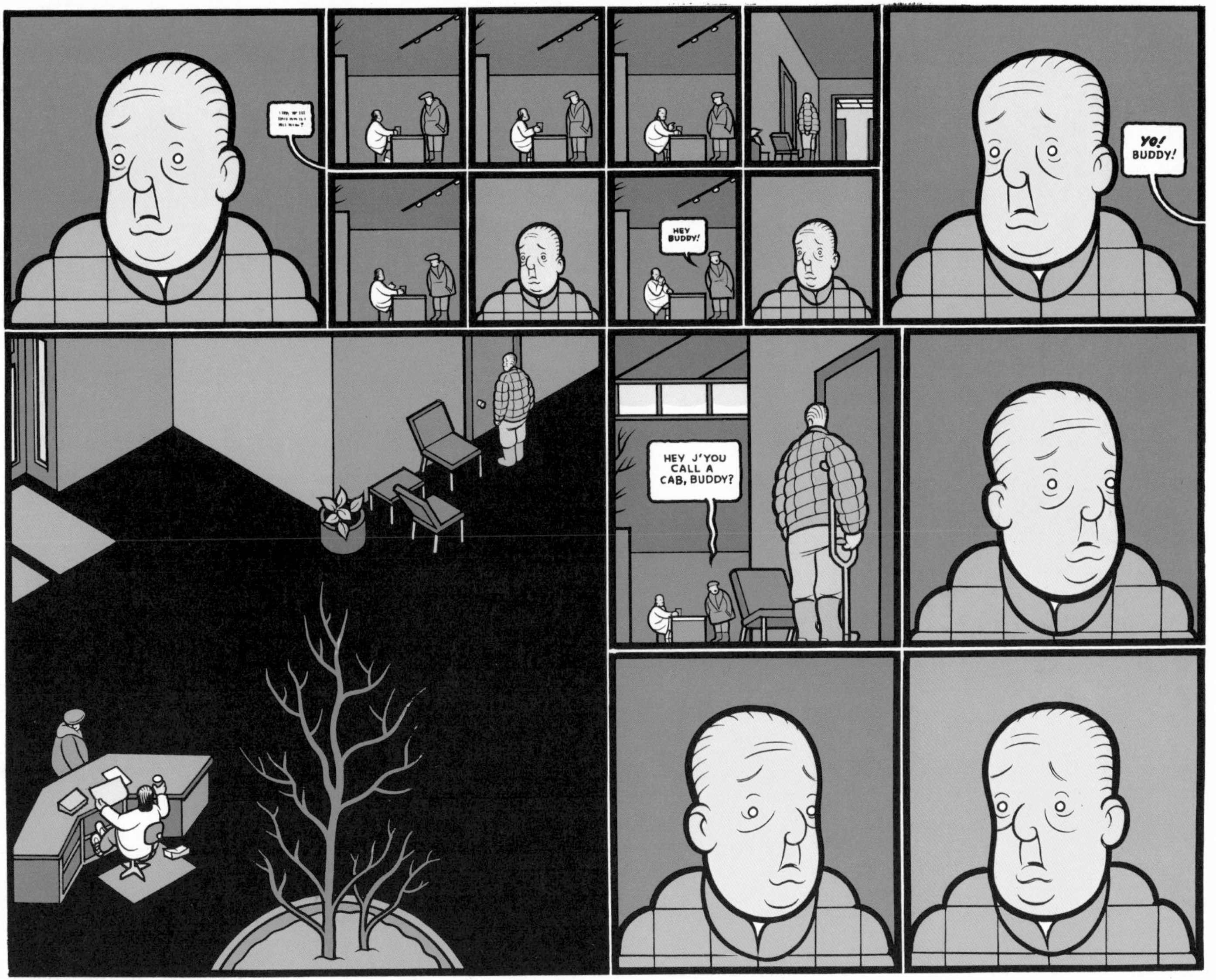
HEY BUDDY!
YO! BUDDY!
HEY J'YOU CALL A CAB, BUDDY?

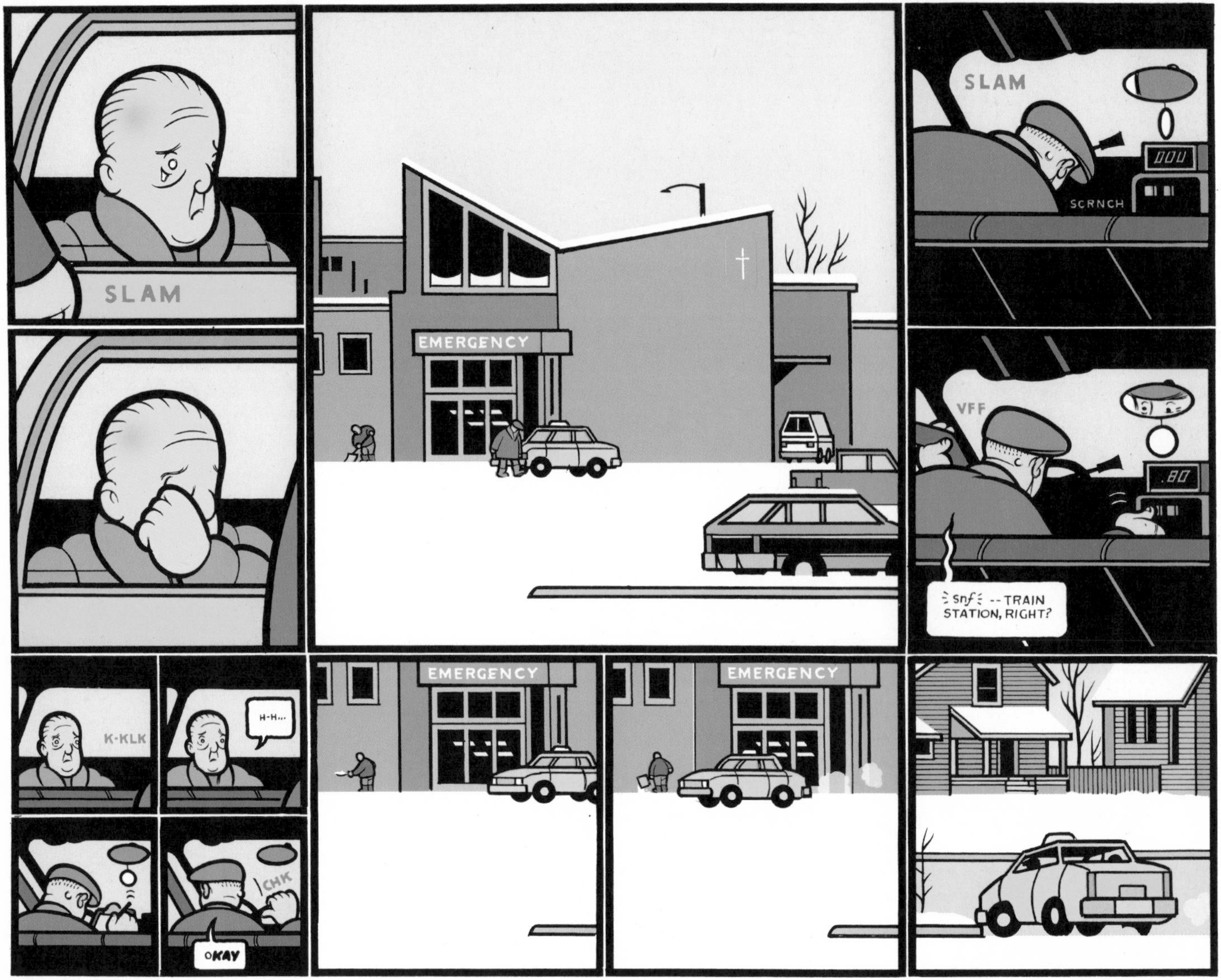
SLAM
EMERGENCY
SLAM
SCRNCH
VFF
.80
snf --TRAIN STATION, RIGHT?
K-KLK
H-H...
CHK
OKAY
EMERGENCY
EMERGENCY

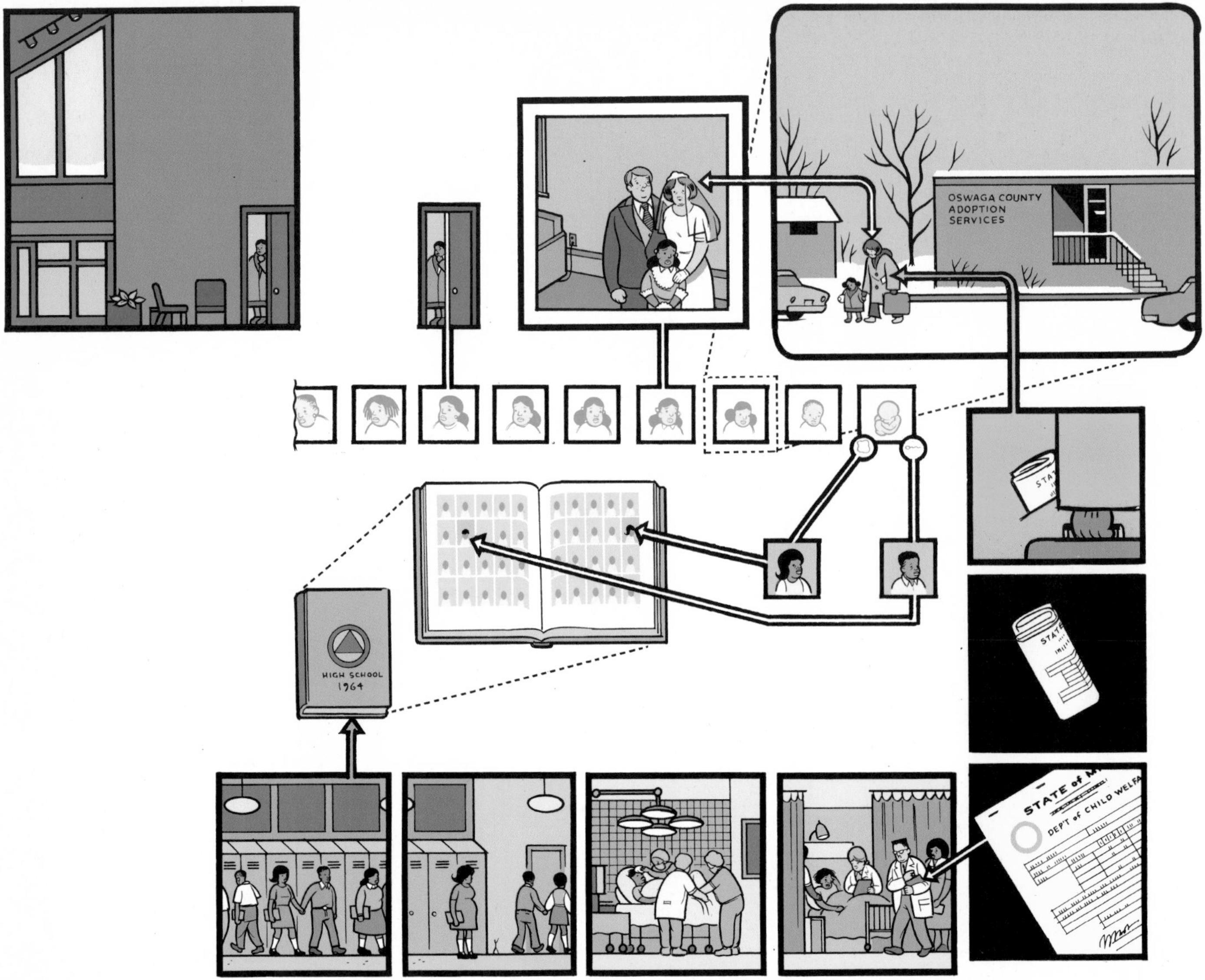

OSWAGA COUNTY
ADOPTION
SERVICES
HIGH SCHOOL
1964
STATE of M
DEPT of CHILD WELFA

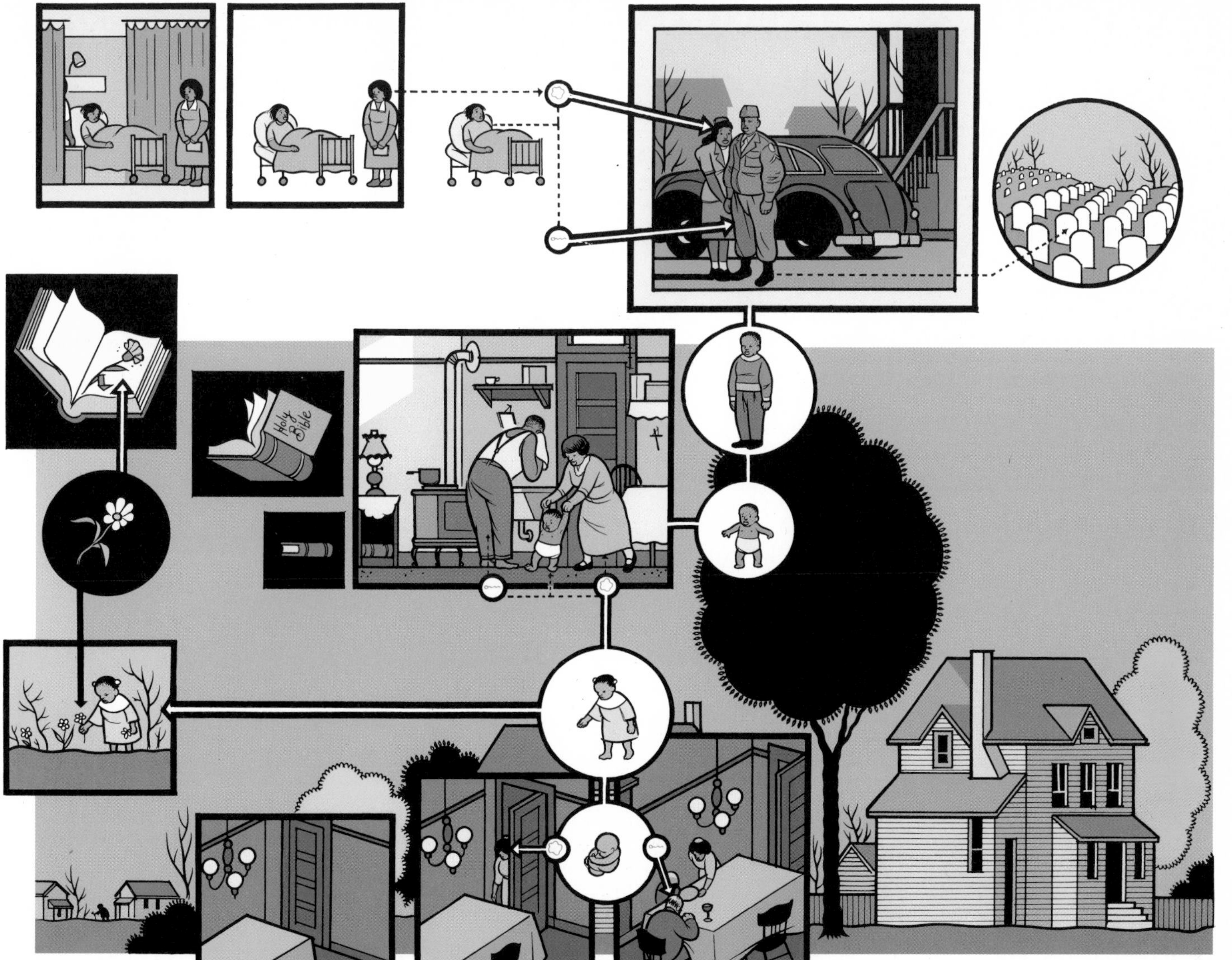
Holy Bible

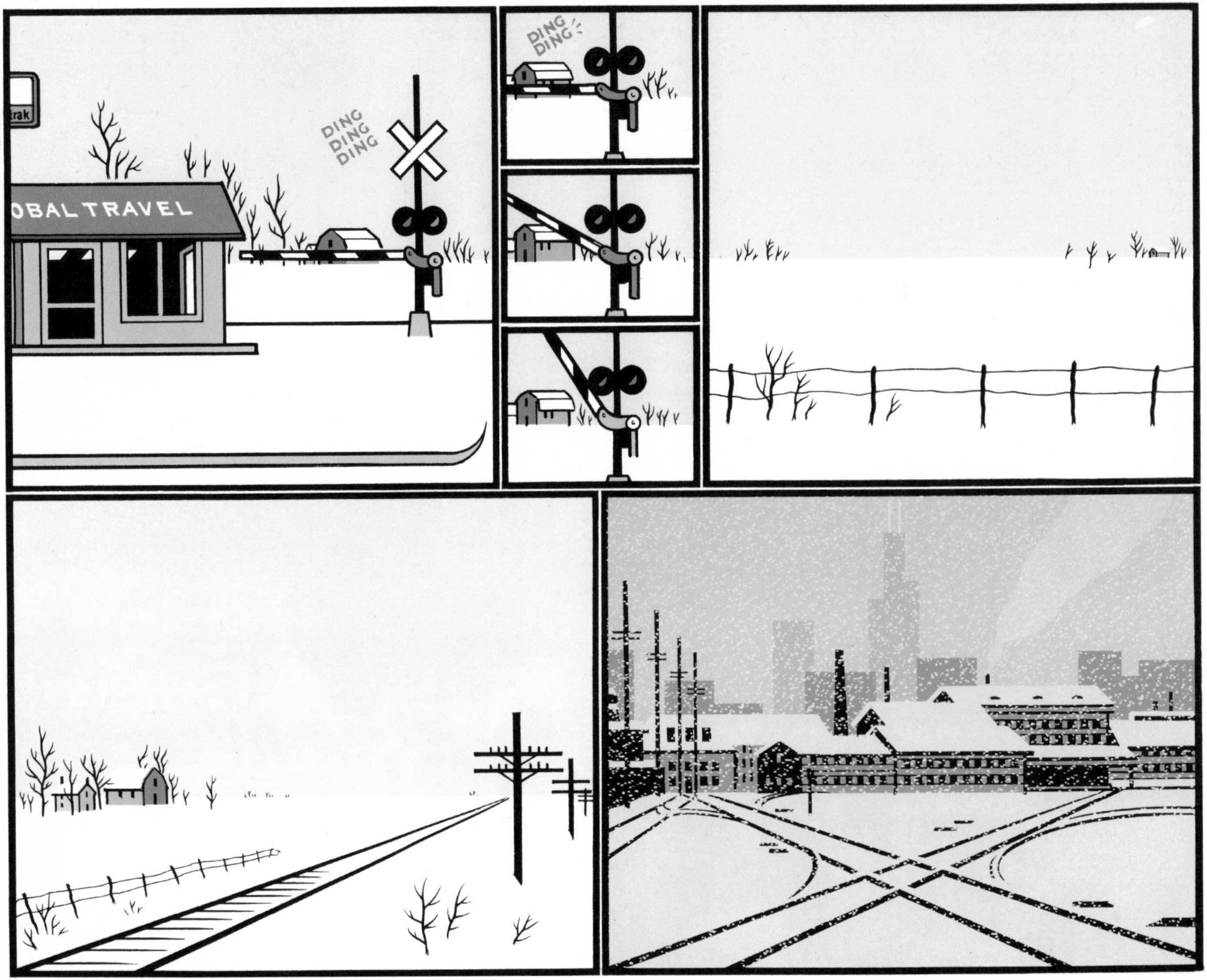
OBAL TRAVEL
DING
DING
DING
DING
DING

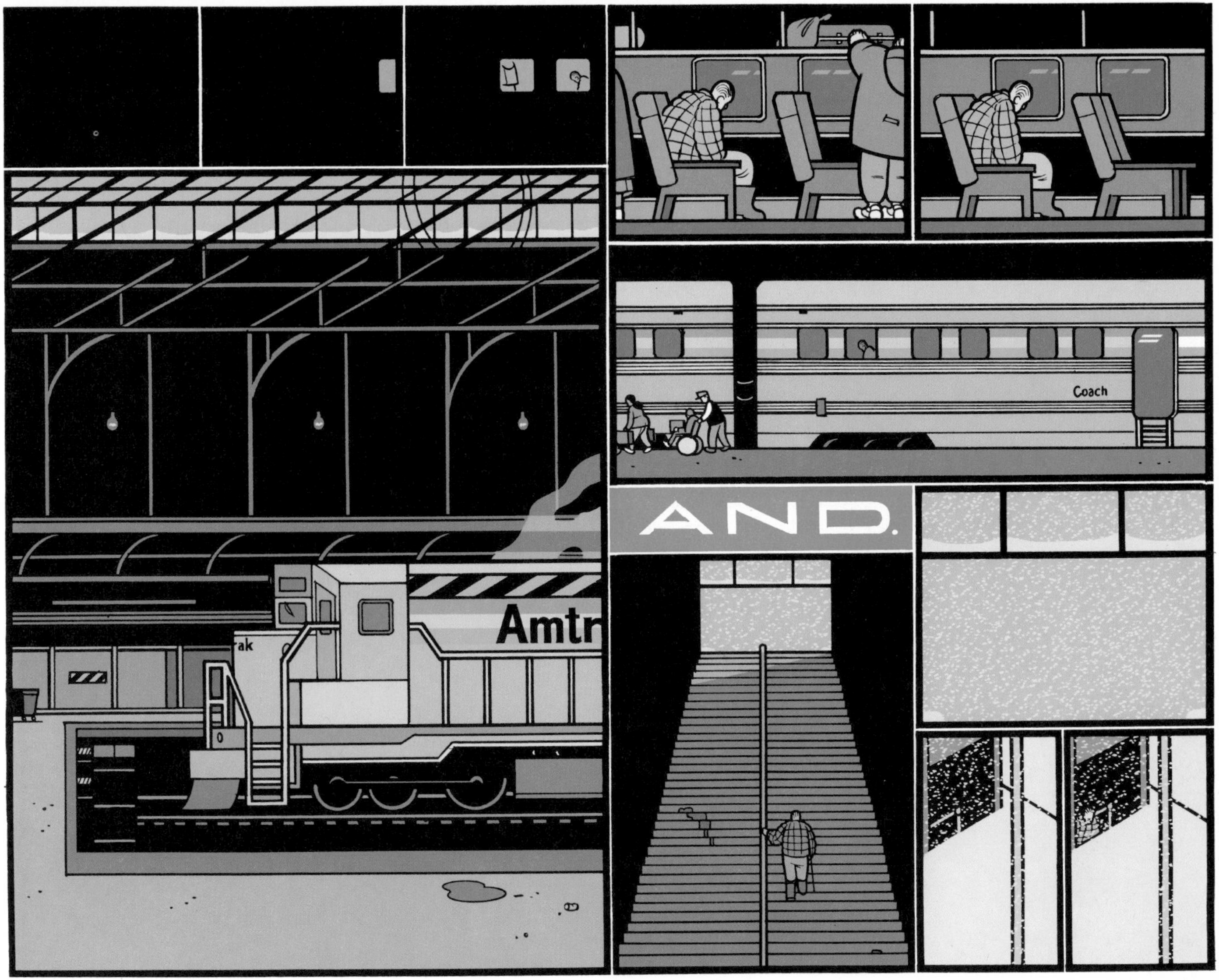
Amtr
rak
Coach
AND.

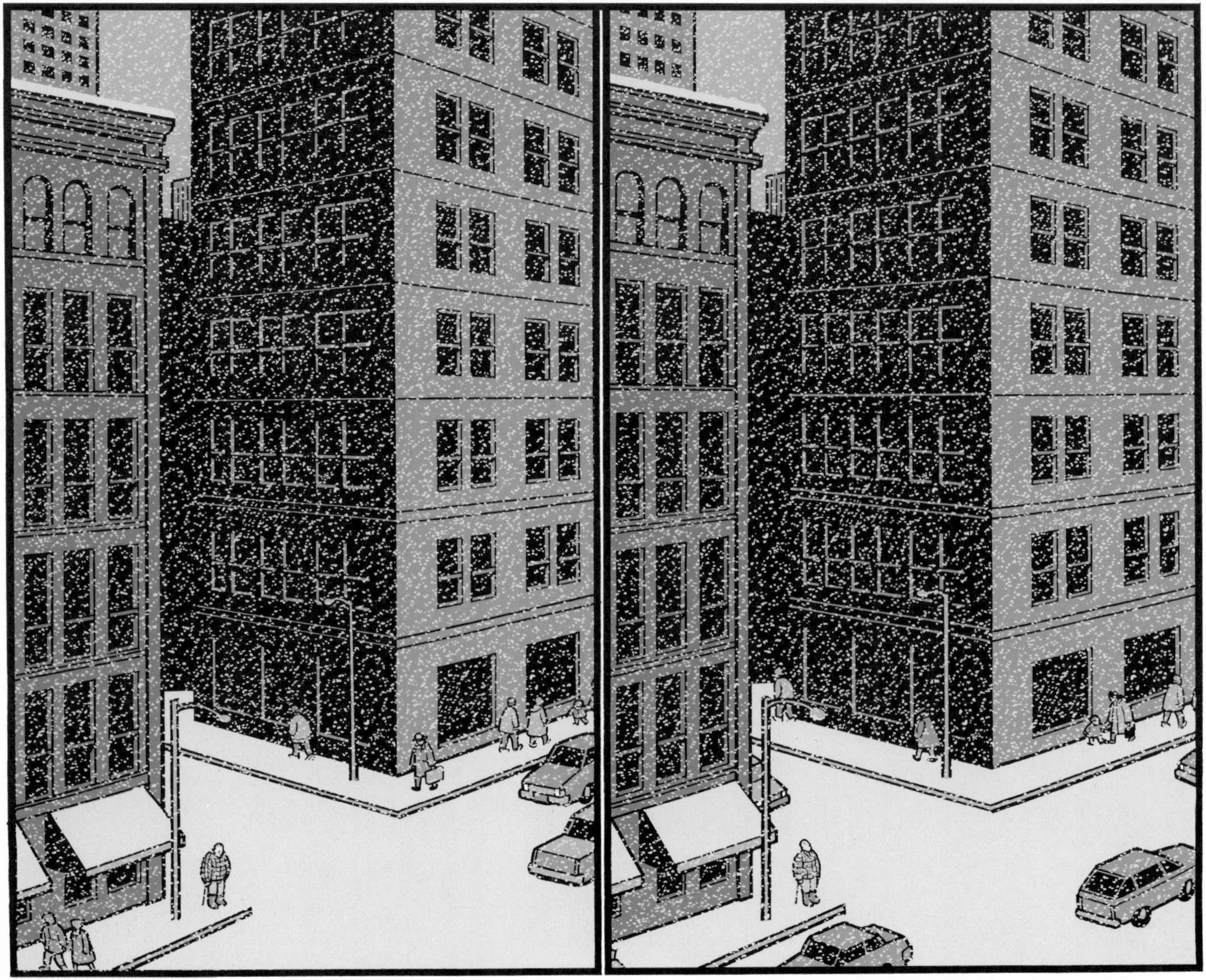

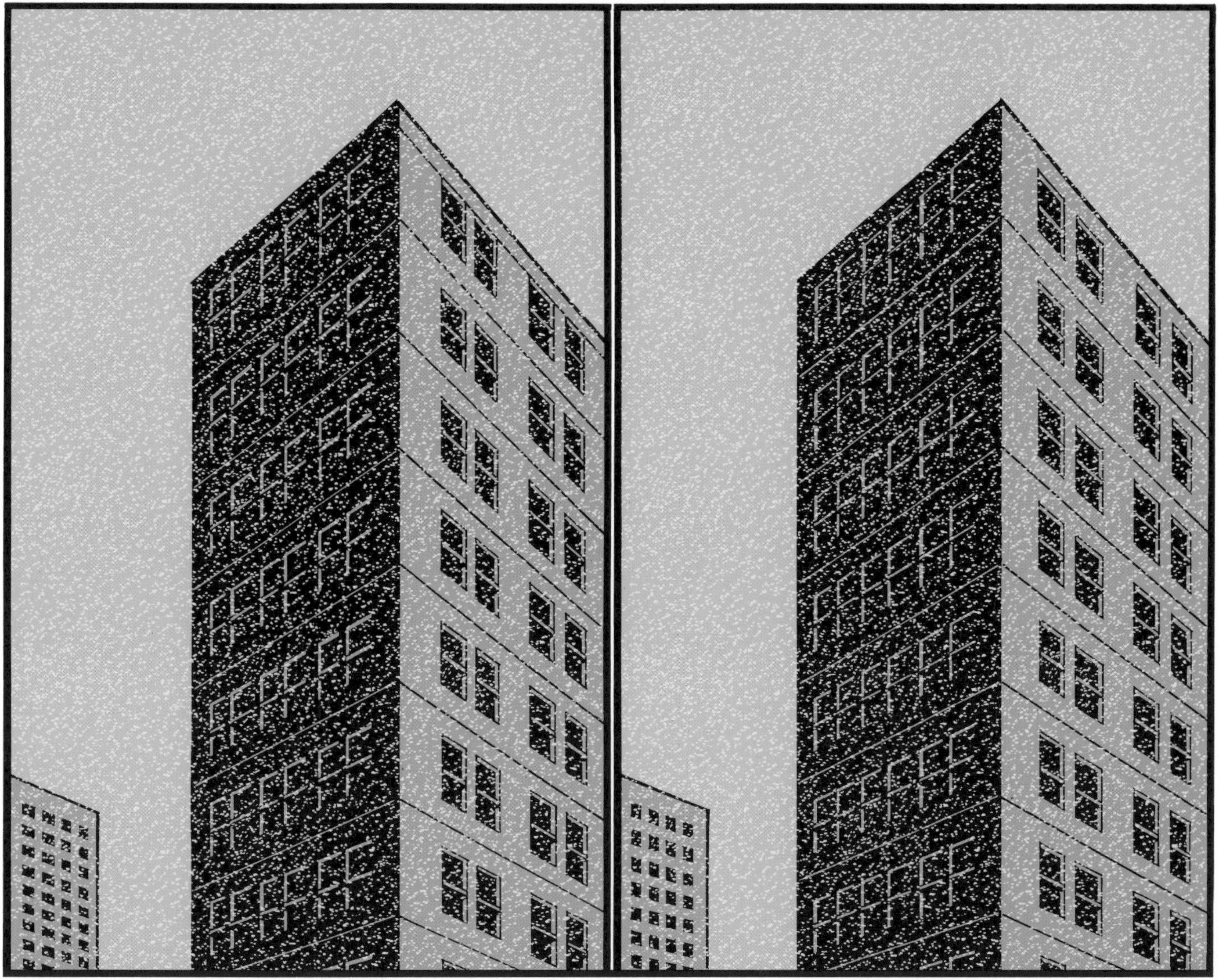

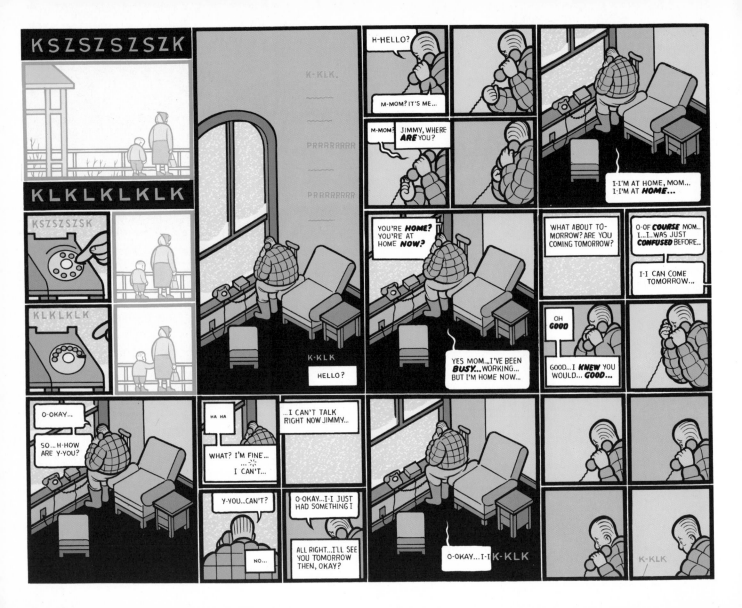

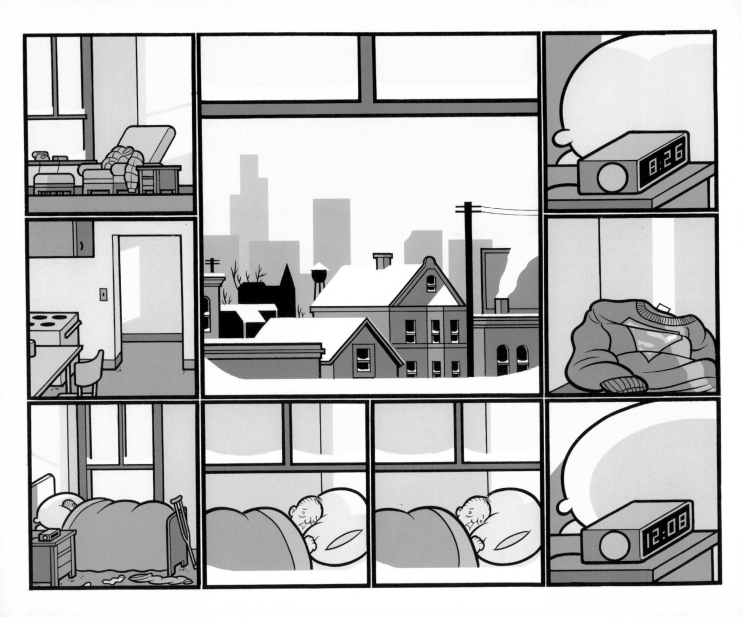

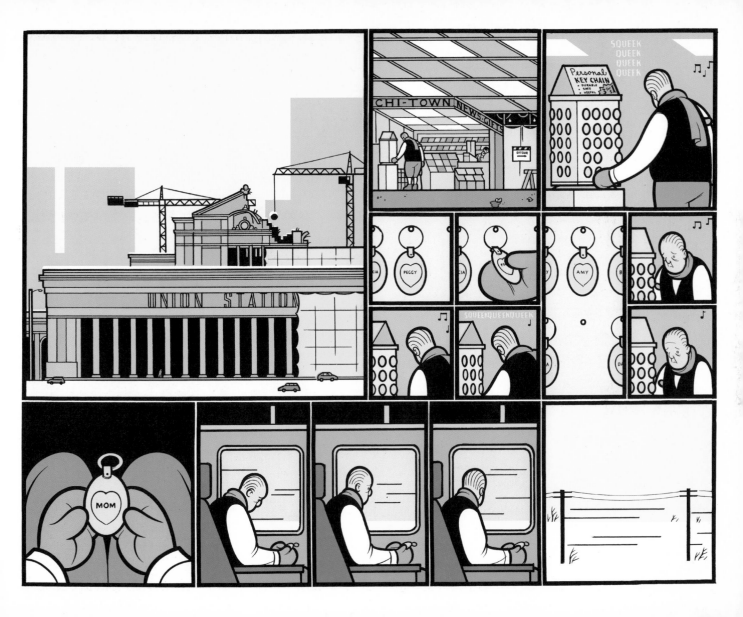

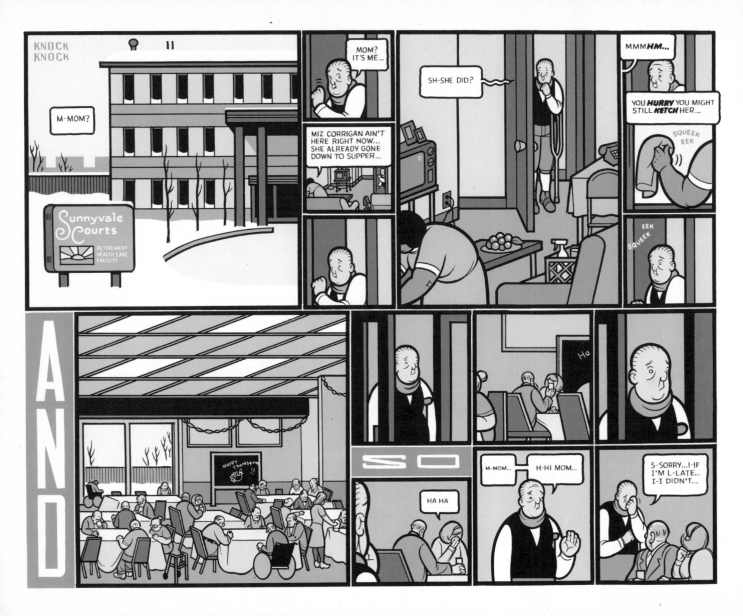

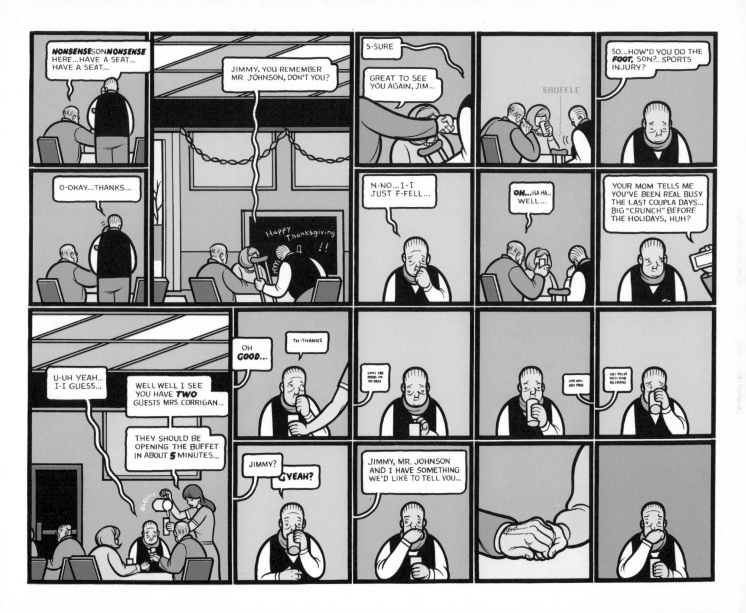

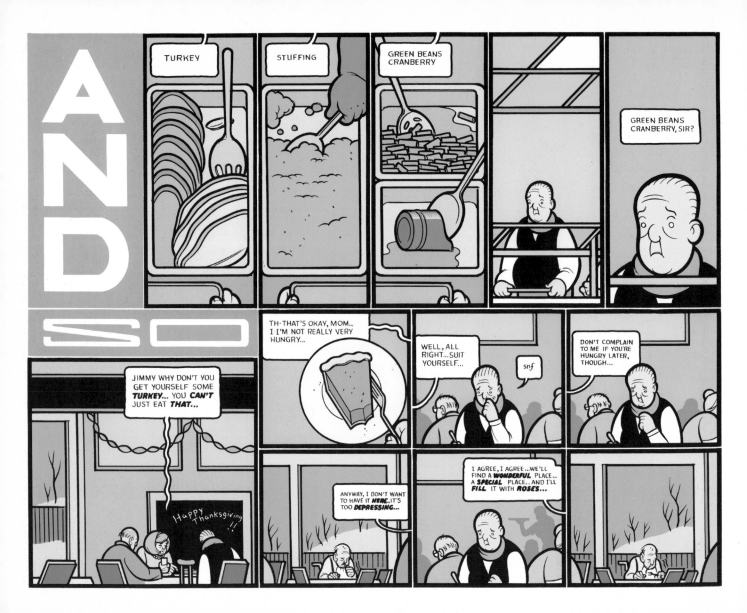

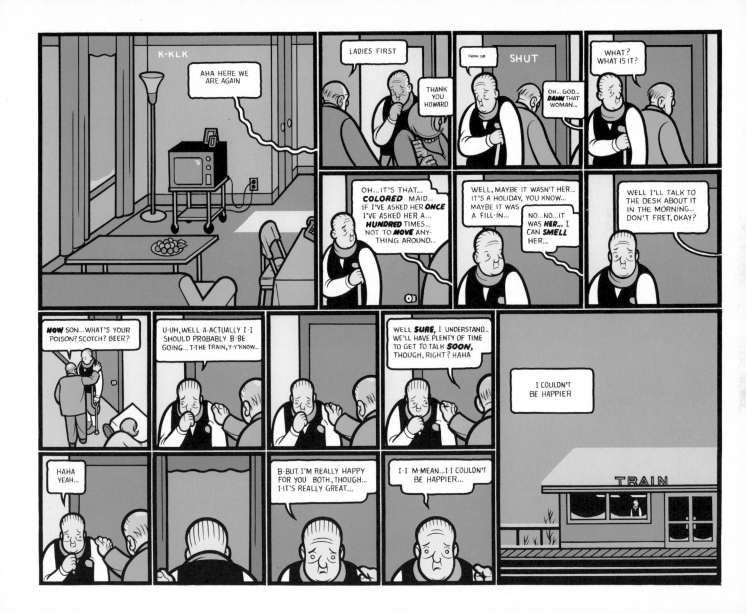

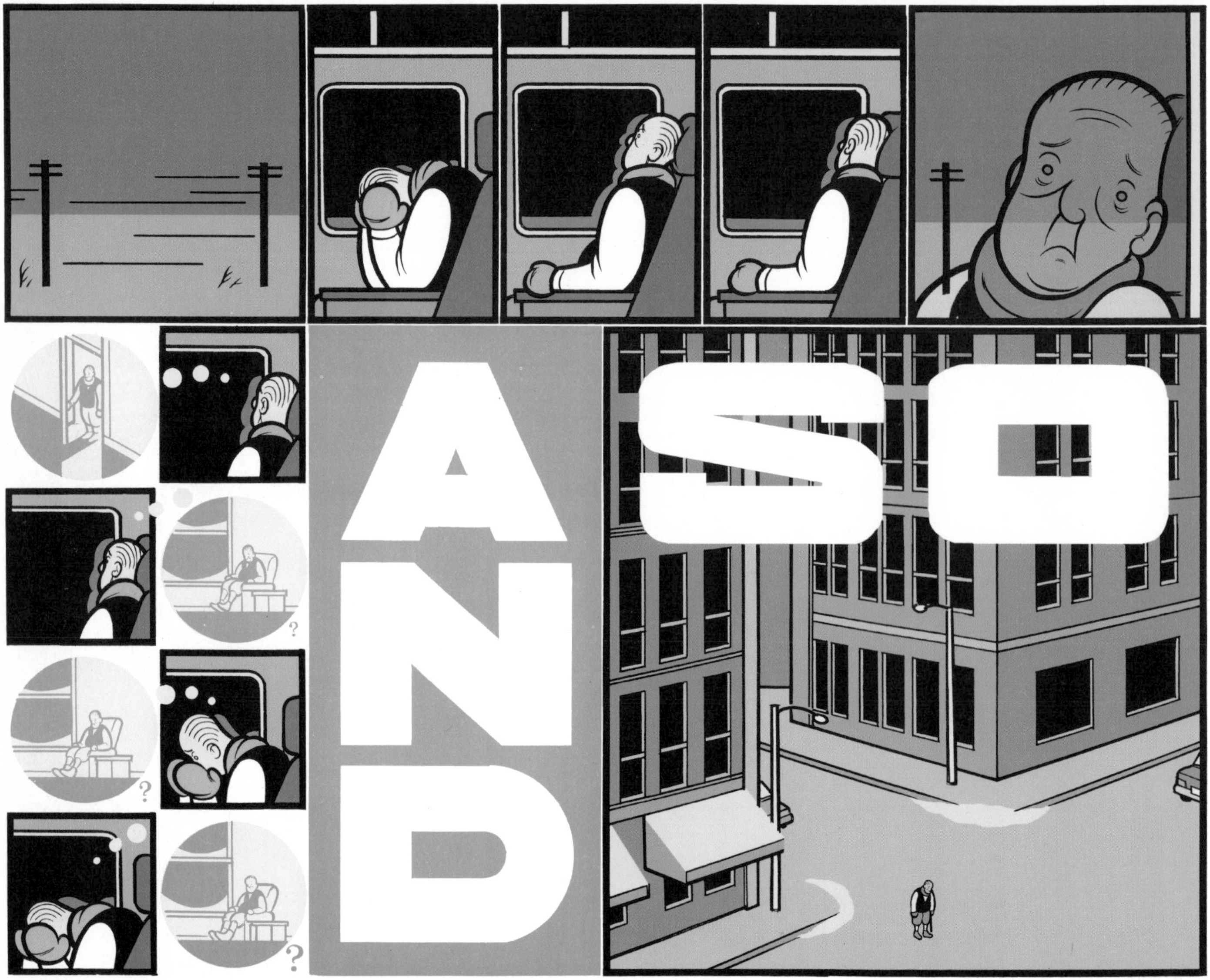
?
?
?
AND
SO

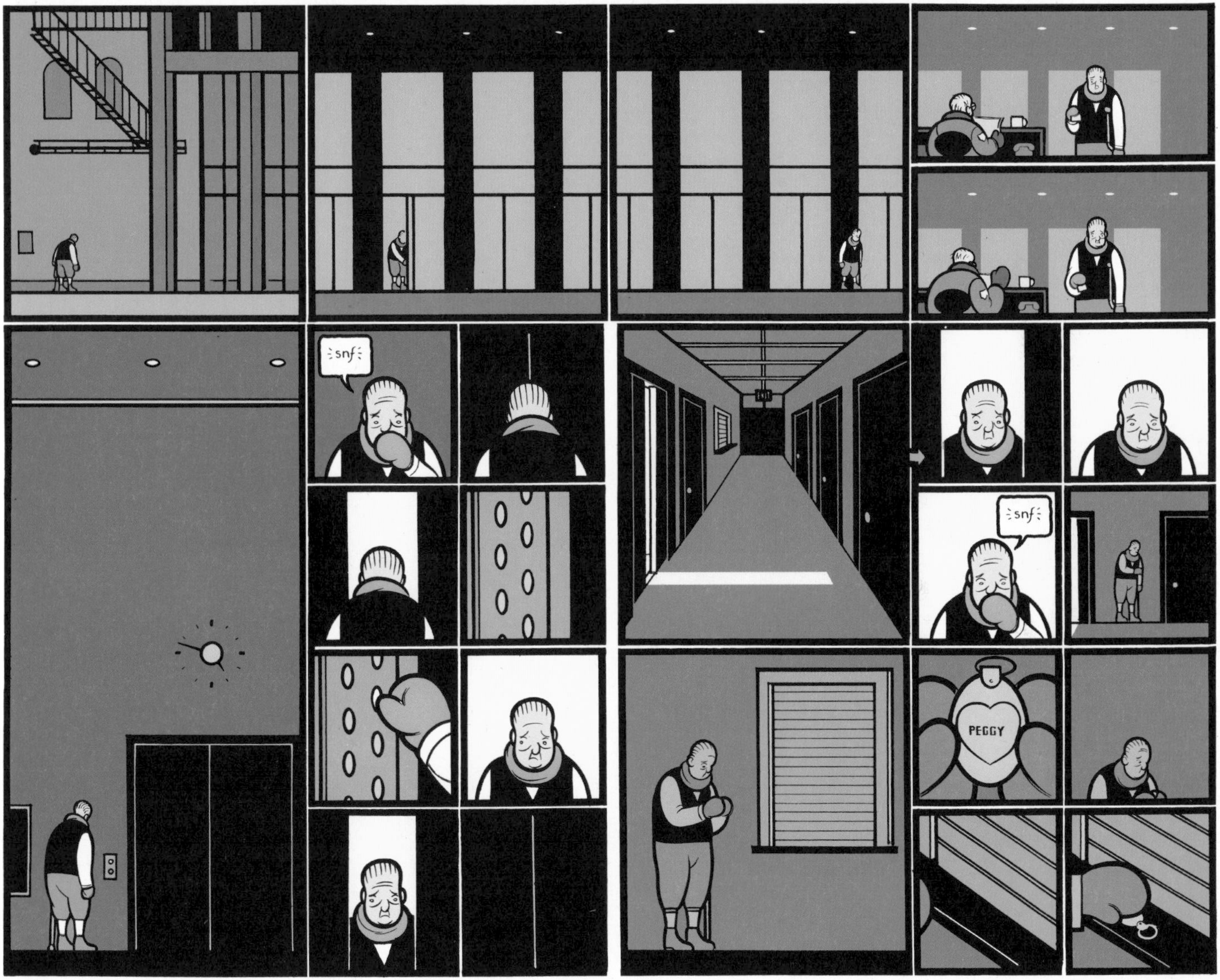
snf
EXIT
snf
PEGGY

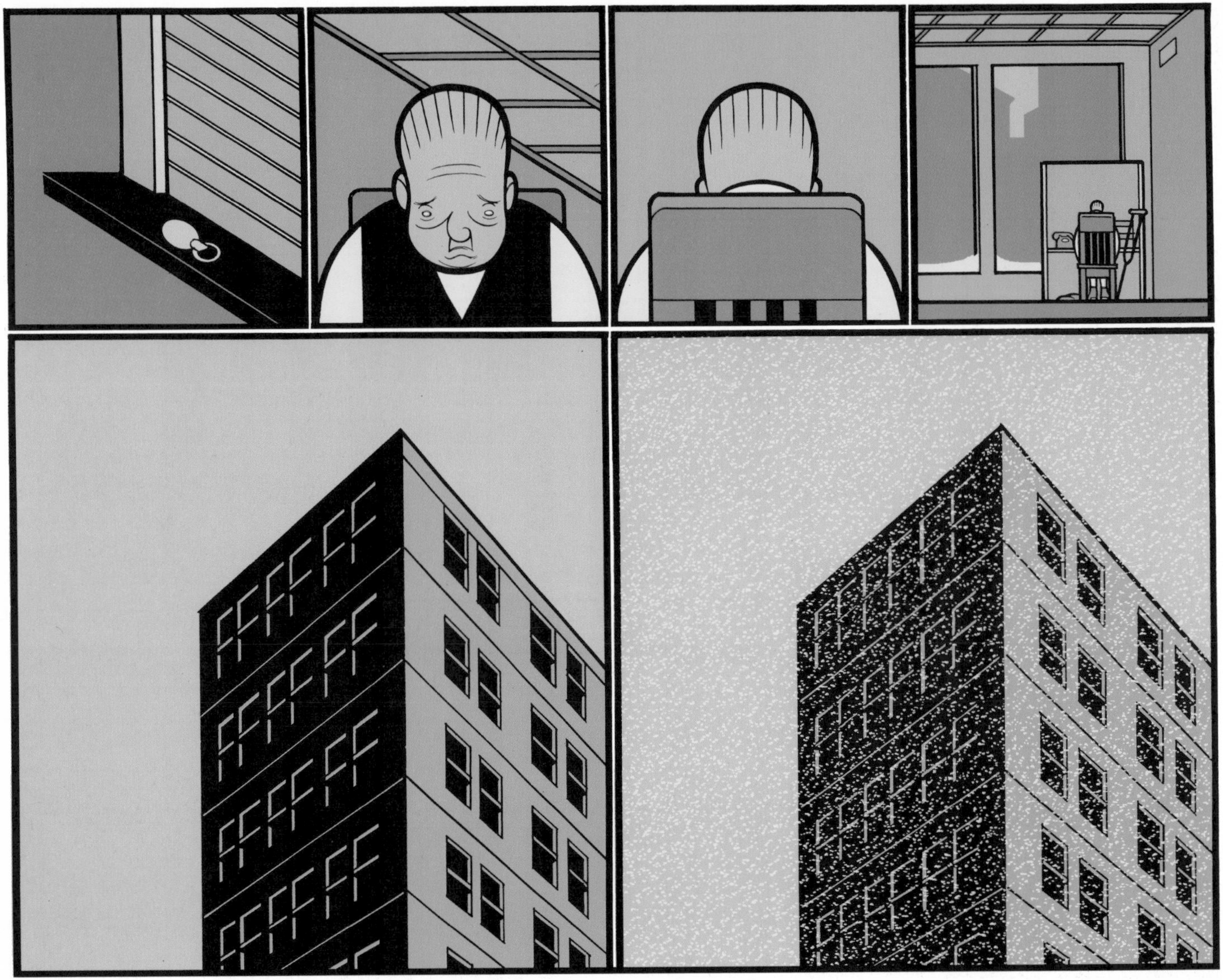

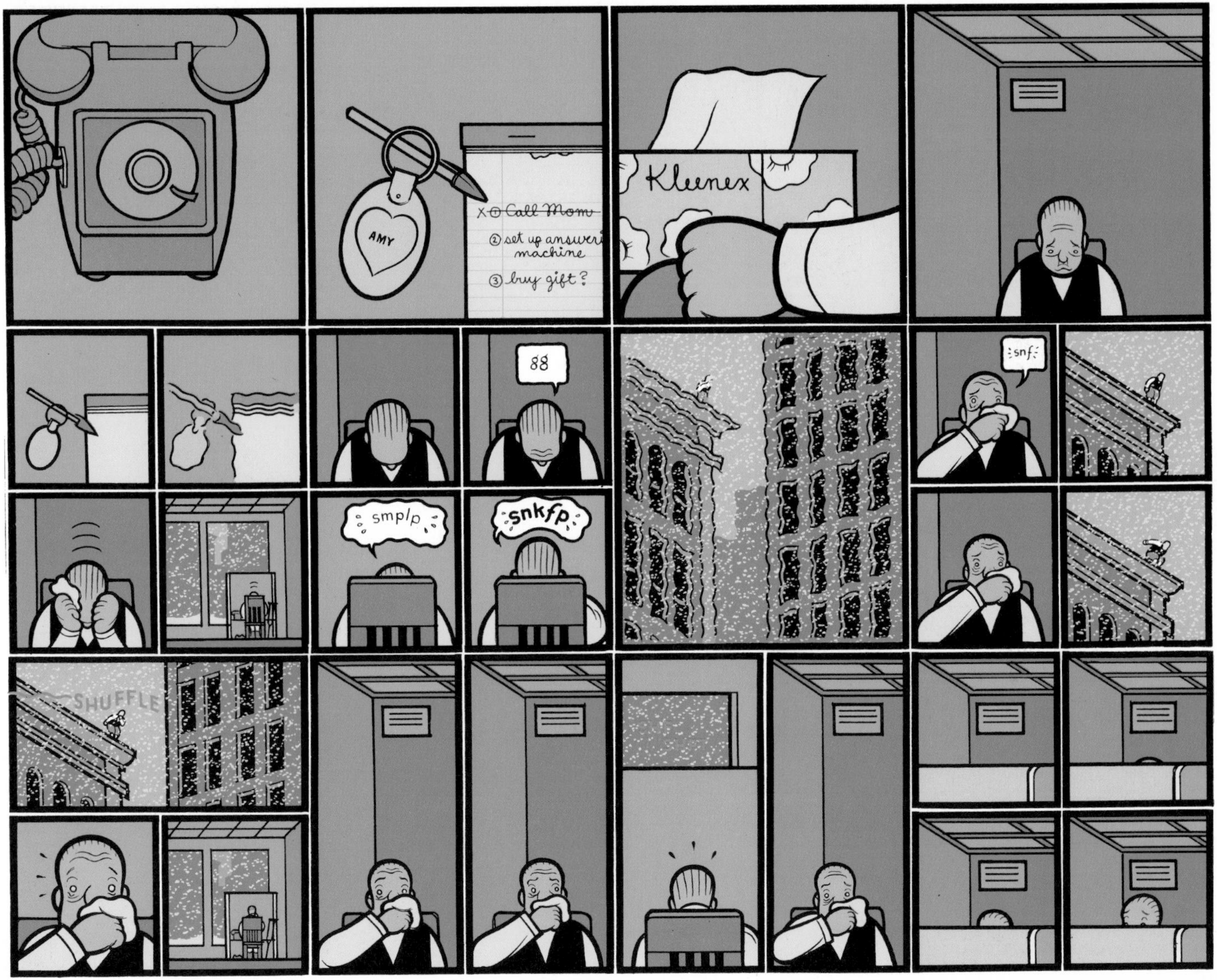

AMY
Call Mom
set up answering machine
buy gift?
Kleenex
88
snf
smplp
snkfp
SHUFFLE

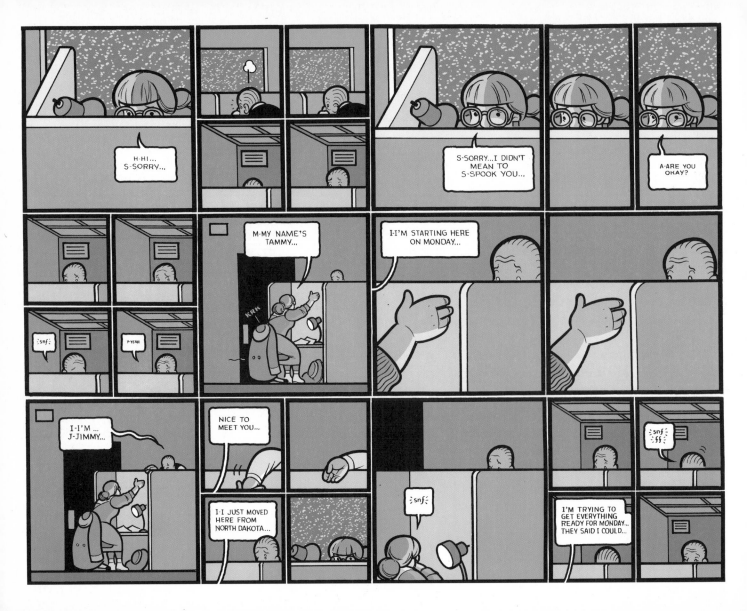

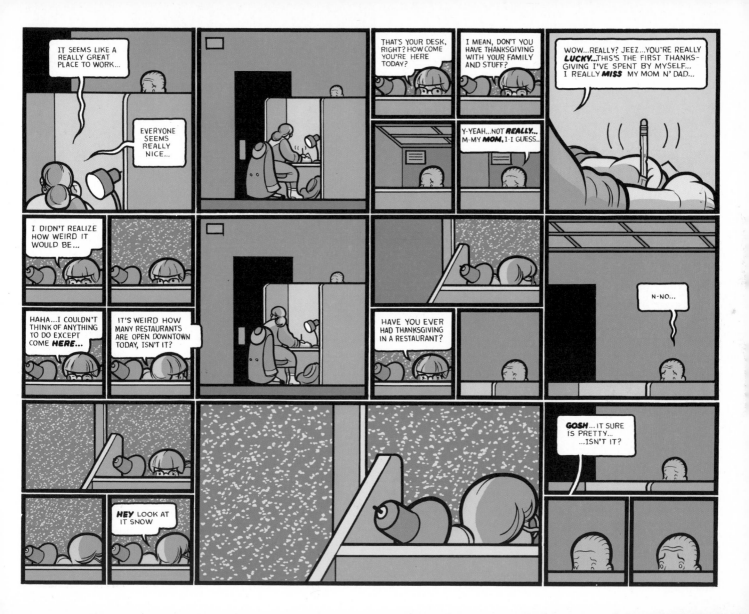

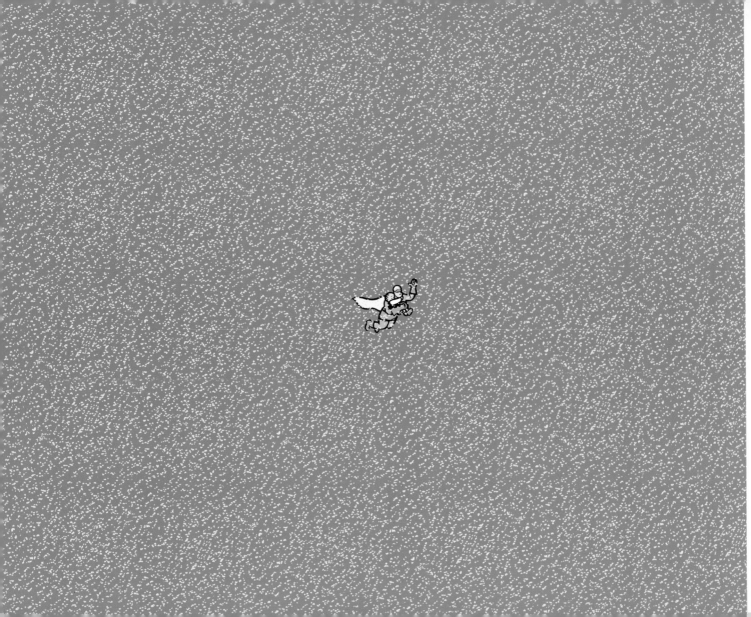

The End

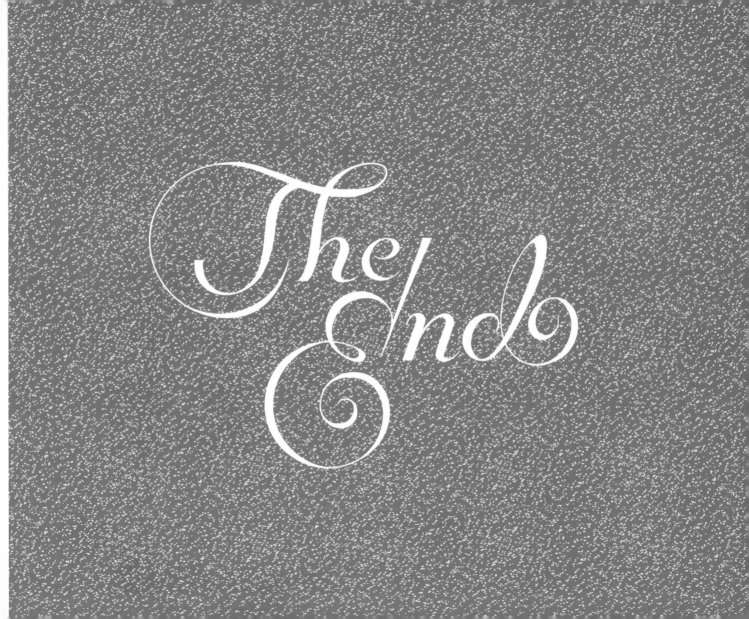

CORRIGENDA

(kôr-ə-jĕn'də) n. pl. A LIST OF ERRORS WITH THEIR CORRECTIONS, IN A BOOK. [LATIN, gerundive of CORRIGERE, to CORRECT.] ARRANGED ALPHABETICALLY.

APOLOGY

(ə-pŏl'ə-jē) n. ALSO **POSTSCRIPT.** I BEGAN THIS STORY IN 1993 AS A WEEKLY COMIC STRIP IN A VERY TOLERANT AND FORGIVING CHICAGO NEWSPAPER, "NEW CITY." IT WAS PLANNED PURELY AS AN IMPROVISATORY EXERCISE, TO TAKE NO MORE THAN A SUMMER TO COMPLETE, AND TO HOPEFULLY PROVIDE A SEMI-AUTOBIOGRAPHICAL SETTING IN WHICH I COULD "WORK OUT" SOME OF THE MORE EMBARRASSING PROBLEMS OF CONFIDENCE AND EMOTIONAL TRUTHFULNESS I WAS EXPERIENCING AS A VERY IMMATURE, AND NOT TERRIBLY FACILE, CARTOONIST. I'D POKED INTO THE SUBJECT BEFORE—THAT OF MEETING AN ESTRANGED PARENT—BUT I WANTED TO TRY A MORE RESPECTABLE "STAB," BY SHOVING MY HAPLESS AND POORLY-WRITTEN "ALTER EGO" OF THE MOMENT, "JIMMY CORRIGAN," THROUGH THE STARTING GATES FIRST. I HAD SPENT MY ENTIRE LIFE AVOIDING CONTACT WITH MY OWN FATHER, AND I GUESS I THOUGHT THAT ONCE THIS STORY WAS FINISHED, I WOULD SOMEHOW HAVE 'PREPARED' MYSELF TO MEET THE REAL MAN, AND THEN BE ABLE TO GET ON WITH MY LIFE. OF COURSE, REAL LIFE IS MUCH MORE BADLY PLOTTED THAN THAT.

ROUGHLY FIVE YEARS LATER, AFTER THOROUGHLY MIRING MYSELF IN THE SWAMPY MUCK OF A "STORY" WHICH NOW SEEMED TO HAVE NO END IN SIGHT, AND, EVEN WORSE, LIKELY NO POINT TO THE POOR MOVIEGOERS AND "SWM"S WHO HAD TO WADE AROUND IT EVERY WEEK TO SWIM IN THE FRESHER WATERS OF THE FILM REVIEWS AND PERSONAL ADS, I RECEIVED A TELEPHONE CALL, WITHOUT WARNING, FROM A MAN CLAIMING TO BE MY FATHER. AT FIRST I THOUGHT IT A JOKE, PERPETRATED BY A DISGRUNTLED AND MEAN-SPIRITED NEWSPAPER READER, BUT THE SHAKY, DECISIVE, RIDICULOUSLY UNFAMILIAR VOICE TOLD ME THAT HE WASN'T TRYING TO BE FUNNY. I WILL NOT CATALOG OUR CONVERSATION HERE, NOR WILL I DETAIL HOW HE LOCATED ME, NOR WILL I TRY TO DESCRIBE THE EMBARRASSING SENSE OF FRUSTRATION AND OUTRAGE THAT I FELT BY HIS BREAKING OUR THIRTY YEAR SILENCE, INSTANTLY LAYING TO REST THE SELF-PITYING IDENTITY I'D UNCONSCIOUSLY CULTURED AND INVESTED INTO A STORY THAT I WASN'T EVEN DONE WITH YET. IN OUR TWENTY MINUTES OF TALK, HOWEVER, I WAS SURPRISED TO DISCOVER THAT, AT LEAST COMPARED TO THIS MAN WHO HAD SUDDENLY STEPPED FORWARD TO CLAIM MY CO-AUTHORSHIP, I WAS THE BETTER WRITER, FOR THE PAINFULLY AWKWARD AND INAPPROPRIATELY FAMILIAR PHRASES WITH WHICH HE TRIED TO LIGHTEN HIS MONOLOGUE WERE MUCH MORE ILL-CONSIDERED AND NONPLUSSED THAN ANYTHING I HAD EVER PUT INTO JIMMY'S DAD'S MOUTH.

HE CALLED ME TWO OR THREE MORE TIMES OVER THE NEXT YEAR, ALWAYS SUGGESTING THAT WE "GET TOGETHER SOMETIME," I ALWAYS VAGUELY AGREEING WITHOUT COMMITTING TO ANY TIME OR PLACE. I DIDN'T LIKE HIS INSISTENCE, AND I WASN'T SURE IF I EVEN WANTED TO MEET WITH HIM YET. WHY, I DON'T KNOW. BUT ONE DAY, ABOUT A YEAR AFTER OUR FIRST "CONTACT," HE CALLED TO SAY THAT HE'D BE VISITING CHICAGO SOON AND ASKED IF I WOULD CONSIDER MEETING HIM AND HIS WIFE AT A RESTAURANT FOR DINNER — NO PRESSURE — JUST DINNER. MY WIFE, WHO HAD UNDERGONE A SIMILAR EXPERIENCE YEARS BEFORE, RIGHTFULLY ENCOURAGED ME. I AGREED. WHAT ELSE WAS I SUPPOSED TO DO?

I DREADED THE DAY, HAVING ATTRIBUTED SO MUCH IMPORTANCE TO IT FOR NEARLY MY ENTIRE LIFE. FUNDAMENTALLY, I GUESS I WAS JUST AFRAID --THE WORST FEAR OF ALL-- THAT HE SIMPLY WOULDN'T LIKE ME. BUT IT WAS EASY: WE MET. I SAW HIM FROM ACROSS THE RESTAURANT: A SMALL, LARGE-HEADED MAN WHOM I WOULDN'T HAVE EVER PICKED OUT OF A CRIMINAL LINE-UP OF A THOUSAND FATHERS. HE WAS PLEASANT, AND SEEMED AS HUMBLED BY MY PRESENCE AS I WAS BY HIS. WE TALKED, OR TRIED TO—I WAS RELIEVED, AT THE VERY LEAST, TO GLEAN FROM HIS REMARKS THAT HE'D NEVER SEEN MY STUFF, THE INVISIBLE AND UNIVERSALLY UNFASHIONABLE WORLD OF THE COMIC STRIP HAVING LEFT ME THANKFULLY UNREAD. GRADUALLY, THE SUBLIME OUTRAGEOUSNESS OF OUR EVENING ERODED INTO TWO PEOPLE SIMPLY RUNNING OUT OF THINGS TO SAY TO EACH OTHER. WE WEREN'T FATHER AND SON ANYMORE, JUST A PAIR OF REGRETFUL MEN. AFTER ABOUT THREE HOURS, WE SAID GOODBYE, SOMEWHAT AFFABLY AGREED TO MEET AGAIN, AND GOT ON WITH OUR LIVES.

THAT CHRISTMAS, I FINALLY WORKED UP THE NON-COURAGE TO CALL HIM AND WISH HIM A HAPPY HOLIDAY, THOUGH HIS ANSWERING MACHINE WAS BARELY AUDIBLE SO I WASN'T SURE IF THE CONNECTION WAS GOOD. I LEFT A MESSAGE ANYWAY. I DIDN'T HEAR FROM HIM AGAIN UNTIL THE FOLLOWING SPRING; HE SAID HE'D BE IN TOWN AGAIN, AND AGAIN ASKED IF I WOULD LIKE TO GET TOGETHER, AND SO I AGAIN AGREED, MARKING THE DATE ON MY CALENDAR SOMEWHAT RELUCTANTLY. HE SAID HE'D CALL WHEN HE GOT INTO TOWN. THE DAY CAME, AND WENT, AND THE TELEPHONE NEVER RANG.

IN THE ENSUING MONTHS I "FINISHED" THE STORY, SHINING IT UP TO THE BEST OF MY ABILITY, GENUINELY SURPRISED THAT IT MIGHT GRADUATE FROM THE EXILE OF NEWSWEEKLIES AND COMIC BOOKS INTO THE "REAL WORLD" OF BOOKSTORES, REMAINDERED TABLES, AND RUMMAGE SALES, DESPITE ITS AWFUL FLAWS. I RESOLVED THAT ONCE IT WAS PUBLISHED AS A BOOK I WOULD PRESENT IT TO MY FATHER, FOR BETTER OR WORSE; AT LEAST IT WOULD BE A MORE PREFERABLE MEANS OF DISCOVERY FOR HIM THAN AT A GARAGE SALE, OR IN A NURSING HOME LIBRARY. UNFORTUNATELY, HOWEVER, I WILL NOT HAVE THAT OPPORTUNITY, AS HE DIED OF A HEART ATTACK IN JANUARY. I MENTION NONE OF THIS TO TRY AND ALIGN MYSELF WITH THE SEEMINGLY UNSTOPPABLE SWARM OF PERSONAL MEMOIRISTS WHO POPULATE THE EXTRA-CURRICULAR BOOK-LISTS OF MULTIPLE SELF-HELP PROGRAMS, BUT TO ADMIT THE CHASM WHICH GAPES BETWEEN THE RIDICULOUS, ARTLESS, DUMBFOUNDEDLY MEANINGLESS COINCIDENCE OF "REAL" LIFE AND MY WEAK FICTION -- NOT TO MENTION MY INABILITY AT KNITTING THEM TOGETHER. IN OTHER WORDS, I WISH I COULD'VE DONE A BETTER JOB. MAYBE I SHOULD'VE JUST TRIED TO BE A MEMOIRIST, OR, MORE EFFECTIVELY, SIMPLY KEPT MY INK BOTTLE CAPPED.

REGARDLESS, IN RACING THROUGH THIS STORY FOR ITS FINAL "EDIT," SKIDDING PAST ALL THESE ERRORS, OMISSIONS, AND MISTAKES, IT OCCURRED TO ME UPON CLOSING THE "MANUSCRIPT" THAT THE FOUR OR FIVE HOURS IT TOOK TO READ IS ALMOST EXACTLY THE TOTAL TIME I EVER SPENT WITH MY FATHER, EITHER IN PERSON OR ON THE TELEPHONE. ADDITIONALLY, AND AT RISK OF SOUNDING MELODRAMATIC, ITS FINAL PRINTED SIZE SEEMS NEARLY EQUAL IN VOLUME TO THE LITTLE BLACK BOX, OR URN, BEFORE WHICH I BRIEFLY STOOD THIS JANUARY, BENEATH A COLOR PHOTO OF THE MAN ITS LABEL CLAIMED TO CONTAIN.
--C. WARE, CHICAGO, MARCH, 2000.

CRUTCH

A SUPPORT, USED by THE LAME or INFIRM AS A WALKING AID, esp. FOLLOWING A LOCOMOTIVE INJURY, viz:

DEDICATION

(dĕd'ə-kā'shən) n. IN THIS SEMI-AUTOBIOGRAPHICAL WORK OF FICTION, I FEAR I MAY HAVE POTENTIALLY IMPUGNED (AT LEAST, PERHAPS, IN A CARELESS READER'S COMPREHENSION OF THE BOOK) SOME "REAL-LIFE" ALTER-EGOS, MOST NOTABLE OF WHOM MIGHT BE MY MOTHER, WHO, BEING A THOUGHTFUL, INTELLIGENT, AND SUPPORTIVE WOMAN THUS BEARS NO RESEMBLANCE WHATSOEVER TO THE MISERABLE WRETCH WHO DOMINATES POOR JIMMY. AS SUCH, THIS BOOK IS DEDICATED TO HER, ESPECIALLY AS IT IS WHOLLY CHARACTERIZED BY HER ABSENCE.